D0787914

THE PAPERS OF DANIEL WEBSTER

CHARLES M. WILTSE, EDITOR-IN-CHIEF

SERIES ONE: CORRESPONDENCE

THE UNIVERSITY PRESS

OF NEW ENGLAND

Sponsoring Institutions

BRANDEIS UNIVERSITY

BROWN UNIVERSITY

CLARK UNIVERSITY

DARTMOUTH COLLEGE

UNIVERSITY OF NEW HAMPSHIRE

UNIVERSITY OF RHODE ISLAND

TUFTS UNIVERSITY

UNIVERSITY OF VERMONT

The Papers of

Daniel Webster

Correspondence, Volume 5

1840–1843

HAROLD D. MOSER, EDITOR

PUBLISHED FOR

DARTMOUTH COLLEGE BY THE

UNIVERSITY PRESS OF NEW ENGLAND

HANOVER, NEW HAMPSHIRE AND

LONDON, ENGLAND 1982

*The edition of the Papers of Daniel Webster, of which this is volume five
in the Correspondence series, has been made possible through grants
from the Program for Editions of the National Endowment for the Humanities, an independent Federal agency, and through the continuing
support, both administrative and financial, of the National Historical
Publications and Records Commission. The edition is sponsored and published by Dartmouth College.*

Contents

*For the page number on which each document of
the Papers begins, see the Calendar.*

A section of illustrations follows page 290

Acknowledgments

The deep indebtedness of the editors to libraries, archives, historical societies, and individual collectors has been many times acknowledged as new volumes of Webster Papers have appeared. As in earlier volumes the source of each individual letter printed or calendared is indicated by the standard location symbol; to each of these depositories, and to the patient men and women who administer them, our most sincere thanks are once again extended. A small sampling of major institutions has continued to supply documents and to answer questions as we have called upon them. These are the Library of Congress, where Manuscript Historian John McDonough has been most helpful; the National Archives, where we are under special obligation to Mary A. Giunta and Richard N. Sheldon; the Massachusetts Historical Society; the New Hampshire Historical Society; and, most important of all, Baker Library of Dartmouth College. Our obligation at Baker, where the project itself is housed, extends to virtually every member of the staff, but is greatest to Virginia Close, Reference Librarian; Patricia A. Carter, Interlibrary Loan Officer; Walter W. Wright, Chief of Special Collections; and Kenneth C. Cramer, Archivist.

To those who have supplied the generous financial support that has kept us working, our obligation is certainly of equal magnitude; Dartmouth College, the National Endowment for the Humanities, the National Historical Publications and Records Commission, and a handful of individual donors.

To various other individuals who have contributed in countless tangible and intangible ways, we may single out for particular mention Leonard M. Rieser, Dartmouth Provost and former Dean of the Faculty of Arts and Sciences, who has added the administration of the Webster Papers to an already overwhelming schedule; William B. Durant, Executive Officer to the Faculty of Arts and Science, who has from the inception of the project handled our finances; George F. Farr, Jr., Assistant Director of the Research Materials Program, National Endowment for the Humanities; and Kathy Fuller, Program Specialist; James B. Rhoads, retired Archivist of the United States and former Chairman of the National Historical Publications and Records Commission; Frank G. Burke, its Executive Director and Roger Bruns, its Publication Program Director.

Finally, we must acknowledge the substantial contribution to this volume by others on the Webster Papers staff, in particular former Ass'stant Editor Rexford G. Sherman, Editorial Assistant Robyn Bem, and Assistant to the Editor-in-Chief, Mary V. Anstruther. We have also been able to call at all times upon the special skills of Legal Editors Alfred S. Konefsky and Andrew J. King, Diplomatic Editor Kenneth E. Shewmaker, and Assistant Diplomatic Editor Kenneth R. Stevens.

Foreword

The four years spanned by this fifth volume of the Correspondence of Daniel Webster were years of contention, fateful alike for Webster and for the country. The campaign of 1840, the first of many in which showmanship transcended issues and personalities, began an era that historians might well have called "the age of Webster" had not Harrison's too-early death tilted the sectional balance to the South. Webster remained at the head of the Cabinet for more than two years, contributing in masterly fashion to America's foreign relations, but losing at an accelerated pace his influence on domestic policy. When he retired in May 1843 because he could not concur in the annexation of Texas, Tyler turned for the support he so desperately needed to the slaveholding states. As a consequence the already visible sectional rift grew wider, foreshadowing the overt conflicts of the 1850s. At the same time there were uneasy rumblings from the multiple levels of friction beneath the outwardly calm surface of the national life.

In addition to the growing sectional differences, there were factional splits within both Whig and Democratic parties. There were also disruptive economic divergencies between those who favored and those who opposed a central bank, between tariff and free trade advocates, and among manufacturing, mercantile, and agricultural interests. Perhaps the implications to be drawn from these various undercurrents were no clearer to Webster than they were to any of his contemporaries; but in the letters he wrote and those he received from friends and supporters in the early 1840s one may trace a certain logic and an ominous inevitability, well exhibited in Professor Moser's judicious selection of documents. As heretofore a calendar serves to give continuity and a measure of completeness to the materials here reproduced. It should be noted, however, that Webster's activities in the sphere of foreign policy, as distinct from his domestic role in the Harrison-Tyler Cabinet, appear in a companion volume reproducing the more important diplomatic papers generated during his first term as Secretary of State.

Charles M. Wiltse

Introduction

This fifth volume of Webster's correspondence spans most of the years of the first Whig ascendancy, from 1840 to 1843. In 1840, the country was deep into a depression; for three long years money had been scarce, food had been in short supply, and countless persons had failed financially. Webster and the Whigs, led by William Henry Harrison and John Tyler, were engaged against their Democratic opponents in the "log cabin and hard cider" campaign that was to sweep them into power and take Webster from the Senate into the State Department. The volume closes in 1843 with Webster once again a private citizen, having resigned his post and left Washington and the Tyler administration for retirement at his beloved Marshfield home.

For Webster, for the Whigs, and for the country, these were trying years. As opponents of Van Buren's hard money policy, Webster and other Whigs spent most of 1840 in trying to defeat the President and his measures by pledging a return of prosperity if elected. Adapting themselves to the campaign tactics that had worked so well for the Jacksonians in the past, the Whigs succeeded. But President Harrison and his party inherited from their Democratic predecessors a troubled economy. The country was far from recovery; indeed, throughout 1841 and 1842, and on into early 1843, the depression became worse.

Once in office, the enthusiasm and cooperation that had characterized the Whig's presidential campaign evaporated. They disagreed as much among themselves as they did with their Democratic opponents. At bottom, the issue was over who controlled the Whig party and determined its policy—Clay and Congress, or the President and his cabinet. The lines along which the battles were to be fought had been formed early, even before Harrison's death on April 4. With Tyler's accession, the fighting intensified, as Tyler, Clay, and the Whigs in Congress disagreed over presumed pledges made during the campaign. Congress and President Tyler could agree on repeal of the subtreasury, bankruptcy legislation, and federal loans, but they could reach no agreement on a new bank—a national bank, a fiscal bank, a fiscal corporation, or exchequer—whatever they proposed to call it or wherever they planned to establish it. As bitterness over a bank intensified, other issues, such as the tariff and distribution of the proceeds from the sale of the public lands, became points of dispute between the Clay Whigs and Tyler. All of Tyler's cabinet except Webster resigned in disgust and anger in September 1841, and the Whig majority in Congress read Tyler out of the party.

In this showdown between Congress and the Executive, Webster sided with President Tyler. The correspondence of this volume covers and elucidates his split with Clay and a whole Whig faction; his role as dispenser of patronage for personal and political gain; and all the intricate ramifications of Tyler's domestic policy, which led finally to Webster's resignation and his efforts to come to terms once more with the other Whigs.

The correspondence also deals with his efforts to cope with international issues and disputes, dominated between 1841 and 1843 by relations with Great Britain (issues covered more at length in volume one of the *Diplomatic Papers*). War was narrowly avoided in 1841 over the McLeod case, but through the negotiation of the Webster-Ashburton treaty in 1842, Webster prepared the ground for a lasting peace between Great Britain and the United States. Before he resigned over Texan annexation on May 8, 1843, he had also opened the door for United States trade with China through his instructions to Caleb Cushing, the first United States minister to that country.

Webster was severely battle-scarred when he left Washington after his term as Secretary of State. His personal and political life had been unveiled for public scrutiny. Rumors of scandals growing out of his efforts to recover something from his extensive western land holdings had become a familiar weapon of partisan warfare. Highly regarded for his accomplishments in international affairs, Webster was nonetheless outside the Whig camp. Men who had been supporters and friends looked at him with suspicion, holding him at arm's length. His goal after May became reacceptance and readmission to the Whig party.

PLAN OF WORK

From its inception the Papers of Daniel Webster was planned as an integrated project, using both microfilm and letterpress publication. The persistent pressure of time and the steadily rising cost of book publication were important factors in the choice of the dual media, but the overriding consideration was the desire to bring all of Webster together, without abridgment or gloss, for those who were equipped to use it that way, while providing the less dedicated scholar and the general reader with the essential Webster in convenient annotated form. The microfilm edition, in four different groupings, is as complete as the surviving records permit. Webster's correspondence, including letters received as well as letters sent, together with miscellaneous notes, memoranda, briefs, drafts, formal writings, reports, petitions, and business papers have been issued with printed guide and index as *The Papers of Daniel Webster* by University Microfilms, Ann Arbor, Michigan. *The Legal Papers of Daniel Webster*, also to be issued with guide and alphabetical list of cases by University Microfilms, consists of records drawn primarily from the county courts of New Hampshire and Massachusetts and from the state and lower federal courts in New England. Records of the Department of State and of the Supreme Court are available on film from the National Archives and Records Service of the General Services Administration, but the user must select for himself the reels that may contain Webster material.

The value of this film, including as it does virtually all known Webster papers, cannot be overstated, but its very magnitude makes it unmanageable. It is relatively expensive, requires special equipment to use, is hard on the eyes, and effectively buries the grains of wheat by mixing them unevenly with an enormous amount of chaff. The user of the film, moreover, must decipher for himself often difficult or faded handwriting. He must search out the identity of persons and the nature of events alluded to, and finally he must rely upon his own judgment as to the significance of the given document. In the letterpress edition all this has been done for him, even to the selection of documents in terms of their significance, by editors totally immersed in the time and place and almost as familiar with the central characters as was Webster himself.

The letterpress edition in effect complements and renders more useful these various microfilm collections, whose very existence has made it possible to select more rigorously the documents important enough to be offered to the larger audience reached by the printed book. Each volume of correspondence, moreover, includes a calendar of letters written in the same time period but not selected for publication. For each of these the microfilm frame number is cited, as is volume and page citation for any document now available only in a printed version. Footnote references are also made to the film wherever appropriate. Items found subsequent to publication of the appropriate volume will be calendared at the end of the *Correspondence* Series. For the general reader and for the student of the period rather than of the man, the editors believe the selection of items printed will be ample. The biographer, and the scholar pursuing an in-depth study of some segment of the times, will need the film, to which he will find the printed volumes an indispensable annotated guide.

The letterpress edition is being published in four different series, overlapping in time but not in content, in order to make maximum use of subject matter specialists as technical editors. The edition has been planned to fill a total of fourteen volumes, of which seven are to be correspondence, three to be legal papers, two are diplomatic papers, and two are speeches and formal writings.

The present volume, including the period 1840–1843, is the fifth in the Correspondence series.

EDITORIAL METHOD

Letters and other documents included in this volume are arranged in chronological sequence, irrespective of whether Webster was the writer or the recipient. The only exception is for letters that were sent as enclosures in later correspondence. These have been placed immediately after the document which they accompanied. Date and point of origin have been placed at the upper right of each letter. If all or part of this information has been supplied by the editors, it appears in square brackets, with a question mark if conjecture. The complimentary close, which in the original manuscripts often takes up three or four lines, has been run continuously with the last line of the text.

All letters are reproduced in full except in rare instances where the only surviving text is incomplete or is from a printed source which did not reproduce it in its entirety. Needless to say, texts from printed sources are used only when the original manuscript has not been found, but the letter is of sufficient importance to warrant its inclusion.

The letters themselves have been reproduced in type as nearly as possible the way they were written. Misspellings have been retained without the annoyingly obtrusive "(sic)"; and abbreviations and contractions have been allowed to stand unless the editor feels they will not be readily understood by a present-day reader. In such cases the abbreviation has been expanded, with square brackets enclosing the letters supplied. Punctuation, too, has been left as Webster and his correspondents used it, save only that dashes clearly intended as periods are so written. Superscript letters in abbreviations or contractions have been brought down, but a period is supplied only if the last letter of the abbreviation is not the last letter of the word abbreviated. In all other cases, periods, apostrophes, dashes, and other forms of punctuation have been left as Webster and his contemporaries used them. The ampersand, far more frequently used than the spelled out "and," has been retained, but diacritical marks over contractions have been omitted even where the contraction itself is retained.

Canceled words or passages that are obvious slips, immediately corrected, have been left out altogether; those which show some change of thought or attitude or have stylistic or psychological implications have been included between angled brackets. Interlineations by the author have been incorporated into the text, but marginal passages, again if by the author, have been treated as postscripts and placed below the signature.

In order to keep explanatory footnotes to a minimum, general notes have been interspersed from time to time with the letters that constitute the text of the volume. These serve to indicate what Webster was doing at a particular time or to explain a sequence of events that may help to clarify subsequent correspondence. Footnotes are used to identify persons, places, events, situations, problems, or other matters that help to understand the context of a particular reference.

Individuals are identified only once, generally the first time they are mentioned. For the convenience of the reader who may have missed this first reference, the appropriate index entry is printed in bold face type. Well-known individuals—those in the *Dictionary of American Biography* or the *Biographical Directory of the American Congress*—have not been identified at all unless the context seems to require it. For those in the DAB the index entry is marked with an asterisk, and with a dagger for those in the BDAC. The extent of footnoting has been reduced by adding given names and initials in square brackets where text references are to surnames only.

Immediately following each document is an unnumbered note indicating the provenance of the document and if appropriate, giving some information about the writer or recipient. Symbols used in these provenance notes are the standard descriptive symbols and the location symbols developed by the Union Catalog Division of the Library of Congress. Those appearing in the present volume have been listed under Abbreviations and Symbols below.

Webster Chronology, 1840-1843

1840

January 13	Webster delivered speech on the agriculture of England at the Massachusetts State House.
January 13	Steamboat *Lexington* burned in Long Island Sound; 140 dead.
January 27	Webster introduced in the Senate a resolution calling for improvement of the steamboat navigation laws.
February 10	Queen Victoria married to Prince Albert of Saxe-Coburg-Gotha.
March 17	Nathaniel Ray Thomas, close Marshfield associate, died afer brief illness.
March	Webster attacked by "Junius" for his opinion to the Baring Brothers & Company affirming the constitutional right of the states to contract loans at home and abroad.
April 1	The antislavery movement entered its political phase with meeting in Albany to form the Liberty party; James Gillespie Birney, former Alabama planter and slaveholder, nominated for President.
April 21	Webster addressed the Essex County, Massachusetts, Whig convention.
May 4	Webster and Clay both addressed Whig convention in Baltimore, a gala celebration to ratify the Harrisburg nomination of William Henry Harrison for President and John Tyler, a renegade Democrat, for Vice President.
May 5	Democratic convention convened in Baltimore and renamed Martin Van Buren as candidate for the presidency.
May 10	Webster invited to represent the rebellious slaves of the *Amistad* before the Supreme Court; did not accept.

July 4	Subtreasury bill signed by Van Buren.
July 4	Webster delivered campaign speech at the Barre, Massachusetts, Whig convention.
July 7	Addressed Whig convention on Stratton Mountain, Vermont.
July 8	Delivered campaign address at Bellows Falls, Vermont.
July 9	Addressed Whigs at Keene, New Hampshire.
August 19	Addressed the Saratoga, New York, Whig convention.
August 28	Attended dinner for Caleb Cushing at Salem, Massachusetts.
September 10	Presided at Whig gathering at Bunker Hill; presented Bunker Hill Declaration.
September 22	Campaigned at Patchogue, Long Island.
October 5	Delivered a major campaign address in Richmond, Virginia.
October 20–23	Again campaigned in New Hampshire, addressing Whigs at Francestown and Orford.
November	Harrison and Tyler elected.
December 11	Webster accepted Harrison's invitation to become secretary of state.

1841

February 15	Webster opened negotiations with the Bank of the United States of Pennsylvania for the settlement of his indebtedness of $114,000.
February 22	Webster resigned his Senate seat.
March 4	William Henry Harrison inaugurated.
March 5	Webster unanimously confirmed as secretary of state; assumed duties of office the following day.
March 6	Webster, representing defendant, delivered closing argument before the Supreme Court in *Rhode Island v. Massachusetts*.

March 12	British minister in Washington demanded release of Alexander McLeod, on trial in New York state for murder growing out of the *Caroline* affair.
March 12/ October 12	Webster sought unsuccessfully to persuade Governor Seward of New York to release McLeod.
March 17	Harrison called extra session of Congress for May 31, to consider state of the finances.
April 4	Harrison died.
April 6	Tyler assumed office as President.
April 6	Bank of the United States of Pennsylvania agreed to Webster's proposal for settlement of his account.
April 10	New York *Tribune* began publication, Horace Greeley, editor.
May 31	Congress met in special session to deal with the financial crisis still lingering from 1837.
June 12	Secretary of the Treasury Thomas Ewing, responding to a Senate resolution, submitted a bank bill to Congress.
June 21	Clay reported Ewing's bill, as amended; resembled old BUS.
June 27	Fiscal Bank (Clay's Bill) passed Senate.
July 12	McLeod remanded for trial by New York Supreme Court.
July 21	Treasury Loan authorized.
August 6	Fiscal Bank passed House.
August 13	Subtreasury repealed.
August 16	President Tyler vetoed Clay's bill for a national bank.
August 16	John Minor Botts published his Richmond "Coffee House" letter denouncing Tyler.
August 19	Tyler signed bankruptcy bill into law, a measure Webster strongly supported.
August 20	John Sergeant introduced the fiscal corporation bill before the House of Representatives.

September 4	Tyler signed into law the land (preemption) bill.
September 9	Tyler vetoed a second bank bill, the fiscal corporation measure.
September 10–11	With the exception of Webster, all of Tyler's cabinet resigned.
September 13	Edward Everett confirmed as minister to England.
September 14	Webster published in the *National Intelligencer* his reasons for remaining in the cabinet.
October 4	Rhode Island followers of Thomas Wilson Dorr adopted an unsanctioned constitution.
October 11	Tyler proposed in a letter to Webster the acquisition of Texas by treaty.
October 12	Alexander McLeod acquitted in the New York courts.
November 6	John B. Jones took over the *Washington Madisonian,* converting it into the Tyler organ in Washington.
November 7	Slaves seized coastwise vessel, the *Creole,* and sailed her to Nassau, where they were freed under British law.
November 1841 / August 1842	Webster failed to secure from Great Britain the return of the *Creole* slaves.

1842

January 28	Charles Dickens landed in Boston for three-month visit to the United States.
March 30	Henry Clay resigned his Senate seat.
April 4	Lord Ashburton arrived to commence negotiation of the northeastern boundary; reached Washington on April 5.
April 18	Dorr elected governor of Rhode Island by majority of adult male population, but few were legally qualified to vote.
May 18	Dorr fled Rhode Island when his followers were routed in an attempt to seize an armory.
August 9	Tyler vetoed tariff bill with a distribution clause.

August 9	Negotiations with Lord Ashburton completed; Webster-Ashburton treaty signed.
August 14	The Seminole War ended by General Zachary Taylor.
August 20	The Webster-Ashburton treaty (Treaty of Washington) approved by the Senate.
August 29	Law enacted, drafted by Webster as an outgrowth of the McLeod case, giving federal courts jurisdiction in cases involving aliens charged with crimes committed under authority of a foreign government.
August 30	Passage of tariff bill without distribution clause.
September 30	Reception held for Webster at Faneuil Hall; Webster defended his political conduct.
October 19	Commodore Thomas ap Catesby Jones seized Monterey, California; Webster disavowed incident.
November 30	Violent storm damages Boston harbor and Webster's Marshfield farm.
December 1	Midshipman Philip Spencer, son of Secretary of War John C. Spencer, with two others, hanged for mutiny aboard *USS Somers*.
December 20	Webster closed his correspondence with Lewis Cass on the right of search.
December 30	Presidential message, prepared by Webster, extended the Monroe Doctrine to the Hawaiian Islands and called for commercial relations with China.

1843

February 15	Webster suggested to close friends that he would shortly retire from Department of State.
March 3	Congress passed and President Tyler signed law repealing the bankruptcy act.
March 3	John C. Calhoun resigned his Senate seat.
March 15	George Brown of Massachusetts sent to Hawaii as first United States diplomatic representative.

March 15	New York friends of Tyler held a political meeting in the Tabernacle and renominated him for the Presidency.
March/April	Webster sought advice from close friends about his retirement from the State Department.
May 7	Dorr convicted of treason after collapse of his movement; sentenced to life imprisonment but served only one year.
May 8	Webster issued instructions to Caleb Cushing, U.S. minister to China, which formed the basis of the Treaty of Wanghia of July 3, 1844.
May 8	Webster resigned as secretary of state; Hugh Swinton Legaré appointed to the post ad interim.
May 15	Webster left Washington for retirement at Marshfield, stopping in Baltimore on May 8 to deliver an address.
June 17	Delivered his second Bunker Hill oration.
August 8	Caleb Cushing and Daniel Fletcher Webster, secretary to the mission, sailed for China.
August 23	President Santa Anna of Mexico warned that any attempt to annex Texas would be an act of war.
September 20–21	Webster delivered a major speech at the State Agricultural Fair in Rochester, New York.
December 18	Associate Supreme Court Justice Smith Thompson died.
December 22	Webster delivered an address on the Landing of the Pilgrims before the New England Society of New York.
December	Webster returned to Washington to argue the Girard Will case before the Supreme Court.
December	William Hickling Prescott published his *History of the Conquest of Mexico*.

Abbreviations and Symbols

DESCRIPTIVE SYMBOLS

Abstract	Summary of contents, or a portion thereof, of a letter or document
AD	Autograph Document
AD draft	Autograph Document, draft
ADS	Autograph Document Signed
ADS Copy	Autograph Document Signed, copied by writer
ADS draft	Autograph Document Signed, draft
AL	Autograph Letter
AL draft	Autograph Letter, draft
ALS	Autograph Letter Signed
ALS Copy	Autograph Letter Signed, copied by writer
ALS draft	Autograph Letter Signed, draft
AN	Autograph Note
ANS	Autograph Note Signed
Copy	Copy, not by writer
DS	Document Signed
Extract	Copy of a portion of a letter or document
LC	Letterbook Copy
LS	Letter Signed

LOCATION SYMBOLS

CLU	University of California, Los Angeles
COMC	Mills College, Oakland, Calif.
CSmH	Henry E. Huntington Library, San Marino, Calif.
CaOOA	Public Archives of Canada, Ottawa
CtHi	Connecticut Historical Society, Hartford
CtY	Yale University
DLC	Library of Congress
DNA	National Archives
GHi	Georgia Historical Society, Savannah
H-AR	Public Archives, Honolulu
ICHi	Chicago Historical Society
ICU	University of Chicago

IEN	Northwestern University, Evanston, Ill.
IMunS	Saint Mary of the Lake Seminary, Mundelein, Ill.
Ia-HA	Iowa State Department of History and Archives, Des Moines
InHi	Indiana Historical Society, Indianapolis
InU	Indiana University, Bloomington
KyLo	Louisville Free Public Library, Louisville, Ky.
KyU	University of Kentucky, Lexington
LU	Louisiana State University, Baton Rouge
MAnP	Phillips Academy, Andover, Mass.
MB	Boston Public Library
MBAt	Boston Athenaeum
MBNU	Northeastern University, Boston
MDuHi	Duxbury Historical Society, Duxbury, Mass.
MH	Harvard University
MH-Ar	Harvard University Archives
MH-H	Harvard University, Houghton Library
MHi	Massachusetts Historical Society
MHingHi	Hingham Historical Society, Hingham, Mass.
MNF	Forbes Library, Northampton, Mass.
MSaE	Essex Institute, Salem, Mass.
MWA	American Antiquarian Society, Worcester, Mass.
MWalB	Brandeis University, Waltham, Mass.
MWiW	Williams College, Williamstown, Mass.
MdBP	Enoch Pratt Free Library, George Peabody Branch, Baltimore, Md.
Me	Maine State Library, Augusta
MeB	Bowdoin College, Brunswick, Me.
MeHi	Maine Historical Society, Portland
MePRC	Roman Catholic Diocese of Portland Archives, Portland, Me.
MiAlbC	Albion College, Albion, Mich.
MiD-B	Detroit Public Library, Burton Historical Collection
MiU-C	University of Michigan, William L. Clements Library, Ann Arbor
MnHi	Minnesota Historical Society, St. Paul
MoHi	Missouri State Historical Society, Columbia
N	New York State Library, Albany
NBLiHi	Long Island Historical Society, Brooklyn, N.Y.
NBu	Buffalo and Erie County Public Library, Buffalo, N.Y.
NBuHi	Buffalo and Erie County Historical Society, Buffalo, N.Y.
NCorniCC	Corning Community College, Corning, N.Y.
NEh	East Hampton Public Library, East Hampton, N.Y.
NH	Hamilton Public Library, Hamilton, N.Y.
NHi	New-York Historical Society, New York City

NIC	Cornell University, Ithaca, N.Y.
NN	New York Public Library
NNC	Columbia University
NNPM	Pierpont Morgan Library, New York City
NNU-F	New York University, Fales Collection
NPV	Vassar College, Poughkeepsie, N.Y.
NRU	University of Rochester, Rochester, N.Y.
NTaHi	Historical Society of the Tarrytowns, Tarrytown, N.Y.
NWM	United States Military Academy, West Point, N. Y.
Nc-Ar	North Carolina State Department of Archives and History, Raleigh
NcD	Duke University, Durham, N.C.
NcU	University of North Carolina, Chapel Hill
Ne	Algemeen Rijksarchief, The Hague
Nh	New Hampshire State Library, Concord
NhD	Dartmouth College, Hanover, N.H.
NhExP	Phillips Exeter Academy, Exeter, N.H.
NhHi	New Hampshire Historical Society, Concord
NjMoHP	Morristown National Historical Park
NjP	Princeton University
NjP-Sch	Princeton University, Scheide Library
NmRA	Arthur Johnson Memorial Library, Raton, N.M.
OCHP	Cincinnati Historical Society
OClWHi	Western Reserve Historical Society, Cleveland
OFH	Rutherford B. Hayes Library, Fremont, Ohio
OGK	Kenyon College, Gambier, Ohio
OHi	Ohio Historical Society, Columbus
PCarlD	Dickinson College, Carlisle, Pa.
PHi	Historical Society of Pennsylvania, Philadelphia
PP	Free Library of Philadelphia
PPARA	ARA Historical Foundation, Philadelphia
PPL	Library Company of Philadelphia
PPAmP	American Philosophical Society, Philadelphia
PPiHi	Historical Society of Western Pennsylvania, Pittsburgh
PWbH	Wyoming Historical and Geological Society, Wilkes-Barre
RHi	Rhode Island Historical Society, Providence
RNHi	Newport Historical Society
RNR	Redwood Library and Athenaeum, Newport
ScU	University of South Carolina, Columbia
SpSAG	Archivo General de Indias, Seville
SwSK	Royal Institute of Technology, Stockholm
T	Tennessee State Library and Archives, Nashville
TNF	Fisk University, Nashville

TxGR	Rosenberg Library, Galveston
TxLT	Texas Tech University, Lubbock
TxSjM	San Jacinto Museum of History Association
TxU	University of Texas, Austin
UPB	Brigham Young University, Provo, Utah
Uk	British Library, London
UkBelQU	Queen's University of Belfast
UkLG	Guildhall Library, London
UkLPR	Public Record Office, London
UkLU	University of London
UkOxU-AS	Oxford University, All Souls' College
VeCAL	Archivo del Libertador, Caracas
Vi	Virginia State Library, Richmond
ViHi	Virginia Historical Society, Richmond
ViRVal	Valentine Museum, Richmond
ViU	University of Virginia, Charlottesville
VtHi	Vermont Historical Society, Montpelier
VtMiS	Sheldon Art Museum, Middlebury, Vt.
WHi	State Historical Society of Wisconsin, Madison

SHORT TITLES

Correspondence	Charles M. Wiltse and Harold D. Moser, eds., *The Papers of Daniel Webster: Correspondence*, vols. 1, 2, 4; Wiltse and David G. Allen, eds., vol. 3 (Hanover, 1974, 1976, 1977, 1980).
Curtis	George Ticknor Curtis, *Life of Daniel Webster* (2 vols., New York, 1870).
DNB	*Dictionary of National Biography.*
Diplomatic Papers	Kenneth E. Shewmaker and Kenneth R. Stevens, eds., *The Papers of Daniel Webster: Diplomatic Papers*, 1 (forthcoming).
Fuess, *Cushing*	Claude Moore Fuess, *The Life of Caleb Cushing* (2 vols., New York, 1923).
McGrane, *Correspondence of Nicholas Biddle*	Reginald C. McGrane, ed., *The Correspondence of Nicholas Biddle dealing with National Affairs, 1807–1844* (Boston and New York, 1919).
MHi Proc.	*Proceedings of the Massachusetts Historical Society.*
mDW	Microfilm Edition of the Papers of Daniel Webster (Ann Arbor, 1971). References followed by frame numbers.
mDWs	Microfilm Edition of the Papers of Daniel Webster, Supplementary Reel.
PC	Fletcher Webster, ed., *The Private Correspondence of Daniel Webster* (2 vols., Boston, 1856).
Speeches and Formal Writings	Charles M. Wiltse, ed., *The Papers of Daniel Webster: Speeches and Formal Writings* (2 vols., forthcoming).
Tyler, *Tylers*	Lyon G. Tyler, ed., *Letters and Times of the Tylers* (3 vols., Richmond and Williamsburg, 1884, 1885, 1896).
Van Tyne	Claude H. Van Tyne, ed., *The Letters of Daniel Webster* (New York, 1902).
W & S	James W. McIntyre, ed., *The Writings and Speeches of Daniel Webster* (National Edition, 18 vols., New York, 1903).
Works	Edward Everett, ed., *The Works of Daniel Webster* (6 vols., Boston, 1851).

SERIES ONE: CORRESPONDENCE

VOLUME FIVE: 1840–1843

The Papers, 1840–1843

When he returned from England on December 29, 1839, Webster found that the political scene had changed little since May 18, the day he left the country. He knew at first hand that the nation was still in a deep recession, for he had met with little success in unloading his western lands to English or European investors. The Democratic party, headed by President Van Buren, remained hopelessly split over economic policies. Whigs, on the other hand, appeared to be strongly united. In early December they had met in Harrisburg, Pennsylvania, where they enthusiastically nominated William Henry Harrison for the Presidency and John Tyler for the Vice Presidency.

As revealed in his correspondence below, Senator Webster again played a key role in the planning and execution of the Whig campaign, but he was never able to forget completely his own burdensome financial problems.

FROM ROBERT WICKLIFFE, JR.

Lexington Ky Jan 22nd 1840.

Dear Sir

I congratulate you upon your Safe return to America and trust that ere this you have again taken your seat in the Senate. I take the liberty of sending you by the same Mail with this a Newspaper in which you will find the proceedings of a [William Henry] Harrison Meeting lately held in this City.[1] Having been appointed Chairman of the Committee to draft Resolutions, I took occasion to pay a passing compliment (as you will perceive from the fifth Resolution) to yourself, Mr [Nathaniel Pitcher] Tallmadge Gen [Winfield] Scott &c. Strange to say this mere compliment met with a most violent opposition from one of Mr [Henry] Clay's immediate friends & at his request the Resolutions were referred to the same committee with the addition of two other gentlemen, devoted adherents of Mr Clay. A majority of the Committee instructed me to *strike out* the fifth Resolution. I reported the instruction of the Committee & moved that the House *disagree*. Upon this a warm debate ensued which lasted nearly five hours. The motion to *strike out* was sustained by Gen Leslie Combs & C[assius] M[arcellus] Clay Delegates to the late Harrisburgh Convention, & opposed by R[obert] Nelson Wickliffe, S[amuel?] A. Young (lawyers) Rev Mr [Edward] Winthrop[2] an episcopalian Clergyman & native of New England & Myself. Gen Combs & Mr Clay seemed to think that the meeting would certainly vote down the Resolution, when informed that the personal relations subsisting between Mr Clay & yourself were not of a friendly character & that your influence was thrown at Harrisburgh in favor of Gen Harrison. Notwithstanding this astounding information, I was sustained in my position & the original resolution was passed by an overwhelming majority. The only dissenting voices were from Mr Clay's *relatives & dependants.*

I rejoice that Harrison has received the nomination. It is a great mistake to suppose that Kentucky will yield him a reluctant support. He is my first choice & the first choice of a large & respectable portion of the Whig Party in Ky. He will carry this state by five thousand votes. The old soldiers and comrades are scattered through every corner of the Commonwealth & he has a deep hold upon the affections of this warm-hearted & grateful state.

The small piece of information contained in this letter, I deemed it my duty as a Political & allow me to add, personal friend to give you. If Mrs [Caroline] Webster & Mrs [Julia] Appleton³ are with you in Washington, I would desire to tender them my congratulatory Compliments.

I have the honor to be with sentiments of the highest Regard, yours &c   R Wickliffe Jr

ALS. NhD. Wickliffe (1815–1850; Transylvania College LLB 1837) was a Lexington lawyer, occasional representative in the Kentucky legislature, and chargé d'affaires to Sardinia, 1843–1847.

1. Not found. The Democratic Lexington *Kentucky Gazette*, January 23, 1840, carried an incomplete report on the Fayette County convention of January 19. It did not, however, quote the fifth resolution which Wickliffe discusses.

2. Wickliffe (1805–1855; Transyl-vania College 1822) was a Lexington editor, lawyer, and occasional state legislator. Winthrop (1811–1865; Yale 1831), a native of Connecticut, was an Episcopal clergyman, who in 1842 moved to Ohio. Young (Transyl-vania College LLB 1839) has not been further identified.

3. Caroline Le Roy (1797–1882), whom DW had married on December 12, 1829; and Julia Webster Appleton (1818–1848), his daughter, who had married Samuel Appleton Appleton in London on September 24, 1839.

FROM WILLIAM HENRY HARRISON

Cincinnati 25th Jany 1840

My dear Sir

I congratulate you on your return to your country & upon the honours you received throughout your whole tour. There was one however, which if you received was not publickly announced & which as you are a great admirer of the ladies you must have coveted. I mean that of saluting the fair head of the Young Queen [Victoria]. The lips, I suppose were as much out of the question to you as were those of the daughters of George the III to Doctor [William] Warburton.¹

"Lips that I never kissed & never Shall." I have no doubt that your trip my dear sir will prove advantageous to our Country.

Well! you will have seen that old Massachusetts supported me without wavering from the beginning to the end of the contest at Harrisburgh. It has I am satisfied made a strong impression in Pennsylvania, Ohio & Indiana, & I trust that no one who knows me will think that it was lost upon me.

In relation to the pending contest for the favor of *the Sovereigns* our cause prospers beyond our hopes. There never has been a time when I would not beat V B in Ohio & Indiana. But the majorities will be much larger than they were at the former Election. I have the advantage now, of a general belief that I may be elected. I was voted for before in both States under the general impression that I could not be elected. Illinois is equally safe. Missouri at this time no doubt is adverse to us.

The times are here so hard, as the saying is, that almost every body feels the pressure & no one out of mercantile business more than I do. With a large & valuable property, as much indeed as I want I am so much embarrassed for the want of a few thousand Dollars that I am really unable in consequence of it to perform the duties belonging to the situation in which I have been placed. In the Spring I had a good prospect of clearing myself of debt & making myself comfortable for life. But not foreseeing the difficulties that were approaching I suffered the opportunity for selling a portion of my property to pass without consumating the bargain. I now find that in this country at least there is an impossibility of selling property for money or raising it by mortgage. Under these circumstances I applied to a friend in New York (who having heard of my difficulties was so obliging as [to] propose to me to draw upon him, which I of course declined) either to sell or mortgage a valuable property I have at Vincennes. This gentleman (Alderman [Silas Moore] Stilwell) made an ineffectual attempt to accomplish my wishes of which he has just informed me. Our mutual friend Alderman [Edward] Curtis was made acquainted with the matter & kindly offered his assistance. But as I presume that there is no probability of effecting any thing in New York I ask your opinion, whether I could accomplish my object in Boston.[2] The property which I would sell or Mortgage is at Vincennes Inda. It consists of about 100 lots in an addition to the town which I laid out & upwards of 200 acres of land immediately adjoining the lots. Vincennes has improved the last few years very greatly & promises to become a large & (as it must be from the beauty of its situation) a handsome City. I would not last Spring have taken less than $20,000 for this property. I will now take $15,000. The last sum would clear me of all my difficulties & give me a fund to enable me to go through the expenses of the campaign which from present appearances will amount to much more than I can afford considering that I have four families to maintain besides my own (proper). My office [(] in consequence of the creation of another court with similar jurisdiction in civil cases) has become of so little value that I have given it up entirely to my son in law who performs the duty.[3] I would as lief raise the money I want as above by mortgage. And in either case the payments would answer thus, $5000 within 90 days $5000 at the end of a year & the residue in two years. The money to be repaid at the end of five years but interest not to be *demanded* until the end of the period. If our country should once be again as prosperous as it has been the above property must in a few years become of immense value. I have a Map of it showing its position in relation to the old town, which I will forward if you inform me that there is any chance of succeeding in this negotiation.

I make no appology my dear sir for troubling you with this business as I am convinced it will give you pleasure to assist me if it is in your power. I very rarely come up to this city having my hands full at home in fulfilling contracts made with the Cincinnati & White Water Canal Compy for supplying them with a large quantity of Stone (wood for burning 3 000 000 of bricks) & lime. I continue to work altho I get no money. The compy (which includes the state, it owning half the stock) having stopt payment.[4]

If Mrs Webster is with you present her with my best respects & believe me ever & truly yours   W. H. Harrison

ALS. NjMoHP.

1. (Warburton (1698–1779) was bishop of Gloucester and Alexander Pope's literary executor. In 1754 he became the king's chaplain. *DNB*.

2. Webster's response has not been found. As late as March 11, Jacob Burnet of Cincinnati urged him to

answer Harrison (mDW 16467).

3. Harrison had served as Hamilton County recorder since 1834.

4. The White Water Canal, chartered in 1838 to link Cincinnati and Indianapolis, ran through the Harrison property at North Bend.

FROM HERMAN LE ROY, JR.

New York. Jany 25th. 1840

My dear Sir

I had flattered myself with the hope on your return from Europe, you would have spared me the painfull task, in reminding you with your note, I now hold & past due since Sept. last. At the time it was given, the period of its payment was of your own selection, & under the full conviction it would be punctually paid, I made my financial arrangements. My engagements for the last twelve month's were unusually large, having purchased a house, & in addition the furnishing of the same, & of which I apprized you. In consequence I was compelled to anticipate its payment, by borrowing from a friend, & which I am now called upon to refund. Fully sensible you will at once perceive the very delicate position in which I am placed, & take such immediate steps as will tend to relieve me etc— below is the amt of the same with interest etc to date. I remain yours Respectfully   Herman Le Roy Jr.

1838

Sept	8th Amt note	$2213.90
/39		
D[ebit] [Sept] 8. one years int		154.97
/40		
Jany 25 D[ebit] 4 m[onths] 17 d[a]ys		58.97
		$2427.84

ALS. NhHi. Le Roy (1791–1869) was the fourth child of Herman Le Roy, Sr., and brother of Caroline Le Roy Webster.

TO [GEORGE WALLACE JONES]

Washington Jan. 27. 1840

Dr Sir

I have but just arrived here, & find yr letter of Decr 23rd.[1] I certainly did not expect to be drawn upon, again, for expenses of the [Jordan's] Ferry.[2] You know I have paid heavily already, & I have no accounts, either of the expenditures, or of the receipts, or of the insurance money, which you observed would be recovered for the lost Boats. So frequent & so large disbursements, without any income, are rather discouraging. I am willing, however, to do my part, in providing for all proper & necessary expenditures.

I expect Mr [Nathaniel Ray] Thomas[3] here in a week on his way to the West. He will go prepared to pay at once, on the spot, whatever is justly chargeable to me. Meantime, lest his journey should be delayed, I will thank you to send me a full account, of receipts & charges, respecting the expenses of the ferry, on my part.[4] If Mr Thomas should not proceed to the West, I shall avail myself of your kindness in offering to see to the payment of taxes on my lands. On his arrival here, I shall write you further; in the meantime, I am, D sir, always with much regard Yrs

D. Webster

ALS. Ia–HA.

1. Not found.

2. Jordan's Ferry, of which DW owned one eighth of the stock, operated across the Mississippi River between Iowa and Wisconsin, at Dubuque. See *Correspondence*, 4:210,

219–220. According to Jones's endorsement, the draft was for $1,000.

3. Thomas (1812–1840) was the brother of Charles Henry and had worked at Marshfield. In 1838, Webster had hired him to look after his western investments but was unde-

cided about sending him back. See Nathaniel Ray Thomas to DW, January 20, 1840, mDW 16245; and DW to DFW, February 7, 1840, below.

4. Not found, although Jones's endorsement records that he sent a copy of the account to DW on February 13.

FROM HARMAR DENNY

Pittsburg Jany 31. 1840

Dr Sir

Permit me to congratulate you on your safe return to our country, as I trust in good health, and prepared for again entering into the struggle in behalf of an injured people & an insulted constitution. Our prospects of electing Genl Harrison are highly favorable and brightening every day. My mind is satisfied that we shall carry Penna. for him, unless something which we cannot now anticipate should occur to counteract the movements which are every where being made in his favor among the people. The nomination of Mr [John] Tyler has placed some of your friends in Penna. in rather an embarrassed position. Some of our papers have not yet lowered the Harrison & *Webster* flag, for that of Harrison & Tyler. There was an unwillingness to make this change, particularly during your absence. It is clear that we ought to run but one electoral ticket in Penna. The antimasonic ticket was formed long before the Harrisburg convention. The Penna. delegates to that convention have however adopted Govs. [Joseph] Ritner & [John Andrew] Shulze who were on our ticket, electors at large, & recommended to the people the selection of "electors" in the several districts, & to nominate, or adopt such as have already been nominated. Meetings are in progress through the State with a view to carry out the recommendation made by the delegates to the Harrisburg convention. It is further required that the nominees should pledge themselves to support Harrison & Tyler. Such of us as have been nominated on the electoral ticket by the antimasonic convention if nominated by the friends of the candidates put in nomination at Harrisburg, feel unwilling to give any pledge with regard to Mr Tyler while your name remains before us. As there has been no formal acceptance by you of our nomination, and your friends in Mass: & New England seem disposed to accede to the nomination of Mr Tyler, it is presumed by some that you do not wish to be considered as a candidate. The whigs in this State give their full and active support to Harrison & Tyler. A large portion of the antimasons has also gone into the same measure. The party in its organic form of course adheres to its own nomination. But we cannot have in the field two electoral tickets opposed to the Van Buren ticket. This would be defeat. We are to have a meeting here on the 11 Feby. It is important for us to know something of your views relative to the nomination for V. P. made by the antimasonic convention, Whether it is your desire that we should adhere to it. I have been spoken to by a commee. & asked to attend the meeting & preside at it; it is also I understand contemplated to place my name on the electoral ticket, it being already on the antimasonic electoral ticket. I may attend the meeting but I cannot consent to be placed on the electoral ticket under a pledge to vote for Mr Tyler, under present circumstances, & thus abandon my own choice & that of the antimasonic party without communicating with you on the subject. Will there be any other nomination for V.P. made in northern States? Will they concur in that made at Harrisburg?

Please favor me with an early answer to be made public if you think proper, at our meeting on 11 Feby.[1] Yours Sincerely   Harmar Denny

ALS. DLC.
    1. DW's response has not been found.

TO JAMES WATSON WEBB   Washington Feb. 1. 1840

Dear Sir

I have recd yr letter; & perhaps it will be sufficient, for the present, to acknowledge, in this way, an early communication of your purposes & wishes to me. In such matters, I shall doubtless act with other friends.[1]

You see what little progress is made in public business in the H. of R. In the Senate, Mr [Felix] Grundy's Resolutions, or more properly his Report, on Mr [Thomas Hart] Benton's resolutions, has created an unexpected Debate.[2] There is either among these Gentlemen a great ignorance of the effect of such things on the credit of the States, or else, which it is rather uncharitable to suppose, a willingness to shake and injure that credit.

Our friends here are receiving daily confirmation of their belief that Genl Harrison will be elected President. Yrs truly   Danl Webster

ALS. CtY.
    1. See Webb to DW, January 30, 1840, mDW 16293. Webb had asked for the appointment of postmaster of New York City should Harrison be elected President.
    2. On December 29, 1839, Benton had introduced six resolutions against federal assumption of state debts, which had been referred to a select committee headed by Grundy. When

Grundy reported against assumption, a long and heated debate ensued. Webster spoke against the resolutions but did not vote on March 6, when they overwhelmingly passed the Senate. *Congressional Globe*, 26th Cong., 1st sess., pp. 82–83, 244–245, Appendix, pp. 210–212; *Senate Documents*, 26th Cong., 1st sess., Serial 357, Document No. 153.

TO DANIEL FLETCHER WEBSTER

                        Washington Feb. 7. 1840

My Dear Son

The conveyance to Messrs [Richard Milford] Blatchford & [Samuel

Bulkley] Ruggles was for a temporary purpose, merely, & I rather supposed they would not record it.[1] They had a right, however, to do so, if they chose. I can, at any time, obtain releases to any part, which is necessary to be released; or, if quite important, can obtain a reconveyance of the whole by the first of May. I have concluded, since the receipt of your next preceding letter,[2] that it is best for [Nathaniel] Ray [Thomas] to go to Peru. As soon as we hear of the opening of the Rivers, and he can get over the mountains, we will get him off. I must leave these land affairs to you & him, it being impossible for me to know enough about them to attend to them. When must the mortgage on White Hall be paid?[3]

All money matters on this side of the Allegheny are as bad as possible. Political affairs look encouragingly. Genl. Harrison will be President, if he lives.

Give my love to Caroline.[4] Yr mother (who will be here in a few days) is very anxious to hear from her. Yrs affectionately   Danl Webster

ALS. NhD. Daniel Fletcher (1813–1862; Harvard 1833) was DW's oldest son, living at this time on DW's Salisbury, Illinois, farm and practicing law.

1. In raising funds for his trip to England in May 1839, DW had conveyed much of his land in Wisconsin, Illinois, Indiana, Ohio, and Michigan to Blatchford and Ruggles to cover their loan of $28,000. See *Correspondence*, 4:346, 352–353, 361–362. Shortly before Webster arrived back in the United States, they had recorded some of the transfers. See, for example, deed transferring property in St. Clair County, Michigan, from DW to Blatchford and Ruggles, December 13, 1839, Deed Book K: 290–291, Office of the Register of Deeds, St. Clair County, Port Huron, Michigan, mDWs.

2. Probably DFW to DW, January 20, 1840, mDW 16249.

3. White Hall, which DW had purchased in May 1838, lay adjacent to his Salisbury farm.

4. Caroline Story White Webster (1811–1866), daughter of Stephen and Harriet White, whom Daniel Fletcher had married on November 27, 1836.

TO NICHOLAS BIDDLE

Feb. 9. [1840]

My Dr Sir,

I know no reason to expect any difficulty, of a serious nature, with England, about the Boundary Question. It is thought the Administration people wish to divert public attention from other things, by giving out hints of trouble to be expected in that quarter.[1] At the same time, I do not think the controversy will be likely to be soon finally settled. I think it is managed on both sides as badly as possible. Two men of sense, with the map before them could sit down in London or Washington, and agree on a line, in an hour, that would well enough suit the convenience of both parties. All these ex parte surveys—projects, & contre projects for explorations &c &c, are foolish measures, protracting the dispute, & not in the end likely, by themselves, to terminate it. But I say again, & "tell true"—that there is not, to my knowledge, any ground at present for apprehension.

Gov. [David Rittenhouse] Porter's conduct has done infinite good here. It gives confidence & courage to good men, & has thrown locofocoism quite aback.[2] I begin to recover my respect for Penna. Yrs   Danl Webster

ALS. DLC.

1. Both Maine and New Brunswick forces had continued to make incursions into the disputed territory and some expected another "Aroostook War."

2. In his recent message to the Pennsylvania legislature, Porter had recommended that the legislature support the state's banks and honor, not repudiate, its state debts. *Niles' National Register*, 57 (January 25, 1840): 340–342.

TO CAROLINE LE ROY WEBSTER

Washington, Feb. 9. 1840

My Dear wife

I recd your letter last Evening, & am glad you are all well, but am getting quite impatient to have you come along. I have told every body you would be here *this* week; and I hope you will not stay beyond the *first* of next, unless it be quite necessary.[1] I am paying here, I presume, just as much as if you were here—& as soon as the cause, on account of which you staid, will allow you to come, I hope you will be under way. The weather has much changed. These rains may derange the Rail Roads, perhaps, for a short time, but I think in a week the conveyance will be good. I trust we shall [have] no more of such severe weather.

My cold is better. I went to a party at Mrs [John] Bells,[2] for ten minutes, friday Evening. It was an agreeable party, but the rooms were very full. They occupy the rooms which the poor Commodore [Isaac Chauncey] occupied, & for this occasion, used the other rooms, which Mr [William Campbell] Preston's family occupy.

I have written a letter of condolence to Mrs [Isaac] Chauncey,[3] & one of congratulations to Mrs Mary Anne McEvers Taylor.[4]

I enclose herewith a letter from Mrs. [Margaretta?] Addicks.[5]

Judge [Joseph] Story, who is quite well, is coming in to take a plate with us today at 3 oclock.

I have several cases in Court yet, which occupy my attention.[6]

If I can get a Post Office Book, I will send it to Mr [David Samuel] Jones,[7] without delay. With love to all abt. you, Yrs truly

Danl Webster (over)

I have heard nothing lately of poor Mr [Isaac P.] Davis.[8] Mr [Stephen] White,[9] now at Buffalo, writes me, that he is getting better still. Yrs

D.W.

ALS. NhHi.

1. Letter not found. The exact reasons for Caroline's delay in joining DW at Washington are somewhat unclear. For one thing, her father, Herman Le Roy was sick. There is some evidence also that Caroline may have been ill. On February 24, DW again implored her to hasten to Washington. ". . . I am at a loss," he wrote, "to find out what you really wish, & to understand your reasons. I am afraid either that the *operation* has not been so successful as you expected, or that it requires more time than you expected to get over it properly. If this be the case, then you are right to stay. But if you *are well*, & really mean to come to Washington at all, I think you [ought] to come at once" (mDW 16381). See also DW to Caroline Le Roy Webster, March 4, 7, 1840, below.

2. Mrs. Bell, née Jane Ervin Yeatman, whom Representative John Bell of Tennessee had married in 1835.

3. Mrs. Chauncey, née Catherine Sickles of New York, who had been widowed on January 27, 1840. Letter not found.

4. Probably the daughter of Charles McEvers, prominent New York businessman and partner in the house of Le Roy, Bayard and McEvers. Letter not found.

5. Mrs. Addicks (1822?–1898), wife of John Addicks, Philadelphia politician. Letter not found.

6. During the January 1840 term of the Supreme Court, DW argued six cases. The arguments had been completed only in *Carr* v. *Duval*, 14 Peters 77; and *Rhode Island* v. *Massachusetts*, 14 Peters 210. Remaining to be argued as of February 9 were *Lattimer* v. *Poteet*, 14 Peters 4; *Peters* v. *Warren Insurance Co.*, 14 Peters 99; *Sprigg* v. *Bank of Mt. Pleasant*, 14 Peters 201; and *Lessee of Pollard's Heirs* v. *Kibbe*, 14 Peters 353.

7. Jones (1778–1848; Columbia 1796) had served on the New York City Council (1813–1816) and was at this time county judge of Queens County and a trustee of Columbia College. In 1827 he had married Susan LeRoy, Caroline's sister.

8. Davis (1771–1855) was a Boston manufacturer and businessman. In 1841, through DW's influence as secretary of state, Davis received an appointment as naval officer of Boston, a post he held until 1845.

9. White (1787–1841), Boston merchant, was a long-time Webster friend and financial backer, and father-in-law of Fletcher Webster.

TO CAROLINE LE ROY WEBSTER

Wednesday Eve'
Feb. 12 [1840]

My Dear wife

I recd yr letter,[1] night before last, giving the awful account of poor Mrs [Charles] M[arch]'s conduct.[2] It has made my heart bleed. I have regarded her as an excellent religious woman. She was with our family, in times of affliction, & I had the most grateful & respectful feelings towards her. And her husband—poor Mr [Charles] March[3]—what will he do. He & I were young men together. Our fathers were friends. We were fellow lodgers, at the commencement of life, & have been friends ever since. Many, many years ago, he introduced me to the first circle of NY friends, which I ever had; Mr [Archibald] Gracie, Mr [Robert] Lenox, D[avid] B[ayard] Ogden, John Welles, Sam[ue]l Boyd,[4] &c. &c. I declare

I have had no happiness, since I recd yr letter. The only consolation is, the woman must be crazy. She cannot be so wicked as to do such things in her right mind. Poor Mr M, I fear, will go crazy himself.

I have been busy all day, in preparing some written arguments for the Court, & in passing two or three hours in the Senate. Nothing of importance in the political world has occurred since I wrote you last. Mr [Ogden] Hoffman is said to have made a very good speech today, on some subject, in H. of R.[5] His reputation is fast rising, in Congress. You know he has a son. I have not seen Mrs H.[6]

Night before last, Mr & Mrs [Edward] Curtis[7] went to a party at Mrs [Benjamin] O[gle] Tayloes.[8] Tonight, there is an assembly, which they also attend. Tomorrow Eve', a party at Mr [John] Forsyth's, & very soon another at Mrs Clement Hills.[9] I attend none of them.

I have sent Mr [David Samuel] Jones a P. office Book. My news from Boston is not very fresh, but I had a letter from Julia some days ago. She says Mr [Isaac P.] Davis was rather better.

It is now the middle of Feby, & in six weeks I shall be making a visit to Boston. Pray remember that, & come along as soon as you can. I hope this milder weather is favorable to your father. Pray give my love to him. I do not expect him to take the trouble of answering my letters; but if any thing important occurs, I will write him again soon.

If our friends, the Messrs Whites,[10] have at last reaped the fruits of their conduct, in supporting the outrageous policy of Genl [Andrew] Jackson, in regard to money matters, I shall not be so unchristian as to rejoice in their misfortunes, but I shall pray that this discipline may tend to their improvement, & edification. Adieu!, Yrs always, (with a rascally steel pen)   Danl Webster

ALS. NhHi. Published in Van Tyne, pp. 743–744.

1. Not found.

2. According to Philip Hone, it had been discovered that Mrs. March was a kleptomaniac. Entry of February 25, 1842, Philip Hone Diary, NHi.

3. March (1781–1855), formerly of Greenland, New Hampshire, was a merchant in New York City. While a student at Phillips Exeter Academy, Webster had probably boarded with the March family.

4. Gracie (1755–1829) was a prominent New York merchant and banker; Lenox (1759–1839), a native of Scotland, was a real estate developer and merchant. Welles was most like-ly also a New York merchant; and Boyd (d. c. 1839; Columbia 1787) was one of the "professional rich" of New York City, a trustee of Columbia College, 1826–1835.

5. Noted for his eloquence, Hoffman had spoken for nearly an hour on the manner in which the Cumberland Road appropriations bill had been brought before the House. *Congressional Globe*, 26th Cong., 1st sess., p. 186.

6. Virginia E. Southard, daughter of Samuel L.

7. Mrs. Curtis (d. 1873), née Mary Cramer, daughter of John Cramer.

8. Mrs. Tayloe (1799–1846), née Julia Maria Dickinson, noted for her

hospitality in Washington.

9. Mrs. Hill, née Sarah Ann Parker.

10. The Whites—Robert, cashier and president of the Manhattan Bank, and Campbell Patrick, congressman and former director of the New York branch of the Bank of the United

States—had supported Jackson's anti-Bank policies. At this time the Manhattan Bank was in serious financial difficulty and under investigation by the state banking committee.

TO EDWARD CURTIS

Senate Chamber, Feb. 17. 1840

My Dear Sir,

I enclose an article,[1] which I perceive is going the round of publication in the Administration papers of the North, & to which my attention has been called by letters from various sources,[2] in that quarter.

I have not the slightest recollection of ever having made these remarks, respecting Genl. Harrison, or any others of similar import; nor was it proposed to me, so far as I remember, in 1835, to be placed on the same ticket with him.[3]

I have known Genl. Harrison for nearly twenty five years, & our relations, during that period, both political & personal, have been of the most friendly kind, and I give him my cordial support for the Office, for which he is now a Candidate.

If you think it necessary that any notice should be taken of the article in question, I will be obliged to you to adopt such a course, for that purpose, as you may think proper. I am, Dear Sir, Yrs truly   Danl Webster

ALS. NhD.

1. The article, circulated in administration newspapers, reported: "Mr. Webster, when asked in 1835, if he would be placed on the same ticket with Gen. Harrison, replied, 'I cannot be *guilty* of any act that shall, in the remotest degree, tend to the elevation of a man to the Presidency who is *justly the scorn and ridicule of his foes,* and the *pity and contempt of*

his friends.' " As above, DW denied the statement. *National Intelligencer,* February 22, 1840.

2. See, for example, John Plummer Healy to DW, February 11, 1840, mDW 16334.

3. While there was some talk of a Harrison-Webster ticket for 1836, DW and his backers rather favored a Webster-Harrison ticket. See *Correspondence,* 4: 48.

Webster's speculation in the Clamorgan grant (see Correspondence *4: 220–222) remained a source of embarrassment to him throughout the 1840s. He still owed a considerable sum to Ramsay Crooks, Pierre Chouteau's agent in New York. The grant had not yet been confirmed, but Webster nevertheless had used his stock in the Clamorgan Land Association as collateral for other loans. He had failed while in England to sell his stock, and Virgil Maxcy, his agent, was only now beginning to realize success. In the letters below, Webster tried to establish terms for paying his Clamorgan debts with John F. A. Sanford, a native of Virginia and Chouteau's son-in-law, who served as agent-at-large for the interests of the company.*

TO JOHN F. A. SANFORD

> Miss Polks
> 4 oClock
> Saturday
> [February 22, 1840]

My Dear Sir

I am exceedingly sorry not to have seen you, & have endeavored several times to find you.

What I propose is this—Mr. Maxcy has taken stock to Europe to sell, & left with me an acknowledgment to pay proceeds *to my order*, written on his obligation. He is to make return by first day of April.

I will leave this obligation with Mr Crooks, with an order to pay him so much thereof as shall discharge the balance of my note. If the property returns unsold, I will give a new note, for the aforesaid balance, & interest, at 6 m[onth]s, with securities to be approved by Mr Crooks.

If this meets your views, you may communicate this to Mr Crooks, or Mr Choteau.

If any modification occur to you I will see you this Eve', at your lodgings or mine, at any hour agreeable to you. Yrs very respectfully

> Danl Webster

ALS. NHi.

TO JOHN F. A. SANFORD

> Miss Polks
> Saturday Eve'
> 6 oclock
> [February 22, 1840]

My Dear Sir,

What I mean by "Security," is, bills of Exchange, or Promissory notes, with such names, in addition to my own, as shall be entirely satisfactory to Mr Crooks; & the paper to be payable at Bank[?]. Yrs truly

> Danl Webster

ALS. NHi.

FROM SAMUEL APPLETON APPLETON

> Boston February 29th 1840

My Dear Sir

It is some time since I have had the pleasure of writing to you, but as nothing of the least importance has transpired, I thought I would not trespass so much on your time, as to make you read a letter with nought in it. Business continues dull, and I am afraid will keep so. Men seem disheartened, & afraid, but good may come out of it. Harrison will be elected by it, & then I trust we shall see brighter days. The Legislature have nominated [Edward] Everett again to be Governor, but I hope, as is expected, he will decline. Then John Davis [1787–1854] will be put up, & Massachusetts will give 15,000 Harrison majority in November. We could elect Everett, but it would be up hill work. He has not any popularity, and we cannot afford with the blot on our Escutcheon to risk anything. Live's of Harrison are plenty, & quite the rage. It is strange how little it takes to make a Hero. [Winfield] Scott I presume will take Harrisons Mantle when he throws it off, & then the most deserving of the Cuba Bloodhounds will stand a chance. We expect to get into our House on Monday. Nancy[1] is in there now & presides over the Culinary department with her usual dignity, & I think she can make you as good a Chowder as formerly. Julia has made sundry Forays into your goods & chattels, & what she has left, look very much as Napoleon's Troops did on their retreat from Russia.

My Uncle Nathan [Appleton] has just presented Julia, with a handsome new Piano, so it will be our own fault if we do not have melody in the House. We are anxiously waiting for the arrival of the Switzerland from Havre. She sailed the 10th of January, & brings our China, Clocks &ct. I think she must be off Cape De Gatt[a]. If you have noticed the late passages from Europe, you will perceive that ours was a good one, much better than any since. Had we waited to come back in the [British] Queen, we should have been in a bad way. We were quite fortunate. Do you ever sigh for the cabin of the Mediator. It appears all to me now like a dream. My lot of Dogs increase in size daily, and will move with us. John [Benjamin] Joy[2] was satisfied with your arrangements for him, and with the one I give him, will have quite a pack. Mr. & Mrs [Robert J.] Mackintosh[3] have not yet arrived, but are daily expected, by the way of Pittsfield. Mrs Nathan [Appleton] is getting along well, & her son is said to be quite a remarkable child, and the image of Papa.[4]

This has been quite a gay week here, Partys every night, & we have been to most all of them. Mr [Samuel Turell?] Armstrong gave a large one, no dancing as he has scruples. The [Benjamin William] Crowninshield's gave one for their Son who married Miss [Caroline] Welch.[5] To look at their Supper Table, you would not have dreamt of hard times. The more I see since my return, the more convinced I am that we spend too much on our suppers, & live in too large Houses.

We have been expecting to hear from Edward [Webster][6] every day. A Havre packet is just in but no letters. Julia writes him by the Packet of the 1st of March. The Switzerland may possibly bring some as she comes direct. He must speak French like a native though I do not believe he has forgot Marshfield.

Julia received a letter from Mrs Webster who speaks of her joining you in Washington as very uncertain. If you are coming here in April it would hardly be worth while.

Julia & myself unite, my dear Sir, in sending our best love, & hope you will not forget you have a home at No. 8 Lincoln Street, & as hearty a welcome I am sure as you can get any where's. Believe Yours most affectionately,   Saml A. Appleton

ALS. MHi. Appleton (1811–1861), the son of Eben Appleton and a business partner of James W. Paige and his uncle, Nathan Appleton, was DW's son-in-law. He had married Julia in London on September 24, 1839.

1. Probably the Appleton's cook.

2. Joy (1814–1864) was Stephen White's son-in-law.

3. Mackintosh was a British diplomat who had married Mary Appleton (1813–1889), daughter of Nathan,

on December 25, 1839.

4. The second Mrs. Appleton (1802–1867), née Harriet Coffin Sumner, had given birth to William Sumner Appleton on January 11, 1840.

5. Caroline Welch had married Edward Augustus Crowninshield (1817–1859).

6. Edward (1820–1848; Dartmouth 1841), Daniel's youngest son, who had remained in Europe.

TO CAROLINE LE ROY WEBSTER

Mar. 4. 1840

My Dear Wife

What in the world has become of you. I am really out of all patience, & full of anxiety. If you are sick, why do not friends write? If you are well, why do you not write yourself. It is now ten days since I have heard from you, except by [way] of a scrap,[1] enclosing a letter from Fletcher, but taking no notice of my recent letters to you. Something I am sure, must be the matter. I hasten this off tonight to the cars, to *conjure you* to let me know what has become of you. Yours affectionately

Danl Webster

ALS. NhHi.

1. Not found.

TO CHARLES HENRY THOMAS

Mar. 5. '40

Dear Henry,

I have been so busy that farming is driven out of my head. I hardly know where to begin to talk about it. But I must say something.

1. As to the fat oxen, let them be sold, as soon as may be.

2. As to the land in front of the House, you say we settled to put that all

down to grass, manuring it well. I forget how this was, but if we so settled, so let it be.

3. We will not lay out for much corn.
4. I wrote something about the little piece on Cherry Hill—I forget what—let that be as I wrote.
5. *Where are we to have turnips.* We must [plant?] some acres, & we must manage manure accordingly. I had thought of using for this purpose the land round [Seth] Weston's[1] barn. I think it likely I may receive 3 or 4 more English Sheep—Leicesters—finally intended for Illinois—but which I shall probably keep one year at Marshfield. At any rate, we must try some sheep, on turnips. Near Weston's barn they will be in sight, & easily taken care of. Perhaps a part of this, however, being well limed may go to wheat. I hope the ploughs are already in the ground—let the wheat go in as soon as possible.

p.s. I have been looking & thinking a little, since I wrote the above. You know, we must try some of our English seeds.

1. Rye grass. This should be sown as early as possible—for sheep & cattle, during summer, if pastures fail—to be cut up & eaten green.
2. Spring vetches. These we must try some of, for same purpose.
3. English field bean. These we must try some of, on the strongest clayey ground we have—well manured.

Now, where shall we find manure for all these things—turnips & all— if we cover over the whole land in front of the House, & lay it down to grass.

Had we not better keep a part of the front lot still up?

How would it do to have turnips, carrots, & beets, in front of the House—also a strip of Rye Grass—also a strip of Spring Vetches? These last to be small strips, only 3 or 4 rods wide, as they are experiments only?

As to the field back of the belt—I do not care much what is done with it—but I think it hardly worth while to lay it down to grass. Suppose you sow some rye, & some oats, & manure the north End, where the clayey part is, & put in the beans.

The season is forward, & if we can get these English things in early, I hope some of them will do well.

You must write up for Mr [Timothy] F[letcher][2] to send down what seeds you need, immediately.

If we keep up the land in front of the House, for turnips &c.—it is a good idea to lime the land round Weston's barn, & sow wheat.

I will try to write you again in a day or two. Meantime, use your own discretion a good deal. We must try to do something handsome with these English seeds. Yrs   D.W.

ALS. MHi. Thomas (1807–1894), elder brother of Nathaniel Ray Thomas, was the son of John Thomas (1764–1837), from whom Webster had purchased Marshfield. From 1832 until his death, DW relied upon Henry to manage the property.

1. Weston (1804–1876), a resident of Marshfield, was a carpenter, often employed by DW and Thomas at the Marshfield farm.

2. Fletcher (1774–1842), who also assisted with the Marshfield farm, was a brother of the first Mrs. Webster.

TO CAROLINE LE ROY WEBSTER

Saturday Eve
Mar. 7. [1840]
10 oclock

My Dear Wife,

I have just recd a letter from you, dated Mar. 4. at Morrisiana[1]—in which you speak of a former letter—but which letter *I have not recd.* You say not one word about coming here, or not coming here; & if you had wished to mortify me, you could not have taken a better course. I care nothing of the things about which you write. *Are you coming here, or are you not?*

My Dear Wife, what possesses you, to act as you do? Why do you do not tell me what you mean? I am disappointed—ashamed—mortified. For Heaven's sake, tell me what you mean. I say to every body, that I am looking for you, every day. *This must be explained.* Yrs   D. Webster

ALS. NhHi.
1. Not found. Morrisiana was the home of Caroline's niece, Hannah Newbold Morris.

FROM CHARLES AUGUSTUS DAVIS

New York 7 March 1840.

Dr Sir,

Should the time come round—showing as in times past that a national Bank wd. be the least of Evils, to resort to, I don't know any public man who could carry as much weight as yourself in parting out a system that wd. not only work well in itself but meet the concurrence of our people at large. I am quite sure myself, that unless we do resort to an *organization* of our *Credit power*, we shall gradually go back to a colonial condition. I am the more impress'd with this conviction not only by all I see about me but also by the general aspect of things in Europe as they come to us now by the "Grt. Western" Steamer. There are two distinct interests at work in Europe—One entirely *national* there & the other measureably identified with us. What may suit the Chancellor of the Exchqr. for *Govt. purposes,* may be totally at war with our trading interest—& unless this distinction is drawn, the *advices* from Europe may seriously mislead us all. England *as a Govt.,* is driven into the necessity of crushing our *Credit*, because if our Credit prevail, hers meets a formidable competition—just so it is with Buttons, & Calicoes. Now if she c'd induce our people to abandon the making of the latter or manage to depreciate them it wd be of course a great gain to her. [Thomas] Spring Rice[1] you remember tried to fund £ 3,000,000. & could not do it—but Mr. [Francis Thornhill] Baring[2] his successor, after our Credit got a stab[?], funded £12,000,000. So it was a matter of life & death with the Govt. If we don't organize our *Credit* power, John Bull runs us off the track—hence nothing delights the Chancellor of Exchqr. more than our scheme of Sub: Treasury,—hard currency, &c.—to be sure it crushes Cotton, but what does he care for that.

The Trading Classes who are our friends being part & parcel of us, see the effect & lament it. They tell us that the measures of our Govt. will compel us to sell cotton for *a song*—& they will pay but *a song* for it.

Where does the blame rest?—is it not in us in permitting Powers that be thus to crush us—& cui bono? I am induced simply in writing you this scratch to call yr. notice to what has bothered me frequently in "news from England"—that unless we draw a line of distinction between what suits the *British Govt.* & what suits the People there—we are all in the wind—the former is their Concern, the latter *Ours*. Yr. serv.

Ch. Aug. Davis

ALS. NhHi. Davis (1795–1867) was a New York merchant and political writer. His Jack Downing letters had been printed in the *New York Daily Advertiser.*

1. Spring Rice, Baron Monteagle (1790–1866) was chancellor of the exchequer in Melbourne's second ad- ministration (1835–1839). *DNB.*

2. Baring, Baron Northbrook (1796–1866) had served as lord of the treasury (1830–1834) and joint secretary (1834, 1835–1839) before he became chancellor of the exchequer (1839–1841). *DNB.*

FROM HENRY H. ELLIOTT

New York March 7. 1840

Dr Sir

We are *all* looking with some anxiety, some for one reason & some for others, upon the movements in Congress upon the subject of a Bankrupt Law. I believe that all classes of men here, both creditors & debtors, are satisfied that nothing else will give us freedom; that without such a law, the whole country will continue to struggle like a chained giant, and there is no weighing or measuring the trials & sufferings that will fall upon families here, & I think thru' the whole country, unless some general relief comes, in this form or some other.

In what other form it may come, or *can* come, I cannot anticipate. I think it is *too late* to attempt to *restore*. We must create anew.

Will you favor me with your opinion upon the probability of getting such a law through this session?[1] Yours with great respect

Henry H. Elliott

ALS. NhHi. Elliott, a native of Guilford, Connecticut, was a merchant in New York City.

1. DW's response has not been found. He had long taken an interest in national bankruptcy legislation, and on August 19, 1841, an act "to establish a uniform system of bankruptcy throughout the United States" passed, but Congress repealed it on March 3, 1843. 5 *United States Statutes at Large* 440–449.

TO [ROBERT CHARLES WINTHROP]

Washington Mar. 14. 1840

Dear Sir

I forward with pleasure your communication to Genl. H[arrison].[1]

Well; if the people will have John Davis for Govr. it must be so. I presume he would accept the nomination. His loss, however, will be great to the Senate.

I shall write you in a day or two, on a very important matter, quite *confidentially*. It requires something to be done, which 5 young men, of some means, and who hope to live a good while, and desire to see things go well, *can do.*[2]

I will tell you, shortly, what it is. Yrs   D Webster

ALS. MHi.
1. Not found.
2. DW's follow-up letter has not been found. Most likely he sought Winthrop's assistance in raising money for the Whig campaign.

TO CAROLINE LE ROY WEBSTER

Sunday Eve
9 o clock
[March 22, 1840]

My Dear Wife,

I have just recd your letter, written partly on friday, & partly yesterday.[1] I see that it fell to you, to announce Rays death[2] to [Charles] Henry [Thomas]; & I am quite sure you did it, as well as such a mournful duty could be done. But I am surprised not to hear of your having seen Mr *Haight*.[3] I supposed he would be in N. York on friday Evening. At any rate, I suppose he must have met with Henry, as nothing has been heard of Henry here. Perhaps he had returned, Eastward, before Mr. Haight reached N. York. I have no letter from him, since he left Duxbury.

My health is getting better. Yesterday & today I have been on horseback—a practice which I must follow, as I need exercise very much.

As to the pamphlet, written in N. Y. in reply to my letter to Messrs

Barings, I care nothing about it.[4] Copies have been sent to me, which I do not take the trouble to read. I only regret that such disorganizing & miserable doctrines, should find readers. The tendency of the times is to the lowest radicalism. The war, is agt. property, & industry, & good character, by the needy, the lazy, & the vicious. That is the whole truth of the matter.

We have nothing of interest here, since I wrote you last. Mr [Abbott] Lawrence's family are believed all to be getting better, though I am still anxious about him. Yesterday I breakfasted with Dr. [Harvey] Lyndsley[5] Harriet [Colby Webster][6] is not very well. She has a fever, but I hope not dangerous. For Mr Lawrence, I *do* feel great concern. Yrs affectionately
D. Webster.

ALS. NhHi.

1. Not found.

2. Nathaniel Ray Thomas had died at Brown's Hotel in Washington, D.C., on March 18, 1840.

3. Either Stephen Haight (1784–1841), a native of Vermont and former sergeant-at-arms of the United States Senate, or his son, John T. (1813–1853), a lawyer, surveyor, and land agent who looked after much of DW's land interests in Wisconsin, where he resided.

4. For DW's letter to Baring Brothers & Co., October 16, 1839, see *Correspondence* 4: 404–407. In a pamphlet entitled *Reply to Daniel Webster. A Letter to Daniel Webster in Reply to his Legal Opinion to Baring Brothers and Co. upon the Illegality and Unconstitutionality of State Bonds and Loans of State Credit* (New

York, 1840), "Junius" challenged DW's conclusion as to the power of states to contract debts abroad. The authorship of this Junius pamphlet has generally been attributed to Calvin Colton, but Joshua Bates believed that Charles Jared Ingersoll of Philadelphia wrote it. See Joshua Bates to DW, April [26], 1840, below.

5. Lindsly (1804–1889) was a prominent Washington physician and longtime friend with whom DW occasionally boarded. His wife was Emeline Colby Webster (1808–1892), whom DW generally referred to as "My Dear Cousin." There is, however, no evidence that Emeline and DW were related.

6. Harriet Webster (1818–1896) was Emeline's sister. In 1841 she married the Reverend Peter Parker, missionary to China.

TO NATHANIEL F. WILLIAMS

Washington Mar. 24. '40
My Dear Sir,

I thank you for the No. of the Log Cabin Advocate.[1] It is a paper of good appearance, & its contents well written, or well selected. I wish it circulation & success.

I verily believe, My Dear Sir, that a political revolution is in progress. It seems to me the evidences are plain that Genl Harrison will be elected President, if he live to see Novr. No man can rejoice in this prospect more than I do; for I think the preservation of interests, most valuable to the Country, entirely depend upon it. There is a very bad & reckless spirit abroad; a spirit of disorganization, of hostility to property, of disregard to engagements & contracts; & a spirit quite too indifferent to the obligations of morality & religion.

So far as this is political, a reformed & honest Government would tend to correct it. Our Government, like all other popular Governments, produces a great effect upon the opinions, & modes of thinking of men, by its example & its influence. A honest, upright, Free Govt. is among the greatest of human blessings. I really hope, that we are about to see some stay put, to the rage of party, & a return to the doctrines & the feelings of *honest politics*, and true patriotism.

Is there any thing I can send to you? You have been in the habit, sometimes, of reading my Speeches, when I make any; but at present I do not trouble my friends in that way. We have had a world of *discussion*; the time for *action* among the People has, I think, arrived. Yours always truly

D. Webster

ALS. NhD. Williams (1780–1864) was a Baltimore merchant and lifelong supporter of DW. In 1841, through DW's influence, President Tyler appointed Williams collector of customs for the Port of Baltimore, and in 1851, again through Webster's influence, President Millard Fillmore appointed him appraiser for the same port.

1. *The Log Cabin Advocate* was a Whig campaign newspaper published in Baltimore, March 21–December 15, 1840.

TO JOSHUA BATES

Washington Mar. 26: '40

My Dear Sir

I must not omit writing you by the B[ritish] Q[ueen]—and as I have a half hour's leisure this morning, I may as well enjoy that pleasure now, as to postpone it to a period, nearer to her departure, since you will have all the news from other sources. We arrived, safe & well, in the Mediator, after a voyage of 35 days, the latter part of it rough, & the approach to the land a little difficult from thick weather. Mrs Webster is in N.Y., Mrs [Harriet Story White] Paige[1] & Julia in Boston; & I am here, doing nothing, and among others who do nothing, of any use or importance, in these sad times. The Sub-Treasury Bill will probably get thro, & become a law,[2] incapable, however, of producing much effect, any way, & powerless, altogether, over the real evils which so much afflict us. We shall also authorise the issue of some five or ten millions of Treasury notes, bearing interest for a year, not exceeding 6 percent, but redeemable at a shorter period, on two months notice. These notes will absorb, *protanto*, the unemployed money, in the Cities, which has been kept out of use, from fear. Some of us much prefer a loan, in the common mode, which would bring the money from your side; but the Govt is quite afraid of doing, what they call beginning another National debt, in time of peace. The issuing of T. notes, bearing interest at 6 percent, they do not allow to be *borrowing money*. So much for humbug.

Our revenue, both from imports & land sales, are falling off, even beyond expectation, & into whosever hands the Govt. may fall next March, it is quite probable a considerable debt will exist, in some shape.

Our political affairs wear a very different aspect, from that which I expected, when I left England. There is certainly a popular out-break, for Genl Harrison, and, at this moment, at least an equal chance for his Election. Genl Jackson's personal weight is felt no more; Mr [Martin] V[an] B[uren] never had any personal popularity, & the power of party cohesion is very much weakened, by the state of the times, & by a sort of enthusiasm for a retired old Genl. One is hardly willing to acknowledge any national connexion, between the *fall* of cotton & wheat, & the *rise* of patriotism. But it is certain, nevertheless, that low prices make us a good deal more enthusiastic in our Country's cause. Genl Harrison is an honest man, & an amiable man; & would be likely, I think, to bring good men about him; & if he should be elected, tho' he has something of the self respect of an old soldier, will exhibit nothing of the obstinacy & ignorant presumption, of his *penult* predecessor. The Whigs all go for him, heartily, and, as I have said, his chance is at least an even one. Your neighbor, Mr [Andrew] S[tevenson?] will not believe this, but it is true.

You see our miserable exhibitions, in the Senate, on the subject of State Debts. The discussion was enough to make one heart-sick.[3] Our *locofocoism*, the spirit of which has too much invaded the Govt. itself, is not a whit better than your *socialism*. We need a *Conservative* party, more than you do. As to State Stocks, Mass[achuse]tts you know may always be relied upon; so I think may N.Y. & Ohio; & I think Pa. will come out right. I have much confidence, too, in Indiana. As to the rest, I should advise caution; but this I say to yourself only. Altho' our T. notes *may be* redeemed within the year, I think there is not the least chance they will be. I shall say this to Mr [Thomas Wren] Ward. Mr Ward was here a fortnight since, & staid a day or two. I learned from him that you think of going on to the Continent, in the Spring, instead of coming to U.S. I regret this, as we should all be glad to see you, & none more glad than myself. I had anticipated the pleasure of sitting with you, at the foot of the falls, & of hearing a noise, loud enough to drive the din of politics out of my ears, & the hum of the Exchange out of yours.

I pray you to remember me, with much kindness, to Mrs Bates,[4] & Madam Vande Wyer, & her husband.[5] We never cease to speak of you all, with grateful recollections of your hospitality & kindness. Our session, I fear, will continue to June, or July. I shall write you, occasionally, & should be more happy to hear from you, if I did not know what labors of writing you have to perform.

I had almost forgotten to say a word about the *Boundary question.* I fear some little warmth here, between Mr [Henry Stephen] Fox & Mr [John] Forsyth.[6] Pray *keep cool*, on your side. It is of *much* importance to keep the *Times* cool, & that it should, frequently, repeat the suggestion, of a settlement by *compromise*—giving, & taking. Have you not the means of seeing, that it takes, & preserves, this tone? Yours truly & faithfully,   Danl. Webster

ALS. CaOOA. Published in A.R.M. Lower, "An Unpublished Letter of Daniel Webster," *New England Quarterly*, 12 (June 1939): 360–364.

1. Mrs. Paige (1809–1863) was the wife of James W. Paige and the daughter of Stephen White.

2. Van Buren signed the sub-treasury bill into law on July 4, 1840.

3. There had been an extended debate on the resolutions against the assumption of state debts.

4. Mrs. Bates (d. 1863), née Lucretia Augustus Sturgis, Joshua's wife.

5. Sylvain Van der Weyer, representative of the Belgian government to the Court of St. James, was Bates's son-in-law.

6. Fox (1791–1846) was the British minister to the United States. *DNB*. The disagreements concerned the *Caroline* and continuing raids along the Niagara frontier.

TO SAMUEL JAUDON

Washington Mar 29. '40

My Dear Sir,

I am going to N.Y. in a day or two, to bring my wife to Washington; but lest I should not get there before the Queen sails, I must write you from this place.

The mercantile & financial state of things, other friends will be able to communicate with more accuracy. I will say a few words, upon other topics. And, first & foremost, we have more than an even chance of accomplishing a thorough Revolution in the Administration. Genl Harrison's nomination runs thro' the Country, most astonishingly. Our friends feel confident of the centre, the N. West, & the N. & East. Ken. & Louisa. will be doubtless with us, very probably Tene. & there are even hopes of Va. The first sharply contested Election will be in Connecticut, on the 5th April.[1] It will be a *sign*, to show how the feeling is in N.E. This hopeful state of things gives quite a new aspect to our politics.

The Administration & all its friends are busy, the Globe furious & rabid; but we trust they will not be able to check the current. You see what a *sweep* the Whigs have made, in & about Philadelphia. If the

Legislature at Harrisburg will only adjourn, without doing any thing violent towards the Bank, I believe the State will go clear for Harrison.

You see warm words between Mr [Henry Stephen] Fox & Mr [John] Forsyth. Yet we do not apprehend any serious mischief. It is, however, unpardonable in both Govts. to leave this controversy unsettled.

There is no disposition here, to have war; & I am sure quite as little on your side. The infirmity of the case, in my opinion, is, that neither administration feels strong enough to take decisive measures to terminate the dispute. Lord Palmerston[2] is afraid of the Tories; Mr. V. B. is afraid of Maine & the Whigs.

I had the pleasure to see Mrs [Anne E.] White,[3] after my arrival here; but the Judge [Hugh Lawson White] had gone to Alexandria, & I did not see him. They reached home safely, & recd, as you will have seen, a sort of triumph. His health is feeble; but if he shall be able to show himself to the People, he will make a great impression, &, in all probability carry the State.

Please say to Mr [Richard] Alsop[4] that a melancholy occurrence has prevented me from being ready to write him, on my own business. N. R. Thomas, my agent in regard to Western Lands came here five weeks ago, at my request, was here taken sick, & died at Browns on the 17th [18th]. A good deal worn down by taking care of him, & much affected by his death, for he was almost as near & dear to me, as a son, I have not been able to examine the necessary papers, to make the statement I promised Mr Alsop to send. It shall go by the next Steamer. Thus far, I have got along without your Brother [Charles Baucker Jaudon].[5] But I shall be obliged to call on him this week, on my way to N.Y. As affairs look rather easier in England, perhaps he will find less difficulty in complying with my wishes. I pray you, make my most respectful & kind remembrances to Mr [James] Morison.[6] I shall not forget the kind interest he took in our American affairs. I liked Mr [Ichabod?] Wright,[7] also, very well, & hope you gave him the *hint*, I desired. I should be sorry he should bury a mint of money in the mud of X X. He had a great deal better put $50,000 of it into some of my high & dry excellent lands, for settlement, which will be quite certain to double his investment for him, in five years. It will do him no harm to tell him this; & the first part of the communication will do him good.

We are passing a Bill for the issue of 5 millions T. notes; & shall need another 5, before July. The subject will be up in the Senate tomorrow, & I shall take occasion to make a short Speech, setting forth the state of the revenue, expenditure, &c.[8] Perhaps some extracts from it may get to N.Y. in season for this conveyance.

I pray you, give my love to Mrs J[audon] & the daughters.[9] We talk about you much, & remember all your kindness with grateful hearts. Julia has gone to housekeeping. I may run down from N. Y. & make her a call.

Pray let me hear from you, by return of the Queen, unless she brings you out, so that instead of hearing from you, we can look upon you. Yours always faithfully   Danl Webster

ALS. NHi. Published in *PC*, 2: 79–81. Jaudon (1796–1874; Princeton 1813) was formerly cashier of the Bank of the United States. Since 1837, he had headed the Pennsylvania Bank's agency in London.

1. In the Connecticut elections in April, Whigs won the governorship and majorities in both houses of the legislature.

2. Henry John Temple, Lord Palmerston (1784–1865) was the British foreign secretary. *DNB.*

3. Mrs. White (d. 1847), née Ann E. Peyton, whom Hugh Lawson White had married in November 1832.

4. Alsop (d. 1842) was a New York merchant with ties in Chile and Peru. At this time he was a director of the Bank of the United States in London.

5. Jaudon (1802–1882) was a physician, but he devoted most of his time to banking and finance.

6. Morrison (1790–1857) was a wealthy English merchant, agent of Morrison, Cryder & Company, from whom Jaudon had borrowed money for the Bank of the United States in 1839. *DNB.*

7. Wright was a Nottingham banker.

8. For DW's speech of March 30th on the Treasury Note Bill, see the *Congressional Globe*, 26th Cong., 1st sess., Appendix, pp. 304–308, and *W & S*, 8:278–296.

9. Mrs. Jaudon (1799–1880), née Marguerite Peyton Alricks, daughter of Ann E. Peyton and stepdaughter of Hugh Lawson White, whom Samuel had married in 1823. Their daughters were Annie Peyton (1824–1894), Julia Webster (1826–1901), and Ada Mary Caroline (1839–1929).

TO CAROLINE LE ROY WEBSTER

Monday Morning
[March ? 1840]

Private

My Dear Wife,

Among the things which have worried me for some time, one is the condition of matters at La Salle, & Fletcher's situation. The state of the times, & the rascally & foolish conduct of the Govt. of Illinois has stopped all their public works. The hands have broke off from the canal, as I understand, leaving it unfinished, & probably it may be four [or] five years before it will be resumed.[1] In this state of things, & while it lasts, Peru will be nothing, & it will be impossible that there should be any business there, by which F. could support his family.

Then, again, if there should be a third season, as sickly as the two last, I should hardly expect him to get through it. Ray's fever here was nothing, between ourselves, but a new breaking out of his old illness. The

Physicians found good reason to think he had never been well, since his long confinement at Tonawanda.

All these things give me trouble, but I have not said any thing about them. I wrote to F. in Peru;[2] from N.Y. on the subject of his health & the climate, &c. He has not said much, in reply. Think of things, & keep them to yourself. Yours   D. Webster

ALS. NhHi. Published in Van Tyne, pp. 599–600.

1. As a result of the depression, the Illinois legislature had called a halt to construction on the Michigan and Illinois Canal, whose terminus was just a few yards from the Webster farm in Peru, Illinois. The canal was not completed until the spring of 1848.

2. Letter not found.

FROM DANIEL FLETCHER WEBSTER

Peru April 8th. 1840.

My dear Father,

I have just rec'd your letter of Mar. 22d.[1]

I have been thinking for some time that this would not do for me & had pretty much determined, after another year, if things did not mend, to remove, somewhere. The business here will not support one—all our hopes have been upon the [Michigan & Illinois] Canal, and the consequent growth of the place, but when the Canal will be finished is very doubtful, certainly not for some time, which would be to me almost lost time.

These considerations, together with the unhealthiness of the country, have weaned me of my Western fever. If there were any chance here, or any tolerable prospect for the future, I could stay & wait a reasonable time, but every thing is so bad, that really we all feel discouraged.

Caroline is very anxious to come East. She fears for herself and her children. We have to give little Daniel[2] calomel already, he is so bilious.

If it could be so arranged that I could form some connection in New York, which would give me a good start, I would bring on my family this Summer, stay awhile with you myself, come out to settle up all business here during the Winter and then finally come East in the Spring. But, you will agree with me, that I could hardly bring my family East, without some prospect of making a final settlement there & without some previous arrangement or prospect that would justify the expense. I would scarcely like Boston, but would try it there, if I could do no better. I should prefer New York.

I have thought that perhaps Mr. [Edward] Curtis could suggest some connection there for me, if he would not be disposed to make one himself. Could some such plan be effected, the Sale of my effects here would put me in funds for some time, leaving the lands in Peru to await the course of events & I could come on, without being any expense to you. I think I could do something in New York. There is a field for all exertion & I could probably earn a handsome living there, with your influence. It is as you say, precisely. The blight which has fallen upon every thing seems to render it necessary to change our plans of operation.

I leave the first Boat, for Springfield, on business connected with the Miller Farm & the [Samuel] Lapsley[3] Place. I shall be absent about a week.

In confidence. Mr. Cabots[4] mercantile establishment here has pretty much gone down. They have lost a good deal of money. The Farm is kept up by main force.

I have let the Haight & Warren & Miller Farms[5] for $200 for one year, to a very good man. I will at all events, if I am well, come to see you in July. If a good arrangement meanwhile can be made, I will bring on the family & leave them East while I come out to finish & settle up affairs. Otherwise I shall take them to Chicago & come on myself.

We are all pretty well today.

The Harrison cause is gaining ground daily. We have just had a famous meeting at Ottawa, the County seat. A slight bilious attack prevented me from attending, which I regret very much, as I wanted to give them a speech. I have made three recently to very respectable audiences.

With much love to Mother & all & many thanks for Edward's letter. I remain dear Father your affectionate Son   Danl. F. Webster

ALS. NhHi.

1. Not found.

2. Daniel Fletcher, Jr., was born in Peru, Illinois, on February 10, 1840, and died September 2, 1865. Called Dan by his father, he was often called Daniel Webster, Jr., by his grandfather.

3. Lapsley (d. 1839), a native of Pennsylvania, had settled in La Salle in 1830, where he farmed and ran a sawmill. Miller has not been identified. DW had purchased parcels of both the Miller and Lapsley properties.

4. Most likely Fletcher was alluding to Samuel Cabot, Jr. (1784–1863), a Boston merchant, the grandson of Thomas Handasyd Perkins.

5. Not identified.

TO EDWARD CURTIS

Boston April 20[, 1840]

My Dear Sir

I was about leaving today, but Essex South has come up, to command me to appear at Salem tomorrow. I tried to get off, but could not.[1] There is an excitement, hereabouts, more extensive, more fervent, & more *deep*, than you have any idea of. Set Mass. down for a majority between 15 & 20 thousand—All her 12 members Whig—Every State Senator a

Whig—& only here & there a loco in the H. of R. Look for clean sweeping.

My little speech on the Revenue &c. is getting into a little repute this way.[2] Pray get somebody to do the needful to have a few copies printed in pamphlet. Our best love to Mrs C. Mrs W. is packing up. Yrs   D.W.

ALS. NhD.

1. DW addressed the Essex County Whig convention in Salem on April 21, 1840.

2. For DW's speech on the issuance of treasury notes, delivered on March 30, see *Congressional Globe*, 26th Cong., 1st sess., Appendix, pp. 304–308; and *W & S*, 8: 278–296.

FROM JOSHUA BATES

London [26] April 1840

My dear Sir,

I have to thank you for your valued letter of the 26th March[1] and have carefully observed its contents. I fear it is not in my power to write you any thing in return that is worth your perusal for nothing of any great importance has occurred during the past month. The discussions in Parliament in relation to the war with China you will have read in the newspapers. I am inclined to think the course taken by the Government is the right one and perhaps the only one. The Chinese must be taken down from the stilts on which their vanity has so far taught them to suppose they could walk over all other nations of Barbarians as they call them. The exhibition of Power which Lord P[almerston] has sent forward will make quick work of it and the result will be equally important for the United States and for Great Britain as there will be greater security and liberty of trade and perhaps several additional ports opened to foreign commerce.[2] The stoppage of all their coasting trade which the fleet gone out is quite competent to do cannot fail I think to bring the Chinese to their senses without Bloodshed. The Maine Boundary Question has again become a matter of deep anxiety to all engaged in commercial transactions with the United States and the injury to our country in a pecuniary point of view in every month, to the value of all the wild land in Maine. It depreciates the Stocks of the different States and narrows the facilities by which our citizens have hitherto been the great carriers of the world. I cannot think the two governments can be so unwise as [to] let this question which any honest man can settle in ten minutes lead to hostilities. You mention that it is desirable to keep the "Times" cool and intimate that I have the means of influencing it. I wish I had any influence with that Journal for it is and always has been hostile to my House[3] and to every thing American and the very day your letter was received it contained a violent article on that very question.[4] It has since been engaged against you and your written opinions about

American State Stocks and citing a pamphlet which has recently appeared written I understand by Mr C[harles] J[ared] Ingersoll of Philadelphia. The only means we have found of lessening the bad effect was by asserting thro' the "Chronicle" that the writer of the Pamphlet belonged to the "Fanny Wright" party who considered the obligations to pay debts of marriage vows and all the fixed forms of Religion as tyranny and therefore to be resisted, and that it was amusing to see a church & State paper quoting the opinions of such a set of disorganizers. But if the "Times" is violent and severe what can be said of the New York Enquirer which contains seven columns of abuse of me and my House for which (after having carefully read it) there is not the foundation of the smallest item of truth but there are points in it, that enable me to fix its paternity on one of the Directors of the Bank.[5] Therefore we are bound to take notice of it and I will send you when printed the statement of all our transactions with Mr [Samuel] Jaudon by which you will see how liberal we have been and how little we merit such abuse.[6] It does not trouble me however. Time always sets things right.

You must get things right in regard to your currency. In the north all seems to go steady with your Banks. The South and west perhaps never should have had any money to handle until the States were older; they will probably grow good in time.

I fully intended to have made the visit you mention to the Great falls, but my Doctors say it will be much better for me to go to Switzerland and Germany where the waters of Carlsbad and the absence of business talk cannot fail to restore me to perfect health.

Mrs Bates is not very well but Mr & Mrs Van der Weyer and the Baby who have been at Brussells for two months and return this week, are quite well. Mrs Bates unites in kind regards to yourself Mrs Webster Mr & Mrs [Samuel Appleton] Appleton and Mrs [James W.] Paige with which believe me my dear sir Very truly yours   Joshua Bates

ALS. NhD.

1. See above.

2. Bates was alluding to Britain's "Opium War" with China. With the 1844 Treaty of Wanghia, the United States secured rights and privileges which Great Britain had won in the 1842 Treaty of Nanking. The ports of Canton, Amoy, Foochow, Ningpo, and Shanghai were opened to trade and residence.

3. Baring Brothers & Company.

4. On April 18, 1840, the London *Times* carried an editorial which predicted an imminent war over the boundary and advocated taking up arms if the United States government continued to make "common cause" with Maine.

5. See the *Morning Courier and New York Enquirer*, December 20, 24, 1839.

6. For a discussion of this Jaudon-Barings affair, see Ralph W. Hidy, *The House of Baring in American Trade and Finance: English Merchant Bankers at Work, 1763–1861* (Cambridge, Mass., 1949), pp. 283–288.

FROM JAMES HAMILTON, JR.

New York April 29th. 1840.

(Private & Confidential)

My Dear Sir:

I greatly regret that I had not the pleasure of meeting you in this City. I arrived at midnight on Friday night last & you departed I understand for Washington on Saturday Morng. I wrote you from Philadelphia directing to Boston that my desire was to see you before I embarked in the G[reat] W[estern] on the 9th. for England.[1] I regret that my engagements here will not permit me to visit Washington.

I need not repeat that I recollect & shall remember the conversation which passed between us in Philadelphia last May.

I have no doubt when an opportunity occurred you did us good in Europe. Since that period we have strengthened our Texian negotiation very powerfully & I go out *almost assured* of success. The Country has grown, & we have fortified ourselves both at home and abroad very essentially.

Our Bankers in London & Paris speak in a tone of much confidence to us. But still we must not neglect one subsidiary help.

Mr. [Albert T.] Burnley[2] (My associate) has procured a strong Letter from Mr [Henry] Clay, and I have obtained Letters from Mr [John C.] Calhoun & Mr [Joel Roberts] Poinsett speaking of Texas in the strongest confidence—of the certainty of her maintaining her independence and from her institutions being founded on our own of enjoying internal peace & social order. But last not least from her having a custom House of her own & an immense domain of public Lands affording the largest means for the ultimate redemption of any Loan which her necessities may require her to Contract. As her Custom House will yield a Million of Dollars this year & the fees & Land Tax ½ a Million it is quite obvious she can afford to pay an interest even of 10 percent on a Loan of 5 Millions—With 150 Millions of acres of the finest Land in the World as a capital for the final redemption of her public Debt.

As it would be of immense consequence to us to add to the Letters of the 3 American Statesmen I have named your own I write to beg you will afford it to me. Instead of its being addressed to me, may I beg the favor of your addressing it to Mr. [Alejandro Maria] Aguado,[3] the great Spanish Banker in Paris with whom I understand you became well acquainted. I will thank you for similar Letters to any of your other financial friends either in England or on the Continent who you think might help us. I give you my honor on no account whatsoever shall your Letters appear in print.[4]

Perhaps a full Letter to me stating your opinion of the destiny of Texas, and the solidity of the security she could offer for a Loan with a general summary of the views I have presented to such of your friends in Europe as you might give me Letters would be the best form to put it in.

A Letter to Mr. Aguado, will be of great value—as our Paris Banker M. Ardoise[5] is now engaged in forming a combination of Bankers in that City to take our Loan. The opinions of such an individual as Aguado could not fail to have the most decisive influence.

I have just returned from Texas and assure you on my honor that the "Empire State" itself does not afford higher security for a public Loan than this New Republic.

As this Letter will reach you on Saturday Morning let me earnestly entreat you to devote an hours leisure on Sunday Morng. to a careful preparation of the Letters which I assure you will be duly appreciated & gratefully remembered by Dear Sir With sincere esteem & respect Your obt. sert.   J. Hamilton

ALS. NhHi.

1. Letter not found.
2. Burnley (1800–1861), a native of Frankfort, Kentucky, was a Texas loan commissioner. In the late 1840s, he established the *Republic*, a Taylor-Whig newspaper in Washington, D.C.
3. (1784–1842).
4. DW did write at least two letters

on Hamilton's behalf. One was enclosed in a letter from Hamilton to Verstolk van Soelen in Amsterdam, July 19, 1840. See Mary Katherine Chase, *Négociations de la République du Texas en Europe, 1837–1845* (Paris, 1932), p. 188. The other letter, which DW sent to Samuel Jones Loyd, May 8, 1840, is printed below.
5. Not identified.

TO SAMUEL JONES LOYD

Washington May 8 1840

My Dear Sir

I thank you for your letter,[1] & the copy of your pamphlet,[2] which I have read with much delight, & which has also afforded great pleasure to many friends. It seems to me that your views are demonstrably right, & such alone as can be safe in practice. I have been, for a long time, something of a student in these matters, & acknowledged myself much enlightened, by intercourse with English friends last summer, & this publication of yours. You have so much more practical knowledge than we have, that your opinions take a more definite & exact shape.

I send this by Genl [James] Hamilton,[3] whom you may have already seen in England. He is a very intelligent man, & acted an important part in Congress, some years ago. I suppose he goes out, wholly or partly, on account of our neighbor, the Republic of Texas. That Country, so recent, & of such strangely sudden origin, as an Independent State, seems to be making steady progress in establishing and maturing its Institutions. Nobody here has any expectation of its re-annexation to Mexico. I believe I did it a great favor, by taking ground, early, against its annexation to us. It is a vastly rich Country, naturally, & large enough for a respectable Independent Community. It must be a great cotton producer; & is receiving constant accessions to its population, by those who go to it with a view of pursuing that cultivation. They have a regular custom house, & their importations must be considerable, even this year, as they fabricate nothing for themselves. Genl Hamilton has visited Texas, is personally well acquainted with the leading men in it, & better qualified, than any Gentlemen I know, to communicate accurate & full information, respecting Texas, & its Government.

England, My Dear Sir, does not seem *half as far off*, as it did before I visited it. Although naturally reading & talking of England all my life, my impressions recd. a vividness, as well as a degree of correctness, by even a short visit, which they otherwise could not have obtained. I find in myself a new degree of interest, for every thing with you, which I hope I may keep alive, as a source of pleasure. London—outside & inside—its Parks, & Buildings, its crowds, & its vast rush of business—& Parliament, & the Courts—and its private Society—the sumptuous entertainments, & what is better, the agreeable, intellectual & friendly Breakfast parties—(none of which has left a more agreeable impression than I experienced from those at 22 Norfolk Street)⁴—all these things are yet fresh; and as I regularly see the London papers, I keep you all before my eyes.

I observe that a Commee is appointed in the H. of C. on the subject of Banking.⁵ If you should happen to think of it, I pray you be kind eno. to send me a copy of its report.

We are here on the Eve' of a great popular election, which much agitates the Country. I found on my return, a State of things which I had not expected. Genl Harrison, a worthy, upright, & respectable man, has been nominated for President, in opposition to Mr Van Buren. There *seems to be* a burst of popular enthusiasm in the Genl's favor. The times are hard, prices low, the currency in a very bad state, & indications warrant the belief that the Country, at least a majority of it, is much inclined for a change, both of men & measures.

My Dear Sir, I pray you to present me to Mrs Jones Loyd,⁶ most kindly & respectfully, & keep me in your own remembrance. Yours faithfully

Danl Webster

ALS. UkBelQU. Published in D. P. O'Brien, ed., *The Correspondence of Lord Overstone* (3 vols., Cambridge, England, 1971), 1: 275–277. Loyd (1796–1883), first Baron Overstone (1860), an authority on banking and finance, succeeded to his father's banking business in 1844. *DNB*.

1. Not found.

2. Loyd had probably sent DW a copy of one of the following: *Remarks on the Management of the Circulation and on the Condition and Conduct of the Bank of England and*

of the Country Issuers during the year 1839 (London, 1840); *A Letter to J. B. Smith, Esq., President of the Manchester Chamber of Commerce* (London, 1840); *Effects of the Administration of the Bank of England: A Second Letter to J. B. Smith . . .* (London, 1840); or *Thoughts on the Separation of the Departments of the Bank of England* (London, 1844), the latter of which had been privately printed in early April, 1840. O'Brien,

1: 275–276.

3. According to O'Brien, 1: 276, Hamilton addressed a note of introduction to Loyd, transmitting DW's letter and asking for an interview.

4. Loyd's London address.

5. Loyd was at this time giving testimony before the Select Committee on Banks of Issue.

6. Mrs. Jones Loyd (d. 1864), née Harriet Wright, daughter of Ichabod Wright, a Nottingham banker.

Although the African slave trade had long been outlawed by the Atlantic nations, its profits were high enough to warrant the risk. The case of the schooner Amistad, *which came before the United States courts in 1839–1840, was an instance of the illicit trade. The* Amistad, *with thirty-nine Negroes newly brought from Africa aboard, was hardly clear of Havana when the slaves seized control of the ship. Also aboard were Jose Ruiz and Pedro Montes, who had purchased the Africans in Havana. Ordered to sail to Africa, Ruiz, Montes, and those of the crew who had not been killed managed instead to loiter up the North American coast. After two months at sea, the vessel was seized by a United States coastal survey brig and brought to New London, Connecticut. Once in port, the officers who had taken custody of the* Amistad *sought salvage of the ship and its cargo, while the Spanish owners charged that the Africans were murderers, pirates, and revolted slaves, and they appealed for the restoration of their property.*

Concerned over the fate of the Africans, a group of abolitionists, led by Lewis Tappan, Joshua Leavitt, and Simeon S. Jocelyn of New York formed a committee to raise funds to provide them with a legal defense.

When the case came before the courts, Seth Perkins Staples (1776–1861; Yale 1797), Theodore Sedgwick, Jr., Roger Sherman Baldwin, and John Quincy Adams represented the Africans. In January 1840, Judge Andrew T. Judson of the district court ruled that the Africans were free men who had been illegally kidnapped and sold in Cuba; he ordered that they be turned over to the President of the United States for return to Africa. The circuit court in April affirmed the ruling of the district court, whereupon an appeal went to the United States Supreme Court, to be argued in the January 1841 term.

In preparing for the defense before the Supreme Court, the "Committee appointed to act for the Africans of the Amistad" *sought additional distinguished counsel. They prevailed upon Adams and Baldwin to remain with the case, but Tappan and his committee, as evidenced in the letter below, also tried to retain Webster for the argument. Whether he responded to Tappan's invitation has not been determined. At any rate, Webster, like Rufus Choate who was also invited but declined, did not appear as counsel. The Supreme Court (15 Peters 518, 1841) affirmed the decision of the circuit court, but the Africans were not immediately transported to Africa. The Supreme Court ruling and their return to Africa remained issues for Webster to face as secretary of state. For a discussion of those affairs, see the* Diplomatic Papers, *1.*

FROM LEWIS TAPPAN

New York, May 10, 1840.

Dear Sir,

On behalf of the Committee appointed to act for the Africans of the Amistad I write to inquire 1. If you are disposed to undertake their defense & can do it *con amore?* 2. What your fee will be? We have already incurred an expense of about $1100, and whatever else may be required must come from a benevolent public. The Comee. in the meantime are responsible for the punctual payment of all liabilities.

Messrs Staples & Sedgwick of this city and R. S. Baldwin Esq of New Haven have acted as counsel for the Africans hitherto, but we are requested, from various quarters, to engage other counsel, particularly as the cause is appealed to the Supreme Court of the United States.

In the District Court the Judge decided that the negroes were *Bozale,* that is, recently from Africa, that they had never been, legally, slaves in Cuba; he dismissed the libel of Ruiz and Montes with costs, and decre[e]d that the Africans should be placed in the hands of the Executive (under the law of 1795) to be sent to Africa. All parties, it was supposed, would acquiesce in this decision, although doubts were entertained whether the law referred to, had reference to a case like this. But the Dis. Atty. by order of [the] Govt. on the demand of the Span. Minister,[1] appealed from this decision.

In the Circuit Court recently we moved for a dismissal of the appeal on the ground that neither party had appealed. The Span. minister, as we urged, having volunteered to appeal without the request of Ruiz & Montes or without their having withdrawn their libels. Judge [Smith] Thompson, however, although he intimated that the Africans were detained without the sanction of any law, & although he did not go into the merits of the case, decided that as a correspondence was carrying on between the Govt. and the Span. Minister, with reference to this case, &c decided that it was *expedient* to entertain the appeal that the matter go up to the Sup. Court. At the same time he refused to admit to bail the 4 children, for whom ample security was offered.

It is supposed by Mr Baldwin that the appeal to the Sup. Court cannot be sustained in as much as the "property" (each African appears separately) does not amount to $2000, as is required in appeals to the Sup. Court.

Some believe that all the Africans are entitled to be bailed if security is offered, and that they might be liberated by Habeas Corpus by a judge of the Sup. Court of Con[necticu]t under the Common Law.

The suits brought by some of the Africans against Ruiz and Montes in the courts of this city for assault & battery are entirely distinct from the above.

A strong desire is manifested, in various places, that you should be retained in this cause, and if you are of opinion that the law is on the side of these poor Africans—that a powerful effort should be made on their behalf—and could exert the great talents with which God has endowed you in this most interesting & righteous defense, no pains will be omitted to secure your services.[2] I remain, very respectfully, yr obt. st.

Lewis Tappan

ALS. NhHi.
1. Pedro Alcántara de Argaiz.
2. DW's endorsement of the letter

simply reads: "May 10 Amistead."
No response has been found.

TO JEREMIAH MASON

Washington May 29. 1840

My dear Sir,

You are powerful, when you choose to move; & an occasion exists, which I hope will induce you to make some little effort. The Whig Comees. are sending Mr [Rice] Garland to the North, to try to get some money to pay expenses, incurred here, & to be incurred, for the circulation of Speeches & Documents. I have been here twenty years, & never witnessed a time, when there was a quarter part of the cry & clamour, that now reaches us, from every quarter, for papers and pamphlets, & public documents. The Whig members have printed, & sent, till they have expended a great deal more than most of them can well afford. What is wanted cannot be furnished, from any other quarter; & we have not the means of furnishing it. It is really indispensable that the Whig Commes should be succored, by contributions from abroad. I have written fully to Govr. [Edward] Everett,[1] & a short letter to Mr [Robert Charles] Winthrop.[2] I hope you will see these Gentlemen. You will readily understand the whole case. I pray you, get our leading men of property together, & state to them strongly what you think of the case.

If we can keep the current setting, thro' the Summer, we shall achieve a Revolution, which will *last*, for some time & certainly bring with it a better state of things. The Whigs in Congress are active, zealous, self devoted, & co-operating with entire unanimity. But they are greatly un-provided with the sinews of War.

AL (signature removed). NhHi.   2. See DW to Winthrop, May 29,
   1. Letter not found.   1840, mDW 16709.

TO DANIEL FLETCHER WEBSTER

Washington
May 31. 1840

My Dear Son

I have recd your letter of the 16th of this month, & also Caroline's,[1] enclosing one to her father. I am glad to see that the Whigs are stirring, in your quarter. Your Senators,[2] I believe are still confident that the vote of the State will be given to Mr Van-Buren; but Mr [John Todd] Stuart thinks otherwise. Our intelligence is encouraging, from all quarters, & I have no doubt, or very little, at present, that Genl. Harrison will be elected.

You seem to be hesitating about coming East. No doubt, it is a subject demanding due consideration. You seem also to think that you prefer Peru to any place East, except N York or Washington. I believe you can get a living in N. York, but there is not a very extensive field of local practice, in Washington. It is, however, a good spot for practice in the Supreme Court, & I believe money is occasionally made by attention to claims pending before Congress. But for political objects, neither N.Y. or Washington is so good as Boston, or Lowell. In either of these last, you would go immediately into the State Legislature, & have a chance to show yourself. And in either of these, you could by diligence & hard labor get a living. Middlesex is not full of talent, & I should esteem Lowell quite a good place, for a promising & resolute young man. With you politics must be subordinate to law. Your first study must be to live.

Perhaps you will not find yourself ready or able to make up your mind, definitely, until I see you. Much ought to depend on what you think of the healthfulness of Peru. My property in the West will want attention from somebody, & since Ray's death I have thought of no way but of put-ting it into your management. At any rate, I must see you, in the course of the season, & we must settle upon something. If you could send your family East, at the same or as little expense as you can send them, & support them, at the North, we will find a corner for them at Marshfield till autumn. I do not know the arrangement of your courts, & therefore cannot say when you, yourself, can best leave home. Many things depend on the result of the ensuing election. If that should go against us, I should know pretty well what to do myself, & what to recommend you to

do. If it should go for us, different questions would arise. I hope you will thing of all these things, & write to me often. Yours affectionately
                              Danl Webster

Is there any other place in the West, where you think you can do better than in Peru?

Do you know any thing of Madison City, Wisconsin?[3]

ALS. NhHi. Published in Van Tyne, pp. 222–223.

1. See DFW to DW, May 16, 1840, mDW 16680. Caroline's letter has not been found.

2. John M. Robinson and Richard M. Young.

3. DW owned shares in the Madison-based Four Lake Company, headed by James Duane Doty.

TO CHARLES HENRY THOMAS

                              Washington June 8. 1840
Dear Henry,

If I never do any thing else, I must write you a letter this morning, & I rise early to get time to do it.

Mrs. W. & myself are both well, & are now thinking of the North. Mrs. W. will leave within a week for N.Y. I shall follow her, perhaps a week after, & intend being at Marshfield before June is out. I have partly engaged to go to Barre, Worcester County, on the 4th of July.[1] If I do, I wish you to go with me, & hope you will make no other engagement. It will be a good opportunity of seeing Worcester Co. farming. I know not, & no one knows, when Congress will adjourn. If it should be in Session, after July 4th.—with a prospect of remaining in Session some weeks, I shall have to return. But I hardly think that is probable. I am now coming so soon, I leave many things which I should otherwise write about.

Pray have my Chaise, in good order, & let it be at Boston by the 25 of this month, & Mrs W. will also wish her large waggon to be there, in good order also. I shall write to John Taylor[2] to send down her horses. Pray write John about the manner of sowing turnips & carrots, & see that Mr. [Timothy] Fletcher sends him up some seed, for turnips. I have been too busy to think of these things, & fear John will omit it.

Tell Dr [John] Porter[3] I conversed with Genl. [George Wallace] Jones about our mineral lands,[4] & have written to Fletcher about his business, &c. We have not heard from F. for sometime. Shall write soon again. Yrs
                              D. Webster

ALS. NhD.

1. For DW's own account of the Barre, Massachusetts, Whig gathering, one he sent to John Plummer Healy for newspaper publication, see mDW 16800. The Barre Gazette, July 10, 1840, carried a lengthy report of the "Whig Jubilee." No complete copy of DW's speech has been found, but his "Speech on the Abolition of Slavery," [1840], mDW 17224 (published in W & S, 13: 595–598), ap-

pears to be a part of his address on that occasion.

2. Taylor (1801–1869) was overseer and tenant at The Elms, DW's farm in Franklin, N.H. DW's letter to Taylor has not been found.

3. Porter (1795–1865), a Duxbury physician and Charles Henry Thomas's brother-in-law, often served as DW's land agent in the upper midwest.

4. For a partial listing of the Grant County, Wisconsin, mineral lands in which Porter, Jones, and DW speculated, see deeds transferring land from the United States to DW, February 19, 1839, Deed Book O: 551–552, Office of the Register of Deeds, Grant County, Wisconsin, mDWs.

FROM JOHN LEEDS KERR

Easton, June 16th. 1840.

My dear Sir,

The plan of carrying on the Presidential Canvass, by assembling large masses of people, seems to have been adopted by the Whigs throughout the Union, with what ultimate success is yet to be seen by us. It is a new experiment in the great art of electioneering, in our Country. Before the Great Convention, at Baltimore, it was proposed by our State Central Committee that we should have three Great Gatherings of the Whigs, from all parts of the State,—two of them, on the Western Shore, and one on the Eastern Shore. Some of our more reflecting Citizens, though zealous Whigs, hesitated on the utility of the scheme and it was left long undecided. For several weeks past, the subject has been again much considered and it is now settled that there shall be at least a Grand Convention of Whigs, on the *15th of July, at Easton.* A Committee of arrangement has been appointed and a general invitation will be immediately published to the Whigs throughout the State, to assemble here, on that day, for the purpose of patriotic counsel, under the advice and aid, if we can obtain it, of some of the most distinguished Statesmen, who are to be especially summoned to mingle with us.

Seeing the universal enthusiasm, which now prevails amongst the Whigs, I have no doubt of this Convention being attended by an immense concourse of people from all quarters, and particularly by the numerous bands of ardent patriots, who have associated under the denomination of "Tippecanoe Clubs," &c &c.

The Eastern-Shore-men do not enjoy the privilege of coming constantly *near* to men and things like those, who live in *Cities.* They have a desire to see amongst them some of the most distinguished men of the nation, and they have formed conceptions of "Giants," in these days. I assure you that the highest gratification will be felt by the Whigs of Talbot and of the neighbouring counties, who will be all here congregated, in seeing and communing with their ablest and most distinguished public men, long known to them and admired at a distance. You will be particularly invited as a guest of this people, in their proposed feast of reason and patriotic communion, and will now immediately receive the call. I seize the first opportunity to write, in advance, and to express to you my own strong desire to see you here and to say that I will be highly gratified by having you as inmate in my "Log-Cabin," during the Convention, and a little longer.[1]

You owe, I think, a visit to the Eastern Shore; and although it might so happen that you would be put to some inconvenience by delaying your return homeward, near the close of the session of Congress, I am very sure you would feel remunerated by a sense of the great satisfaction you will have given to your political friends, by your presence at this Meeting here, and of the important and effectual impressions you will have left on the minds of such a Multitude of honest citizens.

I am least of all men given to flattery or indirection. What I have said to induce you to gratify the strong desire of the Whigs to see you here, at this great Gathering, has been dictated by a sense of duty to them. The pleasure I derive from the hope of having you at my house is the selfish part of the office I have assumed by thus anticipating the formal invitation you will very soon receive from the Talbot Committee.

The Steamer Maryland, will leave Baltimore, as usual, at 7 o'c[lock] in the morning of Tuesday, the 14th. day of July and you may reach my house about 5 o'c in the afternoon of that day. I will take care to meet you or have a carriage in waiting for you at the wharf.

I shall be gratified by receiving an early reply to this letter[2] and I shall cherish a confident hope that you will yield to the wishes of so large a portion of your fellow Citizens of Maryland as will seek with great solicitude this opportunity of meeting you here on the 16th of July. I remain, dear Sir, with high respect and esteem, yrs   John Leeds Kerr

ALS. DLC.
1. By one estimate some twenty-five thousand people attended the Whig gathering in Easton, Maryland, on July 15. DW, however, was not present on this occasion. He had addressed the Baltimore Whig convention on May 4 (see *W & S*, 13: 108–109) and was at Marshfield during the Easton meeting.

2. Webster's reply, dated June 22, has not been found. See Kerr to DW, June 25, 1840, below.

TO SAMUEL JAUDON

Washington June 23. 1840

My Dear Sir,

I duly recd your kind letter of the 15 May,[1] by the Unicorn, and I write you now, mainly to say a few words of our political affairs.

The prospect is now very strong that Genl Harrison will be elected. Indeed, we have no doubt of it. We are more deceived than ever men were before if there be not a state of feeling which will bring him in, by a large majority. We have had no elections since that in Virginia, of which you know the result.[2] Louisiana has an election in July, & several important states in August; & others, as you know in October. So that before the actual voting for President, in Novr. we shall see, probably, what result may be expected. My own confidence is great & entire. No pains will be spared on either side, & we shall have a busy summer of it. And now, My Dear Sir, let me say, that if this event shall take place, it will change my condition, though I cannot say exactly how. Indeed, some change—a change—will take place, let the election go either way. If Mr. V. Buren should be re-elected, I shall go back to the Bar—leaving the Senate—& go to work with all my might. If Genl Harrison should be chosen, I shall equally leave the Senate, & you can judge, as well as I, perhaps, whether I shall thence forward have any thing to do with the Government or not. But I have made these remarks, & introduced this subject, for the purpose of expressing to you a hope, that you will return to your own Country, & connect yourself with its affairs. You have capacity to be highly useful to the Government, in either of various situations.[3] All you need is residence for a year or two among us, a re-integration, so to say, of yr national character, & some acquaintance with public men, who as yet may not have seen or known you. I wish to say, that my regard for you is unabated, & my disposition to serve you perfect. I have thought it not impossible, looking to the future, that we might be mutually useful to each other. If you come over soon, as I earnestly wish you may, we can converse on all these things more at length. In the mean time, I pray you, meditate upon them.

Perhaps I ought to add, that I have no present expectation of going abroad.

I write you this letter confidentially, of course, & only for the purpose of calling your attention to a probable state of things, if Genl. Harrison should be elected.

Yr Brother [Charles Baucker Jaudon] will have informed you that he authorized my draft on you for £1000 on security to be given.

I expect to leave Washington in a few days on a visit to Mass. July 4th. I am to meet the People, in Worcester County. July 7, I expect to be in Vermont, & July 15. on the Eastern shore of Maryland.[4] Great conventions of the People, as you see, are all the rage. Thus far they have had powerful effect, & there is yet no abatement of spirit & zeal. We make a business of political addresses, &c. & I shall do little else till fall. If, under the present circumstances of the Country, & with the advantages we now have we cannot change the Administration, it will be useless to renew the attempt hereafter. But we shall change it.

Mrs Webster is in N.Y. Give my best regards & affectionate remembrances to Mrs J. & the young Ladies; & believe me always truly Yr friend   D. Webster

ALS. NHi. Published in *PC*, 2: 87–88.

1. Not found.

2. The Virginia elections, concluded on April 23, gave the Whigs 87 out of 166 seats in the state legislature, a slight gain over 1839. On the basis of this Whig plurality, many Whigs predicted that they would carry the state for Harrison in November.

3. Jaudon returned to the United States in September 1840. Biddle had hoped to make him head of the Bank, but Thomas Dunlap, then president, refused to step down. Shortly, Jaudon returned to London to negotiate another loan for the Bank. Thomas Payne Govan, *Nicholas Biddle: Na-tionalist and Public Banker, 1786–1844* (Chicago, 1959), pp. 376–407.

4. See above, DW to Charles Henry Thomas, June 8, 1840, for a brief discussion of Webster's participation in the Barre convention. His activity at the Stratton Mountain gathering in Vermont on July 7 is treated in Malvaine Cole, *Daniel Webster Spoke on Stratton Mountain* (Jamaica, Vermont, 1965); and in Agnes Fitch, "Daniel Webster in Vermont," Vermont Historical Society, *Proceedings*, 10 (June 1942): 104–109. No copy of his Stratton Mountain speech has been found. DW did not attend the Easton, Maryland, convention.

TO [ROBERT CHARLES WINTHROP]

Washington June 24. 1840

Dr Sir

I recd yours yesterday,[1] & as I hope to see you soon, need not say much about the proposed Sep. meeting.[2] I begin to doubt the utility of these Conventions. But the People, I suppose, must have their own way. If I have any thing to do with it, which I do not desire, I shall suggest some things. However numerously the occasion may be attended by distinguished men, we should have but few speakers. A few Gentlemen, whose voices will be new, & who attend with an expectation of speaking, will do more good than a greater number.

All this, however, for consideration. Yrs   D. Webster

I hope to be in Boston on Saturday.

ALS. MHi.

1. Letter not found.

2. Winthrop had probably written DW about the Whig gathering planned for Bunker Hill on September 10. As president of that general convention of the Whigs of New England, DW presented the "Bunker Hill Declaration" of principles and purposes, which the gathering adopted. See *W & S*, 3: 41–52.

FROM JOHN LEEDS KERR

Easton, June 25th 1840.

My dear Sir,

Yours, of the 22d inst,[1] reached me by the Mail, which has just arrived, this morning. It's substance gives me much satisfaction, because I draw from it a very strong hope that you will not fail, if circumstances will permit, to gratify the ardent wishes of many—very many patriotic Citizens to meet you, here, in Council, on the 15th. of July. After repeating the expression of my great desire to have the pleasure of your Company in my own "Log Cabin," I must go for the great Whig feeling and again venture to urge with you the importance which I attach to your coming to this particular Convention, on the Eastern Shore. I have not yet, since the receipt of your letter, seen the Committee to know whether you have replied to their invitation;[2] but, I have conversed with many others who unite with me in the opinion that such a *speech* as you would, of course, make on a certain topic, with a *Southerner* to respond,—as one would do,—would go with greater power to draw out the fangs of the Monster of Misrepresentation than any other earthly means. You can have no adequate impression of the effect of the Charge of *abolitionism* and the alleged support of the North for that sole reason have on the election of Harrison, first in this middle region, which has always been called, by an unhappy anticipation, *the Netherlands* where the great battle must be fought, if it should ever come to that, between parties, Our arch enemy is constantly at the ear of the Voter, in these Counties, whether for the form of government, or on a more special but fatal issue. with the whisper, boldly & confidently administered, that the nomination of Harrison was carried by *the North* with a single eye to that question. We do all we can by the plainest statement of facts to purge Harrison from the taint of abolitionism & to defend the North against the imputation of the nefarious designs imputed;—but the dog returns to the vomit, &c. Come, amongst us, and, with all your power, exorcise this spirit. Now is the accepted time. All are anxious to hear & to reflect. Many of the vilest hypocrites of the Loco-Focos gravely—nay, solemnly assert their fears & alarms on this point & have *listeners* amongst our Whig friends. These are ready & most desirous to be satisfied. If [William Campbell] *Preston* come here, he may respond to the expression of your sentiments (—which are all well known & understood—) on this particular & most dangerous point, in his best manner, & I think the tongue of Slander may be blistered & paralized.

Then, other topics may be wielded to effect conviction of the necessity of a Change of Administration & a revolution in the mode of operation under our excellent & all sufficient Constitution. Fulfill only the assurance you give me, that *you feel as if you would make a great effort to be with us*, by resolving that you *will* have it so, & you will not fail. Your plan is the *very one*,—if you must go to Massachusetts in the meantime,—for getting here in one season by the Boat from Baltimore on Tuesday, the 14th. July. I do not know what you may have written to the Committee, but I am sure that your declining to come to the Convention will be a great damper to the hopes & wishes of the People for a great effect from the holding a great Council on this Shore. Maryland is so near the corrupting hand of the ruling powers that if we succeed this year, by reason & argument and spreading the light of truth, it will be a great assurance of the disgust which we hope the people have at last taken at the cause of the Spoilers. I confess, however, that my calculations are not very great. It is a measuring Cast, though all of us talk boldly & confidently of the issue. The Locos in this county are a good deal dispirited, though they sustain a brazen front and never cease their labors. By day & by night, such papers as the Democratic Herald of Baltimore, and Republican are delivered & *read* to doubtful Whigs. But we must do all possible—honorable battle to effect a revolution & now is the *Crisis* in our State. If the enemy find one failure,—signally manifested,—in one of these great calls for Conventions of Masses of Whigs & for their distinguished leaders & counselors, they will *walk in upon us* in high style. I have from the first apprehended danger in such a vast experiment as that of keeping up an excitement, however truly patriotic, so long as this is proposed to be continued and must be continued, if not to be a total failure, and many months are yet to come before the November election.

But excuse me, my dear Sir, for this prosing. Having but a poor genius for persuasion, I have gotten into right down begging.

I have received a letter from Mr Clay, in which he tells me conclusively that, for reasons which he specially assigns, he cannot possibly be with us; and I presume he has written to the same effect to the Committee. [Daniel] Jenifer names to me sundry Members of Congress whom he recommends to be especially invited & pressed to attend the Convention, but he presents the view of having you, with Preston & [John Jordan] Crittenden & [Samuel L.] Southard, *causa qua supra*. Jenifer is one of my hey-day-qui vive-bustling but true friends, and ever true to the Cause, and I shall beg him to keep you up to sticking place, for this Eastern shore visit. Jenifer himself will be an efficient adjunct to our Congressional forces in the Counsels of the Convention, for he will talk boldly, bravely & sensibly.

You will, I hope, receive this before you get off for Massachusetts, that it may avail what it can to increase your inclination to give us the benefit and the pleasure of your Company & Counsel. I remain, Dear Sir, with high respect Yrs   John Leeds Kerr

ALS. NhD.
    1. Letter not found.
    2. Neither DW's invitation from

the committee nor his response has
been found.

FROM JAMES BOYLES MURRAY

London June 29, 1840.

My Dear Sir,

Mr. [Virgil] Maxcy has, I believe, written you on the subject of the sale of the Clamorgan shares, which had become quite hopeless, when he explained its position to me, but I am glad to be able to say for the interest of all parties concerned, has been placed in such a train as to give every reasonable prospect of success, if sustained by concessions on the part of owners in America.[1]

The only point at issue is that the consideration money shall be paid in State Stocks instead of cash, which terms have been fixed by Messrs. R[oswell] L[yman] Colt and W[illiam] A[lbert] Bradley[2] as follows, to wit,

at 65 cts per arpent if paid in 5 per ct. State Stocks at par
    60 - - - - - - - 6 - - - - - - - - -
at par, or U.S. Bank Shares at £22.

Mr [Samuel] Jaudon is fully convinced that it will be for your interest to accept these terms rather than retain the shares, & remain subject to the right of assessment which the English purchasers reserve to the extent of *two* shillings sterling per arpent.

If you should decline authorising a sale of your shares at these rates, Mr Maxcy will replace them with Mr. Jaudon, who in the mean time has agreed to deliver them over (58 in number) with those belonging to Mr. Colt & others, believing your interest will be promoted by his so doing.

The passage of the tax bill in the Pennsylvania House of Representatives[3] has had an ameliorating effect on State credit, but transactions are very limited, & the probability of success in the Clamorgan affair is an exception to all private efforts to obtain money for any object in the United States.

Please address your answer to Mr. Maxcy, as I shall hope [to] be on my way homeward before it can arrive. I remain very respectfully, Dear sir, your most obt. Ser'vt. (signed)   Jas B. Murray.

Copy. NHi. Murray (1789–1866) was a New York merchant and financier, a heavy investor in real estate and state bonds.
    1. Maxcy's letter to DW has not been found. In 1838 DW had requested Maxcy to sell a part of his interest in the Clamorgan Land As-

sociation. Maxcy's efforts appeared about to fail, whereupon James B. Murray took an interest in them, buying, selling, and trading the shares, for which DW and others of the land company were to receive state stocks or United States Bank shares. Murray's installment payments for the shares he took dragged on until late 1842. He and Webster found themselves in considerable disagreement over the value of the stocks and shares which Murray transferred to DW. See, for example, James B. Murray to DW, June 9, 1842, mDW 22657. The issue is also discussed in the Murray, Bradley, Maxcy letters of the early 1840s in the Galloway-Maxcy-Markoe Papers, DLC. For a brief discussion of the Clamorgan Land Association, see *Correspondence*, 4: 220–222.

2. Colt (1779–1856), a merchant and banker in New York City, a director of the Savings Bank of Baltimore, and close friend of DW, was a stockholder in the Clamorgan Land Association. Bradley (1794–1867) was former mayor of Washington, D.C., and president of the Bank of Washington. At this time he was president both of the Patriotic Bank and of the Clamorgan Land Association.

3. The Pennsylvania tax bill levied a direct tax on its citizens for the payment of state debts. *Niles' National Register*, 58 (June 6, 20, 1840): 229, 244.

TO CHARLES HENRY WARREN

Boston July 12. 1840

My Dear Sir

Night before last I passed with Genl [James] Wilson, at his own house, & parted with him yesterday at Peterborough, at 10 oClock. I understand a Campaign is arranged, to commence at Taunton, extend to Nantucket, & terminate at Plymouth. I rise, Mr Speaker, to move to strike out "Plymouth", & insert<ing> "Duxbury." Wilson is a field officer, & entitled to a corresponding command. Fix his H.Q., for the day, at Duxbury, & he will embrace in his operations the whole world from Hingham to Plymouth, & back to Hanson, Halifax, &c. [Charles] Henry Thomas is here, going home today, & I shall ask him to correspond with S[olomon] Lincoln.[1] I pray you, put yourself in communication with Mr [Isaac Lothrop] Hedge.[2] On his return from Nantucket, I meet Genl W. & take him, with you, to Marshfield. I should be glad of an opportunity also of inviting F[rancis] Baylies. We will either *take you in*, or *put you out*.

We had a time—& a scene, on the mountains, not to be described.[3] Only think of 3000 men, encamped for two days, on the very top of the ridge of the G. mountains! Nothing but a Na[u]shon Hunt can come up to it, in grandeur and heroism. All things went well also at Keene.[4] Genl. W in all that region, tho like other good kings conceals his authority, is nevertheless a kind of elected monarch.

The general spirit where I have been is extraordinary—marvelous—unprecedented. We are either on the high road to the accomplishment of the greatest civil revolution ever yet achieved in this country, or else we are in enchanted ground, surrounded by fairies, fancies, phantoms, & dreams. May it please your Honor, *judge* how this is. Decide the matter; is it fact, or only fancy's sketch.

"Dispel this gloom, the light of heaven restore,
"Give me to see"—& so I say no more. Yrs truly   D Webster

ALS. NN. Published in *W & S*, 16: 330. Warren (1798–1874; Harvard 1817) was a Plymouth lawyer and businessman, judge of the Court of Common Pleas, 1839–1844. In later life, he was president of the Boston and Providence Railroad (1846–1867) and sat for a term in the Massachusetts Senate (1851).

1. Lincoln (1804–1881; Brown 1822), a state legislator (1829–1841), was a prominent member of the Hingham bar.

2. Hedge (1798–1867; Harvard 1820), a native of Plymouth, was an active Whig campaigner in the election of 1840.

3. DW was referring to the gathering on Stratton Mountain, Vermont, July 7, 1840.

4. En route from Stratton Mountain to Massachusetts, DW addressed citizens in Bellows Falls on July 8 and in Keene on July 9. *Niles' National Register*, 58 (August 1, 1840): 340.

TO JOSIAH WILLIAM WARE

Boston July 20. 1840.

Dear Sir

It gives me pleasure to comply with your request, by sending you a copy of my remarks, last winter, at the Agricultural meeting in this City.[1] I have been connected with farming, from my youth, but yet do not pretend to any considerable knowledge, or ability to instruct others. What I lack in knowledge, however, I try to make up by zeal, & by a profound attachment to the Agricultural interest.

Having referred to the case of Mr Hooe,[2] you desire my opinion, or my understanding of the practice of the Courts of the United States, as to the admission of such evidence as was admitted in that case.

There is no law of Congress on the subject, & I have always understood that the Courts of the United States, sitting in any particular State, have followed, in these respects, the laws & practices of the States in which they sit.

I cannot say I know or recollect any decided case; but such has been my understanding. Mr [Benjamin Watkins] Leigh, or Mr [Robert] Stannard,[3] who have practised long in the Circuit Court of the United States at Richmond, would be very able to say whether any such evidence was ever admitted by the late Ch. Justice [John] Marshall, or whether he did not, as I presume he did, follow the law of the State, & the practice of the State Courts. If there had been any instance to the contrary, I think we should have heard of it.

I do not wonder that you find it impossible to sustain the present administration, although you aided in placing its head in power. Having always been its opponent, it becomes me to speak of it, not disrespectfully, to you who have been its friend. But I must confess I am filled with apprehension, & amazement, when I see the degree of support which has been given to the Sub-Treasury, & other financial measures recommended by Mr Van Buren. It does seem to me that we have before us a most striking & alarming instance of party blindness & credulity. All these ideas of a Sub-Treasury, of Govt. Banks, of a hard-money currency for Govt, & of disregarding, altogether, the general currency of the Country, appear to me to be Anti-American, outlandish schemes & projects, devised as apologies for the neglect of plain & important Constitutional duties.

It is very possible, as you suggest, that you & myself may differ, as to the power of the Genl. Government, and as to its true policy.

As to the first, if Mr [James] Madison may be regarded as an authentic expounder of the doctrines of the Virginia School, there are few tenets of that School, with which I have any fault to find.

And as to the second, I trust you will agree with me in thinking that the general policy of the North, however you may differ from it, in some respects, is, after all, if carried out with moderation & mildness, not quite so bad as the policy of "a Northern man with Southern principles."[4] I am, Dr sir, Yrs with regard, Danl Webster

ALS. OFH. Ware (1802–1883) was a prominent farmer of Berryville, Clarke County, Virginia, noted for his fine horses, cattle, and sheep (see mDW 27671).

1. DW had spoken on the agriculture of England at a meeting in the Massachusetts Statehouse on January 13, 1840. See W & S, 2: 293–307. Ware's letter to DW has not been found.

2. Ware had probably inquired about one of the following cases: Hooe et al. v. Alexandria, 1 Cranch C.C. 90 (1802), 1 Cranch C.C. 98 (1802); or United States v. Hooe et al., 1 Cranch C.C. 116 (1803).

3. Stanard (1781–1846; William and Mary 1798) was a Richmond attorney and judge of the Virginia Court of Appeals.

4. Martin Van Buren.

TO SAMUEL JAUDON

Boston July 30. 1840

My Dear Sir

By the late arrival of the Steamer I recd. a letter from Mr [James B.] Murray, a copy of which I now enclose,[1] and the main object of this is to signify my confirmation of the disposition which appears to have been made of my 58 Shares of the Clamorgan Stock. You will perceive that he desired a communication to be made to Mr Maxcy, hoping, himself, to be on his return to U.S. soon. I have written Mr Maxcy, to your care,[2] confirming the sale. I do not know whether Mr Murray will bring the Stocks home, or leave them with you. If the latter, can I draw, to any amount on the strength of them, or how shall I best deal with them?

In the present state of the market for such things in England, I think I could probably do better with them here. I have sundry more shares of Clamorgan, which I should like to dispose of.

If Mr Murray should be still in England, I will thank you to make known to him the contents of this. Yours truly always   Danl Webster

ALS. NHi.   29, 1840.
    1. See above, Murray to DW, June   2. Letter not found.

TO ELISHA WHITTLESEY ET AL.

Boston Aug. 3. 1840

Gentlemen,

I have the honor to acknowledge the receipt of your communication of July 27th.[1]

No one can appreciate more highly than I do the great objects, intended to be advanced, by the proposed meeting at Warren, on the 25th. of this month.[2] The distress of the Country is great; the maladministration of the Government, especially in all that relates to currency, finance, & revenue, in my opinion apparent, & flagrant. I know no apology, for much which has been done; I know no preventive of future evils but a change of men. When your friends of Trumbull County, & of the neighboring Counties of Ohio & Pennsylvania shall be assembled, on the 25th. at Warren, I hope there will be among them many who have heretofore supported the present Administration, but who are honest & candid inquirers after truth; and I hope all such will suffer themselves to be asked, with sobriety & kindness, "How has all this difficulty arisen? Why is the currency so much deranged? Why is all business so stagnant? Why is the price of labor, and of products so low? May it not be that all this has come from injudicious meddling with the currency? Was it so in former times, when other counsels prevailed? Were not these consequences foreseen, & clearly pointed out, when the Govt. began with its experiments? And is there now any hope of permanent relief, but by a change of men, & a change of measures?"

Gentlemen, your own noble State, young, vigorous, & already powerful, has much to do in producing such change. Let me cordially exhort, you & your friends, when you separate at Warren, to remember that, like other good citizens, you have a high duty to perform; a duty of disseminating truth, a duty of convincing honest opponents, & a duty of rescuing the administration of the Government, from the hands of those whose measures have proved so prejudicial, & of restoring it again to its ancient principles, and its well approved policy. I am, Gentlemen, with much regard, your friend   Danl Webster

ALS. MHi. Published in W & S, 16: 332.

1. Not found.

2. Some 15,000 to 20,000 people (according to the *Cleveland Herald*) attended the gathering in Warren, Trumbull County, Ohio, which was

called to promote Harrison for President and Thomas Corwin for governor. *Niles' National Register*, 59 (September 12, 1840): 21.

FROM WILLIAM PITT FESSENDEN

Portland. August 6. 1840

Dear Sir,

On Tuesday, the 25th of this present month, the Whigs of Cumberland County and District are to hold a general convention in Portland, for the nomination of Senators to the State, and a Representative to Congress. I write you, at the request of our County Committee, and of many other Whigs, to solicit the favour of your personal attendance upon the occasion.

Aside from our strong desire to see and hear Mr. Webster, we are anxious to have you present for many good reasons connected with the cause. On the election in this County will depend the character of our State Senate, and, consequently, the question whether a Whig, or a Loco, is to take the place of Mr [John] Ruggles. It is very important, too, that the Whigs should have the ascendancy in one branch of our next Legislature, as upon that Legislature will devolve the duty of apportioning Senators and Representatives for the next five, or ten, years. After the Gerrymandering of 1830, we are somewhat anxious & sensitive on this point.

Again—we are anxious to defeat Albert Smith.[1] He is exceedingly unpopular, and more so now than when elected in 1838. At that time he was elected by only 15 majority, and the Whigs fell short, in the County & District, about 150 votes. Since that year, we have undoubtedly had accessions to our ranks, in many of the towns. Our friends are in high spirits, & our adversaries manifestly in trouble. *At present* every thing looks favourable. It is *important* to produce a strong impression at the convention. We want a great convention, and to have its members go home in good heart. We have no doubt that the expectation of seeing & hearing you will render the first of these objects certain of accomplishment, and we shall trust to you, & others who will be present, to fix the Second.

Allow me to add, on my own account, this hope, that you will take this opportunity of making me, & others of your personal friends here, your long promised visit. Mrs Webster's engagement to the same effect is yet in full force, & Mrs Fessenden,[2] with myself, would be most happy, and would expect, to have you bring her with you, and make our house your Head-Quarters, during your stay in town, if such an arrangement would be satisfactory to both of you.

The boat, as you may be aware, leaves Boston on Saturday Evening, & arrives in P. on Sunday morning. It also leaves here on tuesday wednesday & friday Evenings. We could not, probably, let you off on tuesday Evening, at any rate. I mention these facts in order that you may take them into account, while coming to a decision.

The Committee are desirous of receiving an answer as soon as may be convenient to yourself, in order that they may regulate themselves, & make their arrangements, accordingly.[3] If your conclusion is favorable to us, you will oblige me by stating the time when we may expect you, and your mode of conveyance.

With sincere respect & regard, for Yourself & Mrs Webster, I remain, truly Yr friend & Servt.   W. P. Fessenden

ALS. NhD.
1. Both Ruggles and Smith were defeated. Fessenden succeeded to Smith's seat.
2. Mrs. Fessenden (d. 1857), née

Ellen Maria Deering, daughter of a Portland merchant.
3. For DW's response, see DW to Fessenden, August 8, 1840, below.

TO WILLIAM PITT FESSENDEN

Boston Aug. 8. '40
My Dear Sir   Saturday morning

I have a real desire to visit Maine, & if I had recd. your communication a week or ten days ago,[1] I certainly would have made arrangements for attending your Convention. But I am now tied down by so many engagements, that I do not see how it is possible. I go today to N.Y. on Professional business, & hardly expected to be back before the 23, or 24. I have promised to attend a meeting at Newburyport, (dinner to Mr [Caleb] Cushing) which may probably be held on the 26. or 27th. or perhaps 25th.[2] If I should return in season, & can possibly get to you, I shall come. I hear from all quarters that you will be nominated for Congress, at which I greatly rejoice, & doubt not your success. I am, D Sir, yours truly
Danl Webster

ALS. NhD.
1. See above, Fessenden to DW, August 6, 1840.
2. The Essex County Whig convention and dinner to Caleb Cushing

were held in Newburyport on August 28. DW spoke on the occasion, but, tired and ill, his words were barely audible. *Boston Semi-Weekly Atlas,* August 29, 1840.

TO ROBERT CHARLES WINTHROP

New York Aug. 10. 1840
Private
My Dear Sir,

As I have come to a definite opinion that I ought not to preside at the Bunker Hill meeting, I have thought it right to make the suggestion to you, thus early, that the attention of the Comee. may be turned in another direction.

You are aware, that I have from the first doubted the utility of this meeting. It is a hazardous thing to bring such a multitude of people together, without some clear & distinct purpose, especially in the immediate neighborhood of a great City. Now there is nothing to be done, nothing to be commemorated, or celebrated, & nothing to be said that one tenth part of those assembled can possibly hear. The substance of the whole must be procession, & parade. And what good will these do? They may gratify the love of splendid show, but will they give us any votes? I think not. They are more likely, I fear, to offend the ardent & the ignorant of our opponents. There is something, in what is proposed, too nearly approaching to festivity, & joyous triumph, for our condition, while we are beseeching the people to relieve the Country from unbearable distress, by a change of rulers.

These have been my general feelings, on the subject; & I have thought, that whether they were right or wrong, it was clear, at least, that the same expense, labor & effort, made & laid out in other places, & other ways might do more good.

But I suppose the thing has gone too far to be stopped, even if wiser heads than mine doubted its expediency, which they do not appear to. I am quite willing, therefore, to give my best aid & counsel to the preparation of the proceedings, & to meet the Comee. for that purpose any time after my return. My decision, as to presiding at the meeting, rests on other grounds.

It is proposed, very properly, I think, that a solemn, imposing, grave and energetic Declaration shall be made, by these immense multitudes, setting forth their own opinions & principles, & stating the general grounds of their dissatisfaction with the administration of the Government. Now I hope it is not presumptuous to say, that such a Declaration is very likely to advance sentiments, such as the Delegation of Massachusetts, & myself as one of them, have asserted & contended for, for the last ten years. The main question must be, between our opinions & the opinions of our opponents; & if a vast popular congregation is to pass upon this question, it is not quite fitting that any of us should appear to take a lead, in procuring that Verdict.

My Dear Sir, I have already said more than was necessary, but I wish to show the Comee. that notwithstanding my opinions, & my declining to preside at the meeting, I am not only willing but desirous to do all in my power to help thro' with the occasion.[1] I am, Dr Sir, Yours truly

Danl. Webster

The Western news comes in gloriously. I go hence into the heart of the Administration Counties of N.J.

ALS. MHi.

1. In accordance with Webster's suggestion, Whigs dispensed with speeches at the Bunker Hill meeting of September 10 adopting instead a manifesto of principles and purposes for the contest. DW did, however, preside at the celebration. For the declaration of Whig principles, see *W & S*, 3: 41–52; and on the celebration, see *Boston Semi-Weekly Atlas*, September 12, 1840.

TO CHARLES HENRY WARREN

N. York Aug. 15. 1840

My Dear Sir

I may as well confess, & give up, first as last. *I cannot go to Na[u]shon the first of September.* I saw Mr [William W.] Swain[1] here, four days ago, & told him my distress. In addition to what I mentioned to him, I am pressed so hard to show myself, in important & doubtful places, that I am obliged to give a strict account, almost upon oath, of my engagements every day, for the next six weeks. And if I were to say, that I intended four days for a hunt, or a recreation, on Na[u]shon, they might shoot me. That they would follow me there, & bring me away, is certain. You never saw such a commotion as is hereabouts. Here came a Comee. from Utica, 250 miles—& as N. Jersey wd. not quit their hold on me, they snatched up Fletcher & carried him off in [an] instant—as ravenous wolves, when they cannot seize the adults of the flock, run away with innocent lambs![2]

I am most *awfully* pressed to meet a Convention of 3 Counties, on the River above us here, on the 3rd.[3] They say "Schoharie Greene & Columbia form a double Congressional District. Our opponents carried it, in 1838. We believe if you will come & address the people, we can carry the District." I have written that I cannot go;[4] but if these good Whigs, who are tugging with all their might, to make up, in part, in their District, for the expected loss of 4 members in this City, should find that I was recreating, in Na[u]shon, they would never forgive me. I must try to keep well with N. York. Pray signify my case, as early as possible, to Mr Swain, as I do not know where to address him. Tell him to spare me, till this fight is over, & then he may throw me into the sea, if he chooses, at Tarpaulin Cove.[5] Yours always truly, though for the present, a good deal mortified

Danl Webster

ALS. NhHi. Published in *W & S*, 16: 334–335.

1. Swain (1798–1858) was a New Bedford merchant and industrialist, and the owner of Naushon Island, the largest of the Elizabeth Islands.

2. Daniel Fletcher spoke at the Utica convention on August 12, and perhaps also at the New Jersey convention.

3. DW spoke at the Saratoga convention on August 19, and at the Patchogue (Long Island) convention on September 22. See *W & S*, 3: 5–36; 13: 114–132. It has not been established, however, that he spoke in New York on September 3.

4. See DW to John Van Cleek, August 15, 1840, mDW 16905.

5. An inlet on the south shore of Naushon Island.

In July 1839, Isaac, a Virginia slave employed as a ship carpenter in Norfolk harbor, attempted to escape. His effort failed, but Virginia officials pressed charges for slave "stealing" against Peter Johnson, Edward Smith, and Isaac Gansey, the three free blacks from New York with whom Isaac worked, and sought their extradition to Virginia for trial. New York officials refused to extradite them, however. On April 6, 1840, Thomas W. Gilmer, recently inaugurated governor of Virginia, again asked for their return and forwarded supporting resolutions by the state legislature. In the letter below, Seward asked for Webster's opinion on the controversy. Webster responded on September 29, asking for more time and suggesting that "taking a view of all the circumstances, some longer delay is true policy" (mDW 16942). Like most Whigs and Conservative Democrats who looked at the Presidential election and hoped in no way to damage Harrison's chances, Seward did not respond to Gilmer's letter until November 9. The controversy between Virginia and New York dragged on for some two years longer, with both sides refusing to yield ground. For Seward's view of the issue, See George E. Baker, ed., The Works of William H. Seward (5 vols., Boston, 1888) 2:449–518.

FROM WILLIAM HENRY SEWARD

Albany August 25th. 1840.

Private

My dear Sir:

I send herewith a copy of the letter I have prepared in compliance with the request of the Governor of Virginia reviewing the ground heretofore taken by me in denying the demand for the surrender of citizens of this state charged with stealing a slave in that state.[1] The Secretary of state will send you the documents relating to the subject.[2] I beg leave to repeat what was communicated to you by him, that without desiring in any way to embarrass you with any concern in the matter, I should deem it a great favor to have your advice on the subject and any suggestions you may think proper to make concerning the manner in which it is discussed. It involves one of the greatest questions which has ever arisen between the States and I <should deem myself deficient in effort to inform myself concerning it if I omitted to avail myself of any advice which I might properly seek> have for obvious reasons been desirous to obtain all the light of which it is susceptible. You were kind enough to propose to consult the Honorable Justice Story on the subject. I need hardly assure you that I shall esteem myself not only fortunate but much indebted to him if he will examine the subject and favor me with his views of the same.

Ill health and more pressing duties have produced much delay in the preparation of the argument, and I am urged by the Governor of Virginia to transmit my reply as early as possible. I trust you will excuse me therefore for asking your answer at as early a day as will be at all convenient for you. I am very respectfully your obedient servant.

William H. Seward

ALS draft. NRU.

1. Seward's copy of the letter to Gilmer has not been found.

2. Neither the documents nor the

letters from John Canfield Spencer, New York's secretary of state, have been found.

FROM JAMES WILSON

Steubenville, Sept. 7, 1840.

My dear Sir,

I was at the great gathering of the people at Wheeling on the 3d.[1] and there saw many of your friends, particularly Mr. [William F.] Peterson[2] of that place & Mr. [George A.?] Bayard[3] of the neighborhood of Pittsburgh. Upon consultation, we came to the conclusion, that the interests of the Whig party would be greatly promoted by your shewing yourself in these parts without delay, and appearing at meetings of the people. The administration appear to be using every means, fair and foul, to make an impression upon this state; and, in addition to their *foreign* forces previously here, have recently sent out [James] Buchanan. It is obvious that they have selected Ohio as their battle ground. They calculate that carrying their governor & a majority in the legislature on the 13th of October, would go far toward securing to them the electoral vote of N. York and Pennsylvania. It is not believed by the Whigs that they can succeed in this—but they must have had strong encouragement, or they would not be making such strenuous efforts. Many of us think, that with your powerful aid, we can counteract them. There is to be a great Convention holden in Pittsburgh on the 5th. of October. What I would suggest, is, that you come into Ohio, visit the parts where your presence may be most needed, and be at said convention on the 5th. The gentlemen named & myself, consider that this movement, upon your part, would also be of much importance in reference to *ulterior operations*. Under the one term system, the moment one president is chosen, his successor will be either spoken of or brought into the field. Upon this subject I need not be more explicit. You know my views. Please acknowledge the receipt of this,[4] & believe me to remain, as ever, Yours   Jas. Wilson

ALS. MHi.

1. The tristate Whig convention, held in Wheeling on September 3, drew an estimated 30,000 persons; DW had been invited, but declined. See J. S. Shriver et al. to DW, July 9, 1840 (mDW 16815); and DW to Shriver et al., August 3, 1840 (mDW

16865).

2. Peterson, a native of Wheeling, was an agent for eastern land speculators. It has not been established where he invested for DW. See DW to Hiram Ketchum, February 7, [1837], mDW 38663.

3. Bayard (1791–1863), a son of

Stephen, was probably engaged in
boat-building in Pittsburgh.
   4. DW's response has not been

found. He did not campaign in Ohio,
however.

TO SAMUEL JAUDON

Boston Sept. 15th. 1840.

My dear Sir,

By the time this reaches New York, I trust you will be there to receive
it and I propose to proceed to the South at the end of this week, chiefly
for the purpose of seeing you, first and chiefly to learn the state of things
respecting the Clamorgan Scrip. I hope the stocks are brought over, or
left behind under such circumstances as that I can draw on you, for
while I have the poverty of Job, my creditors have not his patience.

A second object is of a different nature. Mr. Biddle and I have determined that it is proper on your arrival on your native shores that you
should have a dinner, to be given in New York by those who think well
of your efforts to sustain American Credit abroad or who may have experienced abroad the kindness which you have habitually shown your
countrymen. I think this is justly due to you and that it's effect will be
good.[1]

If this shall find you already in New York please give me a line in
answer[2] as it will be Saturday P.M. before I shall leave this City. Your's
always truly,   Daniel Webster by D.F. Webster.

Dictated letter. NHi.
   1. For a discussion of Jaudon's efforts in London and Paris, see *Correspondence*, 4:392–398, *passim*;
and Thomas Payne Govan, *Nicholas
Biddle, Nationalist and Public Banker, 1786–1844* (Chicago, 1959), pp.

365–375. It has not been established
that the dinner was held. *Niles' National Register*, 59 (October 3, 1840):
80, reported that Jaudon would be returning to England "in the course of
three or four weeks."
   2. Reply not found.

*His support of the Hartford convention proved to be a rumor that Web-
ster never lived down. He was not a candidate for office in 1840, but the
charges against him persisted. In the letter below to Charles William Cutter (1799–1856; Harvard 1818), Portsmouth lawyer, legislator, court
clerk, and reportedly an editor of the* Portsmouth Journal, *Webster again
denied having any connection with the convention. The discussion on
this occasion arose when Portsmouth Whigs alleged that gubernatorial
candidate Henry Hubbard, Isaac Hill, Isaac Waldron (1774–1845), a
Portsmouth merchant, and William Garland, also a merchant, had
worked to send delegates to Hartford from New Hampshire in 1814.
Their efforts, the* Portsmouth Journal *stated, failed because of Webster's
opposition. See the* Portsmouth Journal of Literature and Politics, *September 19, 26, October 3, 1840.*

TO CHARLES WILLIAM CUTTER

New-York, Sept. 28, 1840.

Dear Sir:

In the Portsmouth Journal of the 26th Instant, I see a letter, or note, signed by Mr *Isaac Waldron*, in which, speaking of the *Hartford Convention*, he says:

"It so happened that I was the only person among the then Federal party in Portsmouth, as far as I can recollect, save Mr William Garland, who was opposed to the Hartford Convention; and I recollect, in a conversation with him on that subject, he fully agreed with me in opinion, and condemned the measure in the most unqualified terms. But that Mr. Daniel Webster ever opposed the sending of a Delegate from Portsmouth to the Hartford Convention, will, I think, be news to Mr. Webster as well as to myself,—for such, as far my information extends, is not the fact. I had as good means of knowing the views of Mr Webster, at that time, as almost any other person, and it is my belief, had he not been at that time a member of Congress, he would probably have been a Delegate from New-Hampshire to that Convention ISAAC WALDRON."

I must be permitted to say that Mr Isaac Waldron assumes for himself a knowledge of my opinions, which he never possessed, as I never had any communication with him on the subject, in any form, nor had he ever any other means of knowing them. With Mr. Garland, of whom he speaks, I was in habits of confidential correspondence,[1] *and with him, on this, as on other subjects, I had the most perfect concurrence of opinion.*

But any body, who knows any thing of the subject, knows that I left home to attend my duties in Congress, before the proceedings in the Legislatures of the neighboring States, in relation to the subject, had been had, and that the Convention was over, and dispersed, before the session of Congress terminated. I am, dear sir, your obt. serv't,   Dan'l Webster.

Text from the *Portsmouth Journal of*   1. No correspondence between DW
Literature and Politics, October 3,   and Garland has been found.
1840. Original not found.

TO CAROLINE LE ROY WEBSTER

Franklin Oct. 26. [1840]
Monday Morng.

Dear Wife,

You will perceive, that this letter is in the hand writing of Mr [Charles Brickett] Hadduck; and it is well, that he is with me, for I have been quite unwell for the last three or four days. They carried me from Nashua to Francestown & from Francestown to Orford,[1] in these miserable go-carts, called barouches—all open in front; and, as the wind was from the North West, with much rain, I had to bear the beating of both. I took up Mr

Hadduck at Hanover; and, when I arrived at Orford, on Thursday evening, I felt down sick, and went immediately to bed; and kept it till noon, on Friday, when I went out, & made my speech, returned & went to bed again, & sent for a Physician. This Physician gave me quantities of Calomel, and, on Saturday, morning I felt somewhat better. I was received into the house of Col. [Edward M.] Bissell,[2] a gentleman, whom you saw on the 10th of Sepr. at our rooms, with Mr [Abiathar G.?] Britton.[3] He and his wife are the kindest people in the world, and gave me every attention. I dont know, that I should have escaped a fever, if I had been obliged to take the run of the tavern. Feeling better on Saturday morning, and the gentlemen furnishing a close carriage for Mr Hadduck & myself, we set out for this place, but only reached Andover that day; for when I got there, I was very much fatigued. We arrived yesterday at ten oclock; but, still, I did not feel well. Common medicine, such as magnesia &c. seemed to have no effect. My skin was very dry & hard. I, therefore, sent for a Physician, & told him to give me a powerful emetic, which he did. I have heard of Thompson's Medicines, some called "screw sugar," some called "wild-cat," but I never took any thing, which made such thorough work with me; I feel much relieved this morning, and mean to get up by & by. But I dictate this from my bed. By way of variety & amusement we had a fall of six inches of snow last night! I shall not be able of course, to attend the meeting at Salisbury today. I lament this very much; but it cannot be helped.

I have written to Mr. [John Plummer] Healey[4] to inform all inquirers, that I shall make no more speeches any where, or under any circumstances. I shall keep still, here, today, and amuse myself by looking out upon the snow. And as soon as I feel able, I shall take the stage coach to Nashua, & so home.

Mrs Ezekiel [Webster][5] is about visting Boston. I think I shall meet her at Concord, and bring her along. John [Taylor's] Family are well. He'd a severe fit of illness in the summer, arising I suspect, from overwork; but he is now quite restored. When we saw him, he was fearful, that the drought would much diminish his crops, but they came in better than he expected. He beats all N.H. for turnips & carrots, which important things I thus mention to you, because, when you have all read this letter, in Boston, I wish you to send it to Henry Thomas; and for the particular benefit of Henry, I wish to add, that John will send down the oxen by the first opportunity, and, perhaps, two or three young cattle with them.

And so no more at present. Yours truly   Danl Webster in bed

LS. NhHi. Published in Van Tyne, pp. 670–671.

1. DW spoke at Whig rallies in Francestown on October 20, and in Orford on October 23.

2. Bissell (1800–1857) was an Or-

ford merchant and state legislator.

3. Britton (1776–1853) was an Orford lawyer, businessman, and legislator.

4. Healy (1810–1882; Dartmouth 1835), after reading law with DW, served as his associate until 1852.

Intermittently he also sat in the Massachusetts legislature. For DW's letter to Healy, also dated October 26, see mDW 16971.

5. Achsah Pollard Webster (1801–1896), Ezekiel's widow, then a resident of Concord.

FROM JOHN JORDAN CRITTENDEN

Frankfort—Oct. 27th 1840.

My Dear Sir,

I have just read your Speech of the 5th Inst:, delivered at Richmond. It is a Capital one, & worthy of the occasion. I don't wonder that it has so much pleased the Virginians.[1]

Well, Sir—after all I do not know if Mr. Van Buren's Administration has not, on the whole been beneficial to the Country. It has produced an excitement, enquiry & discussion, that have made the whole people much better acquainted with their Government, & the proper principles of its policy. It has occasioned a communication & intercourse between the Citizens of different sections of the Union, to an extent that never existed before, and has thereby effaced a thousand prejudices & multiplied incalculably the bonds of National kindness & brotherhood. And whatever grievances we have suffered at his (Mr Van Buren's) hands, are we not just now the happiest people on the whole. I am ready, to give him an acquitance, and acknowledge myself fully compensated for my portion of the evils he has brought on us, by the happiness I now enjoy in the prospect of his utter defeat & over throw.

It seems to me that his doom is set[t]led, & certain. Kenty. Indiana, Ohio, &, I believe, Tennessee are surely against him. My opinion is that Illinois & Mississippi will also be against him, as Louisiana certainly will. So stands the case with us. Of other sections of the country I say nothing to you, who are better informed than I am.

Since the World began there was never before in the West such a glorious excitement & uproar among the people. It is a sort of Popular Insurrection, in which patriotism, intelligence & good order, have governed & prevailed in a most exemplary manner.

I am gratified always to hear of your movements & speeches, because I know that your words do not return in Vain.

And now, with my congratulations on the glorious prospects that surround us, I have only to add that I am Yr Friend &c   J J Crittenden

ALS. DLC.

1. An estimated 15,000 attended the Virginia Whig convention in Richmond. DW's speech on the occasion was carried in *Niles' National Register*, 59 (October 17, 1840): 107–111; it is conveniently reprinted in *W & S*, 3: 83–102.

Hard times, hard cider, and hard campaigning resulted in a sweeping victory for the Whigs in November. Harrison won nineteen of the twenty-six states, carrying seven of the southern states and every northern state except New Hampshire and Illinois. With majorities in both houses of Congress, Webster and other Whig leaders with whom he corresponded began to turn their attention to the assumption of the reins of government.

TO NATHANIEL F. WILLIAMS

Boston Nov. 7. '40

My Dear Sir

Your friend has been so busy, I have not been able to see him. But his cash is ready for him, & he is to take it this morning. I did not intend to draw on you again; but when I came home, finding how little time I had, I drew a Bill & sent it to the Bank where I do business, & it was discounted. It will come along for your acceptance, which you will please honor it with. When I go on, I will see you, & we will arrange to wind up this, without giving you further trouble.

Well! My Dear Sir, we have lived to see a great revolution accomplished. I now pause, to reflect—to be grateful—so to contemplate the dangers we have escaped, & the new prospects which are now before us. I need rest; I intend to keep quiet here, till it shall be time to go to Washington. Your noble State has acquitted herself bravely; & the Whigs of your City deserve all praise. Your good old native State [Massachusetts] votes on Monday—never fear her. Yr friend, with a thankful heart,

Danl Webster

ALS. NhD.

FROM GEORGE AUGUSTUS WAGGAMAN

Baltimore 8th. Nov. 1840

My dear Mr. Webster,

Leaving here tomorrow for La, I cannot deny myself the pleasure of offering to you my most hearty congratulations on the glorious result of the late Election. To you Sir, more than any other man is due the Credit of having broken down the political Monster that has well nigh destroyed the energies and morals of the American people.

In the organization of the new administration that people will not be satisfied unless you be the first and foremost in official Station. I well know that to you personally it is not desirable, but that never flinching patriotism that has caused you to devote your unrivalled talents for so long a time, to the Service of your Country will still I ardently hope impel you on in the glorious career.

If you be not at the head of that Cabinet I much fear the loss of the practical benefit of your previous services to the Country. Every thing will depend on the first start; and whether that will be for good or evil will depend on the wisdom and capacity of those who counsel and direct its policy. You well know by whom and how much the head of the government will be surrounded; and how necessary it will be to guard against those errors that would tumble the Party into ruin and irreparable disaster.

Excuse the liberty I have taken and see in it only, the love esteem and respect of your very faithful friend and Servant   George A Waggaman

Take care of [William Cabell] Rives, trust him not, he cannot be your friend.

ALS. NhD.

TO JOHN MIDDLETON CLAYTON

Marshfield, (near Boston)
Nov. 16. 1840

My Dear Sir,

Neither you nor I have occasion to be ashamed of the States in which we live. Massachusetts has done well, though perhaps little more than was expected of her; but Delaware has truly signalized herself. Her previous situation was one of much embarrassment, & the Whigs have extricated her from it, with wonderful success. I congratulate you, My Dear Sir, most heartily, not only on the good conduct of Delaware & Massachusetts, but on the great & glorious general result. The revolution is so extensive, so complete, & so over whelming, that I can scarcely realize it. And now, my Dear Sir, what are the Whigs to do? A very great responsibility is upon them. The revenues of the Country are in a bad state, the currency in a worse, and the manufacturing interest likely soon to be much depressed.

The State of things requires, in my judgment, the deep reflection, & cordial concert of action, of all good men. I can hardly say how much pleasure it would give me to anticipate your appearance, again, in the Senate; though you would hardly expect me to be willing, even for the purpose of securing so desirable an object, to part with your relative, Mr Thomas Clayton, whom I look upon as one of our soundest & best members. At any rate, I shall be most desirous of seeing you, & of consulting with you, at an early day. Can you not make a short visit to Washington, soon after the commencement of the Session? If you defer it till the 4th. of March, or even till late in the Winter, the City will be full of people, & there will be no leisure for conference, & deliberate consultation. I intend to be early at Washington, & shall be happy to hear from you. Yours with true & sincere regard,   Danl Webster

ALS. DLC.

FROM MICHENOR CADWALLADER

Buffalo, Nov. 18th. 1840.

Dear Sir,

Before adverting to the main objects of this letter, permit me to congratulate you, as a true Whig—as an American Citizen, "to the manor born"—upon the auspicious result of the recent Presidential contest. After years of toil, the strong hands and the true hearts, who have been battling it manfully in defence of the Constitution and national liberty, have at length succeeded in achieving a revolution, which I trust will be as lasting and salutary in its effects, as its occurrence has been a signal & merited rebuke to those who sought and attained power by unjust means, only that it might be exercised for unholy, corrupt & selfish purposes. The struggle has been [an] arduous one, and presented features, moreover, that no true friends of the country could desire often again to look upon. Long may it be ere such another effort may be necessary to oust from the bureaus of State unfaithful ministers of the publick affairs! Such another victory, indeed, might be the uprooting of the republic itself.

But to the matter which induced the penning of this sheet.

My experience in political life, has convinced me, that much and serious evil has resulted from the practice which has latterly prevailed of connecting the newspaper press with the publick printing—in as much as thousands of dollars are thus taken from the national treasury to sustain a print purely partisan in its character and objects—and, as experience has latterly shown, totally reckless of the general prosperity of the country, and devoted to the accomplishment of the most unholy purposes. This should not be. A free press is a blessing. A subsidized or pampered press, a curse of the first magnitude. But more especially is the latter the case, when the controlling or corrupting power is the Federal Executive, or those devoted to his will, & having a direct & palpable interest in his continuing to be the chief alimoner[?] of the national treasury. Thus thinking, I have long entertained a belief that an effort should be made to separate entirely the printing of Congress & the Departments from the Newspaper press, so far as is practicable, but so long as the party at present in control of the national affairs was in power, I deemed it to be worse than useless for any person to make an effort to bring about such a desirable result. As new men are soon to come into power, however, in the executive branch of the government, & as a corresponding change will doubtless take place in the legislative branch, a favorable season to broach the subject, &, I hope, to perfect the measure, will be presented, and it ought by all means to be improved.

My plan is, to have a national printing establishment—and I have made an estimate of the probable cost, &c; but which I do not at present deem necessary to submit to you. In this way, I am convinced, a considerable saving might be made—at the same time that the patronage of the government would be much reduced, and the pernicious influence of a partisan press, sustained by direct levies upon the treasury, be cut off— with the additional advantage, that the work would be much better executed. But as you have turned your attention, doubtless, to this matter, & have better means of judging of the feasibility of my project, or of the best course to be pursued in the premises, I have thought it best to communicate with you, before taking any further steps in the matter myself, as you may possibly have matured some plan of your own. At all events you are a better judge as to the time when a movement should be made, if made at all.[1]

There is one thing, however, that may stand in the way of an early accomplishment of a measure of the kind—I mean the *necessities* of Messrs [Joseph] Gales & [William Winston] Seaton. A strong effort will undoubtedly be made by the friends of these estimable gentlemen to give them another benefit. But how far sympathy & friendship for them, however worthy they may be, should outweigh the manifest interests—political, at least—of the people, I will not pretend to decide now. I would be willing to trust them as far, (if not farther,) as any politicians within my knowledge, and would moreover, exceedingly rejoice at their prosperity—but in carrying out a principle, the line of travel should always be a straight-forward one.

Before closing this subject, I would add, further, that I feel more than an ordinary desire for this separation of the State & the Press, at an early day, from an apprehension that I entertain, that we are not far removed from another political convulsion, to grow out of the tariff and land questions, to say nothing of other unsettled questions of not very trifling moment. I know not how parties may, at the onset, be divided in reference to these grave matters—and it is very possible, that an ably conducted press, sustained by thousands taken from the common treasure, might be anything else than an advocate of, or even neutral in respect to, the interests & the rights of the northern portion of our Union. There is many a "far reaching Buckingham" amongst us—many a one who has a longing heart & an itching palm for the truncheon of power—who might feel inclined to take a strange course in regard to the above questions, & who would have no serious objections to the backing of a strong paper, sustained by other means than those derived directly from individual & voluntary contributions. And I, as one of the great family of freemen "north of Mason & Dixon's line"—whose best interests have too long been made the footballs of speculating politicians—feel no desire to run any further risks, from an arrangement of the kind.

The matter here touched upon, is one entirely worthy of cogitations, grave & serious—but as you are far better qualified than I am to trace its various points & bearings, I shall trouble you with no further speculations of mine—And will here close the subject, with the request, that if you think my suggestions & views in reference to a national printing house are well taken, you will favor me with a communication on the subject.[2]

It was my design to have spent the winter at Washington, on account of the necessity there is for my abandoning, for the season, this airy perch, on account of my health—but as my pen is my only means of support, and I could find nothing to do at Washington—I must forego the intention. I shall spend the winter at Albany.

You will pardon this unreasonably long letter. But as I consider the matters touched upon in it, as worthy of the serious attention of every American, whatever may be his standing in the political world, I could not refrain from addressing you on the subject—And the more especially as I felt confident, at the same time, that you would not consider anything as obtrusive, that pointed, ever so remotely, to the preservation of our national happiness, prosperity—& Independence. With much esteem & regard Yours, &c.   M. Cadwallader

ALS. DLC. Cadwallader (1798–1864), a native of Pennsylvania, settled in western New York in the 1820s, where he edited the *New York Journal* (1826), the *Niagara Courier* (1828–1832), and the *Buffalo Whig and Journal* (1836–1838). Later he served as clerk in the Recorder's Court and as city clerk and comptroller.

1. The office of the superintendent of public printing was not created until August 26, 1852.

2. Not found.

TO SAMUEL FROTHINGHAM

Boston Nov 20. 1840.

Dear Sir,

I wish you to write to my friend Mr. Jaudon at London, requesting him to negotiate for Cash the two remaining instalments, on the sale of my 58 Shares in the Clamorgan Co. Stock due in 1841 and 1842 and payable in U.S. Bank Stock, and after deducting there from the £1000. Stg. due from me to him and interest, to remit you the balance of the nett proceeds in gold sovereigns, insuring the same in London. Or if he should receive the U.S. Bank Shares therefor, then to sell enough of them to pay himself the £1000. Stg. and either sell the balance and remit you the gold as above, or send you the remaining U.S. Bank Shares, as he may think best.

It would be well for you to send this to Mr. Jaudon, that he may hand it to Virgil Maxcy Esq as authority for Mr. M. to arrange with and hand over to Mr. Jaudon for the two last instalments as above, should Mr. M not already feel authorized so to do. Yours with much regard,

Danl Webster

LS. DLC.

FROM JOHN MIDDLETON CLAYTON

Dover—Delaware—Novr. 22. 1840.

My dear Sir,

Your letter of the 16th instant[1] was received by me amidst a scene of the greatest exultation and triumph by the Whigs of Delaware. Our official majority for Harrison is 1096, which, numbers considered, exceeds Harrison's majority in Ohio. We have carried our Governour for 4 years, Rep. in Congress *two Senators in Congress* (there's the rub) 3 electors, all the Senators elected in the State Legislature, a unanimous Whig House of Representatives, every Sheriff & coroner in the State, every county & *every officer in every hundred* of each county.

Verily you and I did not expose ourselves in the rain for nothing in that city of Wilmington.

And now you will ask, what shall the Whigs do? You know my views. I am a *Whig*—a believer in the doctrines of George Washington. We ought to go back to the principles of the fathers of the republic and imitate their example by regulating the currency as they did & by encouraging home industry as they did. I cannot give you all my thoughts in a letter. But let me say—have nothing to do with the experiment of the State Banks when the subtreasury is repealed. Disaster and disgrace will follow both. If there is to be no National Bank, all the State Banks will suspend again in two years after the repeal of the subtreasury. As to the revenue, it will be deficient to support the government, and duties must be laid to protect our manufactures agreeably to the spirit & letter of our compromise act of 1833. Why not fund the debt left by Van Buren on the country?

Is it not time to enact some law to carry out the principle of *home valuations* pledged in the compromise act? What do you suppose southern men (anti-tariff) will give as an equivalent for surrendering that and laying new duties on a foreign valuation?

If I can get time, I will come & see you at Washington this winter. Friends here desire me to go back to the Senate, but I have declined & shall adhere to my profession in preference. Yet though in private life, my thoughts are constantly on the state of the country & have been ever since I left the public service. May God bless and reward your noble efforts for our country is the prayer of Yours faithfully   John M. Clayton

ALS. InHi.
   1. See above.

FROM NICHOLAS BIDDLE

Phila. Decr. 9. 1840

My Dear Sir,

   Soon after leaving you yesterday, I found myself struck inwardly by the cold of the last few days in such a manner as obliged me to go to bed —and this morning on repairing to your lodgings <found> learned that <I had missed the chance of seeing you> you had left town. I had previously sent last night for Mr [Thomas] D(unlap)[1] & urged upon him in the strongest manner the resumption of the old & intimate connexion which existed in my time. He was perfectly sensible of the value of that connection & very anxious to renew it—but in reference to the [m]atter about which you & he communicated, he was crossed much to his mortification by two or three little people. Their [interf?]erence & their connexion with the Institution will however [term]inate with <the year &> the present month when he hopes to [be a]t liberty to do what he desires.

   I feel very anxious <to be> about the result of the other matter—the ostracism[2]—& wish <very much> that the moment the course is ascertained you will let me know by an intelligible phrase how things stand. In the mean time I remain Very truly Yrs   N Biddle

ALS draft. DLC.
   1. Dunlap (1792–1864) was a lawyer and at this time president of the Pennsylvania Bank of the United States.
   2. The significance of the "ostracism" reference has not been determined. In response to Biddle's letter,

DW wrote on December 10: "I thank you for your friendly letter. In all that respects one of the subjects, let us wait until next month.
   "On the other—& the more important, what I have to say is, *dismiss all fears—but say nothing*" (mDW 17112).

FROM JULIA WEBSTER APPLETON

Boston, Friday Dec 11th. [1840]

   I thank you dear Father, for your kind letter from Philadelphia, which I received to day, & still more for the verses inclosed in it.[1] I think them beautiful, dear Father, & thank you for associating me in remembrance with my dearest Mother. I have never thought of her so often as since I have had a child of my own;[2] and could I be but half as good a Mother as she was, I might hope to fulfil my duty to my little girl; but her's I fear, was a goodness which I can not attain.

We are all quite well here. My strength increases gradually, and I hope before long to be quite myself again. I wish you could see my baby. She has improved very much since you left; & begins to show some signs of intelligence. Every body says she is a very bright child, but of course every body would tell it's mother so, and she, of course, believes it.

We can not have had as much snow here as there has been further South, for I have not heard of the railroads being impeded. We have had enough however to make poor sleighing, & intolerable walking.

You are now, I suppose, immersed once more in the cares and excitements of public life. Do not let it interfere with your health dear Father. Pray let that be your greatest consideration. Surely you have done enough for your country—did you never utter another word in its behalf—to be considered the best & noblest among the noble sons of America. Has not the fame of your goodness, your greatness, extended to the uttermost parts of the earth? It can not be increased; & do not, dearest Father, wear yourself out for the good of a country ungrateful at best. What is the whole country, to your family, when weighed in the balance with one hour of anxiety or sickness which it causes you? I am no great patriot. I do not love Rome better than Caesar; the advancement of party better than my own dear Father. I delight to think that you have never held an office, a fact which can be pointed to as proof, if proof were wanting of the perfect disinterestedness of your patriotism.

Don't you think you would be happy to live once more, at home, with your old friends. Do come back to us, dear Father, & do not be persuaded to stay in Washington, by persons who may not be altogether disinterested in their motives—who may look to you to advance them further, than their own unassisted efforts could ever do. Do not be angry with me, dear Father, for saying all this; my pen, I fear, has outrun my discretion, but I have thought so much on the subject lately, that I have said more than I intended. I am not naturally suspicious, but I do mistrust some of your friends. I hope I am wrong. You must not think that my husband has influenced me at all; as he does not know of my writing you, & perhaps would think me quite wrong in doing so. You must forgive me if I have said more than a daughter ought.

I hear from Mother frequently. She seems to be having a gay time in New York. Every thing goes on in our quiet town [as when you were] here. The ladies are more interes[ted in the] prospect of "assemblies" than any t[hing else.] Caroline [Story White Webster] & her children are quite we[ll]. Mr [John Benjamin] Joy is shooting deer on the Cape. He sent home a noble one yesterday. I believe they have killed two of the poor things. Mr [Stephen] White & his wife are at the Maverick House.

I hope you will succeed in getting comfortable lodgings in Washington.

Pray remember me to Mrs [Emeline Colby Webster] Lindsley & Harriet [Colby Webster]. Caroline Appleton[3] desires her best love to you, & I am ever, dear Father, Your affectionate daughter   Julia

ALS. NhHi. Published in *PC*, 2: 91–93.

1. Not found.

2. Julia had recently given birth to her first child, a daughter, Caroline

Le Roy Appleton.

3. Caroline, Julia's sister-in-law, was Eben Appleton's youngest daughter.

FROM NICHOLAS BIDDLE

Phila. Decr. 12. 1840

My dear Sir,

Most sincerely do I rejoice at what you intimate.[1] In consequence of it, I shall do two things inspired by these good auspices to the new course. First I shall write to <   > him which I had not yet done, a friendly note of congratulation[2] & second I shall also <advise> urge my brother, Major John Biddle to make an effort to go to the Senate thus strengthening *your* administration. With great regard Yrs   NB.

ALS draft. DLC.

1. See above, Biddle to DW, December 9, 1840, note 2.

2. Perhaps Biddle was referring to

President-elect William Henry Harrison, to whom he wrote on December 13, 1840. See Govan, *Nicholas Biddle*, p. 388.

TO HIRAM KETCHUM

Washington, December 18, 1840.

My Dear Sir,

I received your letter of the 15th last evening.[1] It had already been intimated to me, that a high judicial office was expected to be tendered to you, in the course of the spring and I have often reflected upon the subject.

In my opinion, you should decide this matter according to your liking. If you think you should be pleased with the performance of judicial duties, why here is an office, high in dignity, and respectable in emolument, and ought not to be refused. For my own part, I could never be a judge. Somehow I have always shrunk from the idea of judicial employment. There never was a time when I would have taken the office of Chief Justice of the United States, or any other judicial station. But this is matter of taste or feeling. I believe the truth may be, that I have mixed up so much study of politics with my study of law, that though I may have some respect for myself as advocate, and some estimate of my own knowledge of general principles, yet am not confident of possessing all the accuracy and precision of knowledge which the bench requires. But I am clear that if you like the business, you should not refuse this offer. Such opportunities do not occur every day.

I am aware, my dear Sir, quite well aware, that as a friend of mine, you could do me much more good, off the bench, than on it; and when the probabilty of your appointment was first mentioned to me, I felt unwilling that it should take place. But even while on the bench, we may hope for the benefit of your friendly advice, which I shall always most highly value, if not for your active efforts. As a question as to what is best for you, I can only repeat the opinion, that if you like the duties of the place, take it; there is nothing equally certain in the strife of politics.[2]

You will have heard all that is known here; and I presume little else will be heard until the General comes over the mountains. Mr. Clay is going to New York, and will probably be there when you receive this letter. I know not whether it be business or pleasure which takes him there. I am, dear Sir, very truly your friend,   Dan'l Webster.

Text from *PC*, 2: 95–96. Original not found. Ketchum (c. 1792–1870) was a New York City attorney, a close personal friend of DW, and a leader of the Webster Whigs in that city.
    1. Not found.

2. DW was alluding to Governor William H. Seward's nomination of Ketchum for circuit judge in New York. Before the confirmation, Seward withdrew the appointment.

TO PELEG SPRAGUE

Washington Decr. 19. 1840

Private

My Dear Sir

I cannot wonder that you have felt some indignation at these out-door movements, respecting the formation of the Cabinet. I am not at a loss to account for their origin, but never for a moment believed they would succeed. I knew that General H. himself felt under the greatest obligation to Massachusetts, because he had so expressed himself in his letters; & I have heard from others the same account which you give of the proceedings at Harrisburg.[1]

But I do not think the Genl. had any occasion to strengthen his fair intentions by reference to the transactions of the Convention. He has never thought of over-looking the North. On the contrary, he has acted just as you, & other friends of the writer of this, would have desired him to act.

You will perceive by the correspondence of the letter writers, that *two* places in the Cabinet are understood to be definitely assigned; the Department of State, & the office of Atty Genl.[2] Probably nothing else will be determined upon, until the President arrives. The greatest trouble will be to find a Secretary of the Treasury. Probably that post may fall to Mr. [Thomas] Ewing, Mr. [John] Sargeant, or Mr. John M. Clayton.[3] The necessity of *distribution* will not, I fear, leave the President at perfect liberty in the selection of men. I esteem it particularly important that he should do very liberal justice to the South; as the South, under what is already understood to be arranged, may be jealous of Northern preponderancy, in the public Counsels.[4] It must be confessed, however, that there is difficulty, in finding men in the South Atlantic States, whom even friends in those States will agree in recommending.

I should be glad to learn your opinions, on these matters, as you know the individuals from among whom a choice must be made.

When your time & your eyes will allow you, do me the favor to let me hear from you. I am, Dear Sir, Very truly, your friend   Danl. Webster

ALS. MDuHi.

1. Sprague's account of the Harrisburg convention has not been found.

2. DW had already been designated for secretary of state, and John J. Crittenden, for attorney general.

3. Ewing received the Treasury post.

4. Harrison's two southern appointees were John Bell of Tennessee to the War Department, and George E. Badger of North Carolina to the Navy.

TO [JOHN PLUMMER HEALY]

Washington Decr. 21. 1840

Dear Sir

I have your letter, respecting Mr [Hall Jackson] Kelly's claim,[1] but fear we can do nothing for him, as the indemnity provided for is limited to cases, which have been previously brought to the notice of our Govt, by letters or memorials presented to the Sec. of State. I do not see that this was done, in Mr Kelley's case.

This Board acts strangely.[2] I doubt whether a single claim will be got through. The American & Mexican ministers can agree upon nothing; not even so far as to bring the cases to a condition, for the interposition of the umpire. The Mexicans will not agree that parties shall appear, by themselves or their counsel—nor present any papers or proofs, not already in the office of the Secretary of State. In short, if rightly reported to me, their conduct indicates a disposition to do nothing under the Treaty.

I hope Mr [Franklin] Haven[3] will have recd such information as will satisfy him about the note-—as I am likely to come upon the Parish. Yrs truly   D. Webster

ALS. MHi.

1. See John Plummer Healy to DW, December 16, 1840, mDW 17142. Kelly (1790–1874) had a claim against Mexico for the detention of

goods at Vera Cruz in 1833. His case was not settled until February 22, 1842.

2. DW was referring to the Board of Commissioners established under

the convention with Mexico of April 11, 1839.

3. Haven (1804–1893) was president of the Merchants' Bank in Boston, a position he held for more than forty-five years. DW and Haven had already formed a close social and financial relationship: the Boston banker became an important source of political and financial backing while DW was able to bring governmental business and an occasional appointment Haven's way.

President-elect Harrison offered Webster his choice of either the Treasury or the State Department, and on December 11 Webster indicated that he would take the State Department post. As word of Webster's decision spread, hordes of hungry office seekers approached him, just as they were already approaching Harrison, for a choice appointment. Most had considerably less national influence than Webster's longtime friend and financial backer, Nicholas Biddle, former president of the Bank of the United States, who, in the letter below, sought the Austrian mission. Although Biddle was directly involved at this time in efforts to persuade the officers of the Bank of the United States of Pennsylvania, the old national bank, to cancel Webster's indebtedness of $114,000, Webster turned down Biddle's request. The rejection in no way weakened their relationship, nor did it diminish Biddle's efforts to help Webster with the settlement of his debt. As many of the letters below show, Biddle had several other friends and acquaintances who wanted jobs; some of these Webster accommodated. Furthermore, Biddle still looked to Webster, the foremost Congressional spokesman for the Bank, to lead in bringing the nation back from the verge of financial collapse, perhaps through the creation of another national bank.

TO NICHOLAS BIDDLE

Dec. 24. '40

Private
My Dear Sir

I duly recd your letter, on a certain subject, & have that subject "in all my thoughts."[1] Nothing could be better for the Country—& nothing would be more agreeable to me, than what you suggested. The difficulty will be with the *Tobacco* men. Those Gentlemen got up the Austrian Mission, some years ago, & expected a Marylander or a Virginian to fill it.[2] Mr. V. Buren disappointed that expectation, & appointed Mr [Henry Augustus] Muhlenbergh, because he could talk German so well. Mr M. having returned, a new rally has been making, & one two or three Tobacco raising candidates are in the field already.

Our latest accounts from Genl. H. are, that he may be expected here about the middle of January—stay here a few days, then go to Va. & pass some time with his friends & relatives, & come to Washington again in due season.

As to Cabinet arrangements, I know of but two things which are regarded as settled; they are, the appointment to the State Dept. & that to the office of Atty Genl. The necessity, real or supposed, of *distribution*— somewhat restricts the choice of men. If I hear any thing further, I will let you know. Yrs   D Webster

ALS. DLC. Published in part in Mc-Grane, *Correspondence of Nicholas Biddle*, p. 339.

1. Biddle had requested the appointment as United States minister to Austria. See Biddle to DW, December 13, 1840, mDW 17131.

2. In line with DW's suggestion, Daniel Jenifer of Maryland received the appointment.

TO SAMUEL BULKLEY RUGGLES

Washington Decr. 24. '40

My Dear Sir,

The conception of a large and useful object, & the judicious resort to means calculated to effect that object, constitute merit. This you will admit. Now, I claim this merit. I have in my mind an object of much utility, as I think; & the means which have occurred to me are admirable. You shall see.

1. The object. It is to present a view—a comparative view—of the importance of our foreign trade, & our domestic trade.

The amount of our foreign commerce is easily seen, as the Annual Documents show it.

But how do I propose to get at any tolerable estimate of our domestic Intercourse? This is the difficult point; & here my singular skill manifests itself. I propose to obtain such an estimate *by requesting S. B. Ruggles to make it for me*! There is ingenuity!

Materials

1. Amt. of coasting tonnage, & estimate of the number of voyages annually.
2. An estimate of the freight, earned by coasting vessels.
3. An estimate of Steam Boat transportation, & freight earned.
4. The amount of the annual receipts of canal tolls, in all the U.S.
5. D[itt]o R. Roads.
6. Amt. of cotton, Rice, tobacco, corn, naval stores &c. purchased by the North of the South, as far as can be estimated, or guessed at.
7. Vice versa, the sales of fish, manufactures &c., of the North, sold in the South.

To be serious, My Dear Sir, I am anxious to say something, about the end of next month, upon the subject intimated above, and I would be very glad of any aid you can give me, in getting materials together.[1] Yours truly   Danl. Webster

ALS. MHi. Published in *W & S*, 16: 335–336.

1. For Ruggles's response, dated January 9, 1841, see below. It has not been established that DW delivered a speech using such material in early 1841.

FROM JAMES F. CONOVER

Cincinnati Decr. 24th. 1840

Dear Sir

The paragraph which recently appeared in the N. York Com. Advertiser announcing your appointment to, and acceptance of the Office of Secretary of State, and that of Mr. Crittenden to the Office of Attorney General,[1] was yesterday, in conversation, confirmed by Genl. Harrison, and I cannot forego the pleasure of congratulating both you and the country on the auspicious commencement of the duties of the new President. So far as I have heard, the intelligence gives universal satisfaction in this quarter, and as for myself, I am most highly gratified that the new Administration will have the advantage of your confidential advice, and personal influence and exertions. The commanding position, acknowledge[d] talents, political experience and influence of yourself and Mr. Clay, rendered it out of the question that Genl. Harrison could with propriety for a moment hesitate to offer both of you a choice of the highest and most important offices within his gift. Yours & Mr C's characters, services to the country and the Whig party, demanded from the new President this evidence of his discretion and accurate knowledge of the public voice, as well as a knowledge of what was due to the feelings of such distinguished champions of the Whig Cause. That the General has made such tender also to Mr. Clay, is well understood here, and it cannot but be a source of regret to the country at large that he declines the acceptance of any office, unless it be the consolation derived from the fact that his great talents and influence may be as beneficially exerted in his present position. Many of his warmest friends, however, I know feel gratified in the highest degree by his determination.

The General has been literally overrun with applications for Office, and the tact he has displayed in ridding himself of personal applicants, is alike amusing and pleasing to his best friends here, and shows his fitness for the station he is elected to occupy. His extreme reserve, however, even to his most intimate and influential friends here, as to his intentions respecting appointments, is a subject of some surprise, and I may add disappointment, if not mortification to such friends. Even

Judge [Jacob] Burnet and Col. [Nathaniel Green] Pendleton, I understand, did not know any thing of the offer made to you and Mr. Crittenden until they saw it in the N. York paper.

I regretted very much that my business last Spring and Summer,
while making my Eastern visit, prevented my extending my excursion
as far as Boston, as I had intended. It would have afforded me peculiar
pleasure to visit that place, (as I have never yet been there,) and to have
accepted your kind invitation to call on you.

Please present my best respects to Mrs. Webster, and accept for yourself the assurance of my profound respect and cordial friendship

James F. Conover

ALS. DLC. Conover (d. 1845) was a
Cincinnati lawyer, former publisher
of the *Cincinnati Daily Whig,* and an
official of the Cincinnati Gas and
Coke Company.

1. The New York *Commercial Advertiser,* December 16, 1840, reported:
"On the first day of the present session, *Daniel Webster* was tendered

the situation of Secretary of State, or
Secretary of the Treasury, or any
other post of the new administration
that he might choose. The country
will rejoice to learn that he will take
the former. It is equally certain that
Mr. Crittenden, of Kentucky, will receive the post of Attorney General.
Noble beginnings, these."

FROM DANIEL FLETCHER WEBSTER

Peru. Dec. 28th. 1840.

My dear Father,

I have been quite occupied ever since my return home in preparing my
affairs for my journey East. Your property here has occupied my mind
very much & do what I can it seems to be nothing but paying out. I wrote
you from Chicago about the taxes on Wisconsin property.[1]

I am going to Princeton to-morrow to look after your Bureau [County]
lands & expect to find taxes to pay as also on Rock Island and Prophet's
Town.

I have paid one hundred dollars on White Hall in satisfaction of the
Lien recovered against it last Court & there will be something over another hundred to clear it. I wrote you what I have done with Wood's
Mortgage.[2] The Miller Farm which I sold you gives me much trouble &
there will have to be I fear payments on that. This is a most disagreeable
letter to be sure, but I feel that I ought to let you know how the lands are
situated. I hope that if we hold on to them they may pay for all the
trouble they have caused.

I learn nothing of how affairs are working in a political way, but I
confess what little I see in the papers is any thing but pleasant. I remain
here only to settle up those affairs of yours of which I have the management & hope to leave for the East in three weeks at farthest.

I have sold every thing of mine except books & they bring something over all my debts. Every thing is perfectly dead here. Our Railroad is stopped—the Canal, like a wounded snake, lives & moves in one or two places only.[3] The Legislature means to give it's last kick with all the Locofocoism it can muster.

I learn they are all well in Boston.

I should not receive an answer to this, hoping to leave Peru before it reaches Washington. With my best love to Mother I am, dear Father, Yr. affectionate Son   Danl. F. Webster.

ALS. NhHi.
1. Letter not found.
2. Letter not found.
3. DFW was referring to the Illi-
nois Central Railroad and the Illinois and Michigan Canal under construction at and near Peru.

FROM NICHOLAS BIDDLE

Phila. Decr. 30, 1840

(*Private*)

My dear Sir

I received yesterday your two notes.[1] I shall forthwith see one or two persons whose sledgehammers will hit the nail on the head of that <topic> iron question.

There are two or three things which you had better know—for as you are to steer, you must see the shoals.

1 There was a story <which came> from Washington, that Mr Ewing could not serve because he was connected with Mr Elihu Chauncey,[2] in some large enterprize—& that Mr Chauncey had objected to his leaving the concern. This is a mistake. The concern here belongs to Mr Chauncey & myself. <   > He has intimated no such purpose—& I <have said> <written> <that he not> wrote to him not to let this personal consideration <to outweigh his> prevent his going to Washington. On that subject therefore no private interest operates.

2. I have <just> received a <long> visit of <several> many hours from a friend who has <been> just returned after passing several weeks in the midst of the most confidential circle of the President Elect and his friends—<   > a disinterested cool observer and I have no doubt of the truth of his observations. <What I gather is this important matter> <Among other things which> He says decidedly that in the opinion of all <those confidential persons> that circle Mr W[ebster] is <considered as> the person who will have <much> more influence with the President than Mr. C[lay]. <There is undoubtedly something, not yet expressed but perfectly understood which will make the Prest incline much

more to the counsels of the former than the latter.> You will take care not to repeat that anticipation, but it is well for you to know that it is expected you shall take the lead.

3. Then again he thinks Mr [Thaddeus] Stevens <was> <is> not <at all> likely to succeed. <His opinions and the mode in which he is put forward are against him.> This is understood in the West—and already the progress of alienation may be distinctly seen in the members of the Electoral College <who nominated him> of Penna—of whom my friend saw two.

4 His competitor here does nothing—knows nothing, and is already malcontent, so I understand for I have not seen him.[3] But my friend says that as the taint of abolitionism is what the President is specially anxious to avoid, he does not like the suspicion under which our Phila. candidate labors on that head.

[5.] My friend came full of another idea. He says that the circle in question incline much to avoid if possible the present agitation of the National Bank, & prefer some quiet arrangement with the existing institution[,] that the same knot are great friends of mine[,] that the President himself when lately at Louisville made a very strong & decided eulogium upon me, and that this circle of friends believe that he wishes me to <be the Secy of the> go into the Treasury. When I told him my determination on that head, he concluded with <an aphorism> this declaration, ["]Well I assure you, you can make the Secretary of the Treasury." Now I would not go into the Treasury <   for all> for all the money in it—but if I <can contribute> could help to put a good man there I would do so. But where is the man? If in this turmoil of Pennsylvania candidates, the President wants to get over a difficulty by naming a Penna man <& thereafter not a competitor> & wishes to name me I will refuse by return of mail, and then we can find some competent person. I mention this, that you may understand exactly <how> the footing on which Mr. H. and I are.

So much for my gossip—divided into five heads, which has the advantage of being at least true. <Very truly> <N> With great regard Yrs   N B.

ALS draft. DLC. Published in part in McGrane, *Correspondence of Nicholas Biddle*, pp. 339–340.

1. See DW to Nicholas Biddle, December 28, 1840, mDW 17173, 17177. DW requested price data on iron and reported Harrison's expected arrival in Washington.

2. Chauncey (1779–1847; Yale 1796) was an influential Philadelphia lawyer and financier, at this time president of the Reading Railroad.

3. Rumors circulated that two Pennsylvanians were under consideration for cabinet posts—John Sergeant for the Treasury and Thaddeus Stevens for postmaster general.

FROM CHARLES ANDERSON WICKLIFFE

Bardstown

De. 31. 1840

Dr Sir

Since my last letter to you[1] (a few days since mailed at this place) tho written two weeks ago, I have met with an article in a New York paper which speaks understandingly that you have determined to accept the office of secretary of state.[2] I congratulate the Nation & Genl Harrison upon this subject, tho you must know my old *Jackson* principle is yet entertained that the appointment of members of congress to office was dangerous. Yours may & will form an exception and I informed Genl Harrison that you were the only man whom I could advise him to take from Congress. It seems however that others will be and I hope for one best. Why I trouble you again is that I see one idea gaining ground that a called session of Congress will take place.[3] My dear Sir prevent and avoid this by all means. If Mr Van B. and the present congress will not do their duty but wickedly leave the country in a condition to suffer let them take the responsibility and receive the bitter curses of the people. Let the Sub-Treasury operate until the regular Session, and the conservatives will then join in and give to the Nation a Bank with competent powers to regulate the currency and act as the fiscal agent of the Government.

If Genl. Harrison call congress public expectation will be too high and must be disappointed. The Whigs and conservatives will differ about state and a National Bank and the Locos will *en masse* vote against any measure which may be proposed. By December 1841, the Nation will be more clamorous upon the subject of a Bank. All sensible men must be satisfied that the state Bank system will not do, and Mr. Calhoun (God forgive him) states the question correctly when he says the issue is between a sub-Treasury & *a U.S. Bank.*

Let the Administration of Genl. Harrison have from the 4. March until December to spoil Mr. Van Burens Books. [Levi] Woodbury has kept them badly and much labor is required to make out a complete balance sheet; look into the post office affairs, Indian Beaureau &c &c and the Florida war &c. When congress meets in Dec. you will have materials to operate upon and Reforms enough to propose up and carry out I hope in good faith. Let us have no Jackson faithlessness upon this subject.

Mr Van Buren received his death blow at his called Session. Had he not committed this blunder he would have been reelected and if Genl H. call congress the Whig party will receive theirs rely upon it: but if they will take possession of the Government and await the regular action of the same, act prudently and fulfill their promises all will be well. You may think this is presumptive in one retired and secluded as I am and expect to be[.] I never laid claim to any superior sagacity or talents but I have a stock of common sense that I have found useful to myself if not to others and it has seldom if ever deceived me when called into exercise.

I have looked upon this called Session project as a common sense man and condemn it and shall fear the consequences to us. Let me hear from you. Your friend   C. A. Wickliffe

Who else will be in the Cabinet?

ALS. NjMoHP.

1. Not found.

2. See the New York *Commercial Advertiser*, December 16, 1840.

3. The *Cincinnati Republican*, as reported by the *National Intelligen-* *cer*, December 10, 1840, had suggested the need for a "called session" of Congress to deal with the nation's finances. The editorial had urged western state legislatures to consider the matter.

TO THEOPHILUS PARSONS

Washington Jan. 2. 1840 [1841]

My Dear Sir

I doubt whether I can give you any useful advice, touching the conduct of the Daily [*Advertiser*].[1] It is a very respectable print, conducted with judgment & intelligence. Mr. [Nathan] Hale does not love political strife, nor is he willing to undertake to give a lead to political opinion. He does not think much of us here, & therefore does not, I think, give great room for Congress proceedings.

I wish he had more disposition to seize on great National questions, discuss them, in all their forms, and awaken a livelier interest in the proceedings of the Genl. Govt.

You are undoubtedly right, in supposing that the *finance* question has been the leading cause of the Revolution. Why, then, should not the press keep the thoughts of men turned to that subject? Why, for example, should not the Editor of the Daily, dissect the Message, & the Secretarys Report, exposing errors & enforcing necessary truths? Why should not the necessity of doing something for the currency, be every day urged upon the People? Why should not the people of New England be shown what the condition of their manufactures must now shortly be, by the near approach of the *penult,* & indeed ere long of the *last* great reduction of duties? Why should not the Press raise its voice agt. the miserable policy of letting in free such enormous amounts of foreign luxuries? In short, My Dear Sir, if a paper is intended to be a mere Chronicle, that is one thing, but if it be meant to perform a political part, it must have discussion, spirited paragraphs, & the power, & habit, of presenting great truths in a variety of forms. In a single discourse, repetition is in bad taste. But the press cannot be effective without much of it. It must renew, today, the arguments of yesterday, & thus hold up, constantly, the truths, which it wishes to impress on the public mind. Well conducted efforts of this kind can alone constitute what we call a vigorous Press.

I will endeavor to send you the Documents, & should be most ready to give you any hints, which might be thought useful.

Congress is rather inert. A degree of lassitude seems to have followed the excitement of last session, & the summer & autumn.

I shall be content with whomsoever you send me for a Colleague, as I am sure he will be some good man.[2] Yrs truly   Danl Webster

ALS. MB. Published in *W & S*, 16: 315–316.

1. Skirting a straightforward discussion of national issues, Nathan Hale's *Boston Daily Advertiser* had become the mouthpiece for Abbott Lawrence, DW's chief opponent in the Massachusetts Whig party. For a discussion of the trouble between Webster and Lawrence, see Kinley J. Brauer, "The Webster-Lawrence Feud: A Study in Politics and Ambitions," *The Historian*, 29 (November 1966): 34–59.

2. The Massachusetts legislature elected Isaac C. Bates to finish out the term of John Davis, who had resigned to assume the governorship. Shortly thereafter Bates was elected to a full term of his own.

FROM SAMUEL BULKLEY RUGGLES

New York Jan. 9. 1841

My dear Sir

Since receiving your letter of the 24th December,[1] I have been seeking in various directions for the information which it calls for, but I greatly fear that the materials yet within my reach, are too scanty to enable me to arrive at any satisfactory result. There being no official tables, from which the coasting trade can be computed, the necessary facts could only be collected by correspondence with commercial men scattered over the Union and engaged in the various branches of trade. That would occupy more time than the occasion permits. Intelligent merchants, to whom I have applied, tell me that the thing cannot be done, without the direct action of the Government in requiring accurate returns of our coasting commerce.

The total transportation on the canals & railroads, I shall be able to arrive at with reasonable certainty, when I shall receive answers to sundry letters which have been written for the purpose. But will this item alone of our domestic intercourse, exhibit any thing like a full and comprehensive view of the sum total of our internal trade? Upon the rivers and lakes, and above all upon the *common roads* of the country, there is a vast and ceaseless movement which contributes most largely to the aggregate amount of our internal commerce. In 1839 we passed through the Erie Canal property of all sorts, worth some 73 millions of dollars,—

while the Hudson River, in its own honest way, carried at least a hundred millions. How much was borne upon the Lakes and through the Sound, our friends off West and down East can best judge. Then there is the broad basin of the Mississippi all alive with movement.

The British Parliment some few years ago, directed Commissioners to ascertain the domestic intercourse of Ireland. For that purpose, numerous officers were employed for several months, upon all the leading roads on that island, numbering the persons and products passing from the interior to the Seaboard. The results exhibited were immense—amounting to several millions of tons. They are curiously displayed on the "Traffic Map" made on that occasion.

The French Government push their statistical inquiries to an extent almost ludicrous, for the Minister of Commerce or of the Interior (I forget which) is charged with the duty, among other things, of numbering every egg laid in the kingdom, and yet they have not, to my knowledge, yet been able to gather up into one sum total, the aggregate amount of their internal transportation. To do it in a government so little centralised as ours, must require much time and labour. It is possible however that when the returns to the census of 1840 shall all come in to the Department of State, shewing the *total production*, of the country in its various industrial divisions, its total *transportation* may be tolerably *guessed* at. When that time arrives, unless my own natal New England blood shall refuse to do its office, I shall be willing to assist in such a process.

I consider it fortunate for the country that your attention has been drawn to this subject, and yet I am not particularly desirous that you should bring it forward in a *Speech*, for you will pardon my forwardness I hope, in saying that *a Secretary of State* might do a clever thing for his country if not for himself, by making the vast and prolific theme of our inland trade by land and by water, the subject of an extended *official report*.[2] Such a paper would surely live. Its preparation might be laborious, but the truth it would display, would produce vast and far reaching effects, influencing perhaps the whole future policy of the Government, and permit me also to add, that even if the Minister who should prepare it, were thereby brought into immediate contact with large masses of his countrymen it might be none the worse for them, or for him. Hoping to be pardoned for thus freely speaking I am as ever faithfully yours

Sam B. Ruggles

Canal matters call me for three weeks to Albany, after which I promise myself the luxury of spending a few days at Washington.

ALS. DLC.

1. See above.

2. Other than the census of 1840,

no contemporary report such as Webster and Ruggles envisioned has been found. This census pulled together statistics on manufacturing, agriculture, etc., to a greater extent than any previous one; DW may have had some influence on the collection and presentation of the returns.

TO SOLOMON LINCOLN

Washington Jan: 15. 1841.

My Dear Sir,

You are aware of my intention to vacate my seat in the Senate, in such season as that it may be filled before the third of March.

As this is generally expected, it is natural that the thoughts of members of the Legislature should be turned towards the object of selection of a successor.

With such Elections I have never interfered, nor do I intend to interfere now, any farther than will appear by the Sequel of this letter.

It is obvious, that Mr. [John Quincy] Adams will be among the Candidates, out of whom a choice is to be made. Some years ago, as you well know, an incident occurred, which interrupted intercourse between Mr Adams and myself, for several years, & wounded the feelings of many of my [his] friends, as well as my own.[1] With me, that occurrence is overlooked, & forgotten. I bury all memory of it, under my regard for Mr. Adams' talents, character, & public services; & it is the purpose of this letter to express a hope, that no friend of mine will suffer the recollection of it to influence his conduct. Perhaps I am guilty of presumption, in supposing that any friend might desire this declaration from me; but in that case, it will only be superfluous, not harmful.

Mr. Adams' great knowledge & ability, his experience, & especially his thorough acquaintance with the foreign relations of the Country, & the zeal which he manifests for the good cause of the Country, will undoubtedly make him prominent as a Candidate, & I wish it to be understood that his election would be, personally, altogether agreeable to me. I shall write to nobody else, My Dear Sir, on this subject. You are at liberty to communicate the substance of this letter, wherever you may think it necessary; but I do not wish any publicity about it, nor any use made of it, not called for by circumstances.[2] I am, Dear Sir, with true friendship & regard, yours   Danl Webster

ALS. NhD. Published in Curtis, 2: 56–57.

1. For a discussion of the disagreement between Webster and Adams on the fortifications bill, see *Correspondence*, 4: 77–86, *passim*.

2. The Massachusetts legislature bypassed Adams to elect Rufus Choate to DW's seat.

FROM ROBERT BARNWELL RHETT

Jan. 15th. 1841

Sir

In the National Intelligencer of the 4th. of September last, I find a

Speech published, delivered by you at Saratoga in the State of New York on the 19th. of August previous,[1] containing the following language[:]

"One of the Gentlemen of the South of that Nullifying State Rights Party, that has absorbed the Administration, or been absorbed by it, comes out boldly with the Declaration, that the Period has arrived *for a direct Tax on land*; and among the reasons assigned for this project is this one, *that it will bring the North to the Grindstone.*" The words underscored by me, are italicized in the print. As I am not aware, that any "Gentleman of the South, of that Nullifying State Rights Party," or of any other Party beside myself, has advocat[ed] Direct Taxation in any form, on the Part of the General Government, I am compelled to believe that I must be the Individual to whom you have ascribed this language. If correct in this inference please inform me, when and where I assigned any such reason, or uttered such language.[2]

Perceiving from the Papers, the active Part you were taking in the late Presidential canvass, I was at a loss, where to direct to you, and determined to await our meeting in Washington at the approaching Congress. Ill health has hitherto detained me from my Seat, and I now avail myself of the earliest opportunity to call your attention to this subject.

My friend & colleague, Col. [Thomas DeLage] Sumpter[3] will hand you this, and receive your answer. Your most obt Servt   R Barnwell Rhett

ALS. NhD.
　1. For DW's Saratoga speech, see
W & S, 3: 5–36.

2. DW's response has not been
found.
　3. Sumter.

TO NATHANIEL F. WILLIAMS

Washington Jan. 25. 1841

My Dear Sir

I thank you for your letter.[1] I fear I shall be obliged to come down & see you. My expectation has been to receive, before this time, funds from Mr [Samuel] Jaudon, for property of mine sold abroad. Letters by the late arrival represent things as *in train*, but some delays had intervened.[2] I must contrive to make my acceptance for 90 d[ay]s available, some how, to enable you to take up yours. The Banks here do nothing, & can do nothing.

I take this occasion to say a word to you, *in perfect confidence*, as to an old friend. My ability to remain here, & undertake the duties which it is likely may be assigned to me, depends on being able to make some arrangement of my personal affairs. I have property enough; but latterly have not been able to dispose of it; & to leave my practice, & come here, would embarrass me, unless things should be previously arranged.[3] Yrs truly   D Webster

ALS. NhD.

1. Not found.

2. DW was expecting funds from the sale of his Clamorgan shares in England. For example, see above, James Boyles Murray to DW, June 29, 1840. The specific "letters by the late arrival" have not been found, however.

3. Williams's response has not been found, but he continued to make loans to DW.

TO EDWARD EVERETT

Washington Feb. 2. 1841

My Dear Sir,

Other correspondents, more faithful than myself, kept you acquainted with the course of political events, from the time of your departure from the Country. We are now on the eve of a new administration. Genl. H. was at Pittsburg, at the latest dates, & is expected here in a week. Most things of importance must, of course, remain unsettled, until his inauguration. As to his Cabinet, you will have heard in what manner he proposes to fill the Department of State, & the office of Atty Genl. Beyond these, his purpose, if formed, is not known. It may be that he has made up his mind to place Mr. [Thomas] Ewing at the head of the Post Office, but I have reason to believe that he postpones his decision, respecting the persons to be Secretaries of the Treasury, War, & Navy Departments, until after his arrival at the seat of Govt. Mr. [John] Bell, Mr [Francis] Granger, Govr [John] Owen of N.C.[1] & Mr T[homas] B[utler] King, of Georgia, are mentioned most frequently as those, from among whom the places still vacant are likely to be filled. I should have included in the list Mr Jno M[iddleton] Clayton. Mr. [John] Sergeant is sometimes spoken of, but I think not very much, recently.

I have no idea, at present, of what may be the course which the President will be inclined to pursue, in relation to our public agents abroad. Mr. [Andrew] Stevenson has desired to be recalled, & provision will probably be made in the Appropriation Bill for an outfit for his successor. But how soon he may return, or how soon after his return the President may think fit to fill the Office, remains to be known. I suppose the party, at present in power, will not so far oblige their successors as to provide outfits, except in cases of voluntary retirement, like Mr Stevenson's. Your own position, at the present moment, is quite favorable for keeping you in the eye of your friends, for public service, in some of the missions, as events may be developed, or as circumstances may require. You will not doubt my own disposition to serve you.[2]

It is arranged between the two Governments, that the negotiation with England for the settlement of the Boundary question shall be conducted here. It has made no progress, that I can learn, since the date of the President's message. It is now a mere business of settling the terms of a Convention, for a joint commission of survey, & with an ultimate arbitration, in case of disagreement. I will say to you *in confidence*, that if the business had remained for adjustment in London, I think I should have accepted the mission to that Court, if the President had offered it. And if any thing should occur to break off the present negotiation, or change its basis, & new discussions were to arise in London, I might incline to cross the water once more. The successes which have recently attended the English arms in the Levant, & in China, & the manner in which she has sustained herself, as against France, on the business of the Treaty of the 15th of July, have their influence here, in awakening the attention of the Country to new fears, respecting her disposition to settle *our* question, amicably or speedily.[3]

As to offices, out of the Cabinet, little or nothing is yet known. The richer collectorships, & Attorneyships, are subjects of much competition —so are the Post Offices in the great Cities. I intend to exert my influence to get a snug little place *for I[saac] P. Davis*—& that is all the purpose, relative to such matters, that I have as yet expressed. This, you will say, is modest, & you will agree that I. P. ought to be made comfortable. Judge [John] Davis [1761–1847], it is understood, will resign his seat soon after the 4th. of March, when he will have filled it forty years. Mr. [Peleg] Sprague, Mr [John] Pickering, Mr [Theophilus] Parsons, & Mr C[harles] H[enry] Warren are all spoken of, as his successor. Mr Sprague is much out of health, & has gone to St Augustine for the winter. I fear there is no prospect of immediate restoration.

There is great reason to think it will be necessary to hold a called session of Congress. The Treasury is very low—we live by the temporary issues of Treasury notes, & the power, even for that, created at the present session, will be a slender reliance, or rather a scant one, for the service of the year. If Congress be convoked, they will assemble probably in June, & the four following measures are likely to draw their attention.

1. A tax, or duty, on Wines, silks, worsteds &c.
2. Distribution of the proceeds of the public lands
3. A Bankrupt Bill
4. A Bill creating a Bank of U.S.

The three first of these measures will doubtless pass; & probably the 4th. The Whig majority in the Senate will be 4–5—or 6–& in the House, as is expected, at least 30.

Mr. [Isaac C.] Bates, you will see, is elected to the Senate in place of Mr [John] Davis [1787–1854] & Mr [Rufus] Choate is likely to fill the place, which I now occupy, & which it is my purpose to vacate about the middle of this month.

So much for public affairs.

We hear of you occasionally, thro various channels, & always with great pleasure. A good deal too ignorant to enjoy all that Italy tenders to the taste of the cultivated, & a little too old to learn, I yet feel that it would be pleasant to see, for once, the skies, the mountains, the Lakes, the Cities & the monuments of art, which form so great a part of what literary men, & lovers of scenery, have talked about, & written about, for so long a time. To you, so full & fresh with history & the classics, the pleasure must be particularly great. The accounts which have come to us of your family, from Edward & others, have been very agreeable. I hope Florence will not disappoint Mrs Everett[4] in the great matter of climate, though all climates, now a days, have got a new character for fickleness.

I think it will be best for Edward to come home in the Spring. He has not yet recd his College degree, which seems necessary, before he begins the study [of] a profession. If he shall arrive in his own Country in May or June, he may probably join the class about to graduate at Hanover. As he must prepare himself to live by his own earnings, it is probably wise for him not longer to withhold his attention from those studies, which fit him for business.

Fletcher is at this moment with us. He thinks of trying his fortune in the practice in New York, if he shall be able to form some connexion, which promises to be useful.

Mrs Webster begs you to accept her kindest remembrance, & we both join in love to Mrs Everett & the daughters.[5] I am, Dear Sir, Yours faithfully, Danl Webster

ALS. MHi. Published in part in *PC*, 2: 99–100.

1. Owen (1787–1841; University of North Carolina), a farmer and former state representative and senator, had been governor of North Carolina, 1828 to 1830.

2. DW informed Everett of his nomination as minister to England on July 24, 1841 (mDW 19752). Before he notified Everett, however, DW wrote Peter Chardon Brooks (July 8, 1841; mDW 19598), Everett's father-in-law, asking if Everett would like the post, and Brooks expressed confidence that Everett would take it

(July 13, 1841; mDW 19631). On Everett's appointment, see also *Diplomatic Papers*, 1.

3. France's signature was conspicuously absent from the treaty of July 15, 1841, signed by Prussia, Russia, Austria, and Great Britain for the settlement of the dispute between the Turkish sultan and Mehemet Ali.

4. Mrs. Everett (1800–1859), née Charlotte Gray Brooks, was the daughter of Peter Chardon Brooks.

5. Everett's daughters were Anne Gorham (1823–1844) and Charlotte Brooks (1825–1879).

TO NATHANIEL F. WILLIAMS

Feb. 14. [1841]

Dear Sir,

I enclose you a check for $1000. I shall be obliged, in a day or two, to draw on you again, until I can arrange matters.

Do you wish to be Collector of Baltimore? If you do, say so by return of mail.[1] Yrs   D. Webster

ALS. NhD.

1. Williams's answer has not been found, but on June 6, Tyler—presumably upon DW's recommendation—nominated Williams collector of customs for the district of Balti-more; on June 23, the Senate confirmed him. *Journal of the Executive Proceedings of the Senate . . . 1837, to . . . 1841* (Washington, 1887), 5: 384–393.

Webster hoped to embark upon his new duties as secretary of state with a clean slate, free from the emotional and physical drain of his debts and the inevitable obligations for favors he felt towards his creditors. As soon as Harrison offered him the post, Webster approached Biddle to seek his intervention with the board of the Pennsylvania Bank of the United States for the clearance of his obligation of $114,000, then over-due at that bank's New York and Philadelphia offices.

Webster had built up this indebtedness in the mid- to late 1830s when he, like many other Americans, had contracted land fever and overspeculated on credit. The depression of 1837 caught him with thousands of acres of western land only partially paid for and with but few prospects for its sale either in America or in England. As his creditors exerted pressure for payment, Webster had apparently gone to the Bank for assistance, and Biddle had sustained him by buying up his overdue notes. By early 1841, however, the Bank itself was again experiencing hard times, and, with Biddle no longer heading it, its new officers began to call in loans, of which Webster's was but one.

As indicated in the letter from Herman Cope below, Webster began his hard bargaining with the Bank and its officers in early February. The negotiations, involving Cope, Biddle, James Duane Doty, Richard Smith, and Alexander Lardner, continued until April 6. Webster and the Bank reached an agreement that the secretary of state would transfer with clear titles most of his western land in exchange for the cancellation of his debt.

The clear-title provision proved to be the point that gave Webster the most trouble. He actually owned only a fraction of the land outright; this he immediately transferred to the Bank. For the larger portion, however, either the titles were unrecorded, the land was inaccurately registered, or the deeds stood jointly in Webster's name and that of another person. These titles he had to clear, so for years Webster was engaged off and on in efforts to fulfill this part of the arrangement. He managed to clear the titles to most of the property before he retired from the State Department in 1843, but the methods by which he did so were sometimes question-

able. Early in 1842, for example, he recommended the appointment of Washington Irving as minister to Spain, whereupon Irving's grateful brother-in-law, Moses Hicks Grinnell, together with his associates Richard M. Blatchford and Samuel B. Ruggles, returned to Webster clear title to certain lands previously mortgaged to them (see Grinnell to DW, [February 10, 1842], below). Even so, Webster was never completely able to fulfill his pledge to the Bank: in the late 1840s he still had some $40,000 worth of land for which he had not been able to clear the titles.

FROM HERMAN COPE

Bank of the United States
Suspended debt & Real Estate
Department
February 15th. 1841

Dear Sir

Your Letter of the 12th. inst has been duly received,[1] apprising me of your readiness at any time to carry into full effect the proposition you submitted to the Bank through me, for the settlement of certain of your liabilities to it, not otherwise secured or provided for, by the conveyance of an adequate amount of real estate, at prices to be mutually agreed upon, in full payment; and which proposition was acceded to by the Board of Directors, on the terms and conditions stated in my letter to you of the 10th. inst.[2]

In conferring with the President[3] this morning on the subject of your Letter, I suggested to him, in view of the objections you have made, that as much inconvenient delay would necessarily and unavoidably ensue in sending our Agent at Cincinnati to make a personal examination of the Lands before we consented to receive a conveyance of them from you, whether our Agent at Washington, Mr. Richard Smith,[4] could not obtain, in that place, sufficient information of the situation and probable value of the Lands to insure our present purpose; and whether under all the existing circumstances it would not be most advisable for the Bank to authorise Mr. Smith to receive from you a List of all the Lands offered, and after he shall have informed himself of their probable value, to act on behalf of the Bank in affixing, with you in person, or your authorised Agent, a price for each separate parcel, at which it shall be conveyed to the Bank under the arrangement with you of the 10th inst.

The President assented to my suggestion. And under his instructions I will write to Mr. Smith by the present mail—enclosing to him a statement of your liabilities to be settled by a conveyance of real Estate, with such directions as may seem necessary for carrying our agreement into speedy and full effect.

The only debt at the New York agency which will properly come under the present arrangement, is the note endorsed by Mr. John Connell[5] for $2283. 69/100. The others I understand, are collaterally secured by mortgage &c, and will continue as heretofore under the charge of that agency.

In the hope that you will now be able to bring those matters to a close at an early day and to mutual satisfaction I subscribe myself with high regard Very truly yours   Herman Cope Superin[tenden]t

ALS. MWalB. Cope (1789–1869) had been agent of the Bank of the United States in Cincinnati before he transferred to Philadelphia to become third assistant cashier at its main office. In late 1840 or early 1841, he was promoted to superintendent of the suspended debt and real estate department.

1. Letter not found.

2. According to Cope's letter of February 10, the agreement was "that the Bank would accept from you [Webster] a conveyance of such of the Lands as are described in the list you furnished me, or mentioned in our conversation, as we might select, at the price or value that shall be fixed for them by two persons—one to be chosen by yourself, and the other by the Bank, with a good and sufficient title and *free of all incumbrance*, to an Amount, in the aggregate, that

will cover and pay your liabilities to the Bank, here and in New York. It is not meant to include in this arrangement the amount of $26,700. for which Mr. Hubbard's Bond & Mortgage is held as collateral security. That we will first endeavour to collect from the Mortgage. The balance of the debt will be somewhere about $100,000, for which the Bank will accept Lands on the terms stated above" (mDW 17480).

3. Thomas Dunlap.

4. Smith was cashier of the Washington branch of the Bank. DW agreed to accept Smith as the Bank's representative in the matter.

5. Connell, a merchant of Philadelphia, was a director of the United States Bank of Pennsylvania in 1838, but he had since been dropped from the directorship.

FROM EDWARD WEBSTER

Florence. Feby. 18 1841.

My Dear Father,

I have drawn two drafts on you, one for the remainder, for which I was authorized to send to Mr [Joshua] Bates, and the other I sent to Mr [John] Watson.[1] Mr [Samuel Appleton] Appleton wished me to buy some pictures for him and as I did [not] know in what manner I could get the money here in time except by drawing on you, and getting it accepted in London, I have done so. The amount is two hundred dollars ($200). Mr A will arrange with you, for it. I have allowed about three hundred dollars for travelling expenses, As I think of going to Rome, as I suppose of course, you will have no objection to it, for it seems a pity to be so near it, and not to see it. I have taken up painting, as you know, but have not as yet finished any picture, but I get along quite as well as I expected. We are in the height of the gay season, it being near the end of Carnival, the streets are full of masks. Yesterday I went to see the Grande Duke and the court walking under the Offices, in an immense crowd of masks. He always does it the three great days of the Carnival. The king of the French could not do such a thing, and yet I suppose that in proportion to the inhabitants, there are more Italians against this government, than French against Louis Philippe.[2] The yoke of Austria seems to be a very heavy and galling burden for them; and yet I believe that the Duke as a man, is very much liked, he has public audiences every week, for all those who have any thing to say to him, the lowest class of people are admited the same as the others. There was also what is called the Corso, yesterday, every one drives through certain streets in their handsomest equipages, some with six horses and three footman, and some of them with their servants in fancy dresses. I remember a negro dressed as a Moor. Mr E and family desire to be remembered to you and Mother, and with much love to all the family I remain your most affectionate Son

Edward.

ALS. NhHi.   *Diplomatic Papers*, I.
1. Watson was "a sort of Banker"   2. Louis Philippe (1773–1850),
for DW in London. See DW to Ed-   king of France, 1830–1848.
ward Everett, November 20, 1841, in

TO [?]

Washington Feb. 21. '41

Dear Sir

Yours of the 18th.[1] came to hand last Evening, & I am quite happy to learn that there is so much unanimity in the choice of Senator.[2] Tomorrow will be my last day in the Senate. I confess I feel a kind of sadness, in quitting a place, in which I have been so long, & to which my habits have become so much conformed.

I have no expectation of ever feeling so much at home, any where else.

Your former letters were duly recd. It is not necessary that you should trouble yourself for any more names. Those I have already received will probably never be looked at, but I thought it might be well to have such documents on hand. I am glad to learn that Mr [Abbott] Lawrence is on the way.[3] Yrs truly   Danl Webster

ALS. NhD.   boundary in 1842, and DW may al-
1. Not found.   ready have been discussing the issue
2. With opposition only from a few   of the boundary question with him.
abolitionists, the Massachusetts legis-   DW, perhaps, also wished to confer
lature had elected Rufus Choate to   with Lawrence on the proposed ap-
fill Webster's Senate seat.   pointment of Edward Curtis as New
3. Lawrence served as a commis-   York customs collector. Lawrence and
sioner to settle the northeastern   DW backed Curtis, blocking Clay's

efforts to secure the nomination of
Robert C. Wetmore. Robert Seager II,
And Tyler Too: A Biography of John
and Julia Gardiner Tyler (New York,
1963), p. 145.

FROM NICHOLAS BIDDLE, WITH ENCLOSURE FROM NICHOLAS BIDDLE, FEB-
RUARY 21

Phila. Feby. 21. 1841

(*confidential*)

My dear Sir,

I think you may be interested in knowing what I have done this evening, <in order to serve> with the hope of serving a common friend Mr
[Edward] Curtis & of gratifying you. <I saw our went to friend Mr
E[lihu] Chauncey this afternoon & stated to him my views on the subject of Mr Curtis's appointment,[1] & urged his speaking on the subject
to Mr [Thomas] E[wing] now & my intentions to speak to Mr E. & urged
him to do the same, which he promised to do in a very decided manner.>

<This evening> In conversation with Mr. E. alone I went over the
matter <with Mr. E.> presenting <distinctly> this view which I consider the true <view> one for *him* to take. <I said> Here are two candidates for an office in New York, one of them a decided personal friend of
the Secretary of <the> State <the o> who would undoubtedly obtain it
but for the decided personal opposition of another gentleman not in the
Cabinet, and who stands in a position of scarcely dissembled [po]litical
<opposition> hostility to the Secretary of State.[2] That other gentleman
does not object <at all> to the personal fitness of the candidate—but he
opposes him on grounds of political feelings (<because he thinks that to
him> mainly was owing <the> his not being now President elect—&
because he thinks he will be unfriendly to him <hereafter> at the next
election. The first objection being analysed means that Genl. H. ought not
to appoint Mr C. because Mr C was mainly instrumental in electing Genl.
H. a reproach fitter for any other ear than Genl. Hs. The <first> second
objection ends also in this an unwillingness to see the Office in the hands
of a friend of the Secy of State). The question <then seems> becomes
at last <but a question> between the Secy of State & the other gentleman. Now which of the two is it most <proper> expedient to gratify?
To which ought the Secy of the Treasury & the Cabinet incline? Of the
two gentlemen one declines a connection with the <Cabn> Admn—<he
keeps aloof>. If <the administration> it is popular he claims the merit
of having made it. If unpopular he disclaims all responsibility for it. He
may profit alike by its misfortunes and its prosperity. The other gentleman has staked all his political fortune on the success of the Admn. He
embarks with Genl. H. to sink or swim with him. Now <is not such a
man more to be cultivated>—are not his views as to the selection of offi-

cers to carry out the measures of the Admn more to be regarded by his colleagues—ought not he to be kept in heart for his great work—not thwarted—but gratified when it can safely be done. <Ans> Try therefore <that there shall be no division> to prevent any collision—but if you must decide between them I would take the side of your colleague. <After I had talked it over thus> I requested Mr. E. Chauncey to talk to him in the same strain which he did this evening.

<I left Mr Chauncey with him, & he no doubt presented the same views. All this is   . He returns tomorrow to Washn.>

All this seems to me right in itself & may not be <useless to our friend Mr. C.> without effect. Very truly yrs   N B.

ALS draft. DLC.
1. Tyler nominated Curtis for collector of customs, New York, on June 16, 1841, but because of opposition, the Senate did not confirm him until September 10. *Journal of the Execu-*

tive Proceedings of the Senate . . . 1837, to . . . 1841 . . . (Washington, 1887), 5: 384, 393, 434.
2. Biddle was alluding to Henry Clay.

ENCLOSURE: FROM NICHOLAS BIDDLE

Phila. Feby. 21. 1841

My Dear Sir,

You must pay the penalty of power and be resigned to receive all applications for its exercise. Mr [Joel B?] Sutherland related to me <today> a conversation which he had with you on the subject of appointments. He thinks that the Commissioner of the Land Office should <have the qualifications for which he is himself remarkable> be a person like himself. He goes to Washn tomorrow <& I rely on your discretion to let him know that> & as I told him I would make the intimation, he will know when you see him that I had mentioned his name to you. With great regard yrs   N B

ALS draft. DLC.

FROM JAMES ALEXANDER HAMILTON

New York, February 22, 1841.

Dear Sir:

I have the honor to inclose a letter containing information which seems to me clearly to indicate that Great Britain is preparing to increase her Lake armaments.[1] Whether this is a violation of the letter or spirit of her understanding with us or not, I cannot judge. It, however, proves that she considers the present condition of our differences as tending to the last resort of nations, to which Mr. [Francis Wilkinson] Pickens' report so directly invites her.[2]

I will embrace this opportunity to present to you one or two considerations in connection with this subject that may be of use, taking the chance of their having been anticipated by you.

It was generally understood when I was at Washington that there was to be an extra session for the purpose of providing means to pay the debts, to repeal the Sub-Treasury law, &c., &c. It has occurred to me that there is a higher duty for such a call than any resulting from these objects to which the public mind has been directed, and one which in the future party conflicts will be incapable of being misrepresented by demagogues or by party slang to be used against us with as much effect as those can be. As to the debts to be provided for, they will take issue upon the fact, and refer to Mr. Van Buren's Message and his Secretary's report, and they will insist that Mr. [Henry Alexander] Wise's Treasury Note Bill did all that was necessary, &c. But if to those motives for a call is added and made the most prominent, the necessity for arming the Nation, of defending her against hostile attack, the facts cannot be denied; and party leaders will be afraid, reckless and bold as they are, to go to the people against so patriotic a course. The feelings of our countrymen on this subject have been too clearly indicated to allow party politicians to mistake them, and very few can be found at this day who have firmness, even when their duty may call upon them to do so, to resist war measures; and let me add that to provide the means for defence you must adopt such measures—to obtain money by loan, by revenues, by increasing the duties, to improve the currency and to relieve the States—as are called for by the actual condition of things; and thus those measures will be adopted for a purpose which will more probably unite the Nation than any other.

One other consideration suggested by the subject, and I will no longer intrude upon you.

Two or three years ago, I sent to Mr. Van Buren a statement of the actual condition of the Steam Marine of Great Britain, and intimated to him as worthy of consideration that the employment of this new agent in this manner and to the extent of navigating the ocean had perhaps rendered it necessary to revise our system of coast defences, the position of forts, and to defend our harbors which are to be attacked. Sail ships might be wholly useless where steam vessels are employed, from considerations that will be so obvious to you as to forbid their repetition. I will merely bring to your view a few facts. The Russian Steam Frigate, building in this port, will carry a larger armament than any other in the world. She draws sixteen feet of water, and is supposed to be a match for any 120 gun-ship drawing 27 to 30 feet water. The *Cyclops*, at the bombardment of Acre, carried from Constantinople 1,500 soldiers, and with her complement of men was supposed to have on board when she went to the attack at least 2,000 men. She and her consort did the decisive work in that attack.

Cunard's steamers, drawing twelve feet water, could be made to carry two large guns to 10-inch balls of 90 lbs. each, and four or six smaller ones.

Take the case of Newport harbor. The entrance upon which our fort is to bear is wide, deep, open, and accessible to vessels of all sizes, but there is another entrance around the island which carries throughout twelve feet water, although very narrow. Such vessels as Cunard's steamers can navigate it; and thus command the towns of Newport and Providence with the adjoining country, regardless of our present fortresses. With very great respect, etc.

Text from James A. Hamilton, *Reminiscences of James A. Hamilton; or, Men and Events at Home and Abroad, During Three Quarters of a Century* (New York, 1869), pp. 312–313. Original not found.

1. Not found.

2. Pickens's report from the House Committee on Foreign Affairs, "Burning of the Steamboat Caroline, and the Imprisonment of McLeod," appears in *Reports of Committees*, 26th Cong., 2d sess., Serial 388, Report No. 162.

TO NICHOLAS BIDDLE

[February 1841]
Wednesday 5 Oclock P.M.

My Dear Sir,

We make little progress here, with my affairs, & I am determined, if nothing happen to prevent, to go myself to Phila[delphi]a.[1] It would take Mr [Richard] Smith three months to adjust the matter, proceeding according to what he understands to be his instructions. If nothing unexpected occur, I shall leave this City on Friday morning, & proceed directly to your House. On Saturday, all must be arranged, if it can be arranged —at least so far as this, that the p[ro]p[ert]y shall be selected, and the prices fixed, & an agreement signed, that on making out titles, & clearing incumberances, my papers shall be given up and the account closed.

It is quite impossible for me to go into office here, with this matter unadjusted. I should not think of it. I will ask Mr [James Duane] Doty to go with me, who knows the value of p[ro]p[ert]y in that Country as well as any other man. I have not spoken to him on the subject, but hope he will be able to accompany me. Agreeably to your kind invitation, I shall proceed immediately to your House.[2] Yrs truly   D. Webster

ALS. DLC.

1. DW was alluding to the settlement of his account with the Bank.

2. On February 7, Biddle had written DW offering him the privacy of Andalusia, where he might complete the settlement with the Bank (mDW 17459).

TO FRANKLIN HAVEN

Mar. 13 '41

Private

Dear Sir

If Mr [Jonas Leonard] Sibley had been appointed by the late Administration, he wd. not have been removed. But finding the place vacant on the 4th. of March, it was deemed expedient to appoint another gentleman.[1] Mr Solomon Lincoln is an excellent man of business, & every way respectable. I have requested him to keep his accounts with you.

Mr L[evi] Lincoln will be Collector, on the first of April. So far as he can, by law, use any Bank, he will use yours.

Mr [Thomas] Ewing sees no incompatibility, in a pension agent's being also Rec[eive]r Genl.[2] I think a removal will be made soon; certainly, if it should be concluded not to have a called session. This matter of a called Session is yet uncertain.

This letter is not intended for your Directors—nor for any eye but yours. Let me say, that in regard to all letters of this sort, the best way is to *read & burn*. Yrs truly   D Webster

ALS. MH–H.

1. Sibley (1791–1852) was a Sutton, Massachusetts, attorney and two-term state legislator, who served as United States marshal for Massachusetts from 1833 to 1841. Contrary to DW's statement, President Van Buren had renominated Sibley on December 16, 1840, but the Senate had postponed consideration of the nomination. Sibley's successor was Solomon Lincoln, nominated on March 9 and confirmed a day later. For Lincoln's application for the post, dated March 4, see mDW 17872. *Journal of the Executive Proceedings of the Senate . . . 1837, to . . . 1841* . . . (Washington, 1887), 5: 315, 317, 334, 338, 341, 372–373. Along with Mark Healy, a director of Haven's Merchants' Bank, Haven had written DW favoring Sibley's renomination (see mDW 17799). DW's letter above appears to have been written in response to Haven's note of [March 2].

2. Instead of Haven's appointment as Receiver General of the Public Money at Boston—as suggested by DW—President Harrison nominated Samuel Frothingham, another of DW's banking friends and financial backers. *National Intelligencer*, March 20, 1841.

TO WASHINGTON IRVING

Washington Mar. 16. '41

My Dear Sir,

It came to my knowledge some days ago that it might be agreeable to you, perhaps, to be Consul in Paris.[1] Encouragement had been previously given, however, in another quarter, which could not with propriety be withdrawn. I assure you, My Dear Sir, that I should esteem it a great honor, and a fortunate incident in my public life to have an opportunity of recommending you to a situation, useful to your interests, & in harmony with your tastes & pursuits.

I cherish the hope that such opportunity may ere long present itself; & in the meantime allow me to express to you my warm attachment & regard.   Danl Webster

ALS. RNHi.

1. See Moses Hicks Grinnell to DW, March 5, 1841, mDW 17910.

TO THOMAS EWING

Department of State,
March 20, 1841.

(Circular)

Sir:

The President is of opinion that it is a great abuse to bring the patronage of the general government into conflict with the freedom of elections; and that this abuse ought to be corrected wherever it may have been permitted to exist, and to be prevented for the future.

He therefore directs that information be given to all officers and agents in your department of the public service that partisan interference in popular elections, whether of state officers, or officers of this government, and for whomsoever or against whomsoever it may be exercised, or the payment of any Contribution or assessment on salaries or official compensation for party or election purposes, will be regarded by him as cause of removal.

It is not intended that any officer shall be restrained in the free and proper expression and maintenance of his opinions respecting public men or public measures, or in the exercise, to the fullest degree, of the Constitutional right of suffrage. But persons employed under the government, and paid for their services out of the public treasury, are not expected to take an active or officious part in attempts to influence the minds or votes of others; such conduct being deemed inconsistent with the spirit of the Constitution and the duties of public agents acting under it; and the President is resolved, so far as depends upon him, that while the exercise of the elective franchise by the people shall be free from undue influences of official station and authority, opinion shall also be free among the officers and agents of the government.

The President wishes it further to be announced, and distinctly understood, that from all collecting and disbursing officers promptitude in rendering accounts, and entire punctuality in paying balances, will be rigorously exacted. In his opinion it is time to return, in this respect, to the early practice of the government, and to hold any degree of delinquency on the part of those intrusted with the public money just cause of immediate removal. He deems the severe observance of this rule to be essential to the public service, as every dollar lost to the treasury by unfaithfulness in office creates a necessity for a new charge upon the people. I have the honor to be, Sir Your obt. Servt   Daniel Webster

Circular. NcD.

TO NICHOLAS BIDDLE

Mar. 23. 41

Private

My Dear Sir,

Mr Smith & Mr Doty have come to a point—a sort of alternative proposition—& Mr Smith has agreed to refer this to Mr [Thomas W.] Sutherland,[1] as an umpire between himself & Mr Doty. And Mr Doty will go to Philadelphia tomorrow, to lay the subject before the umpire, the Bank having an opportunity to lay before him also Mr Smith's communication, & to obtain his decision. I *sincerely & most anxiously* desire that this business may be thus closed. Yrs   D Webster

ALS. DLC.

1. Thomas W. Sutherland (d. 1859), the son of Joel B., was a native of Philadelphia. In 1835 he had gone west, and a few years later he determined to settle in Madison, Wisconsin, where he speculated in land. On April 27, 1841, he was appointed United States district attorney for Wisconsin Territory.

FROM NICHOLAS BIDDLE

Phila. March 25. 1841

My Dear Sir,

We are working about Wisconsin. I have seen Mr Cope—& have just parted with Mr [Alexander] Lardner.[1] I trust I shall not work in vain. Faithfully Yrs   NB

ALS draft. DLC.

1. Lardner was cashier of the Bank of the United States of Pennsylvania at this time.

FROM [JAMES DUANE DOTY] TO NICHOLAS BIDDLE

March 25. [1841]

Mr. W. offers to give *all* his property in the west in satisfaction of the debt of $114,000—reserving to himself only 1120 acres of land in Illinois and 1/4th of his mineral lands in Wiskonsan—say 850 acres. This reservation he is compelled to make to enable him to obtain the means to remove the incumbrances upon this and other portions of the property.[1]

I hope he will be allowed to retain the above interest because I know it is absolutely necessary he should, and that he is extremely anxious to do so. Allow me to add that there can be no adjustment made of this matter but upon this condition, and that justice and liberality (certainly in his opinion) does not require more.

The subject is to be laid before a comtee. in the morning and their decision must be final.[2]

The great interest which I am sure you feel for the prosperity of your friend is my apology for troubling you again.

AL. DLC.

1. The $114,000 represented DW's indebtedness to the Bank at Philadelphia and its New York branch. Contrary to Doty's assertion, DW retained, in addition to his farm "Salisbury" near Peru, Illinois, and mineral lands in southwestern Wisconsin, considerable property in Rock Island City, Illinois. In addition, he probably still had some interest in the Clamorgan lands.

2. For the outcome of the committee meeting, see Herman Cope to DW, March 27, 1841, below.

FROM NICHOLAS BIDDLE

Phila. March 26. 1841

My Dear Sir,

There—it is as I hoped—all settled exactly as you wished. I rejoice at this result—& much rejoice that I may have assisted in accomplishing it. Very truly Yrs   NB.

ALS draft. DLC.

FROM HERMAN COPE

Bank of the United States
Suspended debt & Real Estate
Department
March 27th. 1841

Dear Sir

It is under feelings of deep mortification and regret I have to inform you, that at a meeting of the Committee this morning, the subject of the contemplated settlement with you was brought into notice, and in the remarks which followed, I learned with great surprise, that a majority of the Committee considered the offer of Judge Doty to convey all the property mentioned on the list—except the 1120 acres of Improved Land, was intended to cover only the debt of $93,000—and was not meant to include the debt at our Agency in New York for about $21,000. more as I understood and stated in my letter to you.[1] The same papers and documents upon which I formed my opinion of the nature and extent of Judge Doty's proposition were before the committee, and as I believed at the time led them to the same conclusion with regard to the proposition that I had come to myself: that the property was offered in payment of your *whole* debt of about $114,000. It seems now that the Committee did not so understand it. And they have requested me to inform you of the misunderstanding, and to request that the settlement may be suspended for a few days until they can look more fully into it. Their feelings towards you are I believe entirely friendly, and I still believe the proposition can be so modified as to be made satisfactory to both parties.[2] Very respectfully & truly yours   Herman Cope Superin[tenden]t

ALS. MWalB.

1. See above, Cope to DW, February 15, 1841. According to that letter, DW's transfer of land and property was not to cover all of his indebtedness to the New York agency of the Bank. It has not been established when Cope agreed also to cancel the New York branch debt.

2. In a subsequent meeting the committee agreed to accept Doty's and DW's offer. See Cope to DW, April 6, 1841, mDW 18728. Discrepancies exist in the letters between DW and the Bank officers regarding the amount of his indebtedness to the New York agency. See, for example, Cope to DW, February 10, 1841, mDW 14780.

TO THOMAS EWING

Philadelphia
Sunday Eve'
[March 28?, 1841]

My Dear Sir,

I have been detained here this afternoon in consequence of the arrival of the Southern Cars too late to enable me to proceed, today, to N. York.[1]

The delay has given me an opportunity of seeing something of the excitement, which indeed is very great, now prevailing in the City, on the subject of the appointments. It much exceeds my apprehension. There will be great dissatisfaction, if, at this moment, either [Joseph Washington] Tyson,[2] [Bela] Badger,[3] [James] Todd,[4] or [Alexander] Ferguson[5] were made Collector. But of the four, I think Ferguson, while he has the fewest active friends, has also the fewest determined opponents. My present opinion is, that it is expedient to delay; & to signify to the heads of clans, that they must come to some terms, among themselves, before any thing will be done.

If this course be thought not expedient, I will tell you what I would do. It is this.—

I would make Walter Forward Collector.[6] This would undoubtedly, gratify the State, & would not, I am well informed, dissatisfy the City, except the friends of the City candidates, all of whom, probably, would nevertheless, prefer his appointment to that of any one, except their own friend.

I would make Mr Badger Naval officer, & Mr Tyson Surveyor; & then take a little time to arrange subordinates. In this case, Russell[7] must be Comptroller & he will do well in the office, & Todd must be Auditor. I can at present think of nothing so good as this.

I may, possibly, spend Wednesday afternoon here; & in the mean time, a cool-headed friend, independent of all cliques, will *try*, what can be effected in the way of compromise; but I dare not engage for any favorable result, in that way. Yrs truly   Danl Webster

ALS. DLC.

1. On March 30, DW was in New York. See DW to Isaac Rand Jackson, March 30, 1841, mDW 18621.

2. Tyson (1812–1860) was a Philadelphia lawyer, nominated and confirmed as surveyor and inspector of revenue for Philadelphia in June 1841. He was a close friend of Robert Tyler.

3. Badger (1791–1852) was a wine and liquor manufacturer and merchant in Philadelphia whom Tyler nominated on June 6 as naval officer. The Senate rejected Badger's nomination on September 13, 1841.

4. Todd (1786–1863), a lawyer and state legislator, had been appointed attorney general in 1835 and later judge of the Court of General Sessions by Governor Joseph Ritner.

5. Ferguson (c. 1793–1843), a Philadelphia dry goods merchant, was confirmed as naval officer when the Senate failed to confirm Badger.

6. Instead of Forward, who became first comptroller of the Treasury, Tyler nominated and the Senate confirmed Jonathan Roberts as Philadelphia customs collector.

7. Not identified.

Democratic Senator Alfred Cuthbert of Georgia used Webster's resignation from the Senate on February 22 as an occasion to attack the Massachusetts politician on constitutional and moral grounds. His aim, he told his colleagues, was to offer "proofs in relation to the sentiments of Mr. Webster in regard to the constitutional power of the Government over the transportation of slaves from one state to another." His specific purpose, in light of Webster's statements made during the campaign of 1840, was to secure from Webster a retraction of the comment he had made in the Massachusetts Memorial to Congress in 1820—that Congress did have the power to stop the interstate slave trade. Webster was not present in the Senate on February 22 to defend himself, and although Clay, Rives, and Preston did, Cuthbert nonetheless demanded an explanation—a retraction of the 1820 statement—from Webster; as he charged, Webster's stand "has set up doctrines which throw open all the South to her enemies, which leave us no barrier for our defence, and with nothing to prevent the sea from rushing in to overwhelm us." Rives responded to Cuthbert's feisty remarks by urging him to address Webster in a gentlemanly manner. Cuthbert took the advice, and the letter below is a part of the exchange which took place.

FROM ALFRED CUTHBERT

March 29. 1841

Sir

Yours of the 15th[1] did not reach me untill several days after its date. I have suffered it to [lie] by me some days and my reflections still suggest no sufficient reasons why the plain question proposed in mine of the 6th[2] should not be answered. On the 22d. of Feb. in open Senate Mr Rives in the character of your political friend and zealous eulogist and defender, voluntarily declared that he entertained no doubt, that if I should address to you a written communication proposing the enquiry convey[e]d in my note of the 6th, you would return to that enquiry a frank and satisfactory answer; and he plainly prompted me to that course. On the 1st March in open Senate Mr Rives demanded of me whether I had made the enquiry and in the form suggested by him and again stimulated me to do so. On both occasions I pledged myself to address to you such a letter of enquiry as he suggested. I have redeemed my pledge addressing you in such respectful terms as your station and public character made proper. You decline to answer and our correspondence here ends.[3] The country must determine as to the motives of your silence. Your obedient servant

A Cuthbert

ALS. NhD. Published in the Washington *Daily Globe*, April 2, 1841.

1. *Daily Globe*, April 2, 1841.

2. *Daily Globe*, April 2, 1841. The question posed by Cuthbert was "whether in your opinion 'congress has any authority under the constitution of the United States to prohibit the transfer of slaves from one state to another.'" In the Senate discussion of March 1 (*Congressional Globe*, 26th Cong., 2d sess., Appendix, p. 330), Cuthbert alludes to the views expressed by a committee, of which DW was a member, in the Massachusetts *Memorial to the Congress . . . on the Subject of Restraining the*

Increase of Slavery in the New States . . . . (Boston, 1819). See *Correspondence*, 1: 267–268, 270; *Speeches and Formal Writings*, 1.

3. This evidently was not the first occasion on which Cuthbert and DW had disagreed. In the discussion, Cuthbert admitted "that all personal intercourse between him and that gentleman [DW] had ceased for years, as was known to many; for the course of that gentleman, it was clear to his mind, was hostile to the interests of the South." *Congressional Globe*, 26th Cong., 2d sess., Appendix, p. 331.

FROM RICHARD SMITH

Agency of the Bank U States
Washn Mar 29 1841

Dear Sir

I am advised by Mr [Herman] Cope that the Bank of the U States, has closed the arrangement with Judge Doty,[1] & agreed to take the property from you mentioned in the enclosed list—as soon therefore as the proper conveyances are made, & evidence given that the titles are clear of all incumbrances, your liabilities will be credited with the amt. at which the property was to be rated. I am very respy your obt st   Rd Smith AB.

over

In Wiskonsin
    3556 75/100 acres farming lands—
    3290 55/100   "   mineral lands
    undivided 1/12 part of Helena
    1/24 part of Madison—

In Michigan
    280 acres, town of Commerce
    4157 39/100 do—
      80   do coal lands
    ————————
    4517 39/100

In Illinois
    1920 acres farming lands—
      1 undivided 1/16 part Prophets Town
      3   do   1/8 do of land & ferry known as Jordans ferry
    1/10 of Brewster's estate in the town of Peru—this interest comprises
    50 or 60 lots in Peru
    2 undivided acres in lot no 7 of the 20 acre lots laid off as school
    Comm. of Illinois. Sect. 16.T.33.

In Indiana
    SW 1/4 Sec. 29.T.37.R.9.E.   160
    E.   1/2 NE 1/4 Sect. 9.T.37.R.9.E.   80
                        ————
                      240 acres

In Michigan City
    one half of lot no. 5 R No 10 East

In Ohio
    5 acres in Town of Toledo
    9 1/2 SW fractional qr. section 30 & S.W. fractional qr. & W 1/2 S.E.
    1/4 & east 1/2 NW fractional qr. sect. 31.T.9.S.R.3.W 399 17/100
    acres

ALS. MWalB.
  1. See above, [James Duane Doty]
to Nicholas Biddle, March 25, [1841];
and [Doty] to Biddle, March 29, 1841,
below.

FROM JAMES DUANE DOTY TO NICHOLAS BIDDLE
                                Washington
                                March 29. 1841.
Dear Sir,
    Mr. Webster is now absent to the City of New York, and is not expect-

ed to return until Wednesday or Thursday. I am just shewn a letter from Mr. Cope to Mr. W. in which he says there is some difficulty about the settlement concluded with him by me, *with the Committee*, the amount having been misunderstood by the Comtee.[1] The amount stipulated for was $114,000; an arrangement for a less sum could not be accepted by Mr. W. because it would not give the relief desired.

It seems to me that the Commtee. does not appreciate the liberal offer made by Mr. W., and that he is wholly unable to give more. The property which is retained by him is required to liquidate other debts, and especially to relieve some portion of that which is conveyed from the incumbrances.

I am sorry to trouble you again with this subject, but it will give Mr. W. great distress and trouble if the arrangement made on the 26th. is not considered by the Bank as it is by me, as final. With the greatest respect I am most truly yours   J. D. Doty

ALS. DLC.
    1. See above, Herman Cope to DW, March 27, 1841.

TO CAROLINE LE ROY WEBSTER

Philadelphia
Wednesday, Mar. 31 [1841]

My Dear Wife

My fortune today has been better than ours was, going north. I write this at Mr [Isaac Rand] Jacksons,[1] at 3 oclock, having come to a private house to avoid publicity and importunity. There are no cars for Baltimore this afternoon.

You will write me, I trust, daily & advise me of all that occurs. I am just in season to get this short note into the mail. Yrs   D. Webster

ALS. ViU.
    1. Jackson (1804–1842), a native of Newburyport, Massachusetts, had settled in Philadelphia by the early 1830s. A wealthy supporter, Jackson had recently provided DW with funds for the downpayment on a house in Washington, whereupon Jackson received the appointment of chargé to Denmark. See DW to Isaac Rand

Jackson, February 12, 1841 (mDW 17498), [March 19, 1841] (mDW 18380), March 30, 1841 (mDW 18620); Isaac Rand Jackson to DW, February 15, 1841 (mDW 17523), March 17, 20, 1841 (mDW 18345, 18420); Irving H. Bartlett, *Daniel Webster* (New York, 1978), p. 206; and *Diplomatic Papers*, 1.

FROM JAMES DUANE DOTY TO HERMAN COPE

Washington
April 1. 1841

Dear Sir,

Mr. Webster has returned to this City this evening, and desires me to say in reply to your Letter of the 27th. of March last,[1] that he considers the arrangement by you and myself that the Bank should receive his Western Lands, excepting 1120 acres of improved land in Illinois, in full satisfaction of his debt due to the Bank and to your New York Agency, amounting to about $114,000. *as final,* and that he has very good reasons, which he could give you if his time permitted, *why* it is *certainly* for the interest of the Bank that it should be so regarded by the Committee of the Direction.

Upon this point he is very positive, and believing the Comtee. will perceive the propriety of giving to it the weight which in the judgment of Mr. Webster it merits, you will allow me I trust to express the hope that the instructions to Mr. [Richard] Smith may be renewed to close the matter according to the very equitable and just terms of our agreement. With great regard, I remain Your most obedient servant   J. D. Doty

ALS copy. MWalB.
1. See above, Herman Cope to DW, March 27, 1841.

One month after he took office, President Harrison died of pneumonia. It fell upon Webster, the highest ranking government official in Washington, to notify all the heads of the departments, the members of the diplomatic corps, and all foreign diplomats of the death, through letters similar to the one to Thomas Nelson Carr, below. Until Vice President Tyler's arrival in Washington on April 6, Webster was in fact acting President.

TO THOMAS NELSON CARR

Department of State
Washington 4. April 1841

Sir

It has become my most painful d[ut]y to announce to you the decease of Wil[liam] Henry Harrison late President of the United [States.]

This afflicting event took place, at the Executive mansion, in this City, at twe[nty] minutes before one oclock in the morning. I am, Sir, yr: obt: svt: Danl Webster

LS. MHi. Carr, a native of New York, had served in the New York legislature in 1835. In 1838, President Van Buren appointed him consul to Morocco, where he served until his removal on December 29, 1841.

FROM NICHOLAS BIDDLE WITH ENCLOSURE FROM NICHOLAS BIDDLE, APRIL 3

Phila. April 5. 1841

The enclosed (above)[1] has been lying on my desk for <a few> two days—yet as it concerns yourself—I send it.

Today we have a most atrocious report about the Bank which in a most especial manner abuses our friend Mr [Samuel] Jaudon.² <It has done the work however effectually.> I think the Bank now perfectly dead as any stone. But what can you do with insane people who will commit suicide.

I need not say how much I have been shocked & distressed at the death of the President. But for this meeting of stockholders which I am obliged to watch, I would have gone down to join you in the melancholy offices of his interment. With great regard Yrs   NB.

ALS draft. DLC.
1. See below.
2. Along with several other officers who had served under Biddle, Jaudon had been accused of borrowing large sums of money from the Bank for private speculations. Thomas Payne Govan, *Nicholas Biddle: Nationalist and Public Banker, 1786–1844* (Chicago, 1959), pp. 376–387.

ENCLOSURE: FROM NICHOLAS BIDDLE

Phila. April 3. 1841

My dear Sir,

I have an *omnibus* letter to write to you.

1. Do not fail to make Judge Doty write a decided & decisive letter—which will place you at your ease as to your affairs with the Bank.¹

2. Ponder well—whether after all the Committee missions Mr [Joseph Washington] Tyson would not be the best choice for *you*. There is a little of the spirit of *Anti-Curtis* in it.

3. Mr [Robert] Morris of the Enquirer²—<with whom you talked>—adheres strongly to Mr Tyson—but in case Mr T. is not <chosen> appointed he would like some provision for himself—and he says that his paper has been always for Mr Harrison—& is more exclusively for Mr Webster than any other paper in the City.³

4. Mr Jos[eph] R[ipley] Chandler of the U.S. Gazette wishes to be Treasurer of the Mint—but will not ask for it. I think it would be a very good thing to give it to him unasked. He is an excellent person—quite fit & would be very useful.⁴

5. Do you remember my neighbor Mr [Jacob] Waterman who was turned out by [Amos] Kendall for not circulating Extra Globes. I put his petition for reappointment under cover to you.⁵ <See that he is appointed.> It is a just thing in itself & I want him to see your hand in his success.

6. My excellent old friend Mr [William] Fry⁶—the Editor of the National Gazette called to say—that in Mr [Robert] Walsh's time his paper was uniform in the support of Mr Webster & in this late campaign, was early & vigorous in the cause of Genl Harrison. He thinks that ancient remembrances might induce the Department of State to give to that Ga-

zette the great distinction & the small profit of printing the laws. It would be a good & kind act—if practicable. <and now "my story's done" Yrs always NB.>

7. Do not forget sound H. Senter Huntt,[7] the kinsman of Mr Richard Smith. Mr Smith wrote after his first interview with you, that you said you would provide for him & his family rely on that word as on the law & the gospel.

And "now my story's done." Yrs always   NB

ALS draft. DLC.

1. Doty had already written such a letter, which Biddle presumably had not yet seen. See above, Doty to Herman Cope, April 1, 1841.

2. Morris, a native of Philadelphia trained as a physician, pursued literature and journalism as a vocation. For a quarter century he edited the *Pennsylvania Inquirer*.

3. DW appointed the *Pennsylvania Inquirer* publisher of the laws in June. See Jesper Harding to DW, June 23, 1841, mDW 52458.

4. Following the nomination and withdrawal of William Findlay and

the rejection of Joseph Ritner, the Senate confirmed the nomination of Isaac Roach as treasurer of the Philadelphia mint on September 13, 1841.

5. Not further identified. On Waterman, see also Nicholas Biddle to DW, [March 1841], mDW 18641.

6. Not further identified. For other recommendations of the *National Gazette* as public printer, see B. Peters to DW, March 1, 1841, mDW 52238; and Russell H. Nevins to DW, April 20, 1841, mDW 52235.

7. Not further identified. On Huntt, see Nicholas Biddle to DW, [1841], mDW 38260–A.

FROM HERMAN COPE

Bank of the United States.
Suspended debt & Real Estate
Department
April 6th. 1841

My dear Sir

Upon a consideration, by the Committee, of the proposition submitted by Judge Doty[1] for the final settlement of your liabilities to this Bank as well here as at its Agency in New York; a majority of the Committee agreed to report to the Board in favor of the proposed settlement. I therefore prepared a report for them, setting forth the fact of a positive written contract between yourself and the Bank, in which it is stipulated that payment of your indebtedness to the Bank shall be made by you and accepted by it, in certain Lands mentioned therein, at a valuation. And that a proposition had subsequently been made by you, through Judge Doty, to convey all the Lands described in the List to the Bank, in full payment of your whole indebtedness—with a good title and free of all incumbrance—excepting only, and reserving therefore, 1120 acres in Illinois—subject to prior incumbrances, as stated in my letter to you of the 26th March last,[2] and recommended that the officers of the Bank be authorised to carry into effect the settlement proposed through Judge Doty.

The Board of Directors, at a stated meeting this morning, adopted the report as above; and which consequently authorises me to have it carried into effect on the terms stated in my Letter to you of the 26th of March last.

Mr. [Richard] Smith will be instructed accordingly: and I sincerely hope you will not have any other difficulty interposed in the way of a settlement on the terms now agreed upon. With great regard truly yours

Herman Cope Superin[tenden]t

ALS. MWalB.

1. See above, [Doty] to Biddle, March 25, [1841].

2. Apparently Cope was referring

to his letter to DW, March 27, 1841, above. No letter from Cope to DW dated March 26 has been found.

TO CHARLES HENRY THOMAS

April 11. 41

Dear Henry,

In the sorrow and confusion of the times, I have not been able, till now, to write you, & can now only write a single line.

I enclose $100 check for [Seth] Weston—he must live on that until I can get to Marshfield. If he cannot, you may sell a pair of oxen, or two or three cows, as we shall, of necessity, reduce our farming, this year. I hope to see you about the 25th. of this month, or by the first week in May. You must take care of all things. As to farming, our plan must be,

1. To have little corn, or other tillage, to carry on ourselves—thereby diminishing the necessary amount of labor.

2. To let out as many parcels as may be to such persons only as will cultivate well, & cleanly, on shares.

3. To keep as much stock as will consume the hay & grass. This stock should be principally of young & growing cattle.

As to the garden, it must be taken care of, but not [on] any very large scale. Some of us will be there doubtless in the summer, & we shall want vegetables, fruits &c.

The Horses may be sold, except such as we wanted on the farm. Let me know what offer you can get for Mrs Websters horses.

As to Mr [Tilden] Ames[1] I am exceedingly desirous to oblige him, but I do not see at present what can be done. I will see him when I come on.

Pray give my love to all. I shall pray for time, this week to write to some of you.

My head is nearly turned. In five weeks, we have had three Presidents

—beside which I have been hurried from one death bed to another,[2] under very harrassing circumstances. But my health is good, I am happy to say. Adieu! D Webster

ALS. MHi.
1. Ames (1795–1867) was a Marshfield farmer and cattle drover, a close friend of DW.

2. DW was referring to the deaths of Herman LeRoy on March 18 and President Harrison on April 4.

TO LEVERETT SALTONSTALL

April 12. '41

My Dear Sir,

You will have seen the Inaugural.[1] It is generally thought here that things will continue in the expected course. But we have heavy work before us. I am glad you have made up your mind for a vigorous effort, at the ensuing session, & hope all the other Whig members will do the same. We have lost the popularity of a great name, & must now stand, if we stand at all, on our principles and our measures. Yrs truly

D Webster

ALS. NhD.
1. Tyler's inaugural had been delivered on April 9. See James D. Richardson, *A Compilation of the*

Messages and Papers of the Presidents, 1789–1897 (10 vols., Washington, 1900), 4: 36–39.

TO JOHN DAVIS (1787–1854)

April 16. '41

Private

My Dear Sir

I have duly recd your letter of the 9th.[1] It is not wonderful that the whole country should be filled with apprehension at the present state of things. I do not feel able altogether to allay them, although, so far, the Presidents proceedings are satisfactory.

Towards those of [us] who fill the Departments, I believe he feels kind, & confiding. In this respect, we see no difficulty ahead. But the great question, is, his opinion upon measures; & in regard to this I do not think enough is developed to enable us to judge. If it were not for past opinions & commitments, I believe he would be prepared to [go] ahead, in accordance with the general Whig sentiment of the Country. My *hope* is, that he will consider himself *instructed*, not by one single state, but by the *Country*. In the matter of a Bank, my opinion is, he will sign whatever Congress may agree upon, but I fear he would wish the Bank to be in this District, or recommend some other escape from the old question.

Among ourselves, we are quite harmonious, & get on without jarring; but indeed we have done little except settle questions of appointment, &

I do not see when we shall find an end of that most disagreeable business.

You have had some taste of the pleasures of importunity, & know how to pity us.

As to the R.I. & Mass controversy,[2] the first thing I have to say is, that I am ashamed of the Court. These two last questions they have decided *flagrantly* wrong. There is no mistake about it. But an Answer is ordered, & must be prepared. Though a work of some labor, it will not be difficult. The material for framing it is almost entirely to be found in the Plea. I am willing to continue my services in the case, & to consult on forming the answer, but I hardly know whether I should have time to go through the manual service of writing it. Perhaps I might, or it may be necessary to have another hand. To tell you frankly what I think, I do not see any use in retaining the services of the Atty Genl further.[3] If it strikes you satisfactorily, the business may take this Course; the case may be left wholly in my hands, & out of my fees I will pay some body, either here or in Boston, for doing the mechanical part of the work. This will leave Mr Austin nothing to complain [of]. Perhaps I may get a little aid from Mr [Jeremiah] Mason, who has already been spoken to.

I dislike to say any thing about *fees*, but if you approve of what is above said, & think I deserve any thing, you may send it to me. You will see what I have recd already. I have argued the case three times, besides drawing the plea originally, which was a fortnight's work, the Demurrer &c. Public bodies are poor clients, & I do not wish to do any thing, which may subject either you or me to remark, & let me add in conclusion, that if you can arrange the matter better by allowing me to go out of the cause, I am ready to be discharged.

I pray you remember me to your good wife.[4] I hope to go home for a few days about the first of May, & hope to see you. Yrs always truly
D Webster

ALS. MWA. Published in *W & S*, 16: 340–341.

1. Not found.

2. DW was referring to the case involving the Massachusetts-Rhode Island boundary, which was argued before the Supreme Court on several occasions. See *Rhode Island* v. *Massachusetts*, 12 Peters 657 (1838); 13 Peters 23 (1839); 14 Peters 210 (1840); 15 Peters 233 (1841); 4 Howard 591 (1845).

3. James Trecothick Austin, who joined with DW in arguing the case before the Supreme Court in 1838, was attorney general for Massachusetts.

4. Mrs. Davis, née Eliza Bancroft, was the sister of George Bancroft.

Of all the countries and cities with which the United States maintained diplomatic ties, Webster found that relations between the United States and Great Britain were the most strained in March 1841. Two trouble-

some issues had driven these nations almost to the brink of war. The first, dating back to the Treaty of Paris in 1783, involved the north-eastern boundary between the United States and Canada. For several years, bands of settlers and lumberjacks from each side had made forays into territory claimed by the other, engaging in skirmishes which threatened to erupt into open warfare. The other issue involved the Caroline, *an American vessel engaged in ferrying supplies across the Niagara River to the Canadian rebels. On December 29, 1837, Canadian government forces seized the* Caroline *at her pier near Buffalo, set her afire and cut her loose to drift down the river where she sank just short of the falls. In the attack one American member of the vessel's crew was killed. In 1840 an Ontario sheriff, Alexander McLeod, visiting on the New York side of the river, was heard to boast that he had killed the American. He was promptly arrested by New York authorities and indicted for murder and arson. British Foreign Minister Lord Palmerston avowed the raid on the* Caroline *to have been an official act and demanded McLeod's release; but the Federal Government could not and New York State would not dismiss the charges. Once again Great Britain and the United States were drifting toward war when Webster became Secretary of State. John Evelyn Denison, whose letter appears below, was one of many on both sides of the Atlantic who looked to Webster to resolve this and other outstanding issues and maintain the peace.*

McLeod was acquitted by the New York courts in October 1841 and the way was cleared to negotiate the northeastern boundary. For a more detailed examination of the McLeod case see Diplomatic Papers, 1.

FROM JOHN EVELYN DENISON

Ossington, April 16, 1841.

My Dear Sir:

I must not delay another day thanking you for a letter[1] which gave me so much pleasure; and I should not wish to be quite the last (as I fear I may be) in making you my hearty congratulations on the high post to which you have been called; yet these congratulations not to you so much as to your country, and my country, and the civilized world at large, who are all deeply interested in seeing the politics of the United States conducted in a just, candid, and honorable course.

If we had not seen each other so lately, and if you had not had the opportunity of seeing with your own eyes, and hearing with your own ears, how the United States and every thing that belongs to them are regarded in this country, I might perhaps have thought it worth while to enter at some length on that topic, and to tell you, not only how completely all bad and jealous feelings are cured, but how sincere and universal the desire is to cultivate the most friendly and intimate relations with you, our brethen on the other side of the water. But all this to you must be entirely unnecessary. I make no doubt that, among the great body of the American people, the same feeling of good-will toward us prevails, and I cannot therefore entertain a doubt that our differences may be honorably and peaceably adjusted.

I remember Mr. [Thomas] Jefferson saying to me, that it was his entire belief that Mr. [William] Pitt[2] and the governments of those days delighted in war, on account of the plunder they were able to make of the public money in times of high excitement and large expenditure. But those good old days are now gone by, and even this high motive for destroying life and property is now come to an end.

You will now be overwhelmed with business, and I shall not expect any answer to this, and not a word from you till Congress has separated, and the roughest and the heaviest of your work is over, and the days are long, and you have gone down for a holiday to look at your farm. Then, if any Ossington seeds are doing themselves credit, you may find ten minutes to write me a line. Keep peace, too, and let the highway of the seas be assuredly open; and I must see about sending you a good specimen of some short-horns for your farm, but I won't risk such a precious cargo to the chance of privateers and prize-hunters.

We had a very beautiful spring, and one most favorable for all farming operations. I have lately been buying some very good cattle at terrible high prices, and very soon I shall have a herd worth a visit from any of your agriculturists in search of the best short-horns.

I am busy, too, in finishing my house. I have just had over some German painters from Munich to paint my ceilings. I think Mrs. Webster went to Munich, so she will know the style of work there under the patronage of the king. My attempt is the first that has been made to introduce it into England.

My neighbors, to whom you were so good as to desire your remembrances, were greatly flattered by your recollection of them. I had the clerical neighbor from Doncaster here yesterday, to lecture me on some points of farming. I told him how favorably I had imprinted his name on your mind by the story of his picking up the weed while the dog was pointing. He wanted to deny the story, but, soon afterward, he said he remembered, some years ago, finding some thorns cut off a hedge lying on his land, and that he had thrown them over into a neighbor's wheat. One day, while he was standing concealed under his own hedge, he heard the said neighbor coming down his field, and exclaiming, as he picked up the thorns, "D—— the parson, he has been here again!"

Make my best remembrances to the good Judge [Joseph Story]. Lady Charlotte[3] desires to join with me in kind regards to Mrs. Webster. Believe me, yours very sincerely,   J. E. Denison.

Text from Curtis, 2: 92–93. Original not found. Denison (1800–1873), member of Parliament and later Speaker of the House of Commons, had enjoyed a close friendship with DW since 1824–1825.
1. Not found.

2. Pitt (1759–1806) became chancellor of the exchequer in 1782 and prime minister in 1783.
3. Mrs. Denison (d. 1873), née Charlotte Cavendish Bentinck, third daughter of William, fourth duke of Portland.

FROM EDWARD EVERETT

Florence 16 April 1841

My dear Sir,

I duly received some time since your acceptable letter of the 2d of February.[1] As your letters of the same date to Edward[2] advised his return in the Spring, I, of course, made no attempt to detain him; being, in fact of your opinion, that with his views of professional life, he would do well to enter, without further delay, upon his preparatory studies. Unwilling to have him leave Italy, after having been so near Rome, without seeing it, I advised him to make a short visit to the Eternal City, before setting his face westward. He accordingly left us for Rome & Naples, on the first of this month. We have heard from him up to the 11th from Rome, where he had been passing holy week, and was to start the next day for Naples.[3] He expects to take passage for America by the middle of May. If, after his return, he will bestow the requisite pains to keep up his knowledge of the French & Italian languages, particularly the former, I think the acquisition will be worth, in future life, the time he has employed upon it.

I am greatly indebted to you for your information on public affairs. Subsequent accounts came down to the 19th of March. You will please to accept my congratulations on your being placed at the head of General Harrison's Administration, and my best wishes that you may be happy and eminently successful in that arduous & honorable post. You will have a momentous session in May; but I trust a good majority, in both houses, will sustain you against an embittered and unscrupulous opposition. As to the finances of the Country, it is in vain to raise money, till you put an end to that everlasting and disgraceful Florida War. It is a perfect political syphen, with one leg in the treasury and the other in the bottomless everglades. Can you not find some honest and able general, who will put an end to this disgraceful contest, either by negotiation or the sword?[4] I own, I suspect some of those benefitted by it of prolonging, on purpose, this *multis utile bellum*.

I notice with special interest your remarks on the subject of foreign appointments. As the negotiation on the boundary question was transferred to Washington, at the request of the American Government, I suppose it will remain there; at least in the present stage of the question. Should it be removed to London, you ought, by all means, to follow it there. Strange as it may seem, the question, on its original merits, has never been (properly speaking) *discussed* between the two governments. The transactions before the arbiter were rather an exchange of *books written* on the subject; very able books, on our side; but books, in which the points were buried under the proofs and illustrations. I sincerely wish you could get hold of the subject, as you do of a cause before the Supreme Court of the U.S. and bring it to the test of a vigorous forensic argument. I should not be afraid to have you go with it before the Court of Queen's bench; if the judges would leave reasons of state out of the question.

I am truly rejoiced at your purpose of providing for I[saac] P. D[avis].[5] I wish he could have a place beyond the reach of change, but this I suppose is impossible. I wish Chief justice [Roger Brooke] Taney's health would require him to go to Santa Cruz, and that Judge [Joseph] Story might take his place, but having had, in a small way, some experience of the sweets of controlling patronage, I shall limit my interference with your enjoyment of them, to the expression of this wish. I take it our opponents, if the President adopts the liberal policy of non-removal, will pursue the magnanimous one of non-resignation; thus prolonging by his *generosity* what they owed to the *exclusive course* of his predecessors. It is quite convenient to have the benefit of a proscriptive policy when you are in power & a catholic policy when you are out of power.

I have been strongly urged by Mr. [John Baptiste] Sartori, late American vice Consul at Leghorn,[6] to represent his case to you. His friends in America & among them Judge [Samuel L.] Southard will do it in detail. I owe his acquaintance to Gov. [Lewis] Cass' introduction. Mr. Sartori, I believe, is a very worthy & respectable man, and had a right to expect the consulate on the decease of Mr [Thomas] Appleton,[7] if it were given to any person not a native citizen of the United States. Such ought, I think, to be the rule vizt. to appoint none but native citizens. It was announced by the late Administration as their rule; but in violation of it Mr [Joseph A.] Binda[8] was appointed. As between these two gentlemen, I think Mr Sartori had a right to expect the place; but I do not wish to be considered as expressing any opinion, as to any other question raised on the subject of Mr Binda's appointment.

My wife is greatly indebted to you & Mrs W. for your kind remembrance, which we unite in reciprocating. She and my daughters have enjoyed the winter highly, and are yet undecided where we shall pass the summer: Perhaps at Florence.

As I hear through Mrs [Nathan] Hale,[9] that you have two bushels of letters unopened, I shall not expect you to answer,—hardly to read this. I shall occasionally drop you a line for auld lang syne, and always remain, with true attachment, faithfully Yours,   E. E.

I have written a letter by this packet to the President, which he may perhaps show you, which contains some of the views & speculations prevailing here on public affairs.

My address is Messrs Baring, Brothers & Co.

Private and Confidential

As you have mentioned to me the subject of appointments & intimated the purpose of submitting my name to the President for a mission abroad, as events may be developed or circumstances require, you will pardon me perhaps for saying a few words to you on this matter; although it is a topic on which I wish to say very little. I could not with safety take my wife to Berlin or St. Petersburg. If at this critical juncture in the East, the commercial and political interests of the Country should be thought to warrant a full mission to Constantinople the minister to be also accredited to Greece, that place would be acceptable to me. Should the President deem it expedient to send a full minister to two or more of the Italian Governments jointly, (a common practice), that also would be an eligible appointment. You will find our relations with Sardinia in a very bad state, requiring immediate attention; and a commercial treaty with Tuscany is much wanted. There may, however, be reasons against consolidating the accustomed missions of the second class. I am told by friends at home that I have been some times thought of for the mission to London. If the contingency should not arise in which you would think it necessary to assume that station yourself, and should not Mr [John] Sergeant be selected, whom I see talked of, and whose qualifications are by no one more highly estimated than by me I should prefer that place on some accts. to any other;[10] and it might not be undesirable to you to have it in the hands of a confidential friend. Next to London, if there were a vacancy, I should prefer to go to Paris. But I do not wish any vacancy made for me. Provision I see was made, at the late session, for a new minister to Vienna, where, in consequence of my long residence in former days in Germany, I should, as far as the language goes, feel in some degree at home.

To whatever post you may assign me, as I am here at Florence, should no provision be made for direct diplomatic relations with Tuscany, it might be in my power—if authorized for the purpose—before repairing to my station, to conclude a commercial treaty with this Government. The extraordinary personal kindness which the Grand Duke[11] has shown me this winter, would give me some facilities.

I need not say, my dear Sir, that I have written to you, as I write no one else on this subject; and the more unreservedly, as I shall probably, in no event, name it again. Neither you nor the President will ever by me or, with my knowledge, on my account, be troubled with any solicitations for Office; and what I have now said has seemed to me not wholly un-invited by your own observations.

ALS. MHi. Published in part in Paul Revere Frothingham, *Edward Everett, Orator and Statesman* (Boston, 1925), pp. 176–177.

1. See above.

2. Not found.

3. For a discussion of Edward Webster's sojourn, see above, Edward Webster to DW, February 18, 1841.

4. The "honest and able general" who finally ended the Florida war was Zachary Taylor.

5. Through DW's influence, Davis received the appointment of naval officer for Boston.

6. Sartori (c. 1755–1853), a native of Leghorn, became simultaneously in 1797 the first United States consul to Rome and the Papal States consul to the United States. He settled in Trenton, New Jersey, in 1800 and took out American citizenship. He remained there until about 1830, when he returned to Leghorn, where he served as vice consul during the illness of Thomas Appleton. Sartori's efforts to secure the consulship failed.

7. Appleton (1763–1840), the son of Nathaniel Appleton (1731–1798), a Boston merchant, had served as consul at Leghorn from 1798 until his death.

8. Binda (1790–1864), Count Guiseppe Agememnon of Lucca, Italy, had married Fanny Sumter, granddaughter of General Thomas Sumter of South Carolina, in 1825. Two years later Binda settled in New York City, where he was an art dealer. In 1840, one year before he became a United States citizen, he received from Van Buren the appointment as consul, a position he held, except for the years 1849 to 1854, until 1861.

9. Mrs. Nathan Hale (1796–1866), née Sarah Preston Everett, Everett's sister.

10. According to some reports Harrison had offered the British post to John Sergeant, but he declined.

11. Leopold II (1797–1870) had succeeded his father as Grand Duke of Tuscany in 1824 and ruled until 1859.

FROM GRANT & STONE

Phila. 21 April 1841

Sir

Having been instrumental in procuring the situation as Consul at Pictou N.S. for a very worthy man, James Primrose Esqr.[1] now resident there, we have learned with some surprise that Mr. [Thomas Barclay] Livingston[2] a gentleman recently appointed by Mr Van Buren as Consul at Halifax has, or is about making a representation to you with the object of making himself a Consul General for the British provinces, and thereby giving him the power to appoint deputies for all other ports than Halifax, so that all will be under *his* controul and we may unquestionably suppose this consolidation of power and consequent duties to be performed by Mr. L. does not arise altogether from patriotism or disinterestedness, but possibly from an expectation thereby to receive one half the fees arising from his deputies, as we think was the case with his predecessor Mr [John] Morrow;[3] when through our interference that system was broken up, and Mr. Primrose appointed for Pictou, and there resisted by Mr Morrow and his friends, to an extent that caused difficulties between our government & G Britain when Mr P.s action was suspended until our Minister at St James carried the point of special consuls at such ports as our government saw proper. Mr Morrow then contended for the same thing Mr Livingston now wishes to reestablish, and altogether from interested motives, and not the advantage of our commerce & country.

Pictou has more American vessels visit the port annually for Coal than visit Halifax and requires a special Consul with full authority. If Mr Primrose is not a proper man, or does not do his duty faithfully, turn him out, and we have not a word to say—but we believe your department has found him faithful, capable and deserving—if any charges are made against him let him know them and give him an opportunity to be heard.

One objection made to Mr Primrose is that he is a British subject, and this is true, & yet he is a very correct and honourable man—the fees of our consulate are no inducement to any American to reside there and there is no other inducement.

We have considered it an act of kindness toward Mr Primrose to say thus much, as he is not probably aware of any attempt against him—the paper intended to be sent you by Mr Livingston was sent here to one of our merchants to procure signatures, and several were obtained without much thought upon the subject and we also understand the same paper was sent to Boston for more names now you are aware how readily such papers are signed; where no subscription money is required.

All we ask in behalf of Mr Primrose is that he may be heard if neces‑ sary, but we presume you will at once see thro' the whole movement and object, and decide against any change.[4] Very Respectfully Sir Your Mo Obt Servts   Grant & Stone

ALS. NhHi. Grant & Stone, leading Philadelphia mercantile firm and agents of Baring Brothers & Company in that city, had a strong business alliance with James Primrose of Pictou, Nova Scotia. Both Samuel Grant (1783–1872) and Dexter Stone (1791–c.1846), proprietors of the firm, were Massachusetts natives.

1. Primrose, a native of Scotland and business ally of Grant & Stone, had been confirmed as United States consul at Pictou in December 1837.

2. Livingston (1806–1852), a na‑ tive of New York and partner in the mercantile firm of Barclay & Livingston, had been confirmed as United States consul at Halifax on February 3, 1841.

3. Morrow (1795–1862), a native of England and agent of a Liverpool firm in Halifax, had been appointed United States consul at that post in 1833. In 1840, Van Buren removed Morrow and appointed Livingston.

4. The dispute over the United States consulate in Nova Scotia can be traced in the James Primrose,

Thomas B. Livingston, and John Morrow files, in Letters of Application and Recommendation during the Administrations of Martin Van Buren, William Henry Harrison, and John Tyler, 1837–1845 (M–687), Rolls 19, 23, 26, DNA. See also *Diplomatic Papers* 1.

FROM JOHN DAVIS (1787–1854)

Worcester April 23d. 1841

My Dear Sir

I have recd your favor[1] and can well understand that the crisis of Trial is not yet come. Mr. Tyler has many troublesome matters to contend with as any gentleman who has been the exponent of the peculiar doctrines of Virginia must have. The great difficulty is that the policy of that school does not embrace the country and is not adapted to its wants or its business. The foundation is too narrow even for the diversified interests of Va. It is a mistake to suppose there is nothing but wheat tobacco and negroes, and therefore that provision is to be made for nothing else, and no man will be more sensible of this than he who is brought suddenly to the responsible position of being the guardian and protector of the whole country. New motives must spring up, new standards for estimating public duty and obligations must rise in the mind, general considerations must displace local biases, and there will be a moral necessity created for the exercise of greater candor and embracing broader and more comprehensive principles. Virginia can no longer be cherished to the prejudice of New York for both are alike entitled to favorable regard and the local attachments and interests must give way so as to harmonize with the general good. These things must mind—and I cannot doubt that Mr. Tyler whom I believe to be a sincere patriot will <I hope> feel and obey the influences and convictions they opperate with great force upon any just and <honorable> ingenuous will produce. I am aware that he like every man who is forward in sustaining the ultra doctrine of lower Va. will find inconvenient if not impractical opinions on record but the only manly way is to meet and dispose of them instead of sacrificing himself and the country. It appears to me that all this has passed through the mind of Mr. T. that before he came to the Chair he had realized that Va was not the whole country and that there were other places and interests deserving consideration. He was doubtless reminded of all this forcibly when he was in the west and called upon to address the people.[2] I think also I see it laboring in his mind through the guarded phraseology of his most recent and public manifesto.[3] He seems to be strug[g]ling with himself—and to feel that the states ought not to be rival communities, selfish and ambitious, but one harmonious family striving for a common prosperity. I cannot doubt that he will suffer his convictions instead of attachments springing from local views, to lead him—and I hope the country will give him its confidence and cheer him on in the way of well doing. While there is great anxiety here as to his policy there is a disposition to be satisfied with what is said and done and to give him a fair trial. It appears to me that all matters may be easily straightened and prosperity restored. I am more anxious to tranquilize the public mind upon the currency question than about the mode of doing it. A Bank is probably the wisest measure but it is not without serious objections. The recent developments of abuses in the exercise of banking privileges satisfies me that a charter should be drawn in the most guarded manner.

    1. The capital should be small, but not exceed 30M. The merchants will want 100M but, 20M to 30M with the aid of the deposites is enough.

    2d. The amount of discounts and of circulation should be cautiously and safely limited.

    3d. The dividends should be limited to remove all motive to overwork and the surplus earnings if any should either be an accumulating fund belonging to the U States or paid into the Treasury.

    4th. Trade of all sorts—dealing in stocks of every kind—drawing or dealing in foreign bills of exchange or letters of credit should all be strictly prohibited. It is this illegitimate business that has ruined many banks.

    5th. Loans should be limited to short paper not to exceed four months, and all discounts upon stock of any kind, even their own, should be prohibited.

    6th. No one but the board of Directors should be allowed to discount, or to renew paper.

    7th. No bills under $10 or $20 should be issued and none except of prescribed denominations.

    8th. The revenues should be received and disbursed but should be held on conditions safe for the country and so far contingent as always to secure <the> a faithful observance of the provisions of the charter and a rigid adherence to its pure ba[n]king principles. We want no flourish of financial talents—no bank president to give the lead to trade—or to contrive means for men to pay their debts by an issue of bonds or other paper. We want no guardian of state loans or dealer in state stocks, but we want a bank and nothing else—an institution that will cling to the fundamental principle of always providing the means to maintain paper convertable at sight. This through any crisis that may come will prove more efficacious than all the quack medicine that any Emperic can administer.

    9th. I should prefer that the stock should be all held by individuals but the bank must be open to free and unreserved examination and U.

States in consideration of its great interest should place one or more directors on the board.

From such a bank I think nothing need be apprehended as it would be purely a business of money and would sustain a steady & uniform currency. It could not if in the hands of honest men run riot in schemes of finance and trade

AL incomplete. DLC.
1. See above, DW to John Davis (1787–1854), April 16, 1841.
2. Davis was probably alluding to Tyler's address to a group of citizens of Columbus, Ohio, on September 25, one of the few instances in which

Tyler took an active part in the canvass. Oliver Perry Chitwood, *John Tyler: Champion of the Old South* (New York: 1939), pp. 185–186.
3. Davis was referring to Tyler's "inaugural" address delivered on April 9.

TRANSFER OF SHARE IN THE FOUR LAKE COMPANY
Share No 6

For and in consideration of ten thousand dollars, I hereby assign and transfer to Alexander Lardner, Herman Cope and Thomas S. Taylor,[1] all of the City of Philadelphia in the state of Pennsylvania, the survivors and survivor of them and heirs, executors administrators and assigns of such survivors, forever, all my right, title and interest in the within share of the Capital, and the beneficial interests, of the Four Lake Company,[2] subject to all of the provisions, covenants and charges contained in the Indenture constituting said Company or authorized thereby.

Signed and delivered at Washington this twenty eighth day of April A.D. 1841.   Danl Webster
Witness
J. D. Doty
D. F. Webster

ADS. NhD.
1. Taylor was an accountant for the Bank of the United States of Pennsylvania.
2. The landholdings of the Four

Lake Company, in which DW, Doty, and George W. Jones were investors, lay in Madison, the capital of Wisconsin Territory. See *Correspondence*, 4: 216–217.

FROM RAMSAY CROOKS

Office of the American Fur Company
New York, 30 April 1841

Dear Sir

Enclosed we beg leave to hand your account with us to 30 September 1841—balance due on that day $685.50, which we trust will be found correct, and satisfactory.

When this a/c was made up it was our intention to have presented it immediately; but it has been cont'd[?] with a view to your convenience. We however hope you are now prepared to close this transaction which has been already open 3½ years, and shall be happy to hear from you on the subject. I am Dear Sir very Respectfully your ob Servant

Ramy Crooks President Am fur Co

LC. NHi.

TO SAMUEL APPLETON APPLETON, WITH MEMORANDUM

Boston May 12. 1841

Please deliver to the order of Albert Fearing Esq[1] One thousand bottles of wine, out of my wine closet in Mr [Peter Chardon] Brooks House;[2] selected according to the memorandum, which accompanies this. Yours &c.

Memorandum

From Shelves 4. & 5. Sercial . . . . 300 bottles
    This was imported by me, is of the vintage of
    1817, & was bottled in 1825.
    It is sealed with dark brown wax.
From Shelf No. 1 London Madeira 150
    This was brought to Boston from London, & is 20 yrs old,
    or thereabouts. It is sealed with red wax . . . .
From Shelf No. 8—"Haymaker" 50
    Imported by Mr [Isaac P.] Davis—an old & good, but not
    a very rich wine . . . . . . marked "H." on the cork.
From Shelves 8. 9. 10 "C.M." 200
    This was imported for me by Mr. Charles March of New
    York. I think it is about 12 years old—marked "C.M." on
    the cork.   ————

                                                    700

                              Brot up 700

From Shelf No. 2 "Essex" 100
    This was imported by Mr Davis, who praises it, & drinks
    it. It is very good, & about 12 or 14 yrs old. Marked E on
    the cork—
From Shelf No. 8 "Mur[d]ock" 100
    This is from Murdock's House—a mild & agreeable wine—
    now I believe about 10 yrs old. I like it, as well as almost
    any wine I know . . . .
From Shelves No 2. & 3. "Birckhead" 100
    This is like the next preceding, imported for me by Mr
    [Hugh McCulloh] Birckhead[3] of Baltimore.   ————

                                        1000

From Shelf No. 3 . . . . "Rapid" 50

I add 50 bottles of the "Rapid," for distribution, without charge, among the purchasers of the rest. I have been asked to send what I have to N. Orleans, for any price not exceeding ten dollars a bottle. But it is too good to sell. I keep a few bottles in which to drink the health of my friends.

May 12. 1841.

AL. MHi.

1. Fearing (1798–1875), a native of Hingham, Massachusetts, had established himself as a ship-chandler in Boston about 1833, where he became active as a Whig politician.

2. DW also informed Brooks that he was sending some of his wine and books to Washington and that Sam-uel Appleton and Edward Webster would dispose of the rest. See DW to Brooks [c. May 12, 1841], mDW 38283.

3. Birckhead (1788–1858) was a Baltimore merchant with the firm of Birckhead & Pearce. In 1852 he promoted the sale in Maryland of Everett's edition of Webster's *Works*.

FROM GEORGE WILLIAM GORDON

Post Office.

Boston. May 21. 1841.

Sir,

The Atlas Newspaper has passed into the hands of William Hayden Esqr.[1] and Dr Thomas M[ayo] Brewer. The Contract however between Major [Richard] Haughton[2] and Mr. [John Henry] Eastburn,[3] relative to the printing of the Post Office Department, has not been transferred, and Mr James Haughton[4] succeeds to the rights of his brother under it. If therefore the printing[5] be given to Mr Eastburn, Mr James Haughton will claim an equal share of the profits with him, and the present proprietors of the Atlas will have no share in them.

I have thought proper to state this, presuming that you wished the printing, when changed to go to the Atlas, and that can be done, of course, by giving direct to Messrs Hayden & Brewer,—they can then arrange with Mr Eastburn if they choose, as Major Haughton did before his death, & as they probably would.

It is desirable that the printing be changed as soon as convenient to the Department. The community no doubt expect it. Some of the Post Master[s], in the country, in ordering Blanks through this Office, direct the orders to the Atlas, presuming that the proprietors of that paper already have the printing. I need not allude to the importance of this patronage. In addition to the Blanks for this Office, scarcely a day passes when orders are not received for Blanks from offices in the country. I have the honor to be respectfully, Your Obt. Svt.   Geo. Wm. Gordon

ALS. NN. Gordon (1801–1877; Phillips Exeter Academy 1817) alter-nated a mercantile career with one of federal officeholding. His public offices included postmaster of Boston (1841–1843, 1850–1853) and United States consul to Rio de Janeiro (1843–1846).

1. Hayden (1795–1880), a native of Richmond, Virginia, had been educated in Boston, where he subsequently served as city auditor (1824–1841) in the common council and as Boston's representative on the Massachusetts General Court. He also edited the Boston *Atlas*.

2. Richard Haughton (1799–1841;

Yale 1818) had been senior editor and major owner of the Boston *Atlas*.

3. Eastburn (1805–1873), a Boston native, was printer for the city of Boston (1827–1854) and proprietor of the *Atlas* under Haughton.

4. James Haughton (1807–1888), brother of Richard, was a Boston merchant.

5. Gordon was referring to the printing of post office blanks rather than to the printing of the laws.

TO [EDWARD CURTIS]

Tuesday Eve'.
[May 25, 1841]

Dr Sr

—Never fear—I shall be as cool as a cucumber. If I meet T[allmadge] & C[lay] I shall not know that any thing has occurred.[1] At present, I have the upper hand, & I mean to keep [it]. They cannot touch me with X X X. This, they will find out, in good time. Some folks understand all about things.

I shall see Sec. of War tomorrow abt Blankets. Jno. White is here—talks kind, & is willing to be Speaker. Members are coming in, fast & thick.

Julia went away this P.M. & left us all crying. Yrs   D. W.

Love to Mrs C.

ALS. NN.

1. Curtis had probably informed DW of some specific points upon which Tallmadge and Clay opposed his nomination for collector of customs for the port of New York. Curtis's letter—if that was how the information was conveyed—has not been found.

TO [EDWARD CURTIS]

June 10. '41

Dr. Sir

<[Mordecai Manuel] Noah is essentially wicked, & mischievious, full of envy, hatred & malice. There is nothing of fidelity in him, & never was.[1]

I do not believe any thing can endanger you. Mr [Henry] Clay's friends say he will not persevere—that he will, at most, give a silent vote agt. you. This I believe fully is Mr Crittenden's opinion. Still, I expect there will be a controversy in the Senate. Such people as [John] Reynolds will cause opposition to be raised, among the Locofocos, in order to bring Mr Clay out, in hopes that they may get him *warm*. They know his infirmities.

I cannot believe there is the least question of Mr [Willie Person] Mangum's steady friendship. He must see, that to defeat your nomination would break up the Whig party.

—While I write this, (2 oclock) I suppose Buchanan is attacking my letter to Mr [Henry Stephen] Fox[2]—Rives, Choate, [Jabez Williams] Huntington[3] &c are ready for him.>[4]

—As to the time of sending in nominations—I think we shall begin next week, & probably yours will be among the earliest,[5] unless it shall be delayed, awaiting the further progress of the Commissioners.

—My wife is well—we talk of Mrs Curtis & yourself often—& have confessed to each other that we have made a discovery—that is, that we like you a little better than we were aware of, & wish most devoutly you were here with us again. Yrs   D. W.

ALS. NN.

1. Noah had probably attacked Curtis's nomination in the New York *Evening Star*. The specific charges against Curtis have not been established, however.

2. Fox (1791–1846) was envoy extraordinary from Great Britain to the United States, 1835–1843. DW's letter to Fox, April 24, 1841, is printed in *Diplomatic Papers*, 1. Buchanan's speech on the McLeod case and DW's letter appear in *Congressional Globe*, 27th Cong., 1st sess., Appendix, pp. 14–18.

3. The speeches of Rives, Choate, and Huntington on the McLeod question are also printed in the *Congressional Globe*, 27th Cong., 1st sess., Appendix, pp. 110–113, 417–422, 253–257, respectively.

4. All of the letter enclosed in the angle brackets up to this point has been crossed with two large Xs.

5. Tyler submitted Curtis's nomination as customs collector for New York to the Senate on June 16 but he was not confirmed until September 10.

As secretary of state, Webster involved himself as much with domestic issues—particularly legislation relating to the economy—as with foreign affairs. To his mind the two were inseparable: a healthy economy, sound banks, and a sound currency strengthened international ties and promoted foreign investments in the country. The return of prosperity, the only pledge from the Whigs in the recent campaign, was one they all sought to honor. But basic disagreements emerged over how best to meet that pledge. The dispute centered upon the kind of bank the country needed.

Even as Harrison took office, Whigs began to squabble. Longstanding jealousies and disputes over party leadership came into the open. President Harrison disagreed with Senator Henry Clay over the wisdom of a

special session of Congress to deal with the economy, but Clay's view pre-
vailed. Shortly before he died, Harrison called Congress to convene in
Washington on May 31.

Tyler's accession to the Presidency intensified Whig fighting over party
leadership and program. A states rights Democrat, Tyler strongly disliked
much of the standard Whig program, at the heart of which was a new
national bank. But some kind of financial institution was necessary.
Shortly after Congress met, Secretary of the Treasury Thomas Ewing
sent a proposal to the legislature. It called for a bank of discount and
deposit in the District of Columbia with branches in the states which
approved them.

Ewing's plan, called by the editors of the National Intelligencer *"the*
Treasury project," was published in that paper on June 14. An editorial
called attention to it, and endorsed it:

"We do not doubt," the editors wrote, "but that to the mind of almost
every man who has thought at all upon the subject, this bank project
would be more acceptable if some one or more features of it were differ-
ent from what they are. But to any plan that could possibly be proposed,
objections of detail would arise in different minds according to their par-
ticular views. We do not say that the Treasury plan is perfect, or even
the best that could have been devised. We would ourselves willingly see
one or two of its features changed. But the change of those features
would perhaps repel two friends to the measure for one that it would
attract; and for the mere gratification of a personal wish, we should
never dream of hazarding the success of a great measure."

Seemingly in direct response to this comment, Webster wrote a series
of three editorials which were published, as usual without attribution, in
the National Intelligencer *for June 15, 16, and 17, 1841. In these edi-*
torials, printed below, Webster took the position of mediator, urging both
sides to agree to some measure, even if it were less than each wanted. He
knew that Tyler did not wholeheartedly endorse the Treasury project—
called a "fiscal bank"—but he knew also that the President disliked even
more Clay's countering offer of a bank with unrestricted branching privi-
leges. He was in effect appealing to the President as well as to the two
Whig factions in Congress to accept some sort of compromise for the
sake of the country. In this he failed. Tyler vetoed the measure, and an-
other that followed it, paving the way for the disruption of the cabinet
and a split within the Whig ranks that would not be healed.

REMARKS ON THE FISCAL BANK

[June 14, 1841]

Before offering a few remarks on the plan of the Secretary of the Treasury, for a Bank of the United States, it may be proper to recur to the

general history of the country, for some time past, in regard to the currency, & to state its present condition.

In 1832 President Jackson negatived the Bill for continuing the charter of the Bank of the United States, & in September 1833, now nearly nine years ago, President Jackson, through the instrumentality of the Secretary of the Treasury, removed the public moneys from their then existing lawful deposite. From that moment to this, the currency of the country has been thoroughly deranged. This none can deny. Even if the cause may be disputed, the fact cannot. Those who so please may ascribe the deplorable state of things which has been brought upon us, & which still continues, to the multiplication of State banks between 1832 & 1836, to a spirit of speculation which seized upon the Public, to the maladministration of the late Bank of the United States, after it had ceased to be a National Institution, or to other causes; thus opening the inquiry, whether supposing these causes, or any of them, ought now to be regarded as the immediate productive agents of this mass of public evil, they are not themselves derivative, & secondary, all owing their existence & their power of mischief, to the original acts of the Executive Government.

Without discussing any of these questions, it is enough to say, that since 1833, the currency, the exchanges, & the general moneyed affairs of the Country have been such as greatly to impair the public prosperity. This notorious & lamentable truth, is the first element, to be regarded, in the consideration of the subject.

In the next place, it is true & notorious, that the successive plans for relief & remedy, which the Govt. has prepared & adopted since 1833, have all signally failed, & have only led great & important public interests, day by day, from a bad condition to a worse condition; till, at this moment, the local banks over three quarters of the country, are in a state of suspension, all the circulating paper over the same space greatly depreciated, & much of it hardly more than fifty cents to a dollar.

The next great & notorious fact is, that the policy of the Government, in relation to the currency, has been the main topic of dispute, between political parties, & that, on this point, chiefly, the contest of 1840 turned; & the result of that contest has fully shown that a vast majority of the People rejects & repudiates all the doctrines, all the schemes, & all the experiments, of the last two Administrations.

A new Administration has now come into power, & a new Congress is assembled, for the great purpose of reforming this state of things, & endeavoring to restore the public prosperity by placing the revenue, the currency, & the finances of the Country on a proper footing.

As might have been naturally expected, those who compose the Administration, & the majorities of the two Houses, while all agreeing in the necessity of adopting immediately some efficient measures, are not, perhaps, entirely of the same opinion as to any particular measure, or modification of measure. On the subject of a Bank, especially, it is well known there has existed much difference of opinion, among those who have acted together, most cordially, in opposing & overthrowing the policy of the preceding administrations. The sentiments of the President, for instance as they have been well known, & constantly maintained for the last fifteen years, are not, in all respects, such as the Secretary of the Treasury, & other members of the Cabinet are equally well known to have entertained & expressed. These differences chiefly respect the extent of the Constitutional authority of Congress, in the creation of a Bank, and clothing it with powers.

What, then is the line of duty, naturally recommending itself to those, who with these differences of opinion, find themselves called on to discharge high obligations to the Country? Is it their duty to beat the field of constitutional argument all over again, in the vain hope of coming to a perfect unity of opinion, on all particulars in the end? Is it not, rather, to consider how far they differ, & how far they agree; & to inquire, with candor & honesty, whether that on which they do agree, may not be made efficient for relieving the Country?

It is in the spirit of this last proposition, that the Administration appears to have acted. The particular plan before Congress, on the call of the Senate, & which is now submitted to the wisdom of the two Houses, is the plan of the Secretary [of the Treasury]; but it is reasonable to suppose that it has been considered, & its general outline approved, by others.

It may be presumed, then, that is the opinion of those, connected with the Executive Administration, that such a bank as is proposed, will be useful & efficient, as a fiscal agent of Government, & beneficial also to the Exchanges & currency of the Country. That it does not contain all the provisions, which some would have wished, is very probable; but the objections to it, whatever they may be, are of this negative kind. It may be taken for granted, that there is nothing [in] it, which those who have concurred in it, regard as positively hurtful. And while some might be of the opinion, that with other provisions, it would be more efficient, yet the question naturally presenting itself, was, is it not best for the Country, that we go on, in this measure, just so far as we can go cordially, together, and stop there? Is it not best to have a measure before us, which all, without the violation of any principle, or any consistency, may unite in supporting. Shall we propose something, in which friends can agree, or shall we propose that, which some of these friends cannot support, & thus by division throw ourselves at once into the power of the common adversary?

Poorly, poorly indeed, would the party now in power fulfil the high expectations entertained by the country, if they should not, with a seriousness becoming the solemn crisis of the Country, lay aside the pride of private opinion, give up personal predilections, & with singleness of heart, & under a full sense of the responsibility which rests upon themselves, UNITE their counsels, fairly & cordially, & make a *vigorous* effort to relieve the Country.

That this has been the governing motive in preparing the plan now laid before Congress, there is no doubt; that it will be the governing motive with the Whigs in both Houses, there is no doubt; because they must know that they act in the presence of disappointed & eager adversaries, whose eyes are keen to discern party advantages, & who will be ready, at the show of disorder or division in the ranks of the Whigs, to break in upon them, as squadrons of well-trained cavalry break in & overthrow the column, however great, which exhibits a broken line, or an opening for attack. The only security for the Whigs, is coolness in action, and the compactness of the HOLLOW SQUARE.

AD. NN. Three lines, beginning with "Poorly, poorly indeed," and continuing to "entertained," have been torn from the bottom of one page, but the missing fragment is at NTaHi. The manuscript is endorsed June 14, 1841. It appears, with very minor changes, in the *National Intelligencer* for June 15, and is also published in *W & S*, 15: 123–126.

[THE PROPOSED FISCAL BANK—NO. II]

[June 16, 1841]

The new Bank is proposed to be established in the City of Washington. Most of the friends of a Bank, naturally looking to the institutions of that kind which have heretofore existed, as models, expected it to have its locality in one of the large Cities of the north. The first Bank was placed in Philadelphia, a City, which at that time had the double advantage of being the wealthiest commercial City of the Union, & of being also selected as the Seat of the Government for the next years. Five & twenty years afterwards, when the second Bank was incorporated, it was thought advisable to give it the same location, although the Seat of the Government had been, for ten years, established at Washington. That there are advantages, for the administration of such an institution, in great commercial Cities, which are not to be found elsewhere, is certain. The daily & hourly intercourse of its Governors & Directors with commercial men, the greater facility in noting every change & shade of change, in the condition of the money market, the presence of other well conducted institutions, the benefits of being in the very centre of foreign commerce, & foreign correspondence,—all these, it must be admitted, are great aids, in keeping the judgment of men well informed, while conducting an institution, the operations of which require such an intelligent & careful oversight.

On the other hand, for such an Institution as is *now* proposed, there are reasons of no small weight for desiring its locality to be at the Seat of Government. The main character of the new Institution is that of a fiscal agent; an Institution, that is to say, which is expected to be useful to Government, in the collection, safe keeping, & disbursement of the Revenue. Its proximity to the operations of Government, is, therefore, of itself, some degree of advantage. But there is another, & yet more important view of the question. It is not to be denied, that in the discontinuance of the late Bank of the United States, & in the popular support which followed that measure, ignorance & prejudice had a powerful agency. Loud clamor ag[ains]t monopolies, ceaseless railings against the secret operations of a monstrous monied institution, cries, enough to rend the heavens, against a corporation, which was represented as a master over the Government, & as standing up with authority to overawe & put down the Representatives of the People, were the modes of political discussion, which have brought the country to its present condition. These forms of argument may be resorted to again, for there will always be some degree of ignorance & prejudice in the Community, especially on such subjects, and there will always be demagogues, who have neither principle nor self respect, sufficient to restrain them from turning these elements to their own profit. We take it for granted, that a sample of this way of discussing questions of finance & currency, will be exhibited, before our eyes, while the question of creating the institution itself, is going on.

As one means of counteracting these evils, & of defeating the designs of that low selfishness, which founds its hopes on alarming the prejudices & passions of the people, the Bank is to be established here—here, in the very presence of the Representatives of the people, its proceedings to be made public, & every week, or every day indeed, capable of being examined & scrutinized, by those who are entrusted with the Government of the Country. The Executive Government is to have no power of Control over it, or of interference with it, but to Congress, to the Representatives of the People & of the States, it is to be constantly accountable, & here it is to be, in the midst of them, conscious of their presence, & inviting their examination. Clamor is most easily raised, & groundless fears excited, against whatever is distant, & unknown. The best way to allay the fright of children, who think they have seen a ghost, is to lead them up, & show them that it is not a ghost. And the best way to put down the power of demagogues, who cry out that *they* see a monster, which the People do not see, is to give the people an opportunity to look also.

This object, as far as it is capable of being attained at all, is to be attained by placing the Institution here, in the centre of the Country, & at the Seat of Government, where public men, & others, may become acquainted with its operations, & watch its purposes.

One cannot but think, how much would have been lost, of that rare eloquence, which has for so many years at least stunned, if it has not delighted, the ears of its auditors, with exclamations against monsters, if the object denounced had been concealed neither by secrecy, nor distance, but had existed, before the eyes of these auditors, subject to their inspection, & inviting their examination.

But while the general control of the Institution is to be here, its principal monied operations must doubtless be conducted in the Cities of the North, the South & the West. Among all these its capital will be distributed & in them all its business of discount, exchange, & collection will be carried. The officers at these places will of course possess the same means of mercantile knowledge, as the most intelligent of the local institutions; thus uniting the largest & most accurate practical knowledge with the advantages of a comprehensive & wise general superintendence. It is not altogether unimportant to add, that while between the great cities of the North there might be rivalry & competition, sometimes even assuming the character of jealousy & dislike, none can be either envious or jealous of our humble City of Washington, & each will see, that by placing the general direction here, none of the great rival Cities is to enjoy, over its neighbours, the great advantage of having the establishment of the institution within its own walls, & the distribution of its capital in a great degree subject to its own discretion.

The value of the foregoing remarks may be differently estimated, by different persons; but there remains another, to which all must attach importance. The Bank *can* be established in the District of Columbia; it is *doubtful* whether it could be established elsewhere. It is of little use to discuss the Constitutional question. The question does exist, it exists between friends, conscientious & patriotic friends, who, if they cannot convince one another, do not revile one another, but feeling how much is expected from their joint counsels, make it matter of sacred duty to agree, so far as they can agree, & not to disappoint the best hopes of the country, by pertinacity to particular opinions. Congress may make a Bank which shall not entirely satisfy all the Whigs; but if it should not make *some* Bank, it will be sure to *dissatisfy* all. The Country will pardon those in power, for not doing what they cannot do; but it will not pardon them for weakening their power, by *disunion*. That fault,—one may almost say—that crime, will [not] be held excusable.

AD. NN. Published in the *National Intelligencer*, June 16, 1841; and in W & S, 15: 126–129. Manuscript endorsed June 16.

[June 17, 1841]

The plan submitted by the Secretary proposes, that Branches of the Bank, or offices of Discount & Deposite, may be established in the several States, *with the assent of the States.*

Objections are likely to be raised to this provision of the Bill, by some of those who are, generally, in favor of a National Institution. These objections will probably be, first, that the making of the assent of the States necessary to the establishment of Branches, surrenders, by implication, an important power of the Government; & second, that it is doubtful whether the States will assent, & if they should not, the whole measure would essentially fail.

Let these questions, which are admitted to be important, be considered with candor. Under the present circumstances, he is not wise who hastens to either of these, from the mere impulse of preconceived opinion.

On the first point, it must be admitted, that the practice of the Government is against the Secretary's proposition. The two former Banks were authorised to establish Branches within the States, without the assent of such States. The power has thus been asserted, repeatedly, by Congress, & its exercise by Congress has been sanctioned by the highest judicial tribunal. It is not now proposed to declare that the power does not exist; it is only proposed not now to exercise it; & therefore the true question, in this case, is, how far mere non user is equivalent to surrender.

It is notorious, that there are those who doubt the power, & always have doubted it. They doubt, against repeated decisions of all branches of the Government, & they will continue to doubt, if all these branches should renew their decisions.

The fair implication, therefore, arising from the omission to exercise the power, on this occasion, goes no farther than the well known fact. From not exercising the power, (if it is believed to be useful) the true inference is only that it is a doubtful, as a doubted, power; and it is no new thing, especially in our system, to forbear from exercising an authority which is doubted, & which is not considered as indispensable.

Our legislation is full of instances of such forbearance, & of subsequent exercise of the power from necessity. These instances need not be enumerated. They will occur to every man familiar with the Statute book. So that if it should be deemed necessary, a year hence, to exercise the power now forborne to be exercised, the agreement, so far as it depended on matters of historical fact, would stand thus. Those who should be against the power would say, "it was not granted, in the original law, & therefore the inference is that Congress did not suppose it to exist"; and to this it would be answered, "the power has been repeatedly exercised, in times past, but being doubted by some, & deemed not essential, was not inserted in this law; but subsequent events have shown that it is essential, & therefore the question comes back upon its original ground, & upon former precedents." That there may be *some degree* of implication against the power, from omitting its exercise in the proposed plan of the Secretary, may be admitted; but it cannot be said, on the other hand, that any thing more is implied, than is notoriously true, or that the omission amounts to a surrender of an important principle of the Constitution.

It is undoubtedly the true theory, in our systems of Government, to regard each as independent of the other, revolving in its own orbit, performing its own duties, & fulfilling its own purposes, without either aid, or obstruction. This is the theory, & although all constitutional provisions do not entirely coincide with it, the public good requires that it should be observed, as far as possible. But, as has now been intimated, there are exceptions. There are things, which the States may do, with the assent of Congress, & other things which Congress may do, with the assent of the States. What is now proposed, therefore, is not altogether an anomaly.

On the whole, it is not clear, that the passing of this Bill, in either form, would change the posture of the Constitutional question, or affect the strength of either side of it. If the provision of the Bill requiring the assent of the States should be struck out, & the Bill should pass in that form, it would only reaffirm what has been repeatedly decided, but leaving just as many doubts as exist now; & if it should pass with the provision in, none of those who suppose that Congress may establish branches without the consent of the States, will have changed this opinion.

The second question is the important & practical one; is it likely that any, or many of the States will refuse their assent?

Those who recommend the measure in its present shape, have no fears on this head. That same public opinion which shall carry the measure through Congress will ensure the assent of the States. What State will find its interests in refusing its assent? In such an inquiry, we naturally look first to the large Commercial States, & first of all to New York. Will New York refuse her assent? There will be offered to her great City a Branch, with a very large assignment of Capital, to be managed by those, among the most discreet & skilful in such things, of her own citizens. Will she refuse it? Boston is but twelve hours beyond her. That City, distinguished for noiseless enterprise & far-seeing sagacity, & already in the possession of such advantages, and making such steps of progress, as render her no contemptible rival of her great sister, will be quite ready to take what she rejects. If New York prefers that the "centralization," of which so much was said, some time ago, should be broken up, & another orb formed, of large magnitude, though still less than herself, to which, as their centre, a great proportion of the Commercial & monied affairs of the Country should hereafter tend, it is not probable that Boston would excite herself into any strenuous or heated opposition, to such a course of things. Philadelphia is but six hours from New-York, & there is little reason to suppose that the offer of a branch, with something more than her just proportion of the Capital, would be disagreeable, either to her, or to the State of Pennsylvania. Nor would the State of New Jersey think it any disrespect to her Broad Seal, if she were offered a Branch, with a large Capital, at Jersey City, where the "fiscal agent," not admitted into the City of New York, could very conveniently discharge its functions? We may look to the South, & ask whether Virginia or South Carolina, States in one of which opinion is adverse to a Bank, & in the other divided, prefer, after all, that their parts should go to Maryland & North Caro lina. If the principles of Alabama lead her to refuse, Louisiana would sooner submit to the burden of taking what might properly belong to both States, than to see the measure fail. We may expect, perhaps that the stern sentiments of Missouri will hardly relent & know not, what course Illinois might think it her interest to pursue. But a specie-paying Bank, with a handsome capital & furnishing the country with a perfectly sound currency is not likely to be regarded as a great evil by Ohio, Indiana & Michigan.

There is no doubt, that the States, with one or two exceptions, perhaps, for the present, & with no exceptions, in a short time, will readily give the necessary assent. Indeed the practical difficulty will be on the other side. The danger is, that more branches will be applied for, both by States & individuals, than it will be convenient or perhaps safe for the institution to establish.

AD. NN. Published in the *National Intelligencer*, June 17, 1841; and in *W & S*, 15: 129–133. The manuscript, endorsed June 17, is labelled "The proposed fiscal bank.—No IV" in the handwriting of Joseph Gales, senior editor of the *National Intelligencer*, but the printed version is correctly numbered III.

TO HIRAM KETCHUM FROM DANIEL FLETCHER WEBSTER

Washington June 25th. 1841.

My Dear Sir,

I have just received your letter of yesterday.[1] I showed it, at once, to the Secretary.

He told me to say that there is no man, for whom he feels more kindness & friendship, than Mr. [Charles] King—that he desires to aid him in every way, but that, nevertheless he has not felt it safe to do so, in a public manner, lately.

Mr. King is hasty and inconsiderate, though almost always right. In this very recent affair of the Bank project for instance, he did not, as it would seem, stop to consider that neither Gen. Harrison, nor Mr. Webster is President.[2]

It was thought best, in regard to that great question, to present such a project for a Bank as it was ascertained that the President would approve, "Little it might no better be," than to attempt anything which he might, or would, refuse to sanction.

Mr. King, without waiting to hear a word from Washington, is the first man to come out against this project &, known, or supposed, to be the intimate personal & political friend of the Sec. of State, by so doing, placed him in a very awkward position in regard to the President, which distressed him a good deal.

As events have turned, too, it seems to throw Mr. King into the ranks of one opposed to the Administration on this point & particularly opposed to *one member* of it.

However, as far as any private exertions can go the Sec. will most heartily join Mr. King's friends, & the letters you suggest will be written immediately.[3]

He only regrets that, under present circumstances, he cannot do more.

I feel, & so does he, very much indebted to you for your timely and friendly letter.

I hope, my dear Sir, that you will continue to address me whenever you have occasion, or inclination, being assured that I take it as a kindness & a valuable compliment when you do so. I remain very truly yours
Fletcher Webster.

ALS. NhD.
1. Not found.
2. For King's position on the Bank project, see, for example, the *New York American*, June 16, 1841.

3. Ketchum may have requested DW to write letters for publication. See DW to Hiram Ketchum, [July 18?, 1841], below.

FROM NICHOLAS BIDDLE

And[alusi]a. July 4, 1841

My dear Sir

Do not let the nomination of Mr [Charles Bingham] Penrose be opposed in the Senate if you can prevent it. He is I have no doubt a good officer—& very much your friend—& his rejection would in some quarters be considered as a triumph over your influence.[1]—Very faithfully yrs
N Biddle

ALS draft. DLC.
1. The Senate had confirmed Penrose's appointment as solicitor of the treasury on July 3.

TO [HIRAM KETCHUM]

Monday July 12. '41

Dr Sir

I have seen Webbs two articles,[1] & despise them. I have not noticed the letter you mention in the American of Friday Eve'.[2]

If I see any thing in that paper disrespectful to me, I shall of course stop the paper, & all intercourse with its Editor.

I really wish these over-wise people would say, what we, the Cabinet, ought to have done.

We did not elect Mr Tyler—that was the work of the Whigs—especially of Mr C[lay]'s friends—who made an effort, at Harrisburg, & succeeded in it, to put Mr T. on the Ticket instead [of] D.W. proposed by Mass.

Mr. Tyler did not derive his Anti Bank doctrines from us, but as he says from Mr C[lay] himself.

Now, having shown how far he will go, and where he will stop, pray what does Mr. [Charles] King expect me to do?

Would he have me leave the Govt.—wd. he have us all quit our places —upon the question of the coercive power of branches, in a Bank Charter? If he wd. not have us do this what does he complain of? He is not weak enough to suppose that we could change Mr T's opinions.[3]

I suppose nobody in N.Y. will reply either to Mr Webb—or Mr King's letter writer—very well. Yrs   D. W.

N.B. I pray you omit no *useful* employment, in order to answer my notes.

ALS. NhD.

1. In the *Morning Courier and New York Enquirer*, July 9, 10, 1841, Webb had featured two editorials which accused DW, Ewing, Granger, and other cabinet members of sacrificing their Whig principles and program in order to retain their cabinet positions. Webb specifically attacked them for supporting the fiscal bank plan instead of a full-fledged national bank modelled after the Second Bank of the United States.

2. The letter in the *New York American* has not been identified.

3. The attitudes DW expressed above concerning Tyler and the cabinet's relationship to the Executive are strikingly similar to the views expressed in the allegedly forged letter of July 18 from Washington. See DW to Hiram Ketchum, [July 18?, 1841], below.

TO HIRAM KETCHUM

Washington, July 17, 1841.

My Dear Sir:

The power of Congress to establish a bank rests on two propositions:

1. That a bank is a necessary and proper agent, in the collection and disbursement of revenue.

2. That it is a proper and useful means of regulating commerce be-

tween the several States, and with foreign nations, by furnishing currency and exchange.

There is no other lawful object for a bank, because the constitutional power extends to no other object. Revenue and commercial regulation comprise the whole power. A constitutional bank, then, must be limited to these purposes.

For revenue a bank is necessary: 1. For the safe-keeping of the public money; 2. For its cheap transmission from place to place; 3. For furnishing a convenient circulating paper medium, equivalent to specie, and which shall be of equal and uniform value, in every part of the country, and which may safely be made receivable in debts and dues to Government:

These are the uses of a bank, as connected with the operations of the Government itself, and, I conceive, no others. *And only one of these is provided for in Mr. Ewing's Bill.*[1]

To the general commerce of the country a bank is useful, and in my opinion indispensable, in three respects:

1. By dealing, on a considerable capital, in domestic exchanges, it keeps these exchanges steady and at low rates. Our experience has sufficiently shown the incalculable value of a well-conducted national institution in this respect.

2. By issuing paper, or notes, for general currency and circulation, having a national stamp, and therefore everywhere of equal value, most essentially benefits the currency of the country.

3. By repressing, through the gentle and quiet means of its own circulation in our business, the issue of local institutions, it tends to secure the whole mass of circulating paper against excess.

Now, Mr. Ewing's bill gives the power of dealing in exchanges, without limit, and it gives also the power of issuing paper for circulation. In what then, is it wanting? It wants the power of *local discount,* or the loaning on local notes, without the consent of the States, and the omission of this power *is said* to be a *surrender of a great principle.* Let us examine this. The bank can buy and sell exchange, and it can issue its own notes for currency. It may deal in exchanges to the amount of many millions a year, as the late bank most usefully did; it may receive deposits at its agencies as well as at the bank itself, and it may issue its own notes, for deposits, for specie received, and for any of its own debts. *But it cannot make a local loan.* It cannot establish a branch in Wall Street, and there *loan money* on a note given by one Wall Street merchant to another Wall Street merchant; and, because this power is denied, it is said a great constitutional question is ignominiously surrendered!

That this may be a useful power (most useful to the people and to the State) I fully believe, but is no respect due to that intellect which cannot perceive how this power of local lending is a national power, or how it is connected with the duties of Congress? Suppose Congress were to establish a bank with no other power but this, viz., a power to establish an office in the States, and to loan money on notes, given by one citizen of the State to another, would anybody say that the creation of such a bank was within the authority of Congress? Certainly not. If the same power, then, be inserted among other powers, which are constitutional, does this power itself thereby cease to be unconstitutional? I do not mean to say that these questions cannot be answered by those who seem in such hot haste to ride rough-shod over the supposed opinions of the President; but I say that they require clear reasoning, the cue of distinct ideas and fair exposition; and that they are not to be disposed of by a contemptuous sneer. And so, I think, the people will decide.

It is now admitted that the power of creating local corporations, both for the purpose of loaning money and circulating bills, does belong to the States. The States, in fact, exercise this power, and many of them derive a great part of their revenue from it. In the Eastern States, for example, bank capital is taxed. This capital is employed mostly *in these very local loans*. To put five millions of *untaxed* capital into Boston, there to be used in these local loans, diminishes by so much the capital on which the State of Massachusetts levies her tax, and to that extent directly affects her public revenue; this does not prove that the power does not exist, I admit; but it shows that there are considerations connected with the subject, which wise and moderate men ought to respect. I will not conceal my opinion that the power may be defended on the ground of its being necessary to the efficient execution of the other powers; but I could never put it on any other ground than that, and have always been aware that strict interpreters of the Constitution insist that this mode of reasoning is dangerous, as it attaches one incidental power, raised by argument, to another incidental power, previously raised by argument, and may thus run on indefinitely, till it draws along all sorts of powers in its train. My own opinion is, however, that whatever is *necessary*, must be taken to be granted. And this brings us back at once to General Harrison's ground, and calls upon us to decide whether this *is* necessary. Now, there are those who think it is not, and therefore think that its exercise cannot be justified. Or, if it be, that objections from the States, or many of them, are not to be expected; and, therefore, that the difficulty may in that way be avoided. On this last point, the probability of the States objecting or not objecting, I know nothing which can enlighten your own opinion, but for myself, notwithstanding I foresee some embarrassments, I fully believe that, if the Whig party chose to take up the matter energetically, they can carry it through, and put the bank into successful operation in a few months. But while they continue to differ and to discuss their differences, while some adhere to what they call (erroneously, I think) principle, and others exert themselves, but are obliged to exert themselves without the aid of their brethren, for what they think *practicable* and *attainable*, while one says he is of Paul, and another that he is of Apollos, not only does time run by, leaving nothing done, but a wily and reckless adversary is heading in upon our ranks and is very likely to be able to thwart every thing. Union, decision, and energy, are all indispensable. But UNION is first. If we will but UNITE, we can form decisive purposes and summon up our energies. But how can we rally one set of friends against another set of friends? Of what use are decision and energy in our own family differences? My dear sir, there is but one path out of this labyrinth. There is but one remedy for the urgent necessities of the country, but one *hope* of the salvation of the Whig party—it is *union*, immediate UNION. Let us try such a bank as we can agree upon and can establish. If it fails for want of any particular power, then the necessity for such power will have been ascertained and proved, and Congress will meet again in the winter, with power to revise their own work. The season is advancing and the weather is hot—but nothing, nothing should induce Congress to rise, leaving this great work wholly undone. Yours with constant regard,   D. Webster.

Text from Curtis, 2: 75–77. Original not found. Published anonymously with editorial changes, perhaps made by Ketchum, in the New York *Commercial Advertiser*, July 21, 1841.

1. Ewing's bill, submitted to Congress on June 12, called for a central bank in the District of Columbia with offices of discount and deposit in consenting states.

TO [HIRAM KETCHUM]

Sunday Eve'
[July 18?, 1841]

My Dear Sir,

I send you, under other cover, two *quasi* letters.[1] If you will run over the manuscript, & shall think them of any value, you may have them published, in the Commercial, or *Journal of Commerce*, as letters from a Gentleman in Washington to his friend in N. York—or any other paper, except the American[2] which I think it is best not to trouble, at present. Alter any thing, which you think wrong. I could give a *third* letter,[3] upon some particulars in Mr Ewing's plan, if you think it advisable—especially on the matter of the last Indictment, under the Deposite Act. Be free in your corrections, if you cause them to be published—for they were both written in an hour & a half—& quite defective. Yrs   D. W.

Mr C[lay] has come to a standstill.[4] *Now is the time to rally the press, for*

Ewing, with amendments.

☞ Let no one know the writer of the letters.⁵　D. W.

ALS. NhD.

1. The second of the *"quasi* letters"—DW to Hiram Ketchum, July 17, 1841—appears above. The New York *Commercial Advertiser* printed the first, dated July 16, on July 20, 1841 (also printed in Curtis, 2:72–75), and the second on July 21, without naming sender or recipient. They were promptly reprinted in other New York papers and in the Washington *Madisonian.*

2. The *New York American*, edited by Charles King.

3. During the same week of July 18 to 24, 1841, New York Whig newspapers carried a third item, dated "Washington, July 18, 1841." It called for "Union—Immediate Union" among the Whigs in Congress and in the cabinet and encouraged them to work with President Tyler. Several editors attributed the authorship of all three essays to Daniel Webster,

and the *Morning Courier and New York Enquirer* immediately attacked the reputed author for the "abandonment of those great constitutional landmarks with which his name and fame are so intimately interwoven." This angry Whig response to the third letter led immediately to its being labelled a forgery from the pen of William Leete Stone of the New York *Commercial Advertiser.* For this third letter and a discussion of its authorship, see the *Morning Courier and New York Enquirer*, July 24, 29, 1841; the *National Intelligencer*, July 24, 1841; and the Washington *Madisonian*, July 27, 1841.

4. In his efforts to substitute his own bank plan for Ewing's.

5. DW was named as the author of the three letters in the *Morning Courier and New York Enquirer*, July 24, 1841.

TO EDWARD EVERETT

July 28. 1841

Private

Dr Sir

I must thank you cordially for all your kindness to Edward.¹ He arrived safely, the early part of June, & has gone to D. College to get his Degree.² I suppose he will then go into some Lawyers Office. He speaks gratefully & affectionately of your family; & has I think a good deal improved, under your friendly protection.

Mrs Webster desires me to remember her to Mrs Everett, & your family, as well as to yourself. Her health is good, though she has felt the heat, which has been great for the last month.

The Senate yesterday engrossed a Bill for a Bank. It's shape is the result of many compromises, but it may still be doubtful whether it will become a law. Probably it may pass both Houses, but whether the President will approve it, is a question which I hardly dare ask myself.³ If he should not, I know not what will become of our Administration.

29. The Bk Bill passed the Senate yesterday. It will doubtless pass the

House, & if it meets no Veto, we shall go on swimmingly. Yrs cordially
Danl Webster

ALS. MHi. Published in *PC*, 2: 106.

1. Edward, who had gone to England in 1839 with Samuel Appleton, his prospective brother-in-law, had remained in Europe to study and travel. Everett, also in Europe, had served as Edward's guardian and adviser during this period.

2. Edward graduated from Dartmouth College with the class of 1841.

3. Tyler vetoed the Bank Bill on August 16.

TO HIRAM KETCHUM FROM DANIEL FLETCHER WEBSTER

July 28th. 1841.

Private

Mr [William C.] Rives having voted against Mr. Clay's bill as it has been amended & passed, some doubt exists as to whether the President will sign it.[1] It will pass the House & come to him for Signature I have no doubt. If he should refuse to sign the bill it is not probable that the present Cabinet could consent to hold their places. It is therefore on all grounds very desirable that a strong expression of public sentiment should be made in favour of this bill by everybody. All the Whigs can go heart & hand for this & opinion should be brought to bear most strongly on the President. You see, no doubt, where the pinch is & how important it is that a break up should be avoided as well as that a Bank should be chartered.

Don't let either the American or any body else go wrong this time.[2] Here is a bill passed, in which enough is conceded to State rights & Constitutional scruples. The President has too much patriotism not to sign it. We believe that John Tyler will do so &c.

You will see the necessity of speaking out & at once. Most truly yr's
F. W.

ALS. NhD.

1. Clay's report on the Ewing Bank Bill was in fact a new bank bill. It called for the establishment of a parent bank in Washington with branches in the states. State assent was not required for branches. Rives, previously one of Tyler's chief Democratic opponents in Virginia, had renounced his Democratic party allegiance in 1840 and joined the Whig party. In the Senate he had emerged as one of Tyler's staunchest defenders, one of "the Corporal's Guard," Clay called him. Many observers, with Fletcher, saw Rives's vote against Clay's bill as reflective of Tyler's attitude as well.

2. The *New York American* supported Ewing's bill and presumed that President Tyler would sign it. Should he refuse, however, the *American* urged the cabinet officers to remain at their posts: "We can better do without a Bank altogether, than run the risk of losing such men from the guidance of our public affairs as now surround the President." *New York American*, July 30, August 2, 4, 9, 1841.

ΓΟ [HIRAM KETCHUM?]

Aug. 13. '41

Private

My Dear Sir,

Do what we can, & all we can, I fear we shall have a *Veto*. It will come, however, if it come at all, not before Monday.[1] This gives time to prepare for the blow. My notion is, to preach moderation, & forbearance—let the papers urge the Whigs to hold together, on other great measures, & not lose them also, by reason of the difficulty about the Bank. If the Whigs cannot agree on every thing, let them agree on as much as they can. The Country can look for any thing good, no where else.

All yr Cities papers of Monday, in anticipation of a possible Veto, should put forth these sentiments, as I think fully, & strongly.[2] The Bank is only *one* measure. The Bankrupt Bill, the Land Bill, the Duty Bill—why should all these be lost.[3] Besides until the Veto message be seen, who can tell how far Congress & the President differ about a Bank?—&c. &c. Yrs   D. W.

I shall keep cool, & do nothing abruptly.

ALS. DLC.

1. As DW feared, Tyler's veto of Clay's bill came on Monday, August 16.

2. For editorials in line with DW's recommendation, see the *New York Herald*, August 17, 1841; the *New York American*, August 17, 1841. The *Morning Courier and New York En-* *quirer*, August 18, 1841, strongly attacked the President.

3. These three measures met with Tyler's approval. Tyler signed the national bankruptcy bill on August 19, the land bill on September 4, and the duties bill on September 11. 5 *U.S. Statutes at Large* 440–449, 453–458, 463–465.

TO CAROLINE LE ROY WEBSTER

Monday Morning
Aug. 16. 1841

Dear Caroline

A week has run away, with out my writing to you. It has been an anxious week, on acct. of the Bank Bill; but the question is settled, & a Veto will be sent in today. I hardly know what may [be] the consequences, but the general feeling is not so much irritated as it was a week ago. They may perhaps try another Bill, with modifications.[1] Some of Mr Clay's friends are particularly angry, & this makes it doubtful whether any thing will be done. It is feared, also, that the fate of this measure may have a bad influence on the fortunes of the Bankrupt Bill, & other measures. On the whole, we have an anxious & unhappy time, & I am sometimes heart sick. I hope Congress will get away in a fortnight.

I send you the Intelligencer of this morning, that you may read the account of our trip to Annapolis.[2] The President did not go, as the Senate did not adjourn over, & he was much engaged. There were very few Ladies—Mrs [John J.] Crittenden,[3] Mrs [John Chamberlain?] Clark,[4] Miss White,[5] Miss [Emma?] Yeatman,[6] &c.

Yesterday morning I rode out to Mrs [John] Aggs,[7] as the day was cool & agreeable. I generally ride to the Office, in the morning, & sometimes walk home when it is not too hot. My health is good, except that my rheumatic shoulder troubles me a good deal.

I have thought it best to invite the Whig members to a *man* party, to-morrow, in order to keep them in good temper. Charles [Brown][8] is to buy some hams, & bread, &c.—no ices, & no fruits—& set them on the table down stairs where people may help themselves.

The House gets along, pretty well.[9] Of course the painting inside is not yet finished, as it takes time for the paint to dry.

I notice what you say about papering the rooms. You may have it arranged as you please. I will write tomorrow, saying what day Mr [Edward] Stubbs[10] will be in N.Y. about the carpets. He has been sick, & is now out again.

Fletcher may find it necessary to go to N.Y. on account of Mr [Stephen] White's death[11]—but he has not yet made up his mind, not having heard from Mr [James William] Paige.[12]

It is likely that Capt [Robert] Clements[13] will break up here, the first of next month. When I shall go, if I cannot go North by that time, I know not. If Mr Whitwell[14] takes the house, as is expected, I presume your things can all remain where they are.

I will try to write you again tomorrow. Yrs ever,   D Webster

ALS. NhHi. Published in Van Tyne, pp. 235–236.

1. The Whigs did "try another Bill," the Fiscal Corporation Bill, which Tyler vetoed on September 9, two days before all the cabinet except Webster resigned.

2. Webster and others had gone to Annapolis to visit the ship *Delaware*. *National Intelligencer*, August 17, 1841.

3. Maria Knox Crittenden (1796–1851), née Innes, had first married John Harris Todd. Following Todd's death, she and John Jordan Crittenden had married in 1826.

4. Not further identified.

5. Not identified.

6. Emma Yeatman was the daughter of Henry C. of Tennessee and the stepdaughter of John Bell.

7. Mrs. Elizabeth Agg, née Blackford, was the wife of John Agg, a Washington newspaper correspondent.

8. Brown, a former slave whose freedom Webster had purchased, was Webster's personal servant for many years.

9. With financial assistance from Isaac Rand Jackson, who was appointed chargé to Denmark, DW had recently purchased the Swann house, facing Lafayette Square.

10. Stubbs was a career clerk in the State Department. During DW's tenure as secretary he was the chief disbursing agent.

11. White (1787–1841), a Boston merchant, was Fletcher's father-in-

law. White had died in New York on August 10.

12. Paige (1792–1868), a Boston merchant, and a half brother of Grace Fletcher Webster, was also a son-in-law of Stephen White.

13. Clements, a magistrate in Washington, occasionally rented rooms in his Pennsylvania Avenue house to congressmen and other government officials. Perhaps DW was staying at Clements until the Swann House was ready for occupancy.

14. Not identified.

[VETO OF THE BANK BILL]

[August 16, 1841]

An article for tomorrow— announcing Veto—

—shd. be consd. calmly, & dispassionately—well weighed & examined.

We (Editors) belong to the whole Whig Party—& no section.

We wish to maintain its counsels &c—

What is to be done?—no good can come from violence & outbreak— excitable minds might make a mistake, in this particular—such a course would weaken, disunite, & finally destroy the Whig party, & with it the best hopes of the Country.

[Should] Such a catastrophe be allowed to follow the Veto—?

The President, no doubt, has acted from pure & conscientious motives. His conduct, we are well assured, throughout the whole consideration of the subject, has been frank, courteous, & perfectly satisfactory to every member of his Cabinet, & to all others with whom he has held communication.

We think, therefore, that there is no cause, in what has happened, to weaken the confidence of the Whig Party in President Tyler. He is a Whig, attached to all the great principles of the party, & endeavoring to carry them out, fully & honestly. He knows that nothing else can restore the prosperity of the Country.

We may gather from the message itself that he is now ready to sanction a Bank, such as shall adapt itself to the real wants of the Country.

We trust therefore, that candor & patriotism will be the ruling spirit of the occasion, & that Congress will not only carry out all its other great measures, but make a further trial for a Bank, at this Session. Possibly it may not be accomplished till next winter, but we think it worth a trial. The House of Representatives has shown how much important work may be done, in a short time. Let it try its hand on this subject.

Let union & confidence animate the party—& above all let not the miscarriage of a single measure defeat the high raised hopes of the Country, in regard to others.

Papers at a distance make themselves busy with expected resignations in the Cabinet. We give no heed to such gossip. Why should the Cabinet resign? They have, we presume, given the President their honest advice;

he has recd it respectfully & kindly, & if he feels bound by his own Constitutional opinions to decide agt it, we see not any ground of resignation on that account. The power of approving & disapproving Bills is one which is peculiarly attached to the office of the President, himself; it is hardly an administration matter; & our old fashioned notions are such, that we should no more think of any right in the Cabinet to control the President in this matter, so exclusively his own, than we should of embracing the other heresy, which we took some pains yesterday to expose,[1] which would make him the author of every thing done by one of the Heads of Administration, & responsible for it, &c &c.

AD draft. NN. Published in *W & S*, 15: 135–136. The general views which DW expressed in this draft appeared as an editorial in the *National Intelligencer*, August 17, 1841.

1. For DW's previous essay, "The 'Strange Doctrine,'" see the *National Intelligencer*, August 17, 1841.

TO [THOMAS EWING]

Thursday Morning
5 O'clock
[August 19, 1841]

My Dear Sir,

I learn that the Whig Senators are to have a meeting this Eve', & that a proposition is to be submitted, by Mr [John Macpherson] Berrien, in effect like your own original proposition; viz, that Branches shall be established by the Bank, whenever requested by Congress, &c.

It appears to me that the policy of going upon this, deserves much consideration.

1st. Because the proposition affirms the right of Congress to establish branches, without the consent of the States, which is exactly what the President objects to.

2. Because, to be productive of any good, he would be required to sign just such a law, as he objects to, now.

3. And, therefore, the practical result, if he should sign the bill with such a provision, (as I think he would not) would be, that we should get no branches.

I am above all things anxious that when the Senate starts again, it may so start as to get through the race.

I wish you would look over your Bill, & make it quite clear that the *agencies* may deal in Exchange.

My notion then would be, either to say nothing about affairs of discount at all, (which I believe is about as well as any way) or take the [Richard Henry] Bayard proposition.

The more I think of it, the more I am convinced we can get along with *agencies*, without offices of Discount, *by name*. Yrs   D Webster

ALS. DLC.

TO JOHN TYLER

11 o'clock, August 20th. [1841]

My Dear Sir:

I am promised a copy of the paper (the bill)[1] by twelve o'clock, or a few minutes after, and have left a messenger to bring it immediately to me. It is uncertain whether anything will be done to day, but I understand there is a strong desire for immediate action. The alterations which I suggested were assented to at once, so far as the gentleman himself was concerned to whom the suggestions were made.[2] *I have done or said nothing as from you or by your authority, or implicating you in the slightest degree. If any measure pass, you will be perfectly free to exercise your constitutional power wholly uncommitted, except so far as may be gathered from your public and official acts.* I am, most truly and faithfully, yours, Daniel Webster.

Text from Tyler, *Tylers*, 2: 85–86. Original not found.

1. The Fiscal Corporation Bill, which John Sergeant introduced in the House of Representatives the same day, August 20.

2. Webster had met with Sergeant and John Macpherson Berrien, the House and Senate sponsors of the bill, on August 18. "Diary of Thomas Ewing, August and September, 1841," *American Historical Review*, 18 (October 1912): 102. See also above, DW to Thomas Ewing, [August 19, 1841]. According to Lyon G.

Tyler (Tyler, *Tylers*, 2:86), his father, President Tyler, endorsed the letter: *"The alterations were of no moment, and affected no principle. The bill was to have been submitted for my alterations, and an opportunity to make them was not allowed."* Webster, however, in "Memorandum on the Banking Bills and the Vetoes," [1841], below, recorded that he showed the proposed bill to Tyler. See also [Memorandum on the President and the Fiscal Corporation Bill, September 1841], below.

TO [HIRAM KETCHUM]

[c. August 20, 1841]

Private

I see that our friend King will continue to advise us to go ashore, all standing, & be drowned together. I must say, his course quite surprises me. Might he not take it for granted, that *we* have learned, exactly, *what* can be done, & *all* that can be done; & have acted accordingly? If he wishes to assist X X[1] in breaking up the Admn, & *in getting no Bank,* he acts wisely to that end.

However, it is not my wish that you should say a word to him—that wd. do no good. My only purpose is to express the *pain*—the *deep* pain—with which I notice his remarks.[2]

After all—my opinion is, that we shall have a Bank, essentially on

Mr Ewings plan, & I fully believe it will be a better Bank than we ever have had. I do not mean, that the coercive Branches would not be useful—but I do mean, that taking the Bank as a whole, it will work better than its predecessors. Such is my opinion. I may be wrong; but in one point I can hardly be mistaken; *we shall have some such Bank or none at all.*

There are doubtless many persons, in N.Y. connected with State Institutions, who, whatever they say, would not be *very* sorry, if there were to be no National Bank. These persons' designs are not conc[eale]d. so deep as they think. Yrs   D. W.

ALS. DLC. Published in Curtis, 2: 71–72.
   1. DW was alluding to Clay.
   2. For DW's attitude toward King's position, see above, Daniel Fletcher

Webster to Hiram Ketchum, June 25, 1841. The specific "remarks" of King to which DW referred have not been found.

TO CAROLINE LE ROY WEBSTER

My Dear Wife—

Saturday Eve'—8 oclock
[August 21, 1841]

We have passed three or four more very anxious & excited days. Congress is in a state of great fermentation, & the President appears to me to be a good deal worried. I know not what it is all to come to. Another Bank Bill is brought into Congress, & is likely to pass both houses.[1] If that, also, should receive the Veto, I can not speculate on the consequences. I am with the President a good deal. He seems quite kind, but is evidently much agitated. I am nearly worn down with labor & care, & shall be most happy when these things shall be settled, one way or the other. There is now a breach between the President & Mr Clay, which it is not probable can ever be healed. You will see a strange letter also from Mr [John Minor] Botts, which makes a great deal of talk.[2] For my part, I keep cool; discharge my daily duties as well as I can, & say nothing, or at most but little.

I go to the House[3] but seldom, as little is doing now, but finishing off the inside painting. What is done looks well, & the whole I think will be quite handsome. Mr [Edward] Stubbs means to be at Astor House, Wednesday morning.[4] The chimney pieces are all up, & the grates in.

I have not seen Mrs [Emeline Colby Webster] Lindsley nor hardly any one else. F[letcher] & I eat our solitary dinner, every day. I pray, give my love to all the family where you are. I want to see you, very much, & am most anxious to get out of this present state of perplexity.

My health continues good. Your shower bath does wonders. I use it every morning—& think how you used to make the water spatter. Chs

Brown sends his love to you & Grace.[5] F. is gone to walk with Mr [William Pitt] Fessenden. Yrs ever   D. W.

ALS. NhHi. Published in *PC*, 2: 109–110.

1. The Fiscal Corporation Bill.

2. Botts's letter, dated August 16 and addressed to a Richmond coffee house, had appeared in the Washington *Madisonian*, August 21, 1841. Botts wrote: "Our Captain Tyler is making a desperate effort to set himself up with the loco-focos, but he'll be headed yet, and I regret to say, it will end badly for him. He will be an object of execration with both parties; with one for vetoing our bill,

which was bad enough—with the other for signing a worse one, but he is hardly entitled to sympathy."

3. The Swann House.

4. Stubbs was in New York to purchase carpets for the Webster house. It is possible that he had also gone there on official state department business.

5. Grace Fletcher (August 29, 1837–February 7, 1844) was DW's granddaughter, the daughter of Fletcher.

TO HIRAM KETCHUM

Sunday Eve'
[August 22, 1841]

My Dear Sir

I believe the land Bill will pass the Senate tomorrow,[1] & the Bank Bill the House, tomorrow or on Tuesday.[2] Beyond that, I can foresee little. The President is agitated. Mr Clay's Speech,[3] & Mr [John Minor] Botts' most extraordinary letter,[4] have much affected him. At the same time, there is no doubt that violent assaults are made upon him, from certain quarters, to break with the Whigs, change his Cabinet, &c. &c.[5]

Another week will enable us "to see what we shall behold." I try to keep cool, & to keep up courage, as the agony will soon be over. We are on the very point of deciding, whether the Whig party & the President shall remain together; & at this critical juncture some of our friends think it very opportune to treat him with satire & disdain. I am tired to death, of the folly of friends. Newspapers, supposed to be friendly to me, are, *for that reason*, sent to the President, every day, containing articles derogatory to him!

I must do Col. [William Leete] S[tone] the justice to say he shows sense, & prudence.[6] Yrs   D. W.

ALS. DLC. Published in *PC*, 2: 109.

1. The land bill, providing for the distribution of the proceeds from the sale of the public lands to the states and granting preemption rights, passed the Senate on August 23. Tyler signed the measure into law on September 4, 1841. 5 *U.S. Statutes at Large* 453–458.

2. The Fiscal Corporation Bill passed the House, 125 to 94, also on August 23.

3. Clay's speech, in response to Tyler's veto of the Fiscal Bank Bill, came on August 19. See *Congressional Globe*, 27th Cong., 1st sess., Appendix, pp. 222–224.

4. See above, DW to Caroline Le

Roy Webster, [August 21, 1841].
5. On the cabinet breakup, see, for example, the *New York Herald*, August 20, 1841.

6. Stone was editor and publisher of the New York *Commercial Advertiser*.

TO ISAAC CHAPMAN BATES AND RUFUS CHOATE

August 25. 1841.

Private & Confidential.

Gentlemen,

I should not volunteer my opinions to you, in any matter respecting the discharge of your public duties, in another Department of the Government; but as you spoke last evening of the general policy of the Whigs, under the present posture of affairs, relative to the Bank Bill, I am willing to place you in full possession of my opinion, on that subject.

It is not necessary to go further back, into the history of the past, than the introduction of the present measure into the House of Representatives. That introduction took place, within two or three days after the President's disapproval of the former Bill; and I have not the slightest doubt that it was honestly and fairly intended as a measure likely to meet the President's approbation. I do not believe that one in fifty of the Whigs had any sinister design whatever, if there was an individual, who had such design. But I know that the President had been greatly troubled, in regard to the former Bill, being desirous, on one hand to meet the wishes of his friends, if he could, and on the other, to do justice to his own opinions. Having returned this first Bill with objections, a new one was presented in the House, and appeared to be making rapid progress. I know the President regretted this, and wished that the whole subject might have been postponed. At the same time, I believe he was disposed to consider calmly and conscientiously, whatever other measure might be presented to him.

But in the mean time, Mr. Botts' very extraordinary letter, made its appearance. Mr. Botts is a Whig, of eminence and influence in our ranks. I need not recall to your mind the contents of the letter. It is enough to say, that it purported that the Whigs designed to circumvent their own President, to "head him," as the expression was; and to place him in a condition of embarassment.[1] From that moment, I felt that it was the duty of the Whigs to forbear from pressing the Bank Bill further, at the present time. I thought it was but just in them, to give decisive proof that they entertained no such purpose, as seemed to be imputed to them. And since there was reason to believe, that the President would be glad of time, for information and reflection, before being called on to form an opinion on another plan for a Bank—a plan somewhat new to the Country, I thought his known wishes ought to be complied with. I think so still. I think this is a course, just to the President, and wiser on behalf of the Whig party. A decisive rebuke ought, in my judgment, to be given to the intimation, from whatever quarter, of a disposition among the Whigs to embarrass the President. This is the main ground of my opinion; and such a rebuke, I think, would be found in the general resolution of the Party to postpone further proceedings on the subject to the next session, now only a little more than three months off.

The Session has been fruitful of important Acts. The wants of the Treasury have been supplied;[2] provisions have been made for Fortifications, and for the Navy;[3] the repeal of the Sub-Treasury has passed:[4] the Bankrupt Bill, that great measure of justice and benevolence, has been carried through;[5] and the Land Bill seems about to receive the sanction of Congress.[6] In all these measures, forming a mass of legislation, more important, I will venture to say, than all the proceedings of Congress for many years past, the President has cordially concurred.

I agree, that the currency question is, nevertheless, the great question before the Country: but considering what has already been accomplished, in regard to other things; considering the differences of opinion which exist upon this remaining one; and considering, especially, that it is the duty of the Whigs effectually to repel and put down any supposition, that they are endeavouring to put the President in a condition, in which he must act under restraint, or embarrassment, I am fully and entirely persuaded, that the Bank subject should be postponed to the next Session. I am, Gentlemen, Your friend, & Obt. Servt.   Danl Webster

LS. DLC. Published in the *Madisonian*, September 23, 1841; and in *W & S*, 16: 354–356. For the AL draft of this letter, see mDW 20024.

1. See above, DW to Caroline Le Roy Webster, [August 21, 1841].

2. Congress had passed and President Tyler had signed on July 21, 1841, a law authorizing a government loan not exceeding $12 million. 5 *U.S. Statutes at Large* 438.

3. Tyler had signed the bill making appropriations for a home squadron on August 1 and he approved the fortifications bill on September 9. 5 *U.S. Statutes at Large* 438–439, 458–460.

4. The President assented to the repeal of the subtreasury on August 13. 5 *U.S. Statutes at Large* 439–440.

5. The bankrupt bill became a law on August 19. 5 *U.S. Statutes at Large* 440–449.

6. The preemption bill received the President's signature on September 4. 5 *U.S. Statutes at Large* 453–458.

Throughout the long hot summer of 1841, Tyler, his cabinet, and the Whigs in Congress debated the tariff, distribution, and a bank. Congress and the President had agreed upon a treasury loan, repeal of the subtreasury, and bankruptcy legislation. They had worked out their differences, temporarily, on a tariff and distribution. But they were at loggerheads over a bank. Under Clay's strong leadership, Congress had redrawn Ewing's fiscal bank plan and sent it to Tyler, only to have it vetoed. Headstrong, Congress set to work upon another bank bill despite Tyler's solicitations that the question be postponed until later. Long and hard negotiations between Tyler, Congress, and the cabinet ensued. These conferences resulted in a "fiscal corporation" bill, not what most Whigs in Congress or in the administration wanted, but one that had been drafted in consultation with the President and his cabinet, hence supposedly having Tyler's sanction. Then on September 9, Tyler vetoed this second bank measure and the entire cabinet, except for Webster, resigned.

The entire Massachusetts congressional delegation, summoned by Webster, met at the secretary's rooms the evening of September 10. The cabinet breakup was discussed, and Webster explained his reasons for remaining with the President. According to John Quincy Adams, the meeting broke up with "all agreed that Mr. Webster would not be justified in resigning at this time." Charles Francis Adams, ed., Memoirs of John Quincy Adams . . . (12 vols., Philadelphia, 1876), 11: 13–14.

In the letters below, from September 10 to September 13, Webster explored with friends the course he should follow. He received conflicting advice, but he decided, as he explained in the columns of the National Intelligencer *on September 14, to stay in office because of negotiations pending in the State Department and because he had not found "sufficient reasons" for resigning. Later in the month he exposed in the* Madisonian *the inadequacy of the justifications offered by his former colleagues for resigning their posts.*

TO [ISAAC P. DAVIS]

Sep. 10. [1841] 3 oclock.
    Do the Whigs of Mass think I ought to quit—or ought to stay? Yrs
                                D. W.

ALS. NhHi. Published in Van Tyne, p. 237, as addressed to Peter Harvey. It is more likely, however, that the recipient was Isaac P. Davis, whose letter of September 13, 1841, below, seems to be in direct response.

TO HIRAM KETCHUM

Washington, Sept. 11th. 1841.
My Dear Sir;
    I thank you for your kind and friendly letter.[1]
    You will have learned that Messrs. Ewing, Bell, [George Edmund] Badger, and Crittenden, have resigned their respective offices. Probably Mr. Granger may feel bound to follow the example. This occurrence can hardly cause you the same degree of regret which it has occasioned to me; as they are not only my friends, but persons with whom I have had, for some time, a daily official intercourse. I could not partake in this

movement. It is supposed to be justified, I presume, by the differences which have arisen between the President and Congress, upon the means of establishing a proper Fiscal agency, and restoring a sound state of the currency; and collateral matters, growing out of those differences. I regret these differences as deeply as any man; but I have not been able to see, in what manner the resignation of the Cabinet was likely either to remove or mitigate the evils produced by them. On the contrary, my only reliance for a remedy for those evils has been, and is, on the union, conciliation, and perseverance of the whole Whig party; and I by no means despair of seeing yet accomplished, by these means, all that we desire. It may render us more patient under disappointment in regard to one measure, to recollect, as is justly stated by the President in his last message, how great a number of important measures has been already successfully carried through. I hardly know when such a mass of business has been despatched in a single session of Congress.

The annual winter session is now near at hand; the same Congress is again soon to assemble; and feeling as deeply as I ever did, the indispensable necessity of some suitable provision for the keeping of the public money, for aid to the operation of the Treasury, and to the high public interests of currency and Exchange, I am not in haste to believe that the party, which has now the predominance, will not, in all these respects, yet fulfill the expectations of the Country. If it shall not, then our condition is forlorn indeed. But for one, I will not give up the hope.

My particular connexion with the Administration, however, is in another Department. I think very humbly, none can think more humbly— of the value of the services which I am able to render to the public, in that post. But as there is, so far as I know, on all subjects affecting our foreign relations, a concurrence in opinion between the President and myself, and as there is nothing to disturb the harmony of our intercourse, I have not felt it consistent with the duty which I owe the country, to run the risk, by any sudden or abrupt proceeding, of embarrassing the Executive, in regard to subjects and questions now immediately pending, and which intimately affect the preservation of the peace of the Country. I am, Dear Sir, with Constant regard, yours &c. &c.   Danl. Webster

LS. NhD. Published in *W & S*, 3: 184–185, 16: 356–357; and in the *National Intelligencer*, September 16,

1841.
    1. Not found.

TO JOHN MCLEAN

Washington, Septr. 11th, 1841.

(*Private*)

My Dear Sir:

You have been this day nominated for the Office of Secretary of War, and will be confirmed on Monday. This has been done, under an impression, I hardly know whence derived, that it would be agreeable to you to leave the Bench for some such employment.

I confess I do not see how you can be spared from your present place, without immense loss to the Country; but if your inclination or convenience lead to a change, I pray to assure to you that nothing could be more agreeable to me personally, than that you should join the Administration.

In the present state of things the War Department is probably quite the most important of the vacant posts. On the one hand, we are not without danger of War; and on the other, Indian affairs, originally a sort of appendage to the War Department, has grown to be, of itself, a highly important and interesting principal among the subjects of administration.

You are well acquainted with the duties of the Office, in both its branches; and there are other subjects, of a general nature, which belong rather more to another Department, I mean finance, currency, &c. which will, nevertheless, receive attention from all members of the administration, and in regard to which your advice will be important.

When I think of the Court,—and Judge Story—my mind balances to one side—when I think of the success of President Tyler's Administration, it gets a strong lean the other way. You cannot be in both places; but if you are tired out, by long journies, and sick of Bills, Answers, and Demurrers, no one will be more happy than myself to meet you in the Circle of Heads of Departments.[1] I am, Dear Sir, with great regard, Yours affectionately.   Danl Webster

LS. DLC.
    1. For McLean's response, see letter of September 18, 1841, below.

TO [JOSEPH] GALES AND [WILLIAM WINSTON] SEATON
                                    Washington, September 13. 1841.
Gentlemen:
    Lest any misapprehension should exist, as to the reasons which have led me to differ from the course pursued by my late colleagues, I wish to say that I remain in my place, first, because I have seen no sufficient reasons for the dissolution of the late Cabinet, by the voluntary act of its own members.

    I am perfectly persuaded of the absolute necessity of an institution, under the authority of Congress, to aid revenue and financial operations, and to give the country the blessings of a good currency and cheap exchanges.

    Notwithstanding what has passed, I have confidence that the President will co-operate with the Legislature in overcoming all difficulties in the attainment of these objects; and it is to the union of the Whig party

—by which I mean the whole party, the Whig President, the Whig Congress, and the Whig People—that I look for the realization of our wishes. I can look no where else.

In the second place, if I had seen reasons to resign my office, I should not have done so without giving the President reasonable notice, and affording him time to select the hands to whom he should confide the delicate and important affairs now pending in this Department. I am, gentlemen, respectfully, your obedient servant,   Daniel Webster.

Text from the *National Intelligencer*, September 14, 1841. Original not found. Published in Curtis, 2: 81–82.

FROM ISAAC P. DAVIS

Boston, Sept. 13. 1841

My dear Sir

I have heard but one opinion expressed by the *Whigs*, which has been the great desire that you remain in Office.[1]

They see no good reasons why you should quit, except it may be personal, with which they [are] not acquainted. They would consider it the greatest misfortune that could happen if you should find it necessary to leave the Cabinet, at the present time.

During the whole discussion on the Bank & Vetos—they [have] taken little interest, except only so far, as the result should affect you on the question, of holding your Office, & the danger of its leading to such a division as to cause your resignation. In any event I have not any hesitation in saying that the Whigs very generally, without any exception to my knowledge, join most heartily in the wish, that you may continue, if it can be done without too great sacrafice.

Our situation with England at present moment seems, to require the best talents of the country, to bring us out of difficulty. Shall write you again if I have any reason to change my present impression. I was pleased to find Mrs. W. appear so well since her return. She is now on a visit to Julia. Yrs as ever   I. P. Davis

ALS. DLC.
1. See above, DW to [Isaac P. Davis], September 10, [1841].

FROM ROBERT CHARLES WINTHROP

Monday Aft. Septr. 13. 1841.

Private

My Dear Sir,

I cannot leave Washington (as I shall this afternoon) without expressing to you the deep solicitude I feel on the subject of your present position.

I am aware how heavy a responsibility any man takes, who recommends you to resign your post in the existing condition of our foreign affairs. And if it were made plain to the Country that you retained your relations to the President at his request, in opposition to your own impulses, & only with a view to a temporary emergency, I think you might stand safe.

But the idea, which is beginning to prevail, that you intend to connect yourself permanently with his fortunes, to separate yourself from your late associates, & even to lend your name & influence & personal aid in justifying him & condemning them, will subject you to remarks of the most painful character.

I earnestly hope you will not commit yourself to such a course without weighing well the consequences to your own good name & glorious reputation. I cannot believe that anything but *disesteem* (to use the lightest word) awaits Mr. Tyler, among the great mass of those whom you have hitherto had as your friends. It will be impossible to rally any party in his favor, & those who adhere to him, under circumstances like the present, will be regarded, I greatly fear, with even less indulgence than himself.

I write in great haste & with great freedom. I am sure you will attribute my remarks to nothing but the warmest personal regard, & the most sincere wishes for your future fame. I have felt it the more obligatory to address you on the subject, from the report which is in circulation that the Massachusetts Delegation had unanimously advised you to remain where you are, & from the fear that you might have mistaken the views of at least one of them on Friday evening.[1]

I will only add, that, whatever result you may come to, I trust you will not doubt the respect & friendship of Yours truly &c.   Robt. C. Winthrop

ALS copy. MHi. Winthrop endorsed the letter: "(This letter was written at the earnest instigation of Mr. [Leverett] Saltonstall & of Gales & Seaton of the Intelligencer, & I had reason to think that it arrested a manifestation which Mr. Webster was about making.)"

1. Winthrop had been present at the September 10th meeting in DW's rooms which resulted, according to Adams, in unanimous agreement that the secretary should retain his post.

FROM CHRISTOPHER HUGHES

London, Saturday, 18th. Septr. 1841.
3 o'Clock. P.M.
Covent Garden.
at Mr. John Miller's.

Private.
My dear Sir,
    I write this, at the Agent's of the Legation[1] who will close the des-

patches in about an hour. I have walked from Downing Street, in order to seize the only remaining moment, to add a word—& at the only place where it might be done.

I was received with the greatest possible kindness, & I may say, with even distinction by Lord Aberdeen[2]—whom I have just left. As I have said, we are old acquaintances. Our *tete à tete* lasted about ½ an hour. He gave me the American News—for I have seen no paper & *know nothing* by *last* dates. Our conversation was pretty much confined to American affairs. He told me of the President's *Veto*, of the First Bank Bill: — of the modified new, or 2d. Bank Bill, of whose executive fate nothing is yet known here: & about which the greatest possible anxiety is felt, certainly *in part*, from monetary, or financial Considerations; but principally from the influence the fate of this Bill may have upon our Cabinet; any change in which, & especially *your retirement*, is deeply & gravely deprecated by the British Government.

We then spoke of [Alexander] McLeod's case,[3] which Lord Aberdeen thinks the gravest matter in our relations; if that case be got round, or got over (id est—if McLeod be liberated!) He seems to think, that our *other* points of dispute may be so treated & managed as to preserve— what he declares He most ardently desires to preserve—the friendly relations between the Two Countries. He averred to me over & over, that He was & should be animated by the truest spirit of peace & harmony in his course, in the new office to which he is now restored! and said "Mr. Hughes, I know it is the fashion to represent me, as exclusively imbued with Prussian & with Austrian principles of government—with being a despot in my doctrines & feelings &c. &c. I know this:" (he said laughingly) but it is absurd and "nonsensical." I did not at all deny that *such* was his general fame; & I said that we were & very naturally, rather tenacious about our public respect—however, that we were very proud & *would stand no slight*—or offence, in matters of etiquette and proper deference: & that I was rather apprehensive that taunts & sarcasms might be indulged in, so as to generate bad blood—for we were excessively irritable on such matters: —& that though I believed 49 of 50 reasonable men in U.S. sincerely valued & *desired* peace; yet, the 50 would unite where there was any question of national honour, respect or even pride. Lord Aberdeen said—"Such are exactly our *own* propensities & feelings—& they are natural to the people of all popular Governments! as far as I can control, or as it may depend *on me*—you may rely on it— all that sort of course shall be anxiously avoided; and indeed—I may say —that when formerly in this office I was more intimate with the American Minister—than with any other Minister at this Court"; & He then pronounced the most eloquent and emphatic Eulogium on Mr. [Louis] McLane; which I *heard* with pleasure; for nothing can be greater or more sincere, than my personal respect, admiration for & confidence in Mr. McLane: & I said so to Ld. Aberdeen—& he permitted me to repeat to my friend & Townsman—Mr. McLane, what he had said of him, with his kind recollections.

Lord A. spoke again & again of McLeod's affair—& with the deepest alarm and apprehension; of the conflicting jurisdiction between the General & the State Government of N. York! Of *Your* opinion—that if ever McL. were condemned, the Genl. Govt. would demand his surrender to their control—or rather—insist upon an appeal to the Supreme Court: the right or practicability of which is denied, & resisted by the Govr. of of N. York.[4] In a word—Lord A. is full of alarm and apprehension on this McLeod subject; & I verily believe him also to be full of friendly & peaceful feelings & intentions toward U. States.

He then asked me all about Mr. [Edward] Everett;[5] & Mr. Everett was in *good hands*—for I have the highest opinion & greatest respect for Him; and I told Lord Aberdeen that his Lordships peaceful views, and the quality he so especially eulogized in Mr. McLane, of treating even disagreeable matters of business with a mild, calm & conciliating manner & temper, would be fully met & equalled, in the character & by the carriage and conduct of Mr. Everett: that it appeared to me to be impossible for the President to have selected a better or fitter man for London—in our actual relations—than Mr. Everett. Lord A. said—"after what you say of Mr. Everett, Mr. Hughes, I really hope he may be appointed"—& He then told me about some delay or hesitation in the Senate of which, I knew nothing!

We got very pleasant & cheerful in our chat:—for, in *admitting*, that his Lordship had not been wrong in his *own* account of his renown, as to political principles & propensities & as to his being haughty, proud & imperious—(all which he had said of himself & speaking of his untrue fame:) I made him laugh heartily, when I said, "Why Yes, my Lord, when I first (when you were last in power) came down to Downing St. to *see you*—Even one of your own friends"—(I didn't tell him *who*! but I tell *you*, my dear Mr. Webster, it was Lord Strangford)[6] said,—"Hughes —You need not go to see Lord Aberdeen—unless you can talk Greek. Now, Mr. Everett possesses this faculty—and will talk as *much Greek* with you as you like.["] He laughed most good humoredly—& said— "Well, Mr. H. from your acct. of Mr. E. I hope he may come here &c. &c. &c.["]

We then talked over Swedish politicks, and the character of the King of Sweden[7] whom Lord A knows; & various other matters. He asked me many questions about Sweden &c. &c. We shoke hands; & I walked to White Hall, left a Card for Sir Robert Peel;[8] & then to White Hall Place, where I had a half hours very agreeable conversation with one of the oldest and best & most constant friends I have in Europe & one of the best hearted men & one of the very *cleverest men* in G. Britain. He was 20 years ago my Colleague at Stockholm & is one of the greatest personal & political friends and favorites of Sir R. Peel! I mean Lord [William] Vesey FitzGerald;[9] *up* for Ambassador to Paris; He denies it; & thinks it will be Lord Cowley.[10] Lord FitzGerald told me that Sir C[harles] Bagot's appointment to Canada was official[11] though not gazetted; & I said—we could not have a better man, in our neighbourhood—*for us*; & that I was sure, Sir Charles had peaceful, friendly, & of course, *wise* feelings to-wards U.S.—where he had been very & deservedly popular; & that *he understood* our Country exceedingly well; a great desideratum in the Govr. Genl. of Canada & I shall say so to Sir R. Peel, if I see him as I think I may, *seeing*, that I shall be in London about 12 days.

This is all, I have to say: I have said it—running on—as if I were talking—and *"I guess"* you will admit—that I *can* talk.

Mr. Chargé d'aff[aire]s [Isaac Rand] Jackson is here (I hear:) & I shall now go & see him; & *Mr. Stevenson, which*, I have not *yet* been *able* to do!

I sincerely hope to find you in office; & in good dispositions towards me—whether *in*—or out *of* office; for I shall be equally & always yr. sincere friend, Christopher Hughes.

N.B. I don't know what terms you are on with Mr. McLane; but I should like you to send him this Letter to read—if you please; I may add, that I said to Lord Aberdeen—that his opinion of Mr. McLane corresponded exactly with what Lord Grey[12] *had said to me*—of him—adding "Most often I consider Mr. McLane, a very superior man!" & *so do I*. I have a great mind to bring Mr. McLane ("on my own hook") a half a dozen Coats from Shetly & *ruin* him at once!—*Do* send him this letter!

I shall certainly embark—*on 4th. [of ?] Octr. for Boston.* C. H.

This is a horridly confused Letter, I fear; it is written in a shop—& amidst all manner of din & Confusion! Still, perhaps, you'll make out—what I mean to convey. C. H.

I have been about 24 hours in London; & have scribbled half the time; I shan't write another word though, for I go in next ship—myself. C. H.

ALS. NhHi.

1. As stated above, John Miller, otherwise unidentified.

2. George Hamilton Gordon, fourth Earl of Aberdeen (1784–1860) was the British foreign secretary (1841–1846) under Peel's administration.

3. McLeod (1796–1871), Scottish immigrant to Upper Canada about 1825 and later appointed deputy sheriff, had been arrested in September 1840 on charges of murder in connection with the *Caroline* incident. Released for lack of evidence, he was shortly arrested again on the same charge and confined in prison at Lockport, New York, to await trial. On the McLeod case, see *Diplomatic Papers*, 1.

4. William Henry Seward.

5. Everett had been nominated as minister to England; his confirmation came on September 13.

6. Percy Clinton Sydney Smythe, Viscount Strangford (1780–1855), was an English diplomat who had served in various posts at Lisbon, Stockholm, Constantinople, and St. Petersburg.

7. Charles XIV (1764–1844), who had succeeded to the throne of Sweden and Norway in 1818.

8. Peel (1788–1850) was prime minister of Great Britain (August 1841–June 1846).

9. Baron Fitzgerald and Vesey (1783–1843) had been envoy to Sweden (1820–1823) and was president of the board of control (1841–1843).

10. Henry Wellesley, Baron Cowley (1773–1847) served as ambassador to France (1841–1846), having previously held the same post in Spain and at Vienna.

11. Bagot (1781–1843) was governor-general of Canada (1841–1843).

12. Charles Grey, Earl Grey, Viscount Howick, and Baron Grey (1764–1845).

FROM JOHN MCLEAN

Longwood Near Louisville
18th Sept. 1841

My dear Sir,

Your very kind letter was received yesterday,[1] and I was gratified to find that you remain, at this important crisis, in the Department of State. The country look to you with the deepest interest for the maintenance of its honor, and to avoid, if it can be done, the calamity of war. And I take great pleasure in saying, that the nation reposes an unshaken confidence in your wisdom and patriotism. The trust is great and I rejoice to know that, in your hands, it is safe.

The pleasure and advantage I should derive from being associated with you in the cabinet was much considered, before I declined the appointment which the President, in the kindest terms, tendered to me. But you are aware that I am associated with your best friend on the Bench, to be separated from whom would give me great pain.

If I had been certain that we were about to have a war with England, which I hope and believe is not the case, I should have accepted the War Department. It would in that event be a post of the highest peril, and this to me would have been its strongest recommendation. But this office in time of peace, in my view, is not desirable. It is connected with an extensive patronage but not that kind of patronage, which makes a deep impression upon the country. It affords little or no opportunity to the incumbent to give an elevated tone to the action of the government, and to increase its moral power. A certain prospect of contributing to this, and nothing else, could induce me to leave my present position.

The duties of the War Department are generally matters of routine, and can as well be discharged by a chief clerk as any other person. This,

you are aware, is not the case with my present position. I am, dear Sir,
Very truly & Sincerely yours   John McLean

ALS. MHi.
1. See above, DW to John McLean, September 11, 1841.

TO ?

[Washington]
[September 20, 1841]
If you cannot control this Syracuse meeting,¹ the fat will all be in the
fire. Yrs   D. W.

ANS. NN. Endorsed: "Washington.
20. Sept. 1841."
1. The New York Whig state convention was to convene in Syracuse
in early October. New York City delegates to the convention were pro-Clay
and DW feared they might endorse
the Kentuckian for the Presidency.
In its "Declaration" of October 7, the
convention expressed its "disappointment and regret" that Tyler had not
seen fit to sanction Whig banking
measures. Claiming that they were
"anxious to give Mr. Tyler . . . a
hearty support," the delegates expressed their "heartfelt gratitude and
thanks [to Henry Clay] for all his
eminent public services" but without
nominating him for the Presidency.
Albany Argus, October 6, 9, 1841.

FROM GEORGE WASHINGTON PATTERSON

Westfield Chautauqua County N.Y.
Sept 22. 1841
My Dear Sir
Deeply, most deeply do I regret the position into which the Whig party
has been thrown since I parted with you at Washington on the 5th of
March. At that time the battle had been fought, the victory won, and the
people looked to General Harrison and his Cabinet, with the most entire
confidence, that, with the aid of an enlightened Congress all the measures for which they had contended would be successfully carried out.
The death of General Harrison caused many to fear that the policy of
the Whig party would be frustrated by the accession of Mr Tyler to the
Presidency, but when I saw that he retained the able Cabinet selected
by his predecessor, I had the most entire confidence that all would be
right, but in this how sadly have I been disappointed: The first thing
that alarmed me was the apparent confidence the President placed in a
vile paper published in the City of New York¹—a paper that no respectable farmer in western New York would suffer to remain unburn[e]d on
his premises for a single moment. In that filthy sheet were shadowed
forth the views of the President in advance of any other paper. The next
was his refusal or neglect to remove Post Masters at all the most important points in the State. For instance, at New York, Hudson, Troy,
Utica, Syracuse, Rochester & Buffalo, while one and all of these men

came within the rule laid down by him in his Inaugural address. Next came his veto to a bill got up and carried through Congress as a Whig measure, and last and worst of all, refusing his assent to a bill prepared under his advice and with his approbation—passed by both branches of Congress by a party vote, and then met by the arbitrary use of the executive power!! What would every Whig in the Union have said of Jackson or Van Buren, if they had thus set the will of the Representatives of the people at defiance, and after approving the bill repealing the subtreasury, and the state Bank deposite system, and then refuse to charter a National Bank! Why, we would have denounced them as *Tyrants*, intending to wield the sword of the nation in one hand and the purse in the other; and can we say less of John Tyler whom we have unfortunately placed in power? I think not, and there is not a single Whig within my knowledge in western New York—the "free west," who does not agree with me in opinion. Our leading Whig friends at Albany, by not taking open ground against the conduct of the President, came near sharing the fate that awaits him, but by coming forward at last and calling a State convention through which the people can express their feelings, they have saved themselves and I hope the Whig party in this State. Without it all was lost. You will perhaps enquire what the people expect to accomplish by a movement against the course pursued by the President. I answer— They expect to acquire a reputation for honesty (which they most richly deserve) of contending for principle against power and of showing the world that *one man* cannot with their consent govern this nation.

I most sincerely regret the position in which you are placed in the Administration. Your great and valuable services are wanted by the nation and cannot well be dispensed with, but from the course the President has taken with other distinguished members of the Cabinet I cannot but fear that ere long you must share the same fate.

I know from your published letters that you think the President will return to the path of duty and act with his former friends,[2] but with what confidence let me ask, can members of Congress go to work and mature another bill after what has been done with the two former—no man having any regard for his own reputation or the dignity of his place as member of Congress will be found preparing a bill to be met with another veto.

If anything was wanting to satisfy the President that he was on the wrong side it would only be necessary for him [to] witness the rejoicing of the Tory party in this state. Yours Very Truly and Respectfully

Geo. W. Patterson.

ALS copy. NRU.

1. Patterson was probably alluding either to James Gordon Bennett's *New York Herald* or to William Leete Stone's New York *Commercial Advertiser.*

2. Perhaps Patterson was referring to DW's letters which had appeared in New York newspapers in late July.

See DW's letters to Hiram Ketchum of July 16 and of July 17 (printed above).

[THE CABINET CRISIS]

[September 24, 1841]

It is plain enough, that the retiring members take the President at great disadvantage.

They write him letters, which they know he cannot answer, because the President of the U. States cannot enter into such a correspondence. They use weapons, therefore, which they know *he* cannot use.

In the next place, they undertake to state Cabinet conversations, which *he* regards as confidential, & to which *he* cannot refer, without violating his own sense of propriety & dignity. Having thus placed the President in a position, in which he cannot defend himself, they make war upon him; and this we suppose will be called high-mindedness, & "Chivalry!"

We should more readily incline to suppose there might be some reason for the retirement of the four members of the late Cabinet, if they could agree on such reason among themselves. But, unhappily, they entirely differ, each has a ground of his own, & no sooner does one come forth to show his cause, than another follows with a different showing.

Mr. Ewing, who leads off, rejects the Veto, as ground of resignation, & goes out on "personal indignity."

Mr Crittenden follows, & having no complaint to make of personal indignity, he goes out on the Veto.[1]

Then comes Mr Badger, who does not go out, on the Bank question, but because the case is one of "a measure, embraced, & then repudiated—efforts prompted, & then disowned—service rendered, & then treated with scorn & neglect."[2]

That is to say, Mr Badger resigned because the President trifled with his Cabinet.

But now hear Mr Bell.[3]

"Nor was it because the President thought proper to trifle with or mislead his Cabinet, as there is but too much reason to believe he intended to do, in the affair of the late Fiscal Bank that I resigned my place.

"There were other & pre-existing causes for such a course, &c."

What these "other & pre-existing causes" are, or were, Mr Bell does not inform us. In regard to these, the world is yet to be enlightened.

Placed in the shortest form each Gentleman, with his cause of resignation, stands thus—

Mr Ewing......................personal indignity
Mr Crittenden.................. Veto

Mr Badger.................... Trifling with the Cabinet
Mr [Bell]...................... Other & pre-existing causes

Or the matter may be fairly represented, by stating each one of the several alleged causes, & seeing who concurred in it.

In that view, the case thus—

"Personal Indignity"—Assigned by Mr Ewing; not alleged by anybody else.

"Veto." Assigned by Mr Crittenden, expressly renounced by the rest—

"Trifling with the Cabinet"—the substance of Mr Badger's ground; expressly repudiated by Mr Bell, & alleged by nobody else—

"Other and pre-existing causes"; alleged by Mr Bell, alluded to by nobody else, & of which the world is yet in utter ignorance.

We cannot suppose that these Gentlemen could have a weak affectation, each to give a separate reason for himself; and since they so entirely differ among themselves, we think the inference fair, that there was *no* plain, substantial cause, for breaking up the Cabinet, such as the public mind can readily understand & justify. Time will show what opinion the Country may come to; but of one thing we feel entirely confident, & that is, that when the passions of the moment shall have passed away, the revealing of Cabinet secrets for the purpose of attacking the President, is a proceeding which will meet with general condemnation.

AD. NhHi. Published in the *Madisonian*, September 25, 1841, under the caption "The Ex-Members Publications Abbreviated"; and in Van Tyne, pp. 237–239.

1. Ewing's and Crittenden's letters of resignation were published in the *National Intelligencer*, September 14, 1841.

2. Badger's letter, addressed to Joseph Gales and William Winston Seaton rather than to the President, was also printed in the *National Intelligencer*, September 21, 1841.

3. Bell's letter, similarly addressed, appeared in the *National Intelligencer*, September 23, 1841.

FROM ALBERT FEARING

Boston Sept. 25 1841

Private

Dear Sir,

The panic which has existed here, in the Whig ranks for a few days past, is rapidly passing away and we are preparing to buckle on our armour for the approaching contest with spirit and I trust with effect.[1] The prospect a week since seemed to be, that we might lose the State, but I now feel the utmost confidence of a good result.

The removal of [Leonard] Jarvis[2] & [Eliphalet] Case[3] has had great influence and gives much additional strength to the Administration. If a few more removals could be effected immediately, it would have a most happy influence upon our party and tend to produce kind feelings towards the President and lead to a firm determination to support his Administration.

We had a meeting of the State Central Committee last evening.[4] The best feeling animated all the Members and we shall bring out an Address to the Whigs of our State which I think will meet your entire approbation.[5] Of one thing you may rest assured, that there is a strong determination to support you in your present position.

I have been requested by some of our most respectable Merchants to call your attention to the application of Mr. George Latimer[6] for the Office of Consul at St. John's Porto Rico.

I cannot conclude without again expressing my strong conviction that the removal of a few more of the most obnoxious of the Office holders would do more to heal our divisions and cheer up our friends than any other measure that can be adopted.

Hoping to have the pleasure of seeing you here in a few days I am very Respectfully & truly Yours   Albert Fearing

ALS. NhHi.

1. The Massachusetts Whigs were organizing for the gubernatorial and legislative canvass. They had nominated John Davis for governor.

2. Tyler had removed Jarvis, a Van Buren appointee as Navy agent for Boston, and appointed in his stead I. Vincent Brown. Brown's nomination, to be effective from September 20, 1841, and to run for four years, went to the Senate on December 23. *Journal of the Executive Proceedings of the Senate . . . 1841 to . . . 1845* (Washington, 1887), p. 5.

3. Case (1796–1862), former Universalist minister, had turned to politics and emerged as a leading Jacksonian in Lowell, Massachusetts, in the 1830s. In 1840, Van Buren had appointed him postmaster, but Tyler, in September 1841, had dismissed

him and named Jacob Robbins as deputy postmaster for the city. *Ibid.*

4. Fearing was a member of the Whig State Central Committee at this time.

5. The address of the Whig State Central Committee appeared in the *Boston Semi-Weekly Atlas*, October 2, 1841.

6. Latimer, a native of Philadelphia and former Pennsylvania legislator, was a merchant, having previously served as U.S. consul at Mayaguez, Puerto Rico. For other recommendations of Latimer, see Letters of Application and Recommendation During the Administrations of Martin Van Buren, William Henry Harrison, and John Tyler, 1837–1845 (M–687), Reel 19, Frames 169–175, DNA, RG 59.

[MEMORANDUM ON THE PRESIDENT AND THE FISCAL CORPORATION BILL]
[September 1841]

<My note of these conversations; never expecting them to be quoted or repeated out doors—>

It is not my purpose, to examine, in detail, the Statements of Messrs Ewing, Badger & Bell.[1] <I shall enter into no protracted controversy with them.> But I wish to <expose the error> remark upon a few of

<the most important> what I regard errors <& misrepresentations> contained in these representations.

1. <I am> In the first place the President is represented as having "got up" the last Bank Bill. Mr Ewing says it "was formed & fashioned according to <my> his suggestions, & that in the instigation of it he & another member of the Cabinet were made <my> his agents."

Mr Badger says, that this was a measure which he knew was suggested by <myself> the President himself, & which had been, at <my> his instance introduced it into Congress."

And Mr Bell commences his communication to the public by <stating> speaking of the "part taken by the President in getting up the Fiscal Corporation Bill.["]

Now the truth is, as I understand the matter, that the President <I> "got up" no Bill; that no bill was introduced into Congress by <my> his suggestion, & that he <I> had no agent, or agency, in the "initiation" of any such Bill. This will plainly appear I think from facts & dates.

<A Bill> Long before the 18th. of August, a Bill had been pending, & <then> on that day was still pending, in the H. of R., in Comee. of the whole,—introduced by Mr Sergeant, as Chairman of the Special Commee. on Currency—not unlike Mr Clays Bill.

The Veto was on the 16th.

The Senate acted on the Veto.

On Monday Eve', a Caucus—decided to appt. a <new> Commee &c.

In this Caucus, Botts leading Speech.

AD. DLC. Endorsed by Caleb Cushing, among whose papers the item was found, as follows: "Mem. as to letter to Constituents." Most likely DW drafted this memorandum to suggest to Cushing points he would like Cushing to present in his public "Letter to my Constituents," which Cushing distributed in September or October 1841, defending his support for Tyler. See the *National Intelligencer*, October 9, 1841.

1. For DW's earlier published comments on the cabinet resignations, see above, [The Cabinet Crisis, September 24, 1841].

TO EDWARD CURTIS

Marshfield, October 5, 1842 [1841].
Tuesday morning.

My Dear Sir,

I arrived here yesterday, at three o'clock, notwithstanding the storm;[1] found Mrs. Webster and Edward well, and Marshfield looking as well as usual, what little there is left of it. My great elm has furnished wood for the winter, and the garden fences are gone over to Duxbury. We have had a non-such of a blow, for thirty-six hours. Two vessels are ashore close by us. One, a lumberman, came on the beach Sunday night, lost two men; Edward and the neighbors saved the rest. The other got ashore last night, a large schooner. I see her across the meadows this morning, but she seems high and dry, and I hope no lives are lost. Edward has gone to see. I believe there is not an apple or pear on any tree, this side Boston, but then there are plenty on the ground, which are so much handier. The storm is breaking, we shall have fine weather, and shall be all ready for you Saturday, according to contract.

You will see that the Whig committee of Massachusetts are on the right tack.[2] Seth Peterson[3] goes for the President, notwithstanding the vetoes. He says, there is sometimes an odd fish that won't take clams; you must try him with another bait.

Remember Saturday, three o'clock. Mrs. Curtis may expect a salute. Mrs. Webster is delighted you are coming, and is already meditating murderous deeds in the poultry yard. Don't let any of the party fail. Yours, truly, D. Webster.

Text from PC, 2: 151, with date corrected. Original not found.

1. For a brief account of the gale that hit the Massachusetts shore, see the Boston Semi-Weekly Atlas, October 6, 1841.

2. The address of the Massachusetts Whig State Central Committee, though critical of Tyler's vetoes, nevertheless emphasized the accomplishments of the past session of Congress and declared: "We still have a Whig President, who intends to surround himself with Whig advisers, and to conduct his administration upon Whig principles; and until his acts shall establish the contrary, we hold him to be entitled to the support of a Whig people." Boston Semi-Weekly Atlas. October 2, 1841.

3. Peterson (1788–1866) was one of DW's Marshfield employees.

FROM CHILTON ALLAN

Winchester Oct 5th 1841

Dear Sir

Dureing this recess of Congress you may have leisure for a moment, to look at what is passing the mind of one who has long entertained for you the most sincere feelings of friendship; one who has looked upon you as among the foremost in producing the great political revolution of 1840; one who has cherished a high regard for your talents and fame as occupying a broad space in the character and history of our country.

Without stopping to deplore the occurrences which seperated general Harrison's Cabinet I am anxiously looking at the future.

You acted bravely in maintaining your ground, for it is evidently beset with iminent dangers. If the President shall recommend or agree to an act of Congress that shall replace the currency under the controll of the National power and which shall provide for the collection safe keeping &c of the public revenue then your wisdom in holding on will be evident to all, and you will be entitled to the gratitude of your country. The hope that the President will take this wise course, with me, is founded entirely on what you have said in your two published letters;[1] believing that you weigh well your words. I am looking with intense anxiety to the next message of the President. None can be better convinced than you that President Tyler's administration will be a miserable failure without a national currency.

Currencies regulated by state power broke down our old Confederation; crushed the National prosperity from 1811 to 17 and from 1830 until this time. This was the rock on which the formidable party of Genl Jackson was dashed to pieces. If our history has made any truth more apparent than all others, it is that no party can either maintain power or administer the Government to the satisfaction of the country, when the *National power* is withdrawn from the support of the currency. It is an attempt to build prosperity upon paralised labor.

The last hope that the President will not sacrifice himself upon the exploded mad scheme of State Banks, is founded upon your adherance to his cabinet and upon your published letters. If he should recommend such a Measure as is called for by the Nation what new hopes and new joys would be diffused over our land, and what new honors would await his first Minister. On the contrary what gloom is before us; he cannot stand for a moment poised between the two great parties: he must be with one or the other.

If he attempts to get along by the aid of State institutions with the revenue & currency he must abandon the Whigs and it will be impossible that in such a position you can stand by him. God grant that you may come through the trying <position> scenes that are shifting around you with your title of defender of the constitution made brighter. Your Friend   Chilton Allan

ALS. NhD.   Ketchum of July 16 and July 17
   1. See DW's letters to Hiram   (printed above).

FROM HERMAN COPE

Bank of the United States
Trustees (4th Septr 1841)
Department
October 5th. 1841

Dear Sir

Mr. Richard Smith, of Washington, transmitted to the Bank of the United States, some weeks since, sundry deeds of conveyance from yourself to Herman Cope and Thomas S. Taylor and the Survivor of them, for certain Lands in Ohio, Michigan, Wiskonsin, Illinois and Indiana,[1] which by an agreement between you and the Bank on the 12th of February last,[2] the latter was to receive from you, with a good and clear title, free of all incumbrance, in payment and full satisfaction of your indebtedness and liability to it. Of the sufficiency of the title, and freedom of the Lands from all incumbrance, the legal counsel of Mr. Smith, as the agent of the Bank, was to be the Judge.

Mr. Smith transmitted with the deeds, separate statements of Richard S[mith] Coxe Esqr., his Counsel, of his examinations of the titles to the Lands in Illinois, Wiskonsin and Michigan;[3] and pointing out what still seems necessary to be done to render those titles perfect. I enclose those three statements to you at Marshfield, in the hope that you may, while there, find sufficient leisure to examine the imperfections noted by Mr. Coxe, and be prepared, on your return to Philada, to remove them, to the satisfaction [of the?] Counsel here.

Our agent at Cincinnati,[4] who has been appointed [to undertake a ?] visit of inspection of all the Lands in the Northwest in [which the ?] Bank or its Trustees have an interest, waits now only [for those ?] papers connected with your Lands to set out upon his journey; and I should be much pleased could you spare time enough in this City, on your way to Washington, to complete those title papers in such way as will authorise me to close your accounts on the Books of the Trustees before the next semi annual statements of the affairs of the Trust are made out. With great respect very truly yours Herman Cope, agent for Ja[me]s. Robertson[5] et al: Trustees

ALS. MWalB.

1. For the deeds transferring the property from DW to Cope and Taylor, see the entries in the Calendar under date of April 28, 1841.

2. For the memorandum of the February 12 arrangement with the Bank of the United States of Pennsylvania, see mDW 39835–295.

3. For Coxe's memorandum on Wisconsin lands, May 10, 1841, see mDW 39847; on Illinois lands, May 7, 1841, mDW 39851; and on Michigan lands, May 7, 1841, mDW 39854.

4. Not identified.

5. Robertson (1772–1854), who immigrated to the United States about 1798, had been elected to the Board of Directors of the Bank of the United States of Pennsylvania in 1841 with the vote of the proxies Biddle held. Shortly before August 14, he became president of the Bank.

FROM JOHN TYLER

Washington Oct. 11. 1841.

My Dear Sir;

I have pleasure in saying, that the Cabinet is now full. Mr [John C.] Spencer Mr. [Charles A.] Wickliffe and Judge [Abel Parker] Upshur will be here early this week. Each man will go steadily to work for the country, and *its interests* will alone be looked to. I congratulate you in an especial manner upon having such co-workers. I would have each member to look upon every other, in the light of a friend and brother. By encouraging such a spirit I shall best consult my own fame, and advance the public good. My information from all parts of the country is encouraging, and altho' we are to have a furious fire during the coming winter, yet we shall I doubt not, speedily recover from its effects. Our course is too plainly before us to be mistaken. We must look to the whole country and to the whole people.

The letters from [Andrew] Stevenson and [Christopher] Hughes[1] are full of interest. The swearing in the McLeod case is hard against him, but Mr [Joshua A.] Spencer's[2] opening speech inspires me with confidence. That gotten over and you will have the honour of a final adjustment of all other difficulties.[3] I shall truly rejoice in all that shall advance your fame. I gave you a hint as to the possibility of acquiring Texas by treaty. I verily believe it could be done. Could the north be reconciled to it would any thing throw so bright a lustre around us? It seems to me that the great interests of the north would be incalculably advanced by such an acquisition. How deeply interested is the shiping interest? *Slavery*—I know that is the objection—and it would be well founded if it did not already exist among us—but my belief is that a rigid enforcement of the laws against the slave trade, would make in time as many free States, south, as the acquisition of Texas would add of slave States, and then *the future* (distant it might be), would present wonderful results.[4]

I shall leave here in as few days as I can for my quiet home, to meditate in peace over a scheme of finance. In whatsoever you do upon that subject, remember always my difficulty which, Ewing Bell & Co. to the contrary, have given me from the first more pain that either of them can have felt. The day for attempt at compromise has pass'd however, and we must take good care to trim well our sails for the voyage which lies before us. The more simple the agency to be employed the better. We have no surplus nor are we likely to have for some years, and may be regarded as living "from hand to mouth."

I pray you to accept the sincere assurance of my confidence and warm regard   John Tyler

P.S. Since writing the above the proceedings at the Syracuse convention have reached me. What a low and contemptible farce. You were right to remain in the Cabinet, *quoth [Millard] Filmore & Co.*—and yet these very men united in forcing Granger to retire.[5]

I learn by a private letter[6] that in secret session Mr Clay was proposed for the succession and supported by Filmore.

ALS. DLC. Published in Van Tyne, pp. 239–240.

1. Tyler was probably referring to Stevenson's letter to DW of Septem-

ber 18, 1841, and to Hughes's letter, printed above, of the same date. In his despatch, Stevenson had discussed Palmerston's notes on the *Caroline* issue, African seizures, and an interview with Aberdeen on the McLeod case. For Stevenson's letter, see RG 59 (Despatches, Great Britain), M30, R44, DNA.

2. Spencer (1790–1857), lawyer in Utica and later state senator and mayor of the town, served as McLeod's counsel in the New York courts.

3. The McLeod trial was in its closing stages; McLeod was acquitted on October 12.

4. Webster opposed annexation with the result that Tyler did not press for Texas until Webster was about to retire from the State Department. For DW's attitude toward annexation, see his speech at Niblo's Saloon, March 15, 1837, in *Speeches and Formal Writings*, 2; DW to Charles Allen, December 9, 1843, mDW 25499; and *W & S*, 16: 417.

5. The New York Whig state convention, meeting in Syracuse on October 6, had adopted an address and resolutions "condemning Tyler's vetoes and dissolution of the cabinet, but saying they were anxious to give Tyler a hearty support, and that it would be wholly his own fault if they did not." Frederick W. Seward, *William H. Seward: An Autobiography . . .* (New York, 1891), p. 569.

6. Not found.

FROM JOHN CANFIELD SPENCER

Washington, October 16. 1841.

My dear Sir,

With the exception of our Premier, the members of the cabinet are all here, and in full and active employ. I am exceedingly pleased with my associates, and the President evinces the utmost kindness and confidence. He appears really happy in being surrounded by men whom he knows and feels to be his friends. Of course we miss you very much. We trust that this slight relaxation will restore you to all your strength and vigor, and that you will soon return, a refreshed giant.

I am sorry to see that some papers on both sides in N.Y. State are now urging that the government should press its demands for satisfaction for the destruction of the Caroline, an act at last assumed by the British government. I am apprehensive that a popular current may be excited against us on this point, if we are not careful, and trust you will give the subject your best consideration during your absence.

Altho I had nothing of importance to say, yet I thought you would be glad to hear from some of us. There is great difficulty in negotiating the loan.[1] The President and all the heads of departments are well, and will be happy to hear that you are so. With great regard Yours truly

J. C. Spencer

ALS. DLC.

1. The United States government was engaged in an effort to float a loan in Europe, but with states defaulting and threatening repudiation, Europeans were exceedingly

reluctant to invest. Reginald C. Mc-Grane, *Foreign Bondholders and* *American State Debts* (New York, 1935), pp. 30–34.

FROM EDWARD EVERETT

Rome 22 Octr. 1841.

Unofficial

My dear Sir,

Owing I presume to my having been so much in motion during this month, I have no advices from you later than Col. Fletcher Webster's letter of the 5th of August.[1] I was led by that letter to consider the rejection of my nomination as all but certain. I had therefore no motive for prolonging my stay in Florence, with a view to the more prompt reception of your instructions. Accordingly, as my lease expired on the 1st of October, I started with my family on that day for Naples, proposing to pass a month there and the rest of the winter in this city. I arrived in Naples on the 4th inst. On the 12th, among other articles of intelligence received by the Steam-packet of 15th September, I saw it stated, in six words, in Galignani's paper, that my nomination was confirmed.[2] A similar & of course erroneous statement had appeared in the same paper a month before. As no letters by the packet of the 15th have yet reached me, I could not be sure that this report was not as groundless as the former. The same intelligence, however, was contained in several London papers which I saw in the course of the week; and on the 16th I received two letters[3] from Mr. F[rancis] C[alley] Gray then at London, in which the confirmation of my nomination was spoken of as certain. I considered this information as sufficiently authentic to influence my movements, without waiting to hear from you. I hastened my arrangements therefore for leaving Naples, which I did the next day. I should have taken passage in the steamer from Naples to Marseilles, but a part of my family had so lately suffered severely by sea-sickness, on the way from Leghorn, that I did not like to expose them to it again, without a longer interval. I arrived at Rome on the 19th. I shall start on the 25th for Civita Vecchia, and there take the steamboat the next day. If we have a prosperous passage, we shall reach Marseilles on the 29th. It will take me a week or ten days, according to the state of the Rhone, to reach Paris, besides a day or two which will be required at Marseilles to make arrangements for the journey. I hope, at any rate, to be in Paris by the 10th of Novr. I propose to leave my family there for two or three weeks, and proceed myself without delay to London; but I hope before I get there to receive some communication from you.

In repairing with such haste to England, without [waiting] to receive official advice of my appointmen[t,] I am actuated by the desire to conform to what I suppose must be your wishes and those of the President, in the present state of public affairs; without regard to the personal convenience or gratification of myself or family, which would have suggested a different route from one which we had travelled last year, and especially a longer stay in this most interesting city.

Desiring my most respectful remembrance to the President, & awaiting your instructions, I remain, My dear Sir, as ever, your affectionate and faithful friend,   Edward Everett.

My wife joins me in kindest regards to Mrs. W. [&] other members of your family that may be with you.

ALS. MHi.
1. Not found.
2. Everett's nomination on July 16, 1841, as minister to England had been confirmed by the Senate on

September 13. For a discussion of the nomination and confirmation, see *Diplomatic Papers*, 1.
3. Not found.

FROM DANIEL FLETCHER WEBSTER

Nov 7th. 1841

My dear Father,

I hope you will not delay much longer to come on here.

I do not know what is going on, but there is some body at work, doing mischief I fear.

This [John Beauchamp] Jones who has bought the Madisonian is, I think a fellow of Wise's and [Francis] Mallorys "et id omne genus."[1]

Mr. Wickliffe & Mr. Spencer seemed to know nothing of the movement. Mr. Forward & Mr. [Hugh Swinton] Legaré I am confident did not. I don't know that Mr. Upshur did.

I think the Pres. does. Mr. Wickliffe does not, he told me.

The Pres. will be here, about Thursday or Friday, I think. He is to be in Richmond on Monday—(to-morrow). Gen. [Winfield] Scott has flashed in the pan with his letter.

It first made it's appearance in the Globe.[2]

An old soldier like him ought not to have suffered a surprize & let the enemy capture his ammunition.

He was much annoyed.

We all keep well & have sold Duncan for $175. Sorry to let him go so low, but feed is very high & he was eating his head off.

Shall we see you Thursday or Friday? All well at the Dept. Yr. affectionate son   Fletcher

ALS. NhHi.
1. Jones, with financial backing from Wise and other Virginians, had purchased a controlling interest in

the Washington *Madisonian* from Thomas Allen. On November 6, he had taken over the publication of the paper. On the sale, see John Tyler to

Henry A. Wise, September 27, 1841, in *William and Mary Quarterly*, 1st Series, 20 (July 1911): 7; Thomas Allen to N. P. Tallmadge, November 5, 1841, N. P. Tallmadge Papers, WHi; Allen to W. C. Rives, November 6, 1841, Rives Papers, DLC; Washington *Madisonian*, November 6, 1841.

2. Scott's letter of October 25, 1841, outlining his views on executive power and announcing his availability for a presidential nomination, had appeared in the *Washington Globe*, November 4, 1841.

TO CHARLES HENRY THOMAS

Nov. 19. 41

Dear Henry,

I thank you for your letters,[1] & am glad to learn that all is going on well at Marshfield. How did you like my Worcester steers? The 4 yearlings wd. be famous, except that they have not very handsome *horns*. I trust they will all be well kept, & made to grow.

I have lately written to Mr [Seth] Weston, abt. farming &c. As we have now an Eastern rain storm, I am thinking it may be a regular North Easter with you, bringing with it snow, wild Geese, & *Kelp*. Lend a hand to Weston, in the plan[n]ing of a *barn*. Speaking of *barns*, makes me think of *houses*. If I was able to buy your House, & could take it up, & set it down as it now is, north of Asa Hewitts[2] barn, on the road leading to Seth Petersons, on the south side of black Mount, so that I should not be blown away by the Winter winds, I believe I wd. go to Marshfield, for the rest of my life, winter & summer.

Pray give my love to your wife & mother, & the Dr's family. Yrs   D. W.

ALS. MDuHi.
   1. Not found.

2. Hewitt (b. 1776) was one of DW's Marshfield neighbors.

FROM CHARLES MARCH

New York Nov. 20. 1841.

My Dear Sir,

Of the Eight boxes, two are marked "Ceylon." They contain four dozen from my private Stock. It is of an excellent growth, mild, and imported about eight Years ago via Ceylon—hence its name.

The smaller box marked B contains one dozen of the Burgundy Madeira, which you may recollect.

Will you do me the favor of kindly accepting these two little parcels as a token of the regard of Your old friend   Charles March

It will of course occur to you that the Wine having been many years in bottle will be turbid when unpacked, and should remain a couple of months quiet, before it will be fit to decanter.

ALS. MWalB.

FROM ALEXANDER POWELL

Washington Novr. 25th 1841

Sir

In making this a part of my observations on the frontier, the acquital of McLeod has rendered it unnecessary to say much in regard to the trial, it will be I presume sufficient for me to say that during my stay in Utica I very plainly saw that fear of a conviction of the prisoner was entirely unnecessary, although I was aware that men would be brought forward to swear positively to his participation in the Caroline affair, yet from what I saw and knew of the character of that testimony, I was soon convinced that no intelligent jury would hesitate to acquit the prisoner even had their not been any testimony offered for the defence.

During my stay in Utica I saw and became acquainted with William Lyon McKenzie and his son James[1] two of the principle agitators of the Patriot question. These men I led to believe that I favoured and wished to help their cause and so completely deceived them that they very freely stated to me the state of the Hunters Lodges and other matters connected with [the] Cause of the Patriots.[2]

The oath taken by the members of these Lodges is simply this, "Go aid and assist each other in all times of danger and difficulty["] when consistent with their duty to themselves and families and to keep the secrets of the Society.

I found that the Lodges had in their employment about twelve or thirteen persons the names of some of whom I ascertained as follows, one DeWitt, one Platt Smith one Danl Smith one Parker, one Pauling and one Allen, together with one Williamson who is now confined in the State Prison at Auburn N.Y. These men were commanded by the notorious Lett,[3] and employed solely for the purpose of committing depredations upon Canadian property and excite the inhabitants of the Canadian side of the frontier to acts of retaliation thereby hoping to involve the United States and England in a war.

Your excellency may depend upon it, that the main and sole dependence of the Patriots is upon being able through the excitement which they will through such means strive to keep in existence, to throw the two Countries into a war, when it is their intention to create an insurrection in the Canadas and form a seperate Republic in which most of the Leaders aspire to offices of high honor and dignity.

The opinion so prevalent that these Lodges contain such vast numbers of members is entirely incorrect and this error arises from this Cause.[4] During the former troubles of Canada many persons were deluded into joining these Lodges who have since become entirely and totally disgusted with the members and proceedings thereof and have consequently withdrawn from said Lodges and in consequence of which the signs of recognition &c of this society have undergone an entire change.

I must now call your Excellency's attention to one cause of these troubles on the frontier, which I must presume to think would be just grounds for a remonstrance on the part of the United States with England. England has on her Canadian frontier employed as volunteer soldiers a set of men taken from the walks of Civil life and who find their present employment so much more to their liking as to induce them to aid and assist the patriots on this side of the line to keep up the state of excitement hoping thereby to induce the British Government to retain them in her service. I have no doubt that these men have been the instigators of the stealing of powder and cannon from this side of the line. England has given for an excuse in employing such men, that her regular soldiers desert when stationed so near the line. Then why do not those stationed at the Falls and at Queenstown desert. We shall never have a quiet Frontier until England discharges these civilians from her service and her pay.

I can I think assure your Excellency that an outbreak on the frontier need not be feared. The Patriots know full well that they cannot concentrate a sufficient force for any successfull movement into the Canadas, and have fully determined to wait the issue of the difficulties existing between the United States and England being firmly convinced that sooner or later these difficulties must throw the two Countries into a war.

These opinions were formed from searching and dilligent observations on both the American and Canadian sides of the frontier and from Conversations had with men whom I know to be the principles of these Hunter's Lodges and who were under the firm conviction that I was much interested in the success of their cause and who were very anxious that I should join the Lodge and become the Correspondent thereof stationed at Washington D C. Hoping that this report may meet with the approbation of your Excellency I have the Honor to be very Respectfully Your obt svt   Alexr Powell

ALS. NhHi. Powell, a native of Pennsylvania, was an agent of the State Department along the American-Canadian frontier. He was nominated in late March and confirmed in early April as consul at Rio de Janeiro. When rumor spread through Washington the first weekend after his confirmation that he had paid DW for the post, Tyler withdrew the nomination. *Journal of the Executive Proceedings of the Senate . . .* (Washington, 1887), 6: 47–48.

1. Mackenzie (1795–1861), Canadian journalist and leader of the Canadian uprising of 1837, had fled to New York following the uprising's failure. On Navy Island in the Niagara River he established a provisional government. Subsequently, however, he was arrested and imprisoned for violating American neutrality laws. His son James, who had engaged in printing and publishing,

also fled to New York at the same time as his father and established a newspaper.

2. Organized in American cities and towns along the northern frontier in the aftermath of the Canadian uprising of 1837, the Patriots, or Hunter's Lodges, were to be found from Vermont to Michigan. For a further discussion of the Patriots, see *Diplomatic Papers, 1.*

3. None of the "Patriots" Powell names have been identified.

4. The membership of the Lodges was variously estimated at from 15,000 to 200,000.

TO EDWARD CURTIS

Decr 4. 41

Confidential
Dear Sir;

I think the message[1] will be well recd. & if it should be, our friends should seize the occasion for coming out *strong.* It is the best possible chance for T[hurlow] W[eed].[2] I pray you, lose no time in suggesting a good idea to *him.* A word also to the Commercial, & the Express. If they like it, let them give it a hearty approbation.[3] Verbum sat.   D. W.

ALS. NN.
1. DW was alluding to Tyler's message to Congress, to be delivered on December 7. James D. Richardson, *A Compilation of the Messages and Papers of the Presidents, 1789–1897* (Washington, 1900), 4: 74–89.
2. For Weed's response, see Thurlow Weed to DW, December 18, 1841, below.
3. Both the New York *Commercial Advertiser*, December 8, 10, 1841, and the *New York Daily Express*, December 8, 1841, endorsed Tyler's message.

TO HARRIETTE STORY WHITE PAIGE

Washington
Decr. 5. 1841

My Dear Mrs Paige;

I cheerfully comply with your request, & send you a "lock." Ellen [Fletcher?][1] cut it, & I told her to feel carefully for the bumps of respect & affection, & there insert her scissors. Adieu! my good friend, & may all blessings attend You, & Yours!   Danl Webster

ALS. MH–H. Endorsed by Harriette Paige: "Sending a lock of hair to insert, in a previous gift of a broach, from New York."
1. Ellen Fletcher (d. 1866), DW's niece, was the daughter of Timothy.

FROM CHARLES AUGUSTUS DAVIS

New York 8 Decr 1841

My Dr. Sir

I read last night the Message, almost as soon after its Delivery, as the people in Alexandria got it reprinted, & yet many forget the advantages of Rail roads. It is one of the best Papers that has come from Washington for many a long day, & there is more "Day light" in it than I have seen in many years. I have been all this morning stirring round among the talkers of all parties, and have not heard a word but in its praise. Every honest unprejudiced man approves of it & the hope is generally express'd that Mr. Clay will not oppose it. Chs. King of the American will perhaps have a fling at it, or the *financial* portion of it but that will do more good than harm. Opposition in some quarters is sure to secure high praise in another.

I am as proud as a patriot, for tho' a very humble Whig, I have incur'd the displeasure of some of the "would be" leaders of the party here for daring to differ with them in their indiscriminate abuse of "Jno. Tyler & others," & who was inclined to hope & believe when a fair chance was given to said "John Tyler & others" that great good wd. be found in them. My hopes and wishes are all reallized.

We shall have "the odour of Nationality" now on our currency, & I predict that any man can travel to Jerusalem with such currency as he now can with Bank of England notes. And under judicious management they will perform the duty of Exchange in part, in our foreign trade as well as our Domestic: and the money Brokers of London will redeem them & send them back to their sources in Exchanges, for if our Tariff is rightly managed, the Exchanges of the world can't fail to be in our Favour. We are now at par with London & Paris. As bad as times are, if we can limit imports of articles we can better do without, & make such as we want even at a nominal higher cost, we shall soon bring all matters right.

I now wait to see who will oppose the doctrine of this message & the ground of opposition. Unless he shows better reasons than I at present can see, his vote & my vote will be a tie in the ballot box. I have every confidence now that the present voyage of the "Two Pollies" will terminate prosperously, and that the owners & underwriters will see great cause of joy that Capt. Jumper & his 1st. mate Mr. Nye[1] kept together on that last short trip when the crew absconded. Yr. friend & obt Ser

Ch: Augs. Davis

ALS. NhHi.   *Downing, Major . . .* (New York,
   1. Davis was alluding to the ship   1834).
and characters in his *Letters of J.*

FROM THURLOW WEED

Albany, Dec 18. 1841.

Dear Sir,

The President has triumphed not only over his enemies but over himself. It is a great message. Now God grant to Congress the wisdom to act in the spirit of your Letter in the National Intelligencer of A[u]gust,[1] and all will be well.

If [Horace] Greeley, who is "all honest and true' (we can sing again!) takes hold of the Madisonian, he will reflect whatever is useful and salutary from the President, the Cabinet and the Congress, to the People.[2] Very truly yours,   Thurlow Weed

ALS. DLC. Published in Van Tyne, p. 248.

1. Weed's reference is ambiguous and may have been a slip on his part. The most apt conjecture is DW's letter to Hiram Ketchum of September 11, 1841, printed above, which appeared over his signature in the *National Intelligencer* of September 16, rather than any date in August. No other letter or editorial of DW's, or attributed to him at that time, seems to meet the requirements.

2. Greeley, who had begun publishing the *New York Tribune* in May, had been a correspondent for the Washington *Madisonian*. Rumor had it that he was to take charge of the Washington paper in an effort to reconcile the various Whig factions. Convinced after a trip to Washington that Tyler had no interest in reconciliation, Greeley abandoned the project. Glyndon G. Van Deusen, *Horace Greeley: Nineteenth Century Crusader* (Philadelphia, 1953), pp. 86–87.

The settlement of Webster's account with the Bank of the United States of Pennsylvania in early 1841 relieved him of some of his personal financial problems. But difficulties remained; Webster still needed to clear the titles to the land to be transferred to the Bank.

In addition, the indebtedness arising from his speculation in the Clamorgan Land Association remained with him. In the letter below, Webster discusses with Healy, his Boston law office associate, a case about to come before the Massachusetts Supreme Court involving two notes payable to Pierre Chouteau, Jr., and endorsed by Webster, which had been protested. At the time of protest, notice of refusal to pay had been directed to Webster in Washington. In the case, (Pierre Chouteau, Jr. v. Daniel Webster, 6 Metcalf 1, 1843), Healy and J. P. Rogers, who defended Webster, argued that the "notice should have been sent to Boston, where the defendant had his domicil and an agent to attend to his business, and where notice would have arrived one day earlier than at Washington" (pp. 3–4). Chief Justice Lemuel Shaw delivered an opinion in favor of the plaintiff, holding that "the notice was sufficient to charge the indorser" (p. 1).

TO JOHN PLUMMER HEALY

Washington Decr. 28. '41

Dear Sir

I suppose the facts stated within the asterisks in the enclosed letter[1] are substantially true, and could be proved. They may, therefore, I apprehend, be as well admitted. I do not see their bearing. They do not prove actual notice.

Mr. [Richard S.] Coxe, who has just left me, expresses an entire willingness to insert all facts.

Would it not be well to insert on page 2. at A. the following words, "while he had at all times an agent."

I must leave the matter very much with you. My own attention has not been called recently to the cases respecting notice; but notice is certainly —or at least has been—regarded always as a question of law. The Jury can only find specific facts. It would be disturbing things thought to be well settled, to alter this.

It is of some importance to postpone the judgment, or decision, as long as you can, as it *may* be agt us—though I trust not. Yrs truly

Danl. Webster

ALS. MHi.
  1. Not found.

MEMORANDUM ON THE BANKING BILLS AND THE VETOES
[1841]

When the first Bank Bill was before the President, it was discussed at length, in a full cabinet, I think, with the exception that the Atty Genl was absent.

Mr Ewing read a long & able paper, & the rest of us delivered our opinions verbally. We all earnestly recommended to the President to sign the Bill.

Apprehending a Veto, on Sunday morning Aug. 15, I addressed him a short letter. Vid Paper marked A.[1]

The Veto message was sent in, the following day, Monday, Aug. 16. A movement was immediately made [to] bring forward another Bill, & such an one should be free from all the objections, urged against the former.

Mr Berrien was Chairman of the Comee. of the Senate, & Mr Sargent of that of the House.

These Gentlemen had a conference with the President, on the morning of the 17th. & another on the morning of the 18th.

Most of the members of the Cabinet were at the Presidents together, on the 18 soon afterwards the same day. He spoke of the inconvenience of his holding conversation on the Bank subject with members of Congress; & took our opinions, whether it would not be better that he should decline all such conferences. A majority of us were of opinion that it would be; & he therefore declared that he would hold no more conversations with members of Congress on the subject.

It was understood that Mr Sargeant would introduce the Bill into the House. He then requested Mr. Ewing & myself, to see Mr Berrien & Mr Sergeant, &, not committing or pledging him, nor professing to speak by his authority, nevertheless to state what changes, from the last Bill, would in our opinion, lead him to sign the new Bill; & he pointed out those changes. They were, in effect to make a Bank of issues, deposite, & exchanges; without power of discounting promissory notes. And for such a Bank, he did not intimate that he <desired> requested the assent of the States.

This was in the morning, of the 18.

I took a carriage & came immediately to the Capitol, & saw Messrs. B. & S. <& told> suggested to them the provisions & modifications which I supposed would ensure the Presidents signature; & offered an hour for them to meet Mr Ewing in the P. M.

It is proper to say here, that while thus endeavoring to have the Bill altered to his mind, the President frequently expressed an earnest wish that the subject might be laid over till the next session.

Mr S. being about to introduce the Bill, the President wished me to get him a copy, before it was introduced. I did <not> so, went with it to him, & read [it] over with him.[2] Attention was of course most particularly drawn to the provision of the 16th. Art. of the 11th. Section of the Bill. To this he expressed no objection whatever. He made no mention of the necessity of State assent, to a Bank for carrying on Exchanges between the States. But he wished the title of the Bill, & the name of the Corporation altered. <I observed that that could easily be done.> Using a phrase very common with him, that names are things, he said he did not wish it to be called a Bank. I sat down at his table, <struck out B amended the Title> struck out Bank, & wrote the Title as it finally passed. He wished a reduction of Capital, from 30 millions to 20, or 15—prefering the latter—& he wished the <Bank> Corporation to be restrained from selling the U. S. Stocks, except in some emergency or by authority of Congress. And he suggested no other alteration whatever. I went immediately to my Lodgings on Capitol Hill, sent for Mr S. to the H. of R. & he came over—& showed him the proposed alterations. He copied the title, in his own hand writing, & afterwards told me that he reduced the Capital to 21. millions, instead of 20, for more comment & altera[t]ion.

The Bill <made progress in> was introduced into the House.

On friday, the 20th. the President became acquainted with Mr Botts letter. He came to the Department, & sat an hour, & complained very much of the ill-treatment which he recd. from Mr Botts & other Whigs. He appeared full of suspicion & resentment. I began to fear another Veto. He had the <day> 18 before requested both Mr Ewing & myself to give him our views, respectively, of the pending measure. I drew up a paper according[ly], (a copy is herewith marked B) & sent [it] to him, at 9 oclock, Monday morning, the 23. of Aug.[3] Before he had read a word of it, & notwithstanding what he <said> had said about holding no more conversations with members of Congress, on the same morning, viz. the 23, he saw Mr Chittenden & Mr Babcock, members from N. Y. & said to them that he would have his right [arm] cut off, & his left arm too, before he would sign the Bill then pending. These Gentlemen came to the Dept. & told me this, only a little while after my paper could have reached the Presidents Table. When I next saw him, that day, & the next, he was agitated & excited, & wished me to get the Whigs to put off the measure. I told him I could not ask one or two members to join their opponents, in postponing the measure, but if he wished me, as a member of his Cabinet, to make the suggestion to the Whigs generally, I would do so. Accordingly I spoke to such Whig members of the Senate as I saw, & on the 25 addressed to Messrs Bates & Choate the letter marked C.[4] The Bill had then passed the H. of R. & was before the Senate's Commee., & I caused this letter to be communicated to that Commee.

The Senate passed the Bill on the [3 September].

AD. DLC.
1. Not found.
2. See above, DW to John Tyler, August 20, [1841].

3. Not found.
4. See above, DW to Isaac Chapman Bates and Rufus Choate, August 25, 1841.

TO [SETH WESTON]

Washington
Jan: 5. 1842

Dear Sir—

Ice—kelp—cattle. These are things I wish to hear about, as well as to learn that you are all well. You must write once a week. I suppose you must have some leisure, as the Evenings are long, and you have probably done husking.

This is the right [time] of the moon to put up beef & pork. Give me particulars of the weight of the cattle, & pigs, & the amount put up. I expect the ox & cow were found to be good beef. Yrs   D Webster

We are all well. The young Daniel eats so much milk, we have been obliged to buy a cow.

Does Mr Seth Peterson catch any fish?

Is the ditching all done? Do the Buck's county chickens prosper? Has John Taylor sent down the cattle? Has he sent the turkeys?

ALS. NhHi. Published in PC, 2: 111–112.

FROM JOHN STUART SKINNER

Washington 9th Jany 1842

Private

Dear Sir

You are aware that an association has recently been formed here, at

Washington under the name of the "U.S. Agricultural Society" the general scope and purposes of which, may be readily perceived from the accompanying papers.[1] Within the range of these there are few objects more worthy of serious regard than the question, how far we may expect *Cotton* in the culture of which so much capital, and labour are embarked, to continue to be, as now, by far the most valuable of all our agricultural exports. All who have been at all mindful of our chief sources of national wealth must be aware that the nation which has heretofore been our best customer for this great staple of Southern industry, has been lately adopting measures to render her Cotton Manufactories independent of supplies of the raw material from this country. To what extent these measures have been pushed, and how far they are likely to succeed, has become a problem both political and agricultural of obvious and great importance.

Taking it for granted that all our diplomatic functionaries abroad, keep a vigilant eye upon, and carefully report the introduction and growth, in the Countries where they are stationed, of all branches of industry, which threaten to interfere with the long established pursuits of their own Countrymen; it may be that in the Archives of the State Department, there is information to show the actual and prospective results of the means taken to extend the growth of *Cotton in India*.[2] And hence Sir, I take the liberty of soliciting any such information for the use of the Board of Control of the U.S. Agricultural Society. Your well known partiality for rural pursuits, and your habits of observing the Agricultural Capabilities of different States and Countries, embolden me to ask you to grant for the use of our society copies of any communications, which may from time to time reach your Department, indicating danger of overthrow to any important branches of American Husbandry, or which may otherwise throw light upon objects in reference to which our Association has been formed.[3] With great respect Sir Your Obt. Servt.

J.S. Skinner
Cor: Sec. pro tem: U.S. Ag. Society

LS. NhHi.

1. Skinner enclosed a printed copy of the Constitution of the Agricultural Society of the United States. See mDW 21264.

2. The cotton manufacturing interests in Lancashire, England, had exerted pressure on the East India Company to improve the quality and quantity of cotton produced in India. Although other projects had been attempted in previous years, Skinner was probably referring to a scheme which originated in 1838 to entice American experts in cotton culture to go to India to promote the growth of American cotton varieties. Some ten American planters were recruited, despite great hostility within the Society. By 1840 the planters and their equipment had reached India, but the experiment was largely un-

successful. Seth Leacock and David
G. Mandelbaum, "A Nineteenth Cen-
tury Development Project in India:
The Cotton Improvement Program,"

*Economic Development and Cultural
Change*, 3 (July 1955): 338–341.
    3. DW's response to Skinner's re-
quest has not been found.

FROM DUFF GREEN

Paris 24th. January 1842.

Dear Sir

I take the liberty to refer you to letters which I send by the same packet
to the President, for my views in relation, to the present aspect of our
affairs with England.[1] Before I read the Correspondence with Mr Stevenson, & before I came here & examined the subject with the lights cast
upon it, by European Diplomacy—I was of opinion that England was
sincerely desirous of peace. But altho' I believe, that she sincerely desires
to accomplish her purpose by peace, if she can, I as sincerely believe,
that she has made up her mind to accomplish it by war, if it cannot be
done without war.

I take the liberty also to refer you to copies of letters which I enclose
to Mr. [Charles A.] Wickliffe,[2] that you may see what I have done towards
preparing the way for forcing England to recede, because she cannot go
forward, unless she is sustained by the public opinion of her own people,
and will hesitate to do so unless she is sustained by the public opinion of
Continental Europe.

Through the influence of Genl. [Lewis] Cass much has already been
done to arrest the current, which the british press had put in motion
against us[3]—but I hope to be able to do something more through the
french and german press, and at the suggestion of Dr. [Nathaniel] Niles
I will prepare an article for the Review "des deux mondes" in which I will
demonstrate, as I can, that the purpose of England is to render continental Europe dependant on her for the supply of the raw material for the
manufacture of Cotton, and that her war upon slavery is a war on our
commerce and manufactures—through our domestic institutions.[4]

No one is more sincerely desirous of preserving peace than I am, and
it is because I would preserve peace, that I would urge on you & every
friend of America, to prepare for war. We can gain nothing by conces-
sion. If you are firm, England must yield, or if she goes to war she must
forfeat her greatness. We will fight the battles of Europe. Almost every
European state will sympathise with us, they will all see, that we are
fighting their battles & that our trade & resources will increase, while England must lose her colonies.

If I am correct and, I am confident I am not mistaken, the war will be
on New England. This must be understood in New England & this fact

will unite our people. I have read the secretary's report on the issue of Exchequer bills.[5] I look on it as the ablest paper, to which the discussion on the currency has given rise.

I do not see how Mr. Clay or Mr. Calhoun can sustain themselves in opposing it. But the strongest argument in its favor is the strength it will give the government in time of war. We have all the elements of war within ourselves & the Exchequer bills will command them. The Bank of England rests upon the public credit. The Exchequer bills may be made convertable into six per cents or five per cents & we need not go abroad for a dollar.

I repeat that no opposition can resist this bill if the public can be made to realize the views of England. The purposes are so palpable & the intelligence of our people is such, that they cannot fail to see them.

Much, very much depends upon you. And I confidently hope, that babes, yet unborn, are to lisp your praise for the ability & firmness, with which I am sure you will assert & maintain the Interests of our common country.

Prepare for war. This is our only hope. I repeat if you desire peace, prepare for war.

The British government have one or two modes of maintaining their ascendency. One, is by a repeal of their corn laws & a general reduction of taxes, diminish the cost of production, so as to enable her manufactures to compete with us & other rival manufacturing states, the other is —by destroying slavery—to render it impossible for other manufacturing states to obtain the raw material, as cheaply as through her. She prefers the last mode & if she can accomplish it by negociation, she would much prefer to do so. She does not wish war for the sake of war—but she is prepared to accomplish it by war. If she finds that we are prepared for war & that there is cause to apprehend, that instead of rendering the European Continental states dependant on her through her colonies—there is great danger that her colonies will become independant of her, she will hesitate and may be compelled to fall back on the principles of free trade. She will in that event open her ports to our corn & having abandoned her warfare on our manufactures, will cease to annoy our domestic Institutions.

Rest assured that these suggestions are not fancy sketches. I give them to you, relying on your ability to make plain what I can clearly understand myself—but can not so forcibly impart to others.

By all means let our friends urge the fiscal agent as a war measure; and let every friend of the administration—speak out boldly and decidedly on the pressing necessity of preparing for war as the only means of preserving peace. Your obt. servt.   D. Green

LS copy. DLC. Published in Duff Green, *Facts and Suggestions, Biographical, Historical, Financial, and Political, Addressed to the People of the United States* (New York, 1866), pp. 150–152.

1. See, for example, Green to Tyler, January 24, 1842 in *Facts and Suggestions*, p. 152.

2. Not found.

3. Green was referring to Cass's *Examen de la question aujourd'hui pendante entre le gouvernement des Etats-Unis et celui de la Grande-Bretagne; concernant le droit de visite* (Paris, 1842), published in January.

4. Green's article, "England and America, Examination of the Causes and Probable Results of a War Between These Two Countries," appeared in *Le Commerce, Journal Politique et Littéraire*, March 4–30, 1842. Fletcher M. Green, "Duff Green, Militant Journalist of the Old School," *American Historical Review*, 52 (January 1947): 260.

5. For Walter Forward's report on the Board of Exchequer, see *Executive Documents*, 27th Cong., 2d sess., Serial 401, Document No. 20.

FROM JOHN WILSON

New Orleans
27th Jany 1842

Dear Sir

I am this day fifty two years of age. For the last twelve or fourteen years your position had been one of distinction & of much interest either for the weal or woe of this republic. The political scenes that have lately transpired <during this period> have only increased that interest which had been so long felt in any political act of yours. Your course had been so bold, so direct, and so consistant with itself as well as with the interest of the Country (so at least I thought) that I had generally adopted your view as models in the discussions of those most important questions which every one admits as of vital importance to our distressed (I had nearly said ruined) Country. As a Whig as well as a good citizen I had become more than proud of your power in debate and your consistancy in principle. In my limited sphere in Missouri I had long taken great pleasure in attempting to refute the false or unfair statements of your enemies; as also in making known to my neighbors the favourable impressions I had formed not only of your talents but of your integrity as a man as well as Politician and such had continued to be my course till about the time of the dissolution of the Whig Cabinet and with it (I fear) the dissolution of the Whig party & the further consequences of which I also fear will be to continue for a long time to come the distructive measures so signally condemned by the people in the election of General Harrison. At the time alluded to I stated to you before the disolution that I hoped the Cabinet would hold on as long as they might with honor to themselves & benefit to the Country and that if *any* could not remain, that *all* would retire; as they came in: *together*. You will well remember

that after the retireing Secretaries had resigned I called on you under
some degree of excitement or at all events much concerned at the then
state of things and although it was perhaps roughly and awkwardly done
yet my opinions were anxiously & fully expressed; that whatever might
be the pro & con. opinions as to the propriety or not of those resignations
<yet I told you> I was exceedingly sorry you had not also resigned and
further stated <to you> it as my opinion that among friends of the same
political party aiming at the same fundamental end, and in inforcing the
great principles essential to the interests of the country that in the choice
of legitimate and honorable means to accomplish purposes so essential;
that majorities ought to govern & that as the others had been compelled
from a sense of duty to resign that you ought also to have resigned. Your
immediate answer was that no such rule should govern you. I then told
you that my opinion was you were a ruined man that your act had powerfully added to those things already manifestly foreshadowing speedy
dissolution of the Whig party and consequently would have a large
agency in postponing if not intirely defeating those measures calculated
to curb the exhausting evils under which our Country was suffering from
malpractices of the late dominant party. I further stated to you that I was
extremely sorry that you had used that unfortunate expression in your
letter in relation to the resignation of your fellows "That you saw no
cause for their resignation" (This is the substance of that expression I
quote now from memory)[1] and I then suggested the propriety of your
openly disclaiming the construction which was most generally given to
it; this latter you refused rather positively, but explained to me that you
only meant that you saw no cause to induce *you* to resign in the circumstances that had happened & then in an earnest manner assured me you
held on with a view to the good of the country & to keep the President
from going over to the Locofocos & pledged yourself in the most solemn
manner that at the coming session of Congress the President would propose a United States Bank that would be better than any of the propositions on that subject which had been discussed at the special session
and added in a confident tone that every good Whig would be satisfied
with it. I expressed to you the excitement that I thought was felt in the
country on the subject while you gave me every assurance that in your
opinion that would soon abate. Your published letter had given pledges
similar to some of those I have alluded to above. I also heard of your giving such to others. These so given & published my strong faith in your
integrity—a full knowledge that no man better understood or had more
elaborately shewn the necessity for a national Bank than you or that had
shewn himself more anxious for its establishment—all taken together
made me feel ashamed of the distrust of your motives which others had
so freely began to impugn & (to tell you the truth) to which I was be-

ginning to lend an unwilling ear, & therefore I resolved once more to trust him whom on so many thousands of occasions I had held up to my neighbors & others as a pattern of political integrity & left your Room the last time I was there determined to trust yet once more to the flint which in all the disastres of a 12 years war, had never missed fire. How could I have done less. I honestly believed that without a national Bank founded on solid capital, managed honestly free from executive dictation as well as independent of political experiments could alone restore the country from the parallasis into which it had evidently been thrown by the but too successful executive attempts to clutch within its unholy grasp the whole power of the country and not only to ride rough shod over the settled laws & tried institutions of the land but also over the popular will of a free people. I dreaded no misfortune so much; that so far as I could foresee was likely to take place; as a government Bank founded on government revinue & credit & managed under <executive> the direction of every successful political party, which I knew to be a favourite wish with many of those with whom we both had long done battle. These being my fears, views, & wishes, could I distrust the author of the following pointed & eloquent remarks made in the great metropolis of the union before thousands of the most intelligent of the people not yet four years ago especially too <when> as no declaration of a change had escaped the author. <& who after added> In speaking of general Jacksons change of position shortly after his first election you used these words in your speech at Niblos Garden in New York on the 19th. of March 1837. "But, gentlemen, nine months wrought a wonderful change. New lights broke forth before these months rolled away; and, the President, in his message to Congress in Dec. 1829, held very different <language purposes> language & manifested very different purposes. Although the Bank had five or six years of its charter unexpired, he yet called the attention of Congress very pointedly to the subject and declared:

"1 That the constitutionality of the Bank was well doubted by many.

"2 That its utility or expediency was also well doubted.

"3 That all must admit that it had failed in undertaking to establish or maintain a sound & uniform currency; and 4 that the true Bank for the use of the government of the United States would be a Bank which should be founded on the revinues & credit of the government itself. *These* propositions appeared to me, at the time, as very extraordinary, and the *last one as very startling.* A Bank, founded on the revinue & credit of the government, and managed and administered by the executive, was a conception which I had supposed no man, holding the chief executive power in his own hands, would venture to put forth."[2]

These were then your views and I had every reason to believe were still your opinions at the period of our last conference. I at once resolved

to wait & see what <control> your influence would effect—to see what
control *mind* could exercise over *matter*—integrity and firmness of purpose over stupid idolatry towards old & silly opinions at the same time
supposing that any original purpose <of honesty> of political <pur-
pose> honesty which might have been entertained by the president had
given way to the insideous temptation to perpetuate a power which a
melancholly dispensation of providence and not the voice of the people:
had conferred.

But what am I told now; not only that you approve of the Presidents
late recommendation of a government Bank founded on the revenues &
credit of the government; but that you are the author of the secretarys
report sent to Congress as the plan in detail shadowed forth in the
Message!!!3

I have stated my age in the onset of this letter to show you that it is
not likely that this is the production [of] the hasty & intolerent waward-
ness of youth. I have stated the circumstances that gave rise to; and continued; after others had doubted, my confidence in your integrity. I have
stated some of our last conversations to bring them to your recollection
while at the same time I have declared to you what was my then honest
resolve in relation to yourself and now add that it is my habit neither to
flatter a person who is present or to speak ills of one absent which I
would not say to his face on a proper occasion. I am therefore candid in
saying your present position before the country (it seems to me) requires
in justice to yourself, explanation. But be that as it may I think I have
the right which may justify a devoted friend of long standing to seek at
your hands an explanation, *at least*, of the difference between the government Bank so <recommended> proposed by General Jackson <as>
which in the extract of your Speech above given <& which> you then
thought "very startling" and the one lately proposed by the President, with
which it is triumphantly said by *some* of his friends you are intirely satisfied. Or if there is no difference then I earnestly desire to know the
whys and wherefores of the change of your mind to be in favor of a
proposition which in 1829 and at Niblos in 1837 you thought "so very extraordinary." Does it pass the rights of a long devoted friend to enquire
why an opinion so long held & so ably & so ardently maintained has
been changed for one which seems to me to be in the very teeth of all
former professions? It cannot be that it is. I ask this it may be not in a
polished manner but yet with a plain & candid intention of gaining from
you an explanation of those things which it seems to me none could be
expected to explain but yourself & things too which have caused thousands of your former devoted friends; as well as myself, to doubt <of>
the purity of your motives. I give you my most solemn asseveration that

the application is not made with a view of wounding your feelings with a recital of circumstances which however unpleasant, seem to me to call for explanation and I trust you will not consider me to have diserted my old file leader intirely till he is called and has a chance to answer for himself who certainly has rendered much service to the country in the able and ardent advocacy he has given in favour of its tried institutions and against legislative experiments & executive dictation. It were however just to myself; & courteous to you to say, that I fully believe my convertion to the doctrine of a "government Bank founded on the revinues & credit of the government" Will be exceedingly slow, but if once accomplished my support to the measure will be none the less ardent & sincere. I now add that these are the candid views of the mind of one fully anxious to do justice to <one whom> him whom he had long considered to have boldly stood forward as the champion not only of private but political honesty in the circumstances I have recited that mind has already hesitated to go forward in its wonted career, and now looks anxiously for propelling reasons from the pen of him who has so often given a noon day light to a subject which ere the touch of his power seemed to be enveloped in the mists of the morn or beclouded in the <twilight> hazy twilight of the waneing day. I trust I shall soon receive your answer.[4] Your obt. servt.   John Wilson

ALS. NhHi. Wilson (1790–1877), a native of Fayette, Missouri, and a lawyer, was an uncompromising Whig. Former editor of the *Missouri Intelligencer*, he had run an unsuccessful campaign for Congress in 1838.

1. See above, DW to Gales and Seaton, September 13, 1841.

2. For DW's speech at Niblo's Saloon, see *Speeches and Formal Writings*, 2.

3. Wilson was alluding to the Exchequer Bill. For Forward's report, see *Executive Documents*, 27th Cong., 2d sess., Serial 401, Document No. 20.

4. For DW's response, see DW to John Wilson, February 9, 1842, below.

TO EDWARD EVERETT

Feby. 7th. 1842.

Private

My dear Sir:

I send you eight copies of a pamphlet written by D[aniel] B[ryant] Tallmadge, one of the judges of the Superior Court of the City of New York,[1] reviewing the opinion of Judge [Esek] Cowen,[2] in McLeod's case. You will see that very eminent persons have expressed their entire concurrence in the opinions expressed by Judge Tallmadge.

I should be glad if a copy of the pamphlet could be placed in the hand of Sir Robert Peel, as I have understood that he remarked to Mr. Stevenson, about the time of the departure of that gentleman from London, that "his confidence in Mr. Webster's opinions, as to the law of McLeod's case, was a good deal shaken by learning that Chancellor [James] Kent had expressed opposite sentiments."

You will naturally send a copy to Lord Aberdeen; and please send another to Mr. [Nassau William] Senior;[3] and dispose of the rest at your discretion. Yrs. faithfully,   Danl Webster

LS. MHi.

1. Tallmadge (1793–1847). His pamphlet, *Review of the opinion of Judge Cowen, of the Supreme court of the state of New-York, in the case of Alexander McLeod*, had been published simultaneously in New York and Washington in 1841.

2. Cowen (1787–1844), formerly New York Supreme Court reporter and judge of the fourth circuit, had become associate justice of the New York Supreme Court in 1836.

3. Senior (1790–1864), an economist and barrister, was master in chancery, 1836–1855. *DNB*.

TO JOHN WILSON

Washington
Feb. 9. 1842

Dear Sir

I have recd your letter of the 29th [27th] of January.[1] While I very much lament that you do not approve of recent steps, taken here, in regard to the important subjects of currency & finance, I have no right to complain, nor would I desire you to withhold your opinions, however they may differ from mine. The state of the country is known to us all; we all know the failure, thus far, of all attempts at relief; & yet, for one, I have not thought it a part of duty to give up hope, or relax all effort. I certainly concurred, in the President's recommendation of the plan now before Congress;[2] & this you think inconsistent with former opinions of mine. On this part of your letter, I will say a word or two. Genl Jackson's proposition, so far as it was stated by him, was for a *Bank*, founded on the credit & revenues of the Govt, & to carry on the *common business* of a Bank; that is to say, it was to be a Bank of *Loans & Discounts*.

Now, the plan suggested by the President proposes no *loans*, no *discounts*, in the way of common Bank operations. It seeks to help the country, by furnishing Exchange, as far as its means, & a due regard to safety, will allow. And beyond this, it refrains from all loans or advances to individuals. This distinction appears to me to be very broad & clear.

I cannot help hoping, on the whole, that you will come to the conclusion that the plan before Congress is the most likely to be useful to the Country, of anything that can now be suggested. Yrs respectfully
                                              Danl Webster

ALS copy. NhHi. Published in Van
Tyne, p. 255.

1. See above.
2. The Exchequer Bank.

*Shortly after he took office, Webster secured for Isaac Rand Jackson an
appointment as chargé d'affaires to Denmark, and Jackson obligingly
loaned money for the down payment on the secretary's Lafayette Square
residence. (See* Diplomatic Papers, 1.) *To Webster's critics, this was a
blatant "sale" of public office. So too was the appointment of Washington Irving as American minister to Spain, for quickly thereafter a considerable acreage of western lands held as collateral by Moses Hicks
Grinnell, Samuel B. Ruggles, and Richard M. Blatchford reverted to Webster with clear title, just in time to be deeded to the Bank of the United
States of Pennsylvania as part of his debt settlement. Grinnell engineered
the transfer, as the letter below discloses, and Grinnell was Irving's
brother-in-law. The rumormongers were by no means content, however,
with the "sale" of public office. Webster was publicly accused of lechery,
accepting a bribe, and general misuse of public office and trust. All these
reports, Webster contended, were politically inspired, designed to drive
him from the cabinet. These matters are the subject of the letters in February, March, and early April, below.*

FROM MOSES HICKS GRINNELL

Thursday 3, o'clock
[February 10, 1842]

Private

My Dear Sir

Many thanks, my dear Sir, for your note of the 8th inst.[1] We are all
highly delighted at the nomination of Mr. [Washington] Irving.[2] He is in
town, and has seen your note to me. You know that he is a quiet man,
says but little, yet feels much. He has been taken by surprise, for he had
given up all idea of accepting any thing. Coming however as this does, he
will accept, and forever feel under a deep sense of obligation *to you*—
and now my dear friend, permit me to say, that you have gratified me
beyond measure. Yes, I am happy, and *you* have the thanks of my whole
heart for this generous act of yours.

[Richard M.] Blatchford has got the Deeds all made out, and they are
under [Samuel B.] Ruggles examination.[3] I hope to visit [Washington]
before this month is out. Believe me your Friend   M. H. Grinnell

ALS. MHi.
1. Not found.
2. Tyler had nominated Irving as
minister to Spain on February 8. The
Senate confirmed the appointment on
February 10. *Journal of the Executive
Proceedings of the Senate . . .*
(Washington, 1887), 6: 25.

3. For most of the deed transfers, 11, 1842.
see the Calendar entries of February

FROM THEODORE FRELINGHUYSEN

New York, February 11, 1842

My Dear Sir:

I write to sympathize with your outraged feelings, in the atrocious calumny that has vainly assailed your reputation.[1] It evinces a reach of malignancy that I could hardly have believed it possible to find in our country; but there is a breaking forth of evil in the midst of us, and all over the land, that makes me tremble for our dearest interests. What will become of us if God do not interpose and arrest this lawless and impious daring and violence? My honored friend, this recent blow at your good name is an impressive lesson of what this world is worth—what it is "to trust in man and make flesh our arm." I pray God that your heart may rightly improve it in this respect. You have thirsted for the world's good-will too ardently, I fear, and God now shows you how frail and unworthy of your confidence it is. And what can it do for us in a dying hour? What can it avail us at the judgment-seat? We shall meet then, my dear sir— oh let it be to rejoice together in the redeeming grace of Him that loved us and washed us from our sins in His own blood. I know you will not charge this note to any but the kindest feelings of sincere and anxious solicitude for your eternal welfare. Death has lately been among my friends with sudden visitations, and my mind feels something of the solemnity that should impress us at all times, and, under this feeling, I have written as the heart prompted; and, with best wishes and prayers, Remain very truly yours, Theo. Frelinghuysen.

Text from Curtis, 2: 129. Original not found.

1. Frelinghuysen was alluding to a report carried in the *Louisville Daily Journal* in January 1842 that DW had assaulted the wife of one of the clerks in the State Department when she had applied for a position as a transcriber. The rumor was of course immediately denied by Webster, by various clerks in the Department, by other newspapers, and eventually also by its perpetrator, the *Louisville Daily Journal*. See that paper for January 25 and February 14, 1842, and the New York *Evening Post*, February 10, 1842.

FROM GOUVERNEUR KEMBLE

New York 11 Feby 1842.

Private

Dear Sir,

I was hurried off from Washington by letters from home so suddenly, that I had not an opportunity of seeing you before my departure. The result of all my enquiries both here and at Washington is, that the Bill for the distribution of the proceeds of the public lands must be repealed, and the lands pledged for the payment of the principal and interest of the public debt; until this is done, I think you will neither be able to pass the proposed tariff law, nor to raise money by Loan.[1] You can hardly expect that the Democratic party in Congress, will abandon the vantage ground which they possess in consequence of this law; and after the late defalcations of the States, capitalists, neither in this country, nor in Europe, will Loan of the Government, unless there be some portion of the revenue specially pledged for the payment of the interest. I have letters myself and have seen others from Europe, confirmatory of this opinion.

I am very glad to see that you have thought of my old friend Washg. Irving, but hope that you will restore the rank of the mission, without which, I doubt if he will accept it.[2] I remain with great respect Yours truly   Gouv Kemble

ALS. NhHi.
1. Kemble's suggestion on the tariff and distribution coincided with Tyler's views. After a veto of a provisional tariff bill which included distribution, Tyler signed a higher tariff bill without a distribution rider on August 30, 1842. 5 *U.S. Statutes at Large* 548–567.

2. Until 1839 the United States mission at Madrid had been headed by a minister plenipotentiary, but in 1840 the office had been reduced to the level of chargé d'affaires. With Irving's appointment, the post was restored to its earlier ministerial status.

TO EDWARD CURTIS

Washington
Feb. 24. '42.

Dear Sir,

I have no idea of what the letter writers mean by what they say; only, that I believe they mean to say any thing likely to be read. I never wrote a disrespectful word of the President, in any letter—never mentioned Robt Tyler, in any letter—& every body is at liberty to publish any letter from me, in which he says there is language disrespectful to the President.[1]

Mr Clay's friends are making a great struggle. We shall see what will be the result. His friends are determined, by any means, & at all events, to drive me out of the Cabinet. Let them try that, to their hearts' content.[2]

The "Creole" paper is well recd—& there are those who knash their teeth, at that *fact*.[3]

Mr C[lay] as you observe—did not see the propriety of printing any extra number.[4] Yrs   D. W.

I am willing to recommend Mr [John Lorimer] Graham, if that is be[st?].[5]

ALS. NN. Endorsed "Private."

1. The reports had been publicly circulated and denied that George Poindexter had obtained a copy of a letter from DW to Curtis in which Webster wrote disparagingly of the President and his eldest son and private secretary, Robert Tyler (1818–1877). *New York Evening Post*, February 22, 1842. The alleged letter has not been found.

2. The context in which DW alludes to Clay's friends and to Poindexter in this letter strongly suggests that he saw Poindexter's investigation of the affairs of the New York customs office as politically motivated. See "Report of George Poindexter, Chairman of the Commissioners Appointed to Investigate the Affairs of the New York Custom-House . . ." in *Reports of Committees*, 27th Cong., 2d sess., Serial 409, Report No. 669, pp. 293–297.

3. DW's " 'Creole' paper" was his instruction to Edward Everett of January 29, 1842, which had been submitted to the Senate on February 21 and ordered to be printed on February 23. See *Senate Documents*, 27th Cong., 2d sess., Serial 397, Document No. 137; and *Diplomatic Papers*, 1.

4. Clay had requested that the Senate resolution calling for the printing of 1,000 extra copies of DW's " 'Creole' paper" be referred to the Committee on Printing, in which the Senate concurred. The Committee on Printing recommended and the Senate approved the extra printing on February 23. *Congressional Globe*, 27th Cong., 2d sess., p. 256; *Senate Journal*, 27th Cong., 2d sess., Serial 394, p. 185.

5. To replace John I. Coddington, removed, President Tyler nominated Graham (1797–1897), a New York lawyer, for deputy-postmaster of New York on March 8. The Senate confirmed the appointment five days later.

FROM WILLIAM WOLCOTT ELLSWORTH

Hartford Feby 28th. 1842

Dear Sir

I intended, long since, to have written you, how much I believe the country is indebted to you for remaining at your present post; and I hope and trust nothing will occur to make it necessary or proper for you to abandon it. Although among our Whig friends, here, there was a desire to have an old fashion bank, this expectation has long since been abandoned and we are now ardently desireous of seeing the bill reported by Mr [Nathaniel P.] Talma[d]ge to the Senate, *carried into effect*.[1] This is the general wish among the whigs in Con[necticu]t, so far as I can learn. They will give the trial a sincere cooperation if Congress will allow them the opportunity. Our most esteemed friend, Senator [Jabez W.] Huntington, in his opposition to the Exchequer, I must think, greatly mistook the sentiments of his constituents, for I have not heard one, or seen a single newspaper that coincided with him, in this State.

The Whig party, here, will maintain their ground, as we believe, fully. The abolitionists will take some from both parties, but I think not many. The conservatives have set up a clear ticket, but their number is small, most of them are locos and not a few of them have desired to join that party, openly. We are glad they fight under their own flag; they are made up of discontented office seekers & now as they show their hand we do not fear them. They profess to be the pure friends of the Gen Administration & presume to declare that the Whigs are hostile to the Adminis-[tratio]n. All this is untrue. There are but *two parties in Govt* and there *can be but two.* The Whigs will sustain the administration, but the locos will not & ere long the conservatives will be absorbed in the latter whatever papers & talk they may show to the contrary. We are anxious that our friends at Washington should know how matters are in Con[necticu]t, & be aware of the sinister efforts made & to be made to induce the belief that a new party can be got up here of peculiar friendship for the administration. The Whigs only expect or intend to sustain you. The Patriot & Eagle, a paper published in this City & regularly sent to the President, is edited & supported by men who were [and] have been, if they are not all of them, now, *opposed to the Whigs.* They groaned over the nomination of Gen Harrison & wanted Scott or Clay, and now constantly accuse the Whigs of an opposition to the administration which is wholly false. I believe our delegation in Congress will all of them, unless it be Mr Huntington, vote for the proposed exchequer, & certain I am that this is the general if not universal wish among the Whigs in Govt.

I do most ardently hope Congress will pass the bill of Mr Talma[d]ge. Something *must* be done. State Banks, in the South & West are nearly gone, & what, I ask what can be done if Congress will not interpose. The alternative, is, a specie currency and the exc[h]equer. The first is impossible, the latter is possible, easily obtained &, I believe will relieve the country immensely. With sentiments of Sincere Respect Your Huble Servt

Wm. W Ellsworth

ALS. NhD. Endorsed: "for the President's perusal—Letter from Govr. Ellsworth."

1. The Exchequer Bill. Neither the House of Representatives nor the Senate gave the bill serious consideration. In the session of 1841–1842, the House tabled the measure, and the succeeding session voted it down.

TO [EDWARD CURTIS?]

Saturday Eve' 9 O clock
[February–March? 1842]

Dr Sir

I have recd your note to F[letcher] of last Evening.[1] A letter written this morning[2] gives you what [Robert?] Walker[3] says. *Your* questions were put to him, & he answered them exactly as you could wish. The President thinks your case perfectly strong, so far. All these papers (copies) will go to Poins—but Poins *declines to be prosecutor.* I foresee he will back out.[4]

The Madisonian of Monday shall have such an article as you describe.[5]

Charles King has lost his head, as well as his good feelings. His article of last Evening is all trash. He feels it to be so himself, and talks, therefore, abt. having more to say—when he has nothing to say.

As to Poins being closeted with the President, it is all humbug. He called, but the P. wd not talk abt. his report. Some things indicate a conviction that he may as well be more moderate. I think he feels "headed."[6]

The doctrines of the "Creole" are sound, which is better than to say they are popular. But all Lawyers—all courts, and all the South go for them. Yrs   D. W.

ALS. NN.

1. Not found.

2. Not found.

3. Walker, an Englishman, was an importer of cloth in New York. He had probably been called before Poindexter's committee in the course of its investigation into the New York custom house affairs.

4. Contrary to DW's suggestion,

Poindexter leveled serious charges against Curtis in his report. For the report, see Serial 409, Report No. 669.

5. The article in the Washington *Madisonian* has not been identified.

6. For part of Poindexter's and Tyler's correspondence relating to the investigation, see Serial 409, Report No. 669, pp. 275–297, *passim.*

TO EDWARD CURTIS

Monday Morning
[February–March? 1842]

Private

Dear Sir

I should be willing eno. that Mr Chs King should see the letter I wrote you on Saturday Morning,[1] or, by some accident, become acquainted with a part of its contents.

My reason is, that as I must immediately give directions for no longer sending his Paper abroad, & wish him and his friends to know the true reason. He not only insults me, personally, by saying I have advanced a claim which *I know* to be unfounded, but he takes the side of England, in a matter which he sees is to be very shortly the subject of negotiation between the two Govts. Nothing exceeds my astonishment, at the infatuation of his conduct. Yrs   D. W.

ALS. NN.

1. Not found.

FROM JOHN MCLEAN

29 March 1842

My dear Sir,

Will you give such a direction to the enclosed letter,[1] as shall be most likely to promote my object in writing it.

I have just returned from my Circuit, and I am happy to say that with the considerate and intelligent men with whom I have conversed, your position is better understood than it was some months ago. And if you shall be able to adjust, amicably, our differences with England; in the good done to your Country, you will be more than compensated for the vindictive assaults which have been made upon you.

On your own account, as well as an account of the Country, your friends feel an intense anxiety for your success in your present negotiations. Very truly yours   John McLean

ALS. DLC. Endorsed *"Private."*
1. Not found.

FROM EDWARD EVERETT

London 30 March 1842

(*Private & Confidential*)
My dear Sir,

I had hoped by this packet to have been able to propose some one to you as my secretary, but it is still out of my power to do so definitively. The Office in fact requires a union of qualities not often to be met with. It is a very laborious Office. Mr. [Robert Howe] Gould[1] who is now performing its duties passes five hours daily at his desk, and a few days before the steamers sail has to take home papers to his lodgings to be copied. And yet I spare him all the labor of drafting. All that he has done in that way would not occupy two hours for the last three months. Neither do I call upon him to do out-doors commissions. He is employed five hours daily in writing. To turn off this amount of writing decently, a good hand is absolutely necessary. It would be better that he should belong to the middle or southern states, & highly desirable that the Secretary should have sufficient age, discretion, & capacity for business occasionally to give me something besides mechanical aid; & not less so that he should be a person who would reflect credit on the legation, by being connected with it. The relation between the Secretary and the Minister is so near and intimate that there ought also to be a personal regard existing between them. I must say I have not yet found an individual who unites even the most essential of these conditions. I thought at one time of proposing my nephew N[athan] Hale jun,[2] who in some respects would be all I could wish, but I thought for several reasons it was best to go out of Massachusetts & even New England;—and I really doubt whether it would be true friendship to the young man, to take him away from the profession, by which he is to live. I thought of Mr [George Henry] Calvert —son of the late Mr [George] C. of Bladensburg[3]—but he is a valetudinarian, whom it would assassinate to plant at a desk five hours a day. He has no political claims on us; neither, I think, has his state, which already has Mr [Daniel] Jenifer, Mr [Virgil] Maxcy, Mr Hughes & Commodore [David] Porter in the diplomatic service. I should have preferred a young man from the South, if the proper person could be found. Mr Rives I am told has a very promising son but young.[4] Genl [Abraham] Eustis, who hails I believe from Carolina, had some very fine sons, who were exceedingly industrious and exemplary at college; but I do not know them personally.[5] The locality would be good. There is here a very excellent young man, Mr J[ohn] R[omeyn] Brodhead of Newyork, now employed as agent to obtain copies of historical documents for that State. He is a nephew of Mr [Harmanus] Bleecker now at the Hague. His political principles are sound. He is in all respects a very eligible person for the Office if you are willing to go as far North. He writes an excellent hand. Is laborious, methodical, & conscientious in his work, of pleasing appearance & manners, and unblemished character. There is also at Paris, expected here soon, Mr Alexander Van Rensselaer, a son of the late patroon. Whether he would accept the Office I do not know. His brother Philip,[6] some years ago, declined a similar appointment, offered him by Mr Van Buren. He writes but a tolerable hand;—but if he chose to take the Office, and employ a clerk to do a considerable part of the writing, it would not be a bad arrangement, in reference to the public business, & quite eligible in other respects. It would be entirely agreeable to me to have either of the two last named gentlemen. If you prefer some other candidate at home, I hope you will do me the favor to name him to me, before you give him encouragement.[7]

You understand me *not* to wish the appointment of Mr. Gould, who is now employed in the Office.

It may be satisfactory to you to know a little more distinctly, how it becomes necessary to have so much writing done. When a note is to be addressed to Lord Aberdeen it is drafted by me. This draft must be copied to be sent to Lord A. It must be copied into the letter book of the legation, and a third copy must be prepared for Washington. All this is absolutely necessary, and you perceive from the quantity that comes to Washington how much writing it implies. Of the despatches to you one copy of course is needed but two copies of my draft must still be made, one to be despatched & one retained. Notes from this government are copied into a book & the originals sent to you. I prefer this, by the way, to the former practice of filing the original & sending a copy home. It is immaterial to you whether you have the originals or copies to bind up, & much better here to have a copy in a bound book, than loose originals. One copy of all notes from this Government to me; two copies of all despatches to you, & three of all notes from me to the British Government are therefore absolutely necessary. I have deemed myself authorized for my personal security hereafter, if occasion should arise, to have a copy of all the notes addressed to me by this Government or by me to this government, made for myself; and this is the only service at all personal rendered me by the Secretary. I carry on myself a very voluminous & oppressive correspondence, in which I derive no aid from the Secretary's pen: —So that I pass ten hours at my desk for his five. I mention this only that you need not think I want a man of industry to do my private work.

My office is certainly laborious, but that is no objection to me. The expense is horrid: I am spending far beyond my salary, and yet plaguing myself and all around me with paltry economies! We receive much social kindness. Wherever I go, I hear of you, what it is most pleasant to me to hear, as an American and as your friend. Your retirement from Office would be deemed here a national disaster. That it is frequently said to me that it is a fortunate circumstance that I am here, I ascribe to the fact, that it is taken for granted that I possess your confidence. I dare not write all that has been said to me, on the possible consequences which might have resulted from things going on without a change, in this legation. Anecdotes are daily told me of the indiscretions that were committed, of the coarseness, vulgarity, and profanity of the language used on the most important subjects, which I could not believe, but for the credibility of my sources of information.

Pray let me hear from you how things are going on, if you have ever such a thing as a spare moment, which however I know before hand you have not.

This, of course, is for yourself. To prevent its being hastily shuffled up with other papers, I have given it its running title. Ever yours most faithfully

AL. MHi.

1. Gould, otherwise unidentified, served as interim secretary to the United States legation in London following the resignation of Benjamin Rush and previous to the appointment of Francis Robert Rives.

2. Hale (1818–1871; Harvard 1838) studied law and was admitted to the bar, but like his father he devoted most of his life to journalism.

3. The great grandson and the grandson, respectively, of the fifth Lord Baltimore.

4. William C. Rives's son, Francis

Robert (1822–1891; Virginia 1840), was confirmed as secretary to the London legation on August 24, 1842, and served until 1845, when he returned to New York to practice law.

5. Eustis (1786–1843; Harvard 1804), was a veteran of the War of 1812, the Black Hawk War, and the Seminole War. Everett was most likely alluding to his son, Henry Lawrence Eustis.

6. Alexander and Philip were two of Stephen Van Rensselaer's nine children by his second marriage.

7. To Everett's dismay, Rives re-

ceived the appointment without further consultation with Everett. See Everett to DW, August 3, 1842, and DW to Everett, August 25, 1842, below; and Everett to DW, September 16, 1842, mDW 23429.

FROM JOHN TYLER

March 31 [1842]

My Dear Sir:

I return you Mr. Ketchums letter,[1] and cannot feel otherwise than mortified at the disappointments which he expresses. And yet I am in no way to blame, having made but two appointments in the City of New York viz. the Marshall and P. Master.[2] You know the circumstances attendant upon each. For Mr. K. and his opinions I feel the highest respect—and he will not find me reluctant to manifest this by acts. But there are often difficulties in the way of meeting the wishes of our best friends. Now here is a case in point. Both of us would be gratified to meet Mr. Irvine's wishes, and yet we cannot do so without disappointing most sadly others of our friends.[3]

Should not your own wishes prevail over me in the matter and ought Mr. Irvine to complain—I think not.

Whether he shall or not I cannot help it, and shall always be found ready to sanction your selection for office when the clearest views of policy do not obviously conflict.

I return Mr K.s letter. Truly yrs   J Tyler

ALS. DLC.
1. Not found.
2. Tyler had nominated Silas M. Stilwell for marshal on June 17, 1841, and John L. Graham for deputy

postmaster on March 8, 1842. The Senate subsequently confirmed both.
3. Neither Irvine nor the post Ketchum sought for him have been identified.

Webster's chronic financial distress made him an easy target for rumor and innuendo. One of the more blatant examples—that he had accepted a bribe—circulated in Washington just as Lord Ashburton arrived to discuss the northeastern boundary. Webster was said to be heavily indebted to New Hampshire Governor Henry Hubbard for western lands and the rumor had it that he was about to be hauled into court for nonpayment. Whereupon, the story went, he accepted money from Alexander Powell in exchange for the appointment as consul to Brazil and applied these funds to his Hubbard debt.

Webster discovered that the rumor started with Henry H. Sylvester, Hubbard's brother-in-law and chief clerk in the Pension Office. When he heard the story, Webster asked Secretary of War Spencer to dismiss Sylvester, and Spencer complied. Sylvester's abrupt dismissal provoked

*a congressional investigation, a parade of the charges, and a mild rebuke
of Webster and Spencer for their action. The gossip surrounding the
Powell appointment led President Tyler to revoke it, even after Senate
confirmation. In response to the House investigation, Webster wrote
Cushing a letter (which Cushing requested to be published) and attempted to clarify the matter.*

*The evidence is strong, and is attested by the letter to Cushing, that
Webster did not pay Hubbard anything while the gossip was being circulated. Instead, he and Hubbard's attorney, Henry Morfitt, reached an
agreement whereby Webster would make a payment to Hubbard in December (See DW to Spencer, April 5, 1842; DW to Cushing, August 8,
1842; and DW to Hubbard, December 8, 1842, below. See also Memorandum of DW's account with Henry Hubbard, kept by Morfitt, NhD).*

TO JOHN CANFIELD SPENCER

April 5. 1842

My Dear Sir,

I have to state to you, that Henry H. Sylvester, a clerk in [the] Office
of Commission[er] of Pensions, said yesterday, publicly, in the hearing
of respectable persons, that "he had no doubt that Mr Webster had recd
a bribe for Alexander Powell's appointment as consul."

As I undertake to vouch for the full & exact truth of this, I doubt not
you will see what treatment the case requires at your hands. Yrs truly

Danl Webster

ALS. NhHi.

*When the Whigs took office in 1841, the United States and Great Britain
were at the brink of war. Two issues—the northeastern boundary, and
the question of responsibility for the* Caroline *incident—threatened to
drag them into armed conflict.*

*But political changes in 1841 promised hope for the peaceful resolu-
tion of their differences. In England, the conservative Melbourne ministry
was succeeded by a liberal government formed by Sir Robert Peel, and
the conciliatory Aberdeen replaced the bellicose Palmerston in the Foreign Office. In the United States, a similar development came with the
Whig ascendancy, and particularly with Webster, an Anglophile, replac-
ing John Forsyth, an Anglophobe, as secretary of state. When the Peel
ministry named Lord Ashburton, a personal friend of Webster, as negotiator to Washington, hope for peace brightened.*

*Alexander McLeod's acquittal in New York in October 1841 eliminated
the major obstacle to the commencement of the negotiations, and in
early April 1842, Webster and Ashburton sat down in Washington to*

discuss the differences between the two countries. In some four months the two "friendly negotiators" reached an agreement on the northeastern boundary and other issues. Maine and Massachusetts accepted the boundary compromise, mainly because of the success of Webster and F. O. J. Smith (see letter below) in using the secret service fund, generally employed in foreign intercourse, to promote domestic support for the treaty. On August 20, the Senate ratified it. Much of Webster's correspondence between April and August 1842, below, concerns the Webster-Ashburton negotiations. A fuller discussion appears in Diplomatic Papers, *1.*

FROM FRANCIS ORMAND JONATHAN SMITH

Portland April 16– '42

Dr Sir,

In my letter to you of the 13th inst.[1] you will find explained the motives influencing the omission of the Legislature of this State to act on the Boundary at its late session.

In reply to your favor of the 10th,[2] I am happy to say, that I have had an interview with Mr. [John] Anderson, & he has had one with the Governor, & several political friends of the latter, & the subject of your communication to the Governor was discussed.[3] Mr. Anderson urged, *and will re-urge*, in the most decided and emphatic manner, upon the Governor, & his friends, a special session of the Legislature. The Governor's party are being divided in regard to him, & he therefore is timid tho' inclined, Mr. A. informs me to the propriety of an extra session. Some of his party oppose it on the grounds that the *Whig party* will turn it to political account. But to meet this apprehension, I have written an article which will appear editorially in the Portland Advertiser of Monday next,[4] which Mr. Anderson feels confident will settle the objection they pressed upon the Governor. I have no doubt that he will convene the Legislature as early as needed, after he shall see a supporting manifestation from the Whig Journals of the State—and that he will have without delay. Allow me to say, that any suggestions you may make for action in this session I will see promptly observed—being well satisfied that "the present is the accepted time" to end the dispute. With great esteem I have the honor to be Your Obt Servt   Francis O. J. Smith

ALS. NhHi.

1. See F. O. J. Smith to DW, April 13, 1842, mDW 22153.

2. See DW to [F. O. J. Smith], April 10, 1842, mDW 22107, in *Diplomatic Papers, 1.*

3. See DW to John Fairfield and John Davis (1787–1854), mDW 22110.

4. For Smith's editorial, "The Settlement of the Boundary," see the *Portland Daily Evening Advertiser,* April 18, 1842.

TO JOHN EVELYN DENISON

Washington April 26. 1842

My Dear Sir

Though culpably negligent, in the duty of correspondence, I have not forgotten the *great horns*. Fellows with leather shirts, flat hats, long beards & rifles, are now on the Yellow Stone, & the Platte, looking out for *big horns*. They shall ere long adorn the Halls of Ossington.

Well, Lord Ashburton is here,[1] and we are trying to adjust certain little matters of difference, between you & us. I hardly know how we shall get along, but I can say that a pair of more friendly negotiators never put their heads together. He is a man of business, & of apparent candor & frankness; & it will give me much pleasure if we shall be able to smooth away all frowns & scowls from the faces of the two Governments, & the two countries, & set them to looking upon each other with the most gracious smiles.

I have looked over the principal Speeches in Parliament, this session, down to April 5. Really, the condition of the two Countries is in many respects the same. You have a new administration; so have we. You have a deficit; so have we. You propose a new Tariff; so do we. But then we have neither China, nor India, nor the Quintuple Treaty on our hands. The wreck & ruin of American credit is dreadful. It has caused a sort of paralysis of all the productive powers of the Country. Fortunately, every body has enough to eat & drink; but the earning or accumulation of wealth stopped, in 1837; & it has scarcely moved an inch since. We need two things, & must have them; first, a firm & undisturbed peace; 2. suitable provisions for revenue; while you are, perhaps, the most *taxed*, we are the most *untaxed*, people in the world. With peace, & a just revenue system, we shall begin to better our conditions.

If I shall be more fortunate, or more virtuous, than I have been, in the performance of the duties of friendly correspondence, I shall write you, in a week or two, about our *political domestic* condition, which is bad enough.

Remember me most kindly to Lady Charlotte, & your mother's family. What do you hear from your part of the Colony of New-Zealand? Yrs, with the utmost regard & attachment   Danl. Webster

ALS. ViU.

1. Alexander Baring, Lord Ashburton (1774–1848), financier, had arrived in Annapolis on April 3, and Washington April 4, as special envoy from England to negotiate the northeastern boundary.

Domestic problems, as well as international relations, demanded Webster's attention. The most serious of these domestic issues was the Dorr rebellion in Rhode Island. Still governed under the Royal Charter of 1663 with its highly restrictive franchise, citizens of the state had, to no avail, long petitioned the legislature for manhood suffrage. In October 1841, the disfranchised majority, under the leadership of Thomas Wilson Dorr, called a convention and drafted a new constitution. The state legislature responded later in the year with a more liberal charter, but this was defeated in a popular referendum. Both factions conducted elections in the spring of 1842 and installed officers, each claiming to be the duly authorized government of the state. Armed warfare threatened when the government under the old constitution imposed martial law and called out the state militia to sustain its authority. In the correspondence below, Webster and others discuss the Rhode Island situation, concluding with President Tyler to support the government under the old constitution headed by Samuel W. King. By mid-May the Dorr rebellion collapsed after its forces made an unsuccessful raid upon the state arsenal. A year later Rhode Island adopted a new constitution that met most of the "People's Party's" demands. Dorr himself was convicted of treason, but served only one year of a life sentence.

FROM JOSEPH STORY

Cambridge April 26. 1842.

Dear Sir,

The State of things in Rhode Island is growing every day more and more critical; and there is very great danger that the *free suffrage constitution* will be forced upon the people by intimidation and military force; and if so, the regular old charter Govt. will sustain itself by the like force. I suppose there cannot be any doubt, that the whole proceeding of the so called "free suffrage" convention and constitution makers are without law and against law. And it is the duty of all good men to avert the resort to arms; which may involve the most serious consequences.

The President's letter to Govr. [Samuel Ward] King is as far as it goes, approved by the Mass of thinking men.[1] But it is not sufficient to meet the exigencies which have since arisen. It is true, as he suggests, that under the Act of 1795, he is not authorized to call forth and employ the Militia to suppress any insurrection until there is actual insurrection; nor to issue a proclamation to Insurgents to disperse &c. until there is an actual Insurrection. But this is not his whole power. He has an unquestionable right to issue orders to the Governors of the adjacent States to detail portions of the Militia, so as to have them *prepared* to be called forth at a moment's warning if an insurrection should take place; and I have no doubt that Governor [John] Davis would at once, upon such an order, issue the proper orders to detail the Militia and to have them ready for service. The President, too, may send two or three companies of regular U.S. Troops to Newport, to remain in garrison in the Forts there, and to wait for the orders, if the exigency should arise. You may observe, that while Congress has authority "to call forth the Militia &c. to suppress insurrections" &c. that it is not the whole power given under the Constitution on the subject; another article provides that the U. States shall *"protect"* the states from "domestic violence" upon the call of the Governor or Legislature. "To protect" necessarily means to guard *before* the domestic violence is committed. It presupposes a state of things, requiring protection against a violence which may be threatened, not that has been already committed. The President is to execute the laws of the United States; and the Constitution is the Supreme law. He may therefore and ought to take all steps, which are prudent and necessary to make the *protection* effectual, as *preliminaries.*

I think also, that the President could do a great good, and probably stop all bloodshed by a Proclamation (a preliminary Proclamation) warning all persons not to attemp[t] to carry any measures into effect by military power, or by insurrectionary movements; and stating that under existing circumstances, he has deemed it his duty to take precautionary measures to avert all insurrectionary movements and intimidations, and that he shall hold the militia in readiness to be called forth at the first moment, where an insurrectionary movement shall exist. In this way I think, that probably the crisis might go off peaceably; otherwise in the exasperated state of parties I have many fears, that there will be open warfare. If there should be any such evils, the Administration will be blamed vehemently, even although it may be unjustly and without cause.

It appears to me that a Proclamation with an order to two or three companies of regular Troops to go to Newport, in readiness to act, would compel the parties to pause until better counsels could prevail.

I have written these hasty lines to you, because from what I privately learn from the best sources the dangers are imminent. Of course, I do not wish to be known in this matter; and my sole object is peace. Believe me most truly yours,   Joseph Story

Copy. NhHi.
    1. Tyler to King, April 11, 1842, in Tyler, *Tylers*, 2: 194–196.

TO MRS. EDWARD CURTIS
                                        Washington, May 4, 1842.
(*Private. ☞ Be Particular.*)
My Dear Lady,

    I must tell you, as one of the secrets of diplomacy, but a secret which all the world I believe already knows, that I am to be your way two or three days hence, on a flying visit to Massachusetts. The "candid public" suppose, doubtless, that I am going to confer with Governor Davis and others on the boundary question;[1] to consult the shipping interest of the North about the right of search, &c., whereas I am really going for the change; to get away from my table for a few days, see a few friends in New York, as many in Boston, and as the great object of all, see Seth Peterson, and catch one trout. I shall probably arrive in New York late in the evening, and shall go to the Astor House. The Boston boat not going till evening of the next day, I shall have a long morning. My purpose is to avoid seeing people; and so I shall set out to go to Morrisania, but shall be very likely, nevertheless, to stop at your house, and if you can keep your husband at home, we can have a little talk. I will give him notice, if possible, one day previous to my departure. In truth, I am waiting principally for news from Rhode Island.

I have a number of things to talk over with Mr. Curtis. I believe he will live a thousand years, and triumph over all his enemies.

My wife is well. The two boys are well. Edward is going to be somebody, if one of the Miss Bayards does not deprive him of intellect.[2] They are beautiful girls; but still, the mother is like the mother of mankind,

"The fairest of her daughters, Eve;"

see Milton, not Shakespeare. They have all gone to ——, but to return in June.

But, to resume the thread of my discourse, by the way, threads often become long yarns, Caroline [Story White Webster] is well; her babies are well; and Master Dan[iel F. Webster, Jr.] is another Judge Story. Miss [Ellen] Fletcher is well; the nurse is well; we are all well, down even to my noble collection of cacklers in the poultry yard. But the season advances; summer is coming, according to the almanac, and yet our only warmth is before a good fire. But still, as May is here and June in sight, we all begin to think of flight!! It is merciful in Providence to change the seasons, so that men, and even women too, may find some excuse for change also.

Mrs. Webster talks of New York and Boston; Julia, of Marshfield; Caroline, of Nahant, Newport, Watertown; Fletcher, of staying where he is; Edward of Marshfield. Adieu; I must close this letter in two and a half minutes or lose the mail. Read [George] Poindexter; such men as "Curtis and Webster."[3] Yours, Daniel Webster.

Text from PC, 2: 125–126. Original not found.

1. See DW to John Whipple, May 9, 1842, below.

2. DW was probably alluding to one or more of Richard Henry Bayard's five daughters.

3. For a discussion of Poindexter's report, see above, DW to Edward Curtis, February 24, 1842, and [Feb-

ruary–March? 1842]. DW's allusion is to a letter from Poindexter to Tyler, February 9, 1842, denouncing "all the devices put in requisition by such men as Curtis and Webster, to destroy me in your estimation. . . ." "Report of George Poindexter . . . ," *Reports of Committees*, 27th Cong., 2d sess., Serial 409, Report No. 669, p. 296.

FROM AMBROSE DUDLEY MANN

Cincinnati, May 6, 1842.

Dear Sir;

Since my arrival I have seen many, indeed nearly all the prominent Whigs of this city, and I have availed myself of every suitable occasion to ascertain their opinions in relation to yourself and your connexion with the government. It affords me the highest gratification to assure you, that I have not met with a solitary individual, who countenances the attacks made upon you by the "Globe," and other violent and reckless journals. The feeling is as indignant as it is general, against the merciless ferocity, by which you have been personally and otherwise assailed. In all well regulated communities, there is a paramount obligation, on every member composing it, to repress rude and slanderous publications. This is the only safeguard against the licentiousness of a corrupt and prostituted Press. Your reputation, notwithstanding the fiery ordeal through which it has passed, remains entirely unscathed.[1] *False political friends,*—unprincipled and unrelenting enemies, may continue their unhallowed purpose of endeavoring to hunt you down, but their poisoned arrows will fall harmless at your feet.

Go on—go on, in your honest and patriotic efforts to serve your country: Your reward ere-long will be found in the smiles of a nation of freemen. They will soon discover, that for the *Stone* they have given you, you have returned them *Bread*. If our "vexed questions" with Great Britain, are satisfactorily adjusted under your auspices, you will acquire a popularity "behind the mountains," in the "Great West" which will be as durable as its fertile vallies. Can I, after witnessing your devotion to the public interests, doubt your triumph? Is there a *true friend* to the late sage of North Bend by whom it is not desired? For this purpose, more than any other, he selected you. Could he visit the sphere from which he was called, he would tell his old kindred spirits with what fidelity you are discharging it.

Yesterday I had a long conversation with Josiah Lawrence,[2] the oldest and most influential merchant in the West. He is to Cincinnati what Abbott Lawrence is to Boston—was a zealous advocate for a Bank—and opposed President Tyler on account of his vetoes. After satisfying him with regard to your position I asked him to state to me frankly his opinion of the proposed Exchequer. He replied "Congress should not hesitate a moment about establishing it. It is loudly called for by the peculiar condition of the country. The stock could not now, nor perhaps for the next ten years, be taken in a U.S. Bank, even under a charter as favorable as that enjoyed by the old one. The Exchequer would regulate the Exchanges which is all that can be required from the General Government." (You will find among my Letters, on file in the Department, one from this excellent gentleman.) The opinions expressed by Mr. L. are such as are entertained generally, and you may depend upon it, the *Projet* recommended by the Executive is destined, *in less than a twelve-month, to prostrate its most clamorous enemies in Congress.*

The "Republican," I fear, will not be able to sustain itself. It has no strength in its Editorial Department. [George] Graham's[3] Letters from Washington excite no interest, and in all respects the Paper is so puny as not to merit public patronage. I believe on this account it will lose its subscribers. But in addition to this, there is a prejudice against it, occasioned by its Editors wishing to monopolize all the offices under the Government. [Charles Stewart] Todd has been made a Minister.[4] Graham wants to be a *Charge*!!! And [Henry E.] Spencer[5] is an applicant for the Surveyor General's place. The advocacy of the "Republican" is worth less to the Administration than the neutrality of the "Gazette"; but the Chronicle has more cleverness than either—dignified and decorous in its course. The "Louisville Journal" is about to lay down its weapons against you: The last numbers have been silent.[6]

To-morrow I go to the Northern District of Kentucky, and from thence to Louisville. Wherever I go you may rely there will be one *faithful* tongue to "speak of you as you are." If you think of any thing I can do to serve you command me through the Post-office at Cincinnati, where your communications will be received. When we seperated you said "BE FAITHFUL." *Faithful* you shall ever find me. I have the honor to be with the highest regard, Your obt. servt.   A. D. Mann.

ALS. NhHi.
1. Mann was probably alluding to DW's rumored impropriety with a lady job-applicant in the State Department offices; to Sylvester's charge of bribery; and to the Poindexter investigation, all discussed above.
2. Lawrence was a Cincinnati banker, and incorporator of the Cincinnati and White Water Canal Company.
3. Graham (1798–1881) had settled in Cincinnati about 1822, where

he played an increasingly prominent role in local Whig politics.
4. Tyler had appointed Todd (1791–1871) United States minister to Russia in August 1841.
5. Spencer, a grocer and leading Whig figure, was elected mayor of Cincinnati in 1843.
6. For the *Louisville Daily Journal's* charges against DW, see above, Theodore Frelinghuysen to DW, February 11, 1842.

FROM NASSAU WILLIAM SENIOR

London May 8. 1842

My dear Sir,

Among the labors, which, much for the advantage of America & of the world are imposed on you, I fear you have little time to read any thing but what is official. I venture however to send to you two papers of mine in the last Edinburg Review which, if you can find time to look at them will I think interest you. One is on the English budget. The other on the national character of America, France, & England.[1]

Many of my English friends think me severe on my own country. I hope you will not think I have pressed too heavily on yours—but in fact all nations, as nations, act so ill that any review of their conduct reads like a satire.

Mrs. Senior[2] was much flattered this morning by a very kind note from Mrs. Webster[3]—& very glad to hear a good account of Mrs Appleton. With our best united regards believe me, my dear Sir Yours very truly

Nassau W. Senior

Lord Ashburton saw the article on America &c in proof—indeed took the proofs with him.

AL. NhD.
1. Senior's two articles, reviews of *Die Deutschen Voelker Persoenlich Betrachtet, Speech of the Right Hon. Sir Robert Peel, in the House of Commons, Feb. 9, 1842*; and *Speech of the Right Hon. Sir Robert Peel, March*

11, 1842, appeared in *The Edinburgh Review*, 75 (April 1842): 1–27, 101–118.
2. Mary Charlotte Mair, whom Senior had married in 1821.
3. Not found.

TO JOHN WHIPPLE

Washington, May 9th. 1842.

Private and Confidential
My dear Sir:

You will see the President's letter to Governor King,[1] transmitted through Messrs. [Richard Kidder] Randolph and [Elisha Reynolds] Potter.[2] If there could be any doubt before, there can certainly be none now, that the Government of the United States pledges itself to maintain the existing constitution and laws, till regularly changed. This clear and unequivocal manifestation places Governor King and the Legislature on such commanding ground that they may now, I think, with great propriety, commence the agreeable duty of conciliation; especially as I do not understand that any of the functionaries of the new constitution is actually exercising the powers of office, that any force threatens the lawful Government, or that assemblies of men, with hostile purposes, any where exist. My opinion, therefore, is very clear that no more arrests should be made; that perhaps existing prosecutions had better be discontinued, and that the assembly, at its June session, should call a committee to amend the constitution. Thus far the law has been asserted; and all must now see that resistance is vain and useless; while there are a good many proud spirits who might be driven to extremities, by measures calculated to degrade and dishonor them, but who would, nevertheless, be glad of a fair chance of honorable retreat. Many misguided men are, after all, doubtless of such respectable character, and possess such respectable connexions, that it would be painful to see them subjected to unnecessary mortification, since parties on both sides are made up of neighbors, family friends, and those who maintain kind social relations with one another.

This recommendation proceeds, of course, upon the ground that the officers elected under the new constitution entirely abstain from exercising any authority by virtue of their supposed offices. But if they do so abstain, I am quite anxious that conciliation and peace should be sought by the measures above recommended. I am, dear Sir, Your's with regard,

N.B. I shall arrive in New York on Thursday evening; and be in that city, Friday forenoon; if any friends choose to meet me there, I shall be able to state more fully what we think here. I shall see the President, both to-day and to-morrow.

Copy. NhHi. Published in *PC*, 2: 127–128. Whipple (1784–1866; Brown 1802) was a Providence lawyer. He had appeared as counsel for Rhode Island (DW represented Massachusetts) in *Rhode Island* v. *Massachusetts*, 15 Peters 233 (1841). Upon DW's death he delivered and later published *A Discourse in commemoration of the life and services of Daniel Webster* . . . (Providence, 1852).

1. Tyler's letter to King, May 7, 1842, is discussed in Arthur May Mowry, *The Dorr War: The Constitutional Struggle in Rhode Island* (Providence, R.I., 1901), p. 158.

2. Randolph (d. 1849) was Speaker of the Rhode Island House of Representatives; Potter, a state senator at the time, later served in Congress. Governor King had sent Randolph and Potter to Washington with the May 4 resolutions of the Rhode Island legislature calling for federal intervention in the Dorr crisis. Mowry, *The Dorr War*, pp. 157–158.

FROM WILLIAM CHANNING GIBBS

Newport 12th. May 1842.

Dear Sir,

Bur[r]ington Anthony of Providence,[1] arrived here this morng. the bearer of [a] letter from yourself to John Whipple Esq.[2] Mr Anthony publicly stated to the citizens & to some of the members of the Legislature that you had written to Mr. Whipple to meet you, and Mr. [Thomas Wilson] Dorr and [Dutee Jerauld] Pearce at the Astor House tomorrow morng. for the purpose of making or proposing a compromise between the two parties in the state—that you considered our Law of treason un-constit[ut]ional & that it must be repealed. Your letter was shown to confirm the fact of your having written to Mr. Whipple altho' the seal was not broken. The object of Mr. Anthony undoubtedly was again to unite & rouse his party to action—they had become depressed and the resignations to their pretended assembly had become very general, so much so that it was our opinion that they would never again be able to form a quorum for action or business. The statement of Mr. Anthony was brought up before our Legislature this morng. and I can do them the justice to say that they would not give credit to it for a moment. For any compromise with a party in open rebellion against the Laws and Government of the State, is entirely out of the question. When peace & tranquility is again established among us, we shall again offer to our people another constitution, which will be adopted and which will give an extension of suffrage & an equal representation. I am not willing that Dorr, Pearce & Anthony should make capital for Mr. Van Buren out of our Domestic disturbances. Their whole object is to obtain power in this State to operate against yourself & the General Government. It is a *political movement* on the part of the leading men, and they have roused the passions of the people to that degree that we are almost daily threatened with the torch & with the sword, neither of which, alarm me, altho' it does our wifes and families. In conclusion, I have felt it my duty to inform you of the injurious effect of Mr. Anthony's statement on yourself & on our Government & I hope you will authorize me or the Governor to contradict it. The good people of our State would be highly pleased to see you in Rhode Island and with the assurances of my most perfect respect I am, Dear Sir Your fr. & obt Servt   W Channing Gibbs.

ALS. NhHi. Gibbs (1790–1871) had served as governor of Rhode Island, 1821–1824.

1. Anthony, former United States marshal for Rhode Island, was at this time a leader of the Dorr faction: he was the "people's sheriff" of Providence, and his residence served as Dorr's headquarters.

2. See above, DW to John Whipple, May 9, 1842.

FROM EDWARD EVERETT

London 20 May 1842

(*Private & Confidential, for yourself alone*)

Dear Sir,

General Cass' protest has been furnished to the Times newspaper as I have reason to believe by himself thro Genl. Duff Green.[1] I am constantly asked whether Genl. C's course in this matter is approved by his government. The French Ambassador & Russian Minister put the question to me yesterday. I have to give evasive answers. I can collect your private opinion from your letter of 26th April[2] & from what I learned from Mr [Washington] Irving. But General Green read me a letter from Judge Upshur,[3] in which Genl. Cass' conduct was most warmly commended & Col. [Charles Stewart] Todd blamed for not pursuing a similar course: & Genl Green said Genl. Cass was well pleased with his letters from Washington.

At the close of his protest you recollect Genl C. tells Mr. [François] Guizot that on the arrival of the next packet he shall be able to announce to him either the President's approbation of his course or his own resignation.[4]

The French papers today & the Paris Correspondents of the London papers say that the President approves the pamphlet & the protest.

You are aware that the pamphlet to which so much importance is ascribed in causing the nonratification by France of the Quintuple treaty, did not appear till after the vote of the Chambers which was the real cause. This fact I know in many ways; it is stated in one of Mr [Robert] Walsh's letters to the Intelligencer.[5] I have no doubt Genl. Cass' pamphlet & protest had considerable effect in heightening the public feeling. He was considered as acting for his gv't. But the appearance of the pamphlet could have had no agency in producing the event.

In Judge Upshur's letter to Genl. Green,[6] Genl G. is requested to institute an enquiry on the subject of a banker for the Navy of the U.S. in Paris war being "probable"; and it being necessary to be prepared for a state of things which would make it impossible for the Barings to continue to act as bankers to the Navy. General Green is directed to sound the Rothschilds, at Paris & London.

It appears to me that these proceedings are of doubtful expediency; & the channel of communication of doubtful discretion.

Can neither general Cass nor I be trusted to do the work of the Government?

The Barings when I last heard from them were greatly in advance to the Navy.

I hope we shall soon have a state of things a little more quiet & better organized, when the foreign ministers will not be expected like good Captain Davis of Acton[7] in 1775 to go to war on their hook but when it will be thought worth while to wait for & obey instructions.

All this is for your eye alone.

LC. MHi.

1. Cass's "An examination of the question . . . concerning the Right of Search" had appeared in the London *Sunday Times*, March 13, 20, 1842.

2. See DW to Edward Everett, April 26, 1842: mDW 22270 and *Diplomatic Papers*, 1.

3. Not found.

4. Guizot (1787–1874) was French minister of foreign affairs, 1840–1848. Cass's letter to Guizot, Febru-

ary 13, 1842, is printed in *Diplomatic Papers*, 1.

5. Walsh regularly contributed to the *National Intelligencer* from Paris, his reports on proceedings in the legislative body and on general affairs of France appearing under the head-

ing "From Our Paris Correspondent." Everett was most likely referring to Walsh's letter in the *National Intelligencer*, April 23, 1842.

6. Not found.

7. Not identified.

FROM AMBROSE DUDLEY MANN

Cincinnati, May 24, 1842.

Dear Sir;

Since I had the honor of addressing you, on the 9th inst.,[1] I have visited Kentucky, and have conversed freely with many prominent politicians there. That there was more dissatisfaction in that state with the President, on account of his Vetoes, than in any other, cannot be doubted; but that public opinion is undergoing a favorable change is just as certain. The leading Whig papers, it is true, continue a warfare against his Administration, but their violence will cease, as soon as the Loco Foco candidates are fairly in the field. This event will speedily transpire: The ex-President, and the ex-Governor of Tennessee,[2] will constitute the ticket. The *"Old Roman"* wills this, and his fiat is as imperious as ever, with the leaders of his party. Against a *"restoration,"* the recent supporters of "Tippacanoe and Tyler too," *will rally to a man. Every* Whig Paper will *have* to support the measures of the Administration, if they continue wholesome, before the next Presidential Election. Their Patrons will force them to this alternative, *volens nolens.*

It is generally conceded that the establishment of a Bank, (even if the sanction of the President could be obtained) is utterly impracticable. *In all the country west of the Alleghany, not one hundred thousand dollars of stock would be subscribed, under the most favorable Charter for shareholders!* A melancholy change has come over the fortunes of those, who were most noisy for an institution of the kind, within the last four months. The commercial class of the community is entirely prostrate, from Pittsburgh to New-Orleans. Men who but yesterday were regarded as millionaires, to-day, are among the applicants, for the benefit of the Bankrupt Act. This has been occasioned by the bloated credit system, which succeeded the downfall of the old Bank. Although a *new* one was looked to, as the Panacea for all the pecuniary ills of the country, it is now willingly admitted by candid persons, that it would not have cured the wounds long since inflicted: For these alas! there was "no Balm in Gilead." Therefore, the necessity of a National Bank, as a *relief* measure, no longer exists. If it came clothed with the power of a "Healing Physician," (which in our desperation we claimed for it) its visit would be useless, because the poor sufferer is dead. Amid the surrounding gloom there is light in the distance. The Bankrupt law will purify the commercial atmosphere; the Tariff will lay a solid foundation to build upon, anew; the Exchequer will equalize Exchanges, and keep our local institutions, and individuals, under proper restraint.

Among the *on dits* we have here, it is stated that Mr. Van Buren's visit to the Hermitage is to effect a reconciliation between Gen. Jackson and Mr. Clay! Mr. Clay invited Mr. Van Buren to Kentucky,[3] and his organ at Louisville, is assailing him with more than its accustomed fierceness. The signs of the times are indicative of some great movement, but let what may come, Mr. Clay *can never transfer the Whigs of the West to Mr. Van Buren.* I cannot, myself, believe that he dreams of any thing of the kind. If he attempts it, he will be his own immolator. The result of the Virginia Elections has dispirited Mr. C. really, as the tone of his Letters clearly shows. Mr. Van Buren will be here soon, and I will give you some account of his sojourn, immediately thereafter. With high regard, I have the honor to be, Yours Faithfully,   A. D. Mann.

ALS. NhHi.
1. Not found.
2. Martin Van Buren and James Knox Polk.

3. Following his visit to Jackson at the Hermitage, Van Buren visited Clay at Ashland in May.

FROM AMBROSE DUDLEY MANN

Cincinnati, May 25, 1842.

Confidential
Dear Sir;

At our last interview, you remarked that you would like for me to write you a Letter, that you could show to the President, as you wished me to stand well with him. If you think proper, you are at liberty to transmit to him the accompanying one—which he must regard as confidential.[1]

In a former note[2] I mentioned Havre. So lucrative a post should not be held so long, by any individual, as that has been by [Reuben C.] Beasley.[3] If this position is not attainable, Bremen or Marseilles would be acceptable. The President, long ago, assured me that he would appoint me to *any place*, for which I could procure your recommendation.[4] If you think my services would be more valuable at home, I can procure any additional testimonials, that may be required, of my fitness for the Head of a Bureau. The Recorder of the Land Office, it is rumored, is to be appointed to the 1st Auditorship. I would not object to fill, for a time, the vacancy occasioned by this transfer. I rely however, altogether on your kindness, to place my name before the President, for such situation as you believe I would be most *useful* in. Before I am nominated converse with Gov. [James Turner] Morehead[5] and [Landaff Watson] Andrews. They are my friends sincerely, and I want them to *feel under obligations to you*. Charge my Appointment to Ohio. I have been a citizen of the state five years: But much of this time I have passed in the south. (over.)

The course of the Executive, in relation to the "Insurgents" of Rhode-Island, is making him many friends: He is applauded by all the Whigs, in this region, and temperate Democrats do not withhold their praise. [William] Allen, the Jacobin of the Senate, has completely immolated himself. Even Loco Focoism in Ohio, rabid as it is, dare not justify his unprincipled speeches.

Since I returned I have been constantly in motion—you have nothing to fear in the West. Go on in your bold and faithful career, and all will soon be right. The people are beginning to appreciate your value in the Cabinet and ere-long you will be in exceedingly good odor with them; in due time, through you, I flatter myself that they will be reconciled to the President,—indeed I am sure of it. The "Cincinnati Gazette" is entirely silent as far as you are concerned. I satisfied its Editors of the purity of your motives. The "Louisville Journal" too is becoming much more passive. For the last ten days it has not uttered a sentence against you. I have been operating upon it *indirectly*. These two Journals give tone to the Whig Press in Ohio and Kentucky. In Louisville, as far as I could learn, [George Dennison] Prentice's slanderous attacks found no favor with his best friends.

In conclusion, I beg you to acknowledge the receipt of my letters,[6] and to communicate unreservedly any suggestions you may wish to make. My last letter I fear reached Washington after your departure to the north. Yours &c. &c.   A. D. Mann.

ALS. NhHi.

1. Mann probably enclosed the letter above of May 24 for Tyler's perusal.

2. Not found.

3. Beasley, former United States agent for prisoners in London, had been appointed consul at Le Havre in December 1816.

4. For recommendations of Mann, see Letters of Application and Recommendation During the Administrations of Martin Van Buren, William

Henry Harrison, and John Tyler, 1837–1845 (M–687), Reel 22, DNA, RG 59. On August 29, 1842, Tyler nominated Mann for United States consul at Bremen, and the Senate confirmed the appointment on the same day.

5. For Morehead's recommendation of Mann to Tyler, December 22, 1841, see *ibid*. (M-687), Reel 22, DNA.

6. DW's letters to Mann, if he wrote any, have not been found.

FROM JOHN TYLER

May 27. 1842.

My Dear Sir,

I had hoped that we were done with Rhode Island, but here comes today, by the hands of a *special messenger*, a call from Govr. King for protection against a supposed plot of Dorr to invade the State with troops from Massachusetts & other States.[1] I can not think otherwise of it, than as a continuance of the game of brag, which I had regarded as at an end. But I have thought that the safer way was to show a desire to treat the letter of the Governor with the respect of instituting an inquiry into the matter by a secret agent of our own, & I write you therefore to take the matter in hand, & to appoint a suitable person quietly & silently to go to the borders of Rhode Island, & ascertain all that the insurgents are about.[2] A Mr. [Henry De] Wolf[3] of Massachusetts is said to be the military commander. The chief scene of operations is about Woonsocket Falls & Cumberland, & on the borders of Massachusetts. They are reported to have a thousand stand of arms—tents for a military encampment & two pieces of cannon. The 1st of June is talked of for the general meeting, & the insurgents boast of having 2500 men enlisted in their Service.

Now I wish you to select a suitable person to get in among the people who will be able to find out their real designs. He will of course act confidentially, & will be selected for his prudence & sagacity. Be assured of my constant regard,   John Tyler

P.S. The town of Thompson in Connecticut is spoken of as Dorr's sometime head quarters.

Copy. MHi.

1. Governor King's appeal to Tyler followed an attempt by the Dorr forces to secure men and arms in New York and to seize the state arsenal in Providence. For King's letter to Tyler, May 25, 1842, and Tyler's response, May 28, see *Executive Documents*, 28th Cong., 1st sess., Serial 443, Document No. 225, pp. 32–34.

2. The identity of the agent Webster appointed has not been established. For DW's communication to Tyler, enclosing information from the secret agent, see *ibid.*, pp. 37–38.

3. De Wolf, not further identified, was a leader of the "people's" forces.

TO VIRGIL MAXCY

Boston May 31. 1842.

Private

My Dear Sir,

I have received, here, your private letter of the 30th of April,[1] & have time to answer it, by the Steam Packet, which departs tomorrow.

As to Tennessee lands, I have a large quantity[2]—I believe 250,000 acres, including all which belonged to the late Mr. [Stephen] Haight. The titles are unquestionable, being direct from the State to him. The quality of the several parcels are certified by the Surveyors, who accompanied their report, in the several cases, with statements respecting the soil, surface, streams, &c. These certificates with the title papers are now at

Washington. I am willing to dispose of these lands upon the same terms, as to price, as those upon which you are authorized to sell Mr. [Oliver Keating] Barrells;[3] & as to your compensation, that is a matter which shall be adjusted to your satisfaction. I hope to hear from you soon, relative to this, as I am desirous of doing something with the lands without delay. Yrs truly   Danl Webster

LS. DLC.
1. Not found.
2. The precise location of DW's Tennessee lands has not been established.
3. Barrell was a native of New Castle, Delaware.

Webster found it impossible to meet the payments for his Washington residence on his salary alone. As indicated by the document below, friends—some of whom had already come to his rescue several times— provided him with the necessary funds. After Webster resigned his post, he leased the property to Sir Richard Pakenham, British minister to the United States.

FROM MOSES HICKS GRINNELL, RICHARD MILFORD BLATCHFORD, AND JONATHAN PRESCOTT HALL

Six Thousand Dollars to be raised and applied by Hon: Daniel Webster to the payment of existing mortgages on his dwelling House in Washington City—thereby the House is to be cleared of all incumbrances, and a new Mortgage for *Seven thousand Dollars* is to be executed. As a security for said *Six thousand Dollars* the House is to be conveyed (subject only to said Mortgage for Seven thousand Dollars) to
to be held in Trust for the payment of said *Six Thousand Dollars*, and as security therefor, with interest.[1]

New York June 4. 1842

Dear Sir,
   The conveyance of your House being made in the manner above named, and approved by R. M. Blatchford, I agree to accept your draft, or the Draft of Richard Smith Esq for you, at Sixty days sight, for Three thousand Dollars. Very truly Yours &c   M. H. Grinnell
   I also agree in the same terms to accept your draft, or the draft of Richard Smith Esq for you, for One Thousand Dollars. Yours &c:
R. M. Blatchford
   I also agree on the same terms to accept your draft, or the draft of Richard Smith Esq for you, for Five Hundred Dollars. Yours &c:
J[onathan] Prescott Hall[2]
   If the nature of the conveyance & the present state of the title make it

inconvenient to execute a new mortgage Mr: Smith may, when the Six Thousand Dollars shall have been paid declare in writing that he holds the whole property for the use of the signers of the within paper & of whoever else may contribute to make up the sum of Six Thousand Dollars aforesaid, Mr. Webster giving his written assent & confirmation to such declaration of Mr: Smith. It being however distinctly understood that there is to be a lien or security on said property to the extent of Seven Thousand Dollars which is to have precedence of said Six Thousand Dollars.

Date June 4. 1842

M. H. Grinnell
R. M. Blatchford
J Prescott Hall

LS. ViU.

1. On March 16, 1844, DW deeded the Swann property in Washington to Richard Smith, trustee for the Swanns, to clear his remaining $7,000 indebtedness to the Swann estate, $3,000 to Grinnell, $500 to Blatchford, and $500 to Hall. DW made several other transfers of the property between 1844 and 1849, when he deeded the property to William W. Corcoran. See deeds from DW to Richard Smith, March 16, 1844, Deed Book 8: 306; Richard Smith and Robert B. Swann to DW, March 14, 1844, Deed Book 8: 307; Richard Smith, DW, Thomas Swann, R. M. Blatchford, and Prescott Hall to Moses H. Grinnell, October 18, 1847, Deed Book 9: 317; Richard Smith and John A. Smith to DW to Corcoran, May 4, 1849, Deed Book 10: 346, Office of the Register of Deeds, Washington, D.C., mDWs.

2. Hall (1796–1862; Yale 1817), a native of Pomfret, Connecticut, was a lawyer in New York City.

TO JAMES BOYLES MURRAY

Washington
June 8. 1842

Private

Dear Sir

I enclose you a copy of a postscript to a letter from Mr Maxcy, of the 3rd of May.[1]

This, you will see, alludes to an important question. In every thing regarding the sale of my Clamorgan Shares, I have placed the most unlimited confidence in yourself & Mr Maxcy, considering you as acting as my agents, under a stipulated rate of compensation.[2] If Mr Maxcy feels at liberty to offer no stock, except such as those on which interest is paid, the same reason, I suppose will extend to the rest. I wish for nothing more from you, than you actually recd for the shares, under the agreement, deducting your compensation, &c. Any thing less, certainly, would not do me justice, & therefore would not be offered by you. Will you please furnish me with an exactment of what was recd, & thus shew what my rights are.[3] Yrs very truly   Danl Webster

ALS copy. NhD.
  1. Not found.
  2. See above, Murray to DW, June

29, 1840.
  3. For Murray's response, June 9,
1842, see below.

FROM JAMES BOYLES MURRAY

New York 9 June 1842

Private

Dear Sir

I have yours of 7th Instt.[1]

You do not precisely apprehend my relation to the Clamorgan affair. Mr. Maxcy held your shares as well as others which he was authorised to dispose of at certain rates, & to receive in payment United States Bank Shares, or State Stock, *at par*, & to retain all he got over the limits for his own compensation.

My interest in the matter was entirely accidental, occurring after Mr. Maxcy had *failed in all his efforts* to sell the Shares, & I made a contract with him for the privilege of *purchasing* them within a fixed period on the above terms payable in the stocks at par at certain instalments, & to allow him one half of any profit I might realise over that rate.

I immediately commenced selling & *trading* them as I best could, & in the course of events received almost all sorts of State Stocks except those which have proved to be good, & also North American Trust Co Shares & United States Bank Shares now almost worthless. The option as to the kind of stock to be delivered was with *me*, but in regard to your first instalment I conceded it to Mr. [Samuel] Frothingham[2] your agent, who although I had the State Stocks on hand, preferred United States Bank for which I paid $68 to John Ward & Co.[3] The second instalment altho also pay[abl]e in Stocks was on Mr. Jaudons earnest solicitation, settled by Mr Maxcy *in money* (without authority from me) at such a rate as made a difference to me of some £500, although still a holder of State Stocks, but as it was done by him in good faith I acquiesced in it, [while?] *legally* he was & is liable to make good to me the difference.

In regard to the third instalment Mr Maxcy with equal solicitude for your interest was desirous that I should pay you in the best description of State Stocks, although even here I had the legal right by my contract with him to pay in *U.S. Bank Shares at par*. I gave you a memo. of what State Stocks I had, out of which you made your selection.

Mr. Maxcy writes me that whatever may be the Settlement I may make with you, he will add enough to make it equal as far as his half goes, to *good interest paying State Stocks*. This would certainly be a most liberal act on his part & he will do it, but it must be remembered that he as an original owner in the association can afford to do what I, who was not so, cannot—but I will cheerfully replace all your Clamorgan Shares if you will refund to me *one half* of what I have paid for them, for I leave not only a large portion returned on my hands, but I have actually sold U.S. Bank Shares at $13 which I took in pay for these shares, at £9.10, & I have on hand N.A. Trust Shares which I took at $100 which would not sell at $3, & my State Stocks average me over $70.

I am so little anxious about the matter that if you will give me an order on John Ward & Co for the $11,000 Illinois Stock I will return your receipt & let the whole matter stand over until Mr. Maxcy's return—only I wish it understood that I am ready & willing to settle according to my contract. I would *vastly* prefer rescinding the whole contract and return the shares, receiving back the money, to being supposed capable of taking any unfair advantage.

Before making any further arrangements with Mr. Ward (which is now in progress) I will wait your reply, remaining with great Esteem & respect Dear Sir, Your mo obt Ser   Jas. B. Murray

ALS. DLC.
   1. Not found. Most likely Murray was referring to DW's letter above of June 8, 1842.
   2. Frothingham (1787–1869) was formerly cashier of the Boston branch of the Bank of the United States.
   3. John Ward & Company was a New York investment bank and brokerage house.

FROM JOSHUA BATES

London 13th. June 1842

Private

My dear Sir,

There was never a duller time in the business world and much distress prevails in the manufacturing districts. In India commercial matters are in a bad way. The difficulty seems to be over production every where so that prices have receded to a very low figure. When we are to see any improvement, I know not. It is some consolation however to think that things cannot get much worse. There is not a single buyer for American stocks[—]the public both here and in Holland seem determined that no new loan whether national or State from your side shall be negotiated in Europe while one of the members of the Republic shall adhere to the Doctrine of repudiation. I argue that it is most injust, because one or two states have repudiated to brand the whole United States with the infamy[—]that the true way is to treat every state on its own merits and give credit only where credit is due[.] Sensible people who understand American institutions agree with me but the mass will not separate the good from the bad, and no one will for the present dare to bring out an United States Loan. The settlement of all the differences by Lord Ashburton and the passing of a good Tariff bill would produce a favorable change if not counteracted by further State defalcations: should Maryland & Pennsylvania cease to pay their dividends then I shall despair of ever reviving the credit of the states. Could not Congress pass some strong Resolutions against repudiation[? H]itherto that body has been silent, although the President has alluded to this subject.

I hear nothing about the negotiations except that the government seems satisfied and so far as one can judge, they have hopes of success, and I pray they may not be disappointed, for there cannot be any doubt but it is as important to Great Britain as to the United States, to have the political relations of the two Countries on a permanently amicable basis. The prosperity of both would then proceed uninterruptedly. The French seem perfectly childish[—]they are so annoyed that they cannot play first in all political questions that their hatred of England and the English knows no bounds but they can do nothing. [A]ll Europe is coalesced against them, as faithless and intriguing, and she cannot move in a hostile way without being crushed. While Belgium England & Germany have been improving their internal communications by rail roads, France has been bragging and spending money on Fortifications, and seems to stand isolated from the rest of Europe and fifty years behind.

Mr. Everett is very much liked here and is himself pleased with his situation[. T]he only drawback for him and for all other Americans residing here is in the lamentations of the sufferers by the United States Bank and other American schemes & stocks.

Sir Robert Peels new Tariff is nearly thro' the Commons[. I]t is calculated to increase the trade with the United States and will particularly benefit the Corn and Cattle growing sections of the Union, and as it will enable the country to import more the Tariff on your side may by & by produce a large sum. I cannot but think it of great importance that the national finances be placed in an easy position in order that the capital of the country may quickly return to the chan[n]els of trade. It is to be regretted that the circumstances above alluded to should operate to prevent the negotiation of the National loan here, could that be done, things would soon come right. We have had a remarkable Spring[—]the last half of May & June so far have been very warm, the last 10 days particularly so, 72 to 74 degrees in the shade. This has bro't the wheat so forward that if good weather continues we shall have harvest 6 weeks earlier than usual which disappoints the corn speculators.

The news from China is unimportant except as shewing that England can have the whole empire if they want it. I have seen a letter from a Gentleman at Ningpho (Ningnho) who writes that he is civil Governor and Judge, and that he proceeds from place to place, in a carriage, with two Chinese, with Bamboos, to clear the road for him of the multitude, and that his decisions appear to be very much liked, and that he governs nearly a million of people without difficulty. The Grand army of 80,000 was approaching Ningpho, but the 2000 English were not in the least dismayed, as they were well prepared. Hongkong Ningpho & Chusan are declared to be free ports, and that the British authorities will give timely notice of any intention to withdraw. The Chinese people it is said offer to return to their usual occupations provided they can have the assurance of the British Commander in chief that he will not abandon them.

I hope the expected Steamer from Boston may bring good news from Maine, in regard to the appointment of one or more Commissioners[. T]he greater the number the higher will be my hopes of an amicable settlement of the Boundary Question. Believe me my dear Sir Very Sincerely yours, Joshua Bates.

ALS. NhD.

TO VIRGIL MAXCY

Washington, June 18, 1842.

Private

My dear Sir:

I feel quite obliged by your friendly communication[1] and offer respecting the last instalment on the sale of the Clamorgan shares. I have seen Col. Murray, and communicated to him what you observed in your letter.[2] In this particular I hope I did not err, although he was fearful I might receive from your letter an impression that he was desirous of doing something less than justice to me.[3] I assured him that I took no such view, and did not doubt he would act fairly and liberally in the matter. He agrees at once to place his payment on as good terms as you propose to place that of your part upon. He has gone through the calculations, and thinks that on the basis of your proposition, he and you ought to pay me, each, fifteen hundred dollars, in cash, or its equivalent. He has made provision, for his own part, upon this basis; and he thinks that it will be agreeable to you to be drawn upon, for the same amount, on your part. I have requested him, therefore, to draw on you for the fifteen hundred dollars, on my account; which I thought better than to draw in my own name. I have had some scruples about this, as I certainly have no direct authority from you to draw; but he thinks there will be no difficulty in the case, and I really happen to want the money. I trust therefore, you will not fail to honor his draft, and if it turns out that there is any thing wrong about it, it shall be put right. He thinks he can cash the bill, in New York, which would be an accommodation to me. Yours truly,

Danl Webster

LS. DLC.

1. Not found.
2. See above, DW to Murray, June 8, 1842.
3. See above, Murray to DW, June 9, 1842.

TO ISAAC P. DAVIS

June 26, 1842.

In the Washington market this morning at five o'clock, I saw for the first time the bonita. He is a long, slender, round fish, a little resembling those good-for-nothing gaunt cod, which we sometimes catch in our waters; or more perhaps that species of cod, which in the north of Europe is called ling. He has a large head, and a very wide mouth. There is a great deal of fin along the lower part of his back. I should think he was a great fellow for chasing and seizing. This specimen was four and a half feet long, and must have weighed sixty-five or seventy pounds.

His flesh is said to be quite good; I have never tasted it; it looked firm and white.

And there was the black drum. He is made something after the fashion of a hog, short, thick, deep. His neck is short, and his head not large. He is an urchin-looking fellow, with thick, stiff scales, each as big as a ninepence. His color is a dark, dull brown. This specimen would weigh thirty pounds.

Then there was his more comely cousin, the red drum, smaller and of brighter appearance, and regarded, I believe, as the better fish. Both, I believe, are rather coarse in their texture, and not the very best in their flavor. Yet they are much used for food, and give sport to the lovers of heavy fishing. They are taken in the lower Potomac. And then there was a sheep's head. I looked at it and thought of the cholera, and passed by, not without some emotion.

I brought along with me white tinned hooks from England, lines boiled in gum from Rio Janeiro, and other craft from Boston and New York, not to mention some beautiful little reels, and some elegant artificial bass and blue fish bait, manufactured at Marshfield.

But all remain dry. There is good angling of a morning for rock fish, weighing from three to five pounds, up at the little falls of the Potomac. But I am afraid of the sun.   D. W.

Text from *PC*, 2: 133–134. Original not found.

TO HIRAM KETCHUM

[c. July 3, 1842]

Dear Sir,

I thank you for yr note, some days ago.[1] The Whig Papers—C. King & the rest—*will not publish* my letter to Genl. [Waddy] Thompson.[2]

You see Congress has made an apportionment of members, upon the principle of *approximation*.[3] This is the very principle, for which I struggled in the Senate, agt. Mr. [Littleton Waller] Tazewell, ten years ago. I succeeded in the Senate, but the H. of R. wd. not concur.[4]

On that occasion, I made a Report.[5] Judge Story, in the next Edition of his Commentary on the Constitution, adopted it, as setting up the right rule. On the strength of that report, the measure was carried, this year; & yet not one Whig Newspaper has alluded to it.

I send you a Document, in which you will find a copy of my Rept. Yrs

D. W.

ALS. NhD.

1. Not found.

2. DW was probably referring to his letter of June 22, 1842, to Thompson, reproduced in Diplomatic Instructions of the Department of State, 1801–1906 (M–77), Reel 111, DNA, RG 59.

3. The apportionment act (5 *U.S.* *Statutes at Large* 491) had been approved on June 25, 1842.

4. On the apportionment bill of 1832, see *Correspondence*, 3: 152–153, 160, 168–169.

5. DW's report appears in *Senate Documents*, 22d Cong., 1st sess., Serial 214, Document No. 119; and in *Speeches and Formal Writings*, 1.

FROM JULIA WEBSTER APPLETON

Chelsea, July 11th. [1842]

You see, My dear Father, I have acted, upon your suggestion, & amused myself by some sad attempt at house building; I send two plans, which may perhaps give you the idea, of an idea, & if so I shall be very glad. If you send one to Mr. Pratt,[1] I must beg you to be generous enough to let it pass for your own handiwork, for as it does not follow that one should draw treaties & houses equally well, he will not presume to smile, if he thinks you deficient in the latter art. But a truce to deprecations & now for definitions. My pictures are much like those of the man, who was obliged to write underneath, "This is a cow." No[.] one is *your* plan; the library has three bow windows; the other rooms none. No[.] two is another plan; the Library in that plan would do as well with a bow window towards the west. I have drawn it with one looking towards the *East* which would be simliar to the *square* projection in No[.] 1.

Perhaps as it is to be two stories; you will not want a bedroom on the ground floor; in that case either plan would do, with the bedroom cut off. I have made no staircase, as I thought the old one would answer while the old house stood, & if that were pulled down, it would be as easy to build a stair case on that side of the addition, as to build a new wall. I have drawn two views of how they would look, if *I built them*. The projecting window of the library in No. 1 ought to be in the middle. I have no idea of the me[a]surement of the old house, & have therefore been obliged to guess at its relative proportions. When you have time to look at them, pray let me know if you approve. I suspect Mother will laugh at us both.

I was very glad to see Fletcher once more although I did not see as much of him as I wished. Danny is a dear little fellow, & Grace much

grown. My little ones are [doing] nicely, & I flatter myself that I am picking up. Your glass, dear Father has proved a great acquisition to us. With
the assistance of a pocket map, I am making great progress in the geog-
raphy of the harbor. I can see Scituate plainly, & shall try to discover
Marshfield. All intermediate places seem within stone's throw. We have
had a great deal of cool weather lately, & much rain. But every thing goes
finely; excepting alas! the money in one's pockets. I meant to write to
Mother today, but as I have nothing to say except that we are well, I will
defer it till tomororw. Neddy is making a famous tour. I go to town but
seldom therefore hear no news. I have trespassed too long on your time,
dear Father,—I must just detain you to desire much love to Mother &
Ellen, & to say that [I] am & shall be ever Your affectionate daughter
Julia Appleton.

ALS. NhHi.
 1. Julia was probably referring to

one of the many Pratts in Boston
who were house builders.

TO [ISAAC CHAPMAN BATES]

Washington July 16th. 1842.

Confidential

My dear Sir,

Although pressed with anxious labours in my own department, I yet
cannot be indifferent to the state of things in Congress, connected with
the revenue and finance of the country. Bad as that state is, I fear it will
grow worse, unless counsels of moderation & forbearance can be listened
to.

It is probable the Tariff bill will pass the House of Representatives,
containing a repeal of that provision of the land distribution bill, by
which it's operation will cease when duties are laid above 20. per. cent.
ad valorem.[1]

I have fearful forebodings of the ultimate consequences of uniting
these two subjects, & not as a member of the Govmt. but as a citizen and
one of your constituents I pray you to consider profoundly the propriety
of passing the bill through the Senate in that shape.

It is true that I very much regret the provision in the land distribution
bill to which I have alluded and I know that it's adoption was a matter of
great pain to you; and I am now convinced it would have been better not
to have passed the bill, with such a feature in it, & if I were in Congress,
I should vote to repeal the restriction as a separate measure, but I should
by no means vote to keep the two measures together.

There is, in my opinion, at the present moment no considerable anti-
tariff party in the United States; all see that duties must be laid for revenue & nearly all admit that in laying duties regard may be had to the pro-

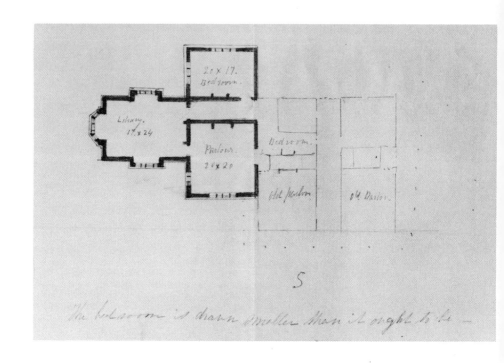

The bedroom is drawn smaller than it ought to be —

South West view of No 1.

Julia Webster Appleton's House Plans, July 11, [1842]

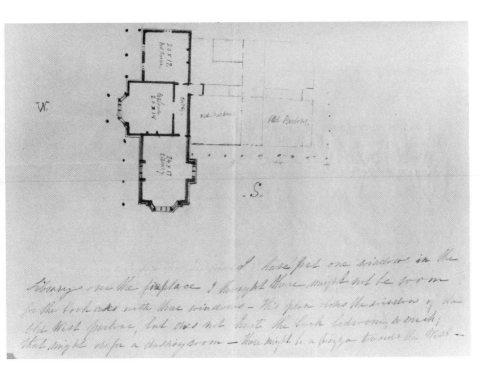

Julia Webster Appleton's House Plans, July 11, [1842]

tection of American Manufactures. I do not think we shall ever have a better opportunity for establishing a Tariff upon just principles & it seems to me that nothing is wanting, to render this opportunity available, but moderation & conciliation.

The present income from the public lands is very inconsiderable & the question of distribution or no distribution of little importance, in my judgment compared with other subjects of vital interest now before Congress.

Although I am for distribution, & if it were in my power would make the act of distribution final & irrepealable, under any circumstances, and in that way put an end to the agitation of such a troublesome question, yet in the present posture of things I cannot think it wise or prudent to put the whole legal provision for the public wants & indeed for carrying on the Govmt. itself, upon the hazard of a connection with another subject, upon which we know that opinions are strongly opposed & warmly excited.

You will excuse me, I know, my dear Sir, for invoking your deepest reflections on this subject, as it appears to me to be one of the greatest moment.

Do me the favour to show this to your colleague. Yrs truly

Draft in DFW's hand. OGK.
  1. The tariff bill, with the clause rescinding distribution, became law on August 30, 1842. 5 *United States Statutes at Large* 548–567.

FROM ISAAC CHAPMAN BATES

Washington July 19th. 1842

My dear Sir,

I recd your letter of the 16th.[1] last eve'g, and I have shown it to my colleague, Mr. Choate, as you desired. With the great respect I have always had for your opinions, and the regard I have for your wishes, and the most anxious desire to do that which, as a senator of Massachusetts, I ought to do in the present crisis of affairs, I see but one course left for me to pursue. You agree with me in opinion, that the proceeds of the public lands ought to be distributed among the states. This you know is the opinion of Massachusetts. The legislature has formally instructed me on the subject. The states, many of them, are deeply in debt. They are in great need of the aid which the public lands will afford them. I cannot give a vote that shall restore them to the treasury, and subject them to the contingencies of the future, and the tariff of duties of consequence, to the fluctuations which their restoration will occasion. Therefore, I cannot vote for a bill that shall have the effect to suspend the distribution indefinitely, without at the same time severing, if I can sever, the connection and dependence upon the tariff of duties, which the proviso in the act of distribution creates. Against that proviso I protested at the time. I gave my vote against it, with the cherished and declared purpose if it was incorporated in the bill, to put an end to it whenever I could.

I share with you fully in the fearful foreboding of the result of the passage of a bill for revenue, adequate to the wants of the government, with a repealing clause of the proviso in it. But my forebodings of the results are equally painful and fearful, if the Senate pass the bill without it. Indeed my conviction is unwavering, that if the Senate should now strip from the House Bill the repealing clause, no bill for revenue will be passed this session. In this position of things pardon me if I repeat that in my judgement there is but one course left for me. In the event contemplated, the responsibility, I think, will not rest upon me. But on the contrary, if I vote against the repealing clause of the Bill, & thereby no bill for revenue or protection be passed this session, I could not answer for it to my own convictions of duty, nor to my own consistency, nor to my own character humble as that may be, and much less could I answer for it to the state that has honored me with its confidence. I have not respect enough for the compromise act as it is called, nor for the proviso in the act of distribution, to be influenced by either. Quite the contrary. I have not forgotten how the one was passed, nor by whom, nor by what combination; nor how the efforts of the others had any tendency to reconcile me to its provisions.

I agree with you entirely that the question of distribution or no distribution, is of little importance, compared with other subjects now before Congress. Therefore it is, that I the more lament it should either impede or prevent the consummation of them. But if of any importance to the Federal Government, it is to the states.

Sir, I cannot express to you the pain it gives me in the present condition of things, to be obliged to act as, according to my present views, I shall act. But I know you will approve the motive that influences me; nor, my dear Sir, will you doubt the sincerity with which I subscribe myself most respectfully & most faithfully Your friend,   I. C. Bates

ALS. NhD. Excerpt published in Van Tyne, p. 272.
    1. See above.

TO [SETH WESTON]

Washington
July 23. 1842

Dear Sir;
    I have recd your letter of the 20th.[1] You appear to be going on well.

You are right in getting a new net. We must follow the fish. Look round, & see our produce this year—& remember what the same land produced when I went first to Marshfield. It is *fish*, *kelp*, & barn manure, [which] have done it. Look at Capt [Asa?] Hewitt's crops. How superior to what they were 10 yrs ago! There is good land enough, if people would but work it well, & manure it.

You do not say where you place the fish—but keep moving. Dont work too hard—nor expose yourself. You have much on your hands—so have I. I keep cool, & hope you will.

Give us an account of [Dr. John] Porter's hay crop. Yrs   D. Webster.

I hear from John Taylor. He goes forward upon the jump!

ALS. NhHi. Published in *PC*, 2: 139–140.
    1. Not found.

TO EDWARD KENT

July 25. 1842

My Dear Sir;

I remember the Concord "Election," very much as you describe it,[1] thro many years; & have pleasure in dwelling on the memory of many valued friends, whom I used to meet on those occasions, & who are now not among us. Where I lived, we were *Country*; Concord was our *City*. It was an exceedingly pleasant village, with a social & friendly set of inhabitants. Your account of Capt [Richard] Ayers[2] is very just. Your recollection does not carry you back to Col Peter Green,[3] & Mr [John] Stevens;[4] although you remember Col [Thomas] Stickney, Dr. [Israel?] Evans, & Mr [George] Hough.[5]

But you must allow me to say, My Dear Sir, that your father's[6] House was for many years quite the center of attraction in our New Hampshire Capital. Its kindness & hospitality have left with me very durable recollections.

We might yet mention a small circle, in & about Concord, of those whom we have known in old times. Mr [Philip] Carrigain, Mr [Abel] Hutchins, Mr [Joseph?] Kimball,[7] & half a dozen others still remain. I occasionally see some of them, & always with pleasure; although I have been absent from that neighborhood so long, & thus have not had the power of forming new acquaintances, as old ones have fallen off, that the change appears to me great, & even sudden. Thus the fashion of the world passeth away, & we pass away with it. Yours truly   Danl Webster

ALS. NhHi.
    1. DW was alluding to Kent's nostalgic essay, "Election Day in Concord, in Olden Times," which had been printed in *Hill's New Hampshire Patriot*, June 9, 1842, and in other

New Hampshire newspapers.

2. Ayer (1757–1831), a native of Haverhill, Massachusetts, had settled in Concord in 1777. In 1814 and 1815 he was a delegate to the New Hampshire legislature.

3. Green (1746–1798), son of Nathaniel Green, was a Concord attorney and state councillor in 1788 and 1789.

4. Stevens (c. 1747–1792) was a Concord merchant.

5. Stickney (c. 1729–1809) was a Revolutionary veteran who had served in the Battle of Bennington; Evans (c. 1747–1807; Princeton

1777) was a Congregational minister in Concord, having served as chaplain in the Revolutionary War; Hough (1757–1830) had set up the first newspaper in Concord in 1789.

6. Edward's father was William Austin Kent (1765–1840), a merchant and banker.

7. Carrigain (1772–1842; Dartmouth 1794) was a Concord lawyer; he had died the previous March 16th. Hutchins (1763–1853) was a clockmaker and tavern-keeper. Kimball (1767–1848), originally from Boscawen, had settled in Newport.

FROM HENRY L. KINNEY

Matamoras July 25th. 1842

My Dear Sir

You will by receiving this be reminded of your friend H L Kinney who remembers you with the affection of a Son. I have written Fletcher frequently and shall now open a correspondence with you should it be agreeable for you to do so.

Whatever your feelings may be towards me will not change the affectionate & friendly attachment I have always felt for you and your family. And when it is in my power to Serve you or them my all Shall be put at Stake to do so. Notwithstanding the horid State of business affairs since I left the U States I have accumilated a verry considerable property in this Country & the verry moment the difficulties are settled between Mexico & Texas I shall be able to realize a large sum of money for a tract of land I come in possession of at the mouth of the Nueces River. For the two years that I have been settled at Corpus Cristi, my place has taken the greatest proportion of the trade from this & other places of account on the coast.

When I first came to this country I petitioned the Mexican Congress through Genl [Mariano] Arista[1] that a law might be passed authorizing Foreigners to hold landed property in this country which law was passed last Congress & it is only within a short time that I have recd my deeds under that act. Genl Arista has shown me much friendship & has been of great service to me in my business in this country. He has more of the American manners & principles than any Mexican I have met.

Genl [Isidro] Reyes[2] who suckseeds Genl Arista is a very good man, but is not thought to possess the talents of Genl Arista. Genl [Antonio López de] Santa Anna[3] is not a favourite of the people.

The U.S. Consul of this place having resigned, I have written Fletcher he could make application for my appointment.[4] In these warlike times that office would give me some protection & assist me in carrying out my business intentions. I have taken no part whatever in the differences between Texas & Mexico although I have been frequently solicited by the Texans to take one of the principal appointments under that Government. I congratulate you for the happy connection made by Miss Julia with Mr Appleton. I have never had the pleasure of an acquaintance with him but I learn from those that know him he is a very good man. It allso gave me great pleasure to hear of your sucksess in the last Presidential struggle. I regret exceedingly the death of Genl Harrison, for I believe his death will retard in a great degree your attaining the Presidency of the U.S.

When you are a candidate for that high office, I shall return to my country & do what I can for you.

I have got a couple of verry curious sheep to send you when an opportunity occurs. Should you write me direct to the care of I. P. S[c]hatzell Matamoros[5]—who is a very wealthy merchant of this place & a particular friend of mine.

Rem[em]ber me kindly to Mrs Webster & Mrs Appleton, & believe me ever your sincere and affectionate friend.   H. L. Kinney

ALS. NhHi. Kinney (1814–1861?), born near Shusshequin, Pennsylvania, moved to Illinois with his father in 1830, where he engaged in farming, mercantile pursuits, and speculation. With Peru, Illinois, as his base he was one of DW's more important land agents in the West in the late 1830s. Broken by the panic, he moved to Texas in the early 1840s and founded Corpus Christi. In the 1850s he organized and led a filibustering expedition to Nicaragua.

1. Arista (1802–1855) was general-in-chief of the northern division of Mexican troops.

2. As stated by Kinney, Reyes (1798–1848) succeeded Arista as general.

3. Santa Anna (1795?–1876) was president of Mexico.

4. Kinney's letter to Fletcher has not been found. Daniel W. Smith, United States consul at Matamoros, was replaced by Richard H. Belt of Indiana in 1844.

5. Schatzell replaced Smith, deceased, as consul in December 1844.

When Webster and Lord Ashburton completed their work on the Treaty of Washington in late July, the question of Webster's resignation resurfaced. Webster received conflicting advice, as in the fall of 1841, but he still had Tyler's confidence and once again chose to remain at his post. That decision, however, severely strained his relationship with the Whigs in his native state and threatened to jeopardize his political future. Much of his correspondence of late August and early September, below, concerns political developments and his standing with the Whig party in Massachusetts.

FROM JOHN MILLS

Washington July 28. 1842

Private

Dear Sir

I am sensible that there is nothing in our acquaintance, or in our past or present political relations, that authorises me, to address to you, this letter. But I offer no apology for doing so, because the subject is one, in which every person may be presumed to feel an interest.

In the course of the last few weeks, I have heard it frequently remarked, by those who, I doubt not are your friends, that when the pending negociation with England is closed, that you *must* consult *your own fame*, and immediately retire from the office of Secretary of State. One gentleman remarked, that the pen with which you placed your name to the treaty, should, before it was again dipped in ink, write the note of resignation.

Were I to presume to give advice on this important subject, it would be the reverse of that, which these friends seem disposed to tender.

That the treaty you are making will augment, even your own reputation as a Statesman, is highly probable: but to resign your office, on the consumation of that act in the present posture of public affairs, without strong and urgent necessity, will not, I apprehend, meet either general approbation, or the expectation of the public. The whole country—men of all parties, know full well, that you mainly sustain the present administration, and although politicians may wish to weaken that administration, *the people generally, have no such desire.* I express no opinion of the executive. But admitting him to be, all that his most bitter enemies have represented, *his administration must be sustained.* And who will the people regard as *their* friend, the men who seek to degrade the President, and to disgrace and weaken his administration, or *the man* who in aiding the President, sustains the honor and interest of the country? I am not the political friend of the President, but hesitate not to say, that the opposition in Congress, and from the Whig press, is producing sympathy for him, which under ordinary circumstances would not be excited. Will that sympathy be lessened, if the "atlantean shoulders," on which he leans for support, are suddenly, and without "good and sufficient cause," withdrawn? I think not.

Heretofore, I have not hesitated to declare, either to political friends or foes, that in my opinion, your conduct was honorable and patriotic, in retaining office, when the other members of the cabinet retired. The reasons for remaining in the cabinet, may not, hereafter, be equally urgent, but they are, and will continue to be powerful, and such as you will find it difficult, I think, to overlook or disregard.

In conclusion, I will repeat that I make no apology for writing, as I know, that I am influenced, in this matter, by motives, free from every taint of interest, personal or political. Indeed, if I were not conscious, of acting from considerations, far above those of a mere partisan character, I should have been spared the labor of writing, and you, Sir, the trouble of reading this letter. I am Sir, very respectfully, yours &c.   John Mills

ALS. NhHi. Published in *PC*, 2: 140–142. Mills (1787–1862), a lawyer, former United States district attorney and Massachusetts legislator from Springfield, was one of Governor John Davis's appointees, along with Charles Allen and Abbott Lawrence, to the northeastern boundary commission.

FROM ABBOTT LAWRENCE

Washington, July 30, 1842.

My Dear Sir:

Since the conversation I had with you upon the subject of your retaining, till the autumn, the "seals of office," I have deliberately considered the consequences that would result to yourself, of delay in this delicate matter—every man should be the judge of his own personal honor—and nothing could have induced me to express an opinion to you, upon a question of so much delicacy, if you had not invited me to do so.

I shall, therefore, without stating the reasons that operate upon my mind, recommend to you, after our treaty shall have been signed, to give notice at once, to the President, that you wish to retire at the termination of the present session of Congress. I feel quite sure you will never retire with so much honor to yourself, as at the present moment. You have achieved all that was expected of you by the country—and your *real* friends, I think, will unanimously agree with me that *now* is the *accepted* time to quit, with honor, your present *responsible* but *disagreeable* position. I pray you to believe that I am now, as I have always been, your sincere friend and obedient servant,   Abbott Lawrence.

Text from Curtis, 2: 131. Original not found.

FROM EDWARD EVERETT

London 3 August 1842.

(*Confidential*)

My dear Sir,

In my despatch[1] I have reported the substance of a conversation, which I had with Sir Robert Peel at Lord Ripon's.[2] In addition to what I have there stated, he said that Lord Ashburton wrote discouragingly of the permanence of our government, thinking it impossible that, with so much disorganization & violence, the system could hold together. I replied in the best manner I could, which was, that we had seen very bad times before, and that when things got very low & very bad, there was always a rally, which brought the country back to a state of greater prosperity than ever. He said he felt confident you were not to blame for the deranged state of things, & he felt sure you were above the influence of the factions, by which the country appeared to be distracted.

I hope you will try, as often as you can, to let me have a few lines confidentially, as to the state of things as far as concerns yourself. I am rejoiced to have you say, in your letter of the 27th June,[3] that you think there is no present prospect of a change in the cabinet. Mr [Charles] Macalester of Pennsylvania is here, and expresses the same opinion, though all sorts of rumors, to the contrary, are, as he says, afloat. Genl. James Hamilton of South Carolina (Texas) is here. He says it is understood that if you go out Mr Stevenson, is to succeed you. He adds that the Presidency lies between Mr Clay, Mr VanBuren, & Mr Calhoun with a leaning, I think, in favor of the prospects of the latter. Genl. [Charles Fenton] Mercer who came in the steamer with Genl. Hamilton appears to share his opinions, as far as the alternative goes between Mr Clay & Mr V. Buren—perhaps from the influence of this recent association. General Duff Green confidently expects, that Mr Calhoun will be the successful candidate.

I informed you, that I had said to Mrs [Stephen] Van Rensselaer,[4] that I should be glad to recommend her son Alexander for appointment, as Secretary of this legation. I have received a letter from Mr Van Rensselaer today, in which he says, that, if he could be permitted to return to the United States, with the family, for a few months, to arrange his affairs, he would be happy to accept the office. To this delay I have no objection. In my letter of the 2d June,[5] I acquainted you with the views, under which I was led to turn my thoughts to him, and I remain of the opinions there expressed, that such an arrangement would conduce to the public service, & the respectability of the mission. I shall be much gratified to have you concur in these views, & recommend to the President, the nomination of Mr V. R.

I send the fourth volume of Madame D'Arblay[6] to Mrs. Webster, to whom & the rest of the family I desire my kind remembrance, being ever, my dear Sir, most truly & Sincerely Yours   E. E.

The cruel Review of Madame D'Arblay in the quarterly is, I understand, by Mr J[ohn] W[ilson] Croker.[7]

ALS. MHi.

1. See Everett to DW, August 1, 1842, Despatches from United States Ministers to Great Britain, (M–30), Reel 45 (Despatch No. 19), RG 59, DNA.

2. Frederick John Robinson, Earl of Ripon (1792–1859), was at this

time president of the board of trade.

3. Everett mistakenly wrote June 27. DW discussed domestic politics in his letter to Everett, June 28, 1842, mDW 22771, and *Diplomatic Papers*, 1.

4. Mrs. Cornelia Paterson Van Rensselaer, daughter of William Paterson.

5. See Everett to DW, June 2, 1842, mDW 22629.

6. Madame D'Arblay, Frances Burney (1752–1840), a novelist. Everett probably forwarded the fourth volume of *Diary and Letters of Madame D'Arblay* (London, 1842).

7. Croker (1780–1857) was a British politician and essayist. The review of D'Arblay had appeared in the *London Quarterly Review*, 70 (June 1842): 134–157.

TO [CALEB CUSHING]

Washington Aug. 8. 1842

Mr [Henry] Hubbard & myself were sureties at the Bank of the Metropolis, for H[enry] L. Kinney, a person from the West, better known to Mr Hubbard than myself, on a note for $3000.

In this note, I had not a particle of interest, any more than Mr Hubbard, but it was my luck to be first indorser. Kinney went off, leaving the note unpaid, Mr Hubbard took it up at the Bank, & called on me, as he had legal right to do, to pay it to him. I remember that a person by the name of [Henry H.] Sylvester, brought me an order for part of the money, which was paid. Who he was I did not know, but supposed him a broker, or man of business in the City. I never complained, or had reason to complain, of his conduct, in this conversation, nor did I treat him with *discourtesy*. He was an entire stranger to me, & called only on a matter of business. Nor when he was removed from his clerkship, did I know, nor had it even occurred to me, that he was the Mr Sylvester who had come to me, on Mr Hubbard's business. I take upon myself cheerfully the responsibility of having said to Mr Spencer, that a person in his Department by the name of Sylvester, had published & circulated in the City gross calumnies agt. me, in regard to the appointment of Alexander Powell, & that I thought he ought to be removed.[1]

I repeat, that at this time, I had not the remotest idea that this Mr Sylvester was the person who had come to me, for Mr Hubbard; nor did I even hear of any thing being said, to my disadvantage, in any way, by that person, in regard to that transaction. My conduct was governed solely, & entirely, by information respecting calumnies uttered by Mr. Sylvester, the Clerk, in regard to Powell's appointment. That information was direct, authentic, from the most credible source; & I believed it, & still believe it, to be strictly, & entirely true.

It is true that Mr [Isaac C.] Bates called on me, but I have no recollection of declining to read any letters, which he desired me to peruse.[2] If he so states it, he is probably correct; but such is not my recollection.

Danl Webster

ALS. DLC. Published in *Reports of Committees*, 27th Cong., 2d sess., Serial 410, Report No. 945, after p. 20.

1. See above, DW to John Canfield Spencer, April 5, 1842. Sylvester's dis-

missal, investigated by the House of Representatives, is discussed in Report No. 945.

2. On Bates's attention to Sylvester's case, see Report No. 945, p. 3.

TO WILLIAM CABELL RIVES

Monday Morning
Aug. 8. 1842

My Dear Sir

For the whole of last week I was intending to call on you, for the purpose of an hour's talk, on pending subjects; but I have been a prisoner, by *lumbago*.

If your convenience will allow you to come round to my house, this morning, soon after breakfast, & favor me with a few minutes of your time, I shall be quite obliged to you. Yrs truly   Danl Webster

ALS. DLC.

FROM JOHN TYLER

Aug. 8. 1842

Dear Sir;

I have delayed sending in this paper to day from a desire that you should look over it before it went.[1] The other gentlemen[2] saw its outline on Saturday when I deeply regretted your absence. Suggest if they occur to you, any amendments on a separate paper.

How deeply do I regret that I cannot have your full concurrence in this procedure. But a Clay Congress can only be met in the way proposed— nor can the independance of the Executive or good of the country be otherwise advanced.

If you could return it to me immediately after reading and suggesting changes it would enable me to have it copied and off of hand this Evening. Most truly yrs   John Tyler

ALS. NhHi. Published in Van Tyne, p. 274.

1. Tyler wished Webster to "look over" his proposed veto of the permanent tariff bill, which had passed Congress on August 5. James D. Rich-

ardson, *A Compilation of the Messages and Papers of the Presidents, 1789–1897* (Washington, 1900), 4: 183–189.

2. Most likely Tyler was alluding to other members of the cabinet.

TO JOHN TYLER

Aug 8th. [1842] 6. o'clock

Confidential

My dear Sir:

I have gone over your paper,[1] twice & must say, that if the thing must be done, you have given the best reasons for it.

But, I must still say, my dear Sir, that in the present awful state of the Country, amidst these violent factions looking to consequences likely to spring up in every quarter I would give almost my right hand if you could be persuaded to sign the bill.

At the same time it is my opinion that the conduct of Congress in uniting these two subjects is wholly indefensible.[2]

What you state, in the first & third head of your reasons, is most just & most important. I feel the force of your remarks on this part of the case & am willing to give you any assurance of my entire disapprobation of the conduct of the two Houses in this respect. It is calculated to give to our legislation a violent, spasmodic, factious character.

Nevertheless in the present state of affairs I should *sign the bill.*

You will find in the accompanying paper[3] some suggestions, which you will look at & give them what weight you think they deserve. Yrs truly

Copy. NhHi. Published in Van Tyne, pp. 274–275.

1. Tyler's veto message of the permanent tariff, sent to Congress on August 9. See above, Tyler to DW, August 8, 1842.

2. The permanent tariff bill retained a distribution proviso while raising the tariff rate above the twenty percent level, a policy Tyler had openly opposed.

3. Not found.

FROM JOHN GRANT CHAPMAN, WITH ENCLOSURE: RESOLUTION OF PORT TOBACCO WHIGS

Port Tobacco Maryland
Augt. 22nd. 1842

Dear Sir

The Convention which assembled at this place on the 18th. inst. instructed me to transmit to you the accompanying Resolution.[1] While it affords me pleasure to be the organ to communicate to you, the approbation of the Whig party of Charles County of your course as a member of the National Cabinet, I may be allowed to say that no one of your friends has viewed your situation with more anxiety or deeper interest than myself, nor is there one who feels a more unwavering confidence that you have continued to look with a single eye to the honor & prosperity of the country. We have seen with mortification & disappointment the President refuse his assent to acts which were passed to carry out principles which the Whigs had regarded as essential to the proper administration of the Government & important to the best interests of the country, & we may sometimes have been at a loss to reconcile your remaining in a Cabinet whose Chief has opposed those measures which you have ever advocated. But permit me to say, that the importance &

delicacy of the negociation lately pending between this Government & that of her Britannic majesty[2] was sufficient to reconcile the great majority of your friends to your retaining a situation where your services could be of paramount importance to our country, & I doubt not that the same wisdom & patriotism will govern your future conduct. I have the honor to be with great respect Yr. friend & servt.   J G. Chapman.

ALS. NhD.
1. See below.
2. The negotiation of the Webster-

Ashburton treaty had been concluded on August 9 and the Senate had approved the treaty on August 20.

ENCLOSURE: RESOLUTION OF PORT TOBACCO WHIGS

At a Convention of Whig Delegates from the several Districts in Charles County, held at Port Tobacco on the 18th. of Augst. among the proceedings was the following—

Resolved that this meeting still retain undiminished confidence in the political integrity of Daniel Webster. And as he has now conducted & concluded our foreign negotiations with an untiring industry & unsurpassed ability, alike honorable to himself & profitable to the nation, this meeting submits with great deference to his judgment, the expediency of his retiring from the station which he now occupies—as the unhappy collisions between the Executive & the Legislature, paralize the efforts of his gigantic mind to promote the public prosperity, & his continuance in office may create unfounded jealousies & distrust in the minds of the great Whig party, unfavorable to his future usefulness, in carrying out the important & patriotic measures of the party.

Resolved that the President of this convention, transmit a copy of the above resolution to Mr. Webster & cause the same to be published.

Copy. NhD.

TO JOHN PLUMMER HEALY

Washington
Aug. 24. 42

Private & Confidential
Dear Sir

My advice to the Whigs of Massachusetts (which I fear they are not likely to have great respect for) would be, *by no means* to commit the State, at this moment, to any body. Events of magnitude are constantly unfolding. Next year at this time will be quite in season—& nothing appears to me to be necessary now but to make a strong rally for the State Govt. Such is Mr Clays present position, that no one can fail to see the awkwardness of pushing him, at the present moment. Such a proceeding can do him no good, & I fear would be sure to give the State to the Loco-focos. It is not to be disguised, that these premature nominations have not helped the Whig cause, in States in which elections have been held, such as N. Carolina, Indiana, Illinois &c. My own opinion is, that equally bad effects would follow from the same policy, if adopted in Massachusetts. I write this in confidence, but you may show it to one or two of the Commee. I never had a stronger opinion, upon any political question.

I pray you, preserve this letter, as I keep no copy. Yrs truly
Danl Webster

ALS. MHi. Published in *W & S*, 16: 389.

TO EDWARD EVERETT

Washington Aug. 25. 1842

Private

My Dear Sir

The President has nominated Francis Robert Rives, son of Mr Rives of the Senate, to be Secretary to the London Mission. This was settled, before the receipt of your last letter, in which, more strongly than heretofore, you recommend Mr. Van Rensselaer.[1] Young Mr. Rives is entirely respectable, & I believe entirely well qualified to discharge the duties of the situation. I do not think, that upon the whole a better appointment could have been made.

Our great distress, at the present moment, is in regard to revenue, & public credit. This day will probably decide whether any revenue Bill at all will pass. It makes me sick at heart to peruse daily the proceedings of Congress. After making all allowances for the consequences of their disagreement with the President, there seems yet little apology for them. The truth is, that the leading friends of Mr. Clay appear to have regarded nothing of so great importance as the promotion of his election, to take place more than two years hence. And it is equally true that sundry persons came into Congress, as Whigs, in the Revolution of 1840, who have nothing of the conservative principles of the Whigs in them, but whose object, on the contrary, appears to be to cut & thrust at any thing which now exists, seeking to distinguish themselves by a rough hand in reforming very small things. Prominent among these, is an old acquaintance of yours from East Tennessee.[2]

I do not know what all these things will come to, but do not wonder that enlightened foreigners begin to doubt of the permanency of our systems. Yrs always faithfully   Danl Webster

ALS. MHi.
1. See above, Everett to DW, Au-

gust 3, 1842.
2. DW was most likely alluding to

Thomas Dickens Arnold, who had served with Everett in the Twenty- second Congress and had been re-elected to the Twenty-seventh.

TO JOHN PLUMMER HEALY

Aug. 26. '42

Confidential

Dear Sir,

I wrote you two days ago,[1] & now will add a word or two more, on the same subject; but this is for your private eye. I have no objection to a Mass. Whig Convention resolving, if they must go so far, tho' they wd. do better to say nothing about it, that "if Mr Clay shall be the leading candidate of the Whigs &c, they would support him cordially &c.["] But to nominate him, or endeavor to *pledge* the Whigs of the State for him, would be little short of insanity. *He has no degree of reasonable prospect of being elected.* Notwithstanding his partizans make so much noise, if you ask where the votes are to come from, nobody can tell. He has not a particle chance in Penna, Virginia, or any Atlantic State South of Va— nor in Alabama, Mississippi, Missouri, Illinois, or Michigan. N.Y. if she support any Whig, will support Scott; & Mr Clay can have no reasonable hope of Connecticut, Maine, or N. Hampshire. He may recon perhaps, on Ken: Tennessee, *Ohio*, & Indiana—but the first of the two last of these are exceedingly doubtful: & Ken: herself has come within an ace of revolution, this month. Depend upon it, the coming elections, wherever they are made to turn on Mr Clay, will terminate disastrously. I advise the Whigs of Massachusetts, therefore, to rally round their State Govts. They are all [united upon] Gov. Davis—or might all agree, I suppose upon Mr [John Quincy] Adams. But they cannot all agree to enter the lists under the Clay banner. I look upon this matter at present only as it is likely to affect the State election, & am anxious, that the Whigs of the Commonwealth should not, by a premature movement on general politics, endanger the result of that election.

These are my opinions, freely given since asked by you, but I do not mean to press them officiously upon others. I pray you regard this, as quite confidential. Yrs truly   Danl Webster

ALS. MHi. Published in *W & S*, 16: 389–390.

1. See above, DW to Healy, August 24, 1842.

FROM JEREMIAH MASON

Boston August 28. 1842

My dear Sir

You are entirely right in the belief that I feel deeply interested in the matter of your treaty, as well for public as personal reasons. In my opinion it is more important to the welfare of the Country than any thing, that has taken place since the Treaty of Ghent. Such I believe to be the public opinion. Your merits in this negotiation are universally admitted to as great an extent as can be desired. What affects you so essentially cannot fail to excite a strong personal interest with me. For be assured, my dear Sir, that there has never been a moment, during our long continued friendship, when I felt more deeply interested in your welfare than I do at the present time. While I most cordially congratulate you on your present success, & the increase of your reputation as a Statesman therefrom, I cannot forbear suggesting my fears & anxiety for the future.

When the late Cabinet so hastily resigned their places, under the supposed influence of Mr Clay, I certainly thought you acted rightly in not going out at his dictation. The emminent services you have since performed will satisfy all, whose opinions are of any value, that you judged rightly in remaining in Office, to enable you to do what you have done. This important affair is now brought to a happy conclusion, & your best friends here think there is an insuperable difficulty, in your continuing any longer in President Tylers cabinet. Having no knowledge of your standing or personal relations with him, or of your views, I do not feel authorized to volunteer any opinion or advise. I presume you are aware of the estimation, in which, the President is held in this region. By the Whigs he is almost universally detested. This detestation is as deep & thorough as their contempt for his weakness & folly will permit it to be. I use strong language but not stronger than the truth justifies. Your friends doubt whether you can with safety to your own character & honor act under, or with such a man.

It is generally understood that Mr. Choate will resign at the end of this session. In that event your old seat in the Senate will be open to you. On some accounts that would not seem to be altogether desirable. I have heard it suggested that you might have Mr. Everetts place in England, & let him go over to France.[1] I repeat that for the reasons already intimated, I give no opinion nor advise as to what is best & most expedient. I hope & trust you will jud[g]e & determine rightly.

Ld. Ashburton has been received here in a manner I presume quite satisfactory to himself. He lauded you publicly & also in private conversation in terms as strong as your best friends could desire.[2] I am my dear Sir as ever Faithfully yours,   J. Mason

ALS. NhHi. Published in *PC*, 2: 148–149.

1. For Everett's comments on DW's interest in the English mission, see Edward Everett to DW, September 16, 1842, mDW 23429.

2. A report of the Boston proceedings in honor of Lord Ashburton appears in the *National Intelligencer*, September 2, 1842.

FROM ALEXANDER BARING, LORD ASHBURTON

N. York 3 Sepr 1842.

My dear Mr Webster

I must at last run away, or rather sail away, without seeing you. This is provoking but I can not help it. I had indeed little to say but it is notwithstanding a mortification to me to leave these shores without first shaking your hand. The pain would be greater if I did not confidently hope to see you in the old world, but for me to benefit by your visit you must make haste for my taper is burning away fast, and I have done my last public work very agreably indeed to my own satisfaction as I have every reason to hope it will prove to the satisfaction of my Royal Mistress.[1] My reception every where has been highly gratifying and when called upon to say something in the great cradle of liberty Faneuil Hall I never longed so much for a few crumbs of your or [Henry Peter] Broughams[2] power to talk to the masses. I did not see [William S.] Derrick[3] but I hope to find him in England. Adieu My Dear Mr Webster. Let me hear from you if you ever have leisure but above all let me see you if you can. Pray remember me most kindly to Mrs Webster and all your family. Yours [sincerely?]   Ashburton

[George Peter Alexander] Healy is to come to take my picture at the Grange in October and pray do not forget that I am to have yours.[4]

ALS. NhHi. Published in *PC*, 2: 157–158 (misdated December 3).

1. Queen Victoria.

2. Brougham (1778–1868), lord chancellor.

3. Derrick, a clerk in the State Department, had been dispatched to England with the official copies of the Webster-Ashburton treaty for ratification.

4. Healy's portraits of Webster and Lord Ashburton are at the New-York Historical Society.

FROM WADDY THOMPSON

Mexico Sep 10. 1842

My Dear Sir.

I have this moment closed my despatch to you[1] in which you will find the note of Mr. [José María] Bocanegra[2] in reply to mine communicating the contents of your two notes to me. I am glad on more accounts than one that the prediction which I made to you at the commencement of this business has been so fully verified. It seems to me that they might have extricated themselves more gracefully. They will be gratified with a proclamation enforcing neutrality and I think now that such a step would be dignified & proper. I should be glad that the arrival of Genl. [Juan Nepomuceno] Almonte[3] in Washington should be signalized by some thing of the kind. He is the head of the liberal party in Mexico & very much attached to our country. He is a patriot & gentleman. If I receive the papers soon I shall make a spanking treaty with these people a different affair from the convention of 1839. Mr. [Brantz] Mayer tells me that he designs shortly to retire from the legation. I wish most sincerely you would send Mr. Fletcher Webster here. If the best intentions and a sincere friendship for you and yours will be a sufficient apology I wd. venture to advise it most strongly. He will never make reputation for himself when he is with you—and no where will he find a better school or a more certain prospect of distinguishing himself than here. I will see that he shall have ample opportunities of doing so. If you have any delicacy in the matter let it be done on my application to the President. If however you & he think otherwise I pray you that a clever man in both the English & American sense be sent out. A member here is surrounded with difficulties & no one to consult with. But I shall clear the docket in a month or two. Most Truly Yr friend   W Thompson.

ALS. NhD. Endorsed by DW: "Private/C.C. to read."
    1. See Waddy Thompson to DW, September 10, 1842, in Despatches from United States Ministers to Mexico, 1823–1906 (M–97), R 12, RG 59, DNA. Thompson was at this time primarily concerned with United States claims against the Mexican govern-ment and the Santa Fe prisoners. On these matters, see *Diplomatic Papers,* 1.
    2. Bocanegra (1787–1862) was the Mexican foreign minister.
    3. Almonte (1803–1869) was the Mexican minister to the United States.

FROM NICHOLAS BIDDLE

Andalusia Sepr. 14, 1842

My dear Sir

I trust by this time your quiet farm life has had its effect upon your health.[1]

I have engaged the Bucks County chickens & shall soon forward them.

I am very glad that you accepted the entertainment offered without the dinner. A dinner requires a speech—& a speech is followed by commentaries which in the present state of affairs it is wiser to avoid.[2]

I hope—& this is the purpose of this memorandum in the shape of a letter—I hope that you will not be influenced by the atmosphere round you, & that in your resolution you will be governed exclusively by your own views of what is due to the country's service & to yourself—without seeking to conciliate or propitiate any party. You have frustrated their purpose—they ascribe to you their failure and every thing which you now do in the way of approximation will be misconstrued into penitence for the past, or apprehension for the future. Neither of these you should feel or show. So decide for yourself.

The industrious acting Secretary has sent to me the Departmental Work, which I shall examine with care.[3]

I understand that there will be a Commee from Boston to examine the Reading Rail Road in the course of a few days.[4] The occasion would be apt for the suggestion of which we spoke.

I am very anxious as to the course you may take in regard to the connection with the administration. It decides all your future political relations, & I wish you to weigh the matter well. With great regard Yrs

N Biddle

ALS. DLC. Endorsed "*Private*."
   1. DW had left Washington for a few weeks' rest at Marshfield and Franklin.
   2. Biddle was alluding to the reception for Webster at Faneuil Hall, scheduled to be held on September 30. An account of the gathering appears in the *Boston Semi-Weekly Atlas*, October 1, 1842.

   3. Fletcher had forwarded to Biddle a copy of *Correspondence between Mr. Webster and Lord Ashburton . . . on McLeod's case . . . on the Creole case . . . on the subject of impressment* ([Washington? 1842?]).
   4. On the Pennsylvania Bank of the United States and the Reading Railroad, see *Correspondence*, 4: 316.

TO CHARLES PELHAM CURTIS

Thursday Eve
Sep. 15. '42

Private & Confidential
My Dear Sir

I hope you have not written for a *reporter*, or that if you have you will counter order the request. Since seeing the proceedings in the Whig Convention yesterday, I perceive it is quite impossible for me to enter into the discussion of material questions, & express my own opinions, without giving offence. It will be better therefore that I should confine myself to a few remarks, in return to the intended friendly welcome, & a few observations on the Treaty, &c. For the same reason, I think, we must give up the idea of a large dinner. There cannot be such a dinner, without toasts: & there cannot be toasts, in which all would concur.[1]

I am sorry for this state of things, but do not see what is to be done but to submit to it. If, on reflection, you think good would come from postponing the meeting, a fortnight or three weeks—or until we hear of the ratification of the Treaty, I should be quite content. Indeed as things now are, I rather dread the occasion. Yrs, most truly,   Danl Webster

ALS. DLC. Published in *W & S*, 16: 383.
   1. DW was alluding to the recep-

tion scheduled at Boston's Faneuil Hall on September 30 to celebrate his successful negotiation of the Treaty

of Washington. His speech on the oc-   *mal Writings*, 2.
casion appears in *Speeches and For-*

Marshfield
Sep. 16. [1842]

Dr Sir

I wish you would find leisure before I come up to look up the Ayes &
Noes in the two Houses, upon the final passage of the Tariff Bill, so as to
show how many Whigs voted agt it, & from what States, & how many of
the other party voted for it, & from what States.[1]

I know not whether it will be best for me to say any thing, at the proposed meeting, beyond a word or two respecting the Treaty.

The tone exhibited by the late Whig convention is so little in accordance with my feelings, that if I say any thing on general politics, I shall
be very likely to give offence. Yrs   D. W.

ALS. MHi.
    1. DW discussed the tariff and votes in his Faneuil Hall speech.

New York Sept. 27th. 1842

Private

My dear Sir,

I regretted very much my absence from town when you passed through
from Washington. I wished, at least, to have taken you by the hand, &
to have rejoiced with you over the admirable Treaty it has been your good
fortune to conclude. I wanted also to tell you that Lord Ashburton in his
private conversation did ample justice to your exertions, without which,
he freely admitted, the Treaty could not have been made. The *proof* of its
equity toward both Countries, is found in the fact, that *ultra* politicians
on both sides, condemn it equally—whilst the great body of the people
here & in the Provinces are satisfied with it! And I will venture to say,
that our grumbling Sister—Maine—could not be tempted *now* to give up
the Treaty for a very large bribe!

My object in writing you today however, is to repeat the wish I expressed one year ago—viz—that neither the abuse of the party press, nor
the solicitations of your personal friends may induce you to surrender
the post you have so ably filled in the Cabinet. There are some other questions of importance to be settled, and as you have hitherto received about
as much abuse as can possibly be heaped upon you, there is nothing very
alarming in the prospect of having to endure it a little longer. I *know*

that R[obert] B[owne] Minturn & M H Grinnell wish you to remain, &
so do many others also, who would tell you, however, that the *Whig party*
would prefer your resignation, if you were to consult them individually!!
I am so disgusted with mere party proceedings, I pay no regard whatever
to the opinions of any man as a *politician*—but I do think in your position just now, you are bound to look to the interests of your Country *first*,
& not to be frightened by any effects upon yourself *politically*, just at this
moment. After the rage of party has spent itself, you will receive the
credit due to your exertions, & people will then rejoice that you had firmness enough to remain in the path of duty, however annoying the company you have met or may meet with may be. Whig *politicians* ask:
"What good can Mr Webster do in such a Cabinet?" I reply—"how can
any one tell, how much evil he may prevent." Some of the very men who
would tell you to resign as a *Whig*, would be much better pleased to see
you remain in, as a *Conservative*. Besides, your department is—foreign
affairs—& in the management of these great Concerns, the President has
certainly given you full power & left everything to yourself. At the very
time that *he* confided in you—how much abuse & detraction did you receive from leading *Whig* presses & from Whig speakers? Therefore, so
far as any claim on your feeling is concerned, I really think Mr Tyler has
the best of the argument. But I put it to you on the ground of *patriotism*
solely, irrespective of mere party, & if I have taken an improper liberty
with you my motive must be my excuse. I write in great haste & with the
full concurrences of our mutual friend Minturn. Yours very truly

Jacob Harvey

ALS. NhHi. Harvey was a merchant in New York City and a close friend to
several prominent English politicians.

MEMORANDUM OF THINGS TO BE PUT IN THE CELLAR

Octr. 15. 1842

To be put into the cellar, for me;

1st. Tub of beef, of abt. 250 lbs; put down with *Liverpool* salt, & a free
use of brown sugar; a little salt petre, but not much. Let the pieces
be well selected, & the whole put in, in the best manner.

2nd. One good hog, well put up in a tub, with Liverpool salt—no salt
petre.

3. One tub hams & shoulders; to be salted in the best manner, with a
free use of brown sugar; when in pickle long enough, to be smoked,
not too much, sowed up in Canvass, & hung up in a cool place the
smaller, the better.

4. 40 bushels of the best of Mr. [Samuel Botsford?] Buckley's kidney,
or Georgia potatos.

5. A barrel or two of the apples now in the corn house; say three.

D. W.

ADS. NhHi.

TO DANIEL FLETCHER WEBSTER

Boston October 19. 1842

Dear Fletcher,

The Britania arrived yesterday, but brought no Mr. Derrick, & no Treaty. I am not a little disappointed at this, as Lord Ashburton arrived out as early as Septr. 23. We have no public despatch from Mr. Everett, but from his private letter I am led to suppose, that the delay, in regard to the ratification, was occasioned, first by Lord Ashburton's proceeding to his own residence, on arriving at Portsmouth, instead of proceeding immediately to London, & secondly by the absence of several members of the Govt. from London, on visits to their respective residences.[1] Mr Everett expresses no doubt of the ratification of the Treaty, altho. it appears that a writer in the Chronicle, supposed to be Lord Palmerston, attacks it vehemently, & calls it Lord Ashburton's capitulation.[2] We may look for Derrick by the next Steam Ship.

I have just returned from N.H. & shall wait no longer for the Treaty, but proceed to Washington next week. Give my best regards to the President. The result of the election in Ohio creates surprise and astonishment,[3] with the proscriptive Whigs in this quarter. But it need surprise no man of sense. New York will follow suit, without doubt; & if Govr. Davis can get thro. in this State, with such a load as he has to carry, he will do well. It is obvious, that the political power in the Country is falling back, into the hands of those who were outnumbered by the Whigs, in 1840. All this was to have been expected, from the violence & injustice which have characterized the conduct of the Whig leaders.

The <present> state of things, now certain to exist three weeks hence, will call on the President, & all who wish well to his administration, to consider deeply & seriously of what shall be done, for the future. Yrs affectionately   Danl Webster

ALS. NhHi. Published in Van Tyne, p. 281.

1. See Everett to DW, October 1, 1842, mDW 23492.

2. The London *Morning Chronicle* had charged that "the treaty was a 'pitiful exhibition of imbecility.' It was 'Lord Ashburton's capitulation.' " As quoted in Howard Jones, *To the Webster-Ashburton Treaty: A Study in Anglo-American Relations, 1783–* 1843 (Chapel Hill, 1977), p. 170. Jones also points out (p. 218) that "there is no doubt of Palmerston's authorship; undated drafts of these articles [in which the attack appears] are in his handwriting . . ."

3. In Ohio, Wilson Shannon, Democrat, had defeated Thomas Corwin, the Whig incumbent, in the gubernatorial election. *Niles' National Register*, 63 (November 26, 1842): 197.

FROM EDWARD EVERETT

London 20 Octr. 1842

(*Private*)

My dear Sir,

I have scarce any thing to add to my private letter of the 17th.[1] I shall hand the ratification of the Treaty to Mr. Derrick today; he sails on the 22d. The seal, which is not in the best condition, was, when I received it, in the plight in which you see it. They have the advantage of us in writing the ratification on Parchment:—we beat them in putting up ours in a neat box.

Mr. [Charles] Dickens' book is out.[2] He hardly alludes to individuals, & speaks, on the whole, unfavorably of the country. I have, however, read but little of it. It is, of course, a hasty gossipping affair. The sale of it will pay the expense of the tour, & that object, I imagine, is what the writer had most at heart.

Mr. [Samuel] Rogers[3] called to see me yesterday. He is the personification of goodness, sense, and kind heartedness:—the Nestor of English literature without the dotage. He is beyond measure delighted with your correspondence with Lord Ashburton.[4] Repeated in cold blood what he says might sound like adulation:—but there is an evident sincerity in his manner, which assures you he feels what he says. He declared he had never read anything so good as your letter on Impressment:—that he had not supposed, till he read it, that there could be such writing now adays. You see in an article in the "Times," a day or two ago, that it had carried conviction into that quarter.[5] I am as ever faithfully Yours   E. E.

ALS. MHi.

1. See mDW 23576 and *Diplomatic Papers*, 1.

2. Dickens (1812–1870), the English novelist, had published his *American Notes*, drawn from his recent tour of the United States.

3. Rogers (1763–1855) was an English poet.

4. *Correspondence between Mr. Webster and Lord Ashburton . . . on McLeod's case . . . on the Creole case . . . on the subject of Impressment* ([Washington? 1842?]).

5. See the London *Times*, October 18, 1842, p. 4.

FROM JOHN HOLMES

Portland 21 Octr 1842

(*Confidential*)

My Dear Sir

While I acknowledge that I am as selfish as others or as many others, still I would not ask a favor of or profess a friendship for one, for whom I did not entertain a favourable opinion. Your late address at Faneuil Hall[1] has inspired me with additional respect & reverence for your talents & patriotism. *You have done right.* There was no need of *your* resigning in a pet because others did & your friends should have been satisfied with your course. You have done thereby great good to your country. If you did it, at some risk of personal popularity, so much more noble was the act.

Whatever may be your future determination I hope & trust that the great national measures to which you allude, will be first matured before you shall leave *the helm*—yes THE HELM for I fear in such a storm, the vessel must sink without *such a pilot*.

Your Bank or *Fiscal Agent* or *Exchequer Bill* or by whatever name you choose to christian it & your *navigation act* are "consummations devoutly to be wished" & it is hoped that you will give such a direction to both, as shall ensure their success. I fear, Sir, that our u[l]tras—Hotspurs & Rowdies have overacted. Would it not have been better for all, to have given President Tyler a fair chance & where they imagined he was wrong to have allowed him an opportunity to correct his error? And after all what are our grounds of complaint? Our *Boundaries & other controversies are satisfactorily* settled. We have a tariff *sufficiently protective*. We have a *general districting law* & a *uniform system of Bankruptcy*, to say nothing of the jurisdiction given to the federal judiciary in national controversaries & many other important act[s], in which the President has cooperated. And after all this, was it necessary to break off from the administration? If there is *blame* in the controversy Congress must take its full share.

You will say that I hold an office & I am arguing to retain it. As much as I need it, I would not justify what I thought wrong to retain a much better office. I own that I owe you for the office I now hold & that I feel grateful for it & I hope for your influence that I may retain it. I can live pleasantly with it & I cannot without it or something like it. If considerations of my having done some good to *my State* & my *country*, have weight—if former friendships shall be regarded, I trust the President will not discard me in the down hill of life. I believe him honest & patriotic &c. I trust I shall not have reason to alter my opinion as to becoming an active partizan at elections. I consider that he has forbidden me. But still I will express an opinion & when I find the President of the U. States abused, as a traitor, robber & pickpocket, I cannot be silent. And when moreover I saw the Queen of G. Britain toasted & at the same time our President *insulted* I did feel my indignation roused.

The truth is our *boys* in Maine & elsewhere have driven on, until they have landed us all in *the ditch*. The premature discussion of Presidential candidates was condemned by the sober & reflecting. But the young men must lead off & here we are. But I am tiring you, with a long epistle & common place thoughts. If you have any leisure write me, if it is but a word. I intended to have seen you in Boston, could I have learnt when you would be there—but this will probably reach you at Washington. I am truly yours   J Holmes

ALS. DLC.

1. The address at Faneuil Hall, delivered on September 30, appeared in the *Boston Semi-Weekly Atlas*, October 1, 1842, and in the *Boston Courier*, October 3. The later pamphlet version differs in many respects, most of them stylistic but some of them significant. See *Speeches and Formal Writings*, 2.

TO NATHANIEL SAWYER

Marshfield, Oct. 27. '42

My Dear Sir,

I duly recd your three letters, the last dated Oct. 14th.[1] Events have proved, that while we judged alike, about the condition of political affairs, & the prospects of the Whig cause, we did not judge wrong. The opinions which I expressed at Faneuil Hall were forced upon me, by the deepest & most honest convictions, & I could not withhold them, altho' I was aware that I should encounter much reproach.

My attachment to true Whig principles is undiminished; but I desire to see more of candor, moderation, & conciliation, in political matters, & especially among men, of all parties. Some weeks ago, I made a visit to our Native State, & native town. One feels, in being among the graves of his ancestors, as if his last home was properly to be by their sides.

I saw your brother Moses,[2] and Mrs [Ezekiel] Webster, & heard of the health & prosperity of others in the family.

Salisbury is improved, in some respects, but not in all. The moral & political tone of the sentiment of the people is, at best, not better than when we were boys. The cause of this, is an interesting question.

If you come to the North, I hope I may see you. Whether I shall again behold the beautiful & rising West, is more than I dare predict, but not more than I hope. I am, D Sir, with sentiments of early & continued friendship, Yours truly   Danl Webster

ALS. NhD. Sawyer (1784–1853; Dartmouth 1805), a native of Salisbury, New Hampshire, had read law with Judge Joseph Story. He began practicing in Newburyport and later moved to Boston. In 1813 he moved west, first stopping in Kentucky and finally settling in Cincinnati, Ohio.

1. None of these letters have been found.

2. Moses Sawyer (1776–1847; Dartmouth 1799) was a Congregational minister who served various churches in New Hampshire, Maine, and Massachusetts.

TO EDWARD EVERETT

Boston Oct. 31. 1842

Private

My Dear Sir

I was sorry the Treaty did not return by the Steamer of the 4th. of this month, as I feared the President would feel some disappointment. I wrote him, however, giving an explanation of the causes of the delay.[1] In three or four days the next Steamer will be here, which I dare say will bring Mr. Derrick & the Treaty.

I believe I have already said to you, that if your last letter on the subject of Secretary, before Mr. Rives' appointment, had been resolved on, had been recd. before that time, your wishes in favor of Mr Van Rennselaer would have been regarded. As it was, I knew no objection to Mr V. R. <*Riv*>; but confess I felt under obligation to Mr Rives, of the Senate, for a manly & able defense of the Treaty, agt. violent assaults made upon it in the Senate. I understood, also, that you had yourself inquired, in a letter to Mr Winthrop, whether Mr. Rives had not a son fit for the place.

We expect Genl. Cass home next month. As I have not seen the President, since the Genl's intention to return to this Country was announced, I can say nothing of any intentions respecting his successor. So far as I am concerned, you may be assured that nothing abrupt will be done, in any matter in which *you* are interested. But how much longer I may be among the Presidents advisers, is quite uncertain. Thus far, every occurrence strengthens the probability of the near approach of that state of things, in which it will become necessary for the President to consider the new position in which he will find himself. I think Mr Cushing will go into the Treasury, either next month, or in the Spring;[2] but have no idea who may be most likely to be my successor. The result of the fall elections, thus far, sufficiently shows the utter folly of having raised Mr Clay's banner. N. York is likely to follow Ohio, & nobody knows what will happen in Massachusetts. The Whig Party cannot hold together, under its present organization, or with the temper which, at present, is manifested by its leaders.

The condition of things is truly discouraging. Business was never worse, its future prospects never more gloomy, while the public counsels certainly manifest little of foresight, or wisdom. But let us hope for better times. When at worst, they say, things must mend. With cordial esteem & regard, I am, D Sir, Yours   Danl Webster

ALS. MHi.
1. Letter not found.
2. On March 2, President Tyler nominated Cushing for the Treasury post, but the Senate rejected the nomination. A few days later Tyler renominated Cushing, but the Senate again refused confirmation.

FROM JOHN HOGAN

Dixon Ills November 14, 1842

Private

Dear Sir,

Permit me to congratulate you, and the country for your very able Speech lately made at Faneu[i]l Hall.

From the many malicious & slanderous charges made against you, since the retirement of the first Cabinet, I had expected you to vindicate yourself as I knew you could, and it is not saying all, that should be said, to assure you, your speech is received by your numerous friends, and by the friends of the administration in this quarter, as a most complete, thorough, and triumphant vindication of yourself and of the administration.

The recklessness of the leaders of the whig party both in referance to Mr Tyler and yourself, is most astonishing. To dash from their lips, the chalice from which they expected a draught of bliss, just at the time of its possession, after years of toil, and, without cause—is to me, most unaccountable.

Every prospect brightened to their gaze, all were enjoying the delights of victory, every thing was moving on pleasantly to the fulfillment of the high expectations, which the country was led to entertain—when in a moment the bond was broken—simply because *One Man*, could not have his wishes gratified in the establishment of an "Old fashioned United States Bank."

Vituperation & malice of his partisans—vented and heaped on Mr Tyler, yourself and many others, who were unwilling to sacrifice the common good to his vaulting ambition—but only sinks him deeper, and places him farther from the object of his wish!

I was pleased at your commendation of the exchequer.[1] I prefer it to any plan hitherto presented. It unites in itself the excellencies of all—the faults of neither.

The people are pleased with it, and men of all parties, whose first wish is for their countries welfare, desire anxiously to see it the law of the land. Many who were friend[l]y to Mr Tyler, have favoured it, from its first presentation but I find a good many more willing, yes anxious to have it pass, since it has publickly received commendation from your master intellect. I do hope it will be pressed at the ensuing Session of Congress, both in the executive message & report from the department, and also by the influence of the cabinet and the friends of the country. I had not intended to have written you so long a letter—knowing how ard[u]ous are your duties, and not knowing whether it would be acceptible to you. I shall therefore omit many things it would gratify me to say & subscribe myself, Your Oblidged & ob Sert and friend   John Hogan

I have taken the liberty to enclose a letter for the Editor of the "Madisonian"[2]—J. H.

ALS. NhD.

1. Hogan was alluding to DW's remarks made at the close of his Fa- neuil Hall speech.
2. Not found.

FROM SAMUEL APPLETON APPLETON

Boston November 22d 1842.

Dear Sir

I have just got a line from you,[1] & in regard to advertising in the Courier; we do not advertise at all, but if we should I will take care that paper has its' share.

Our Election has gone bad enough, much worse than I expected, & I have not the least hope for the Towns that are to try again next Monday, Marcus Morton & his sett will rule in this State for some time to come.[2] The Whig Quarrels will not be healed very easy in my opinion. New Jersey, or Delaware are the only decent States left, & they are not very big ones.

We are all preparing for Thanksg[iv]ing which is tomorrow, Fletcher & Caroline dine with us tomorrow, I have a Turkey for the occasion raised at Chelsea, & wish you were here to try a cut. I have had a Sheep from Marshfield, & it was a nice one, quite equal to anything in the Market.

Edward is pressing his law studies, & enlightens us occasionally on knotty points, he visited Marshfield with Fletcher, but they did not do any serious injury to the Birds in that quarter, the weather to be sure was not very propitious for them.

Julia & the two Small ones are quite well, and send much love to you, Sammy walks quite well, & is quite proud of his performance's.[3]

I suppose you have concluded to hold on till March, I hope it is so, & to judge from the Madasonian, there would appear not any doubt of it.

We do not hear of any more states nominating Clay, that jig is up, Coon Skins are as cheap now.

Hoping to hear from you when you have nothing better to do. I am your affec Son   Saml A. Appleton

ALS. MHi. Endorsed: "Recd. 26. Nov/ Private."

1. Not found.

2. Marcus Morton, the Democratic gubernatorial candidate, had defeated John Davis, the Whig incumbent, by some 1500 votes. In the congressional campaign, the Massachusetts Democrats had also made gains.

3. Caroline Le Roy (1840–1911?) and Samuel (1841–1925) were the Appleton's two children.

TO HIRAM KETCHUM

Nov. 24. '42

Dear Sir

The "Commercial"[1] has ceased coming to me, I suppose in consequence of a public notice from this Depar[tmen]t. I like it, on the whole, as well or better than its cotemporaries—& shall see if I cannot order it. Meantime, say to Col. [William Leete] Stone

1. To take no notice of the paragraphs of the Madisonian at all; but if he finds any important matter in that print to republish it, at once.

2. To take no notice of any little appointments, or removals.

3. Prepare himself for a message, which will, on the whole, please you & him, & take the Country between wind & water—an able, excellent, & well written message.[2] Keep things entirely to yourself, except this hint to him. Yrs   D. W.

ALS. NhD.
1. The New York *Commercial Advertiser.*

2. DW was probably alluding to Tyler's forthcoming second Annual Message to Congress.

TO MARCUS DUVALL

Department of State,
November 26. 1842.

Dear Sir;

The question proposed in your letter of the 24th. instant[1] is quite too extensive to be answered briefly. Persons of great distinction have differed upon it; and perhaps, after all, it must always be subject, in each particular case, to so many qualifications, that an absolute answer, applicable to all cases, can hardly be given.

It is natural to think that the agent is bound to respect the will of his constituents; but, then, on the other side, it is to be considered, that the vote of a representative affects the interest of others, as well as that of his own constituents; and those others may be a nine, and his constituents a one. Shall he, therefore, in giving a vote that is to bind a hundred, follow the wishes and interests of ten, and disregard the wishes and interests of ninety?

That old English parliamentary idea doubtless is, that a representative once chosen, is to act, not exclusively for the interest of his constituents, but for the good of the whole. In this country, both sides of the question have been espoused with ardour, and maintained with great ability. I have never had occasion to discuss the question nor to express any opinion upon it, so far as I remember. Respectfully yours   Danl Webster

LS. DLC. Duvall, a native of Maryland, was at St. John's College, either as a student or member of the fac-

ulty.
1. Not found.

FROM EDWARD EVERETT

London 3 Decr. 1842.

(*Private*)
My dear Sir,

I wrote you a long private letter of the 17th Novr., to go by the Steamer of the 19th, but it was accidentally left out of the parcel of despatches.[1] You observe in your private letter of the 31st,[2] that "You were sorry the Treaty did not return by the Steamer of the 4th Octr. as you feared the President would feel some disappointment." You will have noticed since Mr Derrick's return, that the Queen's ratification of the treaty did not take place, till after the departure of the Steamer. Considering that Lord Ashburton did not arrive till the 23d, and that Sir Robert Peel was then in the Country, where Lord Ashburton went to visit him, it is perhaps as much as Ministers could be expected to do, to get the Queen's signature to the treaty in less than a fortnight. The ratification of the Queen & the Exchange of ratifications has not yet, I believe, been officially announced here. I think this is not done in this Country, till a treaty has been laid before parliament.

I would call your attention to an article in the "Times" today, relative to the Boundary on the Oregon river.[3] I am sorry to see the attempt beginning, to persuade the British public, by such gross misstatements, that the right is all on their side, in this Controversy. It is, however, making trouble for themselves against the day when,—as in the North Eastern boundary,—it becomes necessary to abandon their pretensions, & admit that there are two sides to the argument.

General Cass passed two days in London on his way to Liverpool. I think he goes home, expecting to receive an invitation to become a candidate for the Presidency. Perhaps he has been influenced by General Duff Green's opinion, that the alternative presented is that of General Cass or Mr Calhoun. I see it stated from American information, that Genl. Duff Green carries home *projets* of treaties between the United States and France & G. Britain respectively, drawn up in Concert with M. Guizot & Sir Robert Peel! You will be able to form your own opinion as to the probability, that persons, at the head of the governments of France & England, would commit themselves in this way, with an unauthorized private citizen of a foreign State. Genl. Green was (I believe) introduced to M. Guizot by General Cass, and brought letters from General Cass to London, which procured him introductions to Mr [John] Macgregor,[4] assistant Secretary of the board of trade, to the Earl of Ripon, & Lord Aberdeen. He obtained a letter to Sir Robert Peel, but did not see him. Mr MacGregor inferred (mistakenly of course) from Genl. D. Green's conversation, that he was associated with Mr [Frederick John?] Robinson,[5] in the matter of the loan. Lord Aberdeen told me, that he called on him & talked a great deal: that he (Lord A.) could not comprehend the grounds of the visit; & made no reply beyond words of civility to any thing he said. I have reason to think Gen G. contemplates returning to London, and may try to make the President think, that he has done and is able to do, good. I need not say to you, that no thing would do us more injury in this way, than the belief that the Government of the United States countenanced proceedings so irregular and (according to all European notions) unwarrantable. I send you a map which will enable you to understand the news from China.[6] It is awkwardly drawn, in as much as you must read it sideways. Ever yrs E. E.

ALS. MHi.
  1. See mDW 23734.
  2. See above.
  3. The article, entitled "North-west Boundary," appeared in the London *Times*, December 3, 1842, p. 5.

4. Macgregor (1797–1857) had become joint-secretary of the Board of Trade in 1840.
  5. Earl of Ripon.
  6. Not found.

TO HENRY HUBBARD

Decr. 8. '42

My Dear Sir;
  If you will draw on me for $300, 60 days date, I will surely honor your draft. You propose what is fair, & favorable. This Kinney & Western business has done me infinite harm. It will take two years, at least, to extricate myself, even with better times.[1] Yrs truly Daniel Webster

ALS. CSmH.
  1. On the Hubbard-Webster indebtedness, see above, DW to John

Canfield Spencer, April 5, 1842, and DW to Caleb Cushing, August 8, 1842.

TO [SETH WESTON]

Washington
Decr: 8. '42

Dear Sir;
  I am glad to hear from you, & to learn that you are all well: and will answer your questions.[1]
  Keep the ox & cow, intended for our beef, upon *meal* & hay, till after New Years day. Then slaughter them, the first day of proper weather; & put up the meat, in the very best manner. Perhaps it need not all go into our cellar; but put up enough, & more than enough. I shall run away from Marshfield next Summer, if the provisions are not better than they were last.
  Put me up 300 of clear pork, first quality—in the same nice way. Sometime about the middle of Feby, or 1st of March, put up a small hog, say 180, or 200,—to be pork for boiling. The ribs of this not to be taken out of the middling, as in clear pork, but to be cut thro.
  Salt the shoulders, & hams, & give them a good deal of brown sugar— & have them smoked. Mrs [John] Thomas[2] can tell about this.
  We shall not be able to buy any things, next year, & therefore must have meat to live on.

Provisions are cheaper in the West, than in old Marshfield. A member of Congress tells me, that in Illinois, pork is selling at $1.25 a hundred, beef at two Dollars, & millions of bushels of corn at 8 cents. A good cow may be bought for $4. They say there is plenty of provisions, but the people are likely to starve, for want of money to pay for cooking.

The last news from that quarter is, that the pigs have resolved to make a *strike*, for higher prices; they say that a dollar & a quarter a hundred will not pay for cracking the acorns!

Look out for the first good ice.

I trust the late storm left a good win[d]row of kelp on the Beach. Make the oxen, steers & horses, pay for their keeping, by hauling it up.

I send you a no. of copies of "Capt. Tyler's" Message. Write, once a week.[3] Yrs   D Webster

ALS. NhHi. Published in *PC*, 2: 158–159.
1. Letter not found.
2. Lucy Turner Thomas (1771–

1849) was Charles Henry's mother.
3. For Weston's response, dated December 18, see mDW 23911; and *PC*, 2: 159–160.

TO NATHANIEL F. WILLIAMS

Washington Decr. 8. '42

Private

My Dear Sir;

Will you do me the favor to accept a dr[a]ft, drawn at my request, & for my use, for $1000, at 60 or 90 days?

I am sorry to trouble you, but need some little accomodation of that kind.

You may rely on being placed in funds in season. Let the matter be *entirely within our selves*. I shall get some man of business here to draw the Bill so that my name will not appear.[1] Yrs   Danl Webster

ALS. NhD.
1. On December 10, Fletcher drew on Williams for $1000 (see mDW

39871), but it has not been determined if this draft was made for DW's use.

TO [JOHN PLUMMER HEALY]

Washington Dec 15th/1842

Dear Sir,

I have somewhere a copy in my own handwriting of one of the Sections, I think the sixth of Mr. Clay's compromise Bill as he first drew it and handed it round to his friends, in his own handwriting.

This I have preserved as proof and it is full proof of Mr. Clay's intention to abandon protection altogether after 1842. The copy was made on a sheet of letter paper which was folded crosswise, with a title on the outside, near the end, "Mr. Clay's bill," or "the Sixth Section of Mr. Clay's bill," or some such memorandum. The paper was filed with half a dozen, or a dozen others of various character all tied round with a string.[1]

I have not been able to put my hand upon this paper since the general derangement of things incident to breaking up my household and removing every thing from my library, in going to Europe in '39. There are some boxes of papers taken from the House, which were carried to the office & stand in my little room. One of the boxes, I remember is marked "family papers." I think there are others also. I will be obliged to you at your earliest leisure to make search among these for the paper which I have described above.

Do not devolve this work upon any body else, as these are papers which I do not wish any one else to see. You'rs truly   Danl Webster

LS. MHi. Published in *W & S*, 16: 390–391.

1. On the Clay compromise, see *Correspondence*, 4: 262, 263–265.

FROM FRANCIS LIEBER

Columbia S.C.
Dec. 17. 1842

Private

My dear Sir,

I received your very kind lines of Dec 12, last night, and thank you most cordially for the important documents which you have had the goodness of sending me.[1] They have not yet reached me, but will no doubt arrive in due time. I shall have them bound in one volume and a precious volume it will be. Were I living at Boston, I know I should deliver a course of lectures to the Cambridge Law Students on your letters; and right con amore I should do it. Why has no one yet come out in the North American with an article on your Correspondence worthy of the noble subject, separating the diplomacy from the Law, aye, the Ethics of Nations, as the weft from the warp, and showing the skill, perseverance, delicate irony and sturdy resolution of the one, while freeing the other from all the entwining threads and clearly showing of what good, sound moral stuff the main thread is spun.[2] It is time, it seems to me, that all that which by your Correspondence and Transactions has been gained for the intercourse of civilized nations as international Ethics should be well sifted, clearly stated and be added to the international catechism of our race. But, unfortunately, so it is in almost all cases. We loose in America immeasurable precious time by constant self-laudatory shower-baths and squirting at each other the stagnant contents of pools and gutters.

You have seen, no doubt, what our Legislature here has done in consequence of the resignations of Messrs Calhoun and Preston.[3] What a state of politics! I Corinthians 1.12.

Since I wrote the last line I was visitied by a Rev. Mr [Ernest Lewis] Hazelius, who, a native of Prussia, left it in 1800 and never saw his country again until within a few months. As you may well imagine I put him fairly to the examination rack. In the course of our conversation he mentioned a fact which he authorized me to tell you with his name, when I told him, that I was just writing to you and should desire to mention the fact. It is this, that several German governments, among them to a certainty and his personal knowledge and observation, that of Bremen and Hanover are in the habit of shipping criminals to the U.S. to be let loose here. I knew it had been done once by the Republic of Hamburg; but I knew also that that State was heartily ashamed of it. Here however is a regular thing—a most shameful international outrage. When Lord Ashburton arrived here I ventured to suggest to our common friend Mr Choate that something about pauper-exports should be added to our treaty if there were not already too many subjects to be dealt with. It seems to me, in my humble opinion, that something might very easily be done through our consuls to prevent the importation of crime and vice. Besides the injury done us, the insult is insufferable. Yet, the law ought not to exclude *political* offenders. No wonder *I* plead for them. With the highest regard Your very Obedt Servt   Fr. Lieber

ALS. DLC.

1. On December 4 (mDW 23838), Lieber had requested a copy of *Correspondence between Mr. Webster and Lord Ashburton . . . on McLeod's case . . . on the Creole case . . . on the subject of impressment* ([Washington? 1842?]); and DW had forwarded the document with a covering note on December 12 (see mDW 23873).

2. Jared Sparks shortly published a review essay on the Treaty of Washington and other documents relating to it—though it did not include a review of the above work—in the *North American Review*, 56 (April 1843): 452–496. DW did, however, suggest that Ticknor approach the *North American Review* about Lieber's writing an article. See DW to George Ticknor, December 21, 1842, mDW 23928.

3. The South Carolina legislature had elected James H. Hammond to Calhoun's Senate seat and George McDuffie to Preston's.

FROM JAMES BOYLES MURRAY, WITH ENCLOSURE: DW'S ACCOUNT

Washington December 22. 1842

Dear Sir

I now hand you a statement of my account with you growing out of my agreement to purchase your 58 shares of Clamorgan Stock, payable in United States Bank Stock at par, and by which you will perceive that a very considerable overpayment has been made. The opportunity afforded by the return of Mr. Maxcy, who has brought over all the bankers books as well as the various letters & agreements on which these transactions were founded, enabling me to make up the account & to explain the cause of this overpayment.

As a greater security to the former owners of the Clamorgan Shares contracted for by me, I agreed to allow all the payments from purchasers under me to be placed to the credit of Mr. Maxcy with Prescott Grote & Co the Trustees & Bankers in London.

There was an error in the first instalment being drawn for as being 127 Shares instead of 116, & in the month of November 1840 Mr Jaudon as your agent urged upon Mr. Maxcy to give him a draft for £1470 as being the then market value in London of the 105 U.S. Bank Shares due on the 2d. installment, so as to give him a lien to that extent on the funds altho this money was not yet in the bankers hands but agreeing that the price should be regulated by the market value at the time when the instalments should become payable, which, although Mr. Maxcy was wholly un-authorized by me to vary from our original arrangement, yet, influenced by the desire which he has always evinced to secure your interest, he agreed to do & hence the balance arose which has more than absorbed the whole of the two instalments & shows moreover that the delivery to you of the $11000 Illinois bonds should never have been made. I beg that you will avail yourself of Mr. Maxcys presence in this City with all his papers to become acquainted with all the facts, and then I shall rely upon your doing towards me precisely that which under similar circumstances our positions being reversed, you would have felt justified in requiring at my hands. I remain with great respect Dear Sir Your mo obt Servt

Jas. B. Murray

ENCLOSURE: DW'S ACCOUNT

Hon Danl Webster on a/c Clamorgan Shares in a/c with James B. Murray
1840

Sept 1.	By 58 Shares Clamorgan Stocks purchd. of you through V. Maxcy Esq at $600 pr Share pay[abl]e in U.S. Bank Stock at par in the following Instalments	$34800

1840 Sept	116 Shares	
1841 June	116 do	
1842 March	116 do	
	348	

1840

Octr   To pd. Dr. S[amuel] Frothingham—by
your order 127 Shares U.S. Bk Stock being
116 on 1st Instalment & 11 on a/c of 2d
Instalment leaving 221 Shares due   12700

bal due $22100

payable in U.S. B. Shares at par of these 105 Shares were paye. in June 1841 & 116 do. in March 1842, when the market prices in London were as appears by Mr Jaudons certificate as follows vizt.

105 Shares in June 1841 @ £4   £420

116 do. in March 1842   @   1   116

            £536

Whereas Mr. Maxcy, under whose control the funds
in Prescott Grote & Co were left as a security for
paying the several instalments paid to Mr Saml Jaudon
as your attorney in Feby 1840 £1470 under his indemnity   1470
to your behalf to make good the difference between the
market value of the U.S. Bank Shares as they should become
due & the sum thus paid———

over paid   £934

To which is to be added the value of $11000 Illinois 6 pr. ct. bonds delivered to you under a misapprehension of the state of your a/c.

ALS. DLC. Endorsed *"Private."*   James Boyles Murray to DW, June 29,
   1. For a discussion of the sale of   1840.
the Clamorgan shares, see above,

TO [ROBERT PERKINS LETCHER]

Washington
Decr. 29. 1842

Private & Confidential

My Dear Sir;

I recd this morning your letter of the 23rd,[1] & have lost no time in directing Two Copies of the Census to be sent to you, by mail. The boxes containing the portions of those documents belonging to Kentucky, were shipped near a month ago, I believe, by way of New Orleans.

I assure you, My Dear Sir, I should be most happy to see you, & "talk with you a good deal." I do not believe, that in a free conference, we should differ very widely, as to the causes which have brought things to their present condition. But I am much more doubtful whether either of us could invent a remedy. I have noticed, of course, what has taken place in Kentucky, not omitting the speeches, letters, &c at the Frankfort Barbecue.[2] Very well. It would be affectation in me to pretend, that some of these things, coming from the quarters they did, have not given me pain. They certainly have; while, for others I feel nothing but contempt. But neither those which cause pain, or those which only excite contempt, will be likely to move me, from any purpose which I may entertain.

I am glad you think favorably of the correspondence with Lord Ashburton. I send you herewith a copy of some part of it. I wish it could be generally read, in Kentucky, but I suppose that is hardly probable. I would send you twenty or thirty copies, if you supposed there were so many members of your Legislature, who would be glad to receive one.

I must add, My Dear Sir, that I retain my personal regard & good feeling towards you; never having heard of any personal ill-treatment, on your part, & not at all questioning your right, as well as that of others, to differ from me, politically, as widely as you please. Who thinks most correctly of the present, or who predicts most accurately of the future, are questions which must be left to be solved by time, & events. Yours very truly   Danl Webster

ALS. NcD. Published in Mrs. Chapman Coleman, ed., *The Life of John J. Crittenden* (2 vols., Philadelphia, 1871), 1: 195–196.
    1. Not found.

2. DW was most likely alluding to Kentucky's nomination of Clay for the Presidency. *Niles' National Register*, 63 (November 12, 1842): 169–170.

FROM JOHN TYLER

[December, 1842]

My Dr Sir

Cass's last letter[1] ought to have a reply—beginning with a commentary on the singularity of the whole proceeding and declaring the reply an end of the matter.[2] This is important.

Bentons Speech should be answered seriatim and with power.[3] He stood by with his arms folded during Jackson's and Van Buren's administration, and permitted almost a surrender of the principle involved in the Creole, and now shews wonderful zeal. You remember Mr. Calhoun's resolutions about that time which saved the *principle* from surrender.[4]

A word to you is enough. Truly Yrs   J. Tyler

ALS. DLC. Published in Tyler, *Tylers*, 2: 235.
    1. See Cass to DW, December 11, 1842, in *Diplomatic Papers*, 1.
    2. DW's reply of December 20, 1842, also appears in *Diplomatic Papers*, 1.
    3. Benton's speech against the

Treaty of Washington, delivered in the Senate on August 18, 1842, had only recently been printed. See *Congressional Globe*, 27th Cong., 3d sess., Appendix, pp. 1–27.
    4. *Senate Journal*, 26th Cong., 1st sess., Serial 353, p. 216.

FROM JOSEPH EVE

Galveston January 1st, 1843

Private

Sir

From what I had seen in many of the newspapers published in the United States, I was apprehensive that you intended to withdraw from the State department so soon as the Treaty, made by Lord Ashburton and yourself was ratified by the Government of Great Britain—A Treaty which will perhaps produce more beneficial results to the United States than any act of this or any previous administration, by happily adjusting all the exciting and difficult questions which have heretofore existed between the two governments, and which a year ago all believed would lead to a disastrous and ruinous war.

While a few individuals in the United States arrogate to themselves, the right to find fault with, and condemn every thing which does not originate in their own brain, have the unblushing effrontery to condemn the Treaty;[1] Permit me to congratulate you, and felicitate the friends of the country, upon your success in quieting difficulties that were thought by many to be insurmountable, and to effect which required a union of talents, prudence, candour, patriotism, patience and perseverance rarely to be found in the same individual.

I am truly gratified to learn that you have returned to Washington and have resumed your official Station,[2] and where I most sincerely hope, that it will be compatible with your feelings, and the wishes of the President for you to remain.

With full confidence that so soon as the present political storm passes away, an impartial public will not fail to justly appreciate your important services to the country.

The President's message arived by the last Steamer from Orleans. I consider it an able State paper, as do all others here with whom I have conversed upon that Subject.

I have examined that part of it which speaks of the Exchequer with care, and attention. Believing as I have that a United States Bank was necessary to facilitate the fiscal concerns of the Nation, to regulate exchange and that the commercial and enterprising Spirit of the people of the United States, required the aid of Bank facilities, I have heretofore been a bank man.

But the unfortunate manner which the United States Bank of Pennsylvania has wound up its concerns, the System of Swind[l]ing and robbing so common among the Banks, and the many individuals who have become interested in the local institutions, have all combined to make a national Bank unpopular, so much so, that I believe if the question could be put directly to the people of the United States a majority would vote against it.

With this view of the Subject, were I a member of Congress I would vote for the Exchequer as recommended in the message and give it a fair trial, if it worked well in collecting and disbursing the revinue, in regulating exchange, and affording facilities to commerce, then all should be satisfied with the measure. And if after making a fair experiment it should not meet the expectations of its friends Congress would have the power to repeal it.

The Congress of Texas is still in session, such strong [par]ty feeling prevails among the members, that they have passed no general law, nor are they likely to adopt any mea[sure] calculated to produce union, or, restore confidence[.] With sincere regard and great respect I have the honor to be your obedient Servant   Joseph Eve

ALS. NhD. Published in *Southwestern Historical Quarterly*, 44 (July 1940): 107–108. Eve (1784–1843), a native of Culpepper, Virginia, had settled in Knox County, Kentucky, about 1807. After reading law, he won seats in both the Kentucky house and senate as a Whig. In 1841, Harrison appointed him chargé d'affaires to

Texas, where he served until his death.

1. Eve was most likely alluding to Lewis Cass and Thomas Hart Benton. See above, John Tyler to DW, [December, 1842].

2. Webster and Caroline had been on a short vacation to the northeast and had visited the Elms in Franklin.

FROM EDWARD KENT

Augusta Jany 4 1842 [1843]

(*Private*)

My dear Sir,

I am at this place at this moment, attending to the matter connected with our report & the final close, so far as we are as commissioners concerned, of the long vexed question.[1] I am happy to inform you that our friend [Edward] *Kavanagh* has this day been elected President of the Senate, by a nearly unanimous vote. There was an effort made to place Virgil *Delphini* Parris over him, based upon opposition to the treaty. But it signally failed. I rejoice at this result, particularly as it is evidence that the sober judgment of our people will not endorse the tirade of Mr Benton.[2]

Although there is now a spirit among the trading politicians which would induce them to attempt to manufacture public sentiment, as they do Lowell cotton, by the yard & to order, I think from what I have observed that there is a prevailing feeling of acquiscence and a large majority at heart "rejoice and are glad" at the settlement, and give due credit to all who have been instrumental in effecting the settlement. But, you know, it is safe now, after the treaty is ratified, to be vociferously patriotic and magniloquently warklike [warlike] and some of our *great* men cannot resist the opportunity to figure as champions. Nevertheless, I think our good people do not, at heart, much relish the alternative presented by Mr [Reuel] Williams in his motion in secret session[3] and many say, if War can only be pointed to by those who opposed the treaty, it was folly & wickedness to reject the treaty. Great efforts are making to circulate Benton's speech in Maine, & doubtless it will have some effect, but it cannot shake the strong feeling of satisfaction that the question is settled.

Judge [William Pitt] Preble, who was to draw our report, has not yet arrived. I *hope* it will be such, that we can all sign it and I have but little doubt it will be. At least, I can say that in October he was strong in defence of the treaty.

Our wise executive council refuse to allow us any thing like a reasonable compensation for our services, but that is a small matter in view of the great work accomplished. With true regard your obedient servant

Edward Kent.

ALS. DLC.

1. The Maine commissioners submitted their final report to Governor John Fairfield on January 4, the same day that Kent wrote Webster.

2. For Benton's speech in opposition to the treaty, see *Congressional Globe*, 27th Cong., 3d sess., Appendix, pp. 1–27.

3. On August 19, in the secret session of the Senate on the Treaty of Washington, Williams submitted a resolution which called for the treaty to be sent back to the Committee on Foreign Relations and requested the President "to take immediate possession of the disputed territory." *Congressional Globe*, 27th Cong., 3d sess., p. 1.

TO JOHN PLUMMER HEALY

[Washington, January 9, 1843]

Dr Sir

I must leave Cho[u]teau v Webster[1] to be managed as you see best. Wd. rather avoid a jury trial, if I could—but wd. not, for that object give up any substantial advantage.

In one respect, there seems to be an irregularity. If the Court decide agt me, it is final; but if agt. the Pl[ainti]ff, as he is only to be nonsuited, he may try his luck before another tribunal. Yrs   D. W.

ALS. MHi.

1. *Pierre Chouteau, Jr., v. Daniel Webster*, 6 Metcalf 1–7 (1843), a case which grew out of Webster's indebtedness to the Chouteaus for a portion of the Clamorgan lands. Webster lost the case.

The low point of the depression which started in the late 1830s hit in early 1843. Through authorized loans the federal government had man-

aged to remain solvent, but many state governments were in dire circum-
stances: they were unable to pay the heavy debts they had piled up in
the 1830s for internal improvements and other projects. Some states, like
businessmen, bankers, farmers, and politicians, faced bankruptcy. Many
had already defaulted and others threatened to.

It had been one of Webster's chief objectives as secretary of state to
use his power and influence as an executive officer to promote the return
of prosperity. In much of his correspondence there is a strong suggestion,
never explicitly stated, of something like a pledge to the business and
banking communities—men of wealth who had frequently rescued him
financially—to remain in office until recovery and prosperity returned.
Hopeful that some remedies to the financial crisis could be found which
were acceptable to Tyler, he remained in office until he was convinced of
the futility and failure of his efforts. Ruggles's letter below is typical of
the concern of most promoters and financiers for the economy.

FROM SAMUEL BULKLEY RUGGLES

New York Jan. 9. 1843

My dear Sir

I beg leave to send you a Report we have recently made to the Common Council of this City, touching the Ways & Means of paying its Croton Water debt.[1]

We can hardly flatter ourselves that amid the weighty cases which
press upon your time the fiscal affairs of a mere municipality can excite
much interest,—and yet there are some matters treated of in this paper,
which may possibly attract your favourable notice.

I refer particularly to the ground we take as to the necessity of providing at once, not only for the interest but the principal of the Nineteen
millions which the work has cost us,—& of imposing the whole burthen
upon the present generation. Seeing the sad decline of public character
throughout an extensive portion of the Union, we have felt it peculiarly
incumbent on us as the commercial centre of the North to hold up a
higher standard of public faith to do what we could, in our small way, to
set a wholesome example & efface so far as lay in our power the stain
now resting on the American name. At any rate as honest burghers of
this ancient city, we have felt bound to keep *"the big beaver of the Man-*
hattoes" free from blot or blemish. Repudiation, the Knickerbockers regard as a sordid and unclean thing—a foul beast engendered in the
marshes of the far distant South. We do not intend that its footsteps shall
cross the Hudson—and we live in the hope that ere long *the Strong Man*
will arise and drive it out of the land altogether. In which expectation I
beg to remain always with deep respect   Saml B. Ruggles

ALS. DLC. Endorsed: "Private file."
1. Ruggles probably sent Webster a copy of Charles King, *A Memoir of the Construction, Cost, and Capacity of the Croton Aqueduct . . .* (New York, 1843).

FROM DAVID WEBSTER

Fryeburg Jany. 16. 1843

Respected Sir

Excuse me for trobling you at this time as I expect your business is very presing. After I saw you at Washington I saw Mr [William Pitt] Fessenden at N York & mentioned to him what you told me. He will give me the Bonds of the Ellsworth purchase as they would not be of any use to any one else. Col [John] Black[1] is willing to pay me back in such of the timbered lands as I may choose for what money I advanced him when I made the purchase which was a large amt. as soon as I will produce the Bonds he gave, will not without which I did not expect he would. When I told Mr Fessenden he did not object but said he should see you in a short time would then do it but has not. It will be matter of great value to me to get the original contracts for without them, I cannot recover back what I have paid. Will you have the goodness to give me your opinion—mention the same to Mr Fessenden I will then go to N York and then settle it with him, and you will very much oblg. Your most obedt and humble servt.   David Webster

ALS. DLC. Endorsed: "Private file. / Ansd—declined, till I see the writer." Webster, about whom little is known, was a native of Conway, New Hampshire. He and DW had been—and perhaps still were—partners in the Ellsworth Land and Lumber Company. On the Company, see *Correspondence*, 4: 175.
1. Black (1781–1856), born in London, England, had settled in Maine in 1799 to manage the Bingham lands for Lord Ashburton.

Webster found himself in deep political trouble in early 1843: he had remained too long with the Tyler administration. His influence with Tyler had declined significantly, particularly since the President began to rely increasingly on Democrats for advice. In Massachusetts, Webster had lost support with Whigs because he had continued with the Tyler administration. Many who had previously looked to Webster for leadership now turned to Clay, writing Webster off as lost to the party. Webster's political future was bleak and would become bleaker if he stayed much longer in Washington. He needed to cut his ties with the Tyler administration.

Texas gave Webster the excuse he needed to ease out. Back in October 1841, Tyler had proposed the annexation of Texas, but Webster had been unwilling to pursue it. Now seeking a nomination of his own, Tyler and his confidential advisers turned to Texas annexation as the issue on which they would run his campaign.

In the letter below, Nicholas Biddle alludes to a little known and neglected treaty with Texas—the Treaty of Amity, Commerce, and Navigation—then before the Senate. Webster had concluded the negotiation of this treaty on July 13, 1842. On August 18, President Tyler forwarded it to the Senate for consideration. How Webster, or even Tyler, viewed the treaty—whether as a move to preclude, to postpone, or to hasten the question of annexation—has not been established. At any rate, the Senate first emasculated and then approved the treaty in early March; Webster decided definitely to resign and began to seek advice from Biddle regarding his pending departure.

FROM NICHOLAS BIDDLE

Anda[lusia] Jany. 18. 1843

(*Private*)

My Dear Sir,

I yesterday recd—oddly enough—a letter from a friend in Illinois who says that as he passed thro' Wash[ingto]n recently he learned that Mr Webster intended to insist in the Treaty with Texas now before the Senate, that Texas should pay its debts to Citizens of the U.S. and advising me to see about it, as he knew I had claims.

Now when or where could we have a long talk about Texas? I have been long of opinion that *there* is the true mode of repairing the wrongs of fortune to some of my friends; & the moment I think not far distant. Take it altogether it is the largest question for a statesman now before us. Always yrs   N B.

ALS draft. DLC.

FROM JOHN PLUMMER HEALY

Boston January 31, 1843.

Dear Sir,

Our Supreme Court are now holding a Law Session, to dispose of the cases, which have laid over from the last regular Law term. This is an unprecedented thing, & the Court are enabled to do it, in consequence of the relief they have obtained from the late enlarged exclusive jurisdiction, which has been conferred upon the Court of Common Pleas.

The case of Chouteau vs. Webster was argued yesterday & today, & will now probably be decided, in the course of the coming month. There was nothing in the arguments, that seemed to me to alter the aspect of the case, or to weaken the degree of confidence we have had in a favorable result. On the contrary, the more the case had been scrutinized, the stronger has the defence appeared. As soon as the opinion of the Court shall be delivered, I will communicate it to you,[1] & though I do feel an entire confidence, that the defence will be sustained, I shall be much disappointed if it be not sustained. Mr. [Jonathan Palmer] Rogers,[2] who, as you remember probably, is in the case with me, has an almost undoubting conviction, that our defence can not be shaken.

Mr. [John Jacobus?] Flournoy's[3] letter to you is very different from his letter to me, in all matters of style, & good breeding. Very truly yours,

J. P. Healy.

ALS. MHi. Endorsed: "Private file."

1. Healy's letter informing Webster of the decision of the Court has not been found.

2. Rogers (1802–1846), born in Maine and admitted to the bar there, served as Maine attorney general and state senator. In 1840 he moved to Boston and continued in the legal profession.

3. Flournoy (1808–1879) was a native of Georgia. Somewhat eccentric and a self-styled reformer, he frequently wrote lengthy letters to various United States officials. Neither letter found.

Webster enjoyed the arts and literature and sought to encourage artists and writers by endorsing and subscribing to their works. But, as in his land dealings, he frequently neglected his obligations to them. He was always in debt to Sarah Goodridge for miniatures of him and his family. His failure to pay promptly his debt to John James Audubon is revealed in the letter below.

In 1836, Webster had subscribed to Audubon's Birds of America *in double elephant folio, to be paid in four $200 installments by Webster's friend and financial backer, Isaac P. Davis. Three volumes were delivered to Webster in 1837, but Audubon did not receive any payment until he collected $100 in October 1840. On July 25, 1842, Webster paid him another $100. In response to Audubon's request below, Webster sent him another $200, but there is no record that Webster ever paid off the debt. On Webster and Audubon, see Waldemar H. Fries,* The Double Elephant Folio: The Story of Audubon's Birds of America *(Chicago, 1973), pp. 249–251; and Richard W. Morin, "Statesman and Artist," in* Dartmouth Library Bulletin, *New Series, 10 (November 1969): 2–9.*

FROM JOHN JAMES AUDUBON

New York Feby. 3. 1843.

Private

My Dear Friend,

I will leave this on the 10th. instant on my route to the Rocky Mountains, and am saddly in want of money to assist in the defraying of my expenses; and I wish you would oblige me by sending me the balance of your account, Four hundred and sixty six Dollars 66/100 ($466 66/100) as I should like to take with me all I can to afford me the means of rendering my Journey as compleat as possible in the way of purchasing rare quadrupeds &c &c.[1] I trust that I will find you well on my return, and as Happy as you deserve. Believe me with sincerity and good wishes Your old friend & obt Servant   John J Audubon

P.S. If inconvenient to send me the whole balance, please send what you can spare your old Friend.

ALS. NhD. Endorsed: "Private file."
1. By March 8, DW had sent Audu-

bon a draft for $200. See Audubon to DW, March 8, 1843, mDWs.

TO JOHN PLUMMER HEALY

Washington
Feb. 7. 1843

My Dear Sir

I thank you for your letter, respecting the suit vs me.[1] If I be hired [?] to the kind of men who are fortunate in their private affairs, I should expect success; but I shall feel great concern, till the result is known. However it may terminate, I shall see you & Mr Rogers properly rewarded.

We have extremely cold weather. Yrs   D. W.

ALS. MHi.
1. See above, Healy to DW, January 31, 1843.

FROM ROBERT PERKINS LETCHER

Frankfort 8th. Feb. 1843

My Dear Sir

I thank you, most sincerely for your prompt attention to my request to forward two copies of the Census—they arrived in the "nick of time.["]¹

Your kind favor of the 29th Decr, however, by some accident or other, did not reach me until a day or two since.

Send on fifty copies of your correspondence with Lord Ashburton.[2] They shall be distributed to the members of the Legislature with very great pleasure indeed, and will no doubt be most thankfully recd. This correspondence has been as far as [I] know or believe most favorably spoken of in this country by every body. You have I assure you many warm friends and admirers in this part of the world. It is true many of them regret to differ with you upon some interesting political topics and regret still more, that circumstances have placed you in your present position. If good, hearty, sincere and constant prayers could have the effect to rid you of all difficulties and connections with *men* and *parties* not suited to you in character capacity or usefulness, you would be most speedily relieved, I assure you. You know my dear Sir, how much and how sincerely my attachment has been to you, and I must tell you I have often mourned over the troubles and trials you have experienced. I have wished a thousand times, I could have been near you. I know you have been surrounded with heart-less deceivers, and faithless advisers. I think I understand a few fellows who are pulling the *strings*, and I doubt not you understand these by this time also. Keep cool, be circumspect, and for G—ds sake, use all your efforts to do something for the country in the way of a good currency. If I were the Devil himself and in the place of Jno. Tyler, and felt anxious to punish the country, I would take some other method to do it, than that of inflicting upon it, a bad currency. I have written you, most hastily. I repeat, I should be exceedingly rejoiced to have a long talk with you. Take a mission to England, if the country requires your valuable services. Your faithl. frnd   R P Letcher

ALS. DLC. Endorsed: "Private file."
   1. See above, DW to Letcher, December 29, 1842.
   2. *Correspondence between Mr.*

Webster and Lord Ashburton . . . on McLeod's case . . . on the Creole case . . . on the subject of impressment ([Washington? 1842?]).

FROM GEORGE TICKNOR

Boston Feb. 9. '43

(*Private*)
My dear Sir,
   [Francis Calley] Gray has been ill & much occupied with the Legislative affairs here; so that he has declined writing an article for the N. American Review.[1] [Jared] Sparks, as I learn, this morning, has undertaken it. He had not occurred to me among those who would be likely to do it; but the Editor, Mr. [Francis] Bowen has made application to him, & he has promised to have an article ready in good season, for the next number. He must, therefore, be about it, *immediately.* The points on which, perhaps, I should most differ with him from what I *hear* of his opinions, (for I have not chanced to see him during the last weeks) are whether the line on the so-called Franklin map was probably, the true line or only a mistake of Franklin's; and whether you were bound to show Lord Ashburton this so-called Franklin map. On these points, I hear, he rather *inclines* to the opinion of C[harles] Sumner and others, that the *red* line was the true line of the treaty of '83, & that Lord Ashburton should have had knowledge of it. I mention this merely, that you may, if you deem it advisable, send Mr. Sparks or send me to be given to him, any views, documents or other materials, that may assist him in the matter. I have received nothing from you, since I wrote you about them,[2] & do not wish now to be further concerned in the affair, than you may desire to have me.
   I gave a letter of introduction to Mrs. Webster, two days ago, for our young friend & kinsman, S[amuel] E[liot] Guild.[3] Please to ask Fletcher to be kind to him & if you have opportunity, pray show him kindness

yourself. We are all very fond of him, & he is not only an excellent young man & promising young lawyer, but an agreeable and most *presentable* person, who will do us credit in society any where. Yrs. very faithfully

George Ticknor

ALS. NhD.

1. It has not been determined whether Webster or someone else had asked Gray to write an article on the Webster-Ashburton Treaty for the *North American Review*. On December 21, however, Webster had suggested that he investigate the possibility of Francis Lieber's writing one (see mDW 23928). But Sparks, as Ticknor told Webster, would write

the article. Sparks had in fact written Webster on February 8 (mDW 24309) that he was already engaged in the work. The essay appeared in the *North American Review*, 56 (April 1843): 452–496.

2. Letter not found.

3. Guild (1819–1862; Harvard 1839) was Ticknor's nephew; he studied and practiced law in Boston.

FROM ROBERT PERKINS LETCHER

Frank. 13th. Feb. 1843

My Dear Sir

Our village is greatly distressed at this moment to learn that Geo[rge Bibb] Crittenden a son of Senator Crittenden is now a captive in Mexico. He was a citizen of Texas at the time of his capture. If my dear Sir, you can in any way be instrumental in effecting his release, it will be an act of kindness long and gratefully remembered by his numerous connections and friends. I know whatever you can do, will be done most readily and cheerfully.[1]

I wrote you a hasty letter a few days ago.[2] I still think if your country needs your services in the management of all the delicate and complicated topics which have or may create difficulties with England, you ought not to hesitate a single moment to take the position of *The Negotiator* should it be offered to you. I know nothing of the Cabinet secrets of course, but this much I do know, I should like to see you rid of the miserable concern which surrounds you. I dont see how you can in any way be useful in a suffering country, with such materials as you have to deal with. (However this topic it may not be according to strict order to discuss, and therefore *I drop it.*)

The understanding in this country is that V. Buren having been *reappointed* by Genl. Jackson will again be the candidate of the Loco Foco party. He will be supported in this state by the leading members of that party—in fact he is their first favorite over Col. [Richard Mentor] Johnson and all others. The Col. is exceedingly dissatisfied with the prospects ahead, and so are his particular friends. Mr. Van Buren can now regain his original strength in this state or indeed any where in the west as far as I am informed. Hastily & truly yours with great regard,   R P. Letcher

ALS. DLC. Endorsed: "Private file."
1. Through the efforts of Webster and Waddy Thompson, the Mexicans released Crittenden from his imprisonment in Mexico City. For the Crittenden case and the issue of the Santa Fe prisoners, see *Diplomatic Papers*, 1.
2. See above, Letcher to DW, February 8, 1843.

TO CALEB CUSHING, WITH ENCLOSURE: TO CHARLES ANDERSON WICKLIFFE, FROM DW AND CUSHING, FEBRUARY 15.

[February 15, 1843]

Dear Mr. Cushing

Please put this into your handwriting[1]—bring it to me in the morning for you & me to sign—go with it to the P.M. Genl. *before* he goes to the President. If this be done, something may be attempted in N.H.   D. W.

ALS. DLC.
1. See enclosure below.

ENCLOSURE: TO CHARLES ANDERSON WICKLIFFE, FROM DW AND CUSHING

Washington Feb. 15. 1843

Dear Sir,

We would respectfully, but most urgently, recommend that changes be made in the following Post offices, in N. Hamp: viz, Exeter, Claremont, Newport & Canaan.[1]

In our judgment the public interest requires these changes, without any delay. Yours truly

AL draft. DLC.
1. In all of the post offices mentioned, except Canaan, there were several changes between 1842 and 1844, but whether they resulted from Webster and Cushing's recommendation has not been determined. In Canaan, Jonathan Kittredge was postmaster for the three years, but in Claremont, A. Clossit replaced A. Blodget in 1843 and John J. Prentiss succeeded Clossit in 1844. In Exeter, J. Dearborn succeeded to the postmastership held by J. Robinson, Jr. in 1843; he continued to serve in 1844. In Newport, Calvin Wilcox was postmaster in 1842 and 1844, with B. Nettleton serving in 1843.

One way Webster considered to place distance between himself and President Tyler was to resign as secretary of state and to assume the post of minister to England, hopefully to negotiate a settlement of the Oregon problem. In the fall of 1842, Webster had suggested to Edward Everett, then minister to the Court of St. James's, that Everett head the first United States mission to China. Everett declined, but suggested that he would go to Paris. The discussions between Webster and Everett over the English post led to talk and rumors, but nothing more. Everett was to stay in England, and Tyler sent Caleb Cushing, with Fletcher Webster as secretary, to China. As Webster wrote Letcher below, his "next mission" was to retire to his Marshfield estate.

Washington
Feb: 15. 1843

Private & Confidential
My Dear Sir

I thank you for your letter, & send you 30 or 40 copies of the "correspondence,"[1] & some pamphlets containing Lord Palmerston's articles on the Treaty.[2]

My Dear Sir; be assured nothing shall shake my purpose of *keeping cool*, & waiting events, calmly. I know, that the Country can never prosper till it has a currency; & I verily believe, that we shall not get a Bank, on the old models, in ten years. What, then, is to be done? I think, we must show some *enterprise*, some faculty of invention, or rather of modification. We must make an attempt to adapt old principles, to new forms; & this we could do, if there were among us any union of purpose. But the misfortune is, that there are, on both sides, men who think that their party success depends on carrying certain particular measures. Your Kentucky Whigs, for instance are pledged to a Bank; & tho it is certain that no such thing can be had, for years to come at least, yet they seem willing to make no effort, whatever, for relief from any other measure. See an example of their temper, in the enclosed scrap.[3]

On the other hand, the Locofoco party will have nothing but Sub-Treasury. Next Congress will be locofoco, by a large majority in the H. of R. & a small one, probably, in the Senate. The President, it is very possible, might Veto a Sub-Treasury Bill. I should really hope he would. What is to be done, then, by men, who honestly seek the good of the Country; & who, if they regard their own fame, are more desirous of obtaining distinction by rendering the Country important service, than by merely obtaining high posts?

In my opinion, two things are indispensable:

1st: A currency; & I confess, that while I see no possibility of getting, for many years, any other plan, or measure, my confidence in the beneficial operation of the Exchequer System is Entire, & undiminished.

2. The restoration of public credit; by which I mean the Credit of the States, as well as of the Genl. Govt. This is indispensable. *It cannot be accomplished, but by aid of the Genl. Govt. rendered in some form.* The subject is large, comprehensive, & infinitely more important than our mere party squabbles.

I intend to espouse it, & devote myself to it; & be assured the people are beginning to see & to feel its importance. This matter is large enough for men of some reach to take hold of.

As to "Missions," my next mission, in all probability, will be to Marshfield, Plymo. County, Massachusetts; where sundry acres of very poor land are waiting to see whether I have learned any acts of diplomacy, by which they may be enriched. Very truly Yrs   Danl Webster

ALS. NcD.
1. See above, Letcher to DW, February 8, 1843.

2. *Lord Palmerston on the Treaty of Washington* ([n.p. 1842?]).
3. Not found.

/

TO ROBERT PERKINS LETCHER

Washington
Feb: 21. 1843

Private
My Dear Sir;

I have recd your letter of the 13th.[1] Everything has been done in this Department that could be thought of, useful to young Crittenden. Mr [James T.] Morehead & Mr [Philip] Triplett spoke to me on the subject, & I had great pleasure in doing all, without delay, which seemed to them & to me to be proper & useful. I hope he may be released.

I like to hear you talk about political matters, because I know you usually speak frankly & fearlessly. I doubt not, that on consultation you & I should agree, as fully as ever, on all questions of principle. We both hold to the indispensable necessity of a sound currency, & to the duty of Govt. to furnish it. We think alike, I presume, on the really great & important questions, involved in the contest of 1840.

We may differ, nevertheless, in regard to particular measures, or the particular line of policy, best to be pursued, to accomplish what we think desirable. And we may differ about men.

As to my going abroad, I can truly say I have little desire for it. I am too poor; unless I saw a case, in which I might think myself called upon by a high sense of duty, to make sacrifices. Some of the judgments which you form upon men & things here, I think I could convince you are unjust; but that is a topic upon which I suppose I may as well not write. In my opinion, another twelve months is likely to give a new aspect to public affairs. Yrs always very truly   Danl Webster

ALS. NcD.
1. See above.

FROM C[HARLES?] STANTON ET AL.

New York Febry. 24th. 1843

Dear Sir,

The undersigned have been appointed by the *Executive Committee* of the convention of delegates of this City, who have the superintendance of the mass meeting which is to be held in this City on the 15th. March next to nominate Mr Tyler for the Presidency,[1] To correspond with several of the distinguished Gentlemen, whose position entitles them to the highest consideration of the friends of the Administration in this city.

And your position enables you to know the views of the friends of the President in different parts of the Union, in reference to the mode of nomination of Mr Tyler. Whether it be preferable that the nomination should be made with reference to a democratic or a *Republican convention*, or leave convention or no convention an open question.

An early reply is respectfully solicited to enable the committee to complete the resolutions to be submitted to the before mentioned public meeting.[2] With the highest consideration we are your obt Servts.

> C Stanton
> Chairman,
> 441 1/2 Pearl St   Aaron Swarts
> Alfred Kershaw   J. Hopkins Stewart
> A. H. Bartlett   Thomas W. Pittman[3]

ALS by Stanton, signed also by others. DLC. Endorsed: "referred to Mr Cushing." Stanton was a grocer in New York City.

1. The New York Tyler meeting took place as scheduled at the Tabernacle on March 15; with Caleb Cushing and several other congressmen in attendance, the gathering nominated Tyler for the presidency. *New York Evening Post*, March 16, 1843.

2. Webster's reply has not been found.

3. All were New York City residents: Kershaw, a tailor; Bartlett, a merchant; Swarts, a grocer; Stewart, a lawyer; and Pittman, a speculator.

FROM NICHOLAS BIDDLE

Anda. Feby 27. 1843

My dear Sir,

I beg you to listen to the following oracular sentences which if they have no other inspiration are dictated by a sincere regard for you & for the country.

Do not leave your present position.

If you do, you descend.

You must hereafter be only a King or a King maker.

You can do nothing abroad which you cannot do better while you remain here, & speak thro' your Agents.

As Secretary you are the Government, as a Minister you are the Govt.'s Agent.

Then if you go—who is to take your place?

Some transcendentalist? Some cobweb spinner?

So Stay—stay.

Having delivered myself of these profundities I descend from my tripod—and am Yr friend   N Biddle

ALS. DLC. Printed in McGrane, *Correspondence of Nicholas Biddle*, pp. 344–345.

FROM H[ENRY?] SHAW

Chester, Pa. Feb. 28. 1843

Mr Webster

I called on the P[resident] and he appointed me an interview for the next day—accordingly the next day he gave me an hour, and in that time we ran over the past, and looked at the future. It were needless to attempt a report of all that pass[e]d—for the past, he had done right, and Mr Clay had done wrong—to this I assented only qualifying his position, by the remark that *you also* had done wrong! And I appealed to conviction of the Party, the State of the Country, and the temper of our Leaders as proof, that personal enmities and personal ends had been the guide, when the spirit of Patriotism should have prevailed. For the future—he said he "had *nothing* to expect from the Whigs"—and it was vain to attempt any scheme, in reliance upon them. I suggested, a modification of the Cabinet with a view to Whig policy and a strong movement for the controul of that party—he was utterly faithless in any such plan! Assumption he totally rejected except upon the contingency of a surplus in the Treasury—he fell back constantly upon the "signs of the times," and the N. Jersey movement seemed to fill his vision of the future—he would go for the People—the Parties he despised—would make no attempt to conciliate in any quarter. I spoke of your position—he was full and frank —acknowledged your able support; and said your position was much in your own power—he spoke of the inveterate feelings of the opposition to you, and altho he did not say so, I could not come to any other conclusion, than that your position kept him from receiving the confidence and support of the opposition! I will be frank with you. In my opinion he would feel relieved if you should resign your place, and I am much mistaken if you do not find it impracticable to stay. And yet this inference is drawn against the most emphaticle and reiterated expressions of confidence.

I do not suppose I have told you anything new or that anything was said to me that has not been said to others—my inference also may be wrong. In my opinion the Elements of the Cabinet are insensitive to your future!

I shall not venture to advise, for that you neither need or have desired. This however may be said, for all our expression affirms it, that to hold power in this Government *the man must be strong at home!* Massachusetts waits to replace you at her head—she cannot or will not do so, while *you remain* in your present association. You must determine your own destiny. The glorious old state bears you a love quite as cordial and much more disinterested than those which now surround you! I have strong opinions & strong feelings on the subject, which I shall not fail to express to you if you desire it. My wish and hope is this, that all the essential Elements of the Party so far as moves on command may be brought into harmony, and I should feel deeply gratefull for the occurrence of circumstances that should lead to this result. All have erred, and all must compromise more or less of *feelings* before there can be the least hope of success. Cordially and sincerely your friend   H : Shaw

ALS. DLC. Although this letter is written from Chester, Pennsylvania, the author is probably Henry Shaw, former member of Congress from Massachusetts and unsuccessful gubernatorial candidate in that state in 1845. The letter to DW was presumably written as Shaw was returning to Massachusetts from Washington.

TO [NICHOLAS BIDDLE]

Mar: 2. 1843

My Dear Sir;

I have not the least idea of going abroad, or of taking any appointment, whatever. But I do not expect to remain where I am, more than a month. This, *inter nos.*[1] Yrs   D. W.

I shall see you in 10 days.   D. W.

ALS. DLC. Printed, with deletion, in McGrane, *Correspondence of Nicholas Biddle*, p. 345.

1. Webster was responding to Biddle's letter of February 27, 1843, above.

TO JOHN TYLER

Friday Morning
3 March, 1843

Private.

Dear Sir:

I presume you have not signed the Bankrupt-repeal Bill, yet; and I feel it to be my duty to furnish you evidence, in writing, that I gave you the advice which I did give, yesterday, and that is, *not to sign the Bill.*[1]

For this opinion, I gave my reasons, in brief, yesterday, and need not now repeat them. The Country will not approve, in my judgment, this rash legislation, and these violent changes. If the Bankrupt law be now repealed, it will stand, for all time, a disgrace to our Statute Book; because it will bear the character of a mere sponge. By its operation, thousands of debtors, of the most suspicious character, will have been discharged; while the hasty, ill-judged, and premature repeal of the law, prevents any fair experiment of its just influence and effect, on creditors, honest debtors, and the general interests of the Country.

I assure you, if I were President, the repealing Bill should lie upon my table; and Congress should be left to reconsider this highly important subject, a year hence. Your's truly,

Copy, endorsed by DW. OGK.
1. Tyler signed the bill repealing the bankrupt law on March 3, the

same day that Webster wrote him this letter. 5 *United States Statutes at Large* 614.

TO HENRY WILLIS KINSMAN

Mar. 5. [1843]

Private & Confidential
My Dear Sir;

Under present circumstances,[1] there is no way but for Mr Cushings friends to rally, *in force & spirit*, & return him triumphantly to Congress.[2] This *can be done*, & he will then be in a condition *to protect his friends.* Not a moment's time ought to be lost, in convening a Convention. I pray you to feel the full importance of this movement, *in many bearings*. Yrs truly   Danl Webster

ALS. MHi. Kinsman (1803–1859; Dartmouth 1822), a native of Portland, had read law with Webster and succeeded Alexander Bliss as an associate in Webster's office. In 1837, he moved to Newburyport, opened a law office, and subsequently served in the Massachusetts legislature.
1. On March 2, President Tyler had nominated Cushing for secretary of the treasury, but the Senate on

March 3 rejected the nomination by 27 to 19. Tyler twice resubmitted his name on the same day, but each time the Senate rejected him, by 27 to 10 and by 29 to 2. *Journal of the Executive Proceedings of the Senate . . . 1841 . . . to 1845 . . . .*, 6: 178, 179, 180, 186, 187.
2. Cushing decided not to run in the forthcoming election in Massachusetts. Fuess, *Cushing*, 1: 390–395.

FROM REVERDY JOHNSON

Balt. 8 March, 1843.

Private
My Dear Sir,

I am greatly obliged to you for your kind letter of yesterday,[1] but a part of it, altho you desire no reply, demands one from me. The article you refer to, as having appeared in the American, relative to the late Mr. Robert Smith, was, I suppose, written by me, as I recollect distinctly having, about the period you mention, written in that paper, a vindication of Mr. S. against a hostile & most unjustifiable imputation upon him, in the Madisonian.[2] I have no copy of the article by me, nor can I lay my hands on it, but that it contains any reflection upon your character, when fairly understood, is what I cannot believe. I know, & I am certain you will readily credit it, that from the first of the difficulties which have unfortunately existed in the Whig ranks, & which have given rise to so much abuse of yourself, I have at all times, & upon all occasions, complained of it, as an outrage upon what I thought all would admit, your fervent patriotism, & the invaluable service you had rendered the party, & the country, in the political struggle of the past twelve years. I have denounced it in the strongest terms I could adopt, & often at the hazard of incurring the displeasure of warm personal friends. The course of the Independt. especially, was so grating to my feelings, as regards yourself, that I disagreeably sought an interview with its active editor in Washington, at my own room, & believe, that my persuasion, advice, & remonstrance, had a decided influence upon his subsequent course. With these sentiments towards you as a friend, as well as a public man, I must think, that you have placed a wrong construction upon the article in the American, but if not, I *know*, that nothing was farther from my intention, than to say a word *then*, or at any time, reflecting unkindly, either upon your public or private character. On the contrary, I have ever taken the truest delight, in vindicating you upon all proper occasions, & in every presence, from every imputation I have heard upon either. And in conclusion, I beg leave to assure you, that come what may, if I know myself, you will not find in the circle of numerous personal friends you must have, one who will be more sincere & constant in his hopes, & his efforts to accomplish, as far as it may be in his power, a successful vindication of your character, public & private, from the cruel & most injustifiable imputations that are being cast upon it.

I need not say, My Dear Sir, that I have no motive in this, or in my former letter, except to set myself right, as a *private* man, & a personal friend, in your estimation. If that is accomplished, as I feel it must be, my sole end is attained. Sincerely yr friend   Reverdy Johnson

ALS. InHi.

1. Not found. Webster and Johnson had recently been corresponding about some misunderstanding. See

Johnson to DW, March 6, 1843, mDW 24500.

2. The articles have not been identified.

TO JOHN PLUMMER HEALY

Washington, March 10th, 1843.

Private.

Dear Sir,

This Department has occasion for the services of an intelligent and diligent lawyer, for a period of two or three months. Working as people work here, six hours a day, it would require the longer period; working as you work, ten hours a day, it might be got through in the shorter. Could you so arrange your own business as to come and do it? I should be very much gratified if you could. Some important questions of law are to be studied and considerable masses of papers arranged, analized and abstracts of them made. I suppose we could give you a thousand dollars for the service. The duty is to be performed in the Department and the sooner it is begun the better.[1]

If you cannot come yourself, mention the names of two or three gentlemen, out of which I might make a choice; but do not mention the subject to any of them.

I should much prefer you should come yourself. Please favor me with an early answer.[2] Yours, with much regard, Danl Webster

LS. MHi.
    1. Webster sought Healy's assistance, according to the endorsement on the letter, in preparing a report on Mexican claims.
    2. Not found.

TO THOMAS B. CURTIS

Mar: 13. 1843

Private & Confidential
My Dear Sir

Mr Cushing will be in Boston, on friday morning, at the Tremont House, on his way home. As you may suppose, he feels not only grieved, but indignant, at the treatment which he has recd. from the hands of the ultra Whigs, in the Senate.[1] In this feeling, I, for one most heartily partake; & shall not, & cannot, blame him, for any proper resentment, which he may manifest.

Mr Cushing has been, in my opinion, by far the most efficient friend in Congress of all our N. England interests. Without his unwearied efforts, there would have been no Tariff; & in all great questions, he has pursued, exactly, the principles, upon which the Whigs came into power.

He is now determined, now, to understand what are to be the relations, between him & the Whig Organization of Massachusetts. If the tone which is held towards him, by some of the Whig papers, is to be regarded as sanctioned by the general voice of the Whigs, he only wishes to know it. He asks no favors, of course; but it is no more than right that a clear understanding should exist, all round. There ought no longer to exist a dubious state of relations. Mr. C. will be before the People for reelection.[2] Is he to be opposed, as being no Whig? This is the question.

Mr Cushing will be glad to see you, on friday. Meantime, I have no objection to your reading this letter to Mr [Jonathan] Chapman,[3] chairman of the Whig Genl. Comee. Yrs truly Danl Webster

ALS. MHi. Published in *MHi Proc.*, 45 (November 1911): 161. Curtis was a Boston merchant and banker, a brother of Charles P. Curtis.

1. See above, DW to Henry Willis Kinsman, March 5, [1843].

2. Cushing decided to withdraw from the canvass. See DW to Caleb Cushing, March 27, 1843, below.

3. Chapman (1807–1845; Harvard 1825) was a lawyer. From 1840 to 1842 he served as mayor of Boston.

FROM CHARLES PELHAM CURTIS

[March 23, 1843]

Dear Sir—

I read your letter to my Brother with much interest,[1] and concur entirely in the views you express. I cannot conceive what has had the influence on Mr [Nathan] Hale's mind which is manifest from the complexion of his paper of 18 mos. past—but it is now too late for remedy. If when the first Cabinet abandoned their posts, the D[aily] Advertizer had taken the view of their conduct which I did (& some other Whigs did here) it might have done some—perhaps much—good. Never before in the history of this country, has any Party so completely been the cause of its own ruin as this Whig Party. None but itself can be its parallel. I have read with great pleasure your last letter to Gen Cass.[2] The French will say that he is Cassé. I saw it in the Globe first. Pray how did this happen?

I will ask the favour of you to send me a couple of copies of the *whole correspondence* with Cass, Guizot &c—Also one copy of the Treaty & Correspondence. It is an *on dit*, that Judge Story contemplates resigning his seat on the Bench but *when*, the knowing ones know not.[3] Now, if he would do so before you leave your present place & you could name Mr Choate for his successor I think it would be satisfactory to the Profession. Mr C. is old enough & not too old. He is a *very* acute & excellent lawyer & has excellent temper—which like a low voice in woman is a great grace in a Judge.

Can you give me a hint on this subject—*in pure confidence*—it might enable me to be useful.

I meant to have covered this paper with my ideas—but I have been so interrupted since I began that it is now post time—and you are relieved from any more of my tediousness.

It is understood here that you will soon return to us. We sadly want the aid of Jupiter to get one wheel out of the mire of Locofocoism. Yours very truly & respy   C P Curtis.

ALS. DLC.

1. See DW to Thomas B. Curtis, March 12, 1843, mDW 24628. *Diplomatic Papers*, 1.

2. See DW to Lewis Cass, December 20, 1842, in *Diplomatic Papers*, I.

3. Story remained on the bench until his death in 1845.

TO CALEB CUSHING

Washington
Monday Mar: 27. 43

Private & Confidential
My Dear Sir;

I thank you for your letter, which I recd. two days ago.[1] I believe you have decided right, in withdrawing your name, for the present, as a Candidate for Congress. If there should be again no choice, a different aspect of things might present itself.

So backward & cold is the Season, that it is hardly likely I shall get north earlier than the first of May. In the meantime, I want to see you, much, & think it necessary you should come here, for a day or two. I suppose you care nothing about being at home next Monday; & therefore suppose, you set out for the South, on receipt of this.

Important things, in which you are concerned, are to be thought about, & talked about. I believe the President intends to offer you a Department. I wish you to have *this*. Then, again, there is *China*, if Mr Everett should decline the Mission.[2] It is high time some of these things were settled. I pray you, come & see us, as soon as you can.

The picture has arrived from North Bend.[3] Yrs truly   Danl Webster

ALS. NN. Printed in *W & S*, 16: 401.
1. Not found.
2. Tyler's appointment of Cushing for the treasury post had only recently failed to be confirmed. What other cabinet position Tyler may have had in mind for Cushing has not been determined; but when Everett declined the China mission Tyler named Cushing for it.
3. A portrait of William Henry Harrison.

FROM JOHN POPE

Near Biglick, Roanoke Vir.
March 28th 1843

Dr Sir

I owe you an apology for not calling on you the evening before my Departure from the city as I intended & was very desirous to have done but I assure you that I had not a moment to spare from the many small matters of business which required my attention. Mrs Pope & Miss Booker[1] had packed up their clothes &c prepared to leave & Mrs Pope was too unwell to make a visit. I desired to see you to have a full conversation on the Tariffe & the probable success of a negotiation with G.B. & other powers in relation to commercial intercourse on terms of fair reciprocity. The settlement of the Tariffe on a reasonable & stable basis is of more importance to the Country to the administration & to yourself than other [questions] likely to be agitated for years to come and it is very important to have it adjusted at the next session of Congress. The bank & land bill may be considered as defered for at least six or seven years to come. The regulation & adjustment of the Tariffe is the only leading measure which can agitate or interest the nation before the next Presidential election. Your local position & identity with the manufacturing interest of the north place this subject more within your control & influence than any other man in the nation but I left Washington with some fears that considerations not connected with the national prosperity might have an unfortunate influence on the selection of the individual to accomplish an object so important to the country & the executive administration. I hope my fears may prove to be unfounded. It may be well for all politicians interested in the result of the next Presidential election to understand the prospects of the several aspirants. Cass has come too late to hand for success. The chances for Capt Tyler & Capt Clay are not equal to their own estimates. McLean wishes to be run by the Whigs as does Scott. McLean would be the strongest Whig candidate considering his local position & his connection with the Methodist society throughout the union but I must doubt the success of any Whig candidate at the next election —the current is against them & Clay & the run of the cards can hardly be changed before 1848. When in this state last fall I supposed Calhoun was decidedly the strongest candidate in this state but I incline to think now after full enquiry & observation that Van Buren will be prefered here to Calhoun. If a democrat is to be elected, it must be either V. B. Calhoun or [Richard Mentor] Johnson & Johnson *can* beat either of them if no Whig candidate is run & the contest confined to two democrats & Johnson one of them. If Clay will withdraw or should not be nominated I am disposed to take the stump for Johnson. I have many friends who are for Clay, & I should be sorry to offend them but my feelings & judgment lead me to take Johnson as the safest man & most available candidate. I have explored the whole ground & have full confidence in my own opinion on the subject. In Virginia & N. Carolina the Clay Whigs if they dont openly support V. B. will incline to him rather than Calhoun but they cannot be managed to support V. B. vs Johnson. The whole west & northwest can be to a great extent united on Johnson if he and V. B. should be the only candidates. I desire to see this contest & would take the stump wherever there was a chance to make converts. You are much deeper on many subjects than I am but with regard to elections & the people you must pardon me for claiming to be your Superior. That you may be disposed to quit your present station & be sent to England is my sincere wish. You can I hope do much for yourself & more for the Country.

I have been detained in Virginia longer than I expected by sickness of my family & bad weather. My grandaughter was confined on the road near two weeks by the scarlet fever. I shall leave here tomorrow for Kentucky. I have the honor be with high respect yours &c   John Pope

ALS. KyU. Endorsed by DW: "Private file."
1. Mrs. Pope, the daughter of
Joshua Johnson of Maryland, was Mrs. John Quincy Adams's sister.
Miss Booker has not been identified.

TO FRANCIS BOWEN

Washington April 2. 1843

My Dear Sir;

I am obliged to you for your letter of the 27th. March,[1] which has this moment come to hand, together with a copy of the Review, which I have not opened. I am exceedingly gratified, that Mr Sparks has written an article on the Treaty.[2] The duty could not well have fallen into abler hands.

I commend your idea of obtaining an Article upon Mexico. On that subject, allow me to say, that I expect to be in Boston, ere long, & should be glad to converse with you. Mexico would afford the materials for one interesting Article; our relations with the other American States for another; *China*, for a third.

I cannot but think that the intelligent part of the community would be glad to see each of these subjects fully displayed.

I trust you will persuade Mr Sparks to write a second article, on the right of search, &c. You will have seen in late Nos of the Intelligencer one article on the *Convention [of] 1824*, & one on *Piracy & the Slave trade*.[3]

These you should preserve. I am, with respect, your ob. servt

Danl Webster

ALS. MH–H.
1. See mDW 24745.
2. Sparks's article, "The Treaty of Washington," appeared in the *North*
American Review, 56 (April 1843): 452–496.
3. See the *National Intelligencer*, March 25 and April 1, 1843.

FROM NICHOLAS BIDDLE, WITH ENCLOSURE: MEMORANDUM ON DW'S RESIGNATION

Andalusia 5 April 43

My dear Sir

How unlucky I have been. Your note of ten days ago[1] found me litterally confined to my bed, and I waited the first moment of strength to answer it. Meanwhile your note of the 31 ulto[2] reached Phila[delphi]a Friday afternoon. But my son with whom my letters addressed to Town are left came out to pass his Saturday & Sunday with me and did not return until Monday and the next Tuesday I received it.

I regret very much to have missed the pleasure of the long talk I should have enjoyed with you and especially of chatting with you on the subject which most interests me just now—I mean the mode in which you are to leave Washington.

I shall put down on a separate paper a few ideas I have on that subject which you will take for what they are worth.[3]

As soon as you are settled in private life I have a project which I think may be useful to the Country as well as beneficial to yourself about which I will write to you. Meanwhile I am yours always

AL draft. DLC.
   1. Not found.

2. Not found.
3. See below.

ENCLOSURE: MEMORANDUM ON DW'S RESIGNATION

And[alusi]a April 5, 184[3]

You are going to resign—that you think inevitable. Well. But the matter of resignation is less important than the manner.

In parting with the President the programme will of course be perfectly amiable. Nothing will be visible on either side but reciprocal good will and you are hereafter to be the object of a friendship much cemented by separation. That settled, the next question is what do you retire to? And by what route? You retire of course to absolute private life. Any thing else will be a fall obvious and incurable.

Then by what route do you retire?

If you have any political engagement with any one of the candidates, I have no more to say. You must of course abide his fortunes.

But if you are entirely [un]committed now three routes of retr[eat] are open—the route of Mr. Tyler—the route of the Locofocos, the route of the Whigs.

Now I take the route of Mr. Tyler to be entirely impossible. The moment you leave him, you cease all political sympathy with his administration. The route of the Locofocos is equally impracticable. They will never leave their own leaders—they will never move cordially under the banner of him against whom they have all their lives been fighting.

There remains only the route of the Whigs.

Now I have studied that part of the map—with less judgment of course but with more impartiality perhaps than you have done, because your own sensitiveness has made you more alive to the conduct of that party. They have had jealousies and heart burnings with regard to you. They have treated you unkindly & unjustly.

Coldness there has been—shyness, alienation—soreness at the injury done to them by your ceasing to act with them. But in my judgment there is no bitterness—no wound not easily healed and the prevailing sentiment is rather regret & sorrow than hostility.

Believing therefore that you must fix yourself some where, that seems to be the best place.

And I ha[ve] im[agined this course.]

One of these days, and soon, before your motives are misinterpreted, go to some public meeting—not apparently made for the purpose, and say

Six months ago I told you in Faneuil Hall that I was a Whig unchange-ably. I repeat it now. You separated from me, not I from you, because I staid in power. But I did so, because I thought I could do good. I think I did do good in making the English Treaty and you agreed that I was right. Well, I thought by staying a little longer I could do more good.
I told you so, and I tried.
But I find that I cannot do the good I proposed—and therefore I would not remain in place a moment longer than I could serve the Country.
And so I have come back to you.
I ask nothing. I want nothing. I take my stand in the ranks of the party willing to work with you, to support our measures and our men. Such a step would be decisive—it would be hailed with a shout throughout the Country.
It would make a brilliant retreat—it would extricate you from your pres-ent awkward position and make your future path public and private as smooth as you [could desire.]
Think of this.
I offer it because I wish you to know my own views before I know yours. If you have decided or shall decide otherwise I will bring myself to think it best, but now:
this line of retreat both in a military and civil aspect is the best, in my judgment.
You would think so too, if you studied the retreat [of] Lord Wellington[1] in Spain.
If possible, I would say nothing—or what is equivalent to nothing at parting.
The fear is that you may seem to approve too much of the past—which is much to be avoided.   N Biddle

ALS. DLC.
   1. Arthur Wellesley, first duke of Wellington (1769–1852).

FROM FRANCIS ORMAND JONATHAN SMITH, WITH ENCLOSURE: SMITH TO JOHN TYLER, APRIL 7.

Portland April 7—43.

Dr Sir

I forward above a copy of a letter which by the mail that takes this I have forwarded to the President.[1] I have improved the earliest moment since my return to write it, & I have not had time to revise or amend it —but that it may be in season to be of some possible service, as he in-vited me to write, I send it "with all its imperfections." I hope it may not be wholly without effect—and not displeasing to yourself. Though feebly expressed, it contains God's truths which in time the President will ap-preciate, if he will not now. Truly your friend,   Francis O J Smith

P.S. Doctor [William] Jones, your city P.M.[2] concurs fully in all my views upon the matter, & he is a trust-worthy man, & very much in the President's confidence. I say this, lest you do not know him sufficiently well.

ALS. NhD.

1. See below.

2. Jones, a practicing physician in the District of Columbia and the son-in-law of Thomas Corcoran, Sr., was postmaster in Washington under Jackson and Tyler.

ENCLOSURE: FRANCIS ORMAND JONATHAN SMITH TO JOHN TYLER

Portland April 7th 1843.

Private

Dear Sir

In my late interview with you at Washington, it was my wish to express to you the regret which I felt, in finding the political atmosphere of your City so tainted with hostile prejudices and policy, towards the present organization of your Cabinet, and aiming, especially, to bring about either the *Voluntary*, or *involuntary* retirement of the Secretary of State.

I say "the atmosphere of your City," because it has no sensible prevalence beyond it. Elsewhere it assumes merely the exhibition of an individuality, constituting an exception to the general sense of the mass of the people.

Nevertheless, some there are, I have no doubt, among your well wishers, who sincerely indulge this policy. But, I never entertained a clearer conviction of any one truth in politics, than that all this class, are, in this, the victims of a policy that originates entirely with your most determined & most dangerous enemies—with men who are compassing every influence to consummate the extinction of your political hopes & interests, & covertly to secure to themselves, in the interval, the fruits of a professedly amicable relation to your administration. Will you allow me to express the grounds of my opinions, if only to enable you more deliberately to compare them with the adverse opinion—and time, at any rate, will hereafter determine, which is the true opinion, as well as which is the sincerely friendly & disinterested one.

To proceed, I am fully persuaded, that the perpetuity of your hold upon the support & confidence of *nine tenths* of the moderate & conservative portions of the Whig party in the Middle, & Northern States especially, depends more—yes, almost *in toto* upon the amiable official relations of Mr Webster to your administration.

He it is, & their confidence in his ability, patriotism & sound judgment, tempered by your own, that inspire them with a preference for your Administration over any hopes or interests that has been excited, or attempted to be excited, in favour of Mr. Clay, or in Mr Clay's organized branch of the Whig party proper. But all this portion may be regarded as having, still, a much stronger affinity to Mr Clay's policy & the views entertained by his friends, than they have, or can be made to have, to the ultraism that has, & is destined for some time to have, an ascendancy in the, so called, democratic party. Hence, when they shall be disengaged from your administration—when *the man*, who more than all other men, holds them up to the support of it, shall be severed from it, they will, *ex necessitate rei*, fall back into a reluctant yet actual combination with their old political associates, as the last barrier against loco-foco ultraism. Then, it is manifest, your administration will be forced, *nolens-volens*, to seek its chief support from the radical democracy of the Country. *Their* good will towards you, may at all times be measured by the unexpired term of your administration, & by the spoils they can, in the interim, wrest from it wherewith to build up themselves, & restore their party's nominal, as well as actual ascendency, in the succession to the Presidency.

I have great confidence in the political tact & ability of Mr. [John Canfield] Spencer. But, it would be hypocritical flattery were I to aver, that he has the slightest hold upon any portion of the Whig party in the north & east. He has not. No more has he any upon the ultra portions of the democratic party. Next to Mr Webster, they hate him most. His whole strength is with the moderate & conservative portions of that party, and these, unfortunately, are in minority of their own party, & the *Caucus principle* stifles their voices, & suppresses their policy, in all the resolves of that party, so that, for all practical purposes, except to count numerically for the radicals, against a common adversary, they might as well be out of existence as in their party. It is, then, a mistake, radically & fatally, a mistake, to your administration, to think of holding that great moral & political strength which Mr Webster's relation to your Cabinet represents & controls, when he shall have ceased to maintain that relation before the people. And I can foresee that, however potent the means of Mr Spencer's department may be to protect him against hostile influences & to rally supporters, in ninety days from the separation of Mr Webster from your Cabinet, the same manifestation, from the same sources, that is now being made against Mr Webster, *will be directed against Mr Spencer*. He, too, will be regarded as standing in the way of the radical policy of the mass upon whom your administration will then have been thrown for support; & under various disguised & open pretexts, war will be waged from the camp of your *professed friends & followers*, upon your able & energetic Secretary of the Treasury, as it is now waged upon the Secretary of State. The most fatal condition of things for an administration, is, that which requires much of its energies to be directed to the suppression of discontent *in its own ranks*; to the suppression of adverse & hostile interests, *in its own households*. Most truly may it be said of an administration of government, that, "better is a dinner of herbs where love is—than a stalled ox & hatred therewith." A set of men who make it the condition of their support, that the President shall repudiate a large force of his true friends—manifestly require him to quarrel with his own household. It is the black flag of the pirate, & not the olive branch, that waves over *their* Camp. Their requisition should of itself serve to deter from them, rather than to inspire for them, the confidence of your administration. I am aware, that the idea upon which the opponents of Mr Webster's present relation to your administration, dwell, is, that he may properly be commissioned to the highest representative grade of our government abroad.

Well, this only proves, that it is the influence of his particular place at home, that they covet for destruction, & not that your administration is to be benefited, by actually absolving his connexion with it.

Now it cannot but strike your calm & disinterested friends, as very impolitic for the honor & abiding glory of your administration, to send *the* man *abroad* to negotiate with foreign governments, who has the tact, & ability to bring those governments *here*, to our own shores & to the doors of our own departments, for the purpose of treating with us. When has a higher honor than this, or a better service, been achieved for our government, or any administration of it, *by any man?* Mr. Webster's friends in seeing him sent abroad, if he would consent to go, under such circumstances, could not but think him degraded in both the character & usefulness of his services, rather than exalted. Indeed, those who know him & esteem him as they think he merits, have no idea that Mr Websters own sense of honor & self-respect, would for a moment yield to the thought of going abroad, under such circumstances, or accepting any other position under the government, with the consciousness of having been ejected, against his own judgment of his true position, from his present place.

For many of the passages which I find in the history of Mr Webster's political life, I do not yield even my humble & uninfluential endorsement. But, they are past; & I deem them as having no connexion whatever with the present condition of things, or your administration. Every sensible mind views them in this light. The great question for you & your friends to decide, is, if Mr Webster be driven from us—and go with him thousands & thousands certainly will, in every nor[t]hern & eastern state— what political elements are to be substituted, to the honor & benefit of your administration? Ultraism, alone, must fill up the chasm, or nothing will; and ultraism, whether coming from the Whig, or from the democratic party, *is alike fatal to your administration, & to the hopes of your friends.* It is the *Bohon Upas* in politics, against which the strongest, no less, than the feeblest of your friends, will find it useless to struggle, when the door is once seen to have been opened to its approach, *by your order & assent.*

For one, I am resolved to war upon it, be it represented in whosoever person it may, or in whatever official station. From the dawning of it under Mr Van Buren's administration, to this hour, I have thus warred, sacrificing every personal claim to preferment & without price & without recompense, personally. And with a band of 3,000 co-adjutors *in this State*, actuated by like resolute purposes, who will, *when the proper time arrives*, take the field with me as they did in 1839 & '40, I doubt not that the scale can again be successfully turned against it, here, in spite of organized parties of *30 & 40. thousand strong!* We know our relations— we know well the work necessary to be done, & *we know how to do it.* We look not to the moral courage, or integrity, of purpose, that should actuate the masses—but, we look for these in enough only, for the pur- poses of turning the scale of power into the least dangerous hands; & this number *good sense*, under a bold, manly lead, that has no sinister aims to accomplish & no mere love of spoils will influence, will always be able to find, in an aggregate of 80 or 90,000 voters, who are nearly equal in their divisions & similarly organized. When this shall not be the case, amid the corruptions, always chargeable upon great political parties, human nature must be universally depraved, & moral courage quite extinct.

Yet, I disclaim the practicability of keeping up, between two great leading parties, an *organized third* party, a *tiers etat*, equal to a continu- ous check upon each. I know that is not possible.

The *third party principle*, is more like the outgushing of the torrent— the outbreaking of the volcanic fires of the earth—it is the *occasional* agent of an honest public will, incapable of *continuous* actions; but when periodically started, in the nature of an exception to general influences, it becomes like the lightening of heaven, perfectly overwhelming. The campaign of 1840 is full of illustrations to this point. It was not *the party proper*, on either side, that directed results then; but, those who were ex- ceptions *then,* & who still are exceptions to both of the great parties, wrought those results for the people. The same may happen again in 1844; & if so, it will be roused by the spirit of ultraism in the land & to overwhelm & crush that malign influence once more.

I have unintentionally protracted my suggestions. But, plain & homely, & straightforward as they may seem, I trust you will view them as pro- ceeding from no unfriendly motive, & know that you will reject whatever in them may be inconsistent with the advice of wiser politicians than myself. Most truly your friend   Francis O J Smith

Copy. NhD.

1. John Tyler, by George P. A. Healy, 1842. Corcoran Gallery of Art.

2. Daniel Webster, by George P. A. Healy, 1842. New-York Historical Society.

3. John Jordan Crittenden, by George P. A. Healy, date unknown. Danville Library, Danville, Kentucky.

4. Thomas Ewing, engraved by
A. H. Ritchie from a daguerreotype
by Brady. *American Review*, January 1850.

5. John Bell, engraved by J. C.
Buttre from a photograph by
Brady. Dartmouth College
Library.

6. George Edmund Badger, engraving reproduced in Samuel
A'Court Ashe, ed., *Biographical
History of North Carolina*, Vol. 7
(1908).

7. Rufus Choate, engraved by John Sartain. Dartmouth College Library.

8. Willie Person Mangum, engraved by T. Doney from a daguerreotype by Anthony, Clark & Co. *American Review*, March 1846.

9. William Cabell Rives, lithograph by Charles Fenderich, 1839. Library of Congress.

10. George Evans, engraved by T. Doney. *American Review*, July 1847.

11. John Canfield Spencer, from an engraving in the National Archives.

12. Hugh Swinton Legaré, engraved by T. Doney. *American Review*, July 1845.

13. Abel Parker Upshur, by Sarah M. Peale, 1842. Maryland Historical Society.

14. Isaac P. Davis, engraving in Massachusetts Historical Society, *Proceedings*, May 1869.

15. William Pitt Fessenden, by Asher B. Durand, date unknown. San Antonio Museum Association.

16. Nicholas Biddle, engraving by John Sartain from an unlocated portrait by Jacob Eichholz, 1837. Free Library of Philadelphia.

17. Charles King, by Henry Inman, 1843. New York Chamber of Commerce. Photo courtesy of Pach Bros.

18. William Leete Stone, by Edward D. Marchant, c. 1847. New-York Historical Society.

19. William Winston Seaton, woodcut in *Harper's Weekly*, January 16, 1858.

20. Lord Ashburton, by George P. A. Healy, 1842. New-York Historical Society.

21. Francis Ormand Jonathan Smith, engraved by J. C. Buttre from a photograph by Germon. Maine Historical Society.

22. William Henry Seward, engraved by J. C. Buttre. *Autobiography of William H. Seward* (1877).

23. Edward Everett, by George
P. A. Healy, c. 1842–1843. New-
berry Library.

24. Washington Irving, detail
of original sketch by Daniel
Huntington, 1852. Dartmouth
College.

25. Henry Wheaton, etching reproduced in William Draper Lewis,
ed., *Great American Lawyers*, Vol.
3 (1908).

26. Herman Le Roy, artist
and date unknown. New-
York Historical Society.

27. Caroline Le Roy Webster,
by George P. A. Healy, 1845.
Hood Museum of Art, Dart-
mouth College.

28. Caroline Story White Webster, by Francis Alexander, date unknown. E. Marshall Sargent, Newburyport, Massachusetts.

29. Stephen White, artist and date unknown. Edward H. Harding, Center Sandwich, New Hampshire.

30. George Peter Alexander Healy, self-portrait, 1842. New-York Historical Society.

Cincinnati April 7th. 1843

Dear Sir,

Your favor of the 31st ult.[1] I have received, inclosing the Faneuil Hall speech,[2] for which you will accept my acknowledgements. I trust that you will pardon me, if I state a little more minutely than was stated in my former letter,[3] the present condition of the public feeling in this vicinity.

The ultra men of the Clay school, who, by the way, are not a little reduced in number at present, complain of the unexampled indifference & apathy of the Whigs, & deplore the fact that no method can be hit upon, by which to rouse them to their wonted activity. Such is to some extent the fact, but the cause is not very difficult of detection. The mass of the people are not politicians, and, while they do not comprehend the partizan motives that have governed the factions for the last year, they have become perfectly sick of the performances of their leaders. If those motives were understood, there would be few to tolerate them, but without understanding them, the people have become disgusted with the things done, & with the apparent spirit with which they have been done. It is utterly vain for the ultra press now to attempt anything like a party excitement upon their old plan. All their lucubrations fall flat & insipid upon the public taste. The people are now in that passionless mood in which they would delight more to be told of something promising public & general blessings to the country, than in incense and sacrifices to any human being. Ultraism is the sin now most especially abhorred in this region; and you will seldom hear a man speak upon political subjects, but he will take occasion, before the conversation is closed, to exculpate himself from all sympathy with any thing like partizanship. Time has strengthened the convictions expressed in my former letter, as to the general favor, felt among Whigs of all complexions, for the redemption of State credit. A speech, or a letter from Mr Webster upon this subject, would now be well received, & would probably set the whole mass in motion. The minds of men are in a state of expectation, looking for a conflict upon this precise point. They incline to pause, however, as they would do before a fearful battle, in which they were to engage, & for the result of which they were likely to be held responsible.

One thing may be taken as certain. In this region, President Tyler has no party as a candidate for a second term. Many men feel a strong desire to give the administration countenance & support and disapprove the violence of the opposition. But men, who would go for Mr Tyler, as the next President, are not to be found (perhaps I ought to except some of those who hold office). The idea is regarded as preposterous, and is indulged

only by here & there a dreamy Virginian, who has need to sail to Anti-
chon. It is sincerely regretted, by men who wish Mr Tyler no harm, that
he is now presented before the people, as an expectant for the next Presidency. It must be a wonderful conjunction of strange events, that shall
give Mr Tyler the vote of this part of the country for the Presidency
—a phenomenon in politics: the like whereof has certainly never been
witnessed in this country.

An other matter, I will venture to suggest. It seems to me utterly impossible, that Mr Clay should receive the vote of Ohio for the Presidency,
except perhaps in the event of Mr Calhoun being the only other candidate. There are many reasons which lead me to this conclusion. In the
first place, there is a pretty large segment of the Whig party, which without being Abolitionists, are exceedingly reluctant to vote for a man from a
slave state & a slave holder. They think that the free states have not had
their due proportion of the great offices under the General Government.

Again there is a class of men, not very numerous, it is true, but quite
respectable, particularly in the Northern part of the State who are opposed to Mr Clay as a Duellist. They say that he has done more than any
other man to make that barbarous practice respectable.

Again, there is another class more numerous than either of those,
which I have now named, who are opposed to a United States Bank.
Events well known, that have happened since 1840, among which is the
<deplorable> catastrophe of the Penna. Bank of the United States, have
wrought great changes in the minds of many whigs on that subject.

Another important consideration, which weighs against Mr Clay, is
the extreme party character of his political career, & the denunciatory
course which he has pursued toward the present administration.

For these reasons, & for the additional reason, that Mr Clay was fully
identified with Mr [Thomas] Corwin in our last election, and was fairly
beaten, I cannot suppose that the Whigs of Ohio can triumph under Mr
Clay as their Champion. I will not omit here to say, I am credibly informed, that Mr Clay still makes a U.S. Bank a sine qua non, & gives it
great prominence in his conversation wherever he goes. I omitted to say,
that, among the causes which weigh heavily against the success of the
Whigs under Mr Clay, the Compromise Act cannot be forgotten, in this
State. I was present at the delivery of his Dayton speech, & heard him
declare himself opposed to the Exchequer, as "unconstitutional" &
unwise. This does not appear, nor any mention of the Exchequer, in the
printed speech.

It is this conviction in the minds of our people as to the prospects of
Mr Clay in the next election, which more than anything else encourages
the <Democrats> LocoFocos & dispirits the Whigs. I cannot discover

any changes among men from Whig to Loco Foco principles & prefer-
ences. We have for aught I can see as many Whigs as we had in 1840, &
with a candidate who should combine all branches of the party we
should be as sure of victory now, as we were under General Harrison.
Now Mr Clay cannot combine this great Whig family. Whether it can be
effected under the lead of any man, is indeed uncertain. If Mr Clay were
out of the way, I should not entertain a doubt, but that Mr Webster would
carry the entire strength of the Whig party. The doubt is, whether the
partizans of Mr Clay will see & appreciate the facts which I have named.
They are blind,—they have pledged themselves to him. Our Western politicians have rashly, as I think, made their fortune to depend upon his.
They expect to be great men with him President, but under any other
man, especially under one whom they know they have wronged, they expect little. I am happy however to be able to say that among the better
sort of whigs of this vicinity, there is a manifest relenting for their past
intolerance toward Mr Webster. The jealous flings at him, which are now
exceedingly [few] & only in the most ultra papers are universally received with disgust. The most influential paper by far in this city, if not
in the state, the Cincinnati Gazette, has been cramped & fettered by its
devotion to Mr Clay, till its influence has seemed to be on the wane & its
position has become exceedingly awkward. The publishers, Messrs [S. S.
and R. F.] L'Hommedieu,[4] men of energy, intelligence & wealth, have become indifferent to the success of Mr Clay, & disgusted with the course
which has been pursued. Vaughan the Junior Editor, is in the same
mood. They are ready to do Mr Webster justice, & tired of their position.
Judge [John Crafts] Wright,[5] the senior Editor, alone holds back, professing neutrality. But in his absence, the paper has become at length fully
committed to the plan of relief to the states. The prospect now seems to
be that the paper will grow independent of the influence of Mr Clay &
stand boldly on the great interests of the country, doing justice to Mr
Webster, & ready to espouse his cause for the Presidency in the event of
his being a candidate. The Senior Editor will have to yield, or retire, probably. If the Senior Editor could be purchased out the paper could be depended on for a prudent & efficient support of Mr Webster in the coming
election. This is an important matter, as the whole Whig community in
this region had long been accustomed to be guided by this paper. The
establishment is rich & admirably managed in all its pecuniary affairs.
No new paper would in that event, be necessary to support Mr Webster.
The Republican would hardly oppose you any how, & its influence is
comparatively very small. If you should become disconnected with the
administration, that paper would probably stop. It has lived in very great
measure upon its support of you & the Exchequer. Leave it to praise Tyler

& pap wont save it. The Editor, General Waller,[6] is however an efficient & talented writer. These things I have thought it right to state to you, that you might perceive, that your friends here are in earnest, & that they are not entirely unprepared for action. We regard our cause as a most righteous one, the real cause of our country. It is not our partiality to yourself merely, much as we do admire & approve your character & your career as a statesman & a patriot, but it is our sincere regard for our country, & the deep conviction that you are the only man that can now redeem it, that causes us to trouble you with such communications as this. I am aware that I am liable to be misconstrued in this matter, as acting an officious part. I am not a politician, & I seek no place. My feelings have been strongly enlisted in your behalf & I flatter myself that I have a tolerable conception of the delicacy & difficulty of your position. I have the happiness to agree perfectly in opinion with my friend Mr [Nathaniel] Sawyer as to the matter contained in this letter. We think the tide is now decidedly turning in your favor in this part of the Country. Yours sincerely   A. Taft.

ALS. DLC. Endorsed by DW: "Private file."

1. See DW to Alphonso Taft, March 31, 1843, mDW 24790.

2. Webster had forwarded Taft a copy of the speech he had delivered at Faneuil Hall on September 30, 1842, after the successful negotiation of the Treaty of Washington. For the text of that speech, see *Speeches and Formal Writings*, 2.

3. Not found.

4. The L'Hommedieu brothers had taken over control of the *Cincinnati Gazette* in December 1835.

5. Neither Vaughan nor Wright has been further identified.

6. Not further identified.

TO WARREN DELANO

April 16. 1843
Astor House

My Dear Sir;

I have heard of your kind suggestions to Mr. [Robert Bowne] Minturn, respecting facilitating Mr. Fletcher Webster's proposed visit to China. He will be truly grateful for your countenance, & assistance; I beg leave to express, on my own behalf, my cordial acknowledgements.

I expect to be in my room, this Evening, after 1/2 from 8 oclock. If your convenience should allow you to be in this part of the City, it will afford me pleasure to see You. Yours with regard, Danl Webster

ALS. Rokeby Collection, Barrytown, Dutchess County, N.Y. Courtesy of Richard Aldrich et al. Delano (1809–1898), a native of Massachusetts, was a merchant engaged in the South American and China trade. From 1834 to 1843, he was a commission merchant in China.

FROM EDWARD EVERETT

London, 18 April, 1843.
(Second letter of this date.)[1]

(*Private & Confidential.*)

My dear Sir,

An hour or two only remains, before making up the parcel of dispatches, and I have unfortunately, a very severe headache. I am unable to do more than just to acknowledge the receipt of your letter marked "private and Confidential," of the 29th. March;[2] and to say that I am deeply grieved that Mr [Nathan] Hale should have said any thing to cause you to write it. You do me no more than justice in believing, that it has not been from any prompting of mine.[3] In reference to China, he could not, of course, when he made the remarks to which you allude, (and which I have not seen,) have heard from me, after the news of my appointment reached London; but could the letters I wrote to my sister and other members of my family have been seen by you, you would have found them, *mutatis mutandis*, counterparts of what I wrote to the President and yourself.

Scarcely able as I am at this moment to hold a pen, I must conclude with saying that I am as ever faithfully and affectionately yours,

Edward Everett

P.S. Since receiving your letter, I have thought it would be more agreeable to you that I should make some change in that which I had written to the President. I enclose you the letter as at first written, and send him another, with the omission of the concluding sentences.[4] You can show him the first written letter or not, as you think expedient.

LS. MHi.

1. For Everett's other letter of April 18, see mDW 24893 and *Diplomatic Papers*, 1.

2. See mDW 24767 and *Diplomatic Papers*, 1.

3. Hale was Everett's brother-in-law.

4. Copies of Everett's letters to John Tyler, both dated April 18, appear in the Everett Papers, MHi (Microfilm, Roll 22, Frames 541–542, 544–545).

FROM NICHOLAS BIDDLE

Anda. April 20. 1843

My dear Sir

I inclose the *list* & the *hints*. A half a word to you is as good as thousand.

I am extremely anxious to know whether you are "to be or not to be." With great regard yrs   N B

The *list* was a list of the foreigners holding stock to the amount of

$50000 & upwards in the Penna. funded debt. The hints are as follows:

In August 1843 the principal of the funded debt held in Great Britain will be about 22 millions of dollars of which the annual interest will be $1150. That held in Holland will be about 2 millions, that in France $600,000. Up to the meeting of the legislature in Jany last it was hoped that Provision would be made for the punctual payment of the interest. They adjourned however on the 18th of April leaving things far worse than they were before. For

1. A very little taxation, in addition to what had been already laid, would have been sufficient to pay the interest, if the legislature would only consent to diminish their own useless expenses. But
They would not lay any additional tax—on the contrary
They repealed—that is, they would not renew for another year—one of the existing taxes and
they would make no serious reduction in their own expenses.

2. They have directed that all their Bank & other Stocks which had hitherto been sources of revenue shall be sold, & the proceeds paid to the domestic creditors of course diminishing by so much all resources to pay the stockholders.

3. They have resolved that if a Company will take the public works off the hands of the State, they will accept in payment the Stock. A scheme illusory because it requires a combination of stockholders to the amount of 16 millions to unite in purchasing a series of canals & Rail Roads— which they are to have no share in managing, as they cannot vote by proxy, according to the charter of the company.

The question of the Penna debt is at this moment in a worse position than it ever was—for the State is squandering away its means—and every day blunts its sensitiveness to this dishonorable conduct.

The only way to prevent the loss of the whole is that the Stockholders should rouse themselves and look after their own affairs.

Their great rivals are certain persons to whom the state was, or is said to owe money. These persons with their friends besiege the legislature—they have influence & votes, and naturally obtain the precedence over these distant creditors who are not known, are never heard of, and are presumed to care little or nothing about these distant & merely speculative investments.

These foreign creditors ought to have somebody here to look after their interests—somebody who could represent them before the Legislature— somebody with large powers—who might if necessary to obtain more security for the debt compromise for some abatement of the interest.

Such a course prudent creditors pursue in private life, to their embarrassed debtors, & I much fear that the whole may be placed in jeopardy by this neglect or indifference of the foreign creditors who might find it for their interest to make further advances to complete works now unfinished & unproductive.

ALS draft. DLC.

FROM JARED SPARKS

Cambridge, Apl. 20. 1843

Private

My dear Sir,

In the Intelligencer of the 15th. instant there is a notice which surprises me not a little; namely, that the Vincennes boarded, visited, & examined a Spanish vessel on the coast of Africa, under the suspicion, as it would seem, of being engaged in the slave trade. If this is the *practice* of our vessels, it is idle, and worse than idle, for us to argue against the *right* assumed by Great Britain. One such case, authorized by the government, is enough to confute a volume of arguments. In fact, if such is really the practice of our own vessels, it is not worth while to cite the decisions of judges, or books, or to say any more on the subject.[1]

I am glad to see, that Sir Robt. Peel sets the matter of the map in so proper a light;[2] and I am particularly rejoiced that they have found the same map in the Archives, for I have had strange apprehensions that by some accident or other the map & its red lines might disappear, & thus leave me in an awkward predicament. Excuse these hints & believe me very sincerely yours,   Jared Sparks

ALS. DLC. Endorsed by DW: "*Private files.*"

1. For the full account, summarized above by Sparks, see the *National Intelligencer*, April 15, 1843.

2. For a discussion of the map controversy, see *Diplomatic Papers*, 1.

TO FRANCIS ROBERT RIVES

Department of State.
Washington, 22d. April, 1843.

Sir:

Arrangements have been made, under the President's direction, with the House of Baring, Brothers, & Co. of London, for transacting the business of the United States as their Bankers in Europe, from and after the first of July next. As the accounts of the present Bankers with the United States will be closed at that time, any drafts which you may have occasion to draw after that date, for your salary, will be addressed to Baring, Brothers, & Co. In the meantime, and until the 30th of June next, you will continue to draw on N. M. Rothschild & Sons,[1] as heretofore. I am, Sir, your obedient servant,   Danl Webster

LS. DLC.

1. French bankers.

FROM THOMAS CHAMBERS

Philadelphia, April 24th. 1843

My Dear Sir

It is with the most lively feelings of regret, that I admit, that the late Tariff Law[1] has done nothing, to resuscitate the *Iron business* of our country, but that it is still suffering from severe & heavy embarrassments & that most of our large establishments are suspended & out of operation. The cause I think is to be found in "an unwise & needless Legislation." We have a Tariff; but it is not of the right sort, as it does not command the confidence of the country & no Law can be permanent, which is not generally acceptable to the people. We therefore do not want so much, a *high protective* Tariff, as a stable, fixed & permanent Policy, that will secure the Capitalist a small, but certain reward upon his business & induce him, to expend his money in developing the great resources of the country & how you will naturally ask, is this to be accomplished—by compromise & conciliation with our Southern friends. No. The very diversity of wants & productions, which were evidently intended by the God of Nature, to unite & bind us together & make us, the happiest People upon the face of the Globe, only distracts & seperates us. It can only be accomplished if ever done, by a *Treaty* with foreign Governments. Let our Government propose to England & France to come to some agreement for a just & equal trade & any reciprocal duties, that may be adopted, I answer for it, will be a *sufficient protection*, to our manufacturing industry. It is however the task & work of a master spirit, that must not only teach, but command & soaring high above the party squabbles of the day & devoid of all selfish ambition, seek only the *good* of our entire country. That you possess such a spirit & disposition & are preeminently qualified for such a Task, is my sincere belief & I entertain no doubt, that if you would undertake the task, it would soon be brought to a happy termination.

There never was so propitious a moment, as the present time. The country is sick of politics & politicians. Our agriculture is superabundant; but has *no* market—our manufactures lower, than ever known in the history of the country & *yet* no consumption—our Laborers unemployed & yet *money* abundant.

The advantages which we possess in Penna. & most of the States of this Union, for the Manufacture of Iron of all descriptions, are not surpassed, so far as Nature has bestowed her gifts, by any spot upon the face of the Globe & what do we want, but sound & permanent Legislation, to build up our establishments & enable us to enter into competition with the world. The substitution of Mineral Coal, as a combustible for Charcoal in our Iron establishments has produced a new era in this branch of business, by making our three great & inexhaustible elements of wealth "Coal, Iron, Limestone subserve one common purpose of utility." Large establishments have been erected & are now ready to manufacture, to meet the wants of the country, but from the fear & apprehension, that prevails, that the next Congress will disturb the Tariff Law, most of them are suspended. Such establishments cannot be kept in operation, without large expenditures of money & without accumulating Stock, that in the course of a change of policy must produce the most disastrous results & it is *thus*, that the energies & resources of our country are crippled. It is therefore to put in motion, this great branch of National Industry, that I address you, upon the subject, believing that our Manufacturers, one & all would sacrifice much of the present rates of duties, to procure a permanent Tariff. With great regard & esteem your friend   Thos. Chambers

N.B. I should be pleased to enter into details, in relation to the duties upon Iron, if desirable.

ALS. DLC. Chambers has not been identified.

1. The tariff law had been last re-

vised on August 30, 1842. 5 *United States Statutes at Large* 548–567.

TO [JOHN TAYLOR]

Washington May 1. 1843

Dear Sir

I heard from Mr Weston a few days ago,[1] that you was expected down with the horses, & the cattle also, as he hoped. I trust, that by the time this letter reaches Franklin, you will have got safe back, & be well of your rheumatism, & find all your family well.

And now, my good friend, I am going to write you a straight letter.

First, you did not do right, in not sending down the Stock last fall. This was agreed to; & what is agreed to, *must be done.* That is my way, & there can be no two ways about it. If you were unwell, yourself, you should have sent somebody. You know I never refuse reasonable expenses, in such cases. If you could neither go yourself, nor send by any body else, you ought to have written to me. See the consequence; you are short of hay, to do your springs work, while our barns are yet full. Besides, I shall lose that beautiful little cow, that Mr [George Washington] Nesmith[2] promised me.

Second; you should have driven on the business of the *Wall*, as agreed with Mr Locke,[3] & the preparation for the turnip field. This was all settled, & I expected it would be done; & *it must & shall be done,* yet. I have been at great expense in sending to England for the seed, & have recd it. And that turnip field *shall* be fenced, ploughed, & sowed, this year, if I carry up hands from Marshfield to do it. Now, this is fixed, & there is but one way about it. If you are short of funds, write to me, & I will send you money; *but the thing shall be done.*

Third; I fear you have not built my *Boat*. Now, that also was agreed on, & must be done. If you have not done it, in all this long winter, you cannot do it now. Therefore, do you go immediately, & get some carpenter to make me a boat, of the dimensions which I gave you. Let the boards &c be well seasoned, & let the boat be strong & safe, with good oars & paddles. Let her name be painted on her stern, "Water Lily"; & let her be painted, & in perfect order to be launched, on the 10th day of June. I shall send up a cable & anchor. Now, remember, that this is to be *done*, not merely talked about; but *done.*

4TH. Let Mr Huntoon[4] complete his ploughing; & let that land lie, till I give you further orders. Let the Hancock oxen be well fed, this Spring, with corn; & turn them out to pasture, without too much hard work.

5*th.* And now, one other thing. I calculate, that you have lost money, by trading *in horses.* It is expensive to keep them—& they will sometimes be lame, or sick. Now, *leave off all trading in horses. Keep what you want,* for the farm, & for family use. But have no more changing, & *swapping.* Deal not in horse flesh, beyond your own wants. Put a stake down here, & stand by it; for here, too, there are no two ways. Remember this.

Now, budge not one inch, from any thing which I have said, in this letter. Remember it all, & fulfill it all. If, for the Wall, or the Boat, or any thing else, you need money, let me know it, & you shall have it. But let every thing be done, exactly as I direct, at all events.

I shall be in Boston, by the 20th. of May; & intend to see you, early in June. Mrs Webster & I hope to be with you a good deal, this summer. Now, go ahead; be straight, & come up to the mark, in all things. You have a good wife; a promising family; & shall have the best farm in the Country. Hear my words;

1. Stick to every thing agreed on, & carry it thro'—

2. No more horse trading. Your sincere friend   Danl Webster

ALS. NHD.

1. Weston's letter has not been found.

2. Nesmith (1800–1890; Dart-mouth 1820), a close friend of Webster, was a lawyer in Franklin.

3. Not identified.

4. Not identified.

TO MARY ANN SANBORN

Washington May 3. 1843

My Dear Neice;

I have recd. your letter[1] this morning. I expect to be in Boston, in this month, & will immediately write to Mr [Charles B.] Hadduck to come &

see me, & do all in my power to have a just settlement, immediately. So far as any thing remains due from me, it shall be paid, to your satisfaction. The property (farm) has not been disposed of, nor has it paid its way. But I shall fulfil my engagements.[2] Yours affectionately

Danl Webster

ALS. NhD. Mary Ann Sanborn (1816–1864), Ezekiel Webster's daughter, was the wife of Professor Edwin David Sanborn of Dartmouth College.
1. Not found.

2. Webster was alluding to the settlement of his indebtedness to Ezekiel's family for the Franklin property, still lingering from 1829–30.

TO DAVID SEARS ET AL.

Washington, May 3, 1843.

Gentlemen:

I have received your letter of the 28th of April.[1] You look, gentlemen, with a degree of solicitude which I can well appreciate, to the probability that an adjustment of important questions of international trade between the United States and other countries, especially Great Britain, will be attempted. I fear you estimate quite too highly my own ability to render useful service to the public in such transactions; but, by whomsoever conducted, I should feel the strongest interest in their success, should they take place. I confess that, being truly and sincerely devoted to the protection of American labor and industry, I consider it to be of the highest importance to give to that labor and that industry a security, a steadiness of support, a permanency of encouragement, which they have not lately enjoyed, and which, I fear, they are not likely to enjoy hereafter, unless a more comprehensive policy be adopted than that which has hitherto been pursued. The question of protection has mingled itself to such a degree with questions of supposed local interests, with political questions, and struggles for political power, that it has not been suffered to be at rest on any basis. It has had no repose. This is evidently a great evil. All interests demand a steady and settled policy, and a conviction of the truth appears to be becoming general and strong. Those who possess the means of living desire to feel secure in their enjoyment; and those who have such means to earn must wish, above all things, to know what they may depend upon, when they devote their capital and their labor to particular pursuits or modes of occupation.

It was thought that something was accomplished, and certainly something was accomplished, by the tariff act of last year. Yet, it had hardly passed before events occurred creating the highest probability that the whole subject would be agitated anew in the next Congress. Are we always to be in this fluctuating state? Are we never to be able to look for any thing but a succession of changes? Is there no way of bringing the whole country, and all interests, to an adjustment that may promise some degree of quiet and of general satisfaction? No doubt the various pursuits of the people of this country have really and truly in themselves a strong mutuality of interest. The grain and corn producing States must always find the best market for the surplus of their products in the manufacturing and commercial population of the East; as they will always find the price of manufactured articles, such as they need, kept low, and the quality good, by the productions of Eastern labor. But, so rich and abundant is the grain crop of the country, that, beyond what may be demanded for the consumption of manufacturing and commercial districts, there is still a surplus, for which, or a part of which, a foreign market is desirable. The cotton crop, too, though it finds a market at home, the value of which I think has never been sufficiently appreciated, requires, nevertheless, free exportation, and a large consumption abroad. Cannot those who are concerned in these interests be brought into a harmony and concert of action, proportioned to the real harmony and mutuality which subsist between the interests themselves? For my part, I think the experiment worth trying, and should have great hopes of its success if there were no fear of opposition from collateral or extrinsic causes. My inquiries at the North, and through the Centre, and at the South and West, have been extensive; and the result has led to the conclusion which I have expressed. I would not speak with confidence upon a matter yet untried, and which I know may encounter a variety of objections; but I repeat that, in my opinion, the experiment is worth a fair trial. We may well make one earnest endeavor, even upon slight encouragement, to give permanent support to the industry of the country and stability to the business and pursuits of life.

As to myself, gentlemen, I have no expectation of being concerned, in any manner, in negotiations connected with this subject; and am happy to know that the country has many hands abler than mine to wield such concerns. The Government has eminent ability at its command, both at home and abroad. I have no wish to go abroad on public service. If negotiations should be entered into, there are reasons for desiring that they should be undertaken at Washington; in which case, according to the usual course, they would be conducted by the head of the Department of State, under the direction of the President.

With unfeigned thanks for your manifestation of friendly sentiments, respect, and confidence, I remain, gentlemen, your obliged friend and obedient servant,   Daniel Webster.

Text from the *National Intelligencer*, May 27, 1843. Original not found. Sears (1787–1871; Harvard 1807) was a prominent merchant, land speculator, and social leader of Boston.

1. See David Sears et al. to DW,
April 28, 1843, mDW 25007 (also

published in the *National Intelligencer*, May 27, 1843).

*With Caleb Cushing and Fletcher Webster preparing to leave for China,
Webster resigned his post as secretary of state on May 8; he went back
to Marshfield. From there he watched the Tyler administration move
headlong towards the annexation of Texas and Tyler's nomination for
reelection. Only occasionally during the remainder of the year did he
make public appearances or speeches.*

TO EDWARD EVERETT

Washington May 12. 1843

Private

My Dear Sir;

Your various communications by the last Steam Ship were all regularly recd in this City on the 6th inst. In consequence of your final decision to decline the China mission, which was not unexpected, Mr Cushing was immediately appointed. He will proceed by way of England, &
probably go out about the first of July. I sent nothing of yours to me, to
the President; so he saw only your letter to him.

I resigned my office on the 8th, and Mr [Hugh Swinton] Legaré was
appointed *ad interim*, under the provisions of the Statute. He may probably hold the place some months; & I cannot say who is likely to come in,
when he retires. Possibly, Mr. [Abel Parker] Upshur. The Presidents
range for choice is limited. He is an accomplished lawyer, with some experience abroad, of Gentlemanly manners & character, & not at all disposed to create, or to foment, foreign difficulties. How much of general
comprehensiveness, & practical ability he possesses is yet to be evinced.
I think the President could not, at present, have done better.

I confess, My Dear Sir, I have fears, deep fears, for the future. There
is danger, that the present administration will accomplish little more, of
good. The President has entirely false notions, as I think, of his own
position. He throws himself on the Locofoco Party, & enters into a competition for the favors of that party with Mr Van Buren & Mr Calhoun.
He is sure to be beaten. He has not a particle of strength in that party.
Many moderate Whigs have hitherto felt kindness for him, & these are
the only real friends he has; & these, he is likely to drain off. Well; we
must take things as they come. You will probably be quiet, where you
are; but I confess I do not see who is to be at the helm here, able to instruct you on the important matters of Oregon, & Commercial arrangements.

I leave this place for Massachusetts, the 15th. As to plans for the summer, I have none; but expect to be wafted by the strongest gale. I am

building a room for a Library, at Marshfield, shall there collect my books, & regard that place as home, for the present. But it is very likely I shall be here next winter, partly from Professional motives, & partly for the sake of a milder climate.

I hope you will write me as often as you can, & send me any speeches, or pamphlets, or other fresh publications, of little cost, & let your Secretary keep a minute. Or, what will be better, tell Mr. [John?] Miller[1] to send me any thing which comes out, & which you think I should like to see. Let any thing for me come thro the Mission, but let not parcels, marked for me be under envelopes addressed to the Dept. If they be put into the bag, addressed to me only, I shall get them at Boston. It will be best to send exclusively by way of Liverpool.

Adieu! My Dear Sir. Remember me kindly to Lord Ashburton, & warmly to Lord Brougham, when you see him. Yours always truly,

Danl Webster

ALS. MHi. Published in *PC*, 2: 173.
1. Not further identified.

The editorial below was written by Webster in response to an editorial note in the New York *Journal of Commerce, May 9, 1843. The* National Intelligencer *published Webster's editorial, with minor changes, on May 13, preceded as it is below by the* Journal of Commerce *item.*

EDITORIAL ON DW'S RESIGNATION AS SECRETARY OF STATE
[May 12, 1843]

"There are an abundance of rumors in the newspapers about changes in office, both past and to come. It seems to be expected that President Tyler will throw himself into the ranks of the Democracy, and propitiate the favor of that party by displacing Whigs and appointing Democrats. The Whigs, on the contrary, are indignant that Mr. Tyler should ever displace a man who belongs to 'the party that elected him,' and supply the vacancy from the other side." "Neither the Whigs nor the Democrats will ever, as parties, support Mr. Tyler; and, so far as he has ever done any thing upon any plan of propitiation, he has gone upon a false principle and lost popularity." "Mr. Tyler's only expectation of support was from the favor of the people, to be secured by a just and wise administration." "One thing is certain, he will never be nominated by any Convention called to represent either the Whig or Democratic party. If he be nominated at all, it will be by the spontaneous rising of the people in his favor. But whether he is chosen or even nominated or not, can be of no great moment to him. If he conducts the Administration in a straightforward manner through his term, and does what he can to advance the country in its glorious destiny, he will be honored in any event; but if, stooping from his high position, he should yield himself to political manoeuvres, under the guidance of office-seeking politicians, the people will desert him as completely as the parties have done already. We must think, therefore, that the changes which are made in office, so far as dictated at Washington, are made for other purposes than to secure the favor of any party already in existence."

We cannot concur in all these sentiments, such for instance, as that the Presidents measures of policy have been generally popular. But the article, nevertheless, has much of truth, & strong sense in it, & coming from a quarter, professedly neutral in politics, we would fain encourage the hope that it might prof[f]er influence, in the proper quarter. But we fear much that the infatuation is unconquerable.

That Mr. Tyler can not be nominated by either of the Conventions; that he is proceeding altogether upon a false principle; that he has lost, & is losing popularity; that all these removals without cause are creating a general & a strong feeling of disgust in the Country; & that the idea of making a new party, (deserting the friends who brought him into office) by the patronage of the Government, & by listening to the clamorous demands of hungry office seekers, are truths, in our judgment, most true & manifest. But they will be more manifest, & will receive a still more energetic tone. We see that many of the leading Papers assert, in a positive manner, that the retirement of the late Secretary of State is owing to the fact, that he could not follow the *leader*, & go with *others*, into a desperate plunge, for loco-foco support. We are not in the secret, if there be any secret; but we presume some such course must have led to the Secretarys resignation.

That Mr Webster would have been willing to stay in the Department, & try his hand at other important negotiations, it is natural enough to suppose, if there had not been reasons opposed to his continuance in office, *not connected with the foreign relations of the Country*. That the President would desire to retain Mr Websters services, who can doubt, if other objects & purposes did not thwart that wish? But that is the rub. Every body knows, that the chief emblazonment which the present Administration has placed on the field of its escutcheon is what has been done in foreign negotiations, & Diplomatic intercourse. But we have seen constant intimations, in certain quarters, that when Mr Webster should leave the Cabinet, there would no longer [be] any obstacle, between the President, & the hearty support of what is called the Democratic Party. If such things are said in the Presses, favorable to Mr. Tyler, we have a right to presume that they have been said, much oftener, & with all the earnestness of self interest, & all the importunity which belongs to greedy office seekers, by others who have, in such numerous crowds, had access to him. All this we fully believe to be mere delusion on one side, & nothing less than gross cheating & imposture, on the other.

AD. NN, and *National Intelligencer*, May 13, 1843.

TO EDWARD EVERETT

New York May 28. 43

My Dear Sir,

You know something of Mr. Thurlow Weed, of Albany, the Editor of the Evening Journal, of that City. He makes a trip to Europe, at this time for health & recreation.

Mr Weed is not only an able political writer, but he has also literary tastes, & keeps up with the progress of time & things, in matters of general information. It will do him good to see you, & to talk with you, & to look on his own Country, from the other side of the Atlantic. He is intelligent, & has excellent disposition; and is destined, I think, to act a useful & important part among us. Pray be as kind to him as your convenience will allow. I am, Dear Sir, with the most true regard, Yrs   Danl Webster

ALS. MHi.

FROM JOSHUA BATES

London 30 May 1843

My dear Sir

I have to thank you for your several kind favors to that of the   ,[1] which I should have acknowledged sooner, but that I have been confined to my room for near four weeks by serious illness from which I have now happily perfectly recovered. I have to thank you for having restored to my House the account of the Treasury Department which never ought to have been removed by your predecessors[2] for I am sure a Government was never served more faithfully than the Government of the United States [has] been by Baring Brothers & Co. I do not allude particularly to the period since I have belonged to the House but from the beginning. The principles on which the House is conducted are liberal and honorable towards every body. There is an ambition to do right which makes it very agreeable to belong to such a House. I should have liked very much to have seen you here to settle the remaining difficulties between the two countries. You would have found Sir Robert Peel a complete man of business. As to a commercial treaty I fear it would be impossible to make one. This country has to look to her revenue while the United States must in some degree protect her Iron & Cotton & woollen manufactures which renders it difficult to meet. In retiring from office you have the consolation of having done the State great service. The Ashburton Treaty as it is called here will begin to be appreciated when party hostility shall have exhausted its venom. It is of immense importance to both countries.

Here things do not seem to improve much. Is it not wonderfull that the mighty power of this Country, greater than ever Bonaparte wielded excites so little the attention of European powers. There is a necessity for this Country with her extended dominion a[nd] colonial establishments to be mistress of the seas. She cannot permit any power, to augment her naval force so as to approach her own. At this moment she could send forth 70 or 80 first class steamers. Conquests in China and India seem to follow as a matter of course and all this is going on while Chartists, the corn law repeal, the repeal of the union with Ireland, are agitated with a violence that knows no bounds.

I have written to friend [Thomas Wren] Ward about the Land patents and he will communicate with you on the subject.[3] Can nothing be done for the suffering creditors of the delinquent states—accustomed to consider my country as the model of every thing that was high and honorable, I cannot describe to you how humbled and mortified I feel at the want of good faith in such states as Pen[n]sylvania. A poor state in embarrasment could be pardoned but a wealthy one has no excuse.

Mrs Bates and Mr & Mrs Van de Weyer join with me in kind regards to Mrs Webster and your self, with which I remain very sincerely Yours

Joshua Bates.

ALS. NhD.

1. Bates left the space blank.

2. For one instruction on the restoration of the United States accounts to Baring Brothers & Company, see above, DW to Francis R. Rives, April

22, 1843.

3. The "Land patents" to which Bates referred have not been identified. Ward's communications with DW on the matter have not been found.

FROM JOHN MACGREGOR

Board of Trade
Whitehall
London 17th June 1843

Dear & Esteemed Sir,

I beg leave to thank you for the very valuable returns of the population and agricultural & manufacturing industry of the United States.[1] The papers which I have laid before our Parliament, are I regret all out of print except, the Seventh part (Italy), which I have the honor of to send today through Mr Everett. I have however reprinted them with additional matter in another form, and I beg you to accept the first volume; which as well as the commercial statistics contains my views on the interchange and on taxing commodities.[2]

The parts, which will be continued, & some of them laid before parliament this session, will comprise, the Ottoman Empire, including Egypt and the African states—the Russian Empire, & the remaining states of Europe viz Spain, Portugal, Sweden & Norway—China & the other asiatic states. The United States & other states of America, will also be reprinted and form a second volume similar to the first.

I was much gratified on reading your late speech on Foreign Commerce, and on a projected treaty between England, and the United States of America.[3] I long and seriously, have considered the union of your country, and my own, by moral sympathies and material interests. As far as trade and navigation are in question, I would place the United States upon at least as liberal a footing with England, as our own possessions; and, although I am unable to say so officially I shall continue to impress the advantages to both countries not only now but from generation to generation, to come, without probable limitation of establishing such a system of intercourse, both as respects trade and navigation, between two great countries of the same family. If we accomplished so certain a foundation of peace & of mutual interests, we might compel the world, pacifically, to legislate commercially upon like sound principles.

I have seen a good deal of General [Duff] Green, who seems to me to understand the condition of the United States more comprehensively than most American citizens who have lately visited this country. You have your difficulties, as well as we have ours: but yours are not of so stubborn a character. I am Dear Sir with Sincere respect your's faithfully   J Macgregor

ALS. NhHi.

1. Webster had most likely sent MacGregor a copy of the Sixth Census of the United States or the Compendium (1840).

2. MacGregor probably sent Webster *The Commercial and Financial Legislation of Europe and America, with Revision of the Taxation and Customs Tariff of the United King-* *dom* (London, 1841). Webster later acquired at least two additional works by MacGregor: *Commercial Statistics* (2 vols., London, 1843–1844) and *Progress of America* (2 vols., London, 1847).

3. MacGregor was alluding to Webster's speech of May 18, 1843, at Baltimore, printed in W & S, 13: 150–171.

FROM JOHN TYLER

Washington July 8. 1843

My Dear Sir:

Your letter of the 3. July[1] reached me last night and I delay not to say that the moment I learned your objections to Dr. [Jacob L.] Martin[2] I abandoned all idea of appointing him chief clerk to the State Department. In fact I had been wholly ignorant, at the time I thought of making the appointment of his course towards you. While therefore I may give him some other office, I shall certainly not place him in a position which would imply on my part any dissinclination to comply with your wishes or consult your feelings.

Mr. [Edward H.] Hadducks case stood thus. The public monies had been deposited in an hostile Bank near by the land office. I felt that it was in every way due to the administration to transfer them to the Clinton Bank at Columbus—the order was accordingly made and executed—but in some short time thereafter there appeared in a rabid Press at Cincinnati a communication purporting to give an account of the expense, descending to the minutest particulars attendant on the transfer, the statement however greatly exaggerated, accompanied by an attack upon the administration of a virulent character. It seemed to me at the time to be clearly traceable either to or through the Receiver, and with out knowing any thing of his connexions I felt it was proper to remove him. If the step taken by the govt. in regard to the deposits was wrong, it would have been a source of gratification to me had Mr Hadduck addressed me on the subject—but an attack in the newspapers was more than I could bear.[3]

In furnishing you with this explanation my Dear Sir I give you only an additional proof of my sincere regard for you. In fact no one can possess that feeling towards you in a higher degree. It is for yourself alone—for even if I have been led into error it is too late to correct it by a restoration, altho' I might repair it in some other way.

You will perceive in the newspapers the disclaimer of the British govt. as to the Sandwich Islands—it has been highly gratifying—but inasmuch as there seemed to be an *unnecessary* assertion of right to enforce its claims for indemnity for wrongs committed on British subjects in Mr Fox's letter, it was considered proper in the reply of Judge Upshur to guard against any ambiguous or hidden intent.

I have nothing from England which gives us the hope that any thing will be done by that govt. on the subject of a commercial treaty. Do you get any thing on that subject. Will you permit me in conclusion to say that there is no wish personal to yourself which you may entertain that I shall not be ready most promptly to meet—and any suggestions you may have to make touching our course of public policy will be weighed with the greatest attention.

Be pleased to present me most respectfully to Mrs. Webster and be assured of my constant regard.   John Tyler

ALS. NjMoHP. Published in part in Curtis, 2: 213. Endorsed by DW: "John Tyler. July 8. '43[.] Mr Hadduck's case[.]"

1. See DW to John Tyler, July 3, 1843, in Curtis, 2: 212.
2. Martin, a native of North Carolina, had been chief clerk in the State

Department for eight months when Webster assumed his post as secretary. Webster immediately dismissed Martin and placed Fletcher in his post. In April 1844, Tyler appointed Martin as secretary to the French legation.

3. Haddock (1811–1881), brother of Charles B. and Webster's nephew, had moved to Chicago in 1833 where he became a merchant and banker. Under William Henry Harrison, Haddock had been appointed receiver of public moneys at Chicago. Tyler had dismissed him, as he stated, on the belief that he misused funds.

With the temperance crusade at fever pitch in Massachusetts, a group of Webster's neighbors in nearby Duxbury, led by their minister, Josiah Moore (1800–1881; Harvard 1826), passed resolutions on July 4 requesting Webster's support of their cause through "example" and "eloquence." They asked Webster "to give the subject his serious consideration, and in view of public feeling and sentiment in the region of his residence, and his own social duty, if he be not disposed to take an active part with us, to do nothing at least, which may have the effect to cancel the exertions and retard the progress of this reformation." Webster's caustic response to the resolutions, which he received in mid-August, appears below. The resolutions, DW's response, and Moore's rather labored reply of August 16 (mDWs) are included in Moore to Theodore Parker, February 17, 1853, Theodore Parker Papers, DLC.

TO [JOSIAH MOORE]

Aug. 14 [1843]

This proceeding, which a consciousness of its impropriety seems to have kept so long from me, and which is now recd without a name, is distinguished for want of justice, want of all feelings of neighborly kindness, and want of good manners. I return the paper to its reputed author.

Danl Webster

Copy. DLC.

FROM WADDY THOMPSON

Mexico Aug 24 1843

My Dear Sir

I wrote to you sometime since on the subject of the draft for $3600 for the Santa fe prisoners which had been charged to me.[1] I did not then know that you had retired from the State Dept. and from a letter recently received from the 3d Auditor I am led to believe that it was his own act and not ordered by you. If so, will you do me the favor to write to Mr Upshur on the subject.

I see that the Locofocos are carrying every thing before them. I presume that by this time certain gentlemen have discovered that they are the chief sufferers from having rejected your wise & conciliatory counsels. God grant that you may be able to succeed in yr project of a commercial treaty. I desire it first for its public benefits & next because it will remove the sole objection to you in the South. The north and the south ought to be united and nothing but this Tariff question separates them. They are the wealth the wealthy & the honest partners in the concern—and whilst they are divided they will be plundered by the strong & the unprincipled. This view is to me so obvious that I am only surprized that Jonathan with his usual sagacity has not already seen it and discarded his old opinions of the strong Federal Government—the stronger tho worse for New England. Ever most truly Yrs   W Thompson

ALS. DLC.
1. Thompson was seeking reimbursement for his efforts in securing the release of the Santa Fe prisoners.

TO JOHN TYLER

Boston Aug. 29. 1843.

Private, & entirely confidential.

My Dear Sir,

I have concluded, not without much hesitation, to write you this letter, not expecting or desiring an answer to it, nor wishing that it should be made the subject of conversation, when we meet. But I feel it to be my duty, to suggest to you, frankly & fully, what I think, on some points in the present state of things.

I need hardly say, that I feel great concern, that your administration should go on to its close, successfully & usefully; first, because I have hearty good wishes & feelings towards you personally; & secondly, because I have been, for a short time, a member of the administration, partaking in its general character & fate, for good or evil, & feel therefore something like personal interest in all that affects it.

Now, my Dear Sir, I must declare to you, in all sincerity & truth that I do think there is danger that your administration will terminate with diminished respect, unless you exert firmness, & decision, in resisting the importunities, which I know beset you, from day to day.

You have already so modified your cabinet, as that one half of its members consist of Gentlemen, belonging to the Locofoco, or Democratic party, & who strenuously opposed the movement, which brought Gen Harrison, & yourself, & others, into power. Many subordinate changes have also been made. Yet [it] is evident, that these acts have not, in the least, conciliated the party. Its organs, high & low, are, if possible, more abusive than ever. Witness the Democratic Review, the Globe, &c &c. There is not manifested any disposition at all, in these quarters, to support your administration, nor to support your personal interests hereafter. After all that has been done here, in the North, there is not one paper, of the slightest consequence, belonging to the party, which has committed itself to you. Nor is any such thing intended. Be assured, be assured, my Dear Sir, that those who so much importune you, have no regard to the public good, & no concern, whatever, for your own future fate. I have been of this opinion, all along; & having been now three months among the people, I know it to be well founded. They are governed by mere selfishness & greediness for office; & when you have given them all that you have to give, (& they will be content with no less,) they will not feel the least gratitude or kindness, whatever. In the meantime, it certainly wounds the feelings, & shakes the confidence, of your real friends, that worthy men, standing high with the public, & who bore their full part of the heat & burden of that election, which resulted in placing you in the Presidency, should be removed from office, to make way for those, who were struggling against you, while they were struggling for you. Here is the danger. Will not such a course of things, while it makes no friends any where necessarily cause the administration to lose, in the general estimate of the Country. Is there not danger, exceeding danger, that, two years hence, you will regret the having sacrificed friends, of known worth & fidelity, in the hope of securing the favor of opponents? And will it not be an unhappy thing, if your administration should be known & distinguished hereafter, as one in which patronage of office was relied on, for political & personal support? Is not this against all, that you & I have written, & spoken, & repeated in every form, within the last ten years? I know, my Dear Sir, that I am addressing you freely; but out of the fulness of the heart, the mouth speaketh; & I must repeat, therefore, my conscientious belief, that without the exercise of decision & firmness, in rejecting solicitations for change, your substantial & permanent fame, as President of the United States, is in no small peril.

There are other considerations. It is certain that a majority of the H. of Rep in the next Congress, will be composed of the friends of Mr. Van Buren. Any careful examination of the subject will easily satisfy anyone of this. And no concessions to be made by you, will conciliate that majority. They will thwart you, where they can. And it is now equally certain, that a majority of the Senate will be Whigs, & that they will be exasperated, in a high degree, by the removal of so many of the Whigs of the Country, on political grounds merely. In many cases inquiries will be made into the reasons of these removals; & from what I have lately heard, certain Senators, friends of Mr. Van Buren, have pledged themselves, to go all lengths in these inquiries, & to vote against all nominations, made to fill vacancies, created for merely political purposes. Many rejections must be expected. You will naturally say, let the Senate do as it pleases; & let the Country decide the matter. But is the country likely to be with the Administration, on the question of turning out friends, & appointing opponents, for the purpose of gaining political ends? I think the country will be the other way altogether.

It seems to me, then, that there is but one course to be pursued, likely to redound to the permanent honor of the administration; & that is, to rest its claims, on its great public measures; to seek to recommend itself to the whole People, by its wise policy, domestic & foreign; to remove no man from office but for cause; to hold itself, & keep itself, above the reach of carping & selfish political partizans; to act for the whole country, & to rely on the whole country for support. Such a course would place the two Houses of Congress upon their own responsibility; would leave you high, in general estimation & regard; & would release you, personally, from that importunity incessant & untiring, which I know is the annoyance & torment of your life.

I have thus, My Dear Sir, discharged a duty; & I have done it, because I have felt it to be a duty, & because there is no one, more sincerely desirous for the promotion of your happiness & honor, than I am. Yrs always truly,   Danl Webster

Copy. MHi. Published in *W & S*, 16: 406–408.

FROM ROBERT PERKINS LETCHER

Frankfort K. 2d. Octor. 1843

My dear Sir,

I have this moment, finished reading your speech made at the Agricultural supper in Rochester,[1] and I must say it is a *great*, a *noble*, a *glorious speech*, and one which has afforded me uncommon interest and satisfaction, in its perusal.

You know I have always *loved* you with great sincerity, and have constantly and ardently desired to see you in a position where your talents could be most usefully exerted for the benifit of the country. But I never did like to see you in that miserable Tyler *pack*, more espicially after you had completed the Treaty with England, and I confess on your own account, I was glad you *left it*. All your friends in this country were glad also. The truth is, many of your old friends and warm admirers believe they have good cause to blame you on several accounts, but they all I believe to a man as far as I know, want only some slight pretext to *forgive* and to *forget*, and to like you just as well as ever. The fact is you were born a good Whig, bred a good Whig, and you must die a good Whig and nothing but a Whig. Your strong arm must be constantly raised in defense of the Whig cause, which is the cause of this and all future generations.

If it fail now, I verily believe it will fail forever. Why there is too much at stake, for a man of your powers, your distinction and your patriotism to remain silent and inactive.

I am often askd, what course will Mr. Webster take in the presidential contest? The answer has uniformly been, "I do [not?] certainly know, but I believe just that course which becomes a man of his fame and his character." You know my dear Sir, I am a plain spoken man, and faithful in my attachments, as well as sincere in my councils to my friends. It would distress me, yea, grieve me exceedingly to see you seperated or alienated from the great body of your real friends, or from the cause which you have so long and so ably sustained and advanced by your distinguished abilities. Take ground in due time, maintain your consistency and your principles at all hazards.

I have written you most hastily, and most *freely* as you must acknowledge, but I still have room to tell you, your remarks upon repudiation, *suited my* taste "to a Nats heel." Give it to the rascally Repudiators every where "hot and heavy."[2]

You may write me, just as freely as you please. I never show *papers good or bad*. That's my rule. With great regard your friend   R. P. Letcher

ALS. DLC.

1. Webster's comments at the State Agricultural Fair in Rochester, New York, on September 20 and 21, are

printed in *W & S*, 13: 172–195.

2. Webster had discussed repudiation in his Rochester speech. *Ibid.*, pp. 192–193.

FROM STEPHEN CLARENDON PHILLIPS

Salem October 15. 1843.
(Sunday evening)

My dear Sir,

Your *last* letter was received yesterday morning, but your *first*, which was needed to explain the other, did not reach me till a late hour last evening.[1]

Under the circumstances, I think it expedient that you should accept the invitation of the Committee to address a County meeting, with the understanding that Andover shall be designated as the place of meeting.[2] Although your presence in this quarter would be extremely gratifying, the impulse of a large meeting and your influence are more needed, I think in the other Congressional District; and it seems to me on the whole fortunate that all circumstances should concur in favor of your deciding to go to Andover. The 9th Novr, or any day you may designate, will be agreeable to us—it is very important that you should *now* fix the day.

As soon as your reply is received by the Committee,[3] we shall proceed to make all necessary arrangements; and may safely promise you a nu-

merous attendance and a cordial reception. Yours respectfully & truly
S. C. Phillips

ALS. NhHi.

1. Neither letter found.

2. On September 5 (mDW 25341)
Moses Stuart, as chairman of the
committee, urged DW to address the
Whig convention in Andover. Webster
accepted the invitation and addressed

the Whigs of Essex County on November 9. That speech is printed in
W & S, 3: 159–185.

3. For the acknowledgment of
Webster's acceptance of the invitation, see Samuel Merrill to DW, October 23, 1843, mDW 25403.

TO ROBERT PERKINS LETCHER

Marshfield, (Mass) Octr. 23. 1843

My Dear Sir;

I read your letter of the 2nd instant,[1] not only with interest, but with
emotion. I believe every word you say, of your kind feelings, & friendship
towards me, which I am sure you believe I reciprocate, fully & cordially.
You say I may "write you, freely, as you never show letters, good or bad";
I am quite willing, My Dear Sir, in this confidence, to let you know exactly what I think, & how I feel.

In the first place, you are right in supposing that I must live & die, as
I was born, a "Whig"; as we have understood that term, and especially as
we understood it in the contest of 1840. He is a fool, as well as a foe, who
supposed it possible for me to tread back the steps of my whole political
career, & abandon those principles, the support of which has made me
considerable, in the Country. I am as willing, now, as I ever was, to exert
my faculties for the continued support, & further diffusion, of those principles.

But then, I have some degree of self-respect, & some pride; & shall certainly submit to no sort or degree of ill-treatment. And such, I must confess, I think I have recd. I seldom speak of myself, or my affairs; but as
you invite it, I will be frank. I think, then, that a certain party, a division
of the Whigs, mostly in the West & South, have not extended, in time
past, that cordial respect towards some of us, this way, which they have
ever recd from us. For instance; in 1835, there was no Kentucky candidate before the People; there was a Massachusetts candidate. *How did
Kentucky act?* And, let me add, it was *Kentucky,* & the course adopted by
her in 1836, that gave a new & unexpected direction to Whig Prefer-
ences, *& have kept her own favorite son, from the place in which she
wishes to see him.* I need not *prove* this; reflect upon it, & you will find
it is just so. But let that pass. We all finally concurred in Genl. Harrison's
election. His death blasted our prospects, & we had another man, & another kind of man, to deal [with]. The Whigs were immediately alarmed,

but the universal cry was, "let Genl. Harrison's cabinet keep their places." I kept mine, & yet there are those who will never forgive me for it. The last conversation I ever had with Mr Clay, he said "if I had great national objects, which I supposed I could answer, by staying in the Dept, I was justified in staying." That was my own opinion. I had such objects, & I stayed till they were accomplished.

You regret, that I remained after the Treaty *was completed*. My Dear Sir, when was the Treaty completed? It was ratified at the end of the Session of 1842. The laws, for carrying it into effect, had not passed, & I knew were to be opposed, as they were opposed. They passed, however, at the end of the last Session; & then, & not before, the Treaty was "completed."

I then drew up the papers for the China Mission, a measure which had originated with myself, & then immediately resigned my Office. Now, my Dear Sir, what is there to complain of, in all this, supposing me to have been right, in staying in the Cabinet one hour, after the other gentlemen left it?

There are other things. It is true, that I did not approve of <much> some acts of the Whigs, in the called Session of 1841. I did not approve of the rejection of Mr Ewings Bank Bill; I did not approve of the readiness, not to say eagerness, which was manifested in some quarters to have a quarrel between the Whigs & Mr Tyler. I thought we ought to try, to the last, to hold him, as far as possible, to Whig principles, & a Whig administration; for I was unwilling to lose *all* the great objects of the preceeding contest. I lamented, therefore, the Whig manifesto of 1841, both in regard to its spirit, & its topics.

In Sep. 1842. a proceeding took place, at a Whig Convention in Boston, which I knew was aimed against me. Its object was, to destroy my standing & character, politically, with the Whigs. This object, I determined to defeat, at all hazards, & all consequences; &, thank God, I did defeat it. I defended myself, & nothing more; & if what was done, *necessarily*, on that occasion, reached so far as to be detrimental to others, I am not answerable for that result.

And now, my Dear Sir, let me recal to your recollection a little, the course of events, & the conduct of some leading Whigs. I remained in office, under the circumstances already stated. I got through the negotiation with England, & it does not become me to say how important this was to the country, or whether it was well or ill conducted. But one thing is certain; it never recd. a word of commendation, from certain leading Whigs. They did not complain of its results; but they did not appear to think, that, in its conduct & conclusion, there had been any *merit*, worth speaking of. Very well; no man is bound [to] praise; praise & commendation must be voluntary. But, then, if to withhold approbation be no injury, to be complained of, gross abuse, personal & political, is such an injury; & you know how freely that has been bestowed, on me. You know how I have been attacked & vilified by such men as Garrett Davis, [John Minor] Botts, Jno. C. Clark, [Kenneth] Rayner, & many others, in Congress, all of them being most especial friends of Mr Clay; to say nothing of what has been done out doors, or of the conduct of the scoundrel who publishes the leading Whig Press in Kentucky.

And I must add, that if any attempt has been made by any body, to check this course of atrocious abuse, in & out of Congress, such attempt has never come to my knowledge.

I have now, My Dear Sir, spoken to you, of myself, quite as freely as I ever spoke to any body; I have done so, with entire confidence <in your honor>, & your friendship; & it is time, I believe, to take leave of the subject.

I wish well to the Whig cause, & am ready to make all reasonable sacrifices to insure its success. But those who expect to displace me, from my position, will find, if they have not found already, that they have a work of some little difficulty. I verily believe there is Whig strength enough in the Country to elect a President; but that object can only be accomplished by the exercise of much consideration, wisdom, & conciliation. We must have a hearty *union*, or the prospect is hopeless. That, we must all be convinced of.

Our State elections are now going on, as they should have gone on last year, with a studied abstinence from National topics. The result will be, as I believe, that we shall carry the State, by a strong majority. Massachusetts may then properly speak, on National subjects. At present, she must recon herself among *loco foco* States.

I shall be glad to hear from You, My Dear Sir, freely & fully, as I write you. I go to Boston this week, at which place please address me. With constant & sincere regard, truly Yrs   D. Webster

ALS. NcD. Published in *W & S*, 16: 413–416.
1. See above.

TO SETH WESTON

Washington Novr. 1. '43
Wednesday morning
6 oclock

Mr Weston,

I have a few minutes leisure before other people are stirring, & I employ them in saying a few things to you.

I expect to be in Boston on Monday or Tuesday, the 6th or 7th. But then I have an engagement in Essex County, on Thursday, the 9th. So that it will be Saturday, the 11th. before I can be at Marshfield. And possibly not then, as I must be in Lowell on the 14th.[1] for a week's work. A good many things, therefore, must be looked after, before I see you.

In the first place, put the barns, sheds, &c all in order, to put up the cattle. Winter will [be] upon us soon. The Stantials, or some of them, must be moved a little, in Peleg's barn, so as to bring the calves nearer together. They must all be put up, now, & well kept. Give them turnips and a few oats. Let Peleg[2] take especial care of the fatting sheep. They must have plenty of turnips & oats, or small corn, *with some salt hay, every day,* as well as grass, or English hay. I am to exhibit some of this mutton, both in Boston & N. York; & I shall be shamed, if any thing beats.

I do not know whether any young cattle have been bought, at Brighton; but we shall, some how, fill up all the barns, chock full. Therefore, put the barn at the Winslow House, in proper order—fence the yard, fix the pump, &c.

—I wish you & Henry Thomas would go & look at the wood lot—examine it, see the owner, ascertain the price, & terms of payment.

—Make some calculations about the *Wharf.* Nothing is more wanted, & we must do it, if we do nothing else. See a rough sketch, enclosed.[3] Consider it, & think what alterations of the plan will be best.

—Look after the seine, & take up the reel, & the drying posts.

We shall want some bricks, early in the Spring, & it may be well to give Mr. Chandler[4] notice.

—If you can dispose of the small Harlow oxen, at a fair price, do so.

No matter how soon the steers, destined to be sold for beef, are disposed of.

—Inquire into the barn room, on the Island, and also as to the hay, pumpkins, potatos, & small corn there; to see whether some more steers might not be kept in that barn.

—To give the clay a trial, I think of taking two measured acres, right across the center of the peach orchard, or thereabouts, running from the road back to the pasture; put on 30 loads of clay to the acre, in small heaps, & let it lie till spring, then to be spread, &c. This may be a good time, perhaps, for Daniel Wright[5] to attend to this matter, if there is no kelp to draw. My paper runs out, before I have half done. Yrs

D. Webster

Speak to a Cooper to make 4 nice meat tubs—one large, & three small ones, about two thirds as big as that which came from Washington, & stands in the barn. Let them be nice.

You will of course read all these things over, with Danl. Wright. Let me find a letter in Boston, next Tuesday morning, telling me whether any cattle were bought, in Brighton, & how you like my Pembroke purchase, & other things.

P.S. 2 oclock. P.M. It is barely possible I may be at home, so as to be at Brighton next Monday morning—to see John's cattle. *I shall try.*

ALS. NhHi. Published in *PC*, 2: 175–176.
1. Webster was to argue the Phoenix Bank cases in Lowell. 6 *Law Reporter* 385.
2. Not identified.
3. Not found.
4. Not identified.
5. Wright (1816–1885) was the son of Charles Wright, owner of land adjacent to Webster's farm.

TO EDWARD CURTIS

Washington Wednesday 2 o'clock.
[November 1, 1843]

Dear Sir

I had a very pleasant journey, yesterday from Phila[delphia]. Mrs W. was quite agreeable, & I behaved as well as I knew how.

The business upon which I came is further postponed.[1] I set out, "back again," tomorrow morning. Shall be in N.Y. as I expect, to dine any where, on friday; & shall take the Boat Sat P.M. Yrs, a thousand years, D. W.

ALS. NN.
1. Webster had probably gone to Washington to confer with President Tyler on charges made against Nathaniel F. Williams, for whom Webster had secured the post of customs collector at Baltimore. See John Tyler to DW, [c. November 1, 1843], and DW to Williams, November 10, [1843], below.

FROM JOHN TYLER

[c. November 1, 1843]

My Dr Sir;

Mr. [Nathaniel F.] Williams ought to know that the representations of his enemies have no effect upon me. I regard him as a friend—but the time has come for open and decided action. I am sure he will not falter.[1]
Yrs. Truly   J Tyler

ALS. MHi.
1. On December 16, President Tyler nominated William H. Marriott to succeed Nathaniel F. Williams.

TO NATHANIEL F. WILLIAMS

Nov. 10. [1843]

Dear Sir,

I imagine you are safe. I did all I could for you, & the time is now so

short to the meeting of Congress, I do not believe you will be disturbed.
Yrs truly   Danl Webster

ALS. NhD.

TO EDWARD CURTIS

Lowell, Nov. 17. 1843
friday

Dear Sir

A rumour is rife, that the Annexation of Texas will be recommended,
in the Message.[1] Pray is this true? I wish to know, before hand, as such
a thing would make a great move, hereabouts.

—Pray answer this, if you can, on Saturday, so that I can get your letter in Boston, on Sunday morning.[2]

Andover is dull & documentary;[3] but there is some matter in it, & I
shall endeavor to bring it up, putting most of the quotations into an Appendix. Yrs   D Webster

ALS. NN.

1. In his message to Congress in
December, Tyler pledged his administration to the protection of Texas,
but he and his advisers in the cabinet
were already moving toward annexation. Richardson, *Messages and*

Papers of the Presidents, 4: 260–262.
2. Curtis's response has not been
found.
3. Webster was alluding to his Andover speech of November 9 (*W & S*,
3: 159–185).

TO JOSHUA BATES

Boston Nov. 30. 1843

Private

My Dear Sir

I use one of the earliest hours of a "Thanksgiving" morning, to write
you—to keep myself in remembrance, & to offer the regards & good
wishes of Mrs W. & myself to You & Mrs Bates. We hope your household
is all well, including the *three* generations, which, we presume, still in-
habit it. Mrs W. & myself have had our residence on the Sea Shore, thro
the Summer, or since I left Washington; altho' various occasions have
occurred, calling me to different parts of the Country. We have added a
room or two, to our cold old House at Marshfield, & there we expect to
make our home in times to come, leaving it for a few months in the winter. We stay, now at the Tremont House, & go South in a week or ten
days. No news has yet reached us from Fletcher Webster, who sailed on
the 8th of August for China, via Bombay.[1] Mrs Appleton & family are
living near us, & all well.

We are looking [for] a recommendation of the acquisition of Texas, in his [Tyler's] Message to Congress, next week. If such a thing should happen, a good deal of excitement will be the consequence, perhaps, but no importance ought to be attached to it, as a matter that is likely to affect the stability, or character of the Govt. All the free States will be against annexation, probably without much difference of opinion; & I doubt whether some of the Southern States be not quite cold, on the subject. An immediate & general remonstrance agt. the measure, may be looked for, thro. all this quarter.

There is no kind of doubt, that the President will be able to communicate to Congress a very favorable state of things, respecting our public finances. The receipts at the Treasury have been larger than any body expected. U.S. Stocks, I should suppose, would rise still higher, when the President & Mr Spencer shall have made their showing. As to State Stocks, they ought to rise. I believe, thro. most of the delinquent States, a better feeling begins to exist. The People find themselves getting into better circumstances. They have a new consciousness of ability. No movement has yet been made, however, in the general Govt., & indeed want of *effort*, to bring the public mind right, is the great want in the case. Too many of our leading politicians, on all sides, seem afraid to touch the subject.

I am a bad correspondent, but hope you will not measure your favors, by my merits. It always gives me sincere pleasure to hear from you. I sometimes *dream* of seeing London again, & when this happens you & yours make always part of the vision. I am, Dear Sir, with mo. true regard, Yours   Danl Webster

ALS. NhD.
1. Fletcher was secretary of the Cushing mission to China.

TO EDWARD EVERETT

Boston Nov. 30. '43

Private

My Dear Mr Everett,

We have felt deep & sincere sympathy in the affliction of your family, by the death of your Daughter.[1] The premature blasting of such hopes, causes one of the greatest struggles between affection, & resignation. For my own part, I can speak not without experience, tho' my loss was of the yet only opening bud. Mrs W. intended to write Mrs Everett, by this conveyance, but she is only recovering from a sharp attack of influenza, or *gripe*, as they call it here, which came suddenly upon her, four days ago. She desires the most affectionate remembrance to Mrs Everett, & the other members of your family. We have had our home at Marshfield, since I left the Department. The change is something, but not altogether disagreeable. Farming & shooting have their interests, as well as Diplomacy, & concerns of State. We go to Washington next month, as I have business at the Court.[2] But I always thought ex-Congressmen, ex Secretarys, &c. doleful images, about the Capitol. I keep myself to my work, & limit my stay to the necessity of the case.

We anticipate a recommendation from the President, in his forthcoming message, of the acquisition of Texas. Such was his purpose a week ago. Yesterday, it was rumored here, that he began to doubt; if I hear any thing by tomorrow mornings mail, respecting the matter, I will write you another line.

If such a recommendation be made, & a disposition appear to act upon it, it will create a stir. The measure will be met, in its earliest proposition, by a general remonstrance throughout the North. Presidential candidates will all be put upon their interrogatories, & incidents of interest will not be unlikely to occur. If no excitement from this source, should spring up, the competi[ti]on, I presume, next Nov. will be between Mr Clay & Mr Van Buren. I dare hardly say what I think wd. be the probable result of such a contest. Our Whig politics are sadly mismanaged, all over the Country, & most especially in this State. Young men take the lead, ardent, sanguine, & who seem to think nothing is to be done but to utter warm words of rally to friends, & of unmeasured depreciation of adversaries. A general election has come to be, on all sides, quite too much a matter of mass meetings, of commemorations & celebrations, of banners & trophies. A spirit for such things ran high in 1840, & there seems now quite an attempt to revive it. The Whig cause cannot be maintained, any long time, in Massachusetts, without new counsels. The Liberty party is constantly encreasing, as you will have seen; & to meet this growing danger, nothing is resorted to but a louder cry for the Whigs to "come out!"—but the Whigs go over. We want a paper, prudent, energetic, conciliatory. Such we have not. We need counsels, mild, but comprehensive, & long-sighted; <but> such we have not. Three of our seats in Congress are still vacant, & nobody knows when they will be filled. The Whigs are a minority in the State; yet as they have majorities, in Boston, Lowell, & other large towns, where many Representatives are chosen, *without loss by factions*, they have carried the House, & will doubtless elect a Whig Senate, & a Whig Govr. So far, so good. But this is a frail basis, to rest party hopes upon, for time to come.

It gives me so much pleasure to hear from you, that I hope I may see your hand-writing, even if it [be] but a line by every Boston Steamer. Since June, inclusive, I have made three speeches; vz. Bunker-Hill, Rochester, Andover.[3] These will assume pamphlet form, in a week or two—& I will send you copies. And here, I believe, will be pretty much an end to my practice of making public addresses.

Believe me, Dear Sir, with truly affectionate regard to Your family, Your constant friend,   Danl Webster

ALS. MHi.
1. Everett's daughter, Anne Gorham, had died on October 21.
2. *Vidal* v. *Girard's Executors*, 2
Howard 127 (1844); *Minor* v. *Tillot-
son*, 2 Howard 392 (1844).

3. Webster made his Bunker Hill
speech on June 17 (*W & S*, 1: 259–
283); his Rochester speech on September 20 and 21 (*W & S*, 13: 172–
195); and his speech at Andover, on
November 9 (*W & S*, 3: 159–185).

TO HIRAM KETCHUM

Boston Decr. 2. '43

My Dear Sir;

The articles are both good, but the second, of surpassing excellence.[1] It is strong, close, & to the point. As far as possible, friends will see these articles copied.

Levi C. Turner,[2] signer of the letter which I enclose with this,[3] is a N. Yorker;—seven years ago was a lawyer, in Otsego Co., quite respectable, & thought quite rich. He fell thro, in Illinois & Ohio land speculations, & brought me into some degree of embarrassment with him. For the last two years he has been in Cleveland, in practice, & I believe is going ahead. He is of good manners, & correct behavior, is yet young, & not without ability. I have never corresponded with him on political subjects; but shall answer this letter, in a general way, & think of referring him to you, as a friend on whom he may call, when in N. York, or to whom he might write. I have no doubt he could get any thing republished, in the <Cleveland> Papers, that he might be requested to do.

I have no wish to disturb the present state of things, so far as I am concerned. It does not appear to me there is any move for me to make. The ensuing contest is likely to be entirely between Mr. Clay & Mr Van Buren; & I do not think that my name would materially strengthen the Ticket, bearing the former name. All know the V. Presidency is nothing. The first name is every thing; & I really do not believe that a Ticket, made up of H. C. & D. W. would carry the popular vote of Mass:

My feeling, on the whole, leans much toward an abstinent policy, for the present.

The Printer has my Andover Speech, in Pamphlet form, under hand. It will soon be out. I like the idea of laying your two nos before the members of Congress. I shall ask the Printer to send copies of the Andover Speech to the Washington Booksellers.

You make excellent use of the Resolutions of 1833. I did not think they were so much to the point.

I expect the President will come out strong for Annexation. If he should, the proposition will be met, in this quarter at least, by warm & immediate remonstrances.

Your advice to follow my profession "zealously," is good. I am not without such employment, already, & stick to it, as other young men, who wish to rise, are accustomed to do.

My wife has been sick, of influenza, (so have I) but is fast recovering, & seems pretty well. Yours truly   D Webster

ALS. NhD.
1. Not found.
2. Turner (c. 1805–1867), born in Cooperstown, New York, had served as land agent in the old Northwest for eastern speculators (including DW) in the late 1830s. A lawyer by profession, he also wrote for a Cleveland, Ohio, newspaper in the early 1840s and served as editor and proprietor of the *Cincinnati Gazette* in the 1850s, while he simultaneously wrote editorials for the *New York Tribune*. At the time of his death he was judge-advocate of the army, stationed in Washington.
3. Letter not found.

TO EDWARD CURTIS

Boston Decr. 13. 1843

Dear Sir

I hardly know when I shall reach N.Y. For the last month, or six weeks, I have been busy in my office, & with professional matters. With these, I am now pretty much thro. here, till March. Some preparation is however necessary, in regard to my own affairs, & it would facilitate my movements, hugely, if Mr <Prentiss could cash the other note $10000[?]. If you think that>   [1] would come here. If there is any chance, pray send for him, & give him a talk. He ought to pay the fee *now*, but if I could be authorized to draw on any good name in N.Y. for 4 m[onth]s, it wd. answer the purpose. I have done well, in my line, since May 8th. as I shall show you, when I get along. If I could dispose of the [house] & furniture at Washington,[2] I should get along, without rubbing hard on the rocks. Mrs. Webster will go to N.Y. friday, or saturday, *Edwardo comitante*. I shall follow next week, as soon as I can get away. I should be sorry to miss the 21st. & 22nd. but fear I may. It is *cold*, today. Yrs
D. Webster

ALS. NN.
1. Whether Webster meant Prentiss or someone else has not been determined; at any rate, Webster struck Prentiss and left a blank. Prentiss has not been identified.
2. In 1844, Webster leased his Washington house to Richard Pakenham for three years at $1200 annually. For the lease of February 28, 1844, see mDW 39912.

FROM CHARLES ALLEN

Worcester. Decr. 19th. 1843.

Dear Sir,

I send the letter on the annexation of Texas.[1] Many names of importance have been added, since my last[2] enclosing a copy. You have probably seen, by the papers that resolutions in favor of annexation have been introduced in the Legislatures of South Carolina & Georgia. The papers also publish an interesting article from the Houston Telegraph, giving the sentiments of the Government & people of Texas on the subject.

Since I saw you I have called to mind the tenor of your letter in answer to the New-Hampshire gentlemen.[3] I like it much, & your declaration of the character of the Statesman who should be called to the high office of Prest. of the U.S. The friends of Mr. Clay may not discern all the features of their favorite. But I think they will be obliged to confess that the picture has great merit even where the resemblance fails.

Wishing you a pleasant winter at the South, & success in all your efforts for your own or others good, I remain, very truly, your's,

Charles Allen.

ALS. NhHi.
1. Not found.

2. Not found.
3. Not found.

Calendar, 1840–1843

Items in italics are included in this volume. The diplomatic correspondence from the records of the Department of State has not been calendared here. These materials are discussed in *Diplomatic Papers*, 1.

1840

Jan 1   From Henry Wheaton. ALS. NhD. mDW 16221. Describes his efforts to promote trade with the German states.

Jan 1   Deed transferring certain Marshfield property to Samuel London Frothingham in trust for BUS in New York. DS. MH. mDW 39835–328.

Jan 1   Petition of citizens of Boston for drawbacks on coal consumed by steam packets. DS. DNA, RG 46. mDW 48139.

Jan 3   To Caroline Le Roy Webster. ALS. NhHi. mDW 16225. Discusses his arrival in Boston.

Jan 4   Check for $14.75 to Mr. Mason. DS. NN. mDW 39835–330.

Jan 6   To William Thomas Carroll. AL (signature removed). DNA, RG 267. mDWs. Discusses two Supreme Court cases in which he is involved: *Lessee of Pollard's Heirs* v. *Kibbe* (14 Peters 353, 1840); and *Peters* v. *Warren Insurance Co.* (14 Peters 99, 1840).

[Jan 6?]   To Caroline Le Roy Webster. ALS. NhHi. mDW 16231. Asks why she has not written.

Jan 7   To [?] Farley. ALS. Elliott J. Goldman, Philadelphia, Pa. mDW 16233. Presumes that Treasury notes may be used in payment of any debt to the United States.

Jan 8   From John G. Gamble. ALS. DLC. mDW 16234. Conveys information relative to Florida banks and securities.

[Jan 11?]   To Caroline Le Roy Webster. ALS. NhD. mDW 16227. Reports briefly on his social activity and Massachusetts political developments.

Jan 12–13   To Caroline Le Roy Webster. ALS. NhHi. mDW 16236. Suggests that she accompany him to Washington.

Jan 13   To John Plummer Healy. ALS. MHi. mDW 16239. Demands immediate payment of retainer owed by Samuel Adams.

Jan 14   Promissory note for $200 to the Hancock Bank. DS. NhD. mDW 39835–331.

Jan 17   Receipt for $1.40 for recording and transferring a deed. DS. MWalB. mDW 39835–332.

Jan 19   From Stephen White. ALS. NhHi. mDW 16241. Complains of ill health; discusses his entangled business affairs.

Jan 20   From Charles King. Printed. *Niles' National Register*, 57 (Feb 1, 1840): 359. Encloses DW's notes for his Feb 25, 1833, speech opposing the compromise bill and asks if he would write them out for publication. (See DW to Hiram Ketchum, Jan 20, 1838, *Correspondence*, 4:263–264.)

Jan 20   To Charles King. Printed. *Niles' National Register*, 57 (Feb 1, 1840): 359. Returns notes to King, permitting publication only if without alteration as "notes for a speech."

Jan 20   From Nathaniel Ray Thomas. ALS. NhHi. mDW 16245. Van Tyne, pp. 623–624. Expresses dismay that DW has decided not to send him back to Peru.

Jan 20   From Daniel Fletcher Webster. ALS. NhHi. mDW 16249. Comments on farm work and other activities in Peru.

Jan 22   From Theodore Frelinghuysen. ALS. DLC. mDW 16252. Asks him to address the literary societies of the University of the City of New York.

Jan 22   *From Robert Wickliffe, Jr.*   3

Jan. 23   To Edward Curtis. ALS. NhD. mDW 16259. Blames the weather and Herman Le Roy's ill health for his delay in reaching Washington.

Jan 25   *From William Henry Harrison.*   4

Jan 25   *From Herman Le Roy, Jr.*   6

Jan 26   To Caroline Le Roy Webster. ALS. NhHi. mDW 16267. Reports his arrival in Washington; describes their living quarters.

Jan 26   From Stephen White. ALS copy. NhHi. mDW 16271. *PC,* 2: 72–73. Discusses his health, business affairs, and the state of the nation.

Jan 27   *To [George Wallace Jones].*   7

Jan 27   From Julia Webster Appleton. ALS. NhHi. mDW 16281. Discusses plans for acquiring and furnishing a house on Lincoln Street in Boston.

Jan 27   Motion by DW to amend the steamboat laws. AD. DNA, RG 46. mDW 47956.

Jan 29   To Nicholas Biddle. ALS. DLC. mDW 16284. Expresses hope that Thomas Dunlap will consider a business matter raised in a letter from Richard Mentor Johnson.

Jan 30   From James Watson Webb. ALS. DLC. mDW 16293. Describes the *Courier and New York Enquirer's* financial situation; asks for help in securing appointment as postmaster in New York City should Harrison be elected.

Jan 30   Memorial of the heirs of Thomas Delano for an award for the capture of a vessel by the French prior to 1800. DS. DNA, RG 46. mDW 50727.

Jan 31   To [John Plummer Healy]. ALS. MHi. mDW 12686. Discusses Samuel Adams's retainer fee, congressional matters, Whig presidential prospects.

Jan 31   *From Harmar Denny.*   8

[Jan ?]   To Epes Sargent. ALS. MB. mDW 16296. Asks if Sargent might give his "piece" on the "27th" when the Webster family might be present.

Feb 1   *To James Watson Webb.*   9

Feb 2   To Harriette Story White Paige. ALS. Mrs. Irvin McD. Garfield, Southboro, Mass. mDWs. *PC,* 2: 73–74. Reports on correspondence with Stephen White and trip to Washington.

Feb 5   From Stephen White (enclosure: Stephen White to *Courier and New York Enquirer,* c. Feb 5). ALS. NhHi. mDW 16300. Discusses the destruction by fire of the steamship *Lexington* and suggests corrective legislation.

Feb 6   From Julia Webster Appleton. ALS. NhHi. mDW 16309. Discusses the furnishing of her new house and Boston social life.

Feb 7   To Daniel Fletcher Webster.   9

Feb 8   To [John Plummer Healy]. ALS. MHi. mDW 16316. Discusses
Massachusetts's "immoral" 15 gallon law and Whig prospects.

Feb 9   To Nicholas Biddle.   10

Feb 9   To Caroline Le Roy Webster.   11

Feb 10   To Samuel Rogers. Copy (incomplete). NhHi. mDW 16326.
PC, 2: 74–75. Recalls their brief acquaintance in England and reports on his return voyage; mentions currency situation.

Feb 11   From Edward Everett. ALS. MHi. mDW 16330. Discusses Marcus Morton's administration; declares that he will not accept another gubernatorial nomination.

Feb 11   From John Plummer Healy. ALS. MHi. mDW 16334. Discusses
various business matters; reports that the Massachusetts Van
Buren press has accused DW of unfriendly references to Harrison in 1835.

Feb 11   Receipt for taxes on Londonderry property. DS. NhD. mDW
39835–333.

Feb 12   To J. C. Stickney. ALS. NhD. mDW 16338. Discusses the conspiracy law as it relates to unjust attacks on the property and credit
of a person.

Feb 12   To Caroline Le Roy Webster.   12

Feb 12   Three memorials from citizens of Philadelphia, for an increase
of the duty on silks. DS. DNA, RG 46. mDW 47982.

Feb 13   From Daniel Fletcher Webster. ALS. NhHi. mDW 16343. Discusses the management of DW's property in Illinois and Wisconsin,
the depressed economic conditions around Peru, and the family.

Feb 15   To [John Plummer Healy]. ALS. MHi. mDW 16349. Discusses
his finances, Samuel Adams's fees, and "locofoco" sentiment in the
Senate.

Feb 16   To [Edward Everett]. ALS. MHi. mDW 16352. PC, 2: 75–76.
Comments on radicalism of Marcus Morton and certain United
States senators; discusses gubernatorial contest in Massachusetts
and Whig presidential prospects.

Feb 17   To Edward Curtis.   14

Feb 17   To James Duane Doty. ALS. WHi. mDW 16359. Introduces
Nathaniel Ray Thomas, DW's western agent.

Feb 17   To James Whitcomb. ALS. DNA, RG 49. mDW 57081. Introduces Ray Thomas.

Feb 17   From Zadoc Humphrey. ALS. DLC. mDW 16362. Criticizes
the gag rule and asks DW to present antislavery petitions to the
Senate.

Feb 18   From Daniel Fletcher Webster. ALS. NhHi. mDW 16368. Plans
to campaign for Harrison in northern Illinois; anticipates drawing
on DW for taxes due on Wisconsin property.

Feb 19   From Erastus Root. ALS. DLC. mDW 16372. Regrets that he
is unable to send DW the complete text of his recent speech on the
subtreasury.

Feb 20   To John Pendleton Kennedy (from DW et al.). Printed. Henry T.

Tuckerman, *The Life of John Pendleton Kennedy* (New York, 1871), p. 180. Invite him to a social gathering in Washington.

Feb 20   To James Jay Mapes. Printed. *American Repertory*, 1 (April 1840): 175–176. Van Tyne, pp. 698–699. Congratulates Mapes on the inaugural issue of the *American Repertory* and sends article on "Oram's Compressed Fuel" (*American Repertory*, 1 [April 1840]: 176–177), for publication.

Feb 20   To [Stephen White]. ALS. DLC. mDW 16374. Declines invitation to tour the Great Lakes with White; mentions the desperation of Democrats in Congress.

Feb 20   From Theodore Frelinghuysen. ALS. DLC. mDW 16377. Requests reply to the invitation to address the literary societies of the University of the City of New York.

Feb 22   To John Andrews. ALS. NhHi. mDW 16380. Plans to confer with Thomas Dunlap in Philadelphia as soon as the court adjourns.

Feb 22   To James Whitcomb (by Nathaniel Ray Thomas for DW). ALS by Thomas. DNA, RG 49. mDW 57083. Acknowledges receipt of patents to land in Mineral Point.

[*Feb* 22?]   *To John F. A. Sanford.*   15

[*Feb* 22?]   *To John F. A. Sanford.*   15

Feb 24   To Caroline Le Roy Webster. ALS. NhHi. mDW 16381. Inquires why she has not yet come to Washington.

Feb 24   Petition of citizens of New York for the passage of a general bankrupt law. DS. DNA, RG 46. mDW 47995.

Feb 28   To [John Plummer Healy]. ALS. MHi. mDW 16384. Sends a "draft accepted" and mentions his bankruptcy proposal.

Feb 28   To Daniel Fletcher Webster. ALS. NhHi. mDW 39166. Van Tyne, p. 687. Declares he will not sacrifice his Illinois farms.

Feb 28   From T. J. James. ALS. NhHi. mDW 16385. Proposes changes in DW's bankrupt law.

Feb 28   Petitions against slavery and for the abolition of the slave trade in the District of Columbia or Territory of Florida, from North Yarmouth, Me. (mDW 48078, 48080, 48082); Lockport, N.Y. (mDW 48084); Cincinnati (mDW 48060, 48068), Hamilton County (mDW 48064), Muskingum County (mDW 48070, 48072, 48076, 48088), Trumbull County (mDW 48057, 48074), Ohio; and Philadelphia, Pa. (mDW 48090). ADS. DNA, RG 46.

Feb 28   Petitions of citizens of Cincinnati, Ohio, against the imprisonment in the District of Columbia of blacks claiming to be free. ADS. DNA, RG 46. mDW 48066.

Feb 28   Petition of umbrella makers of Boston, Mass., for a duty on imported silk umbrellas and parasols. DS. DNA, RG 46. mDW 47988.

Feb 28   Petition of Henry Wilson for a pension. DS. DNA, RG 46. mDW 48024.

Feb 28   Memorial from citizens of Philadelphia County, Pennsylvania, for the restoration of a protective tariff. DS. DNA, RG 46. mDW 48016.

Feb 28   Memorial of citizens against the employment of bloodhounds against the hostile Indians in Florida. DS. DNA, RG 46. mDW 48137.

Feb 28   Petition of citizens of Gustavus, Trumbull County, Ohio, against

the admission of any new slave state. ADS. DNA, RG 46. mDW
48062.

Feb 28   Petition of a number of citizens of Athol, Mass., for the establishment of a Congress of Nations to adjust international problems.
DS. DNA, RG 46. mDW 47993.

Feb 29   To Thomas Wren Ward. Copy. CaOOA. mDW 16388. Encloses
note (not found) relative to the titles to land mortgaged to Joshua
Bates.

Feb 29   From Samuel Appleton Appleton.   15

Feb   Petition of citizens of Michigan for an amendment to the act granting preemption rights to settlers on the public lands. DS. DNA, RG
46. mDW 48034.

[Feb ?]   To Caroline Le Roy Webster. ALS. NhHi. mDW 16393. Responds to her proposed departure for Washington; comments on
and urges her to write friends.

Feb [?]   From Erskine Hazard. ALS. DLC. mDW 16397. Offers suggestions on currency reform.

March 1   From John Thurman. ALS. NhHi. mDW 16401. Makes suggestions regarding the proposed bankrupt law.

March 2   From James Barton Longacre. ALS. NhHi. mDW 16403. Van
Tyne, pp. 148–149. Invites DW to subscribe to an engraving of Gov.
[Robert Y.] Hayne.

March 2   Memorial of citizens of New York for the passage of a general
bankrupt law. DS. DNA, RG 46. mDW 48001.

March 3   From Theodore Frelinghuysen. ALS. NhD. mDW 16405. Regrets that DW is unable to speak before the literary societies.

March 4   To Sarah Goodridge. ALS. MHi. mDW 16408. Refers her to
John Plummer Healy for legal counsel in a matter concerning her
brother.

March 4   To Caroline Le Roy Webster.   17

March 4   From Daniel Fletcher Webster. ALS. NhHi. mDW 16412.
States that he has been obliged to draw on DW for $100.

March 5   To Charles Henry Thomas.   17

March 5   To Daniel Fletcher Webster. ALS. NhHi. mDW 16419. PC, 2:
76–77. Congratulates DFW on the birth of a son; reports on Ray
Thomas's illness.

March 5   From Daniel Fletcher Webster. ALS. NhHi. mDW 16423. Asks
DW if he plans to sell his Illinois farms; discusses the possibility
of settling in New York.

March 6   To James Barton Longacre. ALS. NhHi. mDW 16427. Van
Tyne, p. 149. Eulogizes Robert Y. Hayne and asks for a copy of the
engraving.

March 6   To Charles Henry Thomas. ALS. MHi. mDW 16428. Discusses
Ray Thomas's illness.

March 7   To Caroline Le Roy Webster.   19
March 7   From Charles Augustus Davis.   19
March 7   From Henry H. Elliott.   20

[March 8]   To Caroline Le Roy Webster. ALS. NhHi. mDW 16441. Asks
again when or if she plans to come to Washington.

March 9   To Samuel Frothingham. ALS. MHi. mDW 16443. Promises
to try to have $2,500 for him within "20 days."

March 9   To Caroline Le Roy Webster. ALS. NhHi. mDW 16444. Van
Tyne, pp. 624–625. Reports the illnesses of various acquaintances.

March 10   To Charles Henry Thomas. Printed. Curtis, 2: 34. Reports
improvements in Ray Thomas's health.

March 10   From Julia Webster Appleton (with postscript by Samuel
Appleton Appleton). ALS. NhHi. mDW 16448. Comments on home
and family matters and Everett's pending departure abroad.

March 10   From Henry Alexander Scammell Dearborn. ALS. NhHi.
mDW 16452. Discusses government support of industry and Whig
prospects.

March 11   To Charles Henry Thomas. ALS. NhD. mDW 16460. Curtis,
2: 34. Reports Ray Thomas's condition has worsened and urges him
to come to Washington.

[March 11]   To Caroline Le Roy Webster. ALS. NhHi. mDW 16464. Van
Tyne, p. 625. Reports on Ray Thomas's health.

March 11   From Jacob Burnet. ALS. DLC. mDW 16467. Asks DW to
respond to Harrison's appeal for financial assistance.

March 11   From Edward Everett. ALS. MHi. mDW 16469. Commends
DW's tariff speech; reports that he has declined the gubernatorial
nomination and outlines his European itinerary.

March 12   To John Plummer Healy. ALS. MHi. mDW 16473. Mentions
Ray Thomas's illness and a bill which needs paying in Hingham.

[March 12]   To Charles Henry Thomas. ALS. NhD. mDW 16475. Curtis,
2: 34–35. Reports an improvement in Ray Thomas's health.

March 12   To Charles Henry Thomas. ALS. NhD. mDW 16479. Curtis,
2: 35–36. Reports on Ray Thomas's condition.

March 12   To Caroline Le Roy Webster. ALS. NhHi. mDW 16482. Reports on Ray Thomas's condition; complains at not hearing from
her.

[March 12]   To Caroline Le Roy Webster. ALS. NhHi. mDW 16484. Van
Tyne, p. 625. Responds to her letter—not objecting to her decision
to remain in New York but complaining that she had not informed
him earlier.

March 13   To [Mrs. Charles Henry Thomas]. ALS. NhD. mDW 16487.
Curtis, 2: 36–37. Reports that Ray Thomas is worse.

[March 13]   To Caroline Le Roy Webster. ALS. NhHi. mDW 16491. Van
Tyne, p. 626. Reports on Ray Thomas's condition and also on illness in the Lawrence family.

March 13   From Levi C. Turner. ALS. DLC. mDW 16493. Discusses his
financial difficulties—debts and law suits—part of which grew out
of his dealings with Webster.

March 14   To John Plummer Healy. ALS. MHi. mDW 16497. Arranges
for Caleb Rider to draw on him.

March 14   To Mrs. Charles Henry Thomas. ALS. NhD. mDW 16499.
Curtis, 2: 37. Reports improvements in Ray Thomas's condition.

March 14   To [Robert Charles Winthrop].   21

[March 14]   To Caroline Le Roy Webster. ALS. NhHi. mDW 16501. Van
Tyne, pp. 626–627. Reports on Ray Thomas's health.

March 15   From James Jay Mapes. ALS. NhHi. mDW 16503. Thanks
DW for article forwarded to the *Repertory* and expresses hope that
DW may himself contribute from time to time.

March 16 To [Mrs. Charles Henry Thomas]. ALS. NhD. mDW 16505.
Curtis, 2: 37–38. Reports on Ray Thomas's condition.

[March 16] To [Mrs. Charles Henry Thomas]. ALS. NhD. mDW 16509.
Curtis, 2: 37. Reports that Ray Thomas's condition has worsened.

[March 16] To [Mrs. Charles Henry Thomas]. ALS. NhD. mDW 16513.
Curtis, 2: 38. Fears Ray Thomas will not live until morning.

March 16 To Caroline Le Roy Webster. ALS. NhHi. mDW 16507. Reports on Ray Thomas's health; asks again what her plans are.

[March 16] To Caroline Le Roy Webster. ALS. NhHi. mDW 16511.
Reports Ray Thomas is critically ill.

[March 16] To [Caroline Le Roy Webster?]. ALS. NhHi. mDW 16514.
Says Ray Thomas now has convulsions.

March 16 From [Henry Russell Cleveland]. Printed. *Letter to The Honorable Daniel Webster on the causes of the destruction of the steamer Lexington* . . . by A Traveller (Boston, 1840). Comments on the destruction of the steamship *Lexington* and calls for measures to protect travelers.

March 16 From Daniel Fletcher Webster. ALS. NhHi. mDW 16515.
Van Tyne, p. 221. Discusses the rumor that certain friends and family members have failed; comments on Whig prospects.

March 17 To [Mrs. Charles Henry Thomas]. ALS. NhD. mDW 16518.
Curtis, 2: 38. Describes Ray Thomas's condition as desperate.

March [17] To [Mrs. Charles Henry Thomas]. ALS. NhD. mDW 16520.
Curtis, 2: 38–39. Reports that Ray Thomas is receiving constant attention.

[March 17] To Caroline Le Roy Webster. ALS. NhHi. mDW 16523. Van Tyne, p. 627. Reports on Ray Thomas's condition and his own health.

March 18 To [Edward Everett]. ALS. MHi. mDW 16526. *PC*, 2: 77–78.
Offers to assist Everett while Everett is in Europe; comments on Everett's letter to the Whig committee in Massachusetts.

March 18 To Mrs. Charles Henry Thomas. Printed. Curtis, 2: 39. Reports the death of Ray Thomas.

March 18 From John Plummer Healy. ALS. MHi. mDW 16528. Discusses Caleb Rider's French claims account.

March 19 To John Plummer Healy. ALS. MHi. mDW 16531. Gives instructions for paying discount on his note held by Franklin Haven; mentions Ray Thomas's death.

March 19 To Mrs. Charles Henry Thomas. Printed. Curtis, 2: 39–40. Expresses anxiety at not having seen her husband and discusses plans for returning Ray Thomas's remains to Duxbury.

March 19 To Caroline Le Roy Webster. ALS. NhHi. mDW 16532. *PC*, 2: 78–79. Comments on Ray Thomas's death.

March 19 Deed transferring property in Duxbury from Charles Henry Thomas to DW. Copy. Deed Book 210: 120–121. Register of Deeds, Plymouth County, Massachusetts. mDWs.

March 20 To Caroline Le Roy Webster. ALS. NhHi. mDW 16536. Expresses dismay at not having heard from the Thomases at Marshfield; wants to see the bankrupt bill brought forward before he leaves for New York.

March 20 Motion by DW calling on the Treasury Department for in-

formation on the use of Treasury notes. AN. DNA, RG 46. mDW
47967.

March 20   Petition of citizens of Pennsylvania against the admission of
any new slave state into the Union. Printed document, signed.
DNA, RG 46. mDW 48124.

March 20   Petitions of citizens for the abolition of slavery and the slave
trade from Maine (mDW 48120, 48122) and Pennsylvania (mDW
48127). ADS. DNA, RG 46.

March 20   Petition of Rebecca B. Fussell et al. of Pennsylvania for the
repeal of all laws contrary to the Declaration of Independence. DS.
DNA, RG 46. mDW 48149.

March 20   Petition of a number of citizens of Barnstable, Mass., for the
repeal of the naturalization laws. DS. DNA, RG 46. mDW 48142.

March 20   Memorial of Prudence C. Loring, widow of Noadiah Morris,
for a pension. DS. DNA, RG 46. mDW 48030.

March 20   Memorials from citizens of Pennsylvania for the passage of
a bankrupt law. DS. DNA, RG 46. mDW 48004.

March 21   To [George Wallace Jones]. ALS. NhD. mDW 16538. Reports
that because of the recent death of Ray Thomas he will have to make
other plans relative to the ferry account.

[March 22]   *To Caroline Le Roy Webster.*   21

March 22   To Hugh Lawson White. Printed (excerpt). Rosenbach Company, *The History of America in Documents* . . . (3 parts; Philadelphia, 1949–1951), 2: 119–120. Discusses politics and the currency
question.

March 23   From John Evelyn Denison. ALS. DLC. mDW 16543. Curtis,
2: 43–45. States that he will send a design for water meadows;
reminisces about DW's visit and comments on political developments in Great Britain.

March 24   To Henry Russell Cleveland. ALS. NN. mDWs. Thanks him
for a pamphlet on steamboat safety and promises to put it in the
hands of the proper committee.

March 24   To Charles Henry Thomas. ALS. John M. Taylor, San Francisco, Calif. mDW 16548. Curtis, 2: 4–41. Offers condolences and
comfort on the death of Ray Thomas.

March 24   To Caroline Le Roy Webster. ALS. NhHi. mDW 16552. Reports the transfer of Ray Thomas's body to Massachusetts; writes
of friends in Washington, mentioning continued presence in town
of P[eter] and Mrs. Parker.

[March 24]   To Nathaniel F. Williams. ALS. NhD. mDW 16555. Asks
him to "accept & return the above," probably a draft.

March 24   To Nathaniel F. Williams.   22

March 24   From Samuel Appleton Appleton. ALS. MHi. mDW 16561.
Reports on the Boston economic scene and Julia's health.

March 24   Petition of citizens of Bradford, Mass., for the establishment
of a Congress of Nations to adjust international difficulties. DS.
DNA, RG 46. mDW 48151.

March 25   To Caroline Le Roy Webster. ALS. NhHi. mDW 16564. Reports on friends and legislative matters in Washington.

March 25   From Julia Webster Appleton. ALS. NhHi. mDW 16567.

Comments on Ray Thomas's death; gossips about Boston weather
and society.

March 26   *To Joshua Bates.*   23

March 27   To Caroline Le Roy Webster. ALS. NhHi. mDW 16575. Reports that Harriet Colby Webster is gravely ill; thinks of taking new
lodgings in Washington.

March 27   From Herman Le Roy. Dictated letter. NhHi. mDW 16578.
Inquires about a title to land in Milwaukee.

March 28   To the Editors of the Harrisburg, Pennsylvania, *Telegraph
and Intelligencer.* Printed. *National Intelligencer,* April 6, 1840.
Denies the charge that he slurred Harrison in 1835.

March 29   *To Samuel Jaudon.*   25

March 29   From Rufus S. Reed et al. LS. DLC. mDW 16584. Invite DW
to Whig celebration.

March 30   From Daniel Fletcher Webster. ALS. NhHi. mDW 16590.
Discusses his court business, attention to DW's western land interests; reports that he has leased Salisbury and moved into town.

[March ?]   *To Caroline Le Roy Webster.*   27

April 1   Deed transferring property in Marshfield from Eleazer Harlow
to DW. Copy. Deed Book 200: 240. Register of Deeds, Plymouth
County, Massachusetts. mDWs.

April 1   Petitions from citizens of Ohio for the abolition of slavery and
the domestic slave trade in the District of Columbia. AD. DNA,
RG 46. mDW 48130, 48134.

April 1   Petition of citizens of Ohio against the annexation of Texas.
AD. DNA, RG 46. mDW 48153.

April 1   Petition of citizens of Ohio against the admission of any new
slave state. AD. DNA, RG 46. mDW 48132.

April 1   Memorial of citizens of Boston for the passage of a bankrupt
law. DS. DNA, RG 46. mDW 48006.

April 1   Bill (S. 294) to establish a uniform system of bankruptcy. AD.
DNA, RG 46. mDW 47920.

April 2   To Mrs. John Agg. ALS. NhD. mDW 16602. Informs her of his
plans to go to New York; expresses concern over Harriet Colby Webster's illness.

April 2   From Daniel Fletcher Webster. ALS. NhHi. mDW 16605. Expresses shock at the death of Ray Thomas.

April 3   From Edward Everett. ALS. MHi. mDW 16607. Agrees to talk
over plans for Edward Webster's future and comments on Massachusetts politics.

April 6   From John Leverett. ALS. NhHi. mDW 16611. Suggests a compromise which would insure passage of the bankrupt bill.

April 8   To [John Pendleton Kennedy]. ALS. MdBP. mDW 16613. Asks
him to write [Edward?] Curtis as agreed.

April 8   *From Daniel Fletcher Webster.*   28

April 9   From Theodore Dwight. ALS. NhD. mDW 16618. Wants a provision in proposed steamboat legislation which would prohibit the
carrying of gunpowder on vessels.

April 10   Certificate of pew ownership, Village Church, Franklin.
Printed DS with MS insertions. MWalB. mDW 16621.

April 12   From Daniel Fletcher Webster. ALS. NhHi. mDW 16623. Advises DW to sell his canal stock.

April 13   To [Edward Curtis]. ALS. CtY. mDW 16627. Says Mrs. Webster will come to Washington and discusses living arrangements.

April 13   From Robert Lee (enclosure: clipping on bankrupt law). ALS. NhHi. mDW 16629. Asks him for a copy of the proposed bankrupt law.

April 16   From Daniel Fletcher Webster. ALS. NhHi. mDW 16633. Van Tyne, p. 600. Explains why he wants to return to the East and asks DW to help him in getting established in New York.

April 17   To [Young Men of Indiana]. AL draft. MHi. mDW 16635. W & S, 16: 325–327. Declines invitation to attend their Whig convention at Tippecanoe Battlefield.

April 17   From Henry Wood. ALS. NhHi. mDW 39835–335. Instructs DW to pay interest on the mortgage of his White Hall farm.

April 20   To Edward Curtis.   29

April 23–24   From Pliny Freeman. ALS. NhHi. mDW 16643. Makes suggestions concerning the proposed bankrupt bill.

April [26]   From Joshua Bates.   30

April 29   To Joel R. Poinsett (enclosures: Samuel C. Thacher to Poinsett, April 21, 1840; P. O. Thacher to Poinsett, April 25, 1840). ALS. DNA, RG 107. mDWs. Submits papers in support of Samuel C. Thacher's application for an Army appointment.

[April 29]   To [Leverett] Saltonstall. ALS. NhD. mDWs. Suggests he write the secretary of war on behalf of Samuel C. Thacher.

April 29   From James Hamilton, Jr.   32

April 30   Petition of citizens of Beaver County, Pennsylvania, for a national bank and a high protective tariff. DS. DNA, RG 46. mDW 48156.

May 1   To Harmanus Bleecker. ALS. DLC. mDW 16656. Introduces a Mr. Sprague of Massachusetts.

May 1   From James Hamilton, Jr. ALS. NhD. mDW 16658. Proposes to meet with Webster and Biddle for consultations in Philadelphia.

May 1   From Joel R. Poinsett. LC. DNA, RG 107. mDWs. States that Samuel C. Thacher will be invited to take the army qualifying examination.

May 2   To James Hamilton, Jr. Copy. Ne. mDWs. Discusses Texas's future and wishes Hamilton success in Europe on behalf of the Republic.

May 6   To Charles James Blomfield, Bishop of London. ALS. CtY. mDW 26913. Introduces the Reverend Mr. Mason of the American Episcopal Church.

May 8   To Samuel Jones Loyd.   33

May 9   From Edward Everett. ALS. MHi. mDW 16668. Outlines his European itinerary and asks for letters to one or two of DW's English acquaintances.

May 10   From Joseph Story. Printed. William W. Story, ed., *Life and Letters of Joseph Story* (2 vols., Boston, 1851), 2: 330–332. Discusses the problem of including corporations, especially those with state charters, under the bankrupt law.

May 10   From Lewis Tappan.   36

[May 10?] To [Peter Harvey]. ALS. NhHi. mDW 16672. Van Tyne, p. 627. Tells him to send the salmon on.

May 11 From Ebenezer Jesup, Jr., et al. LS. NhHi. mDW 16675. Underscore the need for a national bankrupt law.

May 14 Resolution for appointment of a joint committee to investigate the contract for printing the *Documentary History of the Revolution.* AD. DNA, RG 46. mDW 47968.

[May 15] To Edward Everett. ALS. MHi. mDW 16678. Provides a letter of introduction to Lady Ashburton.

May 16 From Daniel Fletcher Webster (enclosure: John A. Walley to DFW, May 6, 1840). ALS. NhHi. mDW 16680. Describes local political activity; discusses the buying and selling of land.

May 19 Message from House of Representatives naming Stephen Banks Leonard to select committee to investigate the contract to publish *Documentary History.* ADS. DNA, RG 46. mDW 48180.

May 21 From Pearson Cogswell. ALS. NhHi. mDW 16686. Commends DW's speech on the bankrupt bill.

May 22 To Samuel Atkinson. ALS. NPV. mDW 16688. Asks that his respects be conveyed to a Mr. Bourne.

May 22 To William Henry Seward. ALS. NRU. mDW 16690. Recommends John Plummer Healy as "Commissioner to take Depositions" in Massachusetts for New York.

May 22 Insurance policy covering furnishings, etc., of DW's Court Street office. Printed DS with MS insertions. MHi. mDW 39835–337.

May 22 Check for $50 to "self." DS. NN. mDW 39835–339.

May 23 To John Taylor. Printed. Van Tyne, p. 669. Asks Taylor to send for a bill and discusses care of farm matters.

May 24 To Edward Everett. ALS. MHi. mDW 16692. *PC*, 2: 81–82. Expresses appreciation that the Everetts will allow Edward Webster to join them in Europe.

May 24 To [Peter Harvey]. ALS. NhHi. mDW 16696. Van Tyne, pp. 221–222. Reports the safe arrival of the salmon.

May 25 To [Edward Everett]. ALS. MHi. mDW 16697. Thinks he sent him Thomas Hart Benton's report.

May 25 To Samuel Rogers. Printed. *PC*, 2: 82. Introduces Edward Everett.

May 25 Check for $78 to Joseph Williams. DS. NN. mDW 39835–340.

May 26 From Daniel Fletcher Webster. ALS. NhHi. mDW 16699. Discusses the hard times and lack of funds to move back East.

May 26 Check for $300 to "myself." DS. NN. mDW 39835–341.

May 27 From Samuel Morrison (enclosed with DW to John Plummer Healy, [June 19, 1840]). ALS. MHi. mDW 16752. Asks for a copy of the Massachusetts state geological survey.

May 28 Check for $100 to "Mrs Page." DS. NN. mDW 39835–342.

May 29 To Jeremiah Mason.   37

May 29 To Robert Charles Winthrop. ALS. MHi. mDW 16709. Asks him to help Rice Garland raise money for the Whig party.

May 29 Check for $15 to "A B." DS. NN. mDW 39835–343.

May 29 Check for $23 to "P. O." DS. NN. mDW 39835–344.

May 30 From Townsend Haines et al. LS. DLC. mDW 16710. Invite DW to a Harrison convention in Chester County, Pennsylvania, on June 9.

May 30   Check for $10 to "self." DS. NN. mDW 39835–345.

May 31   To Daniel Fletcher Webster.   38

[May ?]   To James Duane Doty. ALS. WHi. mDW 16716. Wants to borrow a book of Indian documents.

June 2   To Samuel Frothingham. ALS. MHi. mDW 16718. Discusses his efforts to pay what he owes.

June 2   Check for $10 to [?]. DS. NN. mDW 39835–346.

[June 3]   From Caroline Story White Webster. ALS. NhHi. mDW 16719. Asks DW to forward a letter to her father and reports briefly on family activity.

June 3   Check for $200 to [David A.?] Hall. DS. NN. mDW 39835–347.

June 5   Check for $25 payable to "self." DS. NN. mDW 39835–348.

June 6   To Nathaniel Silsbee. ALS. CSmH. mDW 16721. Sends letter of introduction for [Jared?] Sparks to the Marquis of Normandy.

June 6   To Samuel Lewis Southard. ALS. NjP. mDW 16724. Asks for information on a point of law.

June 6   From Thomas Dunn English. LS. ViU. mDWs. Invites DW to attend a Harrison meeting in Philadelphia on June 15.

June 6   Deed transferring land in Livingston County, Michigan, from DW to Henry Hubbard. Copy. Deed Book 5: 204–206. Register of Deeds, Livingston County, Michigan. mDWs.

June 6   Deed transferring land in Shiawassee County, Michigan, from DW to Henry Hubbard. Copy. Deed Book E: 122–124. Register of Deeds, Shiawassee County, Michigan. mDWs.

June 6   Deed transferring land in Mineral Point, Wisconsin Territory, from DW to Henry Hubbard. Copy. Deed Book A: 500. Register of Deeds, Lafayette County, Wisconsin. mDW 39835–353 and mDWs.

June 8   To [Samuel Frothingham]. ALS. MHi. mDW 16726. Promises to pay $1,000 on mortgage before end of month.

June 8   To John Plummer Healy. ALS. MHi. mDW 16727. Gives itinerary for June and early July; asks Healy to renew the note signed by Rufus Choate.

June 8   To Charles Henry Thomas.   39

June 8   From Lady Caroline Fitzhardinge Maxse. ALS. DLC. mDW 16732. Thanks DW for a letter and speeches; reports on her family.

June 9   Check for $20 to "self." DS. NN. mDW 39835–354.

June 10   Motion by DW for a reduction of postage on letters. AD with printed notice. DNA, RG 46. mDW 47974.

June 10   Memorial of a number of citizens of New York City opposing an amendment to the proposed bankrupt law. DS. DNA, RG 46. mDW 48039.

June 11   To Samuel Coffin. Printed letter. NhHi. mDW 16740. PC, 2: 82–86. Summarizes the failures of the Democratic administration and urges New Hampshire to support Harrison.

June 11   From Richard Mentor Johnson. Copy. NhHi. mDW 16742. PC, 2: 87. Thanks DW for complimentary remarks in his speech on the bankrupt bill.

June 16   To John Forsyth. ALS. DNA, RG 59. mDW 55561. Recommends Gideon Theodore Snow for U.S. consul at Pernambuco.

June 16   From John Leeds Kerr.   40
June 16   From Josiah Quincy. ALS. DLC. mDW 16747. Sends account of
    DW's speech at the Harvard bicentennial for perusal and correction.
June 17   From Josiah Quincy. ALS. DLC. mDW 16748. Asks him to
    make whatever editorial changes may be necessary in the text
    of his speech.
June 18   Four protested promissory notes, $10,000 each, Henry L. Kin-
    ney to DW. DS. DLC. mDW 39835–181.
[June 19] To John Plummer Healy (enclosure: Samuel Morrison to
    DW, May 27, 1840). ALS. MHi. mDW 16750. Asks Healy to send
    a geology book to Morrison.
June 19   To Nathaniel F. Williams. ALS. NhD. mDW 16754. Asks when
    his note is due.
June 20   To C. A. Repplier et al. ALS. ICHi. mDW 16756. Declines invi-
    tation to attend the National Festival at Philadelphia.
June 22   To [?]. ALS. MHingHi. mDWs. Regrets that a prior engage-
    ment at Barre will prevent his meeting with the Whigs of Boston on
    July 4.
June 22   Draft for $50 by DFW, endorsed by DW. DS. NhD. mDW
    39835–355, 358.
June 23   To Samuel Jaudon.   41
June 24   To [Robert Charles Winthrop].   43
June 25   From Thomas Emory. ALS. DLC. mDW 16764. Thanks DW
    for copy of his address to the Agricultural Society of Massachusetts.
June 25   From John Leeds Kerr.   44
June 28   From Charles Pelham Curtis (enclosure: extracts from bank-
    ruptcy cases). ALS. DLC. mDW 16771. Discusses the proposed bank-
    rupt law.
June 29   To James Miller. ALS. NWM. mDW 16775. Introduces Healy.
June 29   To James Miller. AL draft and LS. MHi and NWM. mDW
    16777. W & S, 16: 329. Asks for an honest appraisal of Harrison's
    "military character."
June 29   From James Boyles Murray.   46
June 30   From James Miller. LS. MHi. mDW 16786. W & S, 16: 329n.
    Summarizes his knowledge of Harrison's military action in the Bat-
    tle of Tippecanoe.
June 30   From Daniel Fletcher Webster. ALS. NhHi. mDW 16790. Van
    Tyne, p. 223. Discusses various property matters and plans to travel
    to the East in August.
[June]   To Nathaniel Pitcher Tallmadge. ALS. NhD. mDW 16798. States
    he will present memorial tomorrow.
July 3   Draft on DW by Patriotic Bank—$421.11. DS. NhD. mDW
    39835–356, 40664.
July 6   To John Plummer Healy. AD. MHi. mDW 16800. Sends account
    (for publication) of speech at Barre, Mass.
July 6   From Thomas Griggs et al. Printed LS. DLC. mDW 16814. In-
    vite DW to a Whig festival at Charlestown, Va.
July 6   Authorization to John Plummer Healy to accept draft for
    $421.11 by Patriotic Bank. DS. NhD. mDW 39835–357.
July 9   From J. S. Shriver et al. ALS by Shriver. NhHi. mDW 16815.
    Invite DW to a Whig convention at Wheeling, Va.

[c. July 9] To John Plummer Healy. ANS. NhD. mDW 39835–358.
Authorizes Healy to pay DFW's draft of June 22, which had been
protested.

July 12 To Charles Henry Warren.   47

July 13 From "An Old School Republican." Printed. *National Intelligencer*, July 18, 1840. Recollects George Washington Prescott's
praise of Harrison's conduct at the Battle of Tippecanoe.

July 14 To Nathaniel F. Williams. ALS. NhD. mDW 16820. Asks him
to renew a note.

July 15 To [?]. ALS. VtHi. mDW 16822. Doubts that he will be able to
visit Bennington, Vt., in August.

July 18 Report from the joint committee on the *Documentary History
of the American Revolution*. AD. DNA, RG 46. mDW 48199.

July 20 To Josiah William Ware.   48

July 22 To Nathaniel F. Williams. ALS. NhD. mDW 16829. Encloses a
draft for $1,000.

July 22 From John A. Corneau. ALS. NhHi. mDW 16831. Asks if remarks DW attributed to John Adams in his eulogy on Adams and
Jefferson were literal quotations.

July 23 From Joshua A. Spencer et al. LS. DLC. mDW 16834. Invite
DW to the dedication of a log cabin at Utica, N.Y., Aug 12.

July 25 From John Plummer Healy. ALS. NhExP. mDW 16836. Introduces a Mr. Harmon.

July 29 To [Edward Curtis]. ALS. NN. mDW 25904. Comments on
James Wilson's campaigning in Massachusetts; expresses his desire
to make a short tour in parts of New York with Curtis.

July 29 To [Caleb Cushing]. ALS. DLC. mDW 16838. Accepts dinner
invitation.

July 30 To Samuel Jaudon.   49

July 30 From Nicholas Biddle. ALS draft. DLC. mDW 16842. Asks for
assistance in preparing a public defense of Pennsylvania's financial
policies.

July 30 From James Gore King (enclosed with Henry J. Ruggles to
DW, July 31, 1840). ALS. MWalB. mDW 16849. Offers DW $250
to represent Illinois in *Illinois* v. *Delafield*.

July 31 To [Thomas and Oliver Lowndes] (enclosed with DW to John
Plummer Healy, Jan 12, 1842). Copy. MHi. mDW 16844. Agrees
to be retained in a suit.

July 31 From Henry J. Ruggles (enclosure: James G. King to DW, July
30, 1840). ALS. MWalB. mDW 16846. Summarizes the case of
Illinois v. *Delafield*, pending in U.S. District Court in New York,
and asks him to appear as counsel for Illinois.

July [?] From Joshua Fifield et al. LS. MHi. mDW 16850. Invite DW
to a political rally at Francestown, N.H.

Aug 1 From Edward Everett. ALS. MHi. mDW 16857. LC. MHi. mDW
16854. Reports that Edward will join them in Florence; discusses
European affairs.

[Aug 2?] To John Plummer Healy. ALS. MHi. mDW 16861. Reports his
imminent departure from Washington.

Aug 3 To Nicholas Biddle. ALS. DLC. mDW 38230. Authorizes publication of his enclosed letter on American credit.

Aug 3   To Nicholas Biddle. Copy. DLC. mDW 16863. Philadelphia *Daily
         Chronicle and General Advertiser*, Sept 1, 1840. W & S, 16: 331.
         Comments on Pennsylvania's fiscal policies and American credit.

Aug 3   To J. S. Shriver et al. LS. OClWHi. mDW 16865. Declines invi-
         tation to appear at Whig rally in Wheeling, Sept 3; elaborates
         on the campaign issues.

Aug 3   To Elisha Whittlesey et al.   50

Aug 4   To [Edward Curtis]. ALS. NN. mDW 16871. Discusses plans for
         going to New York.

Aug 4   To Nathaniel F. Williams. ALS. NhD. mDW 16874. Draws on
         him for $1,000.

Aug 4   Promissory note to Isaac P. Davis for $2,000. DS. MHi. mDW
         39835-359.

Aug 6   To Isaac Chapman Bates. ALS. NIC. mDW 38217. Expresses
         willingness to attend the court for the case mentioned by Bates if it
         should sit in the river counties.

Aug 6   To Caleb Cushing. ALS. NN. mDW 16876. Writes regarding the
         date of the Newburyport meeting.

[Aug 6] To John Plummer Healy. ALS. MHi. mDW 16878. Plans to
         leave for New York in a couple of days.

Aug 6   From William Pitt Fessenden.   51

Aug 7   To [Robert Charles Winthrop]. ALS. MHi. mDW 16884. Dis-
         cusses plans for a political meeting.

Aug 7   From Nicholas Biddle. Printed. Philadelphia *Daily Chronicle
         and General Advertiser*, Sept 1, 1840. Discusses Pennsylvania and
         American credit.

Aug 7   From Charles King. ALS. DLC. mDW 16885. Urges DW to at-
         tend the political meeting at Stanhope, N.J., and to deliver a speech.

Aug 8   To William Pitt Fessenden.   52

Aug 8   From Isaac Chapman Bates. ALS. MHi. mDW 16891. Informs
         DW that the court will sit at Northampton and describes the case
         against the cashier of the Amherst Bank, which he hopes DW will
         argue.

Aug 10   To Robert Charles Winthrop.   52

[Aug 11] To Edward Curtis. ALS. NN. mDW 16899. Acknowledges a
         letter.

Aug 13   From Nicholas Biddle. ALS draft. DLC. mDW 16901. Submits
         draft of his public letter on Pennsylvania and American credit.

Aug 15   To Caleb Cushing. ALS. NN. mDW 16903. Agrees on a date for
         the Newburyport political meeting.

Aug 15   To Joseph Sprague. ALS. NhExP. mDWs. Declines invitation
         to address the Whigs of Hingham.

Aug 15   To John Van Cleek. ALS. ICHi. mDW 16905. Declines invita-
         tion to address Whigs of Greene County, N. Y.

Aug 15   To Charles Henry Warren.   54
Aug 25   From William Henry Seward.   55

[Aug]   From Samuel B. Walcott et al. ALS by Walcott, signed also by
         others. NhD. mDW 16912. Invite DW to address a mass meeting in
         central Massachusetts.

Sept 5   From George Edmund Badger. ALS. NjMoHP. mDW 16916.

Invites DW to address the Whig celebration in Raleigh, N.C.,
stressing the importance of including the South in his campaign.

Sept [6]   To Robert Charles Winthrop. ALS. MHi. mDW 16947. Praises
Winthrop's speech; predicts "a great multitude" at the forthcoming
Bunker Hill rally.

Sept 7   From James Wilson.   56

Sept 9   To Daniel Fletcher Webster. ALS. NhHi. mDW 16923. States:
"I shall be up, tomorrow A.M."

Sept 10   "Bunker Hill Declaration" (with marginal inscriptions).
Printed. NhD. mDWs. Campaign pamphlet by DW.

Sept 15   To Isaac Rand Jackson from DFW. ALS. MdHi. mDWs. Acknowledges Jackson's Aug 30 letter to DW; will send him copies of
the Saratoga speech, to appear in pamphlet form together with the
Bunker Hill Declaration.

Sept 15   To Samuel Jaudon.   57

Sept 15   From William Pennington. ALS. DLC. mDW 25949. Reports
that his friends were delighted with their trip to Boston; expresses
admiration for the Bunker Hill Declaration.

Sept 17   From George Y. Sawyer (enclosure: John Stevens et al. to DW,
Sept [?], 1840). ALS. MHi. mDW 16928. Invites DW to a Whig
rally in Francestown, N.H.

Sept 19   To William Albert Bradley. Dictated letter. NHi. mDW 16933.
Discusses his indebtedness to the Patriotic Bank.

Sept 19   Promissory note to Abraham Tuckerman for $600. ADS. MHi.
mDW 39835-361.

Sept 21   To John Plummer Healy. ALS. MHi. mDW 16934. Asks that a
box of pamphlets—"Bunker Hill Declaration" and his Saratoga
speech—be sent him.

Sept 21   From Silas Wood. ALS. NEh. mDW 16936. Introduces Judge
Richard Conklin; praises DW's Saratoga speech and the Bunker Hill
Declaration.

Sept 23   To Abraham T. Rose and Henry H. Huntting. Printed. *Niles'
National Register*, 59 (Oct 3, 1840): 69. Explains that, contrary to
rumor, he has not been invited to address Senator Silas Wright's
meeting in Patchogue but would not decline if asked.

Sept 23   To Abraham T. Rose and Henry H. Huntting. Printed. *Niles'
National Register*, 59 (Oct 3, 1840): 69. Offers Senator Wright "direct discussion of political topics" at Jamaica or wherever Wright
chooses.

Sept 23   From Abraham T. Rose and Henry H. Huntting. Printed. *Niles'
National Register*, 59 (Oct 3, 1840): 69-70. Report Senator
Wright's inability or unwillingness to discuss publicly with DW in
immediate future.

Sept 25   To John Plummer Healy. LS by proxy. MHi. mDW 16938. Forwards invitations to Whig rallies and asks Healy to decline them
all.

Sept 25   To Abraham T. Rose and Henry H. Huntting. Printed. *Niles'
National Register*, 59 (Oct 3, 1840): 70. Analyzes politics behind
the rival meetings in same location on Sept 22 and 23.

Sept 26   To John Doggett, Jr. ALS. OHi. mDW 16940. Agrees to look
over the proof sheets of [Howard?] Stansbury's report.

Sept 28   To Charles William Cutter.   58

Sept 29   To William Henry Seward. LS. NRU. mDW 16942. Reports that
poor health has caused the delay in answering Seward's letter.

[Sept 29]   To Caroline Le Roy Webster. ALS. NhHi. mDW 16945. Van
Tyne, p. 670. Prepares to leave for the South.

Sept [?]   From S. W. Kent et al. LS. MHi. mDW 16948. Invite DW to a
Whig meeting at Francestown, N.H., in October.

Sept [?]   From John Stevens et al. (enclosed with George Y. Sawyer to
DW, Sept 17, 1840). LS. MHi. mDW 16930. Invite him to a public
meeting in Hillsborough County, N.H.

Oct 1   To Caroline Le Roy Webster. ALS. NhHi. mDW 16951. Van
Tyne, p. 223. Reports his arrival in Wilmington and plans to depart
for Baltimore and Washington.

Oct 3   To Edward Curtis. Printed. *PC*, 2: 88–89. Reports on his
campaigning.

Oct 3   To Caroline Le Roy Webster. ALS. NhHi. mDW 16953. Reports
on Washington friends and on response to his proposed visit to
Richmond.

Oct 7   To Mrs. [?] Norton. AL. ViRVal. mDWs. Thanks her for a bouquet
and card.

Oct 10   To Edward Curtis. Printed. *PC*, 2: 89–90. Reports that he is exhausted after three days' speaking in Richmond.

[Oct 12]   To [Edward Curtis?]. ALS. NN. mDW 16956. Plans to head
north from Washington; comments on political prospects.

Oct 12   To [Edward Curtis?]. ALS. NN. mDW 16959. Reports a Whig
victory in Georgia.

Oct 17   To Edward Curtis. ALS. NN. mDW 16960. *PC*, 2: 90. Reports
on his return to Marshfield and plans for campaigning in New
Hampshire.

[Oct 21]   To John Taylor, Jr. ALS. NcD. mDW 38954. States his intention to visit Franklin, N.H.

Oct 21   To Caroline Le Roy Webster. ALS. NhHi. mDW 16962. Reports
addressing a large crowd at Francestown, N.H.

Oct 22   To William Hebard. Facsimile. NhD. mDWs. Declines invitation to address the Whigs of the Vermont legislature.

Oct 22   To Caroline Le Roy Webster. ALS. NhHi. mDW 16965. Reports
on a large Whig meeting in Claremont, N.H.

Oct 23   Agreement with J. W. Clark & Co. re 500 volumes of DW's law
books, used as collateral for a $500 loan. DS. MHi. mDW
39835–364.

Oct 25   From Hugh Swinton Legaré. ALS. MHi. mDW 16967. Congratulates DW on his reception at Richmond; discusses New York
politics.

Oct 26   To John Plummer Healy. LS by proxy. MHi. mDW 16971. Reports being obliged to curtail his speaking engagements because of
a severe cold.

Oct 26   To George Washington Nesmith. LS. NhHi. mDW 16974. Van
Tyne, pp. 224–225. Reports that because of poor health he will be
unable to attend political rally at Salisbury; urges support for
Harrison.

Oct 26   To Caroline Le Roy Webster.   58

Oct 27   To Caroline Le Roy Webster. LS by proxy. NhHi. mDW 16982.
Van Tyne, pp. 671–672. Reports on his illness and affairs in New
Hampshire.

Oct 27   *From John Jordan Crittenden.*   60

Oct 27   Indenture from the sale of property in Wisconsin to Henry Hubbard of Charlestown, N.H. DS. MiD–B. mDW 39835–349.

[Oct 28]   To Caroline Le Roy Webster (with C. B. Haddock to CLW,
[n.d.]). ALS. NhHi. mDW 16990. Van Tyne, pp. 672–673. States
that he is convalescing at Franklin and expects to be back in
Massachusetts in a few days.

Oct 28   Promissory note by DW and John Taylor to Benjamin Shaw for
$100. DS. NhHi. mDW 39835–365.

Oct 29   From Nathaniel Niles. ALS. mDW 16993. Transmits documentary material on the Bank of France and comments in detail on
the French ministerial crisis.

Oct-Nov   From [Samuel Smith Nicholas]. Printed. *Louisville Journal,*
Oct 31–Nov 18, 1840. Addresses DW on the campaign in a seven-
part series entitled "Letters on the Presidency by a Kentucky
Democrat."

Nov 1   To Nathaniel F. Williams. ALS. NhD. mDW 16997. Begs him to
take up an acceptance "at all events."

Nov 1   From Daniel Fletcher Webster. ALS. NhHi. mDW 16999. Details
a trip down the Ohio to St. Louis; saw Harrison in Cincinnati.

Nov 2   To Nathaniel F. Williams. AL (signature removed). NhD. mDW
17001. Awaits reply from Williams; comments on the exhausting
campaign.

Nov 3   To Thomas Ellicott. ALS. NhHi. mDWs. Sends interest due on
a debt and requests that the principal be allowed to stand.

Nov 5   To Edward Curtis. ALS. NN. mDW 17003. States that he will
meet a payment; discusses the Whig victory in Maine and his concern in the reelection of Moses Hicks Grinnell in New York.

[Nov 6?]   To John Plummer Healy. ALS. MHi. mDW 17006. Sends
check to cover George Wallace Jones's draft.

Nov 7   *To Nathaniel F. Williams.*   61

Nov 7   From Harrison Gray Otis. ALS. DLC. mDW 17014. Invites the
Websters to dinner.

Nov 7   Recommendations from Winfield Scott, for Charles King—postmaster in New York (ALS. NhHi. George C. Whipple, Jr., Carmel,
N.Y. mDW 17012); Elihu Smith, for his son—clerkship in Washington (ALS. MWalB. mDW 17018).

Nov 8   *From George Augustus Waggaman.*   61

[Nov 10]   To [Edward Curtis?]. ALS. NN. mDW 17083. Reports Whig
victory in Massachusetts.

Nov 10   From Daniel Fletcher Webster. ALS. NhHi. mDW 17025. Discusses the Illinois election and his law practice.

Nov 11   From George Poindexter. LS. NhHi. mDW 17027. Congratulates DW on the Whig victory, and discusses the importance of Harrison's selection of advisors.

Nov 13   Insurance policy for $7,000 on wine and library in the Summer
Street House lately occupied by DW. DS. MHi. mDW 39835–367.

Nov 14   From E. S. Davis. ALS. DLC. mDW 17033. Praises DW's Richmond speech; reports solid Whig victories in Tennessee.
Nov 16   To [William Albert] Bradley. ALS. NhD. mDW 17035. Marvels at the Whig triumph; sends check for payment of an account.
Nov 16   To John Middleton Clayton.   62
Nov 18   To [?] Bryant. ALS. NHi. mDW 17047. Suggests that Bryant write him again on the subject raised in his recent letter.
Nov 18   To Thomas Ellicott. Typed Extract. DLC. mDW 17041. Expresses concern over the financial condition of the country.
Nov 18   To W. A. Weeks. ALS. NhD. mDW 17042. Accepts invitation to celebrate Whig victory at Weeks's home.
Nov 18   From Michenor Cadwallader.   63
Nov 19   Recommendation from Nahum Mitchell, for Galen Ames—army paymaster at Springfield (ALS. DNA, RG 156. mDWs).
Nov 19   Promissory note to Ebenezer Trescott for $545.50. DS. MHi. mDW 39835–369.
Nov 20   To [John] Connell. ALS. PHi. mDW 17048. Van Tyne, p. 628. Recalls the fatigue he felt campaigning in New Hampshire; asks Connell to intercede with the directors of the Pennsylvania Bank of the United States concerning his overdue notes.
Nov 20   To Samuel Frothingham.   65
Nov 21   To Harmar Denny. ALS. PPiHi. mDW 17054. Offers congratulations on the Whig victory in Pennsylvania.
Nov 22   From John Middleton Clayton.   66
Nov 23   From John Minor Botts. ALS. NhD. mDW 17059. Blames the Democratic victory in Virginia on "the baneful influence" of William C. Rives.
[Nov 23]   "Revenue and Finances" (editorial). AD. DLC. mDW 17085. *Boston Semi-Weekly Atlas,* Nov 25, 1840.
[Nov 24]   "The Next Senate" (editorial). AD. NhHi. mDW 17097. *Boston Semi-Weekly Atlas,* Nov 25, 1840. Van Tyne, pp. 226–227 (as Dec 3).
Nov 24   Application from William Taggard—navy agent (ALS. DLC. mDW 17063).
Nov 25   To Israel Keech Tefft. LS. GHi. mDW 17065. Accepts honorary membership in the Georgia Historical Society.
Nov 25   From Henry Wheaton. ALS. MWalB. mDW 17067. Trusts that the Whig victory will not precipitate his removal from office.
Nov 26   To John Collins Warren. ALS. MHi. mDW 17071. *Memorial Biographies of the New England Historic Genealogical Society* (9 vols.; Boston, 1880–1908), 3: 54. Relates his high regards for Warren.
Nov 26   From Lewis Cass. ALS. MWalB. mDW 17075. Asks that he be allowed to stay at his post in Paris.
Nov 27   To Edward Everett Hale. AL. MHi. mDW 17080. Asks him to take charge of a letter.
Nov 27   Recommendation from William Crawford et al., for Benjamin Patteson—U.S. marshal for Alabama (LS. MWalB. mDW 17081).
Nov 30   Promissory note for $2,278 to BUS of Pennsylvania. DS. William A. Philpott, Jr., Dallas, Texas. mDW 39835–371.

[Nov?] "And Last Comes Up the Mountain State" (poem). AD. NhD. mDW 17092.

Dec 1 From William Henry Harrison. Copy. NhHi. mDW 17094. *Diplomatic Papers*, 1. Invites DW to accept either the state or treasury department post.

Dec 4 From Feromine A. Sumner. ALS. DLC. mDW 17102. Discusses the tariff.

[Dec 5?] To Nicholas Biddle. ALS. DLC. mDW 17108. Tells him that George Evans is at "the Mansion House."

Dec 9 From Nicholas Biddle. 67

Dec 10 To Nicholas Biddle. ALS. DLC. mDW 17111. Advises Biddle to wait on one matter and not to worry about another.

Dec 10 Patent to land in Rock County, Wisconsin. Typed copy. Register of Deeds, Rock County, Wisconsin. mDWs.

Dec 10 Application from Andrew Webster—Nova Scotia consulate (ALS. NhHi. mDW 17113).

Dec 11 To William Henry Harrison. AL draft. NhHi. mDW 17116. *Diplomatic Papers*, 1. States that he is willing to accept the state department post.

Dec 11 From Julia Webster Appleton. 67

Dec 12 To James Trecothick Austin. ALS. NhD. mDW 17124. Seeks to arrange the time for arguing *Rhode Island* v. *Massachusetts*, 14 Peters 210 (1840).

Dec 12 To Thomas Fessenden et al. LS. NhExP. mDW 17126. Declines invitation from the New England Society of New York.

Dec 12 To John Plummer Healy. ALS. MHi. mDW 17129. Discusses his personal finances.

Dec 12 From Nicholas Biddle. 69

Dec 13 To Harriette Story White Paige. ALS. Mrs. Irvin McD. Garfield, Southboro, Mass. mDWs. *PC*, 2: 94–95. Invites the Paiges to visit him in Washington.

Dec 13 Application from Nicholas Biddle—the Vienna post (ALS draft. DLC. mDW 17131).

Dec 14 To Charles Henry Thomas. AL incomplete. MHi. mDW 17133. Reports his arrival in Washington and discusses Marshfield farming affairs.

Dec 14 Recommendation from Willard Phillips et al., for Thomas P. Jones—commissioner of patents (LS. MWalB. mDW 17135).

Dec 14 Check for $40 to [?]. DS. NN. mDW 39835–372.

Dec 15 To John Plummer Healy. ALS. MHi. mDW 17138. Discusses a note held by Nathaniel Haven.

Dec 15 From Isaac Gibson (with postscript by Simeon Draper). ALS. NhHi. mDW 17140. Writes regarding DW's indebtedness to the Morris Canal and Banking Company.

Dec 16 From John Plummer Healy. ALS. MHi. mDW 17142. Discusses Hall J. Kelly's claim against Mexico.

Dec 16 Check for $50 to Duval & Brothers. DS. NN. mDW 39835–373.

Dec 17 To Elisha Whittlesey. ALS. OClWHi. mDW 17146. Supports the construction of a railroad between LaSalle and Toledo.

Dec 18 To Hiram Ketchum. 69

Dec 19   *To Peleg Sprague.*   70
Dec 21   To [Seth?] Barton. ALS. DLC. mDW 27514. Regrets being un-
           able to spend Christmas with him.
Dec 21   *To [John Plummer Healy].*   71
Dec 21   Check for $131.50 to [Edward?] Curtis. DS. NN. mDW
           39835-374.
Dec 24   *To Nicholas Biddle.*   72
Dec 24   To John Plummer Healy. ALS. MH-H. mDW 17153. Discusses
           the matter of interrogatories involving Henry L. Kinney and Levi C.
           Turner.
Dec 24   To [?] Patterson. ALS. NNPM. mDW 17154. Acknowledges re-
           ceiving a copy of Patterson's address on Primary Education.
Dec 24   *To Samuel Bulkley Ruggles.*   73
Dec 24   *From James F. Conover.*   74
Dec 25   To [Lewis Cass]. Copy. MWalB. mDW 23952. States that there
           will likely be changes in the diplomatic corps but they will not be
           immediate.
Dec 25   To Henry Wheaton. ALS. NNPM. mDW 17164. Reports that
           there will likely be changes in the diplomatic corps but that he
           will try to keep Wheaton.
Dec 25   Check for $50 payable to [?]. DS. NN. mDW 39835-375.
Dec 27   To John Plummer Healy. ALS. MHi. mDW 17168. Expresses
           appreciation for Nathaniel Haven's kindness.
Dec 27   From William Henry Harrison. ALS. NhHi. mDW 17170. *Diplo-
           matic Papers,* 1. Thanks DW for letter accepting state department post.
Dec 28   To Nicholas Biddle. ALS. DLC. mDW 17173. Asks that some-
           one investigate the question of iron duties.
Dec 28   To Nicholas Biddle. ALS. DLC. mDW 17177. Expects Harrison
           in Washington about Jan 15.
Dec 28   To John Plummer Healy. ALS. MHi. mDW 17178. Sends $1000
           to meet Richard S. Coxe's draft.
Dec 28   From John Mercer. ALS. DLC. mDW 17180. Solicits DW's legal
           services in a case involving an estate.
Dec 28   *From Daniel Fletcher Webster.*   75
Dec 30   To James F. Conover. ALS. NhD. mDW 17186. Thinks Harrison
           has acted wisely in dealing with office seekers.
Dec 30   To William Campbell Preston. ALS. NhD. mDW 17189. Pre-
           sents Preston with a pair of Gordon setters and agrees that he
           should take the desk DW is vacating in the Senate.
Dec 30   To Richard Smith. ALS. UPB. mDWs. Offers "immediate &
           final payment" to Bank of the Metropolis by transferring shares in
           the Clamorgan grant.
Dec 30   *From Nicholas Biddle.*   76
Dec 30   Recommendation from William Story, for Augustus Story—
           post in Wisconsin Territory (ALS. MWalB. mDW 17194).
Dec 30   Memorial of Daniel W. Coxe asking that his interest in certain
           lands not be affected by preemption legislation. ADS. DNA, RG 46.
           mDW 48158.
Dec 31   From Beverly Allen. ALS. DLC. mDW 17196. Writes concerning
           the Missouri–Iowa boundary dispute.

Dec 31   From Charles Anderson Wickliffe.   78
Dec 31   Promissory note to the Merchants Bank for $550. DS. NhD.
mDW 39835–376.
Dec   Statement of account with John T. Haight. AD. WHi. mDW
39835–377. Runs to March 1841.
Dec   Petition of citizens of Thomastown, Me., for a general bankrupt
law. ADS. DNA, RG 46. mDW 48048.
1840   To John McKim, Sr., et al from DW et al. LS. NcU. mDW
17198. Seek financial support for the Whig party.
[1840]   To William Woodbridge. ALS. MiD-B. mDW 17202. Sends 100
copies of his Philadelphia speech and offers to send more.
[1840?]   To Nicholas Biddle. AD fragment. DLC. mDWs. Discusses
northeastern boundary.
[1840?]   To Francis Granger. ALS. NhD. mDWs. Excuses himself from
a dinner invitation.
184[?]   Three blank checks on the Merchants Bank, Boston. Printed
documents, signed. MHi. mDW 40679.
[1840–1851]   Inscription to Mary Elizabeth Wilson. Printed. M. E. W.
Sherwood, *An Epistle to Posterity* (New York, 1897), p. 23.

1841

Jan 1   From Edward Everett. ALS. MHi. mDW 17236. Congratulates
DW on the election and discusses his family's activities in Florence,
Edward Webster's studies, the English diplomatic post (which he
thinks DW might take), and relations with Florence, Turin, and
Naples.
Jan 1   From Jonathan Trumbull Warner. ALS. NhHi. mDW 17240.
Urges American attention upon Oregon and the upper Northwest.
Jan 1   Check for $50 to "self." DS. NN. mDW 39835–327.
Jan 2   To Theophilus Parsons.   79
Jan 4   From William Hunter. ALS. NhHi. mDW 17245. Comments on
Brazilian affairs and urges upgrading the U.S. mission there.
Jan 4   From William Plumer, Jr. ALS draft. Nh. mDW 17256. Recom-
mends changes in the Epping, N.H., post office; wants his brother,
George W., appointed postmaster.
Jan 5   To [Thomas Dunlap?]. ALS. NhD. mDWs. States that he is ready
to see Herman Cope and reiterates "that it is expedient to arm Mr
[Samuel] Jaudon against Mr. McCulloch."
Jan 5   To Daniel Fletcher Webster. ALS. NhHi. mDW 17260. Van Tyne,
pp. 668–669. Discusses the purchase of a farm; bank mortgage
on Henry Hubbard.
Jan 5   From Nicholas Biddle. ALS draft. DLC. mDW 17264. States
that Samuel Jaudon has been made a director of BUS and asks DW
to urge him to return to the United States.
Jan 5   From Robert Hanna. ALS. NhD. mDW 17265. Reports on action
of Indiana Assembly concerning public lands.
Jan 6   To John Plummer Healy. ALS. MHi. mDW 17267. Expresses

astonishment at a recent decision by Joseph Story; asks him to see
to it that DFW's bill is not protested.

Jan 6   Check for $30 to "self." DS. NN. mDW 39836.

Jan 6   Recommendation from Stephen Clarendon Phillips, for Richard J. Cleveland—consulate at Havana (ALS. NhHi. mDW 17269).

Jan 7   To Samuel Jaudon. Printed. *PC*, 2: 97–98. Urges him to return to
the United States, noting there is "a disposition" to appoint him
president of BUS.

Jan 7   From Daniel Fletcher Webster. ALS. NhHi. mDW 17275. Discusses tax payments on DW's western lands.

Jan 7   Recommendation from Stephen White, for John O. Charles—
congressional librarian (ALS. MWalB. mDW 17279).

Jan 8   From Ebenezer T. Fogg et al. (with DW to John Quincy Adams,
Jan 13, 1841). ALS by Fogg, signed also by others. MHi. mDW
17299. Ask whether Congress will agree to a survey of the North
River in Massachusetts.

Jan 9   To Samuel Jaudon. ALS. NHi. mDW 17282. Reports Illinois has
paid interest on bonds and will sustain its credit.

Jan 9   To [George Wallace?] Jones. ALS. NhD. mDW 17284. Asks for
advice on a business matter.

Jan 9   From Samuel Bulkley Ruggles.   80

Jan 11   To John Plummer Healy. ALS. MHi. mDW 17290. Asks him to
seek postponement of a court proceeding until after March 3.

Jan 11   From Samuel B. Churchill. ALS. DLC. mDW 17292. Urges
DW to support a preemption bill.

Jan 11   Bill for the relief of the owners of the British brig *Despatch*.
Printed Document (with AN). DNA, RG 46. mDW 47954.

Jan 11   Memorial of citizens of Massachusetts for a general bankrupt
law. DS. DNA, RG 46. mDW 48050.

Jan 11   Petition of Abbott Lawrence et al. of Massachusetts asking that
jurisdiction over offences committed within the admiralty and mari-
time jurisdiction of the United States may be extended to the district courts of the United States. DS. DNA, RG 46. mDW 48161.

Jan 12   Recommendation from William Key Bond, for William H.
Creighton—bearer of despatches to England (ALS. MWalB. mDW
17296).

[Jan 13]   To John Quincy Adams (enclosure in Ebenezer T. Fogg et al.
to DW, Jan 8, 1841). ALS. MHi. mDW 17298. Forwards Fogg's
letter.

Jan 14   To John Henry Clifford. ALS. MHi. mDW 17300. Discusses applicants for a collectorship in Massachusetts.

[Jan 14]   Petition of Henry Brain for reimbursement of money paid to
ransom him from Indian captivity in 1785. DS. DNA, RG 46. mDW
48036.

Jan 15   To Solomon Lincoln.   82
Jan 15   From Robert Barnwell Rhett.   82

Jan 15   Recommendation from Willard Phillips, for Thomas P. Jones—
Patent Office commissioner (ALS. MWalB. mDW 17310).

Jan 16   From Daniel G. Garnsey. ALS. MWalB. mDW 17318. Comments on Whig losses in Illinois and discusses the distribution of
patronage, particularly in Iowa.

Jan 18   From Samuel Appleton Appleton. ALS. MHi. mDW 17322. Encloses inventory of wine from DW's cellar which had been sold to [Samuel Bulkley?] Ruggles.

Jan 19   Petition of citizens of Nantucket, Mass., for indemnification for French spoliations before 1800. ADS. DNA, RG 46. mDW 48169.

Jan 19   Recommendations from Thomas Kinnicutt, for Charles Russell—marshal for Massachusetts (ALS. MWalB. mDW 17325); from William Henry Seward, for a Col. Stone—chargé at some European court (ALS draft. NRU. mDW 17329).

[c. Jan 19]   Memorial of citizens of Ohio for passage of a general bankrupt law. DS. DNA, RG 46. mDW 48052.

Jan 20   Recommendation from David Anthony et al., for Thomas P. Jones (LS. MWalB. mDW 17330).

Jan 21   Check for $50 to "self." DS. NN. mDW 39837.

Jan 23   From Baron de Roenne. ALS. DLC. mDW 17333. Encloses a report on the German Customs Union and also a pamphlet on the progress of agriculture in Germany.

Jan 23   Application from Moses Eastman—clerk in custom house at Boston or Portsmouth (ALS. Fred Courser, Warner, N.H. mDWs).

Jan 23   Petition of citizens of Grand Gulf, Miss., for the passage of a general bankrupt law. DS. DNA, RG 46. mDW 48055.

Jan 25   *To Nathaniel F. Williams.*   83

Jan 25   From Virgil Maxcy. ALS. DLC. mDW 17338. Offers to continue as U.S. chargé d'affaires at Brussels until his negotiations with the Belgian government are completed.

Jan 26   From Charles Francis Adams. ALS. NhHi. mDW 17343. Van Tyne, pp. 228–229. Seeks suggestions for resolutions being drafted by the Massachusetts legislature on the Maine boundary dispute.

Jan 26   Recommendations from Samuel P. Benson, for John D. Kinsman—marshal of Maine (ALS. MWalB. mDW 17345); from Charles Hickling et al., for John A. Webber—military storekeeper, Watertown Arsenal (LS. DNA, RG 156. mDWs).

Jan 27   From Samuel Rossiter Betts. ALS. MWalB. mDW 17347. Introduces Henry H. Elliott.

Jan 28   To Theophilus Parsons. AL draft. NhHi. mDW 17349. LS. MB. mDW 17353. *Diplomatic Papers*, 1. Discusses action in the Massachusetts legislature on the northeastern boundary question.

Jan 28   Recommendation from Parker Cleaveland, for Alfred W. Pike—any office (ALS. MWalB. mDW 17356).

Jan 29   Editorial on speech by Henry Clay. AD. NhD. mDW 17358. *National Intelligencer*, Feb 2, 1841.

Jan 30   To Charles Francis Adams. ALS. MHi. mDW 17361. Van Tyne, p. 230. Comments on the boundary negotiations and thinks a firm but temperate expression by the Massachusetts legislature would be quite satisfactory.

Jan 30   To John Plummer Healy. ALS. MHi. mDW 17364. Expects George Evans to be elected Maine senator; asks him to see Haven about a note.

Jan 30   To Charles Miner. ALS. PWbH. mDW 17366. Charles Francis Richardson and Elizabeth Miner Richardson, *Charles Miner: A*

Pennsylvania Pioneer (Wilkes-Barre, Pa., 1916), p. 131. Thanks
Miner for complimentary remarks in his address of December 4.
Jan 30   From Peter Parker. LS copy. CtY. mDWs. *Diplomatic Papers*, 1.
Strongly urges the sending of a minister plenipotentiary to China.
Jan 30   Recommendations from Ichabod R. Chadbourne, for John D.
Kinsman (ALS. MWalB. mDW 17390); from Charles Stewart
Daveis, for Kinsman (ALS. MWalB. mDW 20069); from Thaddeus
Stevens, for [?]—superintendent, Harper's Ferry (ALS. DNA, RG
156. mDWs).
Jan   Check for $15 to [?]. DS (fragment). NhD. mDWs.
Feb 1   To Solomon Lincoln. ALS. NhD. mDW 17394. Fears a more truc-
ulent British stand on the boundary controversy; discusses patron-
age affecting Plymouth and Boston.
Feb 1   To Nathaniel F. Williams. ALS. NhD. mDW 17397. Discusses
a note due.
Feb 1   Application from John Crafts Wright, for the *Cincinnati Daily
Gazette*—public printer (ALS. DNA, RG 59. mDW 53007).
Feb 1   Recommendations from Harrison Gray Otis, for Allyne Otis—sec-
retary to the London or Paris legation (ALS. DLC. mDW 17399);
from Francis Peabody et al., for Thomas P. Jones (LS. MWalB.
mDW 17402).
Feb 2   To Edward Everett.   84
[Feb 2]   To Harrison Gray Otis. ALS. MHi. mDW 21012. Promises to
present his son's application for a foreign mission to Harrison.
Feb 2   From Nicholas Biddle. Printed. McGrane, *Correspondence of
Nicholas Biddle*, p. 341. Fears that a premature pronouncement on
the recharter of a national bank might have an adverse effect and
asks DW's attention to the matter.
Feb 2   From Nicholas Biddle. ALS. DLC. mDW 17413. Feels that a tariff
reduction on iron would injure the industry.
Feb 2   From Isaac Rand Jackson. ALS copy. MdHi. mDW 17419. Asks
if DW wants to review the English translation of Francis Joseph
Grund's biographical sketch which appeared in the Augsburg *Allge-
meine Zeitung* and asks to publish it in pamphlet form.
Feb 2   Application from Charles Pelham Curtis—district judge of Massachusetts (ALS. DLC. mDW 17415).
Feb 3   To [Theophilus Parsons]. ALS. MB. mDW 17421. Responds to
his inquiry about a post which is to become vacant.
Feb 3   To William Cabell Rives. AL. DLC. mDW 17422. Invites him to
dine.
Feb 3   To Nathaniel F. Williams. ALS. NhD. mDW 17424. Will draw
on him "at 10 days sight"; encloses a check for $1,000.
Feb 3   From Edmund Burke. Copy. DLC. mDW 17426. Asks DW to
clarify a reference to him in his Saratoga speech.
Feb 3   From William Pitt Fessenden. ALS. MWalB. mDW 17430. Discusses patronage in New Hampshire and Maine and makes several
specific recommendations.
Feb 4   To Nicholas Biddle. ALS. DLC. mDW 17434. McGrane, *Correspondence of Nicholas Biddle*, p. 341. Thinks the inaugural address
ought to be confined mainly to a statement of principles.

Feb 4 To Isaac Rand Jackson. ALS. MdHi. mDW 17435. Wishes to review the translation of Francis Grund's biographical sketch before
it is printed.

Feb 4 Recommendations from Robert Hanna, for Thomas B. Johnson—marshal, Iowa Territory (ALS. MWalB. mDW 17436); from
Joseph Healy, for the Concord *New Hampshire Statesman*—public
printer (ALS. DNA, RG 59. mDW 52868); from W. W. Gilliland et
al., for the Charlestown, Indiana, *People's Gazette*—public printer
(DS. DNA, RG 59. mDW 52763).

Feb 5 To [John Plummer Healy]. ALS. MHi. mDW 17438. Asks for the
record of votes cast for him in the congressional elections of 1822,
1824, and 1826.

Feb 5 To Theophilus Rogers Marvin. ALS. MH-H. mDW 17440. Requests copies of Marvin's edition of the Saratoga speech.

Feb 5 Recommendations from Charles G. Loring, for Theophilus Parsons—district judge of Massachusetts (ALS. MWalB. mDW
17441); from Charles B. Penrose, for A. G. Ege—superintendent of
armory, Harper's Ferry (ALS. DNA, RG 156. mDWs).

Feb 6 To [Henry Willis Kinsman]. ALS. NhD. mDW 17444. Discusses
the appointment of a postmaster for Boston.

Feb 6 Application from A. Webster (ALS. NhHi. mDW 17457).

Feb 6 Recommendations from George H. Dunn, for Thomas B. Johnson (ALS. MWalB. mDW 17446); from Rice Garland, for Balie Peyton—district attorney for Louisiana (ALS. MWalB. mDW 17448);
from Gideon Snow, for Gideon Theodore Snow—consulate at Pernambuco (ALS. NhHi. mDW 17450); from Jared Sparks, for Robert Walsh—consulate at Paris (ALS. MWalB. mDW 17453).

Feb 7 From Nicholas Biddle. ALS draft. DLC. mDW 17459. Advises
DW to come to Philadelphia for "the completion of your concerns
with the Bank."

Feb 7 Application from George A. Waggaman—consulate at Paris
(ALS. NhHi. mDW 17460).

Feb 7 Recommendation from [?], for William Wyatt—governor of
Florida Territory (ALS. MWalB. mDW 17462).

Feb [8] To [Nicholas Biddle]. ALS. DLC. mDW 17464. Asks when he
should come to Philadelphia.

Feb 8 Memorial of citizens of Onondaga County, N.Y., asking that
Seneca Indians not assenting to the treaty for the sale of their lands
not be forced to emigrate. DS. DNA, RG 46. mDW 48175.

Feb 8 Recommendations from Milton Stapp, for Thomas B. Johnson
(ALS. MWalB. mDW 17465); from Enoch Train, for James P.
Flint—consul, Buenos Aires (ALS. MWalB. mDW 17467).

Feb 9 Recommendations from William G. Bates, for Samuel H. Walley,
Jr.—marshal in Massachusetts (ALS. MWalB. mDW 17469); from
Thurlow Weed, for Richard Sill—consulship (ALS. MWalB. mDW
17471).

Feb 10 To John Davis (1787–1854). Printed. *W & S*, 16: 338–339.
States that his resignation from the Senate will be announced on
Feb 22.

Feb 10 To [John Plummer Healy]. ALS. MHi. mDW 38549. States that
he will try to send funds to cover Fletcher Webster's acceptance.

Feb 10   From Nicholas Biddle. ALS draft. DLC. mDW 17477. Discusses settlement of DW's account with BUS; urges him to set time for coming to Philadelphia.

Feb 10   From Herman Cope. ALS. MWalB. mDW 17479. Outlines proposal for conveyance of real estate to settle about $100,000 of DW's indebtedness to BUS in Philadelphia and New York (excluding $26,700 for which Henry Hubbard's bond and mortgage are held as collateral and security).

Feb 10   Application from James Watson Webb—postmaster in New York City (ALS. CtY. mDW 17486).

Feb 10   Recommendations from Moses G. Atwood, for Benjamin F. Edwards—marshal for Illinois (ALS. MWalB. mDW 17473); from David Hale, for William B. Taylor—despatch agent (ALS. MWalB. mDW 17778); from Noah Noble, for Thomas B. Johnson (ALS. MWalB. mDW 17482); from David Bayard Ogden, for Samuel M. Ogden—district attorney, Alabama (ALS. MWalB. mDW 17484).

Feb 11   Application from [Richard R.?] Ward—marshal in New York (ALS. MWalB. mDW 17494).

Feb 11   Recommendations from Josiah W. Blake, for George W. Blake—consul at Buenos Aires (ALS. MWalB. mDW 17488); from Josiah Quincy, Jr., for Samuel H. Walley, Jr. (ALS. MWalB. mDW 17490); from John Canfield Spencer, for John A. Tardy—consul at Havre (ALS. MWalB. mDW 17492); from William Leete Stone, for William B. Taylor (ALS. MWalB. mDW 17776).

Feb 12   To Nicholas Biddle. ALS. DLC. mDW 17496. States that he has written to Herman Cope.

Feb 12   To Isaac Rand Jackson. ALS. MdHi. mDW 17498. *Diplomatic Papers*, 1. Asks if Jackson might assist him in financing the purchase of a house in Washington.

Feb 12   Application from Paul Anguera—consul at Barcelona (ALS. MWalB. mDW 17501).

Feb 12   Recommendations from Luther Bradish, for Clark Robinson—marshal in New York (ALS. MWalB. mDW 17504); from W. Sheet, Jr., for Thomas B. Johnson (ALS. MWalB. mDW 17506); from William Singer, for Timothy Darling—consul at Nassau (ALS. NhHi. mDW 17508).

Feb 13   To John Forsyth. ALS. DNA, RG 59. mDW 55457. Asks that papers pertaining to the ships *Franklin* and *Banian* be laid before the Mexican claims commission.

Feb 13   Application from William Leete Stone, for the New York *Commercial Advertiser*—public printer (ALS. DNA, RG 59. mDW 52301).

Feb 13   Recommendations from Franklin Dexter, for Daniel Parkman—marshal in Massachusetts (ALS. MWalB. mDW 17510); from William Hiester, for John P. Hiester—bearer of despatches to Europe (ALS. MWalB. mDW 17511); from Joseph Ritney, for A. G. Ege (ALS. DNA, RG 156. mDWs).

Feb 14   To Nathaniel F. Williams.   86

Feb 14   Recommendation from David Bayard Ogden, for Alfred Seton—a consular post (ALS. N. mDW 17515).

Feb 15   To Solomon Van Rensselaer. Printed. Catharina V. R. Bonney,

A Legacy of Historical Gleanings (2 vols.; Albany, 1875), 2: 158. Invites Van Rensselaer to join him and the president-elect for dinner.

Feb [15]   From Nicholas Biddle. ALS. DLC. mDW 17478. Now thinks DW's bank business can be settled without his coming to Philadelphia; presumes he will be satisfied with the employment of Richard Smith to assess the value of the western lands DW is to convey in partial settlement of his debt.

Feb 15   From Herman Cope.   88

Feb 15   From John Forsyth. Copy. DNA, RG 59. mDW 55680. Informs him that the papers enclosed with his letter of Feb 13 have been laid before the Mexican claims commission.

Feb 15   From Isaac Rand Jackson. ALS copy. MdHi. mDW 17523. *Diplomatic Papers*, 1. Discusses his financial situation and the problems involved in assisting DW to buy a house in Washington.

Feb 15   From J[osiah?] Spalding. ALS. MWalB. mDW 17531. Introduces William Henry Russell.

Feb 15   Recommendations from Luther Bradish, for John A. Tardy (ALS. MWalB. mDW 17517); from Edward Kent, for Timothy Darling (ALS. NhHi. mDW 17525); from Zadoc Long, for Timothy Darling (ALS. NhHi. mDW 17527); from Jeremiah Mason, for Timothy Upham—unspecified post (ALS. MWalB. mDW 17529); from John Pope, for the St. Louis, Missouri, *Daily Commercial Bulletin*—public printer (ALS. DNA, RG 59. mDW 52661).

Feb 16   From Benjamin Ruggles. ALS. NhHi. mDW 17548. Introduces William Duane Wilson.

Feb 16   From John Crafts Wright. ALS. DLC. mDW 17550. Denies rumors of unfriendly editorials about Harrison's cabinet in the *Cincinnati Gazette*.

Feb 16   Recommendations from Samuel Fessenden and Thomas Amory Deblois, for John D. Kinsman (ALS by Deblois, signed also by Fessenden. MWalB. mDW 17533); from Henry Sheffie Geyer, for William Henry Russell—unspecified post (ALS. MWalB. mDW 17535); from G. Hull, for Charles Russell (ALS. MWalB. mDW 17537); from Samuel Longfellow, for John D. Kinsman (ALS. MWalB. mDW 17539); from Jacob McGaw, for Timothy Darling (ALS. NhHi. mDW 17542); from Cyrus Perkins, for Josiah L. James—marshal in Illinois (ALS. MWalB. mDW 17545); from William Bradford Reed, for John P. Hiester (ALS. MWalB. mDW 18023).

Feb 17   From George Edmund Badger. ALS. DLC. mDW 17554. Accepts cabinet post as secretary of the navy.

Feb 17   From William P. Duval. ALS. MWalB. mDW 17557. Urges removal of Robert Raymond Reid as governor of Florida Territory.

Feb 17   From Edward Kent. ALS. NhD. mDW 17566. *Diplomatic Papers*, 1. Warns that Maine is expecting immediate action on the boundary dispute; recommends George Evans for U.S. minister to England.

Feb 17   From Hiram Ketchum. ALS. NhD. mDW 17570. Discusses applicants for government positions in New York.

Feb 17   Recommendations from William A. Crabb, for John P. Hiester (ALS. MWalB. mDW 18022); from Theodore Frelinghuysen, for Asa

Whitehead—district attorney for New Jersey (ALS. MWalB. mDW
17564); from Charles B. Penrose, for John P. Hiester (ALS.
MWalB. mDW 17574); from Charles C. Sullivan, for John P. Hiester
(ALS. MWalB. mDW 18020).

Feb 18   *From Edward Webster.*   89
Feb 18   Recommendations from John Gilmore, for John P. Hiester
(ALS. MWalB. mDW 18018); from Philip Greely, Jr., for John D.
Kinsman (ALS. MWalB. mDW 17576); from Daniel Putnam King
et al., for Charles H. Warren—district judge of Massachusetts (LS.
MH. mDWs); from Joseph M. Sterrett, for John P. Hiester (ALS.
MWalB. mDW 18014); from Robert Wash, for the St. Louis *Com-
mercial Bulletin* (ALS. DNA, RG 59. mDW 52663).
Feb 19   Application from Robert Treat Paine—secretary of legation at
Vienna (ALS. MWalB. mDW 17590).
Feb 19   Recommendations from Nicholas Biddle, for J. C. Montgom-
ery—postmaster in Philadelphia (ALS draft. DLC. mDW 17582);
from Rufus Choate, for Charles Russell (ALS. MWalB. mDW
17583); from Henry H. Fuller, for Charles Russell (ALS. MWalB.
mDW 17585); from Simon Greenleaf, for John D. Kinsman (ALS.
MWalB. mDW 17588); from William L. Storrs, for Gurdon S. Hubbard—marshal in Illinois (ALS. MWalB. mDW 17595); from Thurlow Weed, for Francis Randall—district attorney for Wisconsin
(ALS. MWalB. mDW 15796).
Feb 20   To William Bowen Campbell. ALS. NcD. mDW 17598. Will
relay his letter recommending "Mr. Hall" to Harrison.
Feb 20   To [John Plummer Healy]. ALS. MHi. mDW 17600. States that
certain papers must be in Spanish and English before they are pre-
sented to the commission.
Feb 20   From John Davis (1761–1847). ALS. NhHi. mDW 17603. Discusses his proposed retirement from the bench.
Feb 20   Application from Mattingly & Green, for the *New Albany* (Ind.)
Gazette—public printer (LS. DNA, RG 59. mDW 52768).
Feb 20   Recommendations from Salmon P. Chase, for Andrew Patter-
son—marshal in Mississippi (ALS. MWalB. mDW 17601); from
John Davis (1787–1854), for Charles H. Warren (ALS. MWalB.
mDW 17610); from William Pitt Fessenden, for George W. Cooley—
district attorney in Maine (ALS. MWalB. mDW 17612); from John
Leeds Kerr, for Robert C. Wright—consulate at Rio de Janeiro (ALS.
NhHi. mDW 17614); from Theodore W. Smith et al., for the St. Al-
bans, Vermont, *Franklin Messenger*—public printer (LS. DNA, RG
59. mDW 52810).
Feb 21   *To [?].*   90
Feb 21   *From Nicholas Biddle, with enclosure from Nicholas Biddle, Feb
21.*   91
Feb 21   From Nicholas Biddle. ALS draft. DLC. mDW 17618. Reminds
DW of his desire to go to Europe.
Feb 21   From Calvin Fletcher. Printed. Gayle Thornbrough and Doro-
thy L. Riker, eds., *The Diary of Calvin Fletcher* (Indianapolis,
1973), 2: 288–289. Inquires about state laws governing the resump-
tion of specie payment.
Feb 21   Application from Josiah L. James (ALS. MWalB. mDW 17619).

Feb 21 Recommendation from Nicholas Biddle, for Thomas W. Sutherland—commissioner of the Land Office (ALS draft. DLC. mDW
17617).

[Feb 22] To [Edward Curtis]. ALS. NN. mDW 17623. Suggests that
Curtis ask the *National Intelligencer* to publish DW's letter of
resignation.

Feb 22 To Richard Mentor Johnson. ALS. DNA, RG 46. mDW 48182.
Congressional Globe, 26th Cong., 2d sess., p. 199. Resigns his Senate seat.

Feb 22 From James Alexander Hamilton.   92

Feb 22 From Theophilus Parsons et al. LS. NhD. mDW 17635. Submit
a testimonial in honor of DW's retirement from the Senate.

Feb 22 From Ambrose Spencer. ALS. NhHi. mDW 17641. Introduces
Franklin Townsend.

Feb 22 Recommendations from Thomas Corwin, for John S. Green—
Supreme Court, Iowa Territory (ALS. MWalB. mDW 17625); from
S. Newton Dexter, for Dennis Davenport—military storekeeper,
Rome, New York (ALS. DNA, RG 156. mDWs); from John T. P.
Dumont, for John Ruggles—Patent Office (ALS. MWalB. mDW
17627); from William Dwight et al., for John Howard—superintendent of armory, Springfield, Massachusetts (ALS by Dwight, signed
also by others. DNA, RG 156. mDWs); from Charles Marsh, for
Samuel Prentiss—judge in Vermont (ALS. MWalB. mDW 17629);
from John Otis, for John T. P. Dumont—despatch bearer, Europe
(ALS. MWalB. mDW 17632); from John Scott, for Charles Bogy—
marshal in Iowa (ALS. MWalB. mDW 17639); from John Wilson,
for James H. Birch—unspecified post (ALS. MWalB. mDW 17643).

Feb 23 To Edward Kent. AL draft. DLC. mDW 17648. *Diplomatic
Papers*, 1. Discusses the northeastern boundary question.

Feb 23 From Daniel Putnam King et al. DS. DLC. mDW 17658. Enclose resolutions of the Massachusetts Whig convention.

Feb 23 From William Henry Seward. ALS draft. NRU. mDW 17660.
Introduces S. DeWitt Bloodgood.

Feb 23 From William Henry Seward. ALS draft. NRU. mDW 17661.
Introduces John Romeyn Brodhead, who is about to visit Europe in
search of documents on colonial New York.

Feb 23 Application from James Watson Webb (ALS. CtY. mDW
17672).

Feb 23 Recommendations from Beverly Allen, for the *St. Louis New
Era*—public printer (ALS. DNA, RG 59. mDW 52672); from N. Bow-
ditch Blunt, for Brantz Mayer—secretary of legation, Vienna (ALS.
MWalB. mDW 17654); from Alexander Vietts Griswold, for
George F. Usher—consul, Haiti (ALS. NhHi. mDW 17656); from
Francis Ormand Jonathan Smith, for John D. Kinsman (ALS.
MWalB. mDW 17664); from Samuel Sprigg, for Mordecai Yarnall—
marshal in Virginia (ALS. MWalB. mDW 17668); from John Talia-
ferro, for Waddy Thompson—minister to Mexico (ALS. MWalB.
mDW 17670).

Feb 24 Recommendations from [Thomas?] Dunlap, for Jacob Gratz—
naval officer, port of Philadelphia (LS. DNA, RG 56. mDWs); from

Henry Smith Lane, for various persons and offices in Indiana (ALS. MWalB. mDW 17673).

Feb 25   To Franklin Haven. ALS. MH-H. mDW 17675. Asks him to look after two notes.

Feb 25   To [Franklin Haven]. ALS. MH-H. mDW 17677. W & S, 16: 340. Asks Haven if he would consent to serve temporarily as receiver general in Boston.

Feb 25   To John Plummer Healy. ALS. MHi. mDW 38552. Expresses surprise to hear of dissatisfaction over appointments in Boston, but insists that competence must be the first test of fitness for office.

Feb 25   To Israel Keech Tefft. ALS. GHi. mDW 17678. Acknowledges a certificate of honorary membership in the Georgia Historical Society.

Feb 25   From Samuel Atkinson. ALS. NhHi. mDW 17680. Introduces William Duane Wilson, former publisher of the Pittsburgh *Daily Advertiser.*

Feb 25   Applications from Babcock & Wildman, for the *New Haven* (Conn.) *Palladium*—public printers (LS. DNA, RG 59. mDW 52820); from Gurdon S. Hubbard (ALS. MWalB. mDW 17682); from Peleg Sprague—judge in Massachusetts (ALS. MWalB. mDW 17690).

Feb 25   Recommendations from Joseph Hopkinson, for Jacob Gratz (ALS. DNA, RG 56. mDWs); from Samuel Hubbard and Charles Scudder, for Gurdon S. Coit—despatch agent in New York (LS. MWalB. mDW 17685); from Isaac Munroe, for Brantz Mayer (ALS. MWalB. mDW 17687).

Feb 26   Applications from Beverly Allen—attorney in Missouri (ALS. MWalB. mDW 17693); from Burrington Anthony—marshal in Rhode Island (Facsimile. NhD. mDWs); from Charles Cist—superintendent of the census (ALS. MWalB. mDW 17697).

Feb 26   Recommendations from William Bradford Reed, for Ralph W. Pomeroy—marshal in Pennsylvania (ALS. MWalB. mDW 17701); from Peleg Sprague, for Sylvanus W. Robinson—district attorney in Maine (ALS. MWalB. mDW 17703); from Thaddeus Stevens, for John Dickey—comptroller or auditor (ALS. MWalB. mDW 17705); from Samuel Slaughter, for William B. Slaughter—governor of Wisconsin (ALS. MWalB. mDW 17707); from William H. Tuck, for John Bozman Kerr—secretary to a European legation (ALS. MWalB. mDW 17710).

Feb 27   From Herman Cope. ALS. MWalB. mDW 17713. Encloses a copy of DW's agreement with BUS.

Feb 27   From Jacob Harvey. ALS. NhHi. mDW 17723. Offers to help mediate dispute with Britain in unofficial capacity through his personal acquaintance with Lords Lansdowne and Monteagle.

Feb 27   Agreement with the Bank of the United States. DS. MWalB. mDW 39835-295. Conveyance of DW's western lands to BUS to liquidate indebtedness.

Feb 27   Applications from George Dawson, for the *Detroit Daily Advertiser*—public printer (ALS. DNA, RG 59. mDW 52741); from Joseph Webster Hale—despatch agent (ALS. MWalB. mDW 17719).

Feb 27   Recommendations from William Green, for William B. Slaughter (ALS. MWalB. mDW 17715); from Jacob Harvey, for Mr. Bremner—consul at Paris (ALS. NhHi. mDW 17727).
Feb 28   From John Pendleton Kennedy. Printed. Henry T. Tuckerman, *The Life of John Pendleton Kennedy* (New York, 1871), p. 179. Responds to DW's proposition to make him undersecretary of state.
Feb 28   Recommendations from Nicholas Biddle, for Thomas Hayes—naval agent, Philadelphia (ALS draft. DLC. mDW 17729); from Nicholas Biddle, for Robert E. Griffith—consul at Marseilles (ALS. DLC. mDW 17730); from Richard Thomas, for John Bozman Kerr (ALS. MWalB. mDW 17732).
[Feb]   To Nicholas Biddle.   94
[Feb]   To Nicholas Biddle. ALS. DLC. mDW 17739. Lists the cabinet posts which have been filled.
[Feb]   Memorandum on settlement of DW's account with the Bank of the United States. AD. MWalB. mDW 17740.
Feb   Recommendations from Edward Kent, for Joseph Webster Hale—consulate at Havre (ALS. MWalB. mDW 17741); from William Campbell Preston, for Andrew R. Govan—marshal in Mississippi (LS. MWalB. mDW 17743); from Richard Wigginton Thompson, for Thomas B. Johnson (ALS. MWalB. mDW 17746).
March 1   From Herman Le Roy. LS by proxy. NhHi. mDW 17766. Introduces Brenton Boggs.
March 1   Applications from Charles Miner—governor of Iowa (ALS. MWalB. mDW 17770); from William B. Taylor (ALS. MWalB. mDW 17774).
March 1   Receipt from John Wilson: $18.33 for wood. ADS. NhHi. mDW 39838.
March 1   Recommendations from John Banks, for John P. Hiester (ALS. MWalB. mDW 17748); from John Macpherson Berrien et al., for Ambrose Baber—chargé at Sardinia, and John S. Calhoun—consul at Havana (ALS by Berrien, signed also by others. MWalB. mDW 17750); from Hugh Birckhead, for Brantz Mayer (ALS. MWalB. mDW 17752); from William Crawford, for Samuel T. Brown—district attorney, Alabama (ALS. MWalB. mDW 17754); from John Dennis, for John Pinto—unspecified post (ALS. NhHi. mDW 17757); from Richard Fletcher, for Theophilus Parsons (ALS. MB. mDWs); from Charles King, for Jeremiah H. Pierson—consul at Marseilles (ALS. MWalB. mDW 17759); from James Gore King, for James Hagerty—consul at Liverpool (ALS. MWalB. mDW 17761); from Henry Smith Lane and James Rariden, for Thomas B. Johnson (ALS by Lane, signed also by Rariden. MWalB. mDW 17764); from Josiah S. Little, for John T. P. Dumont (ALS. MWalB. mDW 17768); from Samuel Osgood, for Solomon Warriner—paymaster, Springfield (ALS. DNA, RG 156. mDWs); from B. Peters, for the Philadelphia *National Gazette*—public printer (ALS. DNA, RG 59. mDW 52238); from Marcus Smith, for A. D. Coombs—chargé at Texas (ALS. MWalB. mDW 17772); from James Thomas, for John Bozman Kerr (ALS. MWalB. mDW 17780); from Thomas Washington, for Hardin P. Bostwick—marshal in Tennessee (ALS. MWalB.

mDW 17782); from Thurlow Weed, for the *Albany Daily Advertiser*—public printer (ALS. DNA, RG 59. mDW 52287).

March 2   From George Evans. ALS. NhHi. mDW 17794. Introduces
Abraham Rich.

March 2   Applications from Arthur M. Eastman—auditor, State Department (ALS. MWalB. mDW 17791); from George Kent—secretary
of a legation (ALS. MWalB. mDW 17803); from Cyrus Perkins—
consul, Bordeaux (ALS. MWalB. mDW 17809); from Samuel R.
Spelman—despatch agent, New York (ALS. MWalB. mDW 17995).

March 2   Recommendations from Nicholas Biddle, for James
Robertson—customs officer, Philadelphia (ALS draft. DLC.
mDW 17785); from Nicholas Biddle, for [Thomas L.] McKenney
(ALS draft. DLC. mDW 17786); from William Cranch, for John
Carroll Brent—consul at Paris (ALS. NhHi. mDW 17787); from
Garrett Davis, for Henry Lenba—chargé or secretary of a legation
(ALS. MWalB. mDW 17789); from David A. Hall, for Jacob A. Ben-
der—warden of Washington penitentiary (ALS. MWalB. mDW
17796); from Franklin Haven, for Jonas L. Sibley—marshal, Massa-
chusetts (ANS. MWalB. mDW 17799; from Mark Healey, for
Jonas L. Sibley (ALS. MWalB. mDW 17799); from Edward Kent,
for John T. P. Dumont (ALS. MWalB. mDW 17801); from Benja-
min Watkins Leigh, for John Randolph Clay—chargé, Vienna (ALS.
MWalB. mDW 17806); from Kenneth Rayner, for Daniel Jenifer
(ALS. MWalB. mDW 17812); from Benjamin Swift, for the St.
Albans *Franklin Messenger*—public printer (ALS. DNA, RG 59.
mDW 52817); from Richard H. Vose, for John T. P. Dumont
(ALS. MWalB. mDW 17815).

March 3   From David Bayard Ogden. ALS. NhHi. mDW 17834. Introduces Major White.

March 3   From John Crafts Wright. ALS. NhD. mDW 17842. Asks for
documentation to refute charge that DW supported the Hartford
Convention.

March 3   Applications from Armand Auboyneau—consul, La Rochelle
(ALS. NhHi. mDW 17817); from John T. P. Dumont (ALS. MWalB.
mDW 17828); from William Wyllys Pratt—despatch agent, New
York (ALS. MWalB. mDW 17836); from William Leete Stone, for
the New York *Commercial Advertiser* (ALS. DNA, RG 59. mDW
52299); from Enoch R. Whiting, for the St. Albans *Franklin Messenger* (ALS. DNA, RG 59. mDW 52318).

March 3   Recommendations from Hugh Birckhead, for William O. Niles
et al.—various posts (ALS. NhHi. mDW 17820); from William Key
Bond et al., for the *Cincinnati Gazette*—public printer (ADS. DNA,
RG 59. mDW 53009); from William Leigh Brent, for John Carroll
Brent (LS. NhHi. mDW 17824); from William C. Dawson, for
Waddy Thompson (ALS. MWalB. mDW 17826); from Theodore
Frelinghuysen, for Charles Johnson McCurdy—chargé, Naples
(ALS. MWalB. mDW 17830); from William Henry, for a Bellows
Falls, Vt., paper—public printer (ALS. DNA, RG 59. mDW 52805);
from Willie Person Mangum, for Hardin P. Bostick (ALS. MWalB.
mDW 17832); from William Bradford Reed, for Thomas Connell—

marshal, Pennsylvania (ALS. MWalB. mDW 17838); from Samuel
Sprigg, for Mordecai Yarnall—marshal, Virginia (ALS. MWalB.
mDW 17840); from Charles Vezin, for Arnold Hallback—consul,
Duchy of Baden (ALS. MWalB. mDWs).

[March 4]   To [James Trecothick Austin]. ALS. NhD. mDW 17392. Discusses plans for a court appearance in *Rhode Island* v.
Massachusetts.

March 4   From John Holmes. ALS. MWalB. mDW 17868. Sends proposal on boundary controversy for the President's consideration.

March 4   Applications from Robert Andrews—consul, Paris (ALS.
NhHi. mDW 17847); from Charles Crocker—bearer of despatches
(ALS. MWalB. mDW 17854); from Dobbin, Murphy & Bose, for the
Baltimore American and Daily Commercial Advertiser—public
printer (LS. DNA, RG 59. mDW 52597); from David Kidder—
bearer of despatches (ALS. MWalB. mDW 17870); from Solomon
Lincoln—collector of customs, Boston (ALS copy. MHi. mDW
17872); from Charles Miner (ALS. MWalB. mDW 17875).

March 4   Recommendations from Thomas Adams, for Gurdon S. Coit
(ALS. MWalB. mDW 17845); from Heman Allen, for the St. Albans
Franklin Messenger (ALS. DNA, RG 59. mDW 52815); from Wil-
liam W. Boardman et al., for William R. Hayes—consul, Barbados
(ALS by Boardman, signed also by others. MWalB. mDW 17849);
from William W. Boardman et al., for the Hartford *Connecticut
Courant*, the *New Haven Palladium*, the *Norwich* (Conn.) *Courier*—
public printers (LS. DNA, RG 59. mDW 52824); from Luther Bradish, for Clark Robinson (ALS. MWalB. mDW 17850); from Zadoc
Casey, for William Prentiss—marshal, Illinois (ALS. MWalB.
mDW 17852); from James Dellet, for the Huntsville, Alabama,
Southern Advocate—public printer (ALS. DNA, RG 59. mDW
52639); from James Duane Doty, for Paraclete Potter—secretary,
Wisconsin; for Mortimer M. Jackson—attorney, Wisconsin; for
John F. Potter—marshal, Wisconsin (ALS. MWalB. mDW 17856);
from William Pitt Fessenden, for [?]—clerkship (ALS. MWalB.
mDW 17864); from John Moore, for George Mason Graham—sec-
retary of legation, France (ALS. MWalB. mDW 17877); from John J.
Pearson, for John P. Hiester (ALS. MWalB. mDW 18016); from
Samuel J. Phelps, for John Pettes—marshal, Vermont (ALS.
MWalB. mDW 17879); from Samuel Prentiss et al., for the Mont-
pelier *Vermont Watchman and State Journal*—public printer (ADS.
DNA, RG 59. mDW 52808); from James Rariden, for Lott Bloom-
field—marshal, Indiana (ALS. MWalB. mDW 17881); from Oliver
Hampton Smith and James Rariden, for the *Richmond* (Ind.) *Palladium* and the Indianapolis *Indiana Journal*—public printers
(ALS by Smith, signed also by Rariden. DNA, RG 59. mDW 52759);
from Kenneth Rayner, for Waddy Thompson (ALS. MWalB. mDW
17883); from M. B. Townsend et al., for Timothy Darling (ALS by
Townsend, signed also by others. NhHi. mDW 17886); from Robert Charles Winthrop, for Henry Bass—naval storekeeper, Charlestown, Mass. (ALS. DLC. mDW 17888); from Robert Charles Winthrop, for Nathaniel Amory—consul, Havana (ALS. MWalB. mDW

17890); from Robert Charles Winthrop, for John Langdon Sibley—
congressional librarian (ALS. MWalB. mDW 17892).

March 5   From William Burns (with James Coleman Fisher to DW,
March 6, 1841). ALS. NhHi. mDW 17958. Introduces James Coleman Fisher.

March 5   From Lewis Cass. ALS. NhD. mDW 17894. *Diplomatic Papers*,
1. Warns that Britain would regard the execution of Alexander Mc-
Leod as an act of war and may already be preparing to attack New
York.

March 5   From John Todd Stuart. ALS. NhHi. mDW 17931. Introduces
Silas Reed of Rock Island, Ill.

March 5   Applications from Calvin Colton—Indian commissioner or
consul, Paris (ALS. NhHi. mDW 17900); from James O. Law
(ALS. NhHi. mDW 17919); from Brantz Mayer (ALS. MWalB.
mDW 17921); from John Langdon Sibley (ALS. MWalB. mDW
17925); from George F. Usher (ALS. NhHi. mDW 17934); from
Nathaniel Parker Willis—secretary of a legation (ALS. MWalB.
mDW 17938).

March 5   Commission of DW as secretary of state. Printed document,
with MS insertions. NhHi. mDW 17942.

March 5   Recommendations from James Garland, for T. Stanhope Mc-
Cleland—chargé, Italy (ALS. MWalB. mDW 17908); from Moses
Hicks Grinnell, for Washington Irving—consul, Paris (ALS. NhHi.
mDW 17910); from Ira Haselton et al., for Frederick A. Franklin—
consul, Pictou (LS. NhHi. mDW 17913); from Reverdy Johnson, for
George Huyler—consul, Nassau (ALS. NhHi. mDW 17916); from
R. W. Holman, for Solomon Warriner (ALS. DNA, RG 156. mDWs);
from Josiah Randall, for Ralph W. Pomeroy (ALS. MWalB. mDW
17923); from Edward Stanly, for Waddy Thompson (ALS. MWalB.
mDW 17928); from John Todd Stuart, for Abraham Lincoln—
chargé, Bogota (Copy. MAnP. mDW 17933); from Garret Dorset
Wall, for Daniel C. Croxall—consul, Marseilles (ALS. DLC. mDW
17935); from Robert Charles Winthrop, for Nathaniel Amory
(ALS. MWalB. mDW 17940).

March 5   Senate resolution consenting to the appointments of Daniel
Webster, Thomas Ewing, John Bell, George E. Badger, and John J.
Crittenden. DS. DNA, RG 59. mDW 55161.

March 6   From John Bell. ALS. DNA, RG 59. mDW 54501. Accepts appointment as secretary of war.

March 6   From Alfred Cuthbert. Printed. Washington *Daily Globe*, April
2, 1841. Asks DW his opinion whether Congress has constitutional
authority to prohibit interstate slave trade.

March 6   From Thomas Ewing. ALS. DNA, RG 59. mDW 54480. Accepts appointment as secretary of the treasury.

March 6   Applications from Noyes Barber—commissioner of patent
office (ALS. MWalB. mDW 17948); from Joseph Webster Hale
(ALS. MWalB. mDW 17964); from Samuel R. Spelman (ALS.
MWalB. mDW 17993); from Richard R. Ward (ALS. MWalB. mDW
17996); from T. G. Woodward, for the New Haven *Connecticut Herald*—public printer (ALS. DNA, RG 59. mDW 52829).

March 6   Recommendations from Henry Baldwin, for Henry C. Bos-
ler—marshal, Pennsylvania (ALS. MWalB. mDW 17945); from
James Barbour, for William M. Rives—marshal, Mississippi (ALS.
MWalB. mDW 17951); from Daniel Dewey Barnard, for the *Albany
Daily Advertiser* (ANS. DNA, RG 59. mDW 52289); from David
Paul Brown, for William White—marshal, Pennsylvania (ALS.
MWalB. mDW 17953); from Charles A. Dewey, for Charles H.
Warren (ALS. MHi. mDWs); from James Coleman Fisher, for
Samuel J. Fisher—consul, Paris (ALS. NhHi. mDW 17955); from
John Fitz, for Isaac Fitz—despatch agent, New York (ALS. MWalB.
mDW 17960); from James Garland, for Joseph Marks—consul, La
Rochelle or Rotterdam (ALS. NhHi. mDW 17962); from James
Graham, for the Asheville, North Carolina, *Highland Messenger,*
Raleigh (N.C.) *Register,* and *Newbern* (N.C.) *Spectator*—public
printers (ALS. DNA, RG 59. mDW 52326); from Robert E. Hornor,
for Brantz Mayer (ALS. MWalB. mDW 17967); from John Leeds
Kerr, for Robert C. Wright (ALS. NhHi. mDW 17970); from J. Lee,
for Waddy Thompson (ALS. MWalB. mDW 17971); from John
Moore et al., for George Mason Graham—consul, Paris (LS. MWalB.
mDW 17974); from Samuel Moore, for Samuel J. Fisher (ALS.
NhHi. mDW 17977); from David Bayard Ogden, for Isaac Fitz (ALS.
MWalB. mDW 17979); from Samuel Prentiss, for [?]—marshal,
Vermont (ALS. MWalB. mDW 17981); from Kenneth Rayner, for
Frederick C. Hill—chargé, Venezuela (ALS. MWalB. mDW 17983);
from Kenneth Rayner, for James C. Jones—marshal, Tennessee
(ALS. MWalB. mDW 17985); from Kenneth Rayner, for Z. Collins
Lee—attorney, Maryland (ALS. MWalB. mDW 17987); from James
Rope, for Alexander W. Foster—auditor, Treasury Department
(ALS. MWalB. mDW 17991); from Robert Wickliffe, Jr., for Wil-
liam B. Blackburn, Jr.—marshal, Kentucky (ALS. MWalB. mDW
17998).

March 6   DW's oath of office. DS, with AN. DNA, RG 59. mDW 55176.

March 7   Recommendations from Henry Marie Brackenridge, for William H. Rupp—marshal, Pennsylvania (ALS. MWalB. mDW 18002);
from Alden Bradford, for Thomas G. Bradford—secretary to a legation (ALS. MWalB. mDW 18004); from John H. Eaton, for Joseph R. Croskey—chargé, Central America (ALS. MWalB. mDW
18007); from William Alexander Graham, for C. P. Green—chargé,
Texas (ALS. MWalB. mDW 18009); from William Hiester, for
John P. Hiester (ALS. MWalB. mDW 18001); from J. Glancy Jones,
for William Wyatt (ALS. MWalB. mDW 18024); from William D.
Merrick, for John Bozman Kerr (ALS. MWalB. mDW 18028); from
Waddy Thompson, Jr., for Bushrod W. Bell—marshal, Alabama
(ALS. MWalB. mDW 18031); from Elisha Whittlesey and John
William Allen, for Thomas D. Trebb—despatch bearer (ALS by
Whittlesey, signed also by Allen. MWalB. mDW 18033).

March 8   To Francis Granger. Printed DS with MS insertions. NhD.
mDWs. Encloses Granger's commission as postmaster general.

March 8   From James H. Birch. ALS. MWalB. mDW 18037. Offers suggestions for appointments in Missouri.

March 8   From Henry Stephen Fox. ALS. DLC. mDW 18058. Presents
compliments and encloses a copy of the address he will deliver to
the President.

March 8   From Francis Granger. ALS. DNA, RG 59. mDW 54651. Accepts appointment as postmaster general.

March 8   From Cassius F. Lee. ALS. DNA, RG 59. mDW 54522. Lists
the dates when the commissions of various justices of the peace for
Alexandria are due to expire.

March 8   From Ann Smith. ALS. NhHi. mDW 18077. Introduces her
son, Daniel.

March 8   Applications from John A. Blake—warden, Washington penitentiary (ALS. MWalB. mDW 18039); from George A. Diggs—congressional librarian (ALS. MWalB. mDW 18051); from Alexander W. Foster (ALS. MWalB. mDW 18056); from Thomas P. Jones
(ALS. MWalB. mDW 18060); from John Peters—despatch agent,
New York (ALS. MWalB. mDW 18072).

March 8   Recommendations from Nicholas Biddle, for [Thomas W.?]
Sutherland—surveyor, Philadelphia (ALS draft. DLC. mDW
18035); from Edward Carrington, for Peter W. Snow—consul, Canton (ALS. MWalB. 18043); from Charles W. Cutter and Joel Eastman, for the *New Hampshire Statesman* (ALS by Cutter, signed
also by Eastman. DNA, RG 59. mDW 52866); from William C. Dawson, for William Wyatt (ALS. MWalB. mDW 18045); from William C.
Dawson, for Richard R. Cuyler—district attorney, Georgia (ALS.
MWalB. mDW 18047); from William C. Dawson, for Neil McNair
or Benton Walton—marshal, Georgia (ALS. MWalB. mDW 18049);
from Alexander P. Field, for William Prentiss (ALS. MWalB. mDW
18054); from Dixon H. Lewis, for Bushrod W. Bell (ALS. MWalB.
mDW 18062); from John Strother Pendleton, for C. P. Green (ALS.
MWalB. mDW 18066); from Cyrus Perkins, for Samuel J. Fisher
(ALS. NhHi. mDW 18068); from Charles Scott Todd, for John
Todd—marshal, Illinois (ALS. MWalB. mDW 18087); from Winfield Scott, for Robert Campbell—state department post (ALS.
NRU. mDW 18074); from Richard Smith, for George Mason Graham (ALS. MWalB. mDW 18080); from Thaddeus Stevens, for
Charles Naylor—district attorney, Pennsylvania (ALS. MWalB.
mDW 18083); from Joseph Leonard Tillinghast, for Samuel H. Wal-
ley, Jr. (ALS. MWalB. mDW 18085); from William Wyatt, for the
Tallahassee *Star of Florida*—public printer (ALS. DNA, RG 59.
mDW 52338).

March 9   To Benjamin Rush. LS. NjP. mDW 18089. Informs Rush that
he will be reimbursed for expenses incurred as bearer of despatches
from London to Washington last summer.

March 9   From A. B. Chambers. ALS. MWalB. mDW 18093. Discusses
the distribution of patronage in Missouri.

March 9   From [James Morrison]. AL draft. UkLG. mDW 18098. Reports British parties generally desire peace; discusses efforts in Parliament to revise British import duties.

March 9   Applications from Crum & Bailey, for the Bloomington *Iowa
Standard*—public printer (LS. DNA, RG 59. mDW 52961); from

Jonathan Elliot—consul, Paris (ALS. NhHi. mDW 18097); from William Henry Russell—marshal, Missouri (ALS. MWalB. mDW 18106).

March 9   Recommendations from Elisha Hunt Allen, for John Ruggles (ALS. MWalB. mDW 18091); from George W. Crabb, for the Tuscaloosa, Alabama, *Independent Monitor*—public printer (ALS. DNA, RG 59. mDW 52641); from John W. Crocket, for George A. Sublett—marshal, Tennessee (ALS. MWalB. mDW 18095); from John Davis (1787–1854), for Galen Ames (ALS. DNA, RG 156. mDWs); from James Duane Doty, for the *Milwaukee Sentinel* and *Madison* (Wis.) *Express*—public printers (ALS. DNA, RG 59. mDW 52723); from William Campbell Preston, for Andrew R. Govan (ALS. MWalB. mDW 18102); from William Cabell Rives, for Alexander Spotswood Henry—despatch bearer (ALS. MWalB. mDW 18104); from Richard Henry Wilde, for George W. Greene—consul, Rome (ALS. NhHi. mDW 18109).

March 10   From Samuel Lewis Southard and Jacob Welsh Miller. LS. MWalB. mDW 18144. Ask to be informed in advance of any appointments that are to be made in New Jersey.

March 10   Applications from W. Van Benthuysen, on behalf of Charles King, for the *New York American*—public printer (ALS. DNA, RG 59. mDW 52297); from Pierce Mason Butler—governor, Florida (ALS. MWalB. mDW 18115); from Daniel G. Garnsey—governor, Iowa (ALS. MWalB. mDW 18129); from Isaac Munroe, for the *Baltimore Patriot*—public printer (ALS. DNA, RG 59. mDW 52849); from William W. Norvell—consul, Rio de Janeiro (ALS. NhHi. mDW 18141); from James E. Wharton, for the *Wheeling* (Va.) *Times and Advertiser*—public printer (ALS. DNA, RG 59. mDW 52955).

March 10   Recommendations from Isaac Chapman Bates, for Mr. Schillow—consul, Prussia (ALS. NhHi. mDW 18113); from John O. Choules, for Clark Robinson (ALS. MWalB. mDW 18117); from A. L. Eastman, for John F. Potter (ALS. MWalB. mDW 18371); from William P. Elliott, against Thomas P. Jones (ALS. MWalB. mDW 18119); from William Wolcott Ellsworth, for Henry Leavitt Ellsworth—commissioner of patents (ALS. MWalB. mDW 18122); from George Evans, for John T. P. Dumont (ALS. MWalB. mDW 18124); from Rice Garland, for Taylor Henderson—attorney, Louisiana (ALS. MWalB. mDW 18126); from Rice Garland, for the *Opelousas* (La.) *Gazette* and the Alexandria, Louisiana, *Red River Whig*—public printers (ALS. DNA, RG 59. mDW 52625); from John McLean, for Courtland Cushing—district attorney, Indiana (ALS. MWalB. mDW 18132); from John McLean, for George A. Sublett (ALS. MWalB. mDW 18135); from John McLean, for William Prentiss (ALS. MWalB. mDW 18137); from William D. Merrick, for John Ruggles (ALS. MWalB. mDW 18139); from Oliver Hampton Smith, for John Ruggles (ALS. MWalB. mDW 18142); from Hugh White, for Henry White—marshal, New York (ALS. MWalB. mDW 18146).

March 11   To William Thomas Carroll. AL (signature removed). DNA,

RG 267. mDWs. Requests a certified copy of the Supreme Court's decision in the *Amistad* case.

March 11 To Andrew Stevenson. ALS. DLC. mDW 18148. Introduces W. W. Mann of Georgia.

March 11 From Thomas Sewall. ALS. MWalB. mDW 18166. Introduces F. Garrettson Luckey.

March 11 Applications from Jacob Gratz (ALS. DNA, RG 56. mDWs); from William Henry Russell (ALS. MWalB. mDW 18164).

March 11 Recommendations from Nicholas Biddle, for Kenderton Smith—marshal, Pennsylvania (ALS. MWalB. mDW 18152); from George Evans, for John Ruggles (ALS. MWalB. mDW 18154); from John Henderson, for William Wyatt (ALS. MWalB. mDW 18156); from Willie Person Mangum, for C. P. Green (ALS. MWalB. mDW 18159); from Charles B. Penrose, for H. G. Morrell—secretary, Iowa (ALS. MWalB. mDW 18162); from James Scott, for the *People's Gazette* (ALS. DNA, RG 59. mDW 52761); from James Wilson, for Samuel W. Carr—marshal, Mississippi (ALS. MWalB. mDW 18168); from [William Woodbridge], for J. W. Weston—unspecified post (AL draft. MiD-B. mDW 18171).

March 12 From Horatio Greenough. Printed. Nathalia Wright, ed., *Letters of Horatio Greenough* (Madison, 1972), pp. 302–305. Submits an account of expenses incurred in modeling a statue of Washington commissioned by the U.S. government.

March 12 From Edgerton Vernon Harcourt. ALS. DLC. mDW 18175. Curtis, 2 : 62. Discusses the McLeod and boundary controversies; hopes a rupture between Britain and the United States can be averted.

March 12 Applications from F. Garrettson Luckey—despatch agent, New York (ALS. MWalB. mDW 18205); from Edward D. Mansfield, for the *Cincinnati Chronicle*—public printer (ALS. DNA, RG 59. mDW 52716); from William Bennett Parker—consul, Buenos Aires (ALS. MWalB. mDW 18207); from John H. Williams, for the Frederick, Maryland, *Examiner*—public printer (ALS. DNA, RG 59. mDW 52841).

March 12 Recommendations from William Leigh Brent, for John Carroll Brent (ALS. NhHi. mDW 18172); from James Duane Doty, for the *Iowa Standard* and the Burlington *Hawk-Eye and Iowa Patriot*—public printers (ALS. DNA, RG 59. mDW 52959); from James Duane Doty, for Henry Williams—marshal, Wisconsin (ALS. MWalB. mDW 18180); from William Wolcott Ellsworth, for Thomas Cowles—marshal, Connecticut (ALS. MWalB. mDW 18182); from Nathaniel Torrey, for Solomon Warriner (ALS. DNA, RG 156. mDWs); from John Tyler, for John Strother Pendleton—diplomatic post, South America (ALS. NhD. mDW 18210); from William Woodbridge, for David E. Harbough—district attorney, Michigan (ALS draft. MiD-B. mDW 18212).

March 13 To Franklin Haven.   95

March 13 To Ogden Hoffman. ALS. Noel J. Cortes, Philadelphia, Pa. mDW 18219. Has signed Hoffman's commission as U.S. attorney for southern New York.

March 13 From James D. Graham. ALS. DNA, RG 59. mDW 56732. Presents draft for $1000 to pay for instruments ordered for surveying northeast boundary.

March 13 Application from William Bennett Parker (ALS. MWalB. mDW 18232).

March 13 Recommendations from John William Allen, for Francis Randall (ALS. MWalB. mDW 18220); from William S. Archer, for James Points—marshal, Virginia (ALS. MWalB. mDW 18222); from Thomas Clowes, for Clark Robinson (ALS. MWalB. mDW 18225); from James Duane Doty, for Daniel Hugunin—marshal, Wisconsin (ALS. MWalB. mDW 18228); from Charles Downing, for the Tallahassee *Florida Sentinel* or *Star* and the St. Augustine *News*—public printers (ALS. DNA, RG 59. mDW 52343); from Jonathan McCarty, for Thomas B. Johnson (ALS. MWalB. mDW 18230); from Samuel Prentiss, for John Ruggles (ALS. MWalB. mDW 18234); from Joseph Lanier Williams, for Mr. Grigsby—consul, Bordeaux (ALS. MWalB. mDW 18236).

March 14 To John Jordan Crittenden (with William Henry Harrison to JJC, March 15, 1841). ALS. NcD. mDW 18239. Says that he will furnish Crittenden with instructions and documents relative to the Alexander McLeod case and asks for suggestions.

March 14 Recommendations from Reverdy Johnson, for the *Baltimore American* (ALS. DNA, RG 59. mDW 52593); from Jacob Lendley, for William R. Downing—consul, Canton (ALS. MWalB. mDW 18250); from George H. Proffit, for Thomas B. Johnson (ALS. MWalB. mDW 18252).

March 15 To Henry Clay. LS. DLC. mDW 18254. Deems it essential that consulship at Paris be filled; discusses allowance.

March 15 To John Jordan Crittenden. LS. NcD. mDW 18257. *Diplomatic Papers*, 1. Gives detailed instructions for JJC's mission to New York in connection with McLeod trial.

March 15 From Lewis Cass. ALS. NhD. mDW 18283. *Diplomatic Papers*, 1. Comments on prospect of war with England.

March 15 From Alfred Cuthbert. AN. DLC. mDW 18294. Washington *Globe*, April 2, 1841. Requests a reply to his written communication of March 6.

March 15 To Alfred Cuthbert. Printed. Washington *Globe*, April 2, 1841. Declines correspondence under present circumstances; refers Cuthbert to his past speeches on slavery and to his exchange with John Bolton in 1833.

March 15 Applications from Robert E. Hornor, for the *Princeton* (N.J.) *Whig*—public printer (ALS. DNA, RG 59. mDW 52275); from Jonathan Meredith—attorney, Ohio (ALS. DLC. mDW 18301).

March 15 Recommendations from Nicholas Biddle, for Davis B. Stacey—consul, Liverpool (ALS. MWalB. mDW 18281); from Elihu Chauncey, for Nathan Sargent—unspecified post (ALS. MWalB. mDW 18287); from Thomas W. Chinn, for the St. Francisville *Louisiana Chronicle*—public printer (ALS. DNA, RG 59. mDW 52637); from Thomas Clayton, for John Bozman Kerr (ALS. MWalB. mDW 18289); from William Cranch, for Philip Richard Fendall—attorney, District of Columbia (ALS. MWalB. mDW

18291); from William Hembel et al., for Thomas P. Jones (LS.
MWalB. mDW 18925); from William Hiester et al., for the Harrisburg *Pennsylvania Intelligencer*—public printer (LS. DNA, RG 59.
mDW 52240); from Richard Mentor Johnson, for Isaac Clark—
penitentiary warden, Washington (ALS. MWalB. mDW 18299);
from William Cabell Rives, for John Bozman Kerr (ALS. MWalB.
mDW 18303); from B[enjamin Babcock?] Thurston, for Philip Richard Fendall (ALS. MWalB. mDW 18292); from Weld Jenks et al.,
for John C. Pedrick—consul, Rio de Janeiro (ADS. NhHi. mDW
18523).

March 16   *To Washington Irving.*   95
March 16   From Charles Downing. ALS. MWalB. mDW 18312. Dis-
agrees with the view that reappointing Richard Keith Call governor
of Florida would provoke serious opposition.
March 16   From Horatio Greenough. Printed. Nathalia Wright, ed., *Let-
ters of Horatio Greenough* (Madison, 1972), pp. 306–307. Dis-
cusses the problem of shipping his statue of Washington to the
United States and also the choice of material to be used in a group
sculpture for the Capitol.
March 16   From Charles C. Mills. ALS. MWalB. mDW 18319. Calls for
the removal of Governor Robert Raymond Reid of Florida.
March 16   From Robert Raymond Reid. ALS. MWalB. mDW 18324.
Plans to reply soon to the charges made against him.
March 16   Applications from T. G. Broughton & Son, for the Norfolk,
Virginia, *Norfolk and Portsmouth Herald*—public printer (LS. DNA,
RG 59. mDW 52910); from Stephen Lawson—consul, Nassau
(ALS. NhHi. mDW 18314); from Henry Montgomery, for the *Har-
risburg* (Pa.) *Chronicle*—public printer (ALS. DNA, RG 59. mDW
52250); from M[ichael?] Phillips— appraiser in New York custom
house (ALS. DLC. mDW 18321).
March 16   Recommendations from Nicholas Biddle, for Thomas M.
Willing—consul, Paris (ALS. NhHi. mDW 18310); from W. B. Calhoun, for the *Springfield* (Mass.) *Gazette*—public printer (ALS.
DNA, RG 59. mDW 52900); from William S. Hastings, for the Worcester *Massachusetts Spy*—public printer (ALS. DNA, RG 59. mDW
52897); from Willie Person Mangum, for William Hardiman—marshal, Mississippi (ALS. MWalB. mDW 18317); from W. A. Crabb
et al., for the *Harrisburg* (Pa.) *Chronicle*—public printer (ALS.
DNA, RG 59. mDW 52252); from Joseph Leonard Tillinghast, for
William H. Smith—clerk, State Department (ALS. MWalB. mDW
18326); from Joseph Leonard Tillinghast, for Richard R. Ward
(ALS. MWalB. mDW 18328).
[March 17]   To Joseph Gales, Jr. AL. NhExP. mDW 18330. Accepts dinner invitation.
March 17   To William Henry Seward. Copy, endorsed by DW. NhHi.
mDW 18335. LS. NRU. mDW 18337. *Diplomatic Papers*, 1. Ex-
presses the President's thanks on hearing that WHS considers di-
recting a *nolle prosequi* in the McLeod proceeding.
March 17   From Isaac Rand Jackson. ALS copy. MdHi. mDW 18345.
Diplomatic Papers, 1. Asks about arranging for the remittance of
$2,000.

March 17   From Albert S. White. ALS. MWalB. mDW 18356. Asks that
the Indiana congressional delegation be given time to consult with
constituents concerning appointment of U.S. attorney and U.S.
marshal for their state.

March 17   Applications from Aaron H. Palmer—despatch agent, New
York (ALS. MWalB. mDW 18348); from George P. Putnam—des-
patch agent, London (ALS. MWalB. mDW 18351); from Harman C.
Westervelt—marshal, New York (ALS. MWalB. mDW 18354).

March 17   Recommendations from William S. Archer, for Peachy R.
Grattan—attorney, Florida (ALS. MWalB. mDW 18340); from Nathan Fellows Dixon, for John Jay Hyde—unspecified post (ALS.
MWalB. mDW 18343); from Robert Hanna, for the *Indiana Journal* (ALS. DNA, RG 59. mDW 52751); from Henry Lelar et al., for
John C. Pedrick (ADS. NhHi. mDW 18525); from John McLean,
for George W. Way—consulship (ALS. MWalB. mDW 18346).

March 18   From John Davis (1787–1854). ALS. DNA, RG 59. mDW
54739. Reports that Solomon Lincoln has been given the commission appointing him U.S. marshal for Massachusetts.

March 18   From Ogden Hoffman. LS. DNA, RG 59. mDW 54684. Acknowledges receipt of the commission appointing him U.S. attorney
for the southern district of New York.

March 18   From Solomon Lincoln. LS. DNA, RG 59. mDW 54741. Acknowledges receipt of the commission appointing him U.S. marshal
for Massachusetts.

March 18   From Charles B. Penrose. ALS. DNA, RG 59. mDW 54797.
Accepts appointment as solicitor of the Treasury.

March 18   From George Corbin Washington. ALS. MWalB. mDW
18378. Introduces Jacob Poe of Frederick County, Maryland.

March 18   Applications from Samuel S. Gaskins—clerkship, State Department (ALS. MWalB. mDW 18361); from Richard Henry Lee—
attorney, Pennsylvania (ALS. MWalB. mDW 18364); from John F.
Potter (ALS. MWalB. mDW 18368).

March 18   Recommendations from William S. Archer, for Mordecai
Yarnall (ALS. MWalB. mDW 18359); from Nehemiah Rice
Knight, for Francis M. Demond—consul, Matanzas (ALS. NhHi.
mDW 18363); from James Merrill, for Robert Plunket Maclay—
superintendent of armory, Harper's Ferry (ALS. DNA, RG 156.
mDWs); from George Ticknor, for Samuel Gridley Howe—secretary
of legation, Madrid (ALS. MWalB. mDW 18375); from Albert S.
White, for the *Richmond* (Ind.) *Palladium*, the *Indiana Journal*,
and the *Lafayette* (Ind.) *Free Press*—public printers (ALS. DNA,
RG 59. mDW 52757).

March 19   To Isaac Rand Jackson. ALS. MdHi. mDW 18380. *Diplomatic Papers*, 1. Asks him to send check and to come to Washington.

March 19   From Nicholas Biddle. ALS draft. DLC. mDW 18386. Discusses patronage.

March 19   Application from William Jones—marshal, New York (ALS.
MWalB. mDW 18388).

March 19   Recommendations from William S. Archer, for James Points
(ALS. MWalB. mDW 18382); from James Barbour, for John Strother Pendleton (ALS. MWalB. mDW 18384); from William Pitt

Fessenden, for the *Portland* (Me.) *Advertiser*—public printer (ALS.
DNA, RG 59. mDW 52854); from Nehemiah Rice Knight, for Jo-
siah L. James (ALS. MWalB. mDW 18391); from Daniel Law, for
George W. Greene—consul, Rome (ALS. NhHi. mDW 18394); from
Jeremiah Mason, for Franklin Dexter—attorney, Massachusetts
(ALS. MWalB. mDW 18397); from William Cabell Rives, for John
Strother Pendleton (ALS. MWalB. mDW 18401); from J. Washing-
ton Tyson, for John Williamson—recorder, General Land Office
(ALS. MWalB. mDW 18404); from Henry P. Van Bibber, for Fran-
cis Malbone Auboyneau (ALS. NhHi. mDW 18407); from Thomas
Wilson & Co., for Gideon T. Snow (ALS. NhHi. mDW 18410).

March 20   *To Thomas Ewing.*   96

March 20   To Joseph Hopkinson. ALS. PHi. mDW 18414. Discusses appointments of U.S. attorney and marshal for eastern Pennsylvania.

March 20   From Isaac Rand Jackson. ALS copy. MdHi. mDW 18420.
Diplomatic Papers, 1. Will bring "those papers" with him when he
comes to Washington.

March 20   From Elisha Whittlesey. ALS. DNA, RG 59. mDW 54891. Accepts appointment as auditor of the Treasury for the post office.

March 20   From John Williamson. ALS. DNA, RG 59. mDW 54899. Accepts appointment as recorder of the General Land Office.

March 20   Promissory note for $770.49 to Edward Curtis. ADS. NN.
mDW 39840.

March 20   Applications from Robert Plunket Maclay (ALS. DNA, RG 156.
mDWs); from James Fitz Randolph, for the New Brunswick, New
Jersey, *Fredonian*—public printer (ALS. DNA, RG 59. mDW 52277).

March 20   Recommendations from Elisha Hunt Allen, for John D. Kinsman (ALS. MWalB. mDW 18416); from George Nixon Briggs, for
Joseph K. Hartwell—state department post (ALS. MWalB.
mDW 18418); from Charles G. Loring, for Franklin Dexter (ALS.
MWalB. mDW 18421); from Charles F. Mayer, for Charles W.
Meyer—consul, Bordeaux (ALS. MWalB. mDW 18423); from Wil-
liam Morris Meredith, for Morton McMichael—marshal, Pennsyl-
vania (ALS. MWalB. mDW 18424); from George Poindexter, for
Woodville Latham—department clerk (ALS. MWalB. mDW
18427); from John T. Sargent, for John Langdon Sibley (ALS.
MWalB. mDW 18429); from William Leete Stone, for John F.
Bacon—consul, Nassau (LS. NhHi. mDW 18432).

March 22   From Robert C. Cornell. ALS. DNA, RG 59. mDW 54550.
Accepts commission as receiver general for New York.

March 22   From Joseph Hume. ALS. DLC. mDW 18448. Sends resolutions aproved by 120 members of Parliament endorsing the principle of free trade and asks for DW's views.

March 22   From James Renwick. ALS. DNA, RG 59. mDW 56734. Reports having drawn $1,000 from the account appropriated for the
northeast boundary survey.

March 22   From William Henry Seward. ALS draft. NRU. mDW 18455.
LS. DLC. mDW 18458. *Diplomatic Papers*, 1. Denies that he has decided to direct *nolle prosequi* in the McLeod case.

March 22   From [William Woodbridge]. ALS draft. MiD-B. mDW
18468. Discusses the distribution of patronage in Michigan.

March 22   Applications from Franklin Dexter (ALS. MWalB. mDW
18436); from William C. S. Guinness—despatch agent, New York
(ALS. MWalB. mDW 18446); from James Wilson, for the Steubenville, Ohio, *Western Herald and Steubenville Gazette*—public
printer (ALS. DNA, RG 59. mDW 52697).

March 22   Recommendations from Robert Bennie Cranston, for
George F. Usher (ALS. NhHi. mDW 18434); from Gabriel P. Disos-
way, for F. Garrettson Luckey (ALS. MWalB. mDW 18437); from
William Wolcott Ellsworth and Joseph Trumbull, for Joseph Har-
ris—consul, Matanzas (LS. MWalB. mDW 18440); from Samuel
Emison and John C. Clark, for J. B. Martin—marshal, Indiana
(LS. MWalB. mDW 18442); from John H. Ewing, for John L.
Gow—visitor to West Point (ALS. MWalB. mDW 18444); from
John W. Murdaugh, for the *Norfolk Herald* and the Portsmouth,
Virginia, *Times and Republican*—public printers (AL. DNA, RG 59.
mDW 52943); from Stephen Clarendon Phillips, for William A. Law-
rence—consul, Canton (ALS. MWalB. mDW 18450); from Silas
Reed and Daniel Greene Garnsey, for the Rock Island, Illinois,
Upper Mississippian—public printer (ALS by Reed, signed also by
Garnsey. DNA, RG 59. mDW 52774); from William Cabell Rives,
for William B. Slaughter (ALS. MWalB. mDW 18453); from [Wil-
liam Woodbridge], for James M. Edmunds—chargé, Texas (AL
draft. MiD-B. mDW 18461); from William Woodbridge, for Richard
Butler—secretary, Iowa (ALS draft. MiD-B. mDW 18464); from
William Woodbridge, for Joshua Howard—marshal, Michigan
(ALS draft. MiD-B. mDW 18468).

March 23   To Nicholas Biddle.   97

March 23   From Nicholas Biddle. ALS draft. DLC. mDW 18478. Asks
if Charles Scott Todd might be dissuaded from going to Austria.

March 23   From Moses Hicks Grinnell. ALS. MWalB. mDW 18487. Introduces William H. Trott.

March 23   From John Tyler. ALS. DLC. mDW 18499. Encloses a letter
from Judge Estill and asks that it be shown to the President.

March 23   Applications from Jacob A. Bender (ALS. MWalB. mDW
18476); from Charles Caldwell—despatch bearer (ALS. MWalB.
mDW 18482); from Thomas B. Johnson (ALS. MWalB. mDW
18492).

March 23   Recommendations from Anthony Barclay, for Henry A. W.
Barclay—consul, Rio de Janeiro (ALS. NhHi. mDW 18474); from
N. Bowditch Blunt, for Jacob Acker—marshal, New York (ALS.
MWalB. mDW 18480); from Thomas Clayton, for the Georgetown,
Delaware, *American Republican*—public printer (ALS. DNA, RG
59. mDW 52229); from Andrew Foster et al., for John C. Pedrick
(ADS. NhHi. mDW 18524); from John Gibson, for the New Or-
leans *True American*—public printer (ALS. MWalB. mDW 18485);
from Jonathan Prescott Hall, for Thaddeus B. Wakeman—com-
missioner of patents (LS. MWalB. mDW 18489); from Nathaniel
Pitcher Tallmadge, for John F. Bacon (ALS. NhHi. mDW 18495).

March 24   From Samuel Frothingham. ALS. DNA, RG 59. mDW
54641. Acknowledges receipt of his commission.

March 24   Applications from Francis Joseph Grund, for the Philadel-

phia *Daily Standard*—public printer (ALS. DNA, RG 59. mDW
52243); from William B. Kinney, for the *Newark Daily Advertiser*—
public printer (ALS. DNA, RG 59. mDW 52283); from Essex Ridley Livingston—European consulate (ALS. NhHi. mDW 18515);
from Samuel P. Skilton—naval storekeeper, Charlestown (ALS.
MWalB. mDW 18527).

March 24   Recommendations from Henry Edwards, for Amory Ed-
wards—consul, Rio de Janeiro (ALS. MWalB. mDW 18501); from
Theodore Frelinghuysen, for Elisha W. Chester—despatch agent,
New York (ALS. MWalB. mDW 18504); from William Hiester, for
John P. Hiester (ALS. MWalB. mDW 18507); from Abbott Law-
rence, for George A. Brown—consul, Liverpool (ALS. MWalB.
mDW 18511); from C. L. Mosby et al., for William W. Norvell (LS.
NhHi. mDW 18516); from William Patton, for Elisha W. Chester
(ALS. MWalB. mDW 18518); from John Pedrick, for John C. Ped-
rick (ALS. NhHi. mDW 18520); from John Pedrick et al., for John C.
Pedrick (ADS. NhHi. mDW 18522); from William Winston Seaton,
for Richard J. A. Culverwell—watchman, Washington (ALS.
MWalB. mDW 18643); from Robert Charles Winthrop, for John
Langdon Sibley and Edward Everett, foreign missions (ALS. MWalB.
mDW 18531).

March 25   To John Plummer Healy. ALS. MHi. mDW 18534. Encloses
a draft and asks him to take up an acceptance; complains of being
worn down by the demands of his office.

March 25   From "Amistad Committee." Copy. TNF. mDW 18542. Ask
that the Africans being held in custody by the U.S. marshal be furnished with bedding according to promise.

March 25   From Nicholas Biddle.   97

March 25   From Thomas Ewing. ALS. DNA, RG 59. mDW 54692. Requests that a commission be issued appointing Charles Hopkins solicitor of the General Land Office.

March 25   From [James Duane Doty] to Nicholas Biddle.   97

[March 25]   "The Call of Congress" (editorial). AD. NhD. mDW 18536.
National Intelligencer, March 27, 1841.

March 25   Applications from Albert G. Chadwick, for the St. Johnsbury,
Vermont, *Caledonian*—public printer (ALS. DNA, RG 59. mDW
52321); from Elisha W. Chester (ALS. MWalB. mDW 18546).

March 25   Recommendations from Erastus Brooks, for the *Portland Advertiser* (ALS. DNA, RG 59. mDW 52852); from Timothy Rix, for
the Haverhill, New Hampshire, *Whig and Aegis*—public printer
(ALS. DNA, RG 59. mDW 52861); from William D. Waples, for the
American Republican (ALS. DNA, RG 59. mDW 52231).

March 26   From Nicholas Biddle.   98

March 26   From John Chambers. ALS. DNA, RG 59. mDW 54538. Accepts appointment as governor of Iowa Territory.

March 26   From Theophilus Parsons. ALS. DLC. mDW 18574. Wants
to publish the reply of Massachusetts Whig senators to DW's resignation; discusses state politics.

March 26   Applications from James Bowen—watchman, State Department (ALS. MWalB. mDW 18555); from Charles Lemon—watchman, State Department (ALS. MWalB. mDW 18565).

March 26   Recommendations from William S. Archer, for Samuel T.
Brown (ALS. MWalB. mDW 18550); from James H. Birch, for the
Fayette, Missouri, *Boon's Lick Times*—public printer (ALS. DNA,
RG 59. mDW 52650); from James H. Birch, for William Henry
Russell (ALS. MWalB. mDW 18553); from William B. Calhoun, for
the *Springfield* (Mass.) *Republican*—public printer (ALS. DNA, RG
59. mDW 52895); from Edward Curtis, for Henry A. W. Barclay
(ALS. NhHi. mDW 18557); from Ogden Hoffman, for Robert F.
Winslow—marshal, New York City (ALS. MWalB. mDW 18559);
from Richard Lawrence, for his brother (ALS. MWalB. mDW
18561); from Joshua S. Layton, for the *American Republican* (ALS.
DNA, RG 59. mDW 52233); from Daniel D. T. Leech, for F. Garrettson Luckey (ALS. MWalB. mDW 18563); from James Monroe, for
George W. Slacum (ALS. NhHi. mDW 18569); from James Monroe, for William Whittier—consul, Cowes (ALS. MWalB. mDW
18571); from Leverett Saltonstall, for Levi Bixby—consul, Para-
maribo (ALS. NhHi. mDW 18577).

March 27   To William Hiester. AL draft. MWalB. mDW 18509. Reports
that he still has Hiester's son in mind for despatch bearer.

March 27   To Matthew St. Clair Clarke et al. Printed. *Works*, 6: 542–
543. Asks for a report of work under way on public buildings in
Washington.

March 27   From Herman Cope.   98

[March 27]   From Thomas Ewing. ALS. DNA, RG 59. mDW 54572.
Asks that a commission be issued appointing Jacob De La Motta
receiver general at Charleston.

March 27   From Edgar Snowden and Reuben Johnston. LS. DNA, RG
59. mDW 54836. Accept appointments as justices of the peace for
Alexandria.

March 27   Recommendations from Samuel Rossiter Betts, for Jeremiah H. Pierson (ALS. MWalB. mDW 18579); from Benjamin F.
Brookfield, for the *Newark Daily Advertiser* (ALS. DNA, RG 59.
mDW 52281); from Charles Stewart Daveis, for Essex Ridley Livingston (ALS. NhHi. mDW 18585); from George Fox et al., for
John F. Potter (ALS. MWalB. mDW 18373); from Thaddeus Stevens, for Joseph Ritner (ALS. DLC. mDW 18588); from John Talia-
ferro, for Richard W. Wheat—clerk, State Department (ALS.
MWalB. mDW 18592).

[March 28?]   To Thomas Ewing.   99
March 29   From Alfred Cuthbert.   100
March 29   From Richard Smith.   101

March 29   From William Stirling. ALS. MWalB. mDW 18610. Speaks
critically of his successor as U.S. consul at Barcelona; files a claim
for $75.

March 29   From Otho H. W. Stull. ALS. DNA, RG 59. mDW 54854.
Accepts appointment as secretary of Iowa Territory.

March 29   Applications from John Agg—to compile the *Biennial Register* (ALS. MWalB. mDW 18594); from James A. Young—consul,
Nantes (ALS. NhHi. mDW 18616).

March 29   Recommendations from James Bowen, for James Brooks—
marshal, New York (ALS. MWalB. mDW 18596); from James Col-

lins, Jr., for the *New Albany Gazette* (ALS. DNA, RG 59. mDW
52765); from D. Alonzo Cushman et al., for Fitz Henry McCready—
consul, Baracoa (LS. MWalB. mDW 18599); from Hiram Cutts et al.,
for Frederick A. Franklin (LS. NhHi. mDW 18603); from William
Primrose, for James Primrose—consul, Pictou (LS. NhHi. mDW
18604); from Josiah Sturgis et al., for John C. Pedrick (LS. NhHi.
mDW 18614).

March 29   *From James Duane Doty to Nicholas Biddle.*   102
March 30   To Isaac Rand Jackson. ALS. MdHi. mDW 18620. Plans to
            arrive at IRJ's house tomorrow and asks that his "whereabouts" be
            kept secret.
March 30   From William Barron. ALS. DNA, RG 59. mDW 54492. Ac-
            knowledges receipt of the commission appointing him U.S. marshal
            for Vermont.
March 30   From D. A. Chisholm. ALS. DLC. mDW 18624. Asks DW to
            support his claim against the government.
March 30   From Cornelius Darragh. ALS. DNA, RG 59. mDW 54564.
            Accepts appointment as U.S. attorney for western Pennsylvania.
March 30   From Clark Robinson. ALS. DNA, RG 59. mDW 54824. Ac-
            knowledges receipt of commission appointing him marshal for the
            northern district of New York.
March 30   Applications from Joseph Graham, for the *Cincinnati Repub-
            lican*—public printer (ALS. DNA, RG 59. mDW 52719); from
            Douglas S. Hubbard and Samuel D. Church, for the Pittsfield, Mas-
            sachusetts, *Berkshire County Whig*—public printer (ALS by
            Hubbard, signed also by Church. DNA, RG 59. mDW 52880); from
            William W. Norvell (ALS. NhHi. mDW 18626); from Richard Sut-
            ton—consul, Bermuda (ALS. MWalB. mDW 18628).
March 30   Recommendations from Stevenson Archer, for John Bozman
            Kerr (ALS. MWalB. mDW 18622); from John F. J. White, for the
            Buchanan (Va.) *Journal*—public printer (ALS. DNA, RG 59.
            mDW 52937).
March 31   *To Caroline Le Roy Webster.*   103
March 31   From Samuel Frothingham. ALS. DNA, RG 59. mDW 54643.
            Accepts appointment as receiver general at Boston.
March 31   From Charles Hopkins. ALS. DNA, RG 59. mDW 54690. Ac-
            cepts appointment as solicitor for the General Land Office.
March 31   Applications from Chambers, Knapp & Co., for the St. Louis
            Missouri Republican—public printer (LS. DNA, RG 59. mDW
            52659); from Henry Hubbard, for the *Berkshire County Whig*
            (ALS. DNA, RG 59. mDW 52877); from William H. Trott—consul,
            Bermuda (ALS. MWalB. mDW 18634).
March 31   Recommendations from Daniel Le Roy, for Hamilton Fish—
            marshal, New York (ALS. MWalB. mDW 18630); from Thaddeus
            Pomeroy, for the *Berkshire County Whig* (ALS. DNA, RG 59.
            mDW 52885); from Asher Robbins, for Gideon Theodore Snow
            (ALS. NhHi. mDW 18632).
March   Applications from Richard J. A. Culverwell (ALS. MWalB.
            mDW 18642); from George W. Harper, for the New Lisbon, Ohio,
            Western Palladium—public printer (ALS. DNA, RG 59. mDW
            52713); from Isaac Rand Jackson—diplomatic post (ALS copy.

MdHi. mDW 18644; *Diplomatic Papers*, 1); from John A. King—consul, Buenos Aires (ALS. MWalB. mDW 18646).

March   Recommendations from Jonathan Allen et al., for the *Berkshire County Whig* (ADS. DNA, RG 59. mDW 52882); from Nicholas Biddle, for Jacob Waterman—unspecified post (ALS draft. DLC. mDW 18641); from Nathan Fellows Dixon et al., for the Rhode Island *Providence Daily Journal*, Newport *Herald of the Times*, and Warren *Northern Star*—public printers (LS. DNA, RG 59. mDW 52832); from Thomas Kempshall, for the *Rochester* (N.Y.) *Daily Democrat*—public printer (ANS. DNA, RG 59. mDW 52304); from Samson Mason, for Samuel Eells—consul, West Indies (ALS. NhHi. mDW 18650); from Noah Noble, for William H. Ewing—marshal, Indiana (ALS. MWalB. mDW 18654); from Joseph H. Underwood et al., for Timothy Darling (LS. NhHi. mDW 18664); from Richard H. Vose et al., for Timothy Darling (LS. NhHi. mDW 18666).

[March?]   From John Canfield Spencer to John Jordan Crittenden (Memorandum on McLeod case, endorsed by DW). AD. DLC. mDW 18656.

[March?]   Recommendation from Hiland Hall et al., for the Bennington, Vermont, *State Banner*—public printer (ALS by Hall, signed also by others. DNA, RG 59. mDW 52310).

[March–June]   From Jesse Turner et al. ALS by Turner, signed also by others. MWalB. mDW 24035. Accuse the incumbent U.S. marshal for Arkansas of being a partisan Democrat.

[March–Sept]   To Thomas Ewing. ALS. DLC. mDW 18670. Invites him to dine.

[March–Sept]   Memorandum on appointment of James Hervey Bingham to Land Office with letter of recommendation endorsed by DW. AD. DLC. mDW 18671.

April 1   From W. H. Dillingham. ALS. MWalB. mDW 18678. Tells of correspondence with the clerk of the Canadian House of Commons and asks if it might be of any use to DW.

April 1   Applications from Henry A. W. Barclay (ALS. NhHi. mDW 18674); from W. L. and Q. K. Underwood, for the Helena, Arkansas, *Southern Shield*—public printer (ALS. DNA, RG 59. mDW 52725); from Thomas D. Walpole—marshal, Indiana (ALS. MWalB. mDW 18680).

April 1   Recommendations from Richard H. Bayard, for Robert Jacques—consul, St. Johns, Puerto Rico (ALS. MWalB. mDW 18676); from Lester Filley et al., for the Lenox, Massachusetts, *Eagle*—public printer (ALS by Filley, signed also by others. DNA, RG 59. mDW 52892).

April 1   From James Duane Doty to Herman Cope.   103

April 2   To Mrs. John Agg. ALS. NhD. mDW 16602. Explains why he has been unable to visit her.

April 2   To [George Edmund Badger]. LS. DNA, RG 45. mDWs. Asks for list of employees in the Navy Department to be used in the *Biennial Register*.

April 2   To John Bell. Copy. DNA, RG 99. mDW 57137. Reminds him to submit a list of his department employees for inclusion in the *Biennial Register*.

April 2   From John William Allen. ALS. DNA, RG 59. mDW 52708. Denounces the incumbent printer of the laws at Warren, O.; finds
that Ohio Whigs generally approve of the President's advisers.

April 2   Applications from Samuel F. Coolidge—despatch bearer to England or France (ALS. MWalB. mDW 18684); from Nelson & Bates,
for the Montgomery *Alabama Journal*—public printer (ALS. DNA,
RG 59. mDW 52646).

April 2   Recommendations from John William Allen, for the *Cleveland
Daily Herald*—public printer (ALS. DNA, RG 59. mDW 52705);
from Anthony Barclay, for Henry A. W. Barclay (ALS. NhHi. mDW
18682); from Washington Irving, for George Washington Montgomery—state department post (ALS. NhHi. mDW 18686; Van
Tyne, p. 232); from William Cabell Rives, for Francis Madera—
marshal, Virginia (ALS. MWalB. mDW 18689); from William
Cabell Rives, for Charles J. Cummings—marshal, Virginia (ALS.
MWalB. mDW 18691); from William Cabell Rives, for Mordecai
Yarnall (ALS. MWalB. mDW 18693); from William Cabell Rives,
for Richard Fowks—marshal, Virginia (ALS. MWalB. mDW 18695).

April 3   To Peter Buell Porter. ALS. NBuHi. mDW 18697. Anticipates
"no explosion" over the McLeod affair.

April 3   From Andrew Talcott. ALS. DNA, RG 59. mDW 56736. Has
drawn $1,500 from account for northeast boundary survey.

April 3   Application from Essex Ridley Livingston—consul, Naples
(ALS. NhHi. mDW 18705).

April 3   Recommendations from William S. Archer, for William W.
Warwick—consul, Rio de Janeiro (ALS. NhD. mDW 18699); from
Willam C. Dawson, for the Milledgeville, Georgia, *Southern Recorder*
and *Georgia Journal*, the Augusta *Daily Chronicle and Sentinel*, the
Savannah Republican, the Macon *Georgia Messenger*, the *Colum-
bus Enquirer*, and the Athens, Georgia, *Southern Whig*—public
printers (ALS. DNA, RG 59. mDW 52323); from P. B. Hopper, for
John Bozman Kerr (ALS. MWalB. mDW 18703); from John Leeds
Kerr, for the *Easton* (Md.) *Gazette*—public printer (ALS. DNA, RG
59. mDW 52847); from George Sullivan, for [?]—commissioner of
patents (ALS. MWalB. mDW 18708); from Abraham Warnick &
Co. et al., for William W. Norvell (LS. NhHi. mDW 18710).

April 3   Check to "New York dr[a]ft" for $15. DS. NN. mDW 39842.

April 4   To Thomas Nelson Carr.   104

April 4   To [William Alexander Graham]. Printed Circular. Nc-Ar.
mDWs. J. G. de Roulhac Hamilton, ed., *The Papers of William A.
Graham* (Raleigh, N.C., 1957), 2: 179–181. Notifies him of
Harrison's death and the funeral arrangements.

April 4   Recommendations from Daniel W. Hearne, for his son—clerk,
State Department (ALS. MWalB. mDW 18714); from Richard Mentor Johnson, for Joseph Eve—chargé, Texas (ALS. MWalB. mDW
18716).

April 5   To Epes Sargent. ALS. MB. mDW 18718. Cites his speech on
Jackson's protest for his views of the power of Britain and promises to send Sargent copies of his Richmond speech.

*April 5   From Nicholas Biddle, with enclosure from Nicholas Biddle,
April 3.*   104

April 5   From Henry C. Bosler. ALS. DNA, RG 59. mDW 54518. Accepts office as U.S. marshal for western Pennsylvania.
April 5   From Richard Keith Call. ALS. DNA, RG 59. mDW 54532. Accepts appointment as governor of Florida.
April 5   Recommendations from George Nixon Briggs, for Charles Edwards Lester—consul, southern Europe (ALS. MWalB. mDW 18722); from George Nixon Briggs, for the *Massachusetts Eagle* or the *Berkshire County Whig* (ALS. DNA, RG 59. mDW 52889); from Henry Eddy, for the Shawneetown *Illinois Republican*—public printer (ALS. DNA, RG 59. mDW 52994); from Nehemiah Rice Knight, for Gideon Theodore Snow (ALS. NhHi. mDW 18763); from Edgar Snowden, for John B. Dade—warden, Washington penitentiary (ALS. MWalB. mDW 18724); from John Canfield Spencer, for John S. Rensselaer—chargé, The Hague or Naples (ALS. MWalB. mDW 18726).
April 6   From Herman Cope.   106
April 6   From Jacob Merritt Howard. ALS. NhD. mDW 18730. *Diplomatic Papers*, 1. Describes the activity of Patriots along the Lakes frontier.
April 6   Check for $41 to Charles H. Brown. DS. NN. mDW 39843.
April 6   Recommendations from James H. Birch, for the St. Louis *Commercial Bulletin* and withdrawing his recommendation of John L. Dorsey for chargé d'affaires (ALS. DNA, RG 59. mDW 52668); from James Chestney, for the Tuscaloosa *Independent Monitor* (ALS. DNA, RG 59. mDW 52643).
April 7   From Luther Bradish. ALS. NhHi. mDW 18736. Introduces Vincent Whitney.
April 7   Recommendations from John Macpherson Berrien, for Mr. Hilliard—indefinite post (ALS. MWalB. mDW 18734); from Rufus Choate, for Edward Richardson—consul, Havre (ALS. MWalB. mDW 18738).
April 8   From Isaac Rand Jackson. ALS copies. MdHi. mDW 18746, 18748. *Diplomatic Papers*, 1. Stresses his desire to be named chargé d'affaires in Naples as promised by President Harrison; encloses formal letter which DW may choose to place before President Tyler.
April 8   Application from Robert C. Carman, for the Jackson, Louisiana, *Feliciana Republican*—public printer (ALS. DNA, RG 59. mDW 52628).
April 8   Recommendations from Luther Bradish, for George W. Lay—chargé, Naples (ALS. MWalB. mDW 18740); from Edward Curtis, for William A. Lawrence (ALS. MWalB. mDW 18744); from James Fowler Simmons, for Gideon T. Snow (ALS. NhHi. mDW 18764); from Gideon Snow, for Gideon T. Snow (ALS. NhHi. mDW 18749); from Robert Charles Winthrop, for Robert Swift—consul, St. Thomas (ALS. MWalB. mDW 18752).
April 9   To William Morris Meredith. LS. NhD. mDW 18755. Sends a letter from the U.S. consul at Trinidad describing an incident involving the schooner *Atalanta*.
April 9   To John Tyler (with ANS by Tyler). LS. DNA, RG 59. mDW

56584. Requests authority to pay advances to the commissioners appointed to survey the northeast boundary.

April 9   From Harrison Reid. ALS. DNA, RG 59. mDW 52577. Accepts appointment to print the laws in the *Milwaukee Sentinel.*

April 9   Application from Noyes Barber (ALS. MWalB. mDW 18756).

April 9   Recommendations from Matthew C. Paterson, for William A. Lawrence (ALS. MWalB. mDW 18759); from Robert Rogers, for Gideon T. Snow (ALS. NhHi. mDW 18761).

April 10   From Sam F. Bridge (enclosed with DW to William Alexander Graham, [April 12, 1841]). Printed. J. G. de Roulhac Hamilton, ed., *The Papers of William A. Graham* (Raleigh, N.C., 1957), 2: 187–188. Reports coastwise receipts of grain at Boston from Maryland, Virginia, and the Carolinas.

April 10   From John Chambers. ALS. DLC. mDW 18765. Curtis, 2: 67. Expresses the Harrison family's gratitude for DW's kindness during their bereavement.

April 10   From Reverdy Johnson. ALS. MWalB. mDW 18775. Discusses the various candidates for U.S. attorney in Maryland.

April 10   From William W. Wyman. ALS. DNA, RG 59. mDW 52575. Accepts appointment to print the laws in the *Madison* (Wis.) *Express.*

April 10   Applications from William L. May—marshal, Illinois (ALS. MWalB. mDW 18778); from Vivus W. Smith, on behalf of Charles Scott, for the Columbus *Ohio State Journal*—public printer (ALS. DNA, RG 59. mDW 52700).

April 10   Recommendations from Ichabod Goodwin et al., for Charles W. Cutter—naval storekeeper, Portsmouth, N.H. (LS. NhD. mDW 18768); from Reverdy Johnson, for John Scott—orphan's court, Washington (ALS. MWalB. mDW 18771).

April 11   *To Charles Henry Thomas.*   107

April 11   Recommendation from Nathaniel Greene Pendleton, for Ebenezer Hulse—marshal, Ohio (ALS. MWalB. mDW 18785).

[April 12]   To William Alexander Graham (enclosure: Sam F. Bridge to DW, April 10, 1841). ALS. Nc-Ar. mDWs. J. G. de Roulhac Hamilton, ed., *The Papers of William A. Graham* (Raleigh, N.C., 1957), 2: 186–187. Discusses the importance of trade between Virginia, North Carolina, and Massachusetts.

April 12   *To Leverett Saltonstall.*   108

April 12   To Peleg Sprague. ALS. MDuHi. mDWs. Proposes to recommend Sprague for U.S. judge in Massachusetts.

April 12   From Henderson Taylor. ALS. DNA, RG 59. mDW 54864. Accepts appointment as U.S. attorney for western Louisiana.

April 12   Recommendation from John Stephens, for John Bozman Kerr (ALS. MWalB. mDW 18792).

April 13   From James Primrose (enclosed with Grant & Stone to DW, April 28, 1841). ALS. NhHi. mDW 18958. Defends his official conduct and attacks a proposal for consolidating the consulates at Pictou and Halifax.

April 13   From John Wells, Jr. ALS. DNA, RG 59. mDW 54889. Accepts appointment as justice of the peace in Washington, D.C.

April 13   Application from Nathan Barnes, Jr.—consul, Society Islands (ALS. NhHi. mDW 18795).

April 13   Recommendations from E. B. Estes et al., for William W. Norvell (LS. NhHi. mDW 18797); from C. W. Hanson, for John M. D. Goldsborough—assistant surveyor, northeast boundary line (ALS. MWalB. mDW 18799); from A. J. Jones, for the *Harrisburg Chronicle* (ALS. DNA, RG 59. mDW 52246); from Albert Miller Lea, for John M. D. Goldsborough (ALS. MWalB. mDW 18802).

April 14   To John Tyler. LS draft. MWalB. mDW 18805. Recommends Joshua Howard as U.S. marshal for Michigan.

April 14   From Henry Leavitt Ellsworth. ALS. MWalB. mDW 18810. Requests a ten minute interview to discuss the staffing of the Patent Office.

April 14   Recommendations from George Brink et al., for Levi Bixby (LS. NhHi. mDW 18807); from John H. Kinzie, for Gurdon S. Hubbard (ALS. MWalB. mDW 18813); from Thomas Wheeler Williams, for Noyes Barber (ALS. MWalB. mDW 18815).

April 14   Bank draft by Benjamin Rush for £22 on the Rothschilds, forwarded to DW. ADS. NjP. mDW 39844.

April 15   To Isaac Rand Jackson. ALS. MdHi. mDW 18817. Asks him to come to Washington for a day or two.

April 15   From James Duane Doty. ALS. DNA, RG 59. mDW 54586. Accepts appointment as governor of Wisconsin Territory.

April 15   From George Mason Graham. ALS. MWalB. mDW 18818. Insists he is not an "office seeker."

April 15   From Return J. Meigs. ALS. DNA, RG 59. mDW 54763. Accepts appointment as U.S. attorney for the middle district of Tennessee.

April 15   Application from William Jones—marshal, New York (ALS. MWalB. mDW 18823).

April 16   *To John Davis (1787–1854).*   *108*

April 16   To Joshua A. Spencer. LS. PHi. mDW 18831. *Diplomatic Papers*, 1. Sends copies of correspondence with McLeod's counsel; offers to correspond directly when Spencer confirms that he has joined McLeod's defense.

April 16   From Charles Chapman. ALS. DNA, RG 59. mDW 54544. Accepts appointment as U.S. attorney for Connecticut.

April 16   From D. A. Chisholm. ALS. DLC. mDWs. Asks DW's attention to his claim against the government.

April 16   *From John Evelyn Denison.*   *110*
April 16   *From Edward Everett.*   *112*

April 16   Applications from James C. Doane—naval storekeeper, Charleston (ALS. DNA, RG 156. mDWs); from Alexander P. Field—consul, New Granada (ALS. NhHi. mDW 18845).

April 16   Recommendation from Hiland Hall, for the Montpelier *Vermont Watchman and State Journal* and the Bennington *State Banner*—public printers (ALS with ANS by DW. DNA, RG 59. mDW 52315).

April 17   From Charles Davis. ALS. DNA, RG 59. mDW 54566. Accepts appointment as U.S. attorney for Vermont.

April 17   From Thomas Ewing. ALS. DNA, RG 59. mDW 54793. Requests that William Pelham be commissioned surveyor general of Arkansas.

April 17   From John Holmes. ALS. DNA, RG 59. mDW 54688. Accepts
appointment as U.S. attorney for Maine.

April 17   From Jules von Wallenstein. ALS. NhHi. mDW 18853. Congratulates DW on his appointment as secretary of state.

April 17   Application from Thomas Croxall—commissioner of patents
(ALS. MWalB. mDW 18849).

April 17   Recommendations from Thomas Butler King, for Henry A. W.
Barclay (ALS. NhHi. mDW 18851); from Samuel Prentiss, for the
Vermont Watchman and State Journal and the *State Banner* (ALS.
DNA, RG 59. mDW 52312).

April 18   Recommendations from Etienne Mazureau, for John Gibson
(ALS. MWalB. mDW 18856); from Robert Bowne Minturn et al.,
for Warren Delano, Jr.—consul, Canton (ALS by Minturn, signed
also by others. MWalB. mDW 18858).

April 19   To John Anthon. LS. DNA, RG 76. mDWs. Acknowledges Anthon's letter relative to claims against the Buenos Aires government.

April 19   From John Golden (enclosure: sample of patented credit
check). ALS. DLC. mDW 18865A. Suggests that the government
adopt his patented credit check.

April 19   From A. J. Raines. ALS. MWalB. mDW 18868. Calls for the
removal of Elias Rector, U.S. marshal of Arkansas.

April 19   From Andrew Stevenson. ALS. DLC. mDW 18876. Thinks the
English people are inadequately informed as to the circumstances
of the *Caroline*'s destruction.

April 19   Application from John T. P. Dumont (ALS. MWalB. mDW
18863).

April 19   Recommendations from Simeon Draper, for William H. Trott
(ALS. MWalB. mDW 18861); from Edward Kent, for Samuel Garn-
sey—consul, St. Johns (ALS. MWalB. mDW 18866); from J. W.
Moorhead, for the *Indiana* (Pa.) *Register*—public printer (ALS.
DNA, RG 59. mDW 52258); from A. J. Raines et al., for Thomas W.
Newton—marshal, Arkansas (ALS by Raines, signed also by others.
MWalB. mDW 18872); from F. W. Risque et al., for William W.
Norvell (LS. NhHi. mDW 18874).

April 20   From Horatio Ames. ALS. DNA, RG 45. mDWs. Reports that
his iron business is slow and asks DW to help him obtain contracts,
especially with the navy.

April 20   From Joel Eastman. ALS. DNA, RG 59. mDW 54610. Acknowledges receipt of commission as U.S. attorney for New
Hampshire.

April 20   Applications from Milton Gregg, for the Lawrenceburg, Indiana, *Political Beacon*—public printer (ALS. DNA, RG 59. mDW
52755); from Thomas D. Walpole (ALS. MWalB. mDW 18882);
from Joseph Wood—despatch agent, New York (ALS. MWalB.
mDW 18884).

April 20   Recommendation from Russell H. Nevins, for the Philadelphia *National Gazette* (ALS. DNA, RG 59. mDW 52235).

April 21   From August Belmont. ALS. MWalB. mDW 18886. Sends letters from Rothschild & Sons of London, addressed to Harrison.

April 21   From Grant & Stone.   *115*

April 21   From Sylvester Hartshorn. ALS. DNA, RG 59. mDW 54675.
Accepts appointment as U.S. marshal for Rhode Island.

April 21   From Jacob Harvey. ALS. NhHi. mDW 18897. Gives an extract from a letter from the Marquis of Lansdowne expressing opti-
mism over the chances for a peaceful settlement of Anglo-American
differences.

April 21   From Daniel Hugunin. ALS. DNA, RG 59. mDW 54698. Accepts appointment as U.S. marshal for Wisconsin.

April 21   From Arthur Livermore. ALS. NhHi. mDW 18899. Thanks DW
for the attention given his recent letter.

April 21   From Edward Stubbs. ALS. DNA, RG 59. mDW 56590. Suggests that the agent for the State Department be authorized to make
advances out of the contingent fund.

April 21   Application from John Wheelwright—marshal, New York
(ALS. MWalB. mDW 18903).

April 21   Recommendations from Caleb Cushing, for Frederick A.
Franklin (ALS. NhHi. mDW 18889); from William Pitt Fessenden,
for Horatio Fox—consul, Trinidad (ALS. MWalB. mDW 18890);
from William Henry Seward, for William Duer—consul, Liverpool
(ALS. MWalB. mDW 18901).

April 22   From Francis Granger. LC. DNA, RG 28. mDW 57049. Asks
that a correction be made in the commission appointing John G.
Miller postmaster at Columbus, Ohio.

April 22   From Isaac Otis. ALS. DNA, RG 59. mDW 54785. Accepts appointment as U.S. marshal for the eastern district of Pennsylvania.

April 22   Application from Samuel Eells (ALS. NhHi. mDW 18906).

April 22   Recommendation from Grant & Stone, for the Philadelphia
North American—public printer (ALS. DNA, RG 59. mDW 52264).

April 23   To Josiah Quincy. ALS. CtY. mDW 18910. Asks him to locate
Christopher Gore's manuscript record of the proceedings of the
commissioners appointed under the Treaty of 1794 with England so
that he may examine it.

April 23   To John Tyler. LS. DNA, RG 59. mDW 56588. Requests
authority to make advances and expenditures not exceeding $2,000
out of the fund for the contingent expenses of foreign intercourse.

April 23   From John Davis (1787–1854).   117

April 23   From Alexander P. Field. ALS. MWalB. mDW 18917. Denounces Ferris Forman, U.S. attorney for Illinois, for blatant
partisanship.

April 23   From John J. Roane. ALS. MWalB. mDW 18923. Expresses
extreme mortification at his demotion from office and his treatment
by DW in a recent interview.

April 23   From John Tyler. LS. DNA, RG 59. mDW 56589. Authorizes
advances and expenditures not exceeding $2,000 out of the contin-
gency fund.

April 23   Applications from Essex Ridley Livingston (ALS. MWalB.
mDW 18919); from William Bennett Parker (ALS. MWalB. mDW
18921).

April 24   From James D. Graham. ALS. DNA, RG 59. mDW 56738. Intends making periodic withdrawals of funds needed for the northeast boundary survey.

April 24   From John D. Kinsman. ALS. DNA, RG 59. mDW 54720. Accepts appointment as U.S. marshal for Maine.

April 24   From E. P. Walton and Sons. LS. DNA, RG 59. mDW 52435. Accept appointment to print the laws in the *Vermont Watchman and State Journal.*

April 24   Application from John Ruggles (ALS. MWalB. mDW 18936).

April 24   "Mr. Webster and His Revilers" (editorial). Printed. *National Intelligencer,* April 24, 1841.

April 24   Recommendations from James H. Birch, for the Jackson, Missouri, *Southern Advocate*—public printer (ALS. DNA, RG 59. mDW 52652); from George Howland, Jr., for William H. Allen—collector of customs, New Bedford (ALS. MHi. mDW 18934); from John F. Moses to DFW for the *Knoxville* (Tenn.) *Register and Weekly Times*—public printer (ALS. DNA, RG 59. mDW 52692).

April 25   Recommendation from Isaac L. Hedge, for Henry Evans—superintendent of rope walk, Charlestown, Mass. (ALS. DNA, RG 45. mDWs).

April 26   From George C. Bates. ALS. DNA, RG 59. mDW 54494. Accepts appointment as U.S. attorney for Michigan.

April 26   From Joshua A. Spencer. ALS. DNA, RG 59. mDW 54838. Accepts appointment as U.S. attorney for northern New York.

April 26   Applications from Rufus Beach—despatch bearer (ALS. MWalB. mDW 18940); from John A. King (ALS. MWalB. mDW 18943); from Abner McCarty—marshal, Indiana (ALS. MWalB. mDW 18947).

April 26   Recommendation from Byron Diman, for George F. Usher (ALS. NhHi. mDW 18942).

April 27   From Thomas Ewing. ALS. DNA, RG 59. mDW 54813. Asks for a commission appointing Silas Reed surveyor general for Missouri and Illinois.

April 27   From Israel Webster Kelly. ALS. DNA, RG 59. mDW 54716. Accepts appointment as U.S. marshal for New Hampshire.

April 27   From Alanson Tucker, Jr. ALS. DNA, RG 59. mDW 54886. Accepts appointment as despatch agent at Boston for the State Department.

April 27   From John Tyler. LC. DNA, RG 59. mDW 56918. Authorizes DFW to act as secretary of state during his father's absence.

April 27   Application from Colton & Childs, for the Philadelphia *North American*—public printer (LS. DNA, RG 59. mDW 52260).

April 27   Recommendations from Augustus Seymour Porter, for the *Niles* (Mich.) *Republican*—public printer (ALS. DNA, RG 59. mDW 52731); from Joshua A. Spencer, for George Fisher—chargé, Turin (ALS. MWalB. mDW 18997); from Joseph Leonard Tillinghast, for George F. Usher (ALS. NhHi. mDW 18951).

[April 28] To Isaac Rand Jackson. ALS. MdHi. mDW 18953. Asks Jackson to meet him at the Philadelphia depot.

April 28   To John Tyler. ALS. NcU. mDWs. States that he has seen Elisha Whittlesey "& made all smooth water about young Mr. Green" [a son of Duff Green] who will be promoted as soon as a vacancy occurs.

April 28   From Grant & Stone (enclosure: James Primrose to DW, April

13, 1841). LS. NhHi. mDW 18956. Forwards letter from James
Primrose, U.S. consul at Pictou.

April 28   From Silas Moore Stilwell. ALS. DNA, RG 59. mDW 54850.
Accepts appointment as U.S. marshal for southern New York.

April 28   Application from H. T. Weightman—clerkship, State Department (ALS. MWalB. mDW 18968).

April 28   Recommendations from Nicholas Biddle, for William Ayres—
postmaster, Harrisburg, Pa. (ALS draft. DLC. mDW 18954); from
Samuel Wilkeson, for the Washington *Native American*—public
printer (LS. DNA, RG 59. mDW 52583); from Joseph Trumbull, for
the *Connecticut Courant, New Haven Palladium*, and *Norwich
Courier*—public printers (ALS. DNA, RG 59. mDW 52827).

April 28   Deed transferring land in La Grange and La Porte counties,
Indiana, from DW to Herman Cope and Thomas S. Taylor. Copy.
Deed Book N: 81. Register of Deeds, La Porte County, Indiana.
mDWs.

April 28   Deed transferring land in Allegan County, Michigan, from
DW to Herman Cope and Thomas S. Taylor. Copy. Deed Book 4:
249–250. Register of Deeds, Allegan County, Michigan. mDWs.

April 28   Deed transferring land in Livingston County, Michigan, from
DW to Herman Cope and Thomas S. Taylor. Copy. Deed Book 8:
108–110. Register of Deeds, Livingston County, Michigan. mDWs.

April 28   Deed transferring land in Oakland County, Michigan, from
DW to Herman Cope and Thomas S. Taylor. Copy. Deed Book 25:
311–313. Register of Deeds, Oakland County, Michigan. mDWs.

April 28   Deed transferring land in Shiawassee County, Michigan, from
DW to Herman Cope and Thomas S. Taylor. Copy. Deed Book G:
23–25. Register of Deeds, Shiawassee County, Michigan. mDWs.

April 28   Deed transferring land in Van Buren County, Michigan, from
DW to Herman Cope and Thomas S. Taylor. Copy. Deed Book C:
232–234. Register of Deeds, Van Buren County, Michigan. mDWs.

April 28   Deed transferring land in Green County, Wisconsin, from DW
to Herman Cope and Thomas S. Taylor. Copy. Deed Book A: 334.
Register of Deeds, Green County, Wisconsin. mDWs.

April 28   Deed transferring land in Grant County, Wisconsin, from
DW to Herman Cope and Thomas S. Taylor. Copy. Deed Book D:
60–63. Register of Deeds, Grant County, Wisconsin. mDWs.

April 28   Deed transferring land in Iowa County, Wisconsin, from DW
to Herman Cope and Thomas S. Taylor. Copy. Deed Book B: 273.
Register of Deeds, Lafayette County, Wisconsin. mDWs.

April 28   Deed transferring land in Washington County, Wisconsin,
from DW to Herman Cope and Thomas S. Taylor. Copy. Deed Book
B: 389. Register of Deeds, Washington County, Wisconsin. mDWs.

April 28   Memorandum of DW's conveyances of land in Rock Island
City, Illinois, to Herman Cope and Thomas S. Taylor. AD. DLC.
mDWs.

April 28   Receipt for $1,000 paid by Edward Stubbs. DS. DNA, RG 59.
mDW 56591.

April 28   *Transfer of Share in the Four Lake Company.*   *119*

April 29   From Enoch Davis. ALS. DNA, RG 59. mDW 52437. Accepts appointment to print the laws in the Bennington, Vermont, *State Banner.*

April 29   From Robert Getty. ALS. DNA, RG 59. mDW 54645. Accepts appointment as justice of the peace for Washington, D.C.

April 29   From Andrew Talcott. ALS. DNA, RG 59. mDW 56741. Reports having drawn $4,000 for the purchase of instruments, etc.

April 29   Applications from Nathan Barnes, Jr. (ALS. NhHi. mDW 18970); from Charles W. Brewster, for the *Portsmouth* (N.H.) *Journal of Literature and Politics*—public printer (ALS. DNA, RG 59. mDW 52863).

April 29   Recommendations from J. Scott Harrison, for the Lawrence-burg *Political Beacon* (ALS. DNA, RG 59. mDW 52753); from Reverdy Johnson, for Samuel Barnes—marshal, Maryland (ALS. MWalB. mDW 18972); from William Pennington, for the *Newark Daily Advertiser* and Trenton *New Jersey State Gazette*—public printers (ALS. DNA, RG 59. mDW 52279).

April 30   From Ramsay Crooks.   119

April 30   From Jacob Harvey. ALS. MWalB. mDW 18976. Introduces Sir Joseph de Courcy Laffan.

April 30   From J. Washington Tyson. ALS. MWalB. mDW 18978. Introduces James A. Simpson.

April 30   Application from Nathaniel T. Eldredge, for the *New York Times & Evening Star*—public printer (LS. DNA, RG 59. mDW 52285).

April 30   Recommendation from Augustus Seymour Porter, for the Ann Arbor *Michigan State Journal*—public printer (ALS. DNA, RG 59. mDW 52749).

[April]   To [Caleb Cushing]. ALS. DLC. mDW 18981. Sets time for meeting "Mr. Johnson."

[April]   To [Francis] Granger. ALS. NhD. mDWs. Introduces [L. L.?] Britton, of Orford, N.H.

[April]   From Hiram Ketchum. ALS. NhHi. mDW 18986. Introduces Josiah L. Hale.

[April]   From John Tyler. ALS. InU. mDW 20499. Instructs DW to deliver to Doty his commission as governor of Wisconsin Territory.

[c. April]   To John Tyler. AL draft. NhHi. mDW 19844. *Diplomatic Papers*, 1. Reports on the Patriots.

April   Applications from Daniel R. Sheafe—consul, Pictou (ALS. NhHi. mDW 18989); from Henry B. Stacy, for the *Burlington* (Vt.) *Free Press*—public printer (ALS. DNA, RG 59. mDW 52776).

April   Recommendations from C. S. Bowles et al., for Francis Malbone Auboyneau (LS. NhHi. mDW 18983); from Samuel Judah, for Thomas D. Walpole (ALS. MWalB. mDW 18984).

[April–Sept]   To John Jordan Crittenden. ALS. NcD. mDW 21009. Urges him to make his report on the McLeod affair.

[April–Sept]   From [John Jordan Crittenden]. AD draft. NcD. mDWs. Mrs. Chapman Coleman, ed., *The Life of John J. Crittenden* (2 vols., Philadelphia, 1871), 1: 151–154. Reports on the McLeod affair.

May 1   From Henry Hubbard et al. ALS by Hubbard, signed also by others. DNA, RG 59. mDW 52416. Accept appointment to print the laws in the *Berkshire County Whig.*

May 1   From Balie Peyton. LS. DNA, RG 59. mDW 54801. Accepts appointment as U.S. attorney for eastern Louisiana.

May 1   Recommendations from Theodore Frelinghuysen, for Nicholas Luca Perick—consul, Brousa, Turkey (ALS. MWalB. mDW 18995); from Augustus Seymour Porter, for the *Detroit Daily Advertiser* (ALS. DNA, RG 59. mDW 52747); from Thurlow Weed, for George Fisher (ALS. MWalB. mDW 18998).

May 1   To Thomas Aspinwall from DFW. LS. NhD. mDW 18993. Informs him that DW will be meeting Sir Joseph de Courcy Laffan in New York and wants information on British colonization efforts in New Zealand.

May 2   From Minor Walker. ALS. DNA, RG 59. mDW 54873. Accepts appointment as U.S. marshal for Florida.

May 3   To John Davis (1787–1854). ALS. MWA. mDW 19004. Arranges to meet Davis.

May 3   From John B. Dade. LS. DNA, RG 59. mDW 54558. Accepts appointment as warden of the penitentiary in the District of Columbia.

May 3   From Franklin Dexter. ALS. DNA, RG 59. mDW 54578. Accepts appointment as U.S. attorney for Massachusetts.

May 3   From Absalom Fowler. ALS. DNA, RG 59. mDW 54637. Accepts appointment as acting U.S. attorney for Arkansas.

May 3 [1841–1843]   From John Tyler. ALS. DLC. mDW 19011. Requests interview.

May 3   Application from John Garnier—consul, Nantes (ALS. NhHi. mDW 19005).

May 3   Recommendations from George Pendleton et al., for Frederick A. Franklin (LS. NhHi. mDW 19008); from George W. Sternham, for Armand Auboyneau (ALS. NhHi. mDW 19010).

May 4   From Joshua Howard. ALS. DNA, RG 59. mDW 54696. Accepts appointment as U.S. marshal for Michigan.

May 5   From Justin Butterfield. ALS. DNA, RG 59. mDW 54528. Accepts appointment as U.S. marshal for Illinois.

May 5   From Thurlow Weed. ALS. MWalB. mDW 19014. Introduces Joseph M. Church.

May 5   Recommendations from John M. Scott and G. M. Wharton, for Arthur S. C. [?] Nichols—European consulate (ALS by Scott, signed also by Wharton. MWalB. mDW 19013); from James M. Stewart et al., for the *Indiana* (Pa.) *Register* (LS. DNA, RG 59. mDW 52254).

May 6   From Francis Granger. ANS. DNA, RG 59. mDW 54624. Announces Thomas Finley's appointment as deputy postmaster in Baltimore.

May 6   Application from W. and R. B. Moorhead, for the *Indiana* (Pa.) *Register* (ALS. DNA, RG 59. mDW 52255).

May 6   Recommendation from William W. Norvell, for James Saunders—unspecified post (ALS. NhHi. mDW 19016).

May 7   Memorandum of DW's Illinois lands. Copy. MWalB. mDW 39851.

May 7   Memorandum of DW's Michigan lands. Copy. MWalB. mDW
39854.
May 7   Application from Edward A. Howard, for the *Danville* (Va.)
Reporter—public printer (ALS. DNA, RG 59. mDW 52920).
May 7   Recommendations from Isaac Chapman Bates, for William G.
Woodward—attorney, Iowa (ALS. MWalB. mDW 19017); from
Charles Pelham Curtis, for William G. Woodward (ALS. DLC.
mDW 19019); from Samuel J. Phelps, for John Pettes (ALS.
MWalB. mDW 19021).
[May 8]   To Daniel Fletcher Webster. Copy. NhHi. mDW 19024.
W & S, 16: 382–383. Approves DFW's note to the U.S. marshal of
New York; plans to stay longer in Boston.
May 8   From Robert Hanna. ALS. MWalB. mDW 19025. Discusses the
appointment of a U.S. marshal for Indiana.
May 8   From James Renwick. ALS. DNA, RG 59. mDW 56743. Has
drawn $3,000 for the survey of the northeast boundary.
May 8   Recommendations from John G. Miller, for Samuel Eells (ALS.
NhHi. mDW 19027); from Asher Robbins, for John McLean of
New York—chargé, foreign mission (Copy. DLC. mDW 19031);
from John Canfield Spencer, for Jeremiah Van Rensselaer—unspec-
ified post (ALS. MWalB. mDW 19033); from David Wallace, for
Robert Hanna—marshal, Indiana (ALS. MWalB. mDW 19034).
[May 9]   To John Davis (1787–1854). ALS. MWA. mDW 19036. Ar-
ranges meeting.
May 9   Recommendations from George T. Davis, for William G. Wood-
ward (ALS. MWalB. mDW 19038); from J. G. Marshall, for John
Boggs—marshal, Indiana (ALS. MWalB. mDW 19040); from J.
Sloane, for the *Wooster* (O.) *Democrat*—public printer (ALS. DNA,
RG 59. mDW 52711).
May 10   To Daniel Fletcher Webster. AL. MHi. mDW 19042. *Diplomatic
Papers*, 1. Discusses the federal government's role in the McLeod
trial and insists it will do no more than furnish "proper evidence."
May 10   From Isaac Rand Jackson. ALS copy. MdHi. mDW 19052. In-
vites DW to stay with him so as to avoid the annoyance of visitors
when he comes to Philadelphia.
May 10   From Thomas B. Johnson. ALS. DNA, RG 59. mDW 54706.
Accepts commission as U.S. marshal for Iowa.
May 10   Application from Benjamin Homans—compilation of *Biennial
Register* (ALS. MWalB. mDW 19049).
May 10   Recommendations from Benjamin Robbins Curtis, for Wil-
liam G. Woodward (ALS. MWalB. mDW 19045); from Abijah Fisk,
for Julius O. Harris—consul, Rio de Janeiro (ALS. NhHi. mDW
19224); from William Slade, for the *Middlebury* (Vt.) *People's
Press*—public printer (ALS. DNA, RG 59. mDW 52802).
May 10   Memorandum of DW's Wisconsin lands. Copy. MWalB. mDW
39847.
May 11   To Francis Calley Gray. Copy, endorsed by DW. NhHi. mDW
19053. *Diplomatic Papers*, 1. Wants discreet inquiries made in London to determine if the boundary negotiations might be speeded up.
May 12   To Samuel Appleton Appleton, with memorandum.   120
[c. May 12]   To Peter Chardon Brooks. ALS. NhD. mDW 38283. States

that he is moving some of his books and wine to Washington and thanks Brooks for having provided storage space.

May 12   From Francis Granger. ANS. DNA, RG 59. mDW 54844. Announces Henry B. Stacy's appointment as deputy postmaster in Burlington, Vermont.

May 12   From Horatio Greenough. Printed. Nathalia Wright, ed., *Letters of Horatio Greenough* (Madison, 1972), pp. 312–313. Discusses the problems of shipping his statue of Washington to the United States.

May 12   From Fontaine H. Pettis. ALS. MWalB. mDW 19067. Requests the removal of the incumbent U.S. consul at Bermuda, William T. Tucker.

May 12   From John Henry Shelburne. ALS. NhHi. mDW 19071. Asks for the removal of the incumbent U.S. consul at Pictou.

May 12   Application from J. M. Stuart, for the *Michigan City* (Ind.) *Gazette*—public printer (ALS. DNA, RG 59. mDW 52770).

May 12   Recommendations from William Morris Meredith, for William Meredith, Jr.—secretary, foreign legation (ALS. MWalB. mDW 19061); from Benjamin Pearce, for William John Duane—unspecified post (ALS. MWalB. mDW 19063); from Thomas H. Pettengill and Jonathan P. Webster, for the Concord *New Hampshire Courier*—public printer (ALS by Pettengill, signed also by Webster. DNA, RG 59. mDW 52859); from William Bradford Reed, for William Meredith, Jr. (ALS. MWalB. mDW 19069); from Pierre Van Cortlandt, for Joseph R. Croskey (LS. MWalB. mDW 19072).

May 13   From William W. Stewart. ALS. DNA, RG 59. mDW 54846. Accepts appointment as justice of the peace in Washington, D.C.

May 13   Application from John H. Williams—clerk, State Department (ALS. MWalB. mDW 19076).

May 13   Recommendation from John Gayle, for Joseph White Lesesne—attorney, Alabama (ALS with ANS by DW. MWalB. mDW 19074).

May 14   From Harmanus Bleecker. Copy. DNA, RG 46. mDW 48231. Sends letters of Messrs. Hope & Co. of Amsterdam, holders of Florida stocks.

May 14   From William Prentiss. ALS. DNA, RG 59. mDW 54809. Accepts appointment as U.S. marshal for Illinois.

May 14   Application from Samuel H. Davis, for the *Peoria* (Ill.) *Register*—public printer (ALS. DNA, RG 59. mDW 52988).

May 14   Recommendation from Moses Hicks Grinnell, for Thomas M. Willing (ALS. NhHi. mDW 19079).

May 15   From John B. Eldredge. ALS. DNA, RG 59. mDW 54614. Accepts appointment as U.S. marshal for Connecticut.

May 15   From Thomas W. Newton. ALS. DNA, RG 59. mDW 54779. Accepts appointment as U.S. marshal for Arkansas.

May 15   From John Tyler. ALS. DLC. mDW 19087. *Diplomatic Papers*, 1. Asks DW to read over his reply to Seward and send it along if he has no objections.

May 15   Application from Charles N. Webb, for the Halifax, North Carolina, *Roanoke Advocate*—public printer (ALS. DNA, RG 59. mDW 52146).

May 15   Recommendations from John B. Bibb, for the Russellville, Kentucky, *Logan Herald*—public printer (ALS. DNA, RG 59. mDW 52689); from William D. Merrick, for the Chestertown, Maryland, *Kent News*—public printer (ALS. DNA, RG 59. mDW 52838); from Collin H. Minge, for Julius O. Harris (ALS. NhHi. mDW 19226); from Rogers & Co., for William Whetten—consul, Cowes (LS. MWalB. mDW 19081); from A. C. Rossin & Co., for William Whetten (LS. MWalB. mDW 19082); from John Todd Stuart, for the Springfield, Illinois, *Sangamo Journal*—public printer (ALS. DNA, RG 59. mDW 52984); from George Ticknor, for William G. Woodward (ALS. MWalB. mDW 19083).

May 16   To Daniel Fletcher Webster. Printed. *PC*, 2: 104–105. Describes Joshua A. Spencer's role in the McLeod trial.

May 17   From Luther Bradish. ALS. MWalB. mDW 19089. Introduces Joseph M. Church.

May 17   Recommendations from Rufus Choate, for Samuel Gridley Howe (ALS. MWalB. mDW 19091); from Samuel Denison, for George F. Usher (ALS. MWalB. mDW 19093); from David Bayard Ogden, for William Meredith, Jr. (ALS. MWalB. mDW 19095).

May 17   Deeds transferring lands in Galena, Illinois, from the United States to DW. Copy. Deed Book F: Certificate Nos. 2730–5270, *passim*. Register of Deeds, Bureau County, Illinois. mDWs.

May 18   From David S. Brown. LS. MWalB. mDW 19099. Introduces James McHenry.

May 18   From Ogden Hoffman. ALS. NhD. mDW 19101. Reports developments at the McLeod trial and speculates on the judges' decision.

May 18   From Andrew Stevenson. ALS. DLC. mDW 19108. Insists he must resign by September.

May 18   Recommendations from Mary Barney, for Charles R. Barney—commissioner of patents (ALS. MWalB. mDW 19097); from Abbott Lawrence, for Samuel Gridley Howe (ALS. MWalB. mDW 19104).

May 19   To [Isaac Rand Jackson]. ALS. MdHi. mDW 19112. Asks him to come to Washington at once.

May 19   To Morris Ketchum. ALS. NhD. mDW 19113. Asks whether he still intends "to present the present to Mrs. Webster."

May 19   From Erastus Root. ALS. DLC. mDW 19127. Reports that the New York Senate has approved a resolution urging the establishment of a national bank.

May 19   From Nathan Sufborough. ALS. DNA, RG 59. mDW 54743. Accepts appointment as justice of the peace in Washington, D.C.

May 19   Application from Samuel Gridley Howe (ALS. MWalB. mDW 19120).

May 19   Recommendations from Hugh Birckhead, for the *Baltimore American* (ALS. DNA, RG 59. mDW 52358); from Samuel Denison, for George F. Usher (ALS. NhHi. mDW 19116); from Simeon B. Draper, for James Shaw—consul, Belfast (ALS. MWalB. mDW 19118); from Matthew and R. Maury, for William Whetten (ALS. MWalB. mDW 19122); from William Hickling Prescott, for Samuel Gridley Howe (ALS. MWalB. mDW 19123); from Wight, Sturgis & Shaw et al., for James Shaw (LS. MWalB. mDW 19130).

May 20   To Lewis Cass. LS. RHi. mDW 19132. Introduces Dr. John G.
Tull of North Carolina.

May 20   To Thomas Ewing. Invitation. DLC. mDW 19134. Invites
Ewing to dinner.

May 20   From J. Winthrop. ALS. DNA, RG 59. mDW 54724. Reports the
death of Judge P. K. Lawrence of New Orleans.

May 20   Recommendations from Henry C. De Rham and William
Moore, for William Whetten (LS. MWalB. mDW 19136); from John
Griswold, for William Whetten (ALS. MWalB. mDW 19137); from
G. G. Howland, for William Meredith, Jr. (ALS. MWalB. mDW
19140); from John Pendleton Kennedy, for the *Baltimore American*
(ALS. DNA, RG 59. mDW 52356); from C. Bolton Fox Livingston,
for William Whetten (ALS. MWalB. mDW 19142); from Harrison
Gray Otis, for Jeremiah Van Rensselaer—chargé, Naples (ALS.
MWalB. mDW 19143); from Charles C. Trowbridge, for Robert A.
Forsyth—paymaster, army (Copy. MiD-B. mDW 19147).

May 21   From George William Gordon.   121

May 21   From Abbott Lawrence. ALS. MWalB. mDW 19155. Introduces [Jeremiah] Van Rensselaer.

May 21   From James MacQueen. LS. DLC. mDW 19160. Describes
plans for establishing steamship connections between the West Indies, the United States, and Great Britain, and asks for the U.S.
government's views of the proposal.

May 21   Application from Charles Nichols—consul, Havre or Hamburg
(ALS. MWalB. mDW 19168).

May 21   Recommendations from Ogden Ferguson & Co., for William
Whetten (ALS. MWalB. mDW 19150); from William Edgar Howland and William H. Aspinwall, for William Whetten (ALS.
MWalB. mDW 19154); from J. Lee, for William Meredith, Jr. (ALS.
MWalB. mDW 19157); from John McLean, for Demas Adams—
marshal, Ohio (ALS. MWalB. mDW 19158); from Josiah Quincy, Jr.,
for Jeremiah Van Rensselaer (ALS. MWalB. mDW 19171).

May 22   To Edward Curtis. ALS. NN. mDW 19173. Asks for the date of
Benjamin Clark's death so that arrangements can be made for a
monument.

May 22   To Hiram Ketchum. ALS. MHi. mDW 19176. Declines to enter
in the agreement proposed by David Samuel Jones concerning the
Herman Le Roy will.

May 22   From John H. Overton. Copy. DNA, RG 46. mDW 48771. Describes the work of the party surveying the boundary between Texas
and the United States.

May 22   Application from Matthew Read—despatch bearer (LS.
MWalB. mDW 19182).

May 22   Recommendations from Edward Curtis, for William Whetten
(ALS. MWalB. mDW 19180); from William Bradford Reed, for
James McHenry—consul, Belfast (ALS. MWalB. mDW 19186).

May 23   Recommendation from John Middleton Clayton, for John
McLean (ALS. MWalB. mDW 19188).

May 24   From Isaac Rand Jackson. ALS draft. MdHi. mDW 19194.
Fears that unless a berth is available aboard the *Caledonia*, there
will be a four-week delay in his departure for Denmark.

May 24 Recommendations from Ogden Hoffman, for William Whetten (ALS. MWalB. mDW 19192); from Charles Carter Langdon et al., for Julius O. Harris (LS. NhHi. mDW 19230); from James Franklin Doughty Lanier, for Alexander Ott—consul, Europe (ALS. MWalB. mDW 19190); from Robert C. Wetmore, for Francis Joseph Grund (ALS. MWalB. mDW 19196).

[*May 25*] *To* [*Edward Curtis*]. 122

May 25 To William Henry Seward. ALS. SwSK. mDW 19201. Supposes it is too late to act on a suggestion in Seward's letter of April 29.

May 25 From George William Gordon. ALS. NN. mDW 19209. Thinks the printing of post office blanks should be assigned to the new proprietors of the *Boston Atlas*.

May 25 From Joshua Bates. Copy. DNA, RG 46. mDW 48237. Sends memorial of the proprietors of Mississippi stock in London.

May 25 From Anderson Miller. ALS. DNA, RG 59. mDW 54767. Accepts appointment as U.S. marshal for southern Mississippi.

May 25 From Jesse B. Thomas. ALS. DNA, RG 156. mDWs. Introduces John Francis Hamtramck Claiborne.

May 25 Applications from Thomas J. Holton, for the *Charlotte* (N.C.) *Journal*—public printer (ALS. DNA, RG 59. mDW 52144); from Richard Sutton (ALS. MWalB. mDW 19210); from William Whetten (ALS. MWalB. mDW 19212).

May 25 Recommendations from Hugh Brady, for R. A. Forsyth (Copy. MiD-B. mDW 19203); from S. P. Bullard, for Julius O. Harris (ALS. NhHi. mDW 19206); from William C. Dawson, for the Milledgeville, Georgia, *Southern Recorder*, Augusta *Chronicle and Sentinel*, and *Columbus Enquirer*—public printers (ALS. DNA, RG 59. mDW 52398).

May 26 From William L. Marcy and John Rowan. Copy. DNA, RG 46. mDW 48352. Submit report on the progress of the commission established under the convention with Mexico, April 11, 1839.

May 26 Application from Julius O. Harris (ALS. NhHi. mDW 19221).

May 26 Recommendations from Hugh Birckhead, for William Meredith, Jr. (ALS. MWalB. mDW 19214); from Robert Gilmor, for William Meredith, Jr. (ALS. MWalB. mDW 19216); from Moses Hicks Grinnell, for William Whetten (ALS. MWalB. mDW 19218); from Robert Gould Shaw, for Henry P. Sturgis—consul, Manila (ALS. MWalB. mDW 19233); from Thaddeus Stevens, for Francis J. Grund (ALS. MWalB. mDW 19235).

May 27 From Richard K. Call. ALS. MWalB. mDW 19237. Asks to defend himself against any charges.

[May 27] From Gordon L. Ford. LC. DNA, RG 49. mDWs. Asks whom he should address to obtain a patent to a tract of land in Illinois.

May 27 From James D. Graham. ALS. DNA, RG 59. mDW 56745. Submits a draft of $3,000 to defray the expenses of the survey of the northeast boundary.

May 27 From William Henry Seward. ALS draft. NRU. mDW 19241. Asks that Arthur R. Yulowski, a naturalized citizen of Polish birth, be furnished with identification papers for use during his trip to Europe.

May 27 Application from George Phillips Parker—consul, Italy (ALS. NhHi. mDW 19239).

May 27   Recommendations from Simeon Draper, for Dennis Davenport
—unspecified post (ALS. DNA, RG 156. mDWs); from Jonathan
Prescott Hall, for Dennis Davenport (ALS. DNA, RG 156. mDWs).

May 28   From John L. Boswell. ALS. DNA, RG 59. mDW 52429. Accepts appointment to print the laws in the *Connecticut Courant.*

May 28   From Joseph Tinker Buckingham and Eben B. Foster. ALS by
Foster, signed also by Buckingham. DNA, RG 59. mDW 52418. Accept appointment to print the laws in the *Boston Courier.*

May 28   Recommendation from Nicholas Biddle, for James McHenry
(ALS. MWalB. mDW 19245).

May 29   To John Davis (1787–1854). ALS. MWA. mDW 19247. *W & S,*
16: 341–342. Asks about the Rhode Island suit; comments on organization of House of Representatives.

May 29   From Babcock & Wildman. LS. DNA, RG 59. mDW 52431.
Accept appointment to print the laws in the *New Haven Palladium.*

May 29   From Dudley S. Palmer. ALS. DNA, RG 59. mDW 52412. Accepts appointment to print the laws in the *New Hampshire Courier.*

May 29   Applications from John T. Haight—surveyor, Wisconsin (ALS
copy. NhHi. mDW 19250); from Essex Ridley Livingston (ALS.
NhHi. mDW 19253).

May 29   Recommendations from Nicholas Biddle, for Davis B. Stacey
(ALS. MWalB. mDW 19248); from John Gayle, for Julius O. Harris
(ALS. NhHi. mDW 19228).

May 30   From Lyman Beecher. ALS. MWalB. mDW 19256. Introduces
William Young.

May 30   Application from Samuel D. Marshall, for the *Illinois Republican* (ALS. DNA, RG 59. mDW 52992).

May 30   Recommendations from Rufus Choate, for S. Grafton—unspecified post (ALS. MWalB. mDW 19258); from Rufus Choate, for
J. S. Adams (ALS. MWalB. mDW 19260); from E. H. Gatewood,
for the *Illinois Republican* (ALS. DNA, RG 59. mDW 52990).

May 31   To Nathaniel Pitcher Tallmadge. AL. WHi. mDWs. Invites
Tallmadge to dinner.

May 31   From D. A. Chisholm. ALS. DLC. mDWs. Asks again for a redress for damages from the U.S. government.

May 31   From Dawson & Bates. LS. DNA, RG 59. mDW 52571. Accept
appointment to print the laws in the *Detroit Daily Advertiser.*

May 31   From William S. and James W. Jones. LS. DNA, RG 59. mDW
52496. Accept appointment to print the laws in the Augusta *Chronicle & Sentinel.*

May 31   From Anderson Miller. ALS. DNA, RG 59. mDW 54765. States
that he was born in Virginia.

May 31   From Joseph Weber and John H. Warland. ALS by Warland,
signed also by Weber. DNA, RG 59. mDW 52410. Accept appointment to print the laws in the Claremont, New Hampshire, *National
Eagle.*

May 31   From Daniel H. Whitney. ALS. MWalB. mDW 19262. Warns
that ill-advised appointments are hurting the Whigs in Illinois.

May   From Grieve & Orme. LS. DNA, RG 59. mDW 52494. Accept appointment to print the laws in the Milledgeville *Southern Recorder.*

[May ?] Application from John M. McCreary, for the *Wheeling* (Va.)
Gazette—public printer (ALS. DNA, RG 59. mDW 52935).

[May ?] Recommendations from E. S. Duncan et al., for the Clarksburg, Virginia, *Harrison Whig*—public printer (ALS by Duncan,
signed also by others. DNA, RG 59. mDW 52917); from William
Wolcott Ellsworth, J. H. Brockway, and Joseph Trumbull, for Matthew Read (LS. MWalB. mDW 19185); from Ezra Meech et al.,
for Julius O. Harris (LS. NhHi. mDW 19266).

June 1 To Francis Asbury Dickens. LS. DNA, RG 46. mDW 49424.
Transmits copies of the laws of first and second sessions of the 26th
Congress.

June 1 From John Dunham. ALS. DNA, RG 59. mDW 52433. Accepts
appointment to print the laws in the *Norwich Courier*.

June 1 From R. T. Marks and J. D. Bull. LS. DNA, RG 59. mDW
52498. Accept appointment to print the laws in the *Columbus
Enquirer*.

June 1 From Robert C. Wilson. LS by Proxy. DNA, RG 59. mDW 52553.
Accepts appointment to print the laws in the *Western Herald and
Steubenville Gazette*.

June 1 Application from Samuel Burche—consul, La Rochelle (ALS.
MWalB. mDW 19267).

June 1 Recommendation from John Test, for Julius O. Harris (ALS.
NhHi. mDW 19269).

June 2 To [John Agg?]. ALS. NhD. mDW 19271. Wishes to see him
about the next edition of the *Biennial Register*.

June 2 From Gerrish & Edwards. LS. DNA, RG 59. mDW 52406. Accept appointment to print the laws in the *Portland Advertiser*.

June 2 From Horatio Greenough. Printed. Nathalia Wright, ed., *The
Letters of Horatio Greenough* (Madison, 1972), pp. 313–315. Makes
suggestions for erecting his statue of Washington.

June 2 From Severance & Dorr. LS. DNA, RG 59. mDW 52408. Accept
appointment to print the laws in the Augusta, Maine, *Kennebec
Journal*.

June 2 Application from James E. Wharton, for the *Wheeling Times
and Advertiser*—public printer (LS. DNA, RG 59. mDW 52947).

June 2 Recommendations from Leslie Combs, for William R. Harvey—
marshal, Kentucky (ALS. MWalB. mDW 19272); from William
Leftwich Goggin, for William W. Norvell (ALS. NhHi. mDW
19274); from William Leftwich Goggin, for Virginia newspapers—
public printers (ALS. DNA, RG 59. mDW 52908); from Joseph Rogers Underwood, for the *Logan Herald* (ALS. DNA, RG 59. mDW
52684).

June 3 From Edwards & Smith. LS. DNA, RG 59. mDW 52402. Accept
appointment to print the laws in the *Bangor* (Me.) *Whig & Courier*.

June 3 From Andrew Talcott. ALS. DNA, RG 59. mDW 56749. Reports
having drawn $4,000 from the funds appropriated for the northeast
boundary survey.

June 3 Application from Thomas Croxall (ALS. MWalB. mDW
19277).

June 3 Recommendations from William S. Archer, for the *Wheeling*

Times and Advertiser—public printer (ALS. DNA, RG 59. mDW 52957); from William St. Clair Clarke, for James McHenry (ALS. MWalB. mDW 19276); from Reverdy Johnson, for William Meredith, Jr. (ALS. MWalB. mDW 19280); from Shiplin Knapp, for John Wiley—despatch agent (ALS. MWalB. mDW 19283); from John Stuart Skinner, for Thomas Croxall (ALS. MWalB. mDW 19279).

June 4   From D. P. Holloway. ALS. DNA, RG 59. mDW 52565. Accepts appointment to print the laws in the *Richmond* (Ind.) *Palladium.*

June 4   From Thomas W. Sutherland. ALS. DNA, RG 59. mDW 54858. Accepts appointment as U.S. attorney for Wisconsin.

June 4   From Joseph Livingston White. ALS. MWalB. mDW 19290. Requests the immediate removal of the incumbent U.S. marshal for Indiana, Jesse D. Bright.

June 4   Applications from James McHenry (ALS. MWalB. mDW 19285); from Daniel W. Whitehurst, for the St. Augustine, Florida, *News*—public printer (ALS. DNA, RG 59. mDW 52336).

June 4   Recommendation from Willie Person Mangum, for John McLean (ALS. MWalB. mDW 19287).

June 5   From Benson & Green. LS. DNA, RG 59. mDW 52523. Accept appointment to print the laws in the *Boon's Lick Times.*

June 5   From James H. Craven. ALS. MWalB. mDW 19293. Requests Jesse D. Bright's removal from office.

June 5   Recommendations from Nathan Cummings, for John Ruggles (ALS. MWalB. mDW 19295); from Caleb Cushing, for E. S. Sayre —consul, Matanzas (ALS. MWalB. mDW 19296); from E. W. & C. Skinner et al., for Samuel Denison—commissioner of patents (LS. MWalB. mDW 19298); from John Stuart Skinner, for Pierce Mason Butler (LS. MWalB. mDW 19301); from Henry Alexander Wise, for [William A.] Harrison (ALS. MWalB. mDW 19302).

June 6   From William Woodbridge. ALS. DLC. mDW 19309. Urges that the subject of an extradition treaty be brought forward during the upcoming negotiations with the British government.

June 6   Recommendations from Robert M. T. Hunter, for John J. Roane—clerk, Patent Office (ALS. MWalB. mDW 19304); from William Cabell Rives, for John McLean (ALS. MWalB. mDW 19306).

June 7   To [Samuel Lewis Southard]. AL. NjP. mDW 38853. Declines dinner invitation.

June 7   From William Morris Meredith. ALS. MWalB. mDW 19314. Introduces Charles Vezin.

June 7   From Francis Ormand Jonathan Smith. ALS. NhHi. mDW 19318. *Diplomatic Papers,* 1. Proposes a strategy for reconciling Maine public opinion to a compromise of the boundary controversy.

June 7   From Jared Sparks. LC. MH-H. mDW 19322. Sends copy of Faden map showing the northern boundary of the United States.

June 7   From Joseph Trumbull. ALS. NhHi. mDW 19324. Transmits a letter from the comptroller of the state of Connecticut.

June 7   Recommendations from Willie Person Mangum, for a Mr. Noyes (ALS. MWalB. mDW 19312); from John W. Murdaugh, for

the *Portsmouth* (Va.) *Times & Republican* and the *Norfolk Herald*
(ALS. DNA, RG 59. mDW 52929); from James Fowler Simmons,
for the Rhode Island *Providence Daily Journal, Herald of the Times,*
and *Northern Star* (ALS. DNA, RG 59. mDW 52834); from Charles
Vezin, for Arnold Halbach—consul, Baden (ALS. MWalB. mDW
19326); from R. C. Weightman, for the *Lexington* (Va.) *Gazette*—
public printer (ALS. DNA, RG 59. mDW 52953).
June 8   To Francis Asbury Dickens. LS. DLC. mDW 19329. Informs
   him that certain papers have been referred to Mexican claims
   commissioners.
June 8   To Benjamin Rush. LS. NjP. mDW 19330. Accepts his resignation as secretary to the U.S. legation at London.
June 8   From John Davis (1761–1847). AL copy. MBAt. mDW 19463.
   Asks when he should retire from the bench; praises DW's paper on
   the McLeod case and thinks the President's message was
   "encouraging."
June 8   From Samuel H. Davis. ALS. DNA, RG 59. mDW 52559. Ac-
   cepts appointment to print the laws in the *Peoria Register.*
June 8   From Douglass & Noel. LS. DNA, RG 59. mDW 52569. Accept
   appointment to print the laws in the *Indiana Journal.*
June 8   From John Dowling. ALS. DNA, RG 59. mDW 52567. Accepts
   appointment to print the laws in the Terre Haute, Indiana, *Wabash
   Courier.*
June 8   From Alexander K. McClung. ALS. DNA, RG 59. mDW 54749.
   Accepts appointment as U.S. marshal for Mississippi.
June 8   From William H. Richardson. LC. Vi. mDWs. Acknowledges
   receipt of 750 copies of the acts of the 26th Congress, 2d sess.
June 8   From Samuel Bulkley Ruggles. ALS. DLC. mDW 19337.
   Praises DW's reply to Henry Stephen Fox.
June 8   Recommendations from Elisha Camp, for Samuel Denison
   (ALS. MWalB. mDW 19332); from William Woodbridge to DFW,
   for the *Detroit Daily Advertiser, Niles Republican,* and *Monroe*
   (Mich.) *Gazette*—public printers (ALS. DNA, RG 59. mDW 52744).
June 8   Diploma of honorary membership in the U.S. Naval Lyceum.
   Printed form with MS insertions. NhHi. mDW 19339.
June 8   Receipt for $500 advanced to Francis O. J. Smith from the
   secret service fund. AD by DW, signed by Smith. DNA, RG 59.
   mDW 56624.
June 8   Receipt for $200 paid by Edward Stubbs. LS. DNA, RG 59.
   mDW 56591.
June 8   Application from James Kelly—despatch agent (ALS. MWalB.
   mDW 19335).
June 9   To Virgil Maxcy. LS. ViU. mDW 19346. Transmits a copy of
   Tyler's message to Congress.
June 9   From George Gibbs. ALS. NhHi. mDW 19340. Acknowledges re-
   ceipt of a packet of letters copied in the Department of State.
June 9   From Edgar Anthony Low. ALS. MWalB. mDW 19342. Asks
   that the U.S. government lend its support to an expedition through
   Africa.
June 9   Applications from John Bailhache and S. R. Dolbee, for the

Alton (Ill.) *Telegraph and Democratic Review*—public printer (LS. DNA, RG 59. mDW 52997); from T. C. Prince—messenger or runner (ALS. MWalB. mDW 19348).

June 9   Recommendations from Thomas Sherwood Haymond, for the Morgantown, Virginia, *Democratic Republican*—public printer (ALS. DNA, RG 59. mDW 52139); from Henry W. Hilliard, for the *Alabama Journal*—public printer (ALS with ANS by DFW. DNA, RG 59. mDW 52621); from John Leeds Kerr and Isaac Dashiell Jones, for the *Easton* (Md.) *Gazette* (LS. DNA, RG 59. mDW 52904).

June 10   To [Edward Curtis].   122

June 10   From Charles W. Brewster. ALS. DNA, RG 59. mDW 52414. Accepts appointment to print the laws in the *Portsmouth* (N.H.) *Journal*.

June 10   Application from Edward Eastman, for the Plattsburg, New York, *Clinton County Whig*—public printer (ALS. DNA, RG 59. mDW 52295).

June 10   Recommendations from Beverly Allen, for R. B. Servant—chargé, Granada (ALS. MWalB. mDW 19353); from Thomas Allen, for the *Florida Sentinel* (ALS. DNA, RG 59. mDW 52348); from Caleb Cushing, for Courtland Cushing—attorney, Indiana (ALS. MWalB. mDW 19355); from Richard Lawrence, for his brother—consul, Canton (ALS. MWalB. mDW 19357); from Fred A. Tallmadge, for Charles Nichols (ALS. MWalB. mDW 19359).

June 11   To Caleb Cushing from DW and Caroline Le Roy Webster. AL in Caroline Le Roy Webster's hand. NN. mDW 19361. Invite Cushing to dine.

June 11   From James Atkinson. ALS. DNA, RG 59. mDW 52425. Accepts appointment to print the laws in the Newport, Rhode Island, *Herald of the Times*.

June 11   From Knowles, Vose & Anthony. LS. DNA, RG 59. mDW 52423. Accept appointment to print the laws in the *Providence Daily Journal*.

June 11   From Charles Randall. ALS. DNA, RG 59. mDW 52427. Accepts appointment to print the laws in the Warren, Rhode Island, *Northern Star*.

June 11   From Charles Scott. LS. DNA, RG 59. mDW 52555. Accepts appointment to print the laws in the *Ohio State Journal*.

June 11   From Samuel Weir. ALS. DNA, RG 59. mDW 52484. Accepts appointment to print the laws in the Columbia, South Carolina, *Southern Chronicle*.

June 11   Recommendations from Alexander Barrow, for Samuel Haight—consul, West Indies (ALS. MWalB. mDW 19363); from John Moore, for Samuel Haight (ALS. MWalB. mDW 19373); from William Campbell Preston, for Richard Fitzpatrick—consul, Nassau (ALS. NhHi. mDW 19375); from Thaddeus Stevens, for A. De Kalb Tarr—consul, Tangiers (ALS. MWalB. mDW 19377); from John Todd Stuart, for the *Alton Telegraph and Democratic Review*—public printer (ALS. DNA, RG 59. mDW 52999).

June 12   To Stephen Pleasonton. LS. NhD. mDWs. Requests information concerning the payment of outfits to U.S. diplomats overseas.

June 12   From Francis Granger. LC. DNA, RG 28. mDW 57050. Discusses the laws relating to the mailing weight of public documents.
June 12   From Isaac Rand Jackson. ALS copy. MdHi. mDW 19380.
Diplomatic Papers, 1. Expresses appreciation for his diplomatic
assignment.
June 12   From Samuel C. Reid. Copy. DNA, RG 46. mDW 50212. Asks
that negotiations be reopened with Portugal for indemnification of
the owners of the brig *General Armstrong*.
June 12   From Joseph Ritner. ALS. DNA, RG 59. mDW 54816. Accepts
appointment as treasurer of the U.S. Mint at Philadelphia.
June 12   Applications from John Garnier (ALS. NhHi. mDW 19379);
from J. Knowles, for the *Florida Sentinel* (ALS. DNA, RG 59. mDW
52345).
June 13   Application from Henry Montgomery, for the *Harrisburg
Chronicle*—public printer (ALS. DNA, RG 59. mDW 52248).
June 13   Recommendation from Samuel S. Phelps et al., for the *Middlebury* (Vt.) *People's Press* (LS. DNA, RG 59. mDW 52806).
June 14   From Henry J. Williams. Copy. DNA, RG 46. mDW 48247.
Sends memorial of the London holders of bonds issued by the Bank
of Pensacola.
June 14   Recommendations from Henry Cabot, for John Lothrop Mot-
ley—secretary to legation, France (ALS. MWalB. mDW 19385);
from William Alexander Graham, for Daniel Smith McCauley—
consul, Tripoli (ALS. MWalB. mDW 19387); from William Alexander Graham, for the North Carolina *Raleigh Register*, *Newbern
Spectator*, *Highland Messenger*, and *Charlotte Journal*—public
printers (ALS. DNA, RG 59. mDW 52148); from John Henderson,
for the Mississippi *Natchez Daily Courier*, Jackson *Southron*, and
Holly Springs Conservative—public printers (ALS. DNA, RG 59.
mDW 52674); from John Moore, for B. A. Martel—marshal, Louisiana (ALS. MWalB. mDW 19390); from John Canfield Spencer, for
Samuel Haight (ALS. MWalB. mDW 19392).
[*June 14*]   *Remarks on the Fiscal Bank.*   124
June 15   To E. P. De Marcellin. LS. CtY. mDW 19394. Declines invitation to dine with the New York State Society of the Cincinnati.
June 15   To John Tyler. LS. DNA, RG 46. mDW 48207. Submits issue
to army and navy officers regarding political offenses in elections.
June 15   To John Tyler. LS. DNA, RG 46. mDW 48214. Submits copy
of instructions relating to the investigation of the condition of pub-
lic works in Washington, D.C.
June 15   From Samuel Denison. ALS. MWalB. mDW 19409. Encloses
a letter from Elisha Camp and suggests that inquiries about Camp's
character be directed to Thomas Cotton Chittenden.
June 15   From James Lyons. ALS. NhHi. mDW 19411. Introduces
Philip J. [Barsira?].
June 15   From Prentice & Weissinger. LS. DNA, RG 59. mDW 52551.
Accept appointment to print the laws in the *Louisville* (Ky.) *Journal*.
June 15   From Henry W. Starr. ALS. MWalB. mDW 19415. Denounces
efforts to prevent confirmation of Thomas B. Johnson as U.S mar-
shal for Iowa.
June 15   From Jeremiah Van Rensselaer. ALS. NhHi. mDW 19418. Vin-

dicates the official conduct of George W. Greene, U.S. consul at
Rome.

June 15   Recommendation from John Maynard, for Samuel Haight
(ALS. MWalB. mDW 19413).

June 16   From Charles Carter Langdon. ALS. DNA, RG 59. mDW
52500. Accepts appointment as public printer for the *Mobile* (Ala.)
Advertiser and Chronicle.

June 16   From John Moore. ALS. MWalB. mDW 19422. Reports that
U.S. marshal Charles N. Garrett of Louisiana has left the state.

June 16 [1841–1842]   From John Tyler ALS. DLC. mDW 19424. Asks
DW to review some papers and make suggestions.

June 16   Recommendation from Alexander Barrow, for the *New Orleans Bee*, the *Louisiana Chronicle*, and the *Red River Whig*—public printers (ALS. DNA, RG 59. mDW 52630).

[June 16]   [The Proposed Fiscal Bank—No. II].   *127*

June 17   To John Canfield Spencer. LS. PHi. mDW 19451. *W & S*, 16:
343. Transmits copies of the census reports for two New York
districts.

June 17   From Richard S. Coxe. ALS. DLC. mDW 19452. Agrees to see
DW for a conversation.

June 17   From Simeon Francis & Co. LS. DNA, RG 59. mDW 52561.
Accept appointment to print the laws in the *Sangamo Journal*.

June 17   From Henry Montgomery. ALS. DNA, RG 59. mDW 52456.
Accepts appointment to print the laws in the *Harrisburg Chronicle*.

June 17   From Nelson & Bates. LS. DNA, RG 59. mDW 52502. Accept
appointment to print the laws in the *Alabama Journal*.

June 17   From Albert G. Rhea. ALS. DNA, RG 59. mDW 52547. Accepts
appointment to print the laws in the *Logan Herald*.

June 17   Recommendation from Robert Charles Winthrop, for Joseph
Webster Hale—consul, St. Thomas (ALS. NN. mDW 19454).

[June 17]   [The Proposed Fiscal Bank—No. III].   *130*

June 18   To [Francis Granger]. ALS. NN. mDW 19456. Expresses
pleasure on learning that L. L. Britton of Orford, N.H., may be
given a position.

June 18   From Bullitt, Magne & Co. LS. DNA, RG 59. mDW 52507. Accept appointment to print the laws in the *New Orleans Bee*.

June 18   From Sir Henry Holland. ALS. NhD. mDWs. Curtis, 2: 88.
Reports his discussions with Peter Parker on China.

June 18   From Robert Lucas. LS. MWalB. mDW 19465. Comments on
his dismissal as governor of Iowa Territory.

June 18   Recommendations from Samuel Burche, for Joseph Marks
(ALS. NhHi. mDW 19458); from Rufus Choate, for a Mr. Benson—
consul, Liverpool (ALS. MWalB. mDW 19459); from Caleb Cushing, for Joseph Webster Hale—consul, St. Thomas (LS. MWalB.
mDW 19461); from Nathaniel Pitcher Tallmadge, for Philip Viele—
attorney, Iowa (ALS. MWalB. mDW 19469); from Henry Alexander Wise, for the Clarksburg, Virginia, *Harrison Whig* (ALS. DNA,
RG 59. mDW 52133).

June 19   From John Bausman. ALS. DNA, RG 59. mDW 52454. Ac-

cepts appointment to print the laws in the Washington, Pennsylvania, *Reporter*.

June 19   From Harvey Bell. ALS. DNA, RG 59. mDW 52439. Accepts
appointment to print the laws in the *Middlebury* (Vt.) *People's
Press*.

June 19   From Weston R. Gales. ALS. DNA, RG 59. mDW 52478. Accepts appointment to print the laws in the *Raleigh Register*.

June 19   From Henry B. Miller. ALS. DNA, RG 59. mDW 52753. Accepts appointment to print the laws in the *Niles Republican*.

June 19   Recommendations from Thomas Corwin, for George B. May—
consul, Rio de Janeiro (ALS. MWalB. mDW 19471); from John
Leeds Kerr, for the *Easton* (Md.) *Gazette* (ALS with ANS by DW.
DNA, RG 59. mDW 52902).

June 20   From John I. Pasteur. ALS. DNA, RG 59. mDW 52480. Accepts appointment to print the laws in the *Newbern* (N.C.)
Spectator.

June 21   To John Pendleton Kennedy. ALS. MdBP. mDW 19473. Asks
him to notify the editor of the *Baltimore Patriot* of his selection as
public printer.

June 21   To Augustus Seymour Porter. LS. DNA, RG 46. mDW 50046.
Promises to furnish the chairman of the Senate Judiciary Committee with papers should charges be brought against George C. Bates.

June 21   From Grinnell, Minturn & Co. LS. MWalB. mDW 19477. Introduce Justo Pou.

June 21   From Knowles, Clisby & Smith. LS. DNA, RG 59. mDW 52541.
Accept appointment to print the laws in the *Florida Sentinel*.

June 21   From Brantz Mayer. ALS. MWalB. mDW 19481. Expresses
alarm on hearing that someone other than himself may succeed
John Randolph Clay as secretary of legation at Vienna.

June 21   From James Renwick. ALS. DNA, RG 59. mDW 56750. Accounts for funds withdrawn for the northeast boundary survey.

June 21   From James Thurber. ALS by proxy. DNA, RG 59. mDW
52421. Accepts appointment to print the laws in the Plymouth,
Massachusetts, *Old Colony Memorial*.

June 21   Recommendations from Alexander Barrow, for John Gibson—
consul, Buenos Aires (ALS. MWalB. mDW 19475); from Peter Harmony & Co., for Paul Pou—consul, Barcelona (LS. MWalB. mDW
19479).

June 22   To Thomas Ewing. Copy. DNA, RG 206. mDWs. Encloses the
bond posted by Thomas Hulme, newly appointed consul to Sedan,
France.

June 22   From Margaret Harrison. ALS. MWalB. mDW 19487. Asks
that her husband, Robert M. Harrison, U.S. consul at Jamaica, be
transferred to a more lucrative post.

June 22   From William A. Weaver. LS. DNA, RG 46. mDW 49428. Submits abstract of the Sixth Census.

June 22   Application from William Whetten (ALS. MWalB. mDW
19493).

June 22   Recommendations from John Barney, for William Meredith,
Jr. (ALS. MWalB. mDW 19485); for Augustus Rhodes Sollers et al.,

for John Bozman Kerr (ALS by Sollers, signed also by others. MWalB. mDW 19490).

June 23   To the Senate of the United States. LS. DNA, RG 46. mDW 49426. Transmits abstracts of the census returns.

June 23   From Jesper Harding. ALS. DNA, RG 59. mDW 52458. Accepts appointment to print the laws in the Philadelphia *Pennsylvania Inquirer*.

June 23   From D. B. McAnally. ALS. DNA, RG 59. mDW 52482. Accepts appointment to print the laws in the *Highland Messenger*.

June 23   Application from William H. Trott (ALS. MWalB. mDW 19495).

June 23   Recommendation from James Graham, for the *Highland Messenger* (ALS. DNA, RG 59. mDW 52154).

June 24   To Joshua A. Spencer. LS. CLU. mDW 19497. Doubts he can offer Spencer's son a job at present.

June 24   To John Tyler. LS. DNA, RG 46. mDW 48222. Sends correspondence concerning the payment or assumption of state stocks by the federal government.

[June 24]   To Nathaniel F. Williams. ALS. NhD. mDW 19499. Encloses a draft for $1,000 and asks that he honor a similar draft by Charles Henry Thomas.

June 25   To [Edward Curtis?]. ALS. NN. mDW 19501. Reports the committee is satisfied and "probably things will work along."

[June 25]   From [Edward C. Davis]. LS. DNA, RG 59. mDW 52470. Accepts appointment to print the laws in the *Richmond* (Va.) *Whig*.

June 25   From James Renwick. ALS. DNA, RG 59. mDW 56754. Presents his accounts for auditing.

June 25   From James E. Wharton. ALS. DNA, RG 59. mDW 52472. Accepts appointment to print the laws in the *Wheeling Times and Advertiser*.

June 25   To Hiram Ketchum from Daniel Fletcher Webster.   *132*

June 25   Application from John F. Hamtramck Claiborne—superintendent of armory, Harper's Ferry (ALS. DNA, RG 156. mDWs).

June 25   Recommendation from Benjamin Sprague Cowen, with a memorial from numerous citizens of Wheeling, Va., for the *Wheeling Times and Advertiser* (ALS. DNA, RG 59. mDW 52137).

June 26   To Jeremiah Smith. ALS. MH-H. mDW 19508. Informs him that Jeremiah Robinson has been appointed postmaster at Exeter.

June 26   To John Trumbull. LS. NHi. mDW 19509. Inquires about the diplomatic character of the American commissioners appointed under the Treaty of 1794.

June 26   From A. Graham. ALS. DNA, RG 59. mDW 52468. Accepts appointment to print the laws in the *Easton Gazette*.

June 26   From James Kelly. ALS. MWalB. mDW 19511. Asks for the return of his letter of application and testimonials.

June 26   Application from Thomas M. Willing (ALS. NhHi. mDW 19513).

June 27   From William Bradford Reed. ALS. DLC. mDW 19520. Offers suggestions for the distribution of patronage in Pennsylvania.

June 27   Application from Louis Mark—consul, Bavaria (ALS. MWalB. mDW 19516).

June 28   To Lewis Cass. LS. The Current Company, Bristol, R.I. Introduces Howard Henderson.

June 28   To Edward Everett. LS. MHi. mDW 19527. Introduces James
Colles.

June 28   To the U.S. Senate. LS. DNA, RG 46. mDW 49430. Reports
on the progress of the Sixth Census and asks that the time for its
completion be extended.

June 28   From Oliver P. Baldwin. ALS. DNA, RG 59. mDW 52474. Accepts appointment to print the laws in the *Lexington* (Va.) *Gazette*.

June 28   From Edwin James Foster. ALS. DNA, RG 59. mDW 52519.
Accepts appointment to print the laws in the Holly Springs, Mississippi, *Southern Banner*, formerly the *Holly Springs Conservative*.

June 28   Recommendation from Henry Turner et al., for S. Whitman—
commissioner of patents (DS. MWalB. mDW 19528).

June 29   To Edward Kavanagh. LS. Roman Catholic Diocese of Portland, Me. mDW 19531. Accepts EK's resignation as U.S. chargé
d'affaires to Portugal.

June 29   To John Tyler. LS. DNA, RG 46. mDW 48262. Transmits, for
presentation before the Senate, correspondence with the German
states regarding duties on tobacco.

June 29   From Thomas Walker Gilmer. LS. DNA, RG 59. mDW 55686.
Transmits a resolution requesting a statement of the number of officers and agents employed by the State Department.

June 29   From John F. McJilton. ALS. DNA, RG 59. mDW 52462. Indicates Isaac Munroe will accept appointment to print the laws in the
Baltimore Patriot.

June 29   From John Trumbull. ALS. NH. mDW 19535. States that he
cannot give a "satisfactory answer" to DW's inquiry relative to the
diplomatic status of the American commissioners appointed under
the Treaty of 1794.

June 29   Application from Richard J. A. Culverwell (ALS. MWalB.
mDW 19533).

June 29   Receipt for $800, paid to DW by Edward Stubbs. DS. DNA, RG
59. mDW 56591.

June 29   Receipt to Caleb Cushing for $2,000. ADS. DLC. mDW 39858.

June 29   Recommendations from William Campbell Preston, for the
Calhoun, South Carolina, *Highland Sentinel* or the Cheraw *Gazette*,
the Charleston *Southern Patriot*, the Columbia *Southern Chronicle*,
the *Tallahassee Star*, and the St. Augustine *News*—public printers
(ALS. DNA, RG 59. mDW 52330).

June 30   To [Thomas Ewing]. ALS. DLC. mDW 19537. Advises against
Currier's reappointment as port collector at Newburyport.

June 30   To John Tyler. LS. CSmH. mDW 19539. Recommends the appointment of William B. Blackburn, Jr., or General Thomas Metcalf
as marshal for Kentucky.

June 30   From Benjamin Albertson. ALS. DNA, RG 59. mDW 52517.
Accepts appointment to print the laws in the Jackson *Southron*.

June 30   From Oliver P. Baldwin. ALS. DNA, RG 59. mDW 52476.
Again signifies his acceptance of appointment to print the laws in
the *Lexington Gazette*.

June 30   From Caleb Cushing. LS. NhHi. mDW 19540. Reiterates again his view that Americans ought to be appointed to U.S. consulates.

June 30   From John M. Duffield. ALS. DNA, RG 46. mDW 52515. Accepts appointment to print the laws in the *Natchez Daily Courier.*

June 30   From Francis Harrison. ALS. NhHi. mDW 19542. Discusses American relations with Haiti and makes general suggestions regarding consular agents.

June 30   From Sherman & Harron. LS. DNA, RG 59. mDW 52452. Accept appointment to print the laws in the *New Jersey State Gazette.*

June 30   From Samuel Lewis Southard. LS. MWalB. mDW 19545. Encloses letters dealing with consular matters.

[June]   From John Tyler. ALS. DLC. mDW 21084. Asks him to inform Crittenden of Joseph Eve's appointment.

[June]   From John Tyler. ALS. DLC. mDW 19549. Suggests that DW acknowledge a letter from Edward Kent of Maine.

[c. June]   From John Tyler. ALS. TxSjM. mDWs. *Diplomatic Papers, 1.* Asks if some diplomatic post in South America might be found for General William S. Murphy.

[June?]   From John Tyler. AL. DLC. mDW 22794. Concurs in DW's suggestion regarding the George Johnson case.

[June?]   Memorandum by DW of Waddy Thompson's wish to have the *Highland Sentinel* print the laws. AD. DNA, RG 59. mDW 52332.

June[?]   Recommendation from Edmund Deberry et al., for Charles G. Nelms—district attorney, Mississippi (ALS by Deberry, signed also by others. MWalB. mDW 19547).

July 1   From Marshall & Coulter. LS. DNA, RG 59. mDW 52563. Accept appointment to print the laws in the *Illinois Republican.*

July 1   From John Tyler. ALS. DLC. mDW 19553. Asks for DW's advice concerning a petition for pardon.

July 1   Recommendation from Samuel J. Penn, for John Garnier (ALS. NhHi. mDW 19550).

July 2   To William Alexander Graham. LS. NcU. mDW 19556. Lists the newspapers which have been selected to print the laws in North Carolina.

July 2   From Francis Hall & Co. LS. DNA, RG 59. mDW 52441. Accept appointment to print the laws in the New York *Commercial Advertiser.*

July 2   From Robert E. Hornor. ALS. DNA, RG 59. mDW 52449. Accepts appointment to print the laws in the *Princeton Whig.*

July 2   From Marmaduke D. Johnson Slade. ALS. DNA, RG 59. mDW 52504. Accepts appointment to print the laws in the Tuscaloosa *Independent Monitor.*

July 2   From Francis Ormand Jonathan Smith (enclosure: statement by citizens of Maine regarding northeastern boundary, July 1841). ALS. NhHi. mDW 19559. *Diplomatic Papers, 1.* Outlines specific measures which might be adopted for assuaging Maine public opinion on the boundary issue.

July 2   Recommendation from James Cooper, for Charles Nichols (ALS. MWalB. mDW 19557).

July 3   From Walter Forward. ALS. DNA, RG 59. mDW 54635. Acknowledges commission appointing him first comptroller of the Treasury.

July 3   From E. W. & C. Skinner. ALS. DNA, RG 59. mDW 52443. Accept appointment to print the laws in the *Albany Daily Advertiser*.

July 3   From Silas F. Smith. ALS. DNA, RG 59. mDW 52445. Accepts appointment to print the laws in the Syracuse, New York, *Western State Journal*.

July 3   From Andrew Talcott. ALS. DNA, RG 59. mDW 56757. Explains the delay in his departure for the disputed boundary area; has drawn $5,000 from the account for the northeast survey expedition.

July 3   Application from William H. McCardle, for the *Vicksburg* (Miss.) *Daily Whig*—public printer (ALS with AN by DW. DNA, RG 59. mDW 52678.

July 3   Recommendations from Washington Irving, for James Baker— indefinite post (ALS. MWalB. mDW 19564); from Abbott Lawrence, for Joseph T. Adams—foreign post (ALS. MWalB. mDW 19567); from William Cabell Rives, for A. O. Newton—consul, Matanzas (ALS. MWalB. mDW 19570); from Joseph Lanier Williams, for the *Knoxville Register* (ALS with AN by DW. DNA, RG 59. mDW 52682).

July 4   From Nicholas Biddle.   133

July 5   From Edward Kent. LC. Me. mDW 19580. Protests encroachments on Maine territory by the New Brunswick provincial government; calls for the stationing of U.S. troops at Fish River.

July 5   Application from Charles Nichols (ALS. MWalB. mDW 19585).

July 5   Recommendations from F[elix?] Boudinot, for Francis D. Cummins—commercial agent, Port au Prince (ALS. NhHi. mDW 19574); from William Bowen Campbell, for Thomas R. Jennings— marshal, Tennessee (ALS. MWalB. mDW 19578); from Levi Lincoln, for the Worcester, Massachusetts, *National Aegis*—public printer (ALS. DNA, RG 59. mDW 52872).

July 6   From Phillip Richard Fendall. ALS. DNA, RG 59. mDW 54618. Accepts appointment as U.S. attorney for the District of Columbia.

July 6   From Elisha M. Huntington. ALS. DNA, RG 59. mDW 54700. Accepts appointment as commissioner of the General Land Office.

July 6   From Isaac Munroe. ALS. DNA, RG 59. mDW 52464. Accepts appointment to print the laws in the *Baltimore Patriot*.

July 6   From William B. Kinney. ALS. DNA, RG 59. mDW 52447. Accepts appointment to print the laws in the *Newark Daily Advertiser*.

July 6   From Joshua A. Spencer. ALS. NhHi. mDW 19592. Expects the judges' decision in the McLeod case will be delivered on Monday, July 12.

July 6   Recommendations from John Macpherson Berrien et al., for Andrew L. King—consul, Nassau (LS. NhHi. mDW 19587); from John Jordan Crittenden, for a Mr. Wilson—indefinite post (ALS. MWalB. mDW 19590).

July 7   From L'Hommedieu & Co. LS. DNA, RG 59. mDW 52557. Accept appointment to print the laws in the *Cincinnati Gazette*.

July 7   From Shadrach Nye. ALS. DNA, RG 59. mDW 52535. Accepts appointment to print the laws in the Nashville, Tennessee, *Republican Banner*.

July 7   Recommendations from William Butler, for the *Highland Sentinel* (ALS. DNA, RG 59. mDW 52334); from Joel Wolfe, for Joseph Marks (ALS. NhHi. mDW 19596).

July 8   To Peter Chardon Brooks. ALS. MHi. mDW 19598. *Diplomatic Papers*, 1. Asks if he thinks Edward Everett might like the English post.

July 8   To John Tyler. LS. DNA, RG 46. mDW 48350. Submits report on the progress and condition of the commission under the convention with Mexico, April 11, 1839.

July 8   From John William Allen. Extract. UkLPR. mDW 19602. Reports on activities and suspected intentions of Canadian patriots living in Detroit, Buffalo, and Cleveland.

July 9   From John Tyler. ALS. DLC. mDW 19608. Curtis, 2: 87. Describes measures he has taken to prevent an invasion of Canada by Canadian insurgents living in the United States.

July 9   Recommendation from Isaac Edward Holmes for [?]—consul, La Rochelle (ALS. NhHi. mDW 19606).

July 10   To Deming Jarves. Printed. Frank W. Chipman, *The Romance of Old Sandwich Glass* (Sandwich, Mass., 1932), p. 138. Thanks him for a set of Sandwich glassware.

July 10   From Cosam Emir Bartlett. ALS. DNA, RG 59. mDW 52539. Accepts appointment to print the laws in the Tallahassee *Star of Florida*.

[July 10]   From J. N. Cardozo and James G. Guerry. ALS by Cardozo, signed also by Guerry. DNA, RG 59. mDW 52492. Accept appointment to print the laws in the Charleston *Southern Patriot*.

July 10   From Joshua A. Spencer. ALS. NhHi. mDW 19617. Has learned the New York court will deny motion to discharge McLeod; promises decision will be appealed immediately.

July 10   Application from S. Hull—clerkship (ALS. MWalB. mDW 19613).

July 10   Recommendation from Robert Bennie Cranston, for George F. Usher (ALS. NhHi. mDW 19611).

July 12   To [Hiram Ketchum].   *134*

July 12   To Hiram Ketchum. ALS. NhD. mDW 19623. Asks if Charles King had prior knowledge of a letter signed by a "Delegate to the Harrisburg Convention," which appeared recently in the *New York American*.

July 12   From Cady & Harris. LS. DNA, RG 59. mDW 52525. Accept appointment to print the laws in the St. Louis *Commercial Bulletin*.

July 12   From Absalom Fowler. ALS. DNA, RG 59. mDW 54639. Accepts appointment as U.S. attorney for Arkansas.

July 12   From Thomas T. Russell. ALS. DNA, RG 59. mDW 52537. Accepts appointment to print the laws in the St. Augustine *News*.

July 12   From Shepard & Strong. LS. DNA, RG 59. mDW 52307. Express disappointment on hearing that an appointment to publish the laws was made before the receipt of their application for the *Rochester Daily Democrat*.

July 12   From Joshua A. Spencer. ALS. NhHi. mDW 19628. *Diplomatic Papers*, 1. Discusses strategy which might be adopted in response to the New York court's decision in the McLeod case.

July 12   Recommendation from Nehemiah Rice Knight, for Joseph M. Church—secretary of legation, Naples, Spain, or Austria (ALS. MWalB. mDW 19626).

July 13   To Edward Curtis. ALS. NN. mDW 19632. Advises him to wait for the report of the commission investigating the New York customs house before dealing with William Cairn's case.

July 13   To Thomas Ewing. LS. DNA, RG 217. mDW 57200. Presents Nicholas Philip Trist's views on crew lists and shipping papers.

July 13   From Peter Chardon Brooks. AL draft. MHi. mDW 19631. *Diplomatic Papers*, 1. Expresses confidence that Everett would take the English post.

July 13   From J. P. Reed. ALS. DNA, RG 59. mDW 52488. Accepts appointment to print the laws in the Calhoun, South Carolina, *Highland Sentinel*.

July 13   Recommendation from Stephen White, for Joseph M. Hernandez—governor of Florida (ALS. MWalB. mDW 19634).

[July 13?]   From John Tyler. ALS. DLC. mDW 21111. Introduces William Boulware of whom he has spoken relative to the Naples mission.

July 14   To Peleg Sprague. ALS. MDuHi. mDWs. Reports that he will send Sprague's nomination for U.S. district judge to the Senate the next day.

July 14   From Samuel Fessenden. ALS. NhHi. mDW 19638. Suggests the creation of a commission to settle the Maine boundary dispute.

July 14   From Joshua A. Spencer. ALS. NhHi. mDW 19644. Reports having visitied with McLeod; discusses legal strategy affecting the case.

July 14   Applications from Joseph M. Hernandez (ALS. MWalB. mDW 19642); from Messenger & Rollsten, for the Tuscumbia *North Alabamian*—public printer (LS with AN by DW. DNA, RG 59. mDW 52599).

July 14   Recommendation from Garrett Davis, for John Trimble—attorney, Kentucky. (ALS. MWalB. mDW 19636).

July 15   To Joshua A. Spencer. Copy. NhHi. mDW 19652. *Diplomatic Papers*, 1. States that the McLeod case should go to trial as soon as possible.

July 15   To Nicholas Philip Trist. LS. DLC. mDW 19653. Informs him of his dismissal as U.S. consul at Havana.

July 15   From Nicholas Biddle. ALS draft. DLC. mDW 19659. Introduces James Magee, who is hoping to be appointed British consul at Mobile.

July 15   From George W. P. Curtis. ALS. DNA, RG 59. mDW 54554. Accepts appointment as justice of the peace for Alexandria.

July 15   From Alexander Hill Everett. ALS (not sent). LU. mDW 19663. Defends his investigation and report on the extent of American participation in the African slave trade; elaborates on charges against Trist.

July 15   From Peleg Sprague. ALS. MWalB. mDW 19677. Insists he is in good health and fully able to discharge the duties of U.S. district judge.

[July 15]   From John Tyler. ALS. DLC. mDW 19854. Orders the recall
of Trist from Havana; discusses other appointments.

[July 15]   "English Mission" (editorial). AD. NN. mDW 19654. *National
Intelligencer,* July 15, 1841.

July 15   Recommendations from Caleb Cushing, for Charles D.
Drake—district attorney, Missouri (ALS. MWalB. mDW 19661);
from Isaac Dashiell Jones, for E. Richardson Hooper—clerk, State
Department (ALS. MWalB. mDW 19675); from Nathaniel Pitcher
Tallmadge, for James S. Thayer—despatch agent, New York (ALS.
MWalB. mDW 19681).

July 16   To [?]. ALS. NhD. mDW 19683. Asks that a $700 clerkship be
left vacant until he hears from a friend.

July 16   To Lewis Cass. LS. MiU-C. mDW 19684. Introduces Henry A.
de Forest of Rochester, N.Y.

July 16   To John Davis (1761–1847). LS. MBAt. mDW 19686. Acknowledges his resignation as U.S. district judge for Massachusetts.

July 16   To Hiram Ketchum. Printed. Curtis, 2: 72–75. New York *Commercial
Advertiser,* July 20, 1841. Analyzes conflicting Whig views on the bank
question.

July 16   To Joseph Story. ALS. MHi. mDW 22904. *Diplomatic Papers,*
1. Discusses the McLeod case.

July 16   From Samuel Burche. ALS. NhHi. mDW 19690. States that
the incumbent U.S. consul at La Rochelle does not in fact reside
in that city.

July 16   From John D. Clark. ALS. DNA, RG 59. mDW 54548. Accepts
appointment as justice of the peace for Washington, D.C.

July 16   From [Thomas Walker Gilmer?]. AL. DNA, RG 59. mDW
55719. Transmits a Senate resolution requesting information relative to the printing of the laws and other printing work done by the
State Department.

July 16   From Henry Hart Milman. Printed. Curtis, 2: 89. Introduces
Mr. and Mrs. Charles Lyell, who are about to visit America on a
scientific expedition.

July 16   Contract with Thomas Allen to print the laws. DS. DNA, RG
59. mDW 53539.

July 17   To Hiram Ketchum.   *134*

July 17   From [?]. Copy. NhHi. mDW 19692. Discusses the commercial
potential of Paraguay; suggests himself for appointment as consul
general for the La Plata region.

July 17   From John Henderson. ALS. DNA, RG 59. mDW 52521. Reports that the *Holly Springs Conservative,* designated as public
printer, has changed its name to *Southern Banner.*

July 17   From J. P. Reed. ALS. DNA, RG 59. mDW 52490. Accepts appointment to print the laws in the *Highland Sentinel.*

July 17   From Reuben Johnston. ALS. DNA, RG 59. mDW 54708. Accepts appointment as justice of the peace for Alexandria.

July 17   From William W. Stewart. ALS. DNA, RG 59. mDW 54848.
Accepts appointment as justice of the peace for Washington, D.C.

July 17   Application from William N. Sherman, for the *Woonsocket*
(R.I.) *Patriot*—public printer (ALS with AN by DW. DNA, RG 59.
mDW 52836).

July 17   Recommendation from Nathaniel Briggs Borden, for Julius C.
Anthony—consul, Port au Prince (ALS. NhHi. mDW 19700).

[*July 18?*]   *To Hiram Ketchum.*   137

July 18   From A. R. Porter. ALS. DNA, RG 59. mDW 52527. Accepts
appointment to print the laws in the *Batesville* (Ark.) *News.*

July 18   Recommendation from Edward Cross, for the *Washington*
(Ark.) *Telegraph*—public printer (ALS. DNA, RG 59. mDW
52738).

July 19   From Charles Anthony. ALS. DNA, RG 59. mDW 54488. Accepts appointment as U.S. attorney for Ohio.

July 19   Application from William Bennett Parker (ALS. MWalB.
mDW 19704).

July 19   Recommendations from William Bibb Figures, for the Huntsville
Southern Advocate (ALS. DNA, RG 59. mDW 52352); from Joseph
Leonard Tillinghast, for George F. Usher (ALS. NhHi. mDW
19706); from John P. Van Ness, for Charles W. Van Ness—secretary to the legation, Austria (ALS. MWalB. mDW 19710).

July 20   To Benjamin Tappan. ALS. DLC. mDW 19713. Acknowledges
the copy of a letter from Tappan's son.

July 20   From William Butler. ALS. DNA, RG 59. mDW 52486. Encloses an acceptance letter from the editor of the *Highland Sentinel.*

July 20   From John B. Dade. ALS. DNA, RG 59. mDW 54560. Accepts
appointment as warden of the penitentiary in the District of
Columbia.

July 20   Application from Asa Messenger, for the *North Alabamian*
(ALS. DNA, RG 59. mDW 52601).

July 20   Recommendations from Hiram P. Hunt, for Samuel Haight
(ALS. MWalB. mDW 19715); from David Bayard Ogden, for
Charles Nichols (ALS. MWalB. mDW 19717).

[c. July 20]   From John Tyler. ALS. DLC. mDW 19719. Asks that
copies of the Senate resolution of July 20, 1841, calling for the
names of individuals removed from public office in the federal
government since March 4, 1829, be made and sent to each
department.

July 21   From Porter & Naff. LS. DNA, RG 59. mDW 52466. Accept
appointment to print the laws in the Wilmington *Delaware State
Journal.*

July 21   From Joseph Story. ALS. NhD. mDWs. States he is overwhelmed with business and cannot write a review of Judge [Esek]
Cowen's opinion in the McLeod case; strongly criticizes the opinion.

July 21   From Edward Webster. ALS. NhHi. mDW 19723. Describes
briefly the curriculum of the Harvard Law School; reports visiting
with Julia and finding various family members all well.

July 21   From John Wells, Jr. ALS. DNA, RG 59. mDW 54887. Accepts appointment as clerk of the circuit court for Washington,
D.C.

July 21   Recommendation from Millard Fillmore, for Samuel Haight
(ALS. CSmH. mDW 19721).

July 22   To Hiram Ketchum. ALS. NhD. mDW 19726. *Diplomatic
Papers,* 1. Discusses the pressures of office.

July 22   From Robert Brookhouse and William Hunt. LS copy. UkLPR.

mDWs. Submit a statement of damages and losses sustained by the *Tigris* and *Seamew* as a result of their seizure by British cruisers off the coast of Africa.

July 22   From Francis Granger. ALS. MWalB. mDW 19730. Reports that papers pertaining to the application of F. Garrettson Luckey were transferred to the State Department.

July 22   From J. N. Harker. ALS. DNA, RG 59. mDW 52460. Accepts appointment to print the laws in the Wilmington *Delaware Gazette.*

July 22   From David Levy (David Levy Yulee). ALS. MHi. mDW 19734. Transmits a letter concerning U.S. marshal Joseph Sanchez of Florida.

July 22   Recommendations from John F. Everitt, for Julius O. Harris (ALS. MWalB. mDW 19728); from Thomas Butler King, for Andrew L. King (ALS. NhHi. mDW 19732).

July 23   To John Tyler. LS. DNA, RG 59. mDW 56593. Requests funds to send an agent to Central America and to employ "a suitable person to go to the northern cities."

July 23   From Henry Rowe Schoolcraft (with Schoolcraft to John Tyler, July 23, 1841). ALS draft. DLC. mDW 19742. Submits the prospectus of his book on Indians.

July 23   From Peleg Sprague. ALS. DNA, RG 59. mDW 54842. Accepts appointment as U.S. district judge for Massachusetts.

July 23   From John Tyler. LS. DNA, RG 59. mDW 56594. Authorizes the expenditure of $5,000 from the foreign contingency fund "for objects which it is not now expedient to specify."

July 23   Applications from James Hervey Bingham—clerkship, unspecified post (ALS. NhHi. mDW 19736); from Richard Sutton (ALS. NhHi. mDW 19744).

July 23   Recommendation from Samuel Luckey, for F. Garrettson Luckey (ALS. MWalB. mDW 19738).

July 23   Receipt for $1,000 paid by Edward Stubbs. AD. DNA, RG 59. mDW 56596.

July 24   To William Leigh Brent (with Brent to DW, July 29, 1841). George C. Whipple, Jr. Carmel N.Y. mDW 19746. Reports that the President has agreed to let him look at "the letter"; declines to answer his other questions and warns that he should not infer from this refusal anything unfriendly toward Clay.

July 24   To Caleb Cushing. LS. DLC. mDW 19750. Requests appropriations to cover the salaries and outfits of various U.S. diplomatic representatives abroad.

July 24   To Edward Everett. ALS. MHi. mDW 19752. Curtis, 2: 83–84. *Diplomatic Papers*, 1. Informs Everett of his appointment to the English mission.

July 24   From Courtland Cushing. ALS. DNA, RG 59. mDW 54556. Accepts appointment as U.S. attorney for Indiana.

July 24   From John H. Ransdell and George M. Reynolds. ALS by Ransdell, signed also by Reynolds. DNA, RG 59. mDW 52514. Accept appointment to print the laws in the *Red River Whig.*

July 24   Application from Andrew Webster (ALS. NhHi. mDW 19756).

July 24 Recommendation from George T. Ward, for the Apalachicola
Florida Journal—public printer (ALS. DNA, RG 59. mDW 52340).
[c. July 24] From John Tyler. ALS. DLC. mDW 25548. Returns with
his approval DW's draft of instructions for General William
S. Murphy.
July 25 From Demas Adams. ALS. DNA, RG 59. mDW 54482.
Accepts appointment as U.S. marshal for Ohio.
July 25 From Edward Everett. LC. MHi. mDW 19759. Comments
on Italian reaction to the death of Harrison; believes the conti-
nental powers would side with the United States in the event of
war with England; describes a visit with Joseph Bonaparte.
July 25 Recommendation from William Campbell Preston, for B. W.
Bell—marshal, Alabama (ALS. MWalB. mDW 19763).
July 26 From William Henry Seward. ALS draft. NRU. mDW 19769.
Transmits a report on the McLeod case by the attorney general
of New York.
July 26 Recommendations from Samuel L. Hays, for the Clarksburg,
Virginia, Harrison Whig—public printer (ALS. DNA, RG 59. mDW
52142); from Abraham Rencher, for the Salisbury, North Caro-
lina, Carolina Watchman—public printer (ALS with AN by DW.
DNA, RG 59. mDW 52587).
July 27 From Charles Sumner (enclosure: memorandum on United
States consulate at Rome). ALS. NhHi. mDW 19771. Urges the
development of commercial relations with the Papal States.
July 27 [1841–1842] From John Tyler. ALS. DLC. mDW 19790. Asks
that the enclosed papers relative to "Mr. Martin" be copied.
July 27 From Albert S. White. ALS. MWalB. mDW 19792. Asks DW
to call the President's attention to a letter from Solon Robinson.
July 27 Application from John A. Blake—bookbinding for the State
Department (ALS. MWalB. mDW 19787).
July 28 To Edward Everett.   *138*
July 28 From Albert Crane. ALS. MWalB. mDW 19800. Suggests that
Samuel Denison be sent as a "confidential agent" to watch the
movements of the Patriots along the northern frontier.
July 28 From John Tyler. ALS. DLC. mDW 19810. Writes relative
to the dismissal of a U.S. marshal.
July 28 Applications from Josiah M. Lucas, for the Jacksonville
Illinoian—public printer (ALS. DNA, RG 59. mDW 53001); from
Brantz Mayer (ALS. MWalB. mDW 19808).
July 28 Recommendations from Ogden Hoffman, for Charles Nichols
(ALS. MWalB. mDW 19804); from Hiram Ketchum, for Charles
Nichols (ALS. MWalB. mDW 19806).
July 28 To Hiram Ketchum from Daniel Fletcher Webster.   *139*
July 29 To Samuel Lewis Southard. ALS. NjP. mDW 19811. Asks
him to call on Mrs. Webster.
July 29 From William Leigh Brent (with DW to Brent, July 24,
1841). ALS. George C. Whipple, Jr. Carmel, N.Y. mDW 19749.
Asks that his son be permitted to see "the letter."
July 29 From Joseph Solms. ALS. NhHi. mDW 19816. Introduces
John Devereux.
July 29 Recommendations from Jacob Burnet, for the Davenport

(Ia.) *Gazette*—public printer (ALS. DNA, RG 59. mDW 52963);
from William Pitt Fessenden, for William B. Gooch—consul,
Aux Cayes (ALS. MWalB. mDW 19812).

July 30 To Caleb Cushing. LS. NN. mDW 19819. Transmits an award
made by the Mexican Claims Commission for consideration by
the House Committee on Foreign Relations.

July 30 From Francis Granger. LC. DNA, RG 28. mDW 57051.
Transmits the names of deputy postmasters removed and
appointed since March 4, 1841.

July 30 Application from William Hogan—vice consul, Matanzas
or Hamburg (ALS. MWalB. mDW 19825).

July 30 Recommendation from William Pitt Fessenden, for Francis
Springer—attorney, Iowa (ALS. MWalB. mDW 19822).

July 31 To Francis Granger. ALS. NN. mDW 19828. States that the department heads should report directly to the President and not
to the secretary of state.

July 31 From Franklin Dexter. ALS by proxy. DNA, RG 59. mDW
54580. Accepts appointment as U.S. attorney for Massachusetts.

July 31 From Edwards & Smith. LS. DNA, RG 59. mDW 52404.
Notify the State Department that their interest in the *Bangor
Whig and Courier* has been sold to Messrs. Smith and Sayward.

July 31 From Robert Hanna. ALS. DNA, RG 59. mDW 54665. Accepts appointment as U.S. marshal for Indiana.

July 31 From Joshua A. Spencer. ALS. DNA, RG 59. mDW 54840.
Acknowledges receipt of commission as U.S. attorney for northern
New York.

[July 31] From John Tyler. ALS. DLC. mDW 19834. Suggests that
DW send a letter of condolence to the king of Hanover, whose
wife died.

July 31 From W. L. and Q. K. Underwood. LS. DNA, RG 59. mDW
52529. Accept appointment to print the laws in the Helena,
Arkansas, *Southern Shield.*

July 31 Recommendations from John Devereux, for Gideon T. Snow
(ALS. NhHi. mDW 19832); from Christopher Harris Williams,
for the Huntsville, Alabama, *Southern Advocate* and the *Memphis*
(Tenn.) *Enquirer*—public printers (ALS. DNA, RG 59.
mDW 52350).

[July] To Hiram Ketchum. ALS. NhD. mDW 19836. *Diplomatic
Papers*, 1. Discusses Seward's "contemptible" behavior.

[July] From John Tyler. ALS. DLC. mDW 19852. Thinks "Smith" is
guilty of "great impropriety" but sees no reason to censure
Sanchez.

[July] From John Tyler. ALS. DLC. mDW 25550. Encloses a paper
"written by a Mr. Banks from Honduras."

[c. July] Clause of U.S. bank bill. AD draft. DLC. mDW 19850.

[July? 1841] To Hiram Ketchum. ALS incomplete. NhD. mDW
21731. Is greatly pained by [Charles] King's criticism of the
President.

[July–August] From John Tyler. ALS. DLC. mDW 19856. Comments
that "we shall see what we shall see" if the repeal of the sub-
treasury law should pass the two houses of Congress.

Aug 1   From Charles Pelham Curtis. ALS. NhHi. mDW 19858.
Introduces William Lyman.

Aug 1   From McMahon, Moseley & Dooley. LS. DNA, RG 59. mDW
52543. Accept appointment to print the laws in the *Memphis Enquirer*.

Aug 2   From Cornelius Darragh. ALS. DNA, RG 59. mDW 54562.
Accepts appointment as U.S. attorney for western Pennsylvania.

Aug 2   From George W. Toland. ALS. MWalB. mDW 19860. Introduces
James McHenry.

Aug 2   Receipt for $2,000 disbursed by Edward Stubbs. DS. DNA,
RG 59. mDW 56596.

Aug 3   To Lewis Cass. ALS. The Current Company, Bristol, R.I.
mDWs. Introduces Mr. and Mrs. Daniel Fearing of New York.

Aug 3   To [Samuel Bulkley Ruggles]. ALS. MHi. mDW 19862. Plans
recommending a supplemental bank bill; discusses the alteration
of the original bill by the House of Representatives.

Aug 3   From Charles Chapman. ALS. DNA, RG 59. mDW 54542. Accepts appointment as U.S. attorney for Connecticut.

Aug 3   From Charles Davis. ALS. DNA, RG 59. mDW 54568. Accepts appointment as U.S. attorney for Vermont.

Aug 3   From James G. Edwards. ALS. DNA, RG 59. mDW 52579.
Accepts appointment to print the laws in the *Hawk-eye and
Iowa Patriot*.

Aug 3   From Sylvester Hartshorn. ALS. DNA, RG 59. mDW 54673.
Accepts appointment as U.S. marshal for Rhode Island.

Aug 3   Recommendations from Nicholas Biddle, for James A. Simpson—marshal, New Jersey (ALS. MWalB. mDW 19866); from
Robert Bennie Cranston and Joseph Leonard Tillinghast, for
Francis M. Dimond—consul, Nassau (ALS by Tillinghast, signed
also by Cranston. NhHi. mDW 19872); from William Morris Meredith, for Edward S. Norris—consul, Leghorn (ALS. MWalB.
mDW 19868); from James H. Raymond, for William H. Trott
(ALS. MWalB. mDW 19870).

Aug 3   Receipt for $50 paid to Albert Fitz. ADS. DNA, RG 59. mDW
56609.

Aug 4   To Caroline Le Roy Webster. ALS. NhHi. mDW 19873. Van
Tyne, pp. 234–235. Reports on the Washington scene.

Aug 4   From John Chambers. ALS. DNA, RG 59. mDW 54540. Accepts appointment as governor of Iowa Territory.

Aug 4   From Franklin Dexter. ALS. DNA, RG 59. mDW 54576. Accepts appointment as U.S. attorney for Massachusetts.

Aug 4   From John B. Eldredge. ALS. DNA, RG 59. mDW 54616.
Accepts appointment as U.S. marshal for Connecticut.

Aug 4   From John D. Kinsman. ALS. DNA, RG 59. mDW 54722.
Accepts appointment as U.S. marshal for Maine.

[Aug 4]   Recommendation from William Campbell Preston, for
Richard Fitzpatrick (ALS. NhHi. mDW 19877).

[Aug 5]   To Joseph Gales and William Winston Seaton. ALS. NN.
mDWs. Urge them to reprint an article on Jefferson's constitutional views from the *Southern Literary Messenger*.

Aug 5   To Albert Gallatin. LS. NHi. mDW 19879. Introduces Jules
Lavergne of New Orleans, who is gathering information on commerce and finance.

Aug 5   From [Roger Sherman Baldwin]. AL draft. CtY. mDW 19881.
Summarizes the facts in *United States* v. *William Scovill* in
which a Connecticut button-maker was charged with issuing
counterfeit coins.

Aug 5   Recommendation from Joseph Lanier Williams, for John
Calloway—marshal, Tennessee (ALS. MWalB. mDW 19885).

Aug 6   From James Gadsden. ALS. MWalB. mDW 19887. Urges the
government to support [Achille] Murat's claims against France
and to furnish him with public employment until these claims
are adjusted.

Aug 6   Recommendations from John William Allen, for the *Cleveland
Herald* (ALS with AN by DW. DNA, RG 59. mDW 52702); from
Joseph Lanier Williams, for Matthew Nelson—marshal, Tennessee
(ALS. MWalB. mDW 19891).

Aug 7   To Rufus Choate. LS. NhD. mDWs. Transmits a certified copy
of the agreement providing for the transfer of the George Washington papers to the United States and asks that the requisite fee
be sent to the State Department.

[Aug 7]   To [Thomas Ewing]. ALS. DLC. mDW 20087. Reports that
Richard Milford Blatchford will reach Washington on August 8;
discusses bank bill.

Aug 7   From Balie Peyton. ALS by proxy. DNA, RG 59. mDW 54799.
Accepts appointment as U.S. attorney for eastern Louisiana.

Aug 7   From Otho H. W. Stull. ALS. DNA, RG 59. mDW 54856.
Accepts appointment as secretary of Iowa Territory.

Aug 7   From Andrew Talcott. ALS. DNA, RG 59. mDW 56760. Reports having drawn $3,000 from the account for the exploration
and survey of the northeast boundary.

Aug 7   Recommendation from James Harper, for Philip Banks—
consul, Haiti (ALS. MWalB. mDW 19893).

[Aug 8]   To Richard Milford Blatchford. ALS. NRU. mDW 19895.
Invites Blatchford and "Mr. Bowen" to dine.

[Aug 8]   To Thomas Ewing. ALS. DLC. mDW 19898. Invites Ewing
to dine, along with Richard Milford Blatchford and Francis
Granger.

Aug 8   To Caroline Le Roy Webster. Printed. *PC*, 2: 107–108. Reports
on life in his new Washington house; fears "a great commotion"
should the President veto the bank bill.

Aug 9   To John J. Abert and Peter Force. LS. DLC. mDW 19900. Approves plans for storing the collections of the National Institution in the upper rooms of the Patent Office.

Aug 10   From William Crum. ALS. DNA, RG 59. mDW 52581. Accepts appointment to print the laws in the *Iowa Standard*, removed
from Bloomington to Iowa City.

Aug 10   Application from Robert Treat Paine (ALS. MWalB. mDW
19907).

Aug 10   Recommendations from Charles Carter Langdon, for Julius
O. Harris (ALS. NhHi. mDW 19903); from Thomas P. Trott

et al., for John J. Hyde (ALS by Trott, signed also by others. MWalB. mDW 19910).

Aug 11 To [Thomas Ewing]. LS. DLC. mDW 19913. Notifies him of a cabinet meeting "this morning at 10 oclock precisely."

Aug 11 To [Francis Granger]. LS. Vincent E. Edmunds, Staten Island, N.Y. mDWs. Informs him of a cabinet meeting.

Aug 11 From Andrew T. Judson. ALS. DNA, RG 59. mDW 54712. States that he will deliver the commission of appointment to the U.S. marshal for Connecticut.

Aug 11 From James C. Moses. ALS. DNA, RG 59. mDW 52545. Accepts appointment to print the laws in the *Knoxville Register*.

Aug 11 Application from John H. Williams, for the Frederick, Maryland, *Examiner* (ALS. DNA, RG 59. mDW 52845).

Aug 12 From Silas Moore Stilwell. ALS. DNA, RG 59. mDW 54852. Accepts appointment as U.S. marshal for southern New York.

Aug 12 Application from Walter R. Johnson—commissioner of patents (ALS. MWalB. mDW 19919).

Aug 12 Recommendations from Richard Keith Call, for Richard Fitzpatrick (ALS. NhHi. mDW 19917); from John Leeds Kerr, for the Frederick *Examiner* (ALS. DNA, RG 59. mDW 52843).

Aug 13 To [Hiram Ketchum?].   140

Aug 13 To [Samuel Lewis Southard] (enclosure: estimate of expenses for binding census documents). LS. DNA, RG 46. mDW 49453. Reports that the Census of Pensioners has been taken; recommends that Congress make some provision for binding the census documents.

Aug 13 From Justin Butterfield. ALS. DNA, RG 59. mDW 54526. Accepts appointment as U.S. attorney for Illinois.

Aug 13 From James Douglass. ALS. DNA, RG 59. mDW 52510. Accepts, on behalf of the editor, appointment to print the laws in the *Louisiana Chronicle*.

Aug 13 From Thomas Randall. ALS. MWalB. mDW 19922. Sends information regarding the office of land agent in Florida.

Aug 14 To Caleb Cushing. Invitation. NN. mDW 19924.

Aug 14 To James Fowler Simmons. Invitation. DLC. mDW 19927.

Aug 14 From John Tyler. ALS. DLC. mDW 19929. Asks what he thinks of making [Achille] Murat a judge.

Aug 14 From Thomas W. Sutherland. ALS. DNA, RG 59. mDW 54860. Accepts appointment as U.S. attorney for Wisconsin.

[Aug 15] "The 'Strange Doctrine' " (editorial). Printed. *National Intelligencer*, August 17, 1841.

Aug 16 To Joseph Hopkinson. Printed LS with MS insertions. PHi. mDW 19931. Encloses commission appointing Isaac Otis U.S. marshal for Pennsylvania.

Aug 16 To Caroline Le Roy Webster.   140

Aug 16 Recommendations from Aaron Clark, for John J. Hyde (ALS. MWalB. mDW 19943); from Richard R. Lansing, for Joseph Sanchez—consul, West Indies (ALS. NhHi. mDW 19949); from Francis Mallory, for the *Norfolk Herald* (ALS with AN by DW. DNA, RG 59. mDW 52924).

[Aug 16] Veto of the Bank Bill.   142

Aug 17 Application from George Corbin Washington—commissioner of patents (ALS. MWalB. mDW 19951).

Aug 18 From Nicholas Callan, Jr. ALS. DNA, RG 59. mDW 54536. Accepts appointment as justice of the peace for the District of Columbia.

Aug 18 From David Hoffman. ALS draft. NHi. mDW 19955. Declines appointment as commissioner under the 1839 convention with Mexico.

Aug 18 Recommendations from Landaff Watson Andrews, for the *Vicksburg Daily Whig* (ALS. DNA, RG 59. mDW 52623); from Peter G. Fosdick et al., for Henry Markham—consul, Paita, Peru (LS. NhHi. mDW 20023); from Leverett Saltonstall, for W. G. French—clerk (ALS. MWalB. mDW 19957); from Edward Douglass White, for John J. Hyde (ALS. MWalB. mDW 19959).

[*Aug 19*] *To [Thomas Ewing].*   *143*

[Aug 19] To Caroline Le Roy Webster. ALS. NhHi. mDW 19961. Van Tyne, p. 236. Reports on legislative developments; states that he is "most dreadfully hard worked."

Aug 19 Application from Simrall & Jones, for the Madison, Indiana, *Republican Banner*—public printer (LS. DNA, RG 59. mDW 52772).

Aug 19 Recommendation from John Henderson, for a Mr. Tupper—attorney, Mississippi (ALS. MWalB. mDW 19963).

Aug 20 *To John Tyler.*   *144*

Aug 20 From Cyril C. Cady. Copy. CtY. mDW 19967. Warns of "disastrous" consequences should the Senate fail to confirm Silas Reed as surveyor for Illinois and Missouri.

Aug 20 From William H. Etten. ALS. DNA, RG 59. mDW 52531. Accepts appointment to print the laws in the *Washington* (Ark.) *Telegraph.*

Aug 20 From Thomas B. Monroe. ALS. DNA, RG 59. mDW 54510. States that he has administered the oath of office to William B. Blackburn, Jr., U.S. marshal for Kentucky.

Aug 20 From Stephen Clarendon Phillips (enclosure: Phillips to DW, Aug 20, 1841). ALS. NhHi. mDW 19968. Hopes a satisfactory bank bill may be drafted and presents his ideas in an enclosure which he says may be shown to Tyler.

Aug 20 From Stephen Clarendon Phillips (enclosed with Phillips to DW, Aug 20, 1841). ALS. NhHi. mDW 19971. Bank proposal.

[c. *Aug 20*] *To [Hiram Ketchum].*   *144*

Aug 20 Recommendations from William Butler, for John J. Hyde—chargé, South America (ALS. MWalB. mDW 19965); from Nathaniel Pitcher Tallmadge, for John J. Hyde (ALS. MWalB. mDW 19975); from Thomas Wheeler Williams et al., for John J. Hyde (LS. MWalB. mDW 19977).

[*Aug 21*] *To Caroline Le Roy Webster.*   *145*

Aug 21 From Alexander P. Field. ALS. NhHi. mDW 19985. Explains the delay in arranging for his bond of office.

Aug 21 Application from Charles Nichols (ALS. MWalB. mDW 19990).

Aug 21   Recommendations from James Cooper, for Charles Nichols
(ALS. MWalB. mDW 19983); from Archibald Ladley Linn, for
John J. Hyde (ALS. MWalB. mDW 19988); from Leverett Salton-
stall, for John J. Hyde (ALS. MWalB. mDW 19992); from Silas M.
Stilwell, for John J. Hyde (ALS. MWalB. mDW 19994); from
Joseph Lanier Williams, for the Huntsville *Southern Advocate*
(ALS. DNA, RG 59. mDW 52354).

[*Aug 22*]   *To Hiram Ketchum.*   *146*
[Aug 22]   To Harriette Story White Paige. ALS. MH-H. mDW 19999.
PC, 2: 108. Expresses regret on the death of her father; finds little
good to report on politics and longs for Marshfield.
Aug 22   To Caroline Le Roy Webster. ALS. NhHi. mDW 20005. Van
Tyne, p. 601. Is perplexed by her remaining in New York; com-
ments on the political situation in Washington.
Aug 22   From Shadrach Nye. ALS. DNA, RG 59. mDW 52533. Informs
DW that the Nashville *Republican Banner* has changed ownership.
Aug 22   From Smith & Rhea. LS. DNA, RG 59. mDW 52549. State
that the Russellville, Kentucky, *Logan Herald* is now being pub-
lished as the *Herald and Advertiser.*
Aug 23   From John M. Duffield. ALS. DNA, RG 59. mDW 52676.
Reports that he has not yet received Public Laws No. 1 and No. 2
for publication in his *Natchez Daily Courier.*
Aug 23   From Flint L. Keyes. ALS. DNA, RG 156. mDWs. Claims to
have invented an explosive shell of immense power and asks that
the subject be brought to the attention of the proper authorities.
Aug 23   Receipt for $1,000 disbursed by Edward Stubbs. DS. DNA,
RG 59. mDW 56596.
Aug 23   Recommendation from George Nixon Briggs, for Trowbridge
Ward—consul, Matagorda (ALS. MWalB. mDW 20009).
Aug 24   To William Henry Seward. LS. NRU. mDW 20013. *Diplomatic
Papers*, 1. Encloses extracts from a letter communicated to him by
Henry Stephen Fox warning of a plot to lynch McLeod; urges
precautions to ensure his safety.
[Aug 24]   To Caroline Le Roy Webster. ALS. NhHi. mDW 20019. Van
Tyne, pp. 275–276. Reports there is much "uncertainty and ex-
citement" in Washington.
Aug 24   From Matthew Harvey. ALS. DNA, RG 46. mDW 50014.
Fears that Joel Eastman's nomination for U.S. attorney in New
Hampshire may be rejected on the erroneous assumption that he
is an abolitionist.
Aug 24   Recommendation from Christopher Morgan, for Henry
Markham (ALS. NhHi. mDW 20022).
Aug 25   *To Isaac Chapman Bates and Rufus Choate.*   *147*
Aug 25   Recommendations from Hugh Birckhead, for John F. Ber-
nabeu—consul, Alicante (ALS. MWalB. mDW 20038); from John
H. Eaton et al., for Thomas Cookendorfer—despatch bearer (LS.
MWalB. mDW 20040); from Duncan C. Eldridge, for the *Daven-
port Gazette* (ALS. DNA, RG 59. mDW 52965); from Benjamin
Watkins Leigh, for Bernard F. Carter—secretary, European lega-
tion (ALS. MWalB. mDW 20042).

Aug 25   To Richard Smith from DFW. ALS. UPB. mDWs. Gives status of bill for rechartering the district banks.

Aug 26   To Franklin Haven. ALS. MH-H. mDW 20045. Sees little chance that a bank bill will pass the current session; asks him to take care of a check for $1500.

[Aug 26]   To Willie Person Mangum. Dictated letter. NcD. mDW 20048. Henry Thomas Shanks, ed., *The Papers of Willie P. Mangum* (5 vols., Raleigh, 1950–1956), 3: 221–222. Asks him if Vinson Butler is qualified to be appointed U.S. attorney for western Florida.

Aug 26   Recommendation from Ebenezer Cook et al., for the *Davenport Gazette* (LS. DNA, RG 59. mDW 52360).

Aug 27   To Nathaniel Pitcher Tallmadge. AL. WHi. mDW 20049. Invites Tallmadge to dinner.

Aug 28   To John Macpherson Berrien. ALS. DNA, RG 46. mDW 50011. Encloses a letter relative to the nomination of Joel Eastman for U.S. attorney in New Hampshire.

Aug 28   From Edward Everett. ALS. MHi. mDW 20050. Discusses plans should his nomination for U.S. minister to England be confirmed.

Aug 28   Recommendation from John Todd Stuart, for the Galena, Illinois, *Northwestern Gazette and Galena Advertiser*—public printer (ALS. DNA, RG 59. mDW 52986).

Aug 29 [1841–1842]   From John Tyler. ALS. DLC. mDW 20062. Writes: "The paper is all right and its views of the subject correct."

Aug 30   To Caleb Cushing. AL. NN. mDW 20085. Invites Cushing to dinner.

Aug 30   To Thomas Ewing. AL. DLC. mDW 20064. Invites Ewing to dinner.

Aug 30   To William Cabell Rives. AL. DLC. mDW 20066. Invites Rives to dinner.

Aug 30   From Richard Keith Call. ALS. DNA, RG 59. mDW 54534. Accepts appointment as governor of Florida Territory.

Aug 30   Application from John F. Bernabeu (ALS. MWalB. mDW 20067).

Aug 30   Recommendation from George Evans, for Eben Ritchie Dorr—unspecified post (ALS. MWalB. mDW 20071).

Aug 31   To John James Audubon. LS. NN. mDW 20073. Writes concerning Audubon's application for post as curator general of the National Institution.

Aug 31   From Thomas W. Newton. ALS. DNA, RG 59. mDW 54781. Accepts appointment as U.S. marshal for Arkansas.

Aug 31   Recommendations from Samuel Jaudon, for Louis Marks—consul, Bavaria (ALS. MWalB. mDW 20076); from William Schley, for J. L. M. Smith—consul (ALS. MWalB. mDW 20078).

Aug   To [Caleb Cushing]. ALS. NN. mDW 20081. States that the President will see him in the evening.

Aug   To Caleb Cushing. ALS. NN. mDW 20083. Arranges to see him.

Aug   To [Thomas Walker Gilmer?] (enclosures: lists of attorneys, State Department officials, U.S. marshals, etc.). AL. DNA, RG 59.

mDW 55690. Transmits a list of individuals employed in the State Department.

[Aug?] From [Richard Milford Blatchford et al.]. Copy. NRU. mDW 20093. Argue that the proposed Fiscal Corporation would be supported by capitalists.

Sept 1 From James A. Kelly. ALS. DNA, RG 59. mDW 52512. Accepts appointment to print the laws in the *Louisiana Chronicle*.

Sept 2 From Henry Marie Brackenridge. ALS. DNA, RG 59. mDW 54520. Accepts appointment to the board of commissioners established under the convention with Mexico of 1839.

Sept 2 From Sydney Smith (with ANS by DW). ALS. MHi. mDW 20098. Asks DW to do him "justice" in repeating the story of his introduction of DW to Lord Brougham.

Sept 2 Recommendations from P. Macaulay, for J. L. M. Smith (ALS. MWalB. mDW 20095); from Jonathan Meredith, for J. L. M. Smith (ALS. MWalB. mDW 20096).

Sept 3 From Thomas B. Pottinger. ALS. DNA, RG 59. mDW 54805. Accepts appointment as U.S. marshal for Maryland.

Sept 3 Recommendations from John Macpherson Berrien, for George A. Brown (ALS. MWalB. mDW 20100); from Charles C. Stratton et al., for Marmaduke Burrough—consul, Canton, Lima, or Valparaiso (ALS by Stratton, signed also by others. MWalB. mDW 20115).

Sept 4 To Robert Gould Shaw. LS. NcU. mDW 20117. Recommends Benjamin E. Green, a son of Duff Green.

Sept 4 From William B. Blackburn, Jr. ALS. DNA, RG 59. mDW 54512. Accepts appointment as U.S. marshal for Kentucky.

Sept 4 Application from Marmaduke Burrough (ALS. MWalB. mDW 20120).

Sept 4 Recommendations from William Wolcott Ellsworth, for Joseph Harris (ALS. MWalB. mDW 20123); from William Woodbridge, for Isaiah Thomas and John Griffin—foreign mission (ALS draft. MiD-B. mDW 20128).

Sept 5 Application from Ferdinand Henry Finck—consul, Württemberg (ALS. MWalB. mDW 20132).

Sept 6 Recommendation from Caleb Cushing, for John J. Hyde (ALS. MWalB. mDW 20148).

Sept 7 From John Tyler. ALS. DLC. mDW 20176. Tyler, *Tylers*, 2: 213. Asks that Seward be informed of his approval of the arrangements for McLeod's protection.

Sept 8 Applications from John James Audubon (ALS. MH-H. mDW 20178); from William Handy—temporary employment, State Department (ALS. MWalB. mDW 20180).

Sept 8 Recommendation from James M. Coale, for the *Frederick* (Md.) *Herald*—public printer (ALS with AN by DW. DNA, RG 59. mDW 52210).

[c. Sept 8] From John Tyler. ALS. NjMoHP. mDW 20183. *Diplomatic Papers*, 1. Responds to Fox's notes of Sept 5 and 6.

Sept 9 To John Tyler. LS. DNA, RG 46. mDW 48499. Sends correspondence relating to the convention with Sardinia for transmission to the Senate.

Sept 9   From John Dowling. ALS. DNA, RG 59. mDW 52400. Announces that the Terre Haute *Wabash Courier* has been sold to Messrs. Conard & Harris.

Sept 9   From Andrew Talcott. ALS. DNA, RG 59. mDW 56761. Reports having drawn $3,500 from the account for the exploration and survey of the northeast boundary.

Sept 9   From John Tyler. ALS. DLC. mDW 20192. Asks DW to assist him in gratifying "Judge Baldwin and his son."

Sept 10   To Hiram Ketchum. Printed. *PC*, 2: 110. *Diplomatic Papers*, 1. Reports that several cabinet members will resign tomorrow; promises not to act suddenly or to endanger the country "by any abrupt party proceeding."

Sept 10   From H. D. Saint Anthoine (enclosure: certificate of membership in Institut d'Afrique, Aug 25, 1841). LS. DLC. mDW 20195. Transmits a certificate of membership in the Institut d'Afrique.

[Sept 11]   To Phillip Hone. Copy. NHi. mDWs. Alan Nevins, ed., *The Diary of Philip Hone: 1828–1851* (2 vols., New York, 1927), 2: 560. Announces impending resignation of cabinet members and asks *"whether the Whig public expect me to follow suit, or to hold on a while for the sake or on account of the foreign relations of the country."*

Sept 11   From Israel Webster Kelly. ALS. DNA, RG 59. mDW 54714. Accepts appointment as U.S. marshal for New Hampshire.

Sept 11   Recommendation from Nathaniel Briggs Borden, for the *Taunton* (Mass.) *Whig*—public printer (ALS. DNA, RG 59. mDW 52887).

Sept 12   From John Charles Spencer, Earl of Spencer. Printed. Curtis, 2: 89–91. Reports being defrauded by an adventurer named Monroe Edwards, who forged DW's signature to a letter of introduction.

Sept 13   To Franklin Haven. ALS. MH-H. mDW 20209. Asks that a bank note from Rufus Choate be deposited to his account.

Sept 13   From Nicholas Biddle. ALS draft. DLC. mDW 20210. Invites DW to his country house to talk over recent events.

Sept 13   From John Davis (1788–1878). ALS. DLC. mDW 20215. Advises DW to continue his support of the President.

Sept 13   From Z. Collins Lee. ALS. DNA, RG 59. mDW 54730. Accepts appointment as U.S. attorney for Maryland.

[Sept 13]   From John Tyler. ALS. DLC. mDW 20217. Arranges to meet with DW; discusses appointments.

Sept 13   Recommendation from John P. Van Ness, for Charles W. Van Ness (ALS. MWalB. mDW 20219).

Sept 14   To Joseph Gales and William Winston Seaton. ALS. NN. mDW
20226. *W & S*, 16: 358–359. Inquires about the article stating that
he would remain in the State Department, which appeared in the
National Intelligencer.

Sept 14   To John McLean. Printed LS with MS insertions. DLC. mDW
20229. Encloses commission appointing him secretary of war.

Sept 14   From Eliakim Littell. ALS. DLC. mDW 20237. Urges DW to remain in the State Department; expresses the hope that a satisfactory
banking plan can be worked out.

Sept 14   From Charles B. Penrose. ALS. DNA, RG 59. mDW 54795. Acknowledges appointment as solicitor of the Treasury.

Sept 15   To Nathan Fellows Dixon and James Fowler Simmons. LS.
NhD. mDW 20245. Informs them that the President has postponed
any decision on the appointment of a Providence postmaster.

Sept 15   From Alexander P. Field. ALS. DNA, RG 59. mDW 54622. Accepts appointment as secretary of Wisconsin Territory.

Sept 16   From William Pitt Fessenden. ALS. MWalB. mDW 20261.
Transmits a petition.

Sept 16   From John Sealley et al. LS. NmRA. mDW 20265. Reports that
the Texan invasion of New Mexico has exposed Americans in Santa
Fe to harassment by local authorities.

Sept 16   Application from Samuel Haight (ALS. NhHi. mDW 20263).

Sept 16   Recommendation from Hugh Birckhead, for J. L. M. Smith
(ALS. MWalB. mDW 20259).

Sept 16   Receipt for $150 paid to George Smith. AD by DW, signed by
Smith. DNA, RG 59. mDW 56602.

Sept 17   From Nicholas Biddle. ALS draft. DLC. mDW 20272. Condemns the cabinet resignations.

Sept 17   From Albert Miller Lea (with reply, Sept 20, 1841). True copy.
DLC. mDW 20278. Asks Webster to comment for President Tyler
on the attorney general's opinion in the case of Lt. A. Drane.

Sept 17   Application from Nathaniel Parker Willis—secretary, London
legation (ALS. MWalB. mDW 20285).

Sept 17   Recommendations from George Evans, for Mr. Jewett—consul,
Matanzas—and Timothy Darling (ALS. NhHi. mDW 20274); from
George Evans, for Mr. Ruggles—agent to Louisiana (ALS. MWalB.
mDW 20276).

Sept 18   To Franklin Haven. ALS. MH-H. mDW 20287. Asks that
Haven's bank honor drafts of the U.S. Treasury until he reaches
Boston and arranges for sale of government stock.

Sept 18   To Nathaniel Houghton. LS. NN. mDW 20289. States that
Houghton's passport has been forwarded to the collector of customs
at New York.

Sept 18   To Albert Miller Lea (with Lea to DW, Sept 17, 1841). Copy.
DLC. mDW 20278. Endorses the attorney general's opinion in the
Drane case.

Sept 18   From John Barney. ALS. DLC. mDW 20293. Supports DW's
decision to remain in the State Department and hopes he can persuade the President to adopt some "scheme of finance."

Sept 18   From Christopher Hughes.   *153*

Sept 18   From Theodore H. McCaleb. ALS. DNA, RG 59. mDW 54747.
Accepts appointment as U.S. district judge for Louisiana.

Sept 18   From John McLean.   *157*

Sept 18   From Zachariah Walker. ALS. DNA, RG 59. mDW 54875. Accepts appointment as justice of the peace for Washington, D.C.

Sept 18   Recommendation from William P. Duval, for William A. Davis—attorney, Florida (ALS. MWalB. mDW 20297).

Sept 20   To Sydney Smith. Copy. NhD. mDW 20316. Lady Saba (Smith) Holland, *A Memoir of the Reverend Sydney Smith* (2 vols., New York, 1855), 1: 252. Denies making fun of him and gives assurances of his respect and friendship.

Sept 20   To [?].   *158*

Sept 20   Recommendation from Millard Fillmore, for Thomas M. Foote —postmaster, Buffalo (ALS. DLC. mDW 20320).

Sept 20   Receipt for $1000 advanced to Alexander Powell from the secret service fund. AD by DW, signed by Powell. DNA, RG 59. mDW 56626.

Sept 21   To [Joshua A. Spencer]. ALS. NhD. mDW 20325. Asks about public sentiment in New York regarding the McLeod trial.

Sept 21   To Joshua A. Spencer. Copy. PHi. mDW 20327. *Diplomatic Papers*, 1. Sets forth the "ground of legal defence, in McLeod's case."

Sept 21   From Selah R. Hobbie. LS. DNA, RG 59. mDW 54818. Announces appointments and removals of postmasters at Lowell and Newburyport, Mass., and Auburn, N.Y.

Sept 22   From Thomas Allen. Printed. Washington *Madisonian*, Sept 23, 1841. Asks DW to furnish a copy of his Aug 25 letter to Isaac Chapman Bates and Rufus Choate for publication.

Sept 22   To Thomas Allen. Printed. *Madisonian*, Sept 23, 1841. Sends the requested letter.

Sept 22   From George Washington Patterson.   *158*

Sept 22   From John E. Smith. ALS. DNA, RG 76. mDWs. Presses his claim on the British government in the case of the ship *Portsmouth*, captured in the port of Sierra Leone on Dec 13, 1805.

Sept 22   Application from Henry Markham (ALS. NhHi. mDW 20340).

[Sept 22?]   To Thomas Allen. AN. NhD. mDWs. *Madisonian*, Sept 23, 1841 (incorporated in an editorial entitled "Cabinet Publications"). Draws attention to the secrecy imposed on English cabinet deliberations, as set forth in *Dodd's Parliamentary Companion* for 1841.

Sept 23   To Nicholas Biddle. ALS. DLC. mDW 20352. Proposes to see Biddle in Philadelphia on Sept 27.

Sept 23   From Thomas R. Walker. ALS. DLC. mDW 20358. Asks that E. D. Brown be furnished with letters of introduction to Lewis Cass and Edward Everett.

Sept 23   Receipt for $1,000 paid by Edward Stubbs. DS. DNA, RG 59. mDW 56596.

Sept 24   From John Quincy Adams. LC. MHi. mDW 20375. Asks for a copy of the entire census returns.

Sept 24   From Selah R. Hobbie. LS. DNA, RG 59. mDW 54771. Announces the appointments of postmasters at Louisville, Ky., and Milledgeville, Ga.

Sept 24   From Isaac Otis. ALS. DNA, RG 59. mDW 54787. Accepts appointment as U.S. marshal for eastern Pennsylvania.

Sept 24   From Joshua A. Spencer. ALS. NhHi. mDW 20389. *Diplomatic Papers*, 1. Writes that McLeod's alibi is "impregnable."

[*Sept 24*]   [*The Cabinet Crisis*].   160

Sept 24   Recommendation from Samuel Lewis Southard, for James Hoy—consul, Belfast (ANS. MWalB. mDW 20386).

Sept 25   To Abel Parker Upshur. ALS. PCarlD. mDW 20393. Comments on Marine Lt. [Louis F.?] Whitney's appeal of a court martial conviction.

Sept 25   From Joel Eastman. ALS. DNA, RG 59. mDW 54608. Accepts appointment as U.S. attorney for New Hampshire.

Sept 25   From Albert Fearing.   161

Sept 25   From Selah R. Hobbie. LC. DNA, RG 28. mDW 57053. States that information needed for the *Biennial Register* will be ready by Sept 30.

[Sept 25]   Application from Eli Colby, for the Little Rock *Arkansas Times and Advocate*—public printer (ALS. DNA, RG 59. mDW 52184).

Sept 25   Receipt for $1,000 paid by Edward Stubbs. DS. DNA, RG 59. mDW 56596.

Sept 26   To James L. Edwards. LS. CtY. mDW 20403. Reports finding no record that Reuben Stiles served in the army before Sept 1779.

Sept 26   From Walker Anderson. ALS. DNA, RG 59. mDW 54484. Accepts appointment as U.S. attorney for Florida.

Sept 26   Recommendation from Catherine Chase Oldfield, for her sisters—coloring maps (ALS. MWalB. mDW 20407).

Sept 27   From Samuel Ladd. ALS. DNA, RG 156. mDWs. Asks that a coating he has invented to prevent rusting in fire arms be tested so that he may obtain a patent.

Sept 27   From Joshua A. Spencer. ALS. NhHi. mDW 20421. Reports on the firing from Navy Island upon British ships; describes the preparation of McLeod's defense.

Sept 27   From Charles Anderson Wickliffe. ALS. DNA, RG 59. mDW 54893. Accepts appointment as postmaster general.

Sept 27   Application from William B. Guy—mail carrier (ALS. MWalB. mDW 20410).

Sept 27   Recommendation from Jonathan Prescott Hall, for Thomas Tucker—consul, Bermuda (LS. MWalB. mDW 20412).

Sept 28   From Thomas H. Duval. ALS. DNA. RG 59. mDW 54604. Accepts appointment as secretary of Florida Territory.

Sept 28   From John Holmes. ALS. NhD. mDW 20427. Deplores the Whig divisiveness.

Sept 28   From Daniel A. Webster. ALS. DLC. mDW 20431. Warns that New York City Whigs are greatly disenchanted with the administration's patronage policy and are deserting the party in large numbers.

Sept 28   Recommendation from Daniel Dewey Barnard, for Charles Smyth—consul, Kingston, Ontario (ALS. MWalB. mDW 20425).

Sept 29   From Selah R. Hobbie. LS. DNA, RG 59. mDW 54704. Announces removals and appointments of postmasters at Watertown and Oswego, N.Y.

Sept 29   From Hugh Swinton Legaré. ALS. MHi. mDW 20434. Writes
concerning Waddy Thompson's belief that he had been promised
the U.S. mission to Mexico.

Sept 29   From Daniel Fletcher Webster. ALS. NhHi. mDW 20444. Discusses his revision of a note to Fox and other miscellaneous administrative matters.

Sept 29   Application from Edward Eastman, for the *Clinton County
Whig* (ALS. DNA, RG 59. mDW 52171).

Sept 29   Recommendation from J. Smith et al., for William Mayhew,
Jr.—consul, Bay of Islands, New Zealand (LS. MWalB. mDW
20438).

[Sept 30]   To Daniel Fletcher Webster. ALS. NhHi. mDW 20451. *W & S*,
16: 359. Approves DFW's alterations in the note to Henry Stephen
Fox; reports a general opinion that McLeod will be acquitted.

Sept 30   From John Stuart-Wortley. ALS. DLC. mDW 20457. Curtis, 2:
92. Introduces Lord Morpeth.

Sept 30   Recommendation from Isaac Hull, for Charles Crokat—consul,
Genoa (ALS. MWalB. mDW 20454).

Sept   From Stephen Fairbanks. ALS. DLC. mDW 20464. Reports that
Boston Whigs approve of DW's remaining in office and are generally
satisfied by recent patronage decisions.

[Sept]   [*Memorandum on the President and the Fiscal Corporation Bill*].   *162*

[c. Sept]   To Nathaniel F. Williams. ALS. NhD. mDW 21020. Asks him
to honor a draft for up to $1,500.

[Sept?]   From Isaac Rand Jackson. ALS copy. MdHi. mDW 21051. Presents DW with a gift of wine.

[Sept?]   From John Tyler. ALS. DLC. mDW 21086. Comments on Seward's report on the British steamers and wonders if the United States
ought not to possess "similar boats."

[Sept?]   From John Tyler. ALS. DLC. mDW 21181. Thinks the [Demas?]
Adams appointment (marshal for Ohio) may have been unfortunate.

Oct 1   To Samuel Turell Armstrong. AL. MHi. mDW 20467. Declines
dinner invitation.

[Oct 1]   To John Plummer Healy. ALS. MHi. mDW 20469. Asks him to
inform Thomas Cookendorfer, who is about to leave for England
with despatches, that he has not had time to write further.

Oct 1   To Francis Markoe. ALS. DLC. mDW 20472. Asks him to write
George Griswold about Spanish claims arrangements.

Oct 1   To Daniel Le Roy. Copy. DNA, RG 59. mDW 54738. Appoints Le
Roy despatch agent at New York.

Oct 1   To William Henry Seward. ALS. NRU. mDW 20474. Regrets that
poor health will not permit him to visit Albany as planned.

Oct 1   From Rice Garland. ALS. DNA, RG 59. mDW 54628. Reports on
the circumstances which have prevented Gervais Fontenot from
assuming office as U.S. marshal for Louisiana.

Oct 1   From Joshua A. Spencer. ALS. NhHi. mDW 20477. Reports strong
evidence that McLeod did not participate in the *Caroline* raid.

Oct 1   From John Tyler. ALS. DLC. mDW 20481. Tyler, *Tylers*, 2: 123–
124, 214. Reports an interview he had with John Canfield Spencer

regarding a place in the Cabinet; fears the absence of a witness may postpone the McLeod trial.

Oct 2   To David Samuel Jones. ALS draft. MNF. mDW 20484. Speaks highly of Joseph P. Cogswell, whom Columbia University is considering for an honorary degree.

Oct 2   From Joshua Howard. ALS. DNA, RG 59. mDW 54694. Accepts appointment as U.S. marshal for Michigan.

Oct 2   From Thomas Washington. ALS. MWalB. mDW 20487. Asks that S. B. Marshall, U.S. marshal in Tennessee, be removed from office.

Oct 3   From John Canfield Spencer. ALS. DLC. mDW 20491. Expects he will accept post of secretary of war.

Oct 4   From Ebenezer Dorr. ALS. DNA, RG 59. mDW 54584. Accepts appointment as U.S. marshal for western Florida.

Oct 4   From Joshua Reed Giddings. ALS. NhHi. mDW 20495. Forwards a note (not found) from B. Owen concerning preparations by the Patriots for an armed descent on Canada.

[Oct 4]   From Selah R. Hobbie (enclosure: list of Post Office Department personnel, Oct 5, 1841). LC. DNA, RG 28. mDW 57054. Transmits a list of Post Office employees for inclusion in the *Biennial Register*.

Oct 4   From Benjamin Pickman. ALS. NhHi. mDW 20497. Sends his regards.

Oct 4   Recommendation from Walter Forward, for John H. Peebles—consul, Campeche, Mexico (ALS. MWalB. mDW 20494).

Oct 5   Recommendations from Henry Marie Brackenridge, for John H. Peebles (ALS. MWalB. mDW 20504); from George Gibson, for John H. Peebles (ALS. MWalB. mDW 20509); from Leverett Saltonstall, for John B. Williams—consul, Tangiers (ALS. MWalB. mDW 20511); from Joseph Story, for Henry Ledyard—secretary, French legation (ALS. MWalB. mDW 20513).

Oct 6   To Daniel Fletcher Webster. ALS. NhHi. mDW 20515. Van Tyne, pp. 279–280. Forwards despatches just arrived from England; notes that the English are taking great interest in the McLeod trial.

Oct 6   Recommendation from Oelrichs & Kruger, for Herman Watgen—consul, Angostura (LS. MWalB. mDW 20518).

Oct 8   To Nathan Hale. ALS. MHi. mDW 20521. Thinks that publishing the Earl of Spencer's letter would be the best way to protect the public from the imposter Edwards.

Oct 8   From Miller Grieve. ALS. DNA, RG 59. mDW 52398. Resigns his personal participation in the appointment of the Milledgeville *Southern Recorder* as printer of the laws.

Oct 9   From Daniel Fletcher Webster. ALS. NhHi. mDW 20522. Reports having evaded Tyler's request that he discuss the James Grogan matter with Henry Stephen Fox; states that he has written on the veto question for the *Madisonian*.

Oct 10   Recommendation from William D. Merrick, for Henry W. Baxley—bearer of despatches (ALS. MWalB. mDW 20528).

Oct 11   From Henry O. Sholes. ALS. DNA, RG 59. mDW 52394. Accepts appointment to print the laws in the *Green Bay* (Wis.) *Republican*.

Oct 11   *From John Tyler.*   *166*

Oct 11   From Abel Parker Upshur. ALS. DNA, RG 59. mDW 54868. Accepts appointment as secretary of the navy.

Oct 11   Recommendation from James William McCulloh, for Henry W. Baxley (ALS. MWalB. mDW 20532).

[c. Oct. 12]   From Artemas Hale et al. LS. NhD. mDW 20539. Send resolutions of the Plymouth County Whig convention approving DW's decision to remain in the cabinet.

Oct 13   From Sydney Smith. ALS. NhD. mDW 20548. Lady Saba (Smith) Holland, *A Memoir of the Reverend Sydney Smith* (2 vols., New York, 1855), 1: 252–253. Praises DW's efforts to arbitrate the Anglo-American crisis.

Oct 13   Recommendation from Abbott Lawrence, for Joshua Garsed, Jr.—consul, Hull, England (ALS. MH-H. mDW 20541).

Oct 14   To Nathaniel F. Williams. ALS. NhD. mDW 20552. Asks him to take care of a $1,000 note.

Oct 14   From John Tyler. ALS. DLC. mDW 20556. *Diplomatic Papers*, 1. Suggests modifying DW's instructions to Commodore Charles Morris relative to the Johnson case at Montevideo; reports government stock is selling slowly and asks what he thinks about sending an agent to Holland.

Oct 14   Recommendations from Stephen Clarendon Phillips, for John B. Williams (ALS. MWalB. mDW 20554).

Oct 15   From Walter Forward. ALS. DLC. mDW 20561. Hopes that McLeod's acquittal may bolster the money market.

Oct 15   From Charles Anderson Wickliffe. LS. DNA, RG 59. mDW 54661. Announces the appointment of Charles C. Haddock as postmaster at Buffalo.

Oct 15   Recommendation from N. S. Browning et al., for Henry W. Starr—attorney, Iowa (LS. MWalB. mDW 20559).

Oct 16   To Duff Green. ALS. DLC. mDW 20563. Gives instructions for his mission as despatch bearer to Europe.

Oct 16   To Daniel Fletcher Webster. ALS. NhHi. mDW 20566. Informs him that Duff Green has been appointed a bearer of despatches to England and France and directs Fletcher to forward papers to him.

Oct 16   *From John Canfield Spencer.*   *168*

Oct 17   From James Morrison. ALS. UkLG. mDW 20572. Introduces his son, Alfred Morrison.

Oct 18   Application from B. Alfred Sanders, for the *Davenport* (Ia.) *Gazette*—public printer (ALS. DNA, RG 59. mDW 52362).

Oct 19   From Charles Anderson Wickliffe. LS. DNA, RG 59. mDW 54789. Announces Andrew Palmer's appointment as postmaster at Toledo.

Oct 19   Recommendations from John McLean, for Ambrose Dudley Mann—consul, Malaga (ALS. MWalB. mDW 20575); from James Alfred Pearce, for S. B. Bernabeu—consul, Alicante (ALS. MWalB. mDW 20577).

Oct 20   From Joshua Bates. ALS copy. CaOOA. mDW 20578. Assures him that the British government wants peace; comments on reports in the London *Morning Chronicle* concerning the Hunters' Lodges.

Oct 20   From Samuel James Douglas. ALS. DNA, RG 59. mDW 54590. Accepts appointment as U.S. district judge for middle Florida.

Oct 20   From Gervais Fontenot. ALS. DNA, RG 59. mDW 54626. Accepts appointment as U.S. marshal for western Louisiana.

Oct 20   Application from David Paul Brown—chargé to Texas (ALS. MWalB. mDW 20580).

Oct 22   *From Edward Everett.*   169

Oct 22   From Roger Lawson Gamble. ALS. DNA, RG 59. mDW 52396. Advises that Miller Grieve has resigned as editor of the *Southern Recorder* and asks that the appointment to print the laws be given to Grieve's co-editor, Richard M. Orme.

Oct 22   Recommendations from Isaac Dashiell Jones, for Henry W. Baxley (ALS. MWalB. mDW 20589); from Richard R. Lansing (to DFW), for Joseph Sanchez or Edward A. Lansing—consul, West Indies (ALS. NhHi. mDW 20592); from Morris Ketchum, for Edward A. Lansing (ALS. NhHi. mDW 20595); from William D. Merrick, for Thomas B. Adair—consul, Belfast (ALS. MWalB. mDW 20596); from John G. Stearns et al., for the *Calais* (Me.) *Advertiser*—public printer (LS. DNA, RG 59. mDW 52208).

Oct 23   Recommendations from Timothy Darling to DFW, for the *Calais Advertiser* (ALS. DNA, RG 59. mDW 52204); from Charles F. Mayer, for Henry W. Baxley (ALS. MWalB. mDW 20598); from John Reynolds, for the *Belleville* (Ill.) *Advocate*—public printer (ALS. DNA, RG 59. mDW 52199).

Oct 25   To Daniel Fletcher Webster. ALS. NhHi. mDW 20601. Van Tyne, p. 241. Asks him to inform the secretary of the navy that the incumbent navy agent at Portsmouth, N.H., is entirely trustworthy.

Oct 25   From Henry Markham. ALS. NhHi. mDW 20610. Withdraws his application for the consulship at Paita.

Oct 25   From Andrew Moore. ALS. DLC. mDW 20612. Outlines proposal for a fiscal bank.

Oct 25   Application from James P. Heath—distribution of the laws (ALS. MWalB. mDW 20603).

Oct 25   Recommendations from Washington Irving, for Thomas B. Adair (ALS. MWalB. mDW 20606); from William B. Kinney, for David Ball—marshal, New Jersey (ALS. MWalB. mDW 20608).

Oct 28   From Conrad Hogmire. ALS. DNA, RG 59. mDW 54686. Accepts appointment as justice of the peace for Washington, D.C.

Oct 29   From Miller & Moeller. LS. DNA, RG 59. mDW 52156. Accept appointment to print the laws in the Columbus, Ohio, *Old School Republican*.

Oct 29   From Worthington Snethen to DFW. ALS. DNA, RG 59. mDW 52158. Accepts appointment to print the laws in the New Orleans *Morning Advertiser*.

Oct 30   Application from Bradford A. Manchester—unspecified consulate (ALS. MWalB. mDW 20622).

Oct 30   Recommendation from John R. McMahon, for Henry W. Baxley (ALS. MWalB. mDW 20618).

Oct 31   To Daniel Fletcher Webster. ALS. NhHi. mDW 20624. *Diplomatic Papers*, 1. Asks that his redraft of the orders to Commodore Charles Morris be shown to the President, or, if he is not available, sent along under DFW's signature.

[Oct]   From John Tyler to DFW (enclosures: Blair & Rives to William A. Weaver, Sept 29, 1841; report of the select committee on public printing, Feb 12, 1841). ALS. DLC. mDW 20627. Asks that the enclosed correspondence and Senate report concerning the binding of the Sixth Census be forwarded for DW's consideration.

Nov 1   From Isaac H. Bronson. ALS. DNA, RG 59. mDW 54826. Reports having notified Joseph Simeon Sanchez of the arrival of his commission.

Nov 2   Recommendations from Joshua Jones, for Henry W. Baxley (ALS. MWalB. mDW 20636); from John Gorham Palfrey, for George Wilson—consul, Matanzas (ALS. MWalB. mDW 20639).

Nov 3   To James Miller. ALS. NWM. mDW 20642. Recommends John Minot for a position in the custom house in the Salem and Beverly district.

Nov 4   Application from John B. Williams—consul, Bay of Islands, New Zealand (ALS. MWalB. mDW 20647).

Nov 4   Recommendations from Charles Pelham Curtis, for George Wilson (ALS. DLC. mDW 20663); from Stephen Clarendon Phillips, for George Wilson (ALS. MWA. mDW 20645); from Nathaniel Silsbee, for George Wilson (ALS. DLC. mDW 20664).

Nov 5   From Joseph Simeon Sanchez. ALS. DNA, RG 59. mDW 54828. Accepts appointment as U.S. marshal for eastern Florida.

Nov 6   To Franklin Haven. ALS. MH-H. mDW 20650. Directs his attention to an article signed "Spectator" in the London *Times* of Oct 18.

Nov 6   From Theodore H. McCaleb. ALS. DNA, RG 59. mDW 54632. Advises him that Gervais Fontenot's commission has been delivered; reports himself alive and fully able to perform his judicial duties despite allegations to the contrary.

Nov 6   Recommendations from Caleb Cushing, for Francis M. Dimond (ALS. MWalB. mDW 20652); from Horatio Seymour, for Gilbert T. Thomson—consul, West Indies (ALS. MWalB. mDW 20654).

Nov 7   To Daniel Fletcher Webster. ALS. NhHi. mDW 23690. Van Tyne, pp. 749–750. Reports being delayed by the grounding of his steamer; asks that Charles Mettinger be paid off and dismissed at once.

Nov 7   *From Daniel Fletcher Webster.*   *170*

Nov 8   To Daniel Fletcher Webster. ALS. NhHi. mDW 23693. PC, 2: 152. Thanks him for letters; comments on weather in New York and the recent elections.

Nov 9   Recommendation from George Griswold, for George Wilson (LS. DLC. mDW 20666).

Nov 10   From Samuel C. Reid, Jr. Copy. DNA, RG 46. mDW 50215. Urges the government to press the *General Armstrong* claims against Portugal.

Nov 11   To Harriette Story White Paige. ALS. Mrs. Irvin McD. Garfield, Southboro, Mass. mDWs. Sends present.

Nov 11   Application from George Wilson (ALS. DLC. mDW 20661).

Nov 12 From Charles Anderson Wickliffe. LS. DNA, RG 59. mDW
54504. Announces the appointment of a postmaster at Lewiston,
N.Y.

Nov 12 Application from John Francis Cobb—consul, Antwerp (ALS.
MWalB. mDW 20668).

[Nov 13] To Daniel Fletcher Webster. ALS. NhHi. mDW 20672. Van
Tyne, p. 241. Doubts that he can reach Washington before "Monday"
(Nov 15).

Nov 13 Application from James A. Kelly, for the *Louisiana Chronicle*—
public printer (ALS. DNA, RG 59. mDW 52375).

Nov 14 To Charles Sumner. ALS. NhD. mDW 20674. Suggests that
Lord Morpeth stay at the Washington Hotel while in Philadelphia.

Nov 15 From James Duane Doty. LS. DNA, RG 59. mDW 54588. Acknowledges commission appointing him governor of Wisconsin and
submits his oath of office.

Nov 15 From Algernon Sidney Robertson. ALS. DNA, RG 59. mDW
54820. Accepts appointment as U.S. marshal for eastern Louisiana.

Nov 16 From James Renwick. ALS. DNA, RG 59. mDW 56764. Presents
his expense account as commissioner for the exploration and survey
of the northeast boundary.

Nov 16 Recommendation from Benjamin Merrill, for John B. Williams
(ALS. MWalB. mDW 20678).

Nov 17 From John Tyler (with ANS by Edward Stubbs). LS. DNA, RG
59. mDW 56598. Authorizes the expenditure of $5,000 by the secre-
tary of state "for objects which it is not now expedient to specify."

Nov 17 Recommendation from William Morris Meredith, for Joshua
Garsed, Jr.—consul, Kingston (ALS. MHi. mDW 20680).

Nov 19 To Charles Henry Thomas. AL incomplete. NhD. mDW 20682.
Gershom Bradford, "The Unknown Webster," *Old Time New England*, 44 (Fall 1953): 60. Longs to fish and hunt at Marshfield.

Nov 19 To Charles Henry Thomas. 171

Nov 19 Receipt for $3,000 paid by Edward Stubbs. DS. DNA, RG 59.
mDW 56599.

Nov 20 To Editor of Buffalo *Commercial Advertiser and Journal.*
Printed. *Boston Semi-Weekly Atlas*, Dec 4, 1841. Assures the citizens of Buffalo that he has not been careless of the inscribed silver
plate they presented to him in 1833, as falsely asserted in the *Louisville Gazette.*

Nov 20 To Edward Everett. ALS. MHi. mDW 20688. *Diplomatic Papers,*
1. Discusses the opposition to Everett's nomination.

Nov 20 From Charles March. 171

Nov 20 From Francis Ormand Jonathan Smith. ALS. NhHi. mDW
20694. *Diplomatic Papers*, 1. Describes his plans for winning public
support in Maine for a compromise of the boundary dispute.

Nov 20 From John Tyler. ALS. DLC. mDW 20699. Asks him to inform
[William M.] Blackford "relative to his proposed destination."

Nov 20 Application from John B. Williams (ALS. MWalB. mDW
20701).

Nov 22 From William P. Duval. ALS. DNA, RG 59. mDW 54606. Accepts appointment as law agent in Florida.

Nov 22   From Edward Everett. LC. MHi. mDW 20706. Reports that Lord
Aberdeen is glad DW will remain in office; discusses the appointment of a secretary to the London legation; mentions a conversation
with the Russian ambassador.

Nov 22   From William Morris Meredith. ALS. DLC. mDW 20712. Asks
DW to write an official reply to a letter so as to prevent a challenge
to "my course" by "any mischievous person."

Nov 22   Recommendations from Charles Chapman, for John J. Hyde
(ALS. MWalB. mDW 20704); from Walter Forward, for Philip
Banks (ALS. DLC. mDW 20710).

Nov 23   From John Dunham. ALS. DNA, RG 59. mDW 52392. Reports
having sold the *Norwich* (Conn.) *Courier* to Dorson E. Sykes.

Nov 23   From James Renwick. ALS. DNA, RG 59. mDW 56765. Discusses the expense account of the commissary hired to work with
the northeast boundary survey party.

Nov 23   Recommendation from James F. Babcock et al., for John J.
Hyde (ALS by Babcock, signed also by others. MWalB. mDW
20714).

Nov 25   To John Tyler. Copy. NhHi. mDW 20723. Van Tyne, pp. 241–
242. Discusses the regional distribution of diplomatic appointments.

Nov 25   From Alexander Powell.   *172*

Nov 26   To Franklin Dexter. LS. NhD. mDW 20731. Requests a report
on allegations that a justice of the peace, acting on Dexter's advice,
refused to arrest a deserter from a Swedish brig now in Boston.

Nov 26   Recommendation from Thomas Kinnicutt et al., for George Metcalf—bearer of despatches (ALS by Kinnicutt, signed also by others.
MWalB. mDW 20736).

Nov 27   Applications from Alexander W. Bradford—unspecified South
American post (ALS. MWalB. mDW 20738); from William Bibb
Figures, for the Huntsville *Southern Advocate*—public printer (ALS.
DNA, RG 59. mDW 52213).

Nov 29   From Elliott & McCurdy. LS. DNA, RG 59. mDW 52160. Accept
appointment to print the laws in the *Pennsylvania Intelligencer.*

Nov 29   Application from James E. Wharton, for the *Wheeling Times
and Advertiser*—public printer (ALS. DNA, RG 59. mDW 53245).

Nov 29   Recommendation from S. Chadwick & Co. et al., for George Wilson (LS. DLC. mDW 20741).

Nov 30   To Henry Stephen Fox. ALS. UkLPR. mDW 20743. Encloses an
extract from a letter and thinks Fox can best judge the value of its
suggestion.

Nov 30   From Edward Stanly. ALS. DLC. mDW 20755. Asks that Mrs.
[Daniel Smith] McCauley be informed whether her husband is to be
recalled before she embarks for Tripoli.

Nov 30   Application from Edward Eastman, for the *Clinton County
Whig* (ALS. DNA, RG 59. mDW 52175).

Nov 30   Recommendation from Robert Morris (of Philadelphia) for Dr.
McKelway—marshal, New Jersey (ALS. MWalB. mDW 20753).

[Nov]   From John Tyler. ALS. DLC. mDW 20773. Discusses an appointment for [William M.?] Blackford.

Nov   Receipt for $300 from Albert Fitz. ADS. DNA, RG 59. mDW
56609.

[Nov–Dec]   Draft of presidential message on tariff. AD draft. NhHi.
mDW 20758. Van Tyne, pp. 245–248.

Dec 1   Application from William Bennett Parker (ALS. MWalB. mDW
20777).

Dec 1   Recommendation from William Morris Meredith, for John S.
Riddle—European consulate (ALS. MWalB. mDW 20775).

Dec 2   Recommendation from Nicholas Biddle, for John S. Riddle (ALS.
MWalB. mDW 20780).

Dec 4   To George R. Babcock. LS. NBu. mDWs. Responds to Babcock's
note of Sept 20 about a map supporting the U.S.'s northeastern
boundary claim.

Dec 4   To Edward Curtis.   *174*

Dec 4   From Andrew Talcott. ALS. DNA, RG 59. mDW 56767. Reports
having drawn $1,200 from the appropriation for the exploration and
survey of the northeast boundary.

Dec 5   To Harriette Story White Paige.   *174*

Dec 6   From Oelrichs & Kruger (with ANS by DW). LS. MWalB. mDW
20798. Requests response to their suggestion that a U.S. consul be
appointed to Angostura.

Dec 6   From [Benjamin Tappan, Jr.] (enclosure: Benjamin Tappan, Jr.
to Minister of Foreign Affairs of Ecuador, Feb 22, 1841). AL draft.
DLC. mDW 20800. ALS. DNA, RG 59. mDW 55843. Explains the
difficulties in obtaining ratification of the treaty with Ecuador.

Dec 6   Recommendation from Elisha M. Huntington, for the Lawrence-
burg *Political Beacon*—public printer (ALS. DNA, RG 59. mDW
52371).

Dec 7   From Henry Leavitt Ellsworth. ALS. DLC. mDW 20804. Explains
the need for change in "the examiners department" of the Patent
Office.

[Dec 8]   To [Caleb Cushing]. ALS. NN. mDW 20811. Asks to see him
briefly.

Dec 8   From Charles Augustus Davis.   *174*

Dec 9   To [Samuel Lewis Southard]. LS. DNA, RG 46. mDW 49455.
Transmits an account of State Department expenditures for the year
ending Nov 30.

Dec 10   Recommendation from Samuel Stokely, for the *Western Herald
and Steubenville Gazette*—public printer (ALS. DNA, RG 59. mDW
52386).

Dec 11   Recommendation from Joseph Leonard Tillinghast, for George
F. Usher (ALS. NhHi. mDW 20817).

Dec 12   Recommendations from Calvary Morris, for the *Marietta* (O.)
Gazette—public printer (ALS. DNA, RG 59. mDW 52381); from
John Todd Stuart, for Archibald Williams—chief justice, Iowa
(ALS. NhD. mDW 20819).

Dec 13   To James Trecothick Austin, John A. Lowell, and John Quincy
Adams. LS. MHi. mDW 20821. Promises that the Massachusetts
Historical Society will be reimbursed for maps loaned to and lost at
the State Department.

Dec 13   To Abel Parker Upshur. ALS. CtHi. mDW 20824. Introduces
"Mrs. Auld" and recommends her stepson, William Henry, for a
navy appointment.

Dec 13   Applications from Andrew Foster—consul, Palermo (ALS. NhHi. mDW 20829); from Shepard & Strong, for the *Rochester Daily Democrat* (LS with AN by DW. DNA, RG 59. mDW 52177).

Dec 13   Recommendations from John Macpherson Berrien, for the *Savannah Republican*—public printer (ALS. DNA, RG 59. mDW 52182); from Lewis Condict, for James Lawrence Day—commercial agent, Africa (ALS. MWalB. mDW 20827); from Joseph Lanier Williams, for the *Knoxville Register* (ALS. DNA, RG 59. mDW 52379).

Dec 14   From John Tyler. ALS. DLC. mDW 20830. Suggests that DW write the Committee on Foreign Relations on reviving the "act of 1838."

Dec 15   From Edward Everett. LC. MHi. mDW 20851. AL. MHi. mDW 20857. *Diplomatic Papers*, 1. Reports conversing with Lord Aberdeen on the McLeod issue, reparations for the *Caroline*, the boundary problem, and the Endicott incident at Macao.

Dec 15   From Francis Mallory. ALS. NhHi. mDW 20865. Introduces "Mr. Tucker."

Dec 15   Recommendation from Leverett Saltonstall, for John B. Williams (ALS. MWalB. mDW 20867).

[Dec 16]   A bill to establish a board of exchequer. AD draft. NhHi. mDW 20869.

[Dec 16]   Message on exchequer bill. AD draft. NhHi. mDW 20898.

Dec 17   Recommendations from Alexander Mouton, for the St. Martinville, Louisiana, *Attapakas Gazette*—public printer (ALS. DNA, RG 59. mDW 52377); from Thomas Wheeler Williams, for William Sheffield—consul, Antigua (ALS. MWalB. mDW 20907).

Dec 18   To Edward Everett. LS. MHi. mDW 20909. Introduces Thomas Nelson of Peekskill, New York.

Dec 18   From Thurlow Weed.   175

Dec 20   Recommendations from Thomas A. Tomlinson, for the *Clinton County Whig* (ALS. DNA, RG 59. mDW 52173); from Charles Anderson Wickliffe, for Elisha Smith—despatch bearer to Texas (ALS. MWalB. mDW 20912).

Dec 21   To [Edward Kent]. AL draft. NhHi. mDW 20914. *Diplomatic Papers*, 1. Contends that Maine's opposition is the only obstacle to compromise on the boundary issue and suggests that a commission might help bring the contending parties together.

Dec 21   To Ezekiel W. Leach. LS. MSaE. mDW 20918. Informs him that his passport has been forwarded to the collector of customs at Charleston, S.C.

Dec 21   To [Samuel Lewis Southard] (enclosure: William A. Weaver to DW, Dec 21, 1841). LS. DNA, RG 46. mDW 49493. Transmits a report on the census by the superintending clerk.

Dec 21   From Charles Pelham Curtis. ALS. NhHi. mDW 20919. Introduces George Savage.

Dec 21   From William A. Weaver (with DW to [Samuel Lewis Southard], Dec 21, 1841). ALS. DNA, RG 46. mDW 49489. Discusses problems connected with the preparation of the Sixth Census.

Dec 21   Application from James Dillingham—consul, Bordeaux (ALS. MWalB. mDW 20921).

Dec 21　Recommendations from Richard R. Lansing to DFW, for
　　　　Joseph Sanchez (ALS. NhHi. mDW 20924); from George Savage,
　　　　for Stephen B. Savage—consul, Belize (ALS. MWalB. mDW
　　　　20927).
Dec 21　Receipt for $2,000 paid by Edward Stubbs. DS. DNA, RG 59.
　　　　mDW 56599.
Dec 22　Recommendations from Alexander Barrow, for Samuel Haight
　　　　(ALS. MWalB. mDW 20931); from Archibald Randall, for John F.
　　　　Bernabeu (ALS. MWalB. mDW 20933).
Dec 23　Application from John Neuendorf—consul, Hamburg (ALS.
　　　　NhHi. mDW 20934).
Dec 23　Recommendation from Edward Cross, for the Little Rock *Ar-
　　　　kansas State Gazette*—public printer (ALS. DNA, RG 59. mDW
　　　　52186).
Dec 24　To Franklin Haven. ALS. MH-H. mDW 20936. Thinks of recom-
　　　　mending a friend of [Nathan?] Hale for some post; asks for Haven's
　　　　opinion of the exchequer.
Dec 24　To John Plummer Healy. ALS. MHi. mDW 20939. States that he
　　　　is writing to "Mr. [Peter?] Harvey" by "this post."
[Dec 24]　From Francis J. Grund. ALS copy. ViU. mDWs. Ac-
　　　　knowledges receipt of his appointment as U.S. consul at Bremen;
　　　　urges a new treaty of commerce with this city.
Dec 24　Recommendation from John B. Aycrigg, for David Ball (ALS.
　　　　MWalB. mDW 20941).
Dec 27　From Alexander McCormick. ALS. DNA, RG 59. mDW 55722.
　　　　Inquires, on behalf of the chairman of the Ways and Means Commit-
　　　　tee, about an item appearing in the State Department's estimates.
Dec 27　From John Tyler. ALS. NhHi. mDW 20943. Asks him to look
　　　　into the hardship case of a Mr. Rhind.
Dec 28　To Edward Everett. ALS. MHi. mDW 20945. *Diplomatic Papers*,
　　　　1. Discusses the Maine boundary problem; reports reaction to the
　　　　plan for a fiscal agent.
Dec 28　To John Plummer Healy.　　　　　　　　　　　　　　*176*
Dec 28　From Oliver Pell Secord. ALS. DNA, RG 156. mDWs. Describes
　　　　his invention for firing cannon and musket shot without using gun-
　　　　powder; anticipates an ample reward from "a liberal government."
Dec 28　Check for $54.75 to [John?] Taylor. DS. NjMoHP. mDWs.
Dec 28　Recommendations from David Levy [Yulee], for the *Pensacola*
　　　　(Fla.) *Gazette*, the St. Augustine *Florida Herald*, and the Talla-
　　　　hassee *Floridian*—public printers (ALS. DNA, RG 59. mDW 55216).
Dec 29　To John Tyler. LS. DNA, RG 46. mDW 48537. Informs him, in
　　　　reply to a Senate inquiry, that neither the U.S. nor the British gov-
　　　　ernment has made any proposal since March 4, 1840, concerning
　　　　the right of search.
Dec 29　From Henry Marie Brackenridge and William L. Marcy. ALS by
　　　　Brackenridge, signed also by Marcy. MWalB. mDW 20965. Request
　　　　additional clerical assistance for the board of commissioners ap-
　　　　pointed under the convention with Mexico.
Dec 29　From Henry Stephen Fox. ALS. MH-H. mDW 20967. Encloses
　　　　letters for forwarding by DW's agent to commanding officers in
　　　　upper Canada.

Dec 30 To Demas Adams. LS. OHi. mDW 20970. *Diplomatic Papers*, 1.
Warns that Patriots are preparing to invade Canada and orders him
to be vigilant in upholding the law.

Dec 30 To Charles W. Kelso. LS. PHi. mDW 29276. Expresses his continuing concern over Patriot activities.

Dec 30 From James B. Marshall. ALS. DNA, RG 59. mDW 52162. Accepts appointment to print the laws in the *Louisville* (Ky.) *City
Gazette*.

Dec 30 Recommendation from Alexander H. H. Stuart, for reappointment of the *Lexington* (Va.) *Gazette*—public printer (ALS. DNA,
RG 59. mDW 52180).

Dec 31 From Charles Murray. ALS. DNA, RG 59. mDW 54773. Accepts
appointment as justice of the peace for Washington, D.C.

Dec 31 From James Renwick. ALS. DNA, RG 59. mDW 56771. Plans
transferring money from his appropriation to [Andrew] Talcott's
account.

Dec 31 From John Tyler. ALS. DLC. mDW 20986. Thinks S. DeWitt
Bloodgood ought to be appointed U.S. consul at Bristol.

Dec 31 Promissory note for $1,750 to Isaac P. Davis. DS. MHi. mDW
39860.

[Dec] From John Tyler. ALS. DLC. mDW 21004. *Diplomatic Papers*, 1.
Encloses correspondence relative to the Santa Fe expedition; is inclined to send Leslie Combs.

[Dec] From John Tyler. ALS. DLC. mDW 21002. Fears the exchequer
stands little chance of enactment.

[1841] To Kingston Goddard. Printed. Van Tyne, pp. 740–741. Acknowledges receipt of his sermon and offers some philosophical observations on Christianity and the family.

[1841] To Sarah Goodridge. ALS. MHi. mDW 38398. Asks if she has
found suitable accommodations.

[1841] To [Franklin Haven]. AN. MH-H. mDW 21011. States that Crittenden planned to secure a cabinet post for Abbott Lawrence if he
could.

[1841] To William Cabell Rives. ALS. DLC. mDW 21014. Asks Rives to
meet with Crittenden and himself at the State Department.

[1841] From John James Audubon. AL incomplete. MH-H. mDW
21037. Waldemar H. Fries, *The Double Elephant Folio: The Story of
Audubon's Birds of America* (Chicago, 1973), p. 391. Requests permission to store the copper plates used in printing the illustrations
for *Birds of America* at the N.Y. custom house.

[1841] From George Edmund Badger (memorandum). AD. DNA, RG
59. mDW 52585. List of North Carolina newspapers.

[1841] From E. W. Burr (enclosure: press clippings). ALS. MWalB.
mDW 21039. Discusses the significance of New Zealand to the
United States; urges that the incumbent U.S. consul be replaced by
an American citizen.

[1841] From John Tyler. ALS. DLC. mDW 21078. Asks for a copy of
John Forsyth's letter to Andrew Stevenson which states that the
burning of the *Caroline* is regarded as a public act by the British
government.

[1841]   From John Tyler. ALS. DLC. mDW 21063. Inquires about an
application.
[1841]   From John Tyler. ALS. DLC. mDW 21070. Asks DW to prepare
a letter to the French minister.
[1841]   From John Tyler. ALS. DLC. mDW 21072. Asks if there is any
strong objection to the appointment of Courtland Cushing as U.S.
attorney for Indiana.
[1841]   From John Tyler. ALS. DLC. mDW 21074. Discusses diplomatic appointments for Spain and Russia.
[1841]   From John Tyler. ALS. DLC. mDW 21080. Discusses a note
from Henry Wheaton.
[1841]   From John Tyler. ALS. DLC. mDW 21082. Asks him to look up
papers relative to Minor Walker's application for U.S. marshal in
middle Florida.
[1841]   From John Tyler. ALS. DLC. mDW 21076. Tyler, *Tylers*, 2: 211.
Suggests that an agent be employed to investigate the Patriots.
[1841]   *Memorandum on the banking bills and the vetoes.*   177
[1841]   Receipt for $100 paid to John J. Crittenden from the secret ser-
vice fund to reimburse sums spent in April. ADS by Crittenden.
DNA, RG 59. mDW 56623.
[1841]   Recommendations from Thomas A. Arnold et al., for Robert H.
Hynds—attorney, Tennessee (LS. MWalB. mDW 21035); from
John McLean, for Daniel Goodwin—attorney, Michigan (ALS.
MWalB. mDW 21052); from John Mills et al., forwarded by Calvary
Morris, for the *Marietta* (O.) *Intelligencer*—public printer (LS.
DNA, RG 59. mDW 52721); from [John Pedrick], for his son (AL,
signature missing. NhHi. mDW 21054); from William D. Sewall et
al., for John T. P. Dumont (LS. DNA, RG 59. mDW 21061).
[1841?]   To Nicholas Biddle. ALS. DLC. mDW 21006. Offers to meet
him tomorrow and remain at his disposal until Sunday.
[1841?]   To Sarah Goodridge. AL. MHi. mDW 38405. States that he and
Mrs. Webster will call the next day regarding accommodations.
[1841?]   To Sarah Goodridge. AL. MHi. mDW 38408. Promises to call
at her rooms.
[1841?]   To John Tyler. ALS. DLC. mDW 21015. Reports that his relations with the *National Intelligencer* have been strained since the
appearance of two highly critical editorials and consequently he
doubts that the editors would publish the proposed editorial.
[1841?]   To Daniel Fletcher Webster. ALS. NhHi. mDW 21017. Cannot
say anything today.
[1841?]   To Daniel Fletcher Webster. ALS. NhHi. mDW 21019. Reports
"our business" is drawing to a close.
[1841?]   To Nathaniel F. Williams. ALS. NhD. mDW 21024. Asks for
statistics of tobacco exports.
[1841?]   To [?]. ALS. IMunS. mDW 39336. Praises Clay's speech on
public lands; doubts the House will do much on the tariff.
[1841?]   From Benjamin Schneider et al. LS. MWalB. mDW 21056. Protest the closing of the U.S. consulate at Brousa (Turkish Empire)
and call for Nicholas L. Perick's reinstatement as consul.
[1841?]   Recommendations from Nicholas Biddle, for H. Senter Huntt—

unspecified post (ALS draft. DLC. mDW 38260-A); from Jesse B. Browne et al., for Francis Springer (LS. MWalB. mDW 21038); from Thomas J. Campbell et al., for William M. Inge—marshal, Alabama (ALS by Campbell, signed also by others. MWalB. mDW 21047).

[1841–1842] To [Nathan Hale?]. ALS. MHi. mDW 5870. Reports the land bill will be engrossed, and that efforts in the House to amend the bank bill have failed.

[1841–1843] To Edward Curtis. ALS. NN. mDW 21092. Thinks Clay sent "Genl P" to New York under retainer to harass Curtis; promises a warrant for Curtis's nephew; calls Horace Everett "good for nothing."

[1841–1843] To [George Ticknor]. ALS. NhD. mDW 39076. Sends "notes" for distribution to Lord Brougham and others.

[1841–1843] From John Tyler. ALS. MHi. mDW 21107. Concurs with one of DW's despatches.

[1841–1843] From John Tyler. ALS. MHi. mDW 21113. Asks for a certified record of the case against Samuel A. Suydam.

[1841–1843] From John Tyler. ALS. DLC. mDW 21114. States that it is the government's duty to protect U.S. citizens wherever they may be residing.

[1841–1843] From John Tyler. ALS. DLC. mDW 21116. Agrees to grant an interview with two individuals.

[1841–1843] From John Tyler. ALS. DLC. mDW 21118. Transmits a letter from the U.S. chargé d'affaires at Sardinia.

[1841–1843] From John Tyler. ALS. DLC. mDW 21120. Requests DW to call.

[1841–1843] From John Tyler. ALS. DLC. mDW 21122. States that he will ponder the contents of DW's letter.

[1841–1843] From John Tyler. ALS. DLC. mDW 21124. Admits to "some embarrasment as to the Rio Consulate" and promises that Zachariah Jellison will be provided for.

[1841–1843] From John Tyler. ALS. DLC. mDW 21126. Discusses appointment of consul to Malaga.

[1841–1843] From John Tyler. ALS. DLC. mDW 21129. Returns despatches and agrees to a cabinet meeting.

[1841–1843] From John Tyler. ALS. DLC. mDW 21131. Asks what DW thinks of Abel Parker Upshur's suggestions.

[1841–1843] From John Tyler. ALS. DLC. mDW 21133. Refers to a letter from Iowa Territorial Secretary Otho H. W. Stull.

[1841–1843] From John Tyler. ALS. DLC. mDW 21135. Decides to defer action on an appointment until the close of the session.

[1841–1843] From John Tyler. ALS. DLC. mDW 21139. Asks him to grant Alexander Botts of New York a brief audience.

[1841–1843] From John Tyler. ALS. DLC. mDW 21142. Returns a paper and asks him to confer with John Caldwell Calhoun about it.

[1841–1843] From John Tyler. ALS. DLC. mDW 21145. Enclose a communication for State Department files.

[1841–1843] From John Tyler. ALS. DLC. mDW 21147. Approves a despatch to the U.S. consul at Havana.

[1841–1843] From John Tyler. ALS. DLC. mDW 21152. Inquires about a communication addressed to him by the holders of Mississippi stock.

[1841–1843]   From John Tyler. ALS. DLC. mDW 21156. Encloses some papers with comment.

[1841–1843]   From John Tyler. ALS. DLC. mDW 21158. Agrees to see DW.

[1841–1843]   From John Tyler. ALS. DLC. mDW 21161. Returns a paper and asks him to pursue "the course indicated."

[1841–1843]   From John Tyler. ALS. DLC. mDW 21163. Reports hav- ing referred [John Strother?] Pendleton's letters to Selah R. Hobbie and complains of abuse by the Whig newspaper at Poughkeepsie.

[1841–1843]   From John Tyler. ALS. DLC. mDW 21165. Plans to attend the exhibitions at Georgetown College.

[1841–1843]   From John Tyler. ALS. DLC. mDW 21167. Declares his confidence in "Anderson's statements."

[1841–1843]   From John Tyler. ALS. DLC. mDW 21169. Asks for infor- mation which will enable him to reply to a letter.

[1841–1843]   From John Tyler. ALS. DLC. mDW 21171. Refers to let- ters from Benjamin H. Sheppard.

[1841–1843]   From John Tyler. ALS. DLC. mDW 21173. Suggests he look at the acccompanying letter and throw it in the fire.

[1841–1843]   From John Tyler. ALS. DLC. mDW 21174. Suggests a call during the day.

[1841–1843]   From John Tyler. ALS. DLC. mDW 21177. Requests a translation of François P. G. Guizot's letter.

[1841–1843]   From John Tyler. ALS. DLC. mDW 21179. Encloses a let- ter from "our new judge . . . in Florida."

[1841–1843]   From John Tyler. ALS. DLC. mDW 21183. Calls his at- tention to certain resolutions.

[1841–1843]   From John Tyler. ALS. DLC. mDW 21185. Introduces William Kinney of Virginia.

[1841–1843]   From John Tyler. ALS. DLC. mDW 21189. Asks him to send in a nomination if he concurs.

[1841–1843]   From John Tyler. ALS. DLC. mDW 21191. Comments: "I can see no reason to recommend addition or change."

[1841–1843]   From John Tyler. ALS. DLC. mDW 21193. Encloses letter.

[1841–1843]   From John Tyler. ALS. DLC. mDW 21195. Comments: "Whatever comes from Mr. [Thomas] Aspinwall is interesting."

[1841–1843]   From John Tyler. ALS. DLC. mDW 21197. Refers him to a letter.

[1841–1843]   From John Tyler. ALS. DLC. mDW 21199. Asks him to return John Canfield Spencer's note after reading it.

[1841–1843]   From John Tyler. Mrs. Robert F. Kennedy, McLean, Va. mDW 21205. Plans to visit the Capitol this morning and asks him to notify the members.

[1841–1843]   From John Tyler. Facsimile. George F. Hoar, "Daniel Webster," *Scribner's Magazine*, 26 (July 1899): 78. States: "The old Lion still roars. See Genl Jackson's letter among those which are sent."

[1841–1843]   From John Tyler, Jr. ALS. DLC. mDW 21206. Encloses some papers at the President's direction.

[1841–1843]   From John Tyler, Jr. ALS. DLC. mDW 21208. Encloses a letter for Everett.

[1841–1843]   Opinion regarding President's power to adjourn Congress. AD. ViU. mDW 21096.

[1841–1843]   Recommendation from Nathaniel Silsbee et al., for George Wilson (LS. DLC. mDW 21105).

[1841–1843]   Times employed and expense incurred by State Department clerks. AD. DNA, RG 59. mDW 55806.

1842

Jan 2   From Alexander Baring, Lord Ashburton. Copy. NhHi. mDW 21210. Van Tyne, pp. 252–254. *Diplomatic Papers*, 1. Explains why he accepted the special mission to the United States.

Jan 3   From John B. Aycrigg. ALS. MWalB. mDW 21215. Reports that his congressional colleagues are unwilling to withdraw their recommendations of David Ball.

Jan 3   From Joshua Bates. Printed. Curtis, 2: 95–96. Comments on the impending Ashburton mission; reports Everett is making a good impression in England.

Jan 3   From Edward Everett. AL. MHi. mDW 21221. *Diplomatic Papers*, 1. Comments on the Ashburton mission and the prospects of the United States reaching an agreement with the Five Powers on the right of search; discusses the rental of his London quarters.

Jan 3   From John Beauchamp Jones. ALS. DNA, RG 59. mDW 53474. Accepts appointment to print the laws in the *Madisonian*.

Jan 3   From James Renwick. ALS. DNA, RG 59. mDW 56774. Transmits his quarterly account as commissioner for the survey of the northeastern boundary.

Jan 3   From John Tyler. ALS. DLC. mDW 21228. Asks if anything might be found for "Mr. Burrows" in South America.

Jan 3   Recommendation from Warren Lovering, for John G. Metcalf—bearer of despatches (ALS. MWalB. mDW 21226).

Jan 4   From H[orace] Everett. Copy. DLC. mDW 21229A. Asks for DW's opinion on the petition from Blair & Rives relative to the printing of the census.

Jan 4   Recommendations from William Cabell Rives, for Ambrose Dudley Mann (ALS. MWalB. mDW 21234); from Joseph L. Tillinghast, for William Mayhew, Jr. (ALS. MWalB. mDW 21236).

Jan 4   From Locke & Davis. LS. DNA, RG 59. mDW 53431. Accept appointment to print the laws in the *Savannah Republican*.

Jan 5   To [Samuel Lewis Southard] (enclosure: report on clerks employed at the State Department, Jan 5, 1842). LS. DNA, RG 46. mDW 49494. Transmits a list of clerks employed at the State Department during the past year.

Jan 5   To [Seth Weston].   179

Jan 5   From Alexander McCormick. ALS. DNA, RG 59. mDW 55742. Requests information concerning an appropriation sought by the State Department for incidental and contingent expenses.

Jan 5   From Alexander McCormick. ALS. DNA, RG 59. mDW 55744.
Requests information relative to the appropriation for compensation for the superintendents and watchmen of the northeast
executive building.

[Jan 5]   Memorial of Putnam I. Farnham and Jed Frye in support of a
claim against England. DS. DNA, RG 76. mDWs.

Jan 5   Recommendation from Samuel Lewis Southard (with AN by
DW), for Joseph R. Croskey (LS. MWalB. mDW 21243).

Jan 6   To Caleb Cushing. LS. DLC. mDW 21245. States that an additional appropriation will be needed to complete the survey of
the northeast boundary.

Jan 6   From Charles W. Brewster. ALS. DNA, RG 59. mDW 53371.
Accepts appointment to print the laws in the *Portsmouth
(N.H.) Journal.*

Jan 6   From Silas F. Smith. ALS. DNA, RG 59. mDW 53471. Asks
to be informed whether or not his appointment to print the laws
in the Syracuse *Western State Journal* remains in effect for the
new session.

Jan 6   From Charles Sumner. ALS. DLC. mDW 21248. Encloses a
newspaper article on recent correspondence between Andrew
Stevenson and the British foreign secretary; reports that Lord
Morpeth sympathizes with the Whigs.

Jan 7   To Samuel Lewis Southard. LS. NjP. mDW 21251. Informs
him that no appointments can be made to Central America until
the report of the special agent already sent there has been
received.

Jan 7   From Eben B. Foster & Co. LS. DNA, RG 59. mDW 53375.
Accept appointment to print the laws in the *Boston Courier.*

Jan 7   From Weber & Warland. LS. DNA, RG 59. mDW 53369. Accept appointment to print the laws in the *National Eagle.*

Jan 8   To Thomas Allen. ALS. NhD. mDWs. Demands his attention
to numerous printer's errors in the Blue Book.

[Jan 8]   To Daniel Fletcher Webster (enclosure: DFW to James Holbrook, in DW's hand). ALS. NhHi. mDW 21465. Asks him to
copy and direct the enclosed letter, concerning printing to be
done for the government, to James Holbrook.

Jan 8   From Nathaniel Greene. ALS. DNA, RG 59. mDW 54653.
Accepts appointment as forwarding agent at Liverpool.

Jan 8   From Henry Hubbard and Douglas S. Hubbard. ALS by Henry
Hubbard, signed also by Douglas S. Hubbard. DNA, RG 59. mDW
53379. Accept appointment to print the laws in the *Berkshire
County Whig.*

Jan 8   From William Bradford Reed. ALS. MWalB. mDW 21253.
Advises that care be taken in the choice of U.S. district judge
to succeed Joseph Hopkinson.

Jan 8   From James Thurber. ALS. DNA, RG 59. mDW 53377. Accepts
appointment to print the laws in the *Old Colony Memorial.*

Jan 8   From John Tyler. ALS. DLC. mDW 21256. Directs the appointment of James A. Simpson as U.S. marshal in New Jersey.

Jan 8   From John Tyler. ALS. DLC. mDW 21259. Discusses compensation for Tully R. Wise, U.S. agent at Havana.

Jan 9   To [John Plummer Healy]. ALS. MHi. mDW 21261. Discusses personal finances.

Jan 9   From John Stuart Skinner.   *179*

Jan 9   From John Tyler. ALS. DLC. mDW 21267. Agrees that care should be taken in the selection of a successor to Joseph Hopkinson; proposes that the cabinet meet on Tuesdays and Saturdays.

Jan 10   Recommendations from William Leete Stone, for Charles L. Porter—unspecified post (LS. DLC. mDW 21265); from Samuel Upham, for William Francis Upham—for a marine promotion (ALS. DNA, RG 45. mDWs).

[Jan 11]   To Caleb Cushing. ALS. NN. mDW 21269. Asks him to call at the State Department.

Jan 11   From John Tyler. ALS. DLC. mDW 21279. Returns a paper with his approval.

Jan 11   From Samuel Upton. Printed. *Louisville Journal*, April 13, 1842. Renews his recent application for an interview to settle financial matters; is reluctant to believe DW's neglect of his request was intentional, "after all that has passed between us in former years."

Jan 11   Application from Nathaniel J. Pitcher—reappointment in navy (ALS. DNA, RG 45. mDWs).

Jan 11   Recommendations from Henry W. Hilliard, for B. F. Porter—U.S. attorney, Alabama (ALS. MWalB. mDW 21273); from Charles Scott Todd, for Isaac Shelby Todd—secretary of legation, St. Petersburg (ALS. DLC. mDW 21275).

Jan 12   To John Plummer Healy (enclosure: DW to [Thomas and Oliver Lowndes], July 31, 1840). LS. MHi. mDW 21281. Asks him to identify the addressee of a letter.

Jan 12   To Charles Henry Thomas (enclosure: DW to [Thomas & Oliver Lowndes], July 31, 1840). AL. MHi. mDW 21283. Asks him to identify the addressee of enclosed letter.

Jan 12   From John Quincy Adams. LC. MHi. mDW 21286. Asks, on behalf of the House Foreign Relations Committee, for information relative to the right of search asserted by Great Britain.

Jan 12   From Anne Louisa Baring, Lady Ashburton. ALS. NhHi. mDW 21287. *Diplomatic Papers*, 1. Discusses her husband's mission to the United States.

Jan 12   From Lewis Condict [with ANS by Robert Tyler]. ALS. MWalB. mDW 21295. Asks for the loan of a letter from Theodore Frelinghuysen recommending James Lawrence Day, whom the Colonization Society is considering for governor of Liberia.

Jan 12   From Samuel C. Reid, Jr. Copy. DNA, RG 46. mDW 50219. Requests a reply to his letter of Nov 10, 1841, concerning the *General Armstrong* claims against Portugal.

Jan 13   To Thomas Pennant Barton. LS. MB. mDW 21298. Reports that Benjamin Smith Barton's *Fragments of the Natural History of Pennsylvania* has been deposited in the State Department library.

Jan 13   To Lewis Condict. ALS. DLC. mDW 21299. States that Condict's recommendation, among others, greatly influenced the appointment of Day as U.S. agent on the coast of Africa.

Jan 13   To John Canfield Spencer. ALS. NhD. mDW 21301. Introduces William Pennington of New Jersey.

Jan 13   From Edward Everett. LC. MHi. mDW 21303. Thinks the government should recognize Alexander Hammett's claim against the government for faithful service as U.S. consul at Naples.

Jan 13   From James Hall. ALS. DNA, RG 156. mDWs. Advocates Rock Island as the site for the national armory.

Jan 13   From John Tyler. ALS. DLC. mDW 21305. Promises that any charges against Edward Curtis will be judged strictly by the evidence.

Jan 13   From John Tyler. ALS. NhD. mDW 21307. Introduces Tully R. Wise, who comes to DW for instructions relative to his trip to Havana.

Jan 14   To John Macpherson Berrien. ALS draft. NhHi. mDW 21309. *Diplomatic Papers*, 1. Sends draft of the "McLeod" bill.

Jan 14   To Franklin Haven. ALS. MH-H. mDW 21313. Sends a check for $150 and asks for a statement of his account.

Jan 14   From Edward Everett. LC. MHi. mDW 21315. Recommends that the U.S. mission at Rome be upgraded.

Jan 14   From James Renwick. ALS. DNA, RG 59. mDW 56776. Asks him to honor a draft for $3,000 on the appropriation for the exploration and survey of the northeast boundary.

Jan 14   Application from Josiah M. Lucas, for the *Illinoian*—public printer (ALS. DNA, RG 59. mDW 53480).

Jan 15   To Washington Barrow. Copy. DNA, RG 46. mDW 50220. Asks him to take up the *General Armstrong* claims with the Portuguese government.

Jan 15   To John Quincy Adams. ALS. MnHi. mDW 17303. Sends item (not found) regarding improvements in Scituate, Mass.

Jan 15   To John Tyler (with Tyler to the U.S. Senate, Jan 17, 1842). LS. DNA, RG 46. mDW 48541. Transmits the journal and final report of the commission appointed to mark the boundary between the United States and Texas.

Jan 15   Recommendation from Josiah Randall, for William Rawle— district judge, Pennsylvania (ALS. MWalB. mDW 21319).

Jan 16   To Joseph Gales & William Winston Seaton. ALS. NhD. mDW 21322. Encloses news items from Mexican papers for publication in the *National Intelligencer*.

Jan 16   From John Plummer Healy. ALS. MHi. mDW 21326. Identifies Thomas & Lowndes as the addressees of DW's letter of July 31, 1840.

Jan 16   From Seth Weston. ALS. NhHi. mDW 21328. *PC*, 2: 113. Reports on activity at the Marshfield farm.

Jan 16   Recommendation from Nicholas Biddle, for Robert Taylor Conrad—district judge, Pennsylvania (ALS draft. DLC. mDW 21324).

Jan 17   From George Tyler Bigelow et al. LS lithograph. DLC. mDW

21330. Invite him to a dinner in Boston in honor of Charles
Dickens.

Jan 17   From Hugh Birckhead (enclosure: press clippings). LS.
DLC. mDW 21332. Contends that reciprocity treaties are injurious to American commerce.

Jan 17   From John L. Boswell. ALS. DNA, RG 59. mDW 53389. Accepts appointment to print the laws in the *Connecticut Courant.*

Jan 17   From Thomas Dowling. ALS. DNA, RG 59. mDW 53466.
Accepts appointment to print the laws in the Terre Haute, Indiana,
Wabash Express.

Jan 17   From Francis Hall & Co. LS. DNA, RG 59. mDW 53399.
Accept appointment to print the laws in the New York
Commercial Advertiser.

Jan 17   From William Jay Haskett. LS. DNA, RG 76. mDWs. Encloses papers pertaining to the schooner *Euphrates*, captured
by British cruisers off the coast of Africa.

Jan 17   From Shepard & Strong. LS. DNA, RG 59. mDW 53363. Accept appointment to print the laws in the *Rochester* (N.Y.)
Daily Democrat.

Jan 17   Recommendations from John Todd Stuart et al., for the
Springfield *Sangamo Journal*, the Shawneetown *Illinois Republican*, and the *Peoria Register*—public printers (ALS by Stuart,
signed also by others. DNA, RG 59. mDW 53484); from Thurlow
Weed, for Charles Smyth (ALS. MWalB. mDW 21339).

Jan 18   To John Tyler (with Tyler to the U.S. Senate, Jan 19, 1842,
and copies of correspondence re the brig *Creole*). LS. DNA, RG
59. mDW 48543. Transmits documents pertaining to the *Creole*
incident as requested in a Senate resolution of Jan 11, 1842.

Jan 18   From Babcock & Wildman. LS. DNA, RG 59. mDW 53387.
Accept appointment to print the laws in the *New Haven Palladium.*

[Jan 18]   From John Tyler. ALS. DLC. mDW 21089. Van Tyne, p.
231. Orders the nomination of Algernon Sidney Robertson for
U.S. marshal in Louisiana; will no longer tolerate the *National
Intelligencer* as "the official paper."

Jan 18   Recommendation from Nicholas Biddle, for Thomas Bradford—district judge, Pennsylvania (Copy. PHi. mDW 21342).

Jan 19   To Lemuel Shattuck. LS. CSmH. mDW 21344. Regrets being
unable to furnish him with copies of the Census of 1840.

Jan 19   From Oliver P. Baldwin. ALS. DNA, RG 59. mDW 53415.
Accepts appointment to print the laws in the *Lexington* (Va.)
Gazette.

Jan 19   From Charles P. Smith. ALS. DNA, RG 59. mDW 53403. Accepts appointment to print the laws in the Salem, New Jersey,
Banner.

Jan 19   From Andrew Talcott. ALS. DNA, RG 59. mDW 56778. Reports having drawn $1,800 from the appropriation for the ex-
ploration and survey of the northeastern boundary.

Jan 20   To Oliver Lowndes. ALS draft. MHi. mDW 21345. Discusses
the letter found in the desk of Monroe Edwards.

Jan 20   From J. Coulter. LS. MWalB. mDW 21346. Recommends that

C. Callaghan be sent to negotiate with the Cuban government for interest due claimants under the convention with Spain of 1834.

Jan 20   From Palmer & Bailey. LS. DNA, RG 59. mDW 53373. Accept appointment to print the laws in the Concord *New Hampshire Courier*.

Jan 20   From Abraham G. Randall. ALS. DLC. mDW 21348. Reports that Worcester County Whigs support the financial scheme now before Congress.

Jan 20   From Joseph Richards. ALS. MWalB. mDW 21352. Recommends that C. Callaghan be sent to Cuba to negotiate the claims against Spain under the convention of 1834.

Jan 20   From Dorson E. Sykes. ALS. DNA, RG 59. mDW 53391. Accepts appointment to print the laws in the *Norwich Courier*.

Jan 20   Recommendation from Joseph F. Randolph, for a Mr. Robinson—consul, a Mexican port (ALS. MWalB. mDW 21350).

Jan 21   From Edward Everett. LS. MHi. mDW 21355. *Diplomatic Papers*, 1. Reports discussing with Ashburton the right of search, impressment, and other issues of controversy between the United States and Britain.

Jan 21   From Silas F. Smith. ALS. DNA, RG 59. mDW 53401. Accepts appointment to print the laws in the Syracuse *Western State Journal*.

Jan 22   To John Macpherson Berrien. LS. DNA, RG 46. mDW 50049. Transmits papers pertaining to the nominations of Thomas Claiborne and Joseph Simeon Sanchez.

Jan 23   To Robert Charles Winthrop. ALS. MHi. mDW 21371. Will turn over to him a memorial he is expecting from Boston in favor of the exchequer.

[Jan 24]   From [Lewis Cass]. AL draft (incomplete). MiU-C. mDW 21375. Comments on the prospect of war with Britain.

Jan 24   From Samuel Drury. ALS. DNA, RG 59. mDW 54598. Accepts appointment as justice of the peace in Washington, D.C.

Jan 24   From Robert M. Patterson. ALS. DNA, RG 104. mDW 57142. States there will be a delay in honoring DW's request for copies of the table of coinage executed at the Philadelphia Mint.

Jan 24   *From Duff Green.*   *181*

Jan 24   Recommendations from Elisha W. Huntington, for the *Indiana Journal*—public printer (ALS. DNA, RG 59. mDW 53294); from Nathaniel Pitcher Tallmadge, for Samuel Haight (ALS. MWalB. mDW 21382).

Jan 25   To Henry D. Gilpin. LS. Harry S. Ackerman, Hollywood, Calif. mDW 21384. States that Gilpin's package has been sent to the "Board of Commissioners."

Jan 25   From John Tyler. ALS. DLC. mDW 21394. Concurs in DW's view of the Read case.

Jan 25   From John Tyler. ALS. NhD. mDWs. Discusses the Galveston consulate.

Jan 25   From W. L. and Q. K. Underwood. LS. DNA, RG 59. mDW

53447. Accept appointment to print the laws in the Helena, Arkansas, *Southern Shield.*

Jan 25   Application from Francis Benne—draftsman (ALS. MWalB. mDW 21387).

Jan 25   Recommendations from Jonathan Prescott Hall, for Thomas Tucker (LS. MWalB. mDW 21390); from W. Jones, for Philip Barton Key—despatch bearer, Europe (ALS. MWalB. mDW 21392).

[Jan 25] "British Special Mission" (editorial note on Lord Ashburton). AD. NN. mDW 21385. *National Intelligencer*, March 1, 1842.

Jan 26   To William Morris Meredith. LS. PHi. mDW 21396. Encloses various documents pertaining to the case of the brig *Sophia.*

Jan 26   From Jacob Harvey. ALS. NhD. mDW 21399. Sends letter to be forwarded to Lord Morpeth and comments on the Ashburton mission.

Jan 26   From William Neilson. LS. MWalB. mDW 21401. Asks for early decision on a consular agent for the Somers Islands.

Jan 26   From Jared Sparks. LC. MH-H. mDW 21403. Herbert B. Adams, ed., *The Life and Writings of Jared Sparks* (2 vols., Boston, 1893), 2: 332–333. Asks DW to arrange a location in the State Department for a portrait of Guizot, being presented to the United States by "forty gentlemen" resident in Paris.

Jan 26   From William G. Woodruff. ALS. DNA, RG 59. mDW 53445. Accepts appointment to print the laws in the *Arkansas State Gazette.*

Jan 26   From Henry Wheaton. Copy. NhHi. mDW 21405. Warns that financial reform is essential if foreign confidence in the United States is to be regained; discusses the problem of search and seizure.

Jan 26   Recommendations from B. W. Evers, for Thomas Tucker (LS. MWalB. mDW 21397); from William Wyatt, for Seth P. Lewis—marshal, Florida (ALS. DNA, RG 46. mDW 50062).

Jan 27   From Edward Everett. LC. MHi. mDW 21418. Urges that Horatio Greenough's drafts in payment for a sculpture he is executing for the Capitol be honored by the government.

Jan 27   From Robert M. Patterson. ALS. DNA, RG 104. mDW 57144. Sends copies of the table of coinage executed at the Philadelphia Mint.

Jan 27   From John Wilson.   *183*

Jan 27   Recommendation from Edward Curtis, for Thomas Tucker (ALS. MWalB. mDW 21416).

Jan 28   To [Robert Charles Winthrop]. ALS. MeB. mDW 21428. Forwards memorials received from Boston relative to the exchequer plan.

Jan 28   From Isaac Gibson. ALS. NhHi. mDW 21429. Writes relative to the Morris Canal & Banking Company's claims against DW.

Jan 28   From Joseph Story. ALS. ICU. mDW 21433. Asks for "some pure old brandy."

Jan 28   Application from Philip Barton Key (ALS. MWalB. mDW 21431).

Jan 28   Recommendations from John Reynolds and Richard M. Young
to DFW, for the *Belleville* (Ill.) *Advocate*—public printer (ALS
by Reynolds, signed also by Young. DNA, RG 59. mDW 52202);
from Andrew Scott, for William W. Watts—superintendent, Erie,
Pa. (ALS. DNA, RG 45. mDWs).

Jan 28   To [?]. AL. NhD. mDWs. Stresses urgency of a matter concerning [Charles?] Nichols; asks to be promptly informed *"who
occasions delay."*

Jan 29   To Joshua Bates. ALS. NhD. mDWs. *Diplomatic Papers*, 1.
Expresses satisfaction with Ashburton's appointment; hopes his
own health will stand up during the negotiations.

Jan 29   To [Edward Everett]. LS. MHi. mDW 21434. *Diplomatic
Papers*, 1. Comments on the upcoming Ashburton negotiations;
directs him to take up the "new Nassau case" with Lord Aberdeen.

Jan 29   From Gilman, Small & Co. LS. DNA, RG 76. mDWs. Enclose
documents testifying to the destruction of their property by British
naval forces at Rio Pongo, West Africa.

Jan 29   From John H. Goddard. ALS. DNA, RG 59. mDW 54647. Accepts appointment as justice of the peace for Washington, D.C.

Jan 29   From Harrison Gray Otis. ALS. NhHi. mDW 21438. Introduces
a Mr. Hill of Cambridge.

Jan 29   From Henry Wheaton. Copy. NhHi. mDW 21441. Doubts
France will ratify the Five Power Treaty at present; reports having
written two articles on the controversy in Anglo-American relations.

Jan 31   To Edward Everett. LS. MHi. mDW 21445. Sends a corrected
transcript of his letter of January 29.

Jan 31   To Daniel B. Tallmadge. Printed. John L. Wendell, *Reports of
Cases Argued and Determined in the Supreme Court of Judicature,
and in the Court for the Correction of Errors of the State of New-
York* (Albany, 1842), 26: 703. Asks for copies of the second edition of Tallmadge's review of the opinion in the McLeod case.

Jan 31   From Samuel H. Davis. ALS. DNA, RG 59. mDW 53462. Accepts appointment to print the laws in the *Peoria* (Ill.) *Register*.

Jan 31   From Edward Everett. LS. MHi. mDW 21455. Comments
critically on Stevenson's negotiation with Great Britain; comments
also on Cass's recent pamphlet on "the right of search."

Jan 31   From Samuel D. Marshall. ALS. DNA, RG 59. mDW 53464.
Accepts appointment to print the laws in the Shawneetown
Illinois Republican.

Jan 31   Recommendations from Hugh Birckhead, for Thomas B. Adair
(ALS. MWalB. mDW 21446); from Nathaniel F. Williams, for
Thomas B. Adair (ALS. MWalB. mDW 21463).

[Jan]   From John Tyler. ALS. DLC. mDW 21468. Gives his understanding as to the compensation to be paid Tully R. Wise for his
mission to Havana.

[Jan]   From John Tyler. ALS. DLC. mDW 21137. States that "a like-
ness" of Guizot is being sent from Paris.

[Jan ?]   Recommendation from Samuel Prentiss, for the St. Albans,
Vermont, *Franklin Messenger*—public printer (ANS. DNA,
RG 59. mDW 53348).

Feb 1   To Samuel C. Reid, Jr. Copy. DNA, RG 46. mDW 50222. Informs him that the *Armstrong* claims will be taken up with the
Portuguese government.

Feb 1   From Horace Binney. ALS. NhD. mDW 21471. Declines appointment as U.S. district judge for eastern Pennsylvania.

Feb 2   To George W. Thacher. LS. NhHi. mDW 21474. Declines the
offer of a vessel to carry despatches to Madrid.

Feb 2   To Reuel Williams. AL draft. NhHi. mDW 21475. Van Tyne,
pp. 256–258. *Diplomatic Papers*, 1. Suggests that Maine appoint
commissioners to participate in the boundary negotiations.

Feb 2   From Edward Everett. LC. MHi. mDW 21486. Reports conversation with Ashburton on the right of search, impressment,
and other topics.

Feb 2   From S. Francis & Co. LS. DNA, RG 59. mDW 53460. Accept
appointment to print the laws in the *Sangamo Journal*.

Feb 2   Recommendation from William Pitt Fessenden, for Francis
Springer (ALS. MWalB. mDW 21497).

Feb 3   To Nathaniel F. Williams. ALS. NhD. mDW 21499. Discusses
an acceptance.

Feb 3   Recommendation from George Evans, for Barton Pope—
attorney, Florida (ALS. MWalB. mDW 21502).

Feb 4   To Nathaniel F. Williams. ALS. NhD. mDW 21504. Asks
him to accept a draft by C. J. Nourse for $1,000.

Feb 4   From William Pitt Fessenden to Daniel Fletcher Webster
(enclosed with DW to John Davis, 1787–1854, Feb 1842). ALS
with ANS by DW. MWA. mDW 21716. Asks for William B.
Gooch's commission; thinks Simon Greenleaf would be a poor
judge for Massachusetts (in which DW concurs).

Feb 4   From Joseph Trumbull. ALS. MWalB. mDW 21505. Asks for
the return of John J. Hyde's application papers.

Feb 5   To Charles Anderson Wickliffe (with enclosed affidavits by DW
and clerks of the State Department). Copy. NhD. mDWs. Affidavits published in *Louisville Journal*, Feb 14, 1842. Denies slanderous anecdote reported in the Jan 25 issue of the *Louisville
Journal*.

Feb 5   From Sherman & Harron. LS. DNA, RG 59. mDW 53407. Accept appointment to print the laws in the *New Jersey State
Gazette*.

Feb 5   Recommendations from Joseph L. Tillinghast et al., for Rhode
Island newspapers—public printers (ALS. DNA, RG 45. mDW
53351).

[c. Feb. 5]   From John Tyler. ALS. DLC. mDW 21201. Favors Thomas
Bradford's nomination for district judge in Pennsylvania.

Feb 7   To Edward Everett.   187

Feb 7   To [Samuel Jaudon]. ALS. NN. mDW 21508. Offers to see
Jaudon once "you are out of difficulty."

Feb 7   To William Cabell Rives. LS. DLC. mDW 21509. Transmits
copies of correspondence for the consideration of Congress concerning the salary for a secretary to the U.S. delegation in Turkey.

Feb 7   From Robert E. Hornor. ALS. DNA, RG 59. mDW 53405. Accepts appointment to print the laws in the *Princeton Whig*.

Feb 7 From James Renwick. ALS. DNA, RG 59. mDW 56780. Asks when funds for the survey of the northeast boundary will be deposited in the Bank of America at New York.

Feb 7 Recommendation from Asher Robbins, for William V. Taylor's son—West Point appointment (ALS. DLC. mDW 21511).

Feb 7 U.S. House of Representatives, resolution. DS. DNA, RG 59. mDW 55746. Asks for information re printing furnished under contract to the government departments.

Feb 7 Quitclaim deed transferring property in Grant County, Wisconsin, from Richard Milford Blatchford and Samuel Bulkley Ruggles to DW. Copy. Deed Book, C: 301–302. Register of Deeds, Grant County, Wisconsin. mDWs.

Feb 8 To [William Hickling Prescott]. ALS. DLC. mDW 21514. States that Washington Irving will be sent as minister to Spain.

Feb 8 From Eli Colby. ALS. DNA, RG 59. mDW 53450. Accepts appointment to print the laws in the *Arkansas Times and Advocate*.

Feb 8 Recommendation from Grinnell, Minturn & Co., for P. W. Snow and Warren Delano, Jr. (ALS. MWalB. mDW 21515).

Feb 9 To Francis Asbury Dickens. ALS. DLC. mDW 21517. States that the papers enclosed with his letter of Feb 9 have been sent to the board of commissioners appointed under the convention with Mexico.

Feb 9 To John H. Overton. Copy. DNA, RG 46. mDW 48810. Acknowledges the journal and map drawn by the commission appointed to mark the boundary between Texas and the United States; asks for his correspondence with the Texas commissioners.

Feb 9 To John Wilson.   *188*

Feb 9 From Millard Fillmore. LS. DNA, RG 59. mDW 55761. Reports that the Ways and Means Committee has refused to approve an additional appropriation for the *Biennial Register*.

Feb 9 From Reuel Williams. ALS. NhHi. mDW 21521. Has shown DW's letter of Feb 2 to Governor John Fairfield and promises to make further inquiries today.

[Feb 10] From Moses Hicks Grinnell.   *189*

Feb 10 Recommendations from William Pitt Fessenden, for Francis Springer (ALS. MWalB. mDW 21523); from Robert Field Stockton, for a Dr. Forman—unspecified post (ALS. DLC. mDW 21528).

Feb 10 Certificate of membership on the American Board of Commissioners for Foreign Missions. Printed DS with MS insertions. DLC. mDW 21530.

Feb 11 To Charles Anderson Wickliffe. Copy. DNA, RG 46. mDW 49503. Inquires about mailing copies of the Sixth Census.

Feb 11 From Theodore Freylinghuysen.   *190*
Feb 11 From Gouverneur Kemble.   *190*

Feb 11 From Edward Stubbs. Printed copy. DNA, RG 59. mDW 55749. Gives his understanding of Forsyth's interpretation of the proviso for the *Biennial Register* attached to the appropriation for 1839.

Feb 11 Application from John Forsyth, for the *Mobile* (Ala.) *Daily Ledger*—public printer (ALS. DNA, RG 59. mDW 53332).

Feb 11   Recommendation from Charles Pelham Curtis, for Charles
Robinson—navy post (ALS. DNA, RG 45. mDWs).

[Feb 11]   Review of the opinion of the New York court in McLeod's case
(editorial). AD. NhD. mDW 21531. *National Intelligencer*,
Feb 12, 1842.

Feb 11   Quitclaim deed transferring property in Peru, Ill., from Richard
Milford Blatchford and Samuel Bulkley Ruggles to DW. Copy.
Deed Book 8: 65. Register of Deeds, LaSalle County, Illinois. mDWs.

Feb 11   Quitclaim deed transferring property at Fort Wayne, Ind.,
from Richard Milford Blatchford and Samuel Bulkley Ruggles to
DW. Copy. Deed Book 5: 467–468. Register of Deeds, LaGrange
County, Indiana. mDWs.

Feb 11   Deed transferring property in Eaton County, Michigan, from
Richard Milford Blatchford and Samuel Bulkley Ruggles to DW.
Copy. Deed Book 3: 575. Register of Deeds, Eaton County,
Michigan. mDWs.

Feb 11   Quitclaim deed transferring property in Eaton County, Michigan, from Richard Milford Blatchford and Samuel Bulkley Ruggles
to DW. Copy. Deed Book 5: 506–507. Register of Deeds, Eaton
County, Michigan. mDWs.

Feb 11   Quitclaim deed transferring property in Oakland County,
Michigan, from Richard Milford Blatchford and Samuel Bulkley
Ruggles to DW. Copy. Deed Book 22: 482–483. Register of Deeds,
Oakland County, Michigan. mDWs.

Feb 11   Quitclaim deed transferring property in St. Clair County,
Michigan, from Richard Milford Blatchford and Samuel Bulkley
Ruggles to DW. Copy. Deed Book L: 401. Register of Deeds, St.
Clair County, Michigan. mDWs.

Feb 11   Quitclaim deed transferring property in Portage County,
Wisconsin, from Richard Milford Blatchford and Samuel Bulkley
Ruggles to DW. Copy. Deed Book A: 39. Register of Deeds,
Columbia County, Wisconsin. mDWs.

Feb 11   Deed transferring land in Genessee County, Michigan, from
Richard Milford Blatchford and Samuel Bulkley Ruggles to DW.
Copy. Deed Book 4: 404. Register of Deeds, Genessee County, Michi-
gan. mDWs.

Feb 12   To [Hugh Swinton Legaré]. LS. DNA, RG 60. mDWs. Asks
whether the secretary of state is authorized by law to spend more
than $2,000 for compiling the statistics of the Sixth Census.

Feb 12   To Waddy Thompson. LS. DLC. mDW 21539. Informs him of
his appointment as U.S. minister to Mexico.

Feb 12   From Charles Anderson Wickliffe. Copy. DNA, RG 46. mDW
49504. Explains postal regulations affecting the mailing of packages.

Feb 12   From Reuel Williams. ALS. NhHi. mDW 21548. *Diplomatic
Papers*, 1. Discusses public attitudes in Maine toward a boundary
settlement.

Feb 12   Recommendations from Thomas Brown, for Seth P. Lewis
(ALS. DNA, RG 46. mDW 50056); from John Connell, for Joel Bar-
low Sutherland—comptroller of the Treasury (ALS. MWalB. mDW
21560); from Moses Hicks Grinnell, for Joseph Green Cogswell—
secretary, legation to Spain (ALS. MWalB. mDW 21542); from

George Law, for Thomas B. Adair (Copy. DLC. mDW 21544).

Feb 13 From Lewis Cass. Copy. MiU-C. mDW 21522. Summarizes conversations with Guizot on the Quintuple Treaty and suppression of the slave trade; comments on the upcoming Ashburton negotiations.

Feb 13 From Waddy Thompson, Jr. ALS. DNA, RG 59. mDW 55170. Returns his oath of office as U.S. minister to Mexico.

Feb 13 Recommendations from George Ticknor, for Joseph Green Cogswell (ALS. NhD. mDWs); from Henry Alexander Wise, for Balie Peyton—secretary, legation to France (ALS. MWalB. mDW 21562).

Feb 14 To Samuel Turell Armstrong. ALS. MHi. mDW 21564. *Diplomatic Papers*, 1. Accepts membership on the Board of Foreign Missions.

Feb 14 From Millard Fillmore. LS. DNA, RG 59. mDW 55763. Requests information on past expenditures "for the relief and protection of American Seamen in foreign countries."

Feb 14 From Millard Fillmore. LS. DNA, RG 59. mDW 55765. Inquires, on behalf of the Ways and Means Committee, about the estimates for contingent expenses.

Feb 14 Recommendations from James A. Meriwether, for John Reed—marshal, Florida (ALS. MWalB. mDW 21567); from William Hickling Prescott, for Joseph Green Cogswell (ALS. NhD. mDW 21569); from Edward Stanly, for the *Washington* (N.C.) *Whig*—public printer (ALS. DNA, RG 59. mDW 53478); from Joseph Story, for A. B. Woodward—district attorney, Iowa (ALS. MWalB. mDW 21571).

Feb 15 To [Isaac Chapman Bates and Rufus Choate]. AL draft. NhHi. mDW 21573. Van Tyne, pp. 270–271. Suggests that Massachusetts join Maine in the boundary negotiations.

Feb 15 To Samuel Lewis Southard. LS. DNA, RG 59. mDW 49525. Transmits the report of the superintending clerk of the Sixth Census and suggests that certain points in the law for the distribution of the census be clarified.

Feb 15 To Elisha Whittlesey. LS. OClWHi. mDW 21579. Informs him that congressional committee reports from the Confederation period are available at the State Department.

Feb 15 From Nathaniel Greene. ALS. DNA. RG 59. mDW 54655. Accepts appointment as despatch agent at Liverpool.

Feb 15 From Jared Sparks. LC. MH-H. mDW 21582. *Diplomatic Papers*, 1. Reports on a map of the northeastern boundary he found in the Archives des Affaires Etrangères in Paris.

Feb 15 From John Canfield Spencer and Abel Parker Upshur. LS. DLC. mDW 21588. Urges that the National Institution be granted use of the entire room now partially filled with its exhibits.

Feb 15 From Henry Wheaton. Copy. NhHi. mDW 21590. Reports on developments concerning the Quintuple Treaty; reports also a conversation with the French king relative to the dangers of war between Britain and the United States.

Feb 15 Recommendation from William B. Kinney, for David Ball (ALS. MWalB. mDW 21580).

Feb 16 To Manuel Alvarez. LS. NmRA. mDW 21599. States that the grievances contained in a memorial transmitted with Alvarez's letter of February 2 will be presented to the Mexican government.

Feb 16 To John Macpherson Berrien. LS. DNA, RG 46. mDW 50099.

Encloses recommendations in favor of Thomas Bradford, whose nomination is now pending in the Senate.

Feb 16   To [Hugh Swinton Legaré]. Copy. DNA, RG 60. mDWs. Elaborates on his request for the attorney general's opinion relative to the Sixth Census.

Feb 16   To John M. Leitch et al. LS. MoHi. mDW 21600. *Diplomatic Papers*, 1. Reports that the President has ordered that everything possible be done to secure the release of Thomas S. Lubbock, captured on the Texas expedition to Santa Fe.

Feb 16   To Abel Parker Upshur. ALS. NhHi. mDW 21603. Refers to a matter concerning a Mr. Robinson.

Feb 16   From Millard Fillmore. LS. DNA, RG 59. mDW 55767. Requests information concerning individuals employed by the State Department "who are not clearly provided for by law."

Feb 16   From Washington Irving. ALS. NN. mDWs. Expresses his gratitude on being appointed U.S. minister to Spain; recommends Joseph Green Cogswell for secretary to the legation.

Feb 16   From Richard Rush. AL. DLC. mDW 21604. Acknowledges an English newspaper sent under DW's frank.

Feb 16   Recommendation from William P. Duval, for Hezekiah Hawley—marshal, Florida (ALS. DNA, RG 46. mDW 50032).

Feb 17   From E. Graham. ALS. DNA, RG 59. mDW 53456. Accepts appointment to print the laws in the *Cincinnati Republican*.

Feb 17   From Peleg Sprague. LS. NhHi. mDW 21606. *Diplomatic Papers*, 1. Offers to act as an intermediary in the Maine boundary dispute.

[Feb 17]   From John Tyler. ALS. DLC. mDW 21722. Is willing to oblige DW in John S. Maxwell's appointment as secretary of legation to Russia and agrees to Joseph Green Cogswell's nomination.

[Feb 17]   From John Tyler. ALS. DLC. mDW 21720. Agrees to the nomination of Joseph Green Cogswell.

Feb 17   Application from Joseph R. Chandler, for the Philadelphia *United States Gazette*—public printer (ALS. DNA, RG 59. mDW 53358).

Feb 17   Recommendation from George B. Cary, for Hezekiah Hawley (ALS. DNA, RG 46. mDW 50030).

Feb 18   To George Ticknor. ALS. DLC. mDW 21610. *Diplomatic Papers*, 1. Informs him of Joseph Green Cogswell's nomination for secretary to the U.S. legation at Madrid; thinks the United States is well represented at the major European capitals.

Feb 18   To Seth Weston. ALS. NhHi. mDW 21612. *PC*, 2: 115. Makes comments and inquiries about farming activity at Marshfield.

Feb 18   To Reuel Williams. ALS draft. NhHi. mDW 21615. *Diplomatic Papers*, 1. Warns that Maine and Great Britain must compromise their "insurmountable claims" to the disputed areas.

Feb 18   From Edward Everett. ALS. MHi. mDW 21628. Comments on the *Creole* case; notes the injurious effect news of the Philadelphia banks is having on American credit in England.

Feb 18   From Millard Fillmore (with extract from tabular statement). LS. DNA, RG 59. mDW 55771. Inquires about apparent discrepancies between accounts for the contingency funds.

Feb 18   Recommendation from Washington Irving, for Joseph Green Cogswell (ALS. MHi. mDW 21632).

Feb 18   U.S. Senate Resolution. DS. DNA, RG 59. mDW 55769. Calls for information re agents and commissioners employed by the executive departments without express provision by law.

Feb 19   To Nicholas Biddle. ALS. DLC. mDW 21638. Declares that Thomas Bradford will be confirmed; asks him to see that a note to "W. M. M. our friend" is burned.

Feb 19   To Samuel Rush et al. AL draft. NhHi. mDW 21639. Van Tyne, pp. 261–263. Declines invitation to celebrate Washington's birthday; asks that the Tyler administration be judged by its measures.

Feb 19   To John Tyler (enclosure: DW to Edward Everett, January 29, 1842). LS. DNA, RG 46. mDW 47804. Encloses an extract from his letter to Everett on the *Creole* incident.

Feb 19   From Richard Rush. Copy. DLC. mDW 21646. Renders a bill for his services in securing the Smithson legacy for the U.S. government.

Feb 19   Recommendations from Roger Lawson Gamble, for George W. Crawford—bearer of despatches (ALS. MWalB. mDW 21644); from William D. Merrick, for the *Baltimore Patriot*—public printer (ALS. DNA, RG 59. mDW 53222); from Joseph Leonard Tillinghast, for John I. DeWolf—bearer of despatches (ALS. MWalB. mDW 21658).

[Feb 20]   To Nicholas Biddle. ALS. DLC. mDW 21660. Declares: "Mr *Bradford* will be Judge."

Feb 20–24   From [Lewis Cass]. AL draft. DLC and MiU-C. mDW 21662. Defends secrecy in diplomacy; reports conversations with Guizot and other French officials on the right of search and the suppression of the slave trade.

Feb 21   From Robert C. Nicholas. ALS. DNA, RG 59. mDW 54783. Accepts appointment as U.S. attorney for eastern Pennsylvania.

Feb 21   Application from Thomas H. Willing—secretary to a legation (ALS. MWalB. mDW 21673).

Feb 22   To Nicholas Biddle. ALS. DLC. mDW 21675. Inquires about the "political tendencies" of a Mr. Scott and John Banks.

Feb 22   To Charles Stewart Daveis. Dictated letter. NNC. mDW 21677. Asks to see him at Department of State.

Feb 22   To John White. Printed. DNA, RG 59. mDW 55748. Replies to House inquiry into printing and binding done under contract for the executive departments.

Feb 22   From William M. Blackford. ALS. DNA, RG 59. mDW 53423. Returns his oath of office.

Feb 22   From Henry D. Machen. ALS. DNA, RG 59. mDW 53423. Accepts appointment to print the laws in the *Washington* (N.C.) *Whig*.

Feb 22   Recommendation from Richard Wylly Habersham, for Seth P. Lewis—marshal, Florida (ALS. DNA, RG 46. mDW 50059).

Feb 23   From James Freeman Clarke. ALS. DLC. mDW 21678. Inquires about the truth of an anecdote he has been telling about DW's reply to Hayne.

Feb 23   From Millard Fillmore (enclosure: House resolution of Feb 23,

1842). LS. DNA, RG 59. mDW 55773. Transmits a copy of a resolution on government receipts and expenditures for DW's comment.

Feb 24   To Edward Curtis.   191
Feb 24   To Edward Everett. Extract. DNA, RG 46. mDW 50350. Trans-
mits documents pertaining to the *Seamew* and *Tigris* seizures.
Feb 24   To Peleg Sprague. ALS. MDuHi. mDWs. Solicits comments rela-
tive to proposals he made to some gentlemen in Maine relative to
the boundary negotiations.
Feb 24   From Nicholas Biddle. ALS draft. DLC. mDW 21685. Replies to
DW's inquiry about various candidates for office in Pennsylvania.
Feb 24   Quitclaim deed transferring property in Bureau County, Illinois,
from DW to Alexander Lardner et al. DS. MWalB. mDW 39835-240.
Feb 24   Quitclaim deed transferring land in Peru, Ill., from DW to Alexander Lardner et al. Copy. Deed Book 8: 63. Register of Deeds,
LaSalle County, Illinois. mDWs.
Feb 24   Quitclaim deed transferring land at Fort Wayne, Ind., from DW
to Alexander Lardner et al. Copy. Deed Book 5: 468-469. Register
of Deeds, LaGrange County, Indiana. mDWs.
Feb 24   Quitclaim deed transferring property in Eaton County, Michigan, from DW to Alexander Lardner et al. DS. MWalB. mDW 39862.
Feb 24   Quitclaim deed transferring property in Calumet County, Wisconsin, from DW to Alexander Lardner et al. DS. MWalB. mDW
29835-261.
Feb 24   Quitclaim deed transferring property in Grant County, Wisconsin, from DW to Alexander Lardner et al. Copy. Deed Book C: 302-
303. Register of Deeds, Grant County, Wisconsin. mDWs.
Feb 25. To Samuel Jaudon. ALS. NN. mDW 21687. Rejoices at "deliv-
erance, from the annoyance"; wants to talk with Jaudon.
Feb 25   Recommendation from Josiah Randall, for Thomas Wilkins—
secretary, foreign legation (ALS. MWalB. mDW 21689).
Feb 26   To [Seth Weston]. ALS. NhHi. mDW 21691. *PC*, 2: 115-116.
Discusses Marshfield affairs.
Feb 26   From Morgan Bates. ALS. DNA, RG 59. mDW 53468. States
that he is the new proprietor of the *Detroit Daily Advertiser.*
Feb 26   From Nicholas Biddle. ALS draft. DLC. mDW 21693. Doubts
that the backers of a candidate for the New York post office whom
DW opposes will create much difficulty.
Feb 26   From Vespasian Ellis. ALS. DNA, RG 59. mDW 53441. In-
forms him that the name of the St. Louis *Commercial Bulletin* has
been changed to *Native American Bulletin.*
Feb 27   To the House of Representatives. AL draft. ICHi. mDW 21695.
Recommends that Congress approve compensation for salvage in the
Amistad case despite the Supreme Court's ruling.
Feb 27   Recommendation from Nicholas Biddle, for Archibald Randall—
district judge, Pennsylvania (ALS draft. DLC. mDWs).
Feb 28   From Samuel James Douglas. ALS. DNA, RG 59. mDW 54592.
Accepts appointment as U.S. judge for the middle district of
Florida.
Feb 28   From William Wolcott Ellsworth.   192
Feb 28   Recommendations from Simeon Draper, for James P. Allaire—
sale of steam engines to the government (ALS. DNA, RG 45.

mDWs); from Leverett Saltonstall, for John B. Williams (ALS. MWalB. mDW 21711).

Feb 28   "British Special Mission" (editorial). AD. NN. mDW 21699. *National Intelligencer*, March 1, 1842.

[Feb]   To Caleb Cushing. ALS. NN. mDW 21713. Introduces General Eaton of Buffalo.

[Feb]   To John Davis (1787–1854) (enclosure: William Pitt Fessenden to DFW, Feb 4, 1841). ALS. MWA. mDW 21718. Reluctantly encloses a letter from Fessenden and suggests that it ought to be burned.

[Feb]   To Edward Stubbs. Printed. DNA, RG 59. mDW 55749. Inquires about Forsyth's interpretation of the 1839 proviso for the *Biennial Register*.

[Feb ?]   From Nicholas Biddle. ALS. DLC. mDW 21719. Thinks Randall's conduct toward Jaudon commendable; praises DW's *Creole* letter.

[Feb/Mar]   To [Edward Curtis?]. ALS. NN. mDW 21727. Scoffs at the notion that Poindexter will be first comptroller.

[Feb/Mar]   From John Tyler. ALS. DLC. mDW 21734. Curtis, 2: 183. Expresses approval of Cass's "course"; thinks the Russians must be impressed with the importance of maintaining freedom of the seas.

March 1   From Algernon Sidney Robertson. ALS. DNA, RG 59. mDW 54822. Acknowledges the commission appointing him U.S. marshal for eastern Louisiana.

March 1   From D. Carmichel Wickliffe. ALS. DNA, RG 59. mDW 53454. Accepts appointment to print the laws in the *Lexington* (Ky.) *Observer & Reporter*.

March 1   Application from George F. Usher (ALS. MWalB. mDW 21755).

March 2   From Nicholas Biddle. ALS draft. DLC. mDW 21757. Warns that the "proposed Postmaster in New York" may have information injurious to Edward Curtis.

March 2   From Hugh Swinton Legaré. ALS. MHi. mDW 21760. *Diplomatic Papers*, 1. Asks him to have P. A. de Argaiz, the Spanish minister, notified of the Supreme Court's ruling in the *Amistad* case.

March 2   From Richard Smith. ALS. NhHi. mDW 21673. Encloses a deed to property adjoining DW's Washington residence and asks him to have it properly executed.

March 2   Recommendation from Zadoc Casey, for Dr. Q. C. Alexander—consul, Bombay (ALS. MWalB. mDW 21758).

March 3   To Manuel Alvarez. LS. NmRA. mDW 21764. States that the government must know whether he is an American citizen before it can support his claim against Mexico.

March 3   From Edward Everett. LC. MHi. mDW 21768. *Diplomatic Papers*, 1. Criticizes Cass's protest against French ratification of the Quintuple Treaty.

March 3   From Edward Everett. LC. MHi. mDW 21772. Explains the reasons for his delay in replying to Lewis Cass's letter.

March 3   From Edward Everett. LC. MHi. mDW 21773. Reports a conversation with the Russian Minister Brunnow concerning Cass and French attitudes towards the Quintuple Treaty.

March 3 From Millard Fillmore. ALS. DNA, RG 59. mDW 55775. Inquires about discrepancies concerning expenditures for publishing and distributing the laws.

March 3 Recommendations from David Daggett, for Sereno E. Dwight—bearer of despatches (ALS. MWalB. mDW 21765); from Robert Rogers, for Gideon T. Snow (ALS. NhHi. mDW 21775).

[c. March 3] From John Tyler. ALS. DLC. mDW 24040. States that he has decided on Archibald Randall to succeed Joseph Hopkinson; directs DW to send up three other nominations.

March 4 To Manuel Alvarez. LS? (incomplete). NmRA. mDW 21776. States that the United States cannot support his claim against Mexico because he is not an American citizen.

March 4 To Jared Sparks. LS. MH-H. mDW 21779. *Diplomatic Papers,* 1. States he made a map discovery three years ago similar to that described in Sparks's letter of Feb 15.

March 4 From Millard Fillmore. ALS. DNA, RG 59. mDW 55777. Requests an explanation for discrepancies relative to expenditures for publishing and distributing the laws since March 4, 1829.

March 4 From William Bennett Parker (with AN by DW). ALS. DLC. mDW 21781. Contends that American commerce has suffered under the reciprocal trade arrangement with Great Britain.

March 4 Application from Sanford & Wilson, for the *Mobile* (Ala.) *Register and Journal*—public printer (LS. DNA, RG 59. mDW 53321).

March 5 To Caleb Cushing. AN. NN. mDW 21787. Invitation.

March 5 From Samuel Jaudon. ALS. DNA, RG 45. mDWs. Introduces James G. Stacey, president of the Allaire Company, who wishes to contract with the government for the sale of steam engines.

March 5 From Hiram Ketchum. ALS. DNA, RG 45. mDWs. Introduces James G. Stacey.

March 5 From Dolly Payne Madison. AL. DLC. mDWs. Accepts dinner invitation.

March 5 Recommendations from Horace Everett, for Levi Bixby (ALS. NhHi. mDW 21789); from John Otis, for John T. P. Dumont (ALS. MWalB. mDW 21791); from William W. Watts, for the *Erie* (Pa.) *Gazette*—public printer (ALS. DNA, RG 59. mDW 53353).

[March 6] To [Nicholas Biddle]. ALS. DLC. mDW 22034. Announces Archibald Randall's nomination for U.S. judge in Pennsylvania and expects an early confirmation.

March 6 Recommendation from Nicholas Biddle, for a Captain Henry—Washington post on special navy board (ALS draft. DLC. mDW 21794).

March 7 To Nathaniel Amory. LS. TxGR. mDW 21795. Forwards the Treasury secretary's response relative to duties illegally charged on animals imported from Texas.

March 7 To J. H. Brower. ALS. Mrs. Thomas D. Hewitt, Villanova, Pa. mDW 21796. Thanks him for box of steam candles.

[March 7] To Caleb Cushing. ALS. DLC. mDW 21798. Requests a short-term loan of $1,000.

March 7   To Millard Fillmore (enclosure: statement re publication of the U.S. laws). Copy. DLC. mDW 21801. Explains differences in statements furnished to Fillmore and to Thomas Walker Gilmer concerning expenditures for the publication and distribution of the laws.

March 7   To Thomas Walker Gilmer. LS. DLC. mDW 21805. Encloses a copy of his letter to Fillmore relative to the expense of publishing and distributing the laws.

March 7   To William Plumer, Jr. Printed. PC, 2: 116. Acknowledges a book of poems.

[March 8]   To Robert Field Stockton. ALS. DLC. mDW 22039. Reports the confirmation of Archibald Randall and the nomination of John L. Graham for postmaster in New York; promises "Capt Henry" will never be forgotten.

March 8   From Benson & Green. LS. DNA, RG 59. mDW 53439. Accept appointment to print the laws in the *Boon's Lick Times*.

March 8   From Thomas Dawes Eliot. ALS. NhHi. mDW 21806. Encloses a communication to the President from friends of Samuel R. Blackler, U.S. consul at Otaheite.

March 8   From Forsyth & Ballentyne. LS. DNA, RG 59. mDW 53433. Accept appointment to print the laws in the *Mobile Daily Ledger*.

March 8   From John Grubb. ALS. DNA, RG 59. mDW 54659. Accepts appointment as justice of the peace for Alexandria.

March 8   From Pearce & Bullock. ALS. NhHi. mDW 21810. Urge that American shipping be adequately safeguarded in any commercial agreement reached with Great Britain.

March 8   Recommendation from Robert M. T. Hunter and John Caldwell Calhoun, for Edward Dixon—consul, Antwerp or Matanzas (ALS by Hunter, signed also by Calhoun. MWalB. mDW 21808).

March 9   From William C. Zantzinger. ALS. DNA, RG 59. mDW 54913. Accepts a clerical appointment at the State Department.

March 9   From Elijah Paine. ALS. NhHi. mDW 21813. PC, 2: 116–117. Discusses his plans for retiring as U.S. district judge for Vermont; deplores Whig press attacks on Tyler and DW.

March 9   From Charles Randall. ALS. DNA, RG 59. mDW 53381. Accepts appointment to print the laws in the Warren, Rhode Island, *Northern Star*.

March 9   From Albert G. Rhea. ALS. DNA, RG 59. mDW 53451. Accepts appointment to print the laws in the Russellville *Herald & Advertiser*.

March 9   From James and Robert C. Wilson. LS. DNA, RG 59. mDW 53458. Accept appointment to print the laws in the *Western Herald & Steubenville Gazette*.

March 9   Application from James Brooks, for the *New York Express*— public printer (ALS. DNA, RG 59. mDW 52293).

March 9   Recommendation from James Brooks, for the *Portland* (Me.) *Advertiser*—public printer (ALS. DNA, RG 59. mDW 52857).

March 10   From James Atkinson. ALS. DNA, RG 59. mDW 53383. Accepts appointment to print the laws in the Newport, Rhode Island, *Herald of the Times*.

March 10   From Harvey Bell. ALS. DNA, RG 59. mDW 53393. Accepts appointment to print the laws in the *Middlebury* (Vt.) *People's Press.*

March 10   From Nicholas Biddle. ALS draft. DLC. mDW 21816. Praises Archibald Randall's nomination; urges him to prevent the defeat of J. Washington Tyson's nomination for commissary of purchases.

March 10   From Archibald Ladley Linn. ALS. DNA, RG 59. mDW 55779. Asks for a statement of the cost of printing for the State Department since 1829.

March 10   From Ezekiel Parker Walton & Sons. LS. DNA, RG 59. mDW 53397. Accept appointment to print the laws in the Montpelier *Vermont Watchman and State Journal.*

March 10   Recommendations from Robert Looney Caruthers et al., for John J. Hinton, Hardin P. Bostwick, Samuel M. Blyth—marshal, Tennessee (ALS by Caruthers, signed also by others. MWalB. mDW 21818).

March 11   To Pearce & Bullock. ALS draft. NhHi. mDW 21820. Van Tyne, p. 263. States unofficially that he shares their concern over the reciprocity treaties.

March 11   From Millard Fillmore. ALS. DNA, RG 59. mDW 55790. Seeks information concerning the annual estimates for contingency expenditures.

March 11   From John McLean. ALS. MWalB. mDW 21825. Introduces Polish exile P. Kowalewski.

March 11   From William Henry Seward. ALS draft. NRU. mDW 21828. Asks that something be done for Levi Butler of New York, captured on the Santa Fe expedition.

March 11   Recommendation from Abbott Lawrence, for George Brown—consul, Sandwich Islands (ALS. MWalB. mDW 21823).

March 12   To the [board of] commissioners of the navy. ALS. DNA, RG 45. mDWs. Introduces Messrs. Allaire and Tracy, manufacturers of steam engines.

March 12   From Lewis Cass. AL draft (under date of March 14). MiU-C. mDW 21868. Copy. Uk. mDW 21829. Accuses Britain of duplicity in its opposition to the slave trade and its support of the Quintuple Treaty; summarizes various conversations with French officials on related questions.

March 12   From Henry Wheaton. Copy. NhHi. mDW 21849. Reports that the Quintuple Treaty has placed France in a moral dilemma.

March 12   Application from James May Jones—distributor of public documents in the West (ALS. MWalB. mDW 21845).

March 12   Recommendation from William Sprague, for George F. Usher (ALS. MWalB. mDW 21847).

March 13   To Nathaniel F. Williams. ALS. NhD. mDW 21855. Asks him to accept a $1,000 draft.

March 13   From Edward Everett. ALS. MHi. mDW 21860. LC. MHi. mDW 21856. Discusses duty on rough rice, the transmission of despatches, legation appointments; reports on British affairs and promises to press the *Tigris* and *Seamew* claims.

March 13   Recommendation from Jacob Merritt Howard, for the Marshall, Michigan, *Western Statesman*—public printer (ALS with AN by DW. DNA, RG 59. mDW 53288).

March 14   Recommendation from Andrew Scott, for the *Erie Gazette* (ALS. DNA, RG 59. mDW 53356).

March 15   To Edward Everett. LS. MHi. mDW 21879. Introduces Burwell Boykin.

March 15   From Henry Stephen Fox. ALS. DLC. mDW 21880. Asks that arrangements be made which will allow entry of Ashburton's baggage free of duty.

March 16   From John Quincy Adams. LC. MHi. mDW 21883. Encloses House resolution inquiring as to expediency of reducing the expense of the diplomatic establishment and asks for DW's views.

March 16   From William Bibb Figures. ALS. DNA, RG 59. mDW 53435. Accepts appointment to print the laws in the Huntsville *Southern Advocate*.

March 16   From Archibald Ladley Linn. ALS. DNA, RG 59. mDW 55781. Clarifies his request for information relative to State Department expenditures for printing and advertising since March 4, 1829.

March 16   From McAnally & Christy. LS. DNA, RG 59. mDW 53425. Accept appointment to print the laws in the Asheville, North Carolina, *Highland Messenger*.

March 16   Recommendation from Levi Lincoln (with PS by Abbott Lawrence), for Charles Naylor—foreign consulate (ALS. NhHi. mDW 21885).

March 17   To Joseph Story. LS. MHi. mDW 21889. *Diplomatic Papers*, 1. Comments on the debate in the House of Lords on the *Creole*; asks what legal precedents might be cited in support of indemnification in such a case.

March 17   Application from Philip Hamilton—bearer of despatches (ALS. MWalB. mDW 21891).

March 18   From James H. Causten. ALS draft. DLC. mDW 21893. LS. DLC. mDW 21901. Protests handling of his clients' claims by the board of commissioners appointed under the convention with Mexico.

March 19   From John H. Overton. Extract. DNA, RG 46. mDW 58735. Encloses correspondence between himself and Memucan Hunt relative to the survey of the boundary between Texas and the United States.

March 19   Recommendation from Meredith Poindexter Gentry, for Benjamin H. Sheppard—marshal, Tennessee (ALS. DNA, RG 46. mDW 50078).

March 20   From H. C. Gilman. ALS. NhHi. mDW 21911. Reports that DW's views on the *Creole* incident are generally approved in the South; advises against a proposed tax on postmasters' commissions.

March 20   Recommendation from William D. Merrick, for Joseph Hobson—consul, Valparaiso (ALS. MWalB. mDW 21915).

March 21   From Richard W. Greene. ALS. DNA, RG 59. mDW 54657. Accepts appointment as U.S. attorney for Rhode Island.

March 22   To Millard Fillmore. LS. NhD. mDW 21920. Discusses the case of Levi Butler, who went on the Texan expedition to Santa Fe.

[March 22]   From [Adino Nye Brackett]. AL copy. Helen Brackett Knapp,

Damariscotta, Me. mDWs. Discusses the survey of the northeast boundary and offers to undertake a portion of the survey himself.

March 22 Recommendation from Washington Irving, for his nephew— marine appointment (ALS. Dr. Noel J. Cortes, Philadelphia, Pa. mDW 21922).

March 23 To Elijah Paine. AL copy. NhHi. mDW 21925. *PC*, 2: 118. Acknowledges Paine's plan to retire and congratulates him on his long service as a U.S. judge.

March 23 To Silas Moore Stilwell. LS. NhD. mDW 21927. Encloses a remission of penalty against Frederick B. Meyer and states that the suit against him is to be discontinued.

March 23 From John Tyler. ALS. DLC. mDW 21941. Asks him to call a cabinet meeting.

March 23 Recommendation from Thomas Flournoy Foster, for Robert Howe Gould—secretary, London legation (ALS. MWalB. mDW 21939).

March 24 To Edward Everett. LS. MHi. mDW 21943. Introduces Thomas Lloyd Halsey.

March 24 From John Tyler. ALS. DLC. mDW 21948. Reports being constantly "assailed" by charges against James Duane Doty, but promises to do him justice.

March 24 Recommendations from Nicholas Biddle, for N. Bloodgood— consul, Marseilles (ALS draft. DLC. mDW 21944); from Charles F. Mayer, for James William McCulloh—first comptroller of the Treasury (ALS. MWalB. mDW 21945); from Kenneth Rayner and Augustus Rhodes Sollers, for John L. Dorsey—commissioner to examine lead mines (ALS by Rayner, signed also by Sollers. DNA, RG 156. mDWs).

March 25 To Edward Everett. LS. MHi. mDW 21950. Introduces Charles W. Clifton.

March 25 Application from Theodore Laujoulet—consul, Algeria (ALS. NhHi. mDW 21951).

March 25 Recommendations from Z. Collins Lee, for James William McCulloh (ALS. MWalB. mDW 21957); from Joel Parker, for Salma Hall—chargé, Belgium (ALS. MWalB. mDW 21960).

March 25 From Charles Horace Upton. ALS. NhHi. mDW 21693. *Louisville Journal*, April 13, 1842. Demands payment of an acceptance he contends DW owed his late father.

March 26 To Charles Horace Upton. AL draft. NhHi. mDW 21966. *Louisville Journal*, April 13, 1842. Van Tyne, pp. 726–727. Denies he owed Upton's father anything.

March 26 From Henry B. Humphrey et al. LS. NhHi. mDW 21972. Recommend that the U.S. consul at Rome be elevated in rank and paid a fixed salary.

March 26 From Peleg Sprague. ALS. NhHi. mDW 21980. Reports reaction in Maine to DW's various proposals relative to the boundary controversy.

March 26 From Joseph Story. Copy. NhHi. mDW 21984. *Diplomatic Papers*, 1. Discusses points of international law applying to persons committing crimes upon the high seas.

March 26   Application from Jared Sparks—consul, Belgium (ALS. MWalB. mDW 21976).

March 27   Receipt for $500 from Francis Ormand Jonathan Smith. DS. DNA, RG 59. mDW 56604.

March 28   From Theodore S. Fay. ALS copy. NhD. mDW 21937. Introduces "two German gentlemen, the messieurs Loebzer."

[March 28]   From John Tyler. ALS. DLC. mDW 21996. Calls for the nominations of William Armistead as marshal for Alabama and Richard M. Woods for Tennessee.

March 28   From Charles Horace Upton. Printed. *Louisville Journal*, April 13, 1842. Writes scathing reply to DW's letter of March 26; brings in evidence Samuel Upton's last letter to DW, dated Jan 11, 1842.

March 28   Recommendations from Abbott Lawrence, for Jared Sparks (ALS. MWalB. mDW 21991); from David Levy [Yulee], for Fielding A. Brown—consul, Nassau (ALS. MWalB. mDW 21994).

March 29   To John Prescott Bigelow. LS. MH-H. mDW 21998. States that the President has received the resolutions passed by the Massachusetts legislature.

March 29   From Samuel Joseph May and Edward Moreton. ALS by May, signed also by Moreton. DLC. mDW 22001. *Diplomatic Papers*, 1. Submit a resolution by a Plymouth County, Massachusetts, abolitionist convention urging the free states not to support a war against England in defense of slavery.

March 29   From John McLean.   *194*

March 29   Application from Mace D. Pendleton and John Joseph Bruner, for the Salisbury, North Carolina, *Carolina Watchman*—public printer (ALS by Bruner, signed also by Pendleton. DNA, RG 59. mDW 53325).

March 29   Recommendation from Meredith Poindexter Gentry, for Benjamin H. Sheppard (ALS. DNA, RG 46. mDW 50085).

March 30   To Edward Everett. ALS. MHi. mDW 22005. *Diplomatic Papers*, 1. Speaks of Ashburton's pending arrival, Mexico's threats against Texas, and ascribes present economic difficulties to the compromise tariff of 1833.

March 30   To Jared Sparks. ALS draft. MWalB. mDW 22009. Fears the President has already promised the appointment of chargé d'affaires to Belgium to someone else.

March 30   From Edward Everett. ALS. MHi. mDW 22014. Explains the "narrative" he delivered to Lord Aberdeen on the *Creole* incident; believes Britain sincerely wants to avoid war with the United States.

March 30   From Edward Everett.   *195*
March 31   From John Tyler.   *198*

[March]   To Caleb Cushing. ALS. NN. mDW 22036. Asks Cushing to "send me Kleuber" (Johann Ludwig Klüber, *Droit des Gens moderne*, 1819).

March   To John Tyler (with copies of papers re the demarcation of the boundary line between the United States and the Republic of Texas). LS. DNA, RG 46. mDW 48777. Transmits documents pertaining to the survey and demarcation of the boundary between Texas and the United States, as requested by a Senate resolution of Feb 2, 1842.

April 1 From Robert Brown. ALS. DNA, RG 59. mDW 53443. Accepts appointment to print the laws in Jackson, Missouri, *Southern Advocate*.

April 1 From John McLean. ALS. MWalB. mDW 22042. Discusses the appointment of a successor to the late Jesse L. Homan, U.S. district judge for Indiana.

April 1 From William Bennett Parker. ALS. DLC. mDW 22046. Contends that American shipping has been adversely affected by the reciprocity treaty with Great Britain and calls for government protection.

April 2 To Silas Moore Stilwell. LS. NN. mDWs. Requests a receipt for the remission of penalty recently sent for John Collins.

April 2 To John Tyler. LS. DNA, RG 59. mDW 56605. Asks him to authorize an advance to Thomas Aspinwall, U.S. consul at London, to cover various official expenses.

April 2 From Washington Irving. ALS. ViU. mDWs. Regrets Joseph Green Cogswell's refusal to serve as secretary to the U.S. legation at Madrid; recommends that the position now be offered to Alexander Hamilton, Jr.

April 2 From Robert Perkins Letcher (enclosure: William Adams to Letcher, April 1, 1842). Copy. NhHi. mDW 22059. *Diplomatic Papers*, 1. Encloses an appeal to the government to intervene with the Mexican government on behalf of two imprisoned Americans; urges him to prevent repeal of the land bill.

April 2 Application from George Bass—customs house, Boston (ALS. MWalB. mDW 22057).

April 4 From Richard Keith Call. LS. MWalB. mDW 22066. Accuses former Governor John Branch of North Carolina of creating prejudice against him in Washington.

April 4 Recommendation from William Leftwich Goggin, for William W. Norvell (ALS. NhHi. mDW 22073).

April 5 To Dolly Payne Madison. Copy. DLC. mDWs. Breakfast invitation.

April 5 *To John Canfield Spencer.*   *199*

April 5 From John Tyler. ALS. DNA, RG 59. mDW 56606. Authorizes various advances to the U.S. consul at London.

April 5 From Dolly Payne Madison. AL. NjP. mDW 22079. Accepts breakfast invitation.

April 5 Application from John A. King—consul, Montevideo (AL. NhHi. mDW 22078).

April 5 Recommendation from Henry Cabot, for Gideon T. Snow (LS. NhHi. mDW 22077).

[April 5?] From John Tyler. ALS. DLC. mDW 22080. Arranges to receive Lord Ashburton.

April 6 From James Renwick. ALS. DNA, RG 59. mDW 56784. Transmits his account with the State Department for the quarter ending April 1.

April 6 Application from Josiah A. Noonan, for the *Milwaukee* (Wis.) *Courier*—public printer (ALS. DNA, RG 59. mDW 53281).

April 6 Recommendation from Robert Gould Shaw, for Gideon T. Snow (LS. NhHi. mDW 22082).

April 7   To David Daggett. LS. CtY. mDW 22084. Informs him that the
State Department seldom employs special despatch agents.

April 7   To James Reily. Extract. DNA, RG 46. mDW 52077. Encloses
a copy of the orders concerning Indians sent to the commander of
U.S. troops on the Texas border.

April 7   Applications from Ralph Randolph Gurley—consul, Rio de Janeiro (ALS. NhHi. mDW 22086); from William Hendricks—district
judge, Indiana (and introduces William G. Bright) (ALS. NhHi.
mDW 22088); from Charles Nichols—consul, Bristol, England
(ALS. MWalB. mDW 22090).

April 8   To William Thomas Carroll. AL. DNA, RG 267. mDWs. Asks
whether the Supreme Court has decided a Florida land claim case in
which the United States was a party.

April 8   To Edward Everett. LS. MHi. mDW 22093. Introduces James L.
Ridgley.

April 8   From Francis C. Lowell. ALS. MWalB. mDW 22096. Introduces
George A. Glidden, an applicant for U.S. consul at Alexandria, and
warns of his tendency to exaggerate.

April 8   From George J. S. Walker. ALS. DNA, RG 59. mDW 54870. Accepts appointment as U.S attorney for Alabama.

April 8   Applications from George Gorham Gardner—consul, Rio de Janeiro (ALS. NhHi. mDW 22094); from George Strobel—consul,
Bordeaux (ALS. MWalB. mDW 22098).

April 9   To Joseph Story. ALS. MHi. mDW 22101. *Diplomatic Papers*,
1. Asks him to draft articles for inclusion in the treaty with England.

April 9   Application for Moreau Forrest—consul, Rio de Janeiro (ALS.
NhHi. mDW 22105).

April 10   To [Francis Ormand Jonathan Smith]. ALS. NHi. mDW
22107. *Diplomatic Papers*, 1. Thinks the time has come to press for
a settlement of the boundary controversy.

April 11   To John Fairfield and John Davis (1787–1854). Draft, with
revisions in DW's hand. NhHi. mDW 22110. Announces Ashburton's arrival; emphasizes the importance of a speedy resolution of
the boundary problem and calls on Maine and Massachusetts to participate in the negotiations.

April 11   From Samuel Prentiss. ALS. DNA, RG 59. mDW 54807. Accepts appointment as U.S. district judge for Vermont.

April 11   Application from Robert Howe Gould—secretary to the Russian legation (ALS MWalB. mDW 22121).

[c. April 11]   From John Tyler. ALS. DLC. mDW 22127. Tyler, *Tylers*,
2: 194–196. Asks DW to comment on his draft of a letter to the
governor of Rhode Island relative to the Dorr rebellion.

April 12   To [Samuel Lewis Southard]. ALS. NjP. mDW 22129. Is
unsure what is planned for "Mr. Slacumb" but will inform him
should a vacancy occur.

April 12   To John Tyler (with copies of correspondence re the demarcation of the boundary line between the United States and Texas). LS.
DNA, RG 46. mDW 48734. Transmits correspondence requested by
a Senate resolution of Feb 2, 1842.

April 12   Application from William H. Trott (ALS. MWalB. mDW
22136).

April 12   Recommendations from Hugh Birckhead, for a relative—consul, Rio de Janeiro (ALS. NhHi. mDW 22131); from Thomas Dawes Eliot, for John Stoddard—consul, Rio de Janeiro (ALS. NhHi. mDW 22133); from William Tucker, for William K. Tucker—consul, Rio de Janeiro (ALS. NhHi. mDW 22138).

[c. April 12]   From John Tyler. ALS. DLC. mDW 21149. Discusses the appointment of a surveyor for the Port of Boston.

April 13   To William Adams. AL draft. NhHi. mDW 22139. *Diplomatic Papers*, 1. Assures him that every effort possible will be made on behalf of Adams's sons, captured on the Santa Fe expedition.

April 13   To John Tyler (enclosure: list of accompanying papers). LS. DNA, RG 46. mDW 48986. Transmits papers in reply to a Senate resolution of July 24, 1841, asking for correspondence with any U.S. minister or agent in Austria concerning commercial interests.

April 13   To John Tyler. LS. DNA, RG 46. mDW 48991. Accounts for State Department personnel employed without express provision by law, as requested by a Senate resolution of Feb 18, 1842.

April 13   From William Morris Meredith. ALS. InHi. mDW 22148. Discusses his proposed resignation as U.S. attorney for eastern Pennsylvania.

April 13   From Francis Ormand Jonathan Smith. ALS. NhHi. mDW 22153. Copy. MeHi. mDWs. Reports political views in Maine relative to the boundary negotiations; thinks sentiment is shifting in favor of a compromise.

April 13   From George Welcker. LC. DNA, RG 94. mDWs. Promises that General Dorman will be given careful consideration in the selection of visitors to the Military Academy.

April 13   From George Welcker. LC. DNA, RG 94. mDWs. Acknowledges DW's recommendation of Dr. Hall for visitor to the Military Academy.

April 13   Applications from Mary A. W. Connor—copying (ALS. MWalB. mDW 22142); from Charles Naylor (ALS. NhHi. mDW 22151).

April 13   Recommendations from John F. Everitt, for Julius O. Harris (ALS. NhHi. mDW 22144); from Virgil Maxcy, for John Francis Cobb—consul, Amsterdam (ALS. MWalB. mDW 22146); from Jacob Thompson and William McKendree Gwin, for Edward P. Borden—consul, Rio de Janeiro (ALS by Thompson, signed also by Gwin. NhHi. mDW 22156).

April 14   To Caleb Cushing from DW and Caroline Le Roy Webster. AL in Caroline Le Roy Webster's hand. DLC. mDWs. Invite Cushing to dinner.

April 14   To Edward Everett. LS. MHi. mDW 22158. Introduces George Lampson of Cincinnati.

April 14   From Hugh Birckhead. ALS. MWalB. mDW 22159. Gives a character reference, as requested by DW; hopes the tariff will be acted upon soon.

April 14   Recommendation from George Nixon Briggs, for Charles Edwards Lester (ALS. MWalB. mDW 22161).

[c. April 15]   Recommendation from Henry Hall et al., for William K. Tucker (LS. NhHi. mDW 22193).

April 16   To John Davis (1787–1854). ALS. NhD. mDWs. *PC*, 2: 119–
120. Comments on the boundary negotiations; thinks the U.S. position on the *Creole* incident is "defensible and safe."

April 16   To Alexander Hill Everett. LS. MHi. mDW 22173. Introduces
James O'Hara Denny.

April 16   To David Sears. Printed. *PC*, 2: 120. Acknowledges Sears's
letter on Rhode Island affairs.

April 16   From Lewis Cass. AL draft. MiU-C. mDW 22174. Discusses
French attitudes toward the Quintuple Treaty and insists that he
has done nothing incompatible with his official position.

April 16   From Francis Ormand Jonathan Smith.   200

April 16   Recommendations from John Leeds Kerr, for Pollard E. Birckhead—consul, Rio de Janeiro (ALS. NhHi. mDW 22182); from William Tucker, for William K. Tucker (ALS. NhHi. mDW 22187).

[c. April 16]   From Alexander Baring, Lord Ashburton. Invitation.
MH-H. mDW 22240-A.

April 17   From P. A. de Argaiz (enclosed with DW to Abel Parker
Upshur, April 28, 1842). Copy. DNA, RG 45. mDWs. Reports an
incident in which a Spanish vessel was detained near Tampico by
an armed ship flying American colors and urges the United States
to take steps to prevent the abuse of its flag.

April 17   From David Files. Printed document, signed. DNA, RG 206.
mDWs. Informs DW that Samuel Hopkins has declared bankruptcy.

April 17   Application from William K. Tucker (ALS. NhHi. mDW
22189).

April 18   To Philip Richard Fendall. LS. NcD. mDW 22194. Sends along
petitions for use in preparing Fendall's report and opinion in the
case of William H. Thornbury.

April 18   From John J. Abert. LS. DLC. mDW 22195. Asks that the National Institution be given the upper story of the Patent Office.

April 18   From Henry Leavitt Ellsworth. LS. DLC. mDW 22197. Insists
that the Patent Office needs the National Gallery for its own exhibits and urges that other arrangements be made for the National
Institution.

April 18   Applications from W. W. McGuire—consul, Campeche (ALS.
MWalB. mDW 22213); from William K. Tucker (ALS. NhHi. mDW
22191).

April 18   Recommendations from Abraham Rencher, for the *Carolina
Watchman* (ALS. DNA, RG 59. mDW 53328); from Thomas Clayton, for the Wilmington *Delaware Republican*—public printer (ALS.
DNA, RG 59. mDW 53360); from Edward Everett, for Aaron Vail—
consul, Belgium (ALS. MHi. mDW 22206); from Jonathan McCarty,
for William Monroe McCarty—consul, Rio de Janeiro (ALS. NhHi.
mDW 22210); from Albert S. White, for Isaac Naylor—district
judge, Indiana (ALS. MWalB. mDW 22215).

April 19   From Joseph Story. Copy. NhHi. mDW 22221. *Diplomatic
Papers*, 1. Sends drafts of three treaty articles.

April 19   Recommendation from Joshua A. Spencer, for Jabez W. Gilbert—territorial judge, Wisconsin or Iowa (ALS. MWalB. mDW
22218).

[p/m April 19] Recommendation from [?], for William W. Norvell (AL with signature missing. NhHi. mDW 22366).

April 20 To Edward Everett. ALS. MHi. mDW 22226. Introduces a Mrs. Carroll and asks that she be given every assistance to facilitate her journey to Denmark.

April 20 To Edward Sandford. LS. Donald L. Goldwasser, New Orleans, La. mDWs. States that his passport has been forwarded to the collector of customs at New York.

April 20 From Hiram Ketchum. ALS. NhHi. mDW 22230. Introduces Thomas A. Alexander, the newly elected mayor of Jersey City.

April 20 From John Moore. ALS. DNA, RG 59. mDW 53296. Encloses copies of three Louisiana papers in his district, all desirous of publishing the laws.

April 20 From Jared Sparks. LC. MH-H. mDW 22235. Recommends Anthony Stokes's *A View of the Constitutions of the British Colonies in North America . . .* (London, 1783), for information pertinent to the boundary question.

April 20 Application from James Renwick—surveyor, northeastern and northwestern boundary lines (ALS. MWalB. mDW 22232).

April 20 Recommendation from Henry Dodge, for the *Milwaukee Courier*—public printer (ALS. DNA, RG 59. mDW 53279).

April 20 Draft for $700 by Alfred Fitz. ADS. DNA, RG 59. mDW 56607.

April 21 Application from John M. Macpherson—consul, Rio de Janeiro (ALS. NhHi. mDW 22237).

April 23 To John Tyler. ALS. DNA, RG 46. mDW 50054. Comments on charges against James Duane Doty.

April 23 From James W. and William S. Jones. LS. DNA, RG 59. mDW 53247. Ask whether they should continue printing the laws in the Augusta, Georgia, *Chronicle and Sentinel* under the authority previously granted.

April 23 Application from J. M. Stuart, for the *Michigan City* (Ind.) *Gazette*—public printer (ALS. DNA, RG 59. mDW 53283).

April 23 Recommendation from Lot Clark, for Thomas Douglass—district attorney, Florida (ALS. MWalB. mDW 22241).

April 25 To Lewis Cass. LC. MiU-C. mDW 22243. *Diplomatic Papers,* 1. Explains the U.S. government's position in the Ashburton talks; thinks its stand on the *Creole* has been misunderstood in Europe.

April 25 To Edward Everett. LS. MHi. mDW 22246. *Diplomatic Papers,* 1. Discusses the issues in the boundary disagreement and hopes Aberdeen perceives the need for an amicable settlement.

April 25 To Joseph Story. ALS. MHi. mDW 22253. *Diplomatic Papers,* 1. Explains the U.S. government's position in the Ashburton talks; finds Ashburton well disposed and well informed.

April 25 From Louis Mark. ALS. MWalB. mDW 22256. States that he may resign his post if Baden and Württemberg are not added to the Bavarian consulate.

April 25 From J. H. Clay Mudd. ALS. MWalB. mDW 22258. Reports great dissatisfaction in Iowa with Judge Charles Manson's handling of the Ross murder case.

April 25 From D. Carmichael Wickliffe. ALS. DNA, RG 59. mDW 53330. Asks whether printing a government advertisement for the sale of land in Illinois falls within his responsibility as publisher of the laws.

April 25   Recommendations from Charles Magill Conrad, for I. Garnier—consul, Nantes (ALS. NhHi. mDW 22254); from Samuel Lewis Southard, for T. A. Alexander—consul, Rio de Janeiro (LS. NhHi. mDW 22261).

April 26   To John Evelyn Denison.   201

April 26   To Edward Everett. LS. MHi. mDW 22270. *Diplomatic Papers,* 1. Reports having proposed to Ashburton that a naval patrol be established off the coast of Africa.

April 26   From Joseph Story.   202

April 26   From Nathaniel Wolfe. ALS. DNA, RG 59. mDW 54907. Accepts appointment as U.S. marshal for Delaware.

April 27   To James Knox Polk. ALS. DLC. mDW 22279. States that inquiries will be made concerning Samuel Norvell, captured on the Santa Fe expedition.

April 27   From John Davis (1787–1854). AL incomplete. DLC. mDW 22282. Denounces Great Britain for bullying and international thievery and insists it must either pay for or give up the territory it is demanding in Maine.

April 27   From John Tyler. ALS. DLC. mDW 22290. Encloses letters and hopes Mr. Cary of Virginia can be provided for.

April 27   Applications from Ferdinand Henry Finck (Copy. NcD. mDW 22286); from Charles B. Jaudon—commissary general (ALS. MWalB. mDW 22288).

April 28   To Edward Everett. LS. MHi. mDW 22292. Van Tyne, pp. 268–269. Asks him to explain to Lord Aberdeen the significance of a road now being constructed between Fredericton (N.B.) and the Great Falls of the St. John River.

April 28   To Samuel Lewis Southard. LS. DNA, RG 49. mDW 49498. Presents data concerning passengers arriving in the United States from foreign countries.

April 28   To Abel Parker Upshur (enclosure: P. A. de Argaiz to DW, April 17, 1842). LS. DNA, RG 45. mDWs. Encloses a note from the Spanish minister reporting an "outrage" against a Spanish vessel near Tampico and asks for a full explanation.

April 28   From Samuel Charles. ALS. DNA, RG 59. mDW 53409. Accepts appointment to print the laws in the *Cumberland* (Md.) *Civilian.*

April 28   From Pratt, Cloud, & Brothers. LS with AN by DW. DNA, RG 59. mDW 53411. Accept appointment to print the laws in the *Baltimore Republican and Daily Argus.*

[April 28]   From John Tyler. ALS. DLC. mDW 22293. Asks him to call a cabinet meeting.

April 28   Recommendation from Hiland Hall et al., for the Bennington, Vermont, *State Banner*—public printer (ALS by Hall, signed also by others. DNA, RG 59. mDW 53323).

April 28   Deed transferring property in Iowa County, Wisconsin, from DW to Herman Cope and Thomas S. Taylor. Copy. Deed Book A: 33. Register of Deeds, Columbia County, Wisconsin. mDWs.

April 29   To Thomas Clayton. LS. DNA, RG 46. mDW 50045. Informs him that the State Department has no papers on file relating to the Huntington nomination.

April 29   To Silas Moore Stilwell. LS. NN. mDWs. Encloses a remission of fine for William Murphy and a pardon for Alexander Barron.

April 29   From Roswell L. Colt. ALS. NhHi. mDW 22295. Asks if the claims of the Robert Oliver estate might be put forward in any negotiations for a new treaty with Great Britain.

April 29   Application from Sereno E. Dwight (ALS. MWalB. mDW 22298).

April 30   To Charles H. Bell and John S. Paine. Printed. W & S, 11: 290–291. Makes detailed inquiries about the African slave trade.

April 30   To Edward Everett. LS. MHi. mDW 22300. Introduces Samuel P. Davis.

April 30   To ·Abel Parker Upshur. ALS. DNA, RG 45. mDWs. Recommends Charles C. Hunter for appointment as a midshipman.

April 30   To [?] Young. LS. NhHi. mDW 22301. Invites him to dinner.

April 30   From James H. Causten (enclosures: documents re Mexican claims). Copy. DLC. mDW 22310. Files an elaborate complaint against the commission established to arbitrate claims against Mexico under the convention of 1839.

April 30   From Samuel L. Harris (enclosure: proclamation by the governor of Maine, April 29, 1842). Copy. NhHi. mDW 22363. Encloses Governor John Fairchild's proclamation calling for a special session of the Maine legislature.

April 30   From [Lewis Cass]. AL draft. MiU-C. mDW 22302. Describes sentiment in the French Chamber of Deputies toward the Quintuple Treaty and says that ratification will be an issue in the July elections.

[April]   From John Tyler. ALS. DLC. mDW 21065. Rejoices at the discharge of "this intruder" [John S. Hogan] and hopes the proceedings "will keep [Allan] McNab and his men on the Canada side of the line."

[April]   From John Tyler. ALS. DLC. mDW 21067. Suggests language which might be adopted concerning the form of application for the delivery of fugitives.

[April–Aug]   To Francis Granger. ALS. NhD. mDWs. Invites him to dine with Lord Ashburton and others.

[April–Aug]   To [William Cabell Rives]. ALS. DLC. mDW 38817. Discusses the cost of the survey of the northeastern boundary.

May 2   From Edward Everett. LS with postscript in EE's hand. MHi. mDW 22373. Fears that the leaking to the French press of his April 12 letter to Lewis Cass may compromise his relations with other diplomats; reports strong opposition in France to the Quintuple Treaty.

May 2   From William Henry Seward. ALS draft. NRU. mDW 19001. Asks that a parcel of books be forwarded to the Dutch government.

May 2   From John Tyler (with ANS by Edward Stubbs). LS. DNA, RG 59. mDW 56622. Authorizes the expenditure of $3,000 for agents in Maine "on the northeastern Boundary question and for Mr. Fitz in the West Indies."

May 2   Receipt for $3,000 received from Edward Stubbs. DS. DNA, RG
         59. mDW 56612.
May 3   From Nicholas Biddle. ALS draft. DLC. mDW 22386. Comments
         on the defeat of J. Washington Tyson's nomination for commissary
         of purchases and suggests he might be sent to arrange a loan
         abroad.
May 3   From Gerrish & Edwards. LS. DNA, RG 59. mDW 53367. Ac-
         cept appointment to print the laws in the *Portland Advertiser*.
May 3   Recommendations from William W. Boardman, for Sereno E.
         Dwight (ALS. MWalB. mDW 22387); from William C. Jones, for
         the *Red River Whig* (ALS. DNA, RG 59. mDW 53314).
May 4   To Alexander Baring, Lord Ashburton (enclosure: John Davis
         [1787–1854] to DW, April 27, 1842). ALS. UK. mDW 22389. En-
         closes a letter from James Alexander Hamilton to Tyler and the ex-
         tract of another from Governor John Davis of Massachusetts.
May 4   To Alexander Baring, Lord Ashburton (enclosure: Timothy Dar-
         ling to DW, April 16, 1842). Copy. UkLPR. mDWs. Transmits letter
         from Darling, U.S. consul at Nassau.
May 4   To Mrs. Edward Curtis.   203
May 4   From William Armistead. ALS. DNA, RG 59. mDW 54490. Ac-
         cepts appointment as U.S. marshal for Alabama.
May 4   From Smith & Sayward. LS. DNA, RG 59. mDW 53365. Accept
         appointment to print the laws in the *Bangor Whig & Courier*.
May 4   Recommendation from Henry W. Taylor, for the Marshall,
         Michigan, *Western Statesman* (ALS. DNA, RG 59. mDW 53285).
May 6   From Ambrose Dudley Mann.   205
May 6   From John Tyler. ALS. DLC. mDW 22404. Asks him to call a
         cabinet meeting.
May 7   From John Quincy Adams. LS. MHi. mDW 22406. Van Tyne,
         pp. 288–289. Asks that a proviso in the appropriation bill for contin-
         gent expenses be rephrased.
May 7   To Reuel Williams. LS. DLC. mDW 22410. *Diplomatic Papers*, 1.
         Urges that the Maine boundary commissioners be empowered to act
         on behalf of the state without restriction during the negotiations.
May 7   From Morgan Bates. ALS. DNA, RG 59. mDW 53470. Accepts
         appointment to print the laws in the *Detroit Daily Advertiser*.
May 7   Recommendation from [Thaddeus B.?] Wakeman, for Hezekiah
         Hawley (ALS. DNA, RG 46. mDW 50038).
May 8   From Nassau William Senior.   207
May 8   From John Tyler. ALS. DLC. mDW 22413. *Diplomatic Papers*,
         1. Returns papers received from Everett and Jenifer and discusses
         impressment.
May 9   To Franklin Dexter. LS. NBuHi. mDW 22415. Asks for papers
         concerning Simon Porter, accused of stabbing William Brown, a
         seaman, on the brig *Mermaid*.
May 9   To John Whipple.   207
May 9   From Lewis Fields Linn (endorsed: "Draft of a letter written by
         J. P. Sheldon, at the request [of], and for, Lewis Fields Linn . . .").
         Copy. MiD-B. mDW 22424. Urges that the United States and Britain
         agree not to use Indians in wartime.

May 9   Application from John Hillard—bearer of despatches (ALS. MWalB. mDW 22422).

May 9   Recommendations from Caleb Cushing, for Alfred G. Benson— despatch bearer to England (ALS. MWalB. mDW 22420); from Albert S. White, for Thomas Douglass—attorney, Florida (ALS. MWalB. mDW 22431).

May 10   From Charles H. Bell and John S. Paine. Copy. UkLPR. mDWs. Discuss slave trade on the west coast of Africa.

May 10   Application from David Hines—to deliver copies of the Sixth Census (ALS. MWalB. mDW 22433).

May 11   From Richard M. Woods. ALS. DNA, RG 59. mDW 54909. Accepts appointment as U.S. marshal for Tennessee.

May 11   Application from J. J. Vasques—consul, Switzerland (ALS. MWalB. mDW 22435).

May 12   From William Channing Gibbs.   208

May 12   Recommendation from John Canfield Spencer, for the Michigan *Western Statesman* (LS. DNA, RG 59. mDW 53290).

[May 12]   Editorial on northeastern boundary negotiations. AD. NhD. mDW 22437. *National Intelligencer*, May 13, 1842.

May 13   To Daniel Fletcher Webster. ALS. NhHi. mDW 22444. Asks him to suggest Mr. Nettleton to the President for the Santa Cruz consulate.

May 13   From Philemon Dickerson. ALS. DNA, RG 59. mDW 54832. Acknowledges receipt of a commission for James A. Simpson.

May 13   Recommendation from Robert Smith, for James Donnell—secretary, French legation (ALS. MWalB. mDW 22447).

May 14   To Jared Sparks. ALS. MH-H. mDW 22449. *Diplomatic Papers*, 1. Asks him to go to Augusta "on a confidential mission."

May 14   To Reuel Williams. Copy. DLC. mDW 22451. *Diplomatic Papers*, 1. Warns that imposing constraints on the Maine boundary commissioners would jeopardize the negotiations with Ashburton.

May 14   Recommendation from Francis Mallory, for B. O'Neill—despatch bearer (ALS. MWalB. mDW 22458).

May 16   To Edward Everett. LS. MHi. mDW 22460. *Diplomatic Papers*, 1. Criticizes Aberdeen's response to Everett on the *Creole* incident; fears the intransigent attitudes of Maine and Great Britain may hinder the boundary negotiations.

May 16   To John Fairfield. Printed. Herbert B. Adams, ed., *The Life and Writings of Jared Sparks* (2 vols., Boston, 1893), 2: 401. Introduces Jared Sparks, who carries a confidential communication to Fairfield.

May 16   To Jared Sparks. ALS. MHi. mDW 22464. *Diplomatic Papers*, 1. Encloses a confidential letter to Governor John Fairfield.

May 16   To Daniel Fletcher Webster. Copy. NhHi. mDW 22465. Van Tyne, p. 602. Plans to accompany [Samuel?] Appleton Appleton to Maine; reports that Timothy Fletcher is dying; states that Nathaniel Haven and William Appleton are going to New York to see what can be done about the $3.5 million loan.

May 16   From Jared Sparks. LC. MH-H. mDW 22471. Comments on his mission to Governor John Fairfield; refers to an article by Charles

Butler for an understanding of the British position on the boundary issue.

May 16   To James Larned[?] from Daniel Fletcher Webster. LS. DNA, RG 217. mDW 57233. Replies to queries concerning claims for exemption from tonnage duties and other claims concerning "light money."

May 16   Application from Marmaduke D. Johnson Slade, for the Tuscaloosa *Independent Monitor*—public printer (ALS. DNA, RG 59. mDW 53220).

May 16   Recommendations from Elbridge Gerry (enclosure: W. A. Rhodes to Gerry, July 17, 1841), for W. A. Rhodes—diplomatic agent, Paraguay (ALS. MWalB. mDW 22467); from Abraham Rencher, for the *Carolina Watchman* (ALS. DNA, RG 59. mDW 53250); from Samuel Lewis Southard, for A. Fillippi—consul, Papal State (ALS. MWalB. mDW 22469).

May 17   To Edward Kavanagh (enclosure: DW to [Reuel Williams, May 14, 1842]). LS. MePRC. mDW 22474. Encloses copies of his letter to "a friend" for leaders of the Maine legislature.

May 17   From Edward Everett. LC. MHi. mDW 22479. Reports a conversation with Aberdeen on the boundary issue.

May 17   From Andrew Talcott. ALS. DNA, RG 59. mDW 56785. Encloses a requisition for $6,000 for the expenses of the northeast boundary survey.

May 18   From Peleg Sprague. ALS. NhHi. mDW 22484. Reports that a joint committee of the Maine legislature has approved the appointment of boundary commissioners but it has not yet decided on its range of power.

May 19   From Edward Everett. LC. MHi. mDW 22491. *Diplomatic Papers*, 1. Requests that a search be made for maps.

May 19   From James A. Simpson. ALS. DNA, RG 59. mDW 54834. Accepts appointment as U.S. marshal for New Jersey.

May 19   From Jared Sparks. LC. MH-H. mDW 22498. *Diplomatic Papers*, 1. Reports conversations with Fairfield and leading Maine legislators relative to the boundary commission and their views of a settlement.

May 19   Application from Thomas Dennison—consul, Bristol (ALS. MWalB. mDW 22488).

May 20   From Edward Everett.   209

May 20   From Elisha M. Huntington. ALS. DNA, RG 59. mDW 54702. Accepts appointment as U.S. district judge for Indiana.

May 20   From Peleg Sprague. ALS. NhHi. mDW 22506. Reports on legislative developments in Maine relative to the appointment of boundary commissioners.

May 20   Recommendation from William Wyllys Pratt, for William W. Russell—despatch bearer (ALS. MWalB. mDW 22504).

May 21   To Caroline Le Roy Webster. ALS. ViU. mDW 22510. Expresses concern for her health; reports that all is well at Marshfield.

May 21   To Daniel Fletcher Webster. ALS. NhHi. mDW 22513. *Diplomatic Papers*, 1. Reports Seth Peterson's assessment of the current political situation and that he has "attended . . . thoroughly" to Maine.

May 23 To Caroline Le Roy Webster. ALS. ViU. mDW 22519. Reports
on guests at Marshfield; reports news from Maine and expects
that Davis will appoint good commissioners for Massachusetts.

May 23 From John Davis (1787–1854). ALS. MWalB. mDW 22523.
Thinks "Mr Lunt of Newburyport" is qualified to serve as a boundary commissioner for Massachusetts.

May 23 From Enoch Davis and James G. C. Cook to Daniel Fletcher
Webster. LS. DNA, RG 59. mDW 53395. Accept appointment to
print the laws in Bennington, Vermont, *State Banner.*

May 24 From [?]. AL. NhHi. mDW 22525. Demands the removal of
James Primrose, U.S. consul at Pictou.

May 24 From Ambrose Dudley Mann.   211

May 25 To John Plummer Healy. ALS. MHi. mDW 22531. Writes:
"Look for me early tomorrow."

May 25 From Israel Webster Kelly. ALS. MWalB. mDW 22533. Denies
a "slander" uttered against [George F.] Cutter at a temperance meeting in Portsmouth.

May 25 From Ambrose Dudley Mann.   212

May 25 From James Renwick. ALS. DNA, RG 46. mDW 56787. Reports
having drawn $5,000 from the account for the exploration and sur-
vey of the northeast boundary.

May 25 From Lorenzo Sabine. ALS. NhHi. mDW 22539. Offers suggestions for resolving the northeast boundary controversy.

May 25 From Jared Sparks. LC. MH-H. mDW 22541. States that he
left some papers for DW with James William Paige in Boston.

May 26 To Mrs. Edward Curtis. Printed. *PC,* 2: 129–131. Describes his
Marshfield estate.

May 26 To [Albrecht Elof Ihre]. Copy. DLC. mDWs. Introduces
George W. Lay, newly appointed U.S. chargé d'affaires to Sweden
and Norway.

May 26 From John Otis. ALS. DLC. mDW 22544. *Diplomatic Papers,* 1.
Reports the appointment of the Maine boundary commissioners.

May 26 Recommendation from Jacob Welsh Miller, for Henry D. Maxwell—bearer of despatches (ALS. MWalB. mDW 22542).

May 27 From John Tyler.   213

May 28 To George W. Coffin. AL draft. MHi. mDW 22550. *Diplomatic
Papers,* 1. Makes detailed inquiries about public lands owned by
Maine and Massachusetts.

May 28 To Edward Kent. AL draft. MHi. mDW 22556. LS. NhD. mDW
22560. Hopes that the Maine commissioners can be in Washington
by June 12.

May 28 To John Mills. LS. NhD. mDW 22562. Hopes the Maine commissioners can be in Washington by June 12.

May 28 To Caroline Le Roy Webster. ALS. ViU. mDW 22564. Reports
on family matters and on Samuel Lewis Southard's health.

May 28 From Knowles, Vose, & Anthony. LS. DNA, RG 59. mDW
53385. Accept appointment to print the laws in the *Providence Daily
Journal.*

May 28 Recommendation from Stephen Clarendon Phillips, for Gideon
Barstow—consul, Rio de Janeiro (ALS. NhHi. mDW 22568).

May 30   From Henry O. Sholes. ALS. DNA, RG 59. mDW 53472. Accepts appointment to print the laws in the *Green Bay* (Wis.) *Republican.*

May 30   Recommendation from Charles Sumner, for Theodore S. Fay—secretary, Prussian legation (ALS. MH-H. mDW 22572).

May 31   To Edward Everett. AL draft. MHi. mDW 22576. LS. MHi. mDW 22580. PC, 2: 131–132. Comments on the negotiations with England and domestic politics.

May 31   To Virgil Maxcy.   214

May 31   To Virgil Maxcy. AL copy. MHi. mDW 22590. LS. DLC. mDW 22595. Reports the appointment of Henry W. Hilliard as Maxcy's successor as chargé d'affaires to Belgium; thinks it would be inexpedient to take up the question of renewing the commercial treaty with Belgium.

May   From John Mason, Jr. ALS draft. MiD-B. mDW 22599. Calls on the government to support his clients' claims against Mexico.

June 1   To Edward Everett. ALS. MHi. mDW 22603. Complains about unofficial mail sent in the despatch bags of the Department of State.

June 1   To [Samuel Ward King et al.]. ALS. MHi. mDW 22606. Introduces John Plummer Healy.

June 1   To Jared Sparks. ALS. MH-H. mDW 22608. *Diplomatic Papers,* 1. Is convinced that Sparks' mission to Maine was important and promises to write later concerning his compensation.

June 1   From Thomas H. Blake. ALS. DNA, RG 59. mDW 54516. Accepts appointment as commissioner of the General Land Office.

June 1   Recommendation from Thomas Wheeler Williams, for William K. Tucker (ALS. NhHi. mDW 22618).

June 2   From Edward Everett. LS. MHi. mDW 22623. Reports a conversation with Aberdeen on the *Creole* and *Tigris* and on the boundary negotiations; reports also "unabated" opposition to the American loan and hopes it can be marketed at home rather than in Europe.

June 2   Recommendation from Edward Everett, for Alexander Van Rensselaer—secretary, British legation (ALS. MHi. mDW 22629).

June 3   To P. A. de Argaiz. LS. SpSAG. mDW 22633. Makes suggestions regarding the payment of the next installment due under the Treaty of 1834 between the United States and Spain.

June 3   To Edward Everett. ALS. MHi. mDW 22635. Introduces George W. Whistler, on his way to Russia to superintend the construction of a railroad.

June 3   From Thomas Flournoy Foster. ALS. MWalB. mDW 22638. Withdraws his endorsement of Robert Howe Gould for secretary of the U.S. legation at London.

June 3   From Henry M. Watts. ALS. DNA, RG 59. mDW 54881. Accepts appointment as U.S. attorney for Pennsylvania.

June 3   From Grinnell, Minturn & Co. to DFW. LS. DNA, RG 59. mDW 56614. Inform him that Albert Fitz's draft for $700 has been paid.

June 3   Receipt for $100 paid to John P. Healy from the secret service fund. ADS by Healy. DNA, RG 59. mDW 56627.

June 4   From Moses Hicks Grinnell, Richard Milford Blatchford, and Jonathan Prescott Hall.   215

June 6   From William Maxwell Evarts. ALS. DLC. mDW 22642. Requests a copy of DW's last letter from Earl Spenser for use by the defense in the trial of Monroe Edwards.

June 7   From John L. Dorsey. ALS. DNA, RG 59. mDW 56468. Expects the remaining prisoners from the Santa Fe expedition to be freed on Santa Anna's birthday; reports Mexico is on the brink of revolution.

June 8   To James Boyles Murray.   216

June 9   To Christopher Hughes. LS. MiU-C. mDW 22647. Informs him of his appointment as chargé d'affaires to the Netherlands.

June 9   From John Hastings. ALS. NhHi. mDW 22655. Introduces B. O'Neill.

June 9   From James Boyles Murray.   217

June 9   From John Tyler. ALS. DLC. mDW 22661. Asks if a place can be found for "Capt. Frazier."

June 9   Recommendation from Barker Burnell, for George Gorham Gardner (ALS. NhHi. mDW 22653).

June 10   To William Henry Seward. LS. NRU. mDW 22663. Acknowledges his letter to the President of June 4 concerning the surrender of fugitives.

June 10   To Abel Parker Upshur. LS. DNA, RG 45. mDWs. Will forward instructions relative to the detention of former U.S. Consul Thomas Nelson Carr at Tangiers if it should be necessary.

June 10   From Benjamin Patteson. ALS. DNA, RG 59. mDW 54791. Acknowledges his appointment as U.S. marshal for Alabama.

June 10   Recommendation from Benjamin Glover Shields, for W. W. McGuire (ALS. MWalB. mDW 22665).

June 11   To Sir Charles Bagot. ALS. CaOOA. mDW 22667. Introduces Professor James Joseph Sylvester of the University of Virginia.

June 11   To [Edward Everett]. ALS. MHi. mDW 22669. Introduces Jonathan Prescott Hall.

June 11   From James Renwick. ALS. NhHi. mDW 22672. *Diplomatic Papers*, 1. Reports on the sale value of land in the Aroostook Valley.

June 11   From Reuel Williams. ALS. NhHi. mDW 22674. Gives references for the circumstances of settlement at Madawaska and in the Aroostook Valley.

June 11   Application from Edward P. Borden (ALS. NhHi. mDW 22671).

June 12   To [Henry] Handley. ALS. MBNU. mDWs. Introduces Jonathan Prescott Hall.

June 13   To John Plummer Healy. ALS. MHi. mDW 22676. Asks that a letter from John Stuart Skinner on agricultural topics be sent to him for reply.

June 13   From Joshua Bates.   218

June 13   Recommendations from Hugh Birckhead, for his nephew, James B. Bond—consul, Rio de Janeiro (ALS. NhHi. mDW 22678); from Hugh Birckhead, for John Travers—consul, Rio de Janeiro (ALS. NhHi. mDW 22682); from James Harwood, for John Travers (ALS. NhHi. mDW 22683).

June 13   Senate resolution confirming certain Presidential nominations. ADS by Francis Asbury Dickens. DNA, RG 59. mDW 55157.

June 14   To Edward Everett. LS. MHi. mDW 22684. *Diplomatic Papers,*
1. Comments on the boundary negotiations and on the search for
maps.

June 14   To Edward Everett. LS. MHi. mDW 22686. Introduces William
Thomas Carroll.

June 15   To Edward Everett. LS (with postscript in DW's hand). MHi.
mDW 22687. Discusses English journals and documents needed
by the Department of State.

June 15   To John Tyler (with copies of correspondence concerning U.S.
citizens captured with the Texan Expedition to Santa Fe). LS. DNA,
RG 46. mDW 49063. Encloses correspondence as requested by a
Senate resolution of March 29, 1842.

June 15   Recommendations from Joseph Lanier Williams, for John M.
Lea—district attorney, Tennessee (ALS. DNA, RG 46. mDW
50071); from Thomas Wheeler Williams, for Eli Smith or Jasper
Chasseaud—consul, Beirut (ALS. MWalB. mDW 22691).

June 16   To Christopher Hughes. LS. MiU-C. mDW 22693. Authorizes
a brief delay in his departure for The Hague.

June 16   To Seth Weston. ALS. NhHi. mDW 22696. *PC,* 2: 132–133.
Discusses farm work to be done at Marshfield.

June 16–17   From Edward Everett. ALS. MHi. mDW 22705. Promises
to exclude as much nonofficial mail from the despatch bag as he
can; discusses the boundary negotiations, the *Seamew* case, and the
status of Liberia.

June 16   From Grinnell, Minturn & Co. LS. DNA, RG 59. mDW 56616.
Enclose Albert Fitz's draft for $700.

June 16   From Grinnell, Minturn & Co. LS. DNA, RG 59. mDW 56618.
Acknowledge a $700 payment to cover Albert Fitz's draft.

June 16   From Thomas Spooner. ALS. MWalB. mDW 22713. Asks if his
appointment as purser in the navy has been approved.

June 17   To [Millard Fillmore?] (with note of authentication by Fillmore). ALS. NRU. mDW 22715. Sends the 1842 edition of the
Yearly Journal of Trade and offers to send London papers dealing
with the tariff.

June 17   From A. R. Watson. ALS. MWalB. mDW 21337. Withdraws
his application for warden of the city penitentiary and asks that his
papers be returned.

June 17   Recommendations from Samuel Burche, for John Marks—
consul, La Rochelle (LS. NhHi. mDW 22718); from Thomas J.
Campbell, for John M. Lea (ALS. DNA, RG 46. mDW 50070).

June 18   To [Willie Person Mangum] (enclosures: DW to Charles Anderson Wickliffe, Feb 11, 1842; Wickliffe to DW, Feb 12, 1842).
LS. DNA, RG 46. mDW 49499. Submits information relative to the
printing and distribution of the Sixth Census.

June 18   To Virgil Maxcy.   220

June 18   From William S. Murphy. ALS. NhD. mDW 22727. Expresses
gratitude for DW's approval of his conduct in office.

June 18   From Henry Savage (with John Appleton to Lemuel Shaw,
Jr., April 13, 1859). Extract. MHi. mDWs. Reports the arrival and

abrupt departure of William S. Murphy, special and confidential U.S. agent in Guatemala.

June 18   From John Tyler. ALS. DLC. mDW 22729. Calls his attention to a Senate resolution concerning William Brown Hodgson.

June 19   From John Tyler. ALS. DLC. mDW 22731. Regards as doubtful the extent to which "we can go towards restraining African trade *to a direct trade."*

June 20   To [James Boyles Murray]. ALS. PP. mDW 22733. Expects "the best kind" of Illinois bonds to be left with John Ward.

June 21   To Edward Everett. ALS. MHi. mDW 22735. Introduces a Professor Mitchell.

June 21   To Silas Moore Stilwell. LS. NN. mDWs. Encloses the President's remission of forfeiture and penalties incurred by the barque *Science.*

June 21   To John Tyler (enclosure: list of accompanying papers). LS. DNA, RG 46. mDW 50040. Transmits correspondence requested by a Senate resolution of April 15, 1842, concerning W. B. Hodgson.

June 21   From Tully R. Wise. ALS. DNA, RG 59. mDW 54905. Accepts appointment as first auditor of the Treasury.

June 22   To Edward Curtis. Copy. DLC. mDW 22735-A. Concurs in [Silas?] Wright's interpretation of the law respecting the interest of port collectors in seizures.

June 22   To John Tyler (enclosure: tabular statements of expenses incurred by the Commission of Enquiry into public buildings at Washington, Feb 24, 1842). LS. DNA, RG 46. mDW 48996. Encloses papers in compliance with Senate resolution of Feb 16, 1842.

June 22   To [John Tyler]. ALS. NhD. mDW 22736. States that the nomination for U.S. marshal in Florida was sent to Tyler some two or three months past.

June 22   To [John Tyler]. ALS. MWalB. mDW 22737. Discusses nominations for office in Iowa.

June 22   From Sandy Harris et al. LS. DLC. mDW 22741. Invite DW to an Independence Day celebration at Philadelphia.

June 23   To John Macpherson Berrien. LS. DNA, RG 46. mDW 50064. Transmits papers relative to the fitness of Seth P. Lewis for U.S. marshal in Florida.

June 23   From John Tyler. ALS. DLC. mDW 22743. Asks for an interview.

June 24   From James Renwick. ALS. DNA, RG 59. mDW 56789. Presents a draft for $7,500 and asks that it be paid immediately.

June 24   From John Tyler. ALS. DLC. mDW 22749. Approves a revised despatch.

June 24   Application from Nicholas L. Goldsborough, for himself— appointment in Philadelphia or Baltimore (ALS. MWalB. mDW 22745).

[c. June 24]   From Alexander Baring, Lord Ashburton. Invitation. MH-H. mDW 22744-A.

June 26   To Isaac P. Davis.   221

June 26   From Alexander P. Field. ALS. NhHi. mDW 22751. Explains his sudden departure from Washington.

June 27   To Joaquin Acosta. LS. VeCAL. mDWs. Invites Acosta to the
funeral for Samuel Lewis Southard.

June 27   To [Waddy Thompson]. AL draft. NhHi. mDW 22754. *Diplomatic Papers*, 1. Asks him to inquire discreetly whether the Mexican
government might agree to cede San Francisco in settlement of
claims it owes.

June 27   From Joseph Leonard White. ALS. MWalB. mDW 22762. Asks
that a correction be made in the commission appointing Anthony
Ott U.S. consul at Altona.

June 28   To [Edward Everett]. LS. MHi. mDW 22763. Curtis, 2: 104–
107. Expresses discouragement at the lack of progress in his talks
with Ashburton; feels the British misunderstand the American
position regarding the need for an extradition agreement.

June 28   To Edward Everett. ALS. MHi. mDW 22771. *Diplomatic
Papers*, 1. Discusses domestic politics and the possible failure of the
Ashburton mission.

June 28   From Edward Curtis. Copy. UkLPR. mDWs. Discusses viola-
tions of American laws by British passenger ships.

June 28   From Ambrose Dudley Mann. ALS. NhHi. mDW 22775. Reports on Ohio politics; asks to be nominated to "whatever position
you may determine upon."

June 28   From John Tyler. ALS. DLC. mDW 22777. Wants Dr. Mitchell
appointed a bearer of despatches to Europe.

June 29   From Duncan Kirkland McRae. ALS. DNA, RG 59. mDW
56467. Reports on the Santa Fe prisoners.

June 30   To John Plummer Healy. ALS. MHi. mDW 22779. States that
the "Salisbury notes" may be returned to John E. Hunt.

June 30   To Seth Weston. ALS. NhHi. mDW 22780. *PC*, 2: 134–135.
Gives instructions for spreading fish over his Marshfield land.

June 30   From Edward Everett. LC. MHi. mDW 22782. LS. MHi. mDW
22786. Reports receiving an address at Manchester; reports a conversation with Aberdeen on the question of a cession west of the St.
John River.

June   To Charles William Wentworth, Earl Fitzwilliam. ALS. MBNU.
mDWs. Introduces Jonathan Prescott Hall.

[June]   From John Tyler. ALS. DLC. mDW 22796. *Diplomatic Papers*, 1.
Comments on Bocanegra's "impudent paper" of May 12, 1842.

[June]   Resolution re Mexican claims. AD draft. NN. mDW 22792.

[June?]   From John Tyler. ALS. DLC. mDW 22794. Concurs in DW's
recommendation in the George Johnson case.

[June–July]   From [John Tyler]. ALS. DLC. mDW 22798. Reports a plea
for American intervention to secure a truce between Mexico and
Texas.

[June–August]   From Alexander Baring, Lord Ashburton. ALS. MHi.
mDW 24029. Promises to call on Webster.

July 1   To Thomas Laurie. LS. NhD. mDW 22800. States that Laurie's
passport has been forwarded to the collector of customs at Boston.

July 1   To [?] Lee. ALS. NhD. mDW 22801. Decides against exchanging
or making expensive alterations to his carriage.

July 1   To Silas Moore Stilwell. LS. NN. mDWs. Refers him to Edward

Curtis for information concerning the remission of penalties on the ship *Yazoo.*

July 1   From Alexander Baring, Lord Ashburton. ALS. DLC. mDW 22802. *Diplomatic Papers,* 1. Accuses the commissioners from Maine and Massachusetts of unnecessarily prolonging the boundary negotiations; detests the Washington weather.

July 1   Receipt for $60 paid to Edward Kavanaugh from the secret service fund, for John Andrews. AD by DW, signed by Kavanaugh. DNA, RG 59. mDW 56628.

July 2   To Sandy Harris et al. Printed. *W & S,* 16: 378–379. Declines invitation to the Independence Day celebration at Philadelphia.

July 2   From S. T. G. Hayes (with press clipping). ALS. NhHi. mDW 22809. Queries an anti-labor remark attributed to DW by a Democratic newspaper.

July 3   To Daniel Fletcher Webster. ALS. NhHi. mDW 22815. *PC,* 2: 135. Asks for another pair of waistcoats; reports that the boundary business is not yet "out of the woods."

[c. *July 3*]   *To Hiram Ketchum.*   221

July 4   From Edward Kent (enclosure: memorandum on northeast boundary). ALS. DLC. mDW 22819. Submits memorandum of the Maine commissioners' views concerning the tract of territory proposed for cession to New Brunswick.

July 5   To John Macpherson Berrien. LS. DNA, RG 46. mDW 50016. Transmits papers pertaining to the nomination of George S. Hawkins.

July 5   From James Renwick. ALS. DNA, RG 59. mDW 56793. Transmits his quarterly account.

July 5   From Richard M. Woods. ALS. DNA, RG 59. mDW 54911. Acknowledges commission as U.S. marshal for eastern Tennessee.

July 6   From John F. McJilton. ALS. DNA, RG 59. mDW 53413. Acknowledges appointment of the *Baltimore Patriot* as printer of the laws.

July 7   To Benjamin Watkins Leigh. ALS. ViU. mDW 22828. Thanks Leigh for his "kind attention to my little affair."

July 7   From John Canfield Spencer. ALS. MHi. mDW 22829. Introduces a Mr. Nicolet, who has information to confide relating to Isle Royal and the northeastern boundary question.

[c. July 7]   From [?] to John Tyler (enclosure: press clipping from the *Baltimore Patriot,* June 30, 1842). AL. DNA, RG 59. mDW 53225. Complains that the *Baltimore Patriot* is actively supporting Clay despite patronage received from the Tyler administration.

July 8   From Edward Everett. ALS. MHi. mDW 22834. Reports on the efforts by Cambridge University officials to grant him an honorary degree.

July 8   From Charles March. ALS. NhHi. mDW 22842. Asks that his brother, John March, U.S. consul in the Madeira Islands, be granted a leave of absence.

July 9   To Waddy Thompson. AL draft. NhHi. mDW 22844. *PC,* 2: 136–138. Discusses Mexico's attitude toward Texas and the indemnity question.

July 9   From [?]. AL (signature missing). DNA, RG 76. mDWs. Encloses documents pertaining to Le Roy, Bayard & McEvers's claim against the British government.

July 9   Recommendation from William Tucker, for William K. Tucker (ALS. NhHi. mDW 22855).

July 9   From the Commissioners of Maine. AL. NhHi. mDWs. Return maps and books sent for use during the discussion of the boundary question.

[July 10]   From Alexander Baring, Lord Ashburton. ALS. DLC. mDW 22856. Curtis, 2: 113. Agrees that it seems better to ignore "some coarse insinuations in Mr. Preble's paper."

July 10   From John Tyler. ALS. DLC. mDW 22859. Tyler, *Tylers*, 2: 258. Returns Webster's "admirable" letter to Waddy Thompson and urges Webster to probe Ashburton to see if the British are behind the problems with Mexico.

July 11   To [Jared Sparks]. ALS. MH-H. mDW 22861. *W & S*, 16: 371. Requests an account of the expenses Sparks incurred on his mission to Maine.

July 11   From Julia Webster Appleton.   222

July 11   From John L. Sullivan. ALS. DLC. mDW 22875. Proposes a national banking and railway system to strengthen and unite the country.

July 11   Application from William Bennett Parker (ALS. MWalB. mDW 22873).

July 12   To the Editor of the Shawneetown *Illinois Republican*. Printed. *Boston Semi-Weekly Atlas*, Aug 24, 1842. Expresses his sympathy for the workingman and farmer.

July 12   From Cuthbert Powell. ALS. NhHi. mDW 22879. Introduces a Mr. McRhea of Virginia.

July 12   Application from James E. Wharton, for the *Wheeling* (Va.) *Times and Advertiser*—public printer (ALS. DNA, RG 59. mDW 53243).

July 13   To John Tyler (with copies of correspondence between the Republic of Mexico and the United States in relation to Texas). LS. DNA, RG 46. mDW 49176. Submits papers requested by a Senate resolution of July 11.

July 13   From the Commissioners of Maine and Massachusetts. AL. NhHi. mDW 22881. Express hope that the conference with Webster, Ashburton, and the commissioners can be held as soon as possible.

July 13   From Joseph Harris. ALS. DNA, RG 59. mDW 54671. Accepts appointment as justice of the peace for Alexandria.

July 13   Recommendation from William Wyatt, for George W. MacRae—district attorney, Florida (ALS. DNA, RG 46. mDW 50066).

July 14   From Putnam I. Farnham & Co. LS. DNA, RG 76. mDWs. State that their claim against Britain for the detention of their barque *Jones* at Sierra Leone has been ignored.

July 14   From Edward Kent. ALS. NhHi. mDW 22883. Discusses the compensation which should go to Maine in connection with the boundary settlement.

July 15   To Rufus Anderson. ALS. MH-H. mDWs. Inquires about E. A. Webster, who has been removed from his post as consul, Bombay.

July 15   To Seth Weston. ALS. NhHi. mDW 22886. *PC*. 2: 138. Discusses farming and reports on family activity.

July 15　From Edward Kent. ALS. NhHi. mDW 22890. Requests the return of his notes on the value of territory proposed to be surrendered.

July 15　From Jared Sparks. LC. MH-H. mDW 22894. Herbert B. Adams, ed., *The Life and Writings of Jared Sparks* (2 vols., Boston, 1893), 2: 275. Offers to sell to the Department of State Dr. Thaddeus Mason Harris's index to the Washington papers for $450.

July 16　To [Isaac Chapman Bates].　　223

July 16　To [Seth Weston]. ALS. NhHi. mDW 22906. *PC*, 2: 139. Discusses farm operations at Marshfield.

July 16　From Charles Anderson Wickliffe. Copy. DNA, RG 28. mDW 57061. Requests a copy of a recent act of Congress establishing certain mail routes.

July 16　Recommendation from Benjamin Randall, for William K. Tucker (ALS. NhHi. mDW 22909).

July 17　From Peleg Sprague. ALS. DLC. mDW 22914. Gives an account of time and money expended on his mission to Augusta.

July 17　From John Tyler. ALS. DLC. mDW 19702. Requests the nomination of Benjamin H. Sheppard as marshal for middle Tennessee.

July 18　From Edward Everett. ALS. MHi. mDW 22916. Comments on the boundary negotiations and the *Creole* debate in the House of Lords.

July 18　From Edward Everett. ALS. MHi. mDW 22940. Comments on the "horrid state" of American politics and discusses the choice of a secretary to his legation.

July 19　To [George Nixon?] Briggs. LS. NhD. mDW 22950. Suggests that the franking law be modified to permit him to delegate his franking privilege to others at the Department of State.

July 19　To Abel Parker Upshur. LS. DNA, RG 45. mDWs. Transmits the President's instructions concerning duties collected on articles deposited at Mahon, Spain, for the U.S. Mediterranean squadron.

July 19　From Isaac Chapman Bates.　　226

July 19　From Adoniram Chandler. Copy. DLC. mDW 22952. Applies to bid on the printing of the stereotype edition of the U.S. laws.

July 19　From John Tyler. ALS. DLC. mDW 19708. Suggests that George W. MacRae be nominated for U.S. attorney in Florida.

July 19　From John Tyler. ALS. DLC. mDW 22957. Asks that William J. Davis be informed of the charges against him.

July 19　Recommendation from Simeon Draper, for W. H. Robinson— despatch bearer to Mexico (ALS. MWalB. mDW 22954).

July 19　Secret service fund account. DS. DNA, RG 59. mDW 56620. Copy. NhHi. mDW 22959. *Diplomatic Papers*, 1. Statement of disbursements totalling $4460.

July 20　To Virgil Maxcy. LS. NN. mDW 22962. Accepts his resignation as chargé d'affaires to Belgium and asks him to turn over the property of the legation to his successor, Henry W. Hilliard.

July 20　To Silas Moore Stilwell. LS. NN. mDWs. Encloses the President's remission of forfeitures and penalties against five British vessels.

July 20　From John Canfield Spencer. Copy. CaOOA. mDW 22963. Encloses an intelligence report which contains information he thinks DW might wish to bring to the attention of British authorities.

July 21　From Thomas Courtney Donn. ALS. DNA, RG 59. mDW 54582. Accepts appointment as justice of the peace in Washington, D.C.

[c. July 21]   To Joseph Reed Ingersoll. ALS. MeHi. mDWs. Asks him to consult with Edward Stubbs regarding the bill "legalizing certain payments & for other purposes."

July 22   To John Macpherson Berrien. AL. DNA, RG 46. mDW 50076. Transmits papers pertaining to the nomination of Benjamin H. Sheppard for U.S. marshal in Tennessee.

July 22   From Charles Allen. ALS. NhHi. mDW 22968. States that the Maine commissioners will accept the terms of the northeastern boundary treaty.

July 22   From Patrick Gaines Goode. ALS. DNA, RG 59. mDW 53231. Asks to be informed if the *Wheeling Times and Advertiser* will be reappointed to print the laws.

July 22   From John Canfield Spencer. ALS. MHi. mDW 22971. States that Mr. Nicolet has been requested to come to Washington immediately.

July 23   To Victory Birdseye. LS. NBLiHi. mDW 22973. Informs him that the U.S. minister to Mexico will inquire into Robert D. Phillips's case and attempt to secure his release.

July 23   To John J. Palmer. ALS. NhD. mDW 22976. Encloses $2,000 for deposit in Merchants' Bank of New York.

July 23   To [Seth Weston].   227

July 24   Testimonial for John James Audubon. Printed. *The Auk*, 25 (April 1908): 170–171.

July 25   To Alexander Baring, Lord Ashburton. ALS copy. NhHi. mDW 22981. PC, 2: 140. Asks that American vessels be granted the right of navigation at the mouth of the Detroit River.

July 25   To Edward Kent.   228

July 25   From Henry L. Kinney.   229

July 25   Recommendation from George Nixon Briggs, for John Taltock—bearer of despatches, Great Britain (ALS. MWalB. mDW 22989); from Thomas Wilson & Co. et al., for George S. Roy—consul, Port au Prince (LS. MWalB. mDW 22994).

July 26   To Edward Everett. Copy. DNA, RG 46. mDW 50386. Transmits documents pertaining to the detention of the American barque *John A. Robb* by *H.M.S. Waterwitch* and directs him to bring the case to the attention of the British government.

[July 26]   From Alexander Baring, Lord Ashburton. ALS. DLC. mDW 23005. Curtis, 2: 117. Argues against the inclusion of a provision for compensating Maine and Massachusetts in the treaty.

July 26   Recommendation from Samuel Ward, for Charles Frederic Mensch—professor, National Institution (ALS with ANS by DW. MWalB. mDW 23013).

July 27   From Dillon Jordan. ALS. DNA, RG 59. mDW 54710. Acknowledges commission appointing him U.S. district judge for western Florida.

July 27   From William Kinney. ALS. DNA, RG 59. mDW 54718. Accepts appointment as U.S. attorney for western Virginia.

July 27   From John Tyler. ALS. DLC. mDW 23016. Asks if the U.S. consul at Havana was authorized to leave his post.

July 27   From John Tyler. ALS. DLC. mDW 23019. Tyler, *Tylers*, 2: 264. Suggests that the release of Americans imprisoned at Van Diemen's land be requested "as a boon" rather than insisted upon as "a right."

July 28   To John S. Young. LS. T. mDWs. Asks that a copy of the laws of
Tennessee for 1837–1838 be sent to the Department of State library.

July 28   From John Mills.   231

July 28   From John Otis. ALS. DLC. mDW 23025. States that he and
Edward Kent will call for a copy of the treaty articles on the free
navigation of the St. John and the disputed territory fund.

July 28   From John Tyler. ALS. DLC. mDW 23009. Approves, with some
suggested modifications, Ashburton's note on the *Caroline.*

July 29   To John Macpherson Berrien. LS. DNA, RG 46. mDW 50068. Encloses papers pertaining to the nominations of George W. MacRae and
John M. Lea.

July 29   From Hugh Swinton Legaré. ALS. MHi. mDW 23027. *Diplomatic
Papers*, 1. Suggests changes in DW's *Creole* letter.

[July 30]   To [Alexander Baring, Lord Ashburton]. AL draft. MWalB. mDW
23031. Argues vigorously against the practice of impressment.

July 30   To [John Tyler]. ALS copy. NhHi. mDW 23056. Van Tyne, p. 272.
Expresses mortification over libelous references to Lord Ashburton in the
Madisonian.

July 30   To Abel Parker Upshur. LS. DNA, RG 45. mDWs. Sends him a roll
of charts with a pamphlet of sailing instructions sent from London by
Everett.

July 30   From Thomas Douglass. ALS. DNA, RG 59. mDW 54594. Acknowledges appointment as U.S. attorney for eastern Florida.

July 30   From Edward Everett. LC. MHi. mDW 23058. Writes concerning
British publications to be sent to the Department of State.

July 30   From Abbott Lawrence.   232

July 30   From John Tyler. LS. DNA, RG 59. mDW 55835. Authorizes
DW to negotiate with the chargé d'affaires of Texas.

July 31   From Alexander Baring, Lord Ashburton. ALS. NhHi. mDW
23061. *Diplomatic Papers*, 1. Thinks the *Creole* and extradition
issues are related and would be best resolved in London.

[July]   To [Caleb Cushing]. ALS. NN. mDW 23064. Arranges for Cushing to
call upon him.

[July]   From Alexander Baring, Lord Ashburton. ALS. DLC. mDW 23066.
Diplomatic Papers, 1. Expresses amazement that DW could adopt the
views of the Maine commissioners as his own; reports a satisfactory conversation with Edward Kavanagh; likes the cruising convention.

[July]   From Alexander Baring, Lord Ashburton. ALS. NhD. mDWs.
Curtis, 2: 119. Asks for the revised draft of the cruising convention.

[July]   From Alexander Baring, Lord Ashburton. Printed. Curtis, 2:
120. *Diplomatic Papers*, 1. Will be seeing Calhoun regarding the *Creole*;
finds Legaré's proposal unsatisfactory; has informed the Maine commissioners that they must come to a decision regarding "our line."

[July–Aug]   From John Tyler. AD incomplete. DLC. mDW 23070. Discusses
the impressment question.

Aug 1   From George S. Curson. ALS. DNA, RG 59. mDW 56473. Expects to
be detained at New Orleans until the arrival of the cutter that will carry
him to Vera Cruz.

Aug 1   From John Tyler. ALS. NhHi. mDW 23089. Van Tyne, p. 273. Approves DW's impressment letter, but suggests that the principle be extended to cover similar problems on land.

Aug 1   From John Tyler. Copy. DNA, RG 59. mDW 55834. Authorizes DW to
conclude the treaty with Great Britain.

Aug 1   Application from George S. Roy (ALS. MWalB. mDW 23087).

Aug 1   Recommendations from Henshaw, Ward & Company, for Thomas
McGuire—consul, Rio de Janeiro (LS. NhHi. mDW 23161); from
John Otis, for John T. P. Dumont—despatch bearer, England (ALS.
MWalB. mDW 23084).

Aug 2   To [Seth Weston]. ALS. NhHi. mDW 23091. *PC*, 2: 142. Discusses
his Marshfield farm business.

Aug 2   From Edward Everett. LC. MHi. mDW 23093. Discusses conversations with British officials and the selection of a secretary.

Aug 3   To Silas Moore Stilwell. LS. NN. mDWs. Encloses a remission
of fine for Albert Slater.

Aug 3   From Edward Everett.   232

Aug 3   From John Tyler. ALS. DLC. mDW 23100. Suggests an amendment to DW's *Caroline* case letter.

Aug 4   From Matthew St. Claire Clarke (with DW to Willie Person
Mangum, Aug 6, 1842). Copy. DNA, RG 46. mDW 49512. Reports
that his audit of Thomas Allen's bill for printing the compendium
to the Sixth Census has found it correct.

Aug 4   Recommendations from Mordecai Manuel Noah, for Charles A.
Miller—consul, Dundee, Scotland (ALS. MWalB. mDW 23103); from
Robert C. Wetmore, for Charles A. Miller (ALS. MWalB. mDW 23105).

[Aug 5]   To Caleb Cushing. ALS. NN. mDW 23106. Asks him to bring over a
copy of "Garrett Davis' Report in Sylvester's case."

Aug 5   From Hugh Swinton Legaré. ALS. MHi. mDW 23108. Reports a successful negotiation with Ashburton on the protection of American shipping in the Bahama channel and on the extradition article.

Aug 6   To Willie Person Mangum (enclosures: Thomas Allen to DW, Aug 6,
1842; Auditors' Report, July 22, 1842; Expense Account, June 18, 1842;
Clarke to DW, Aug 4, 1842; W. Hickey to Clarke, Aug 3, 1842). LS. DNA,
RG 46. mDW 49508. Transmits documents, Thomas Allen's bill for printing the compendium of the Sixth Census.

Aug 6   From Thomas Allen (with DW to Willie Person Mangum, August 6,
1842). ALS by proxy. DNA, RG 46. mDW 49507. Submits a bill for printing 20,000 copies of the compendium of the Sixth Census.

Aug 7   From John Tyler. ALS. DLC. mDW 23112. *Diplomatic Papers*, 1. Recommends some changes in Ashburton's proposed note on the *Creole*.

Aug 8   To [Caleb Cushing].   234
Aug 8   To William Cabell Rives.   235
Aug 8   From John Tyler.   235
Aug 8   To John Tyler.   235

Aug 8   From George Evans. ALS. DNA, RG 59. mDW 55792. Inquires
about arrangements for paying for the printing of the compendium
of the sixth census.

Aug 8   From John Tyler. ALS. NhHi. mDW 23130. *Diplomatic Papers*, 1.
Offers congratulations on the completion of the treaty, but wonders if
there should be "separate conventions for each subject."

Aug 9   From George S. Hawkins. ALS. DNA, RG 59. mDW 54677. Accepts
appointment as attorney for the Apalachicola district of Florida.

Aug 9   From Johan George Hülsemann. AL draft. DLC. mDW 23133. Announces the appointment of Daniel J. Desmond as provisional Austrian vice consul at Philadelphia.

Aug 9   Recommendation from Robert James Walker, for Charles A. Miller (ALS. MWalB. mDW 23138).

[c. Aug 9]   From John Tyler. ALS. NhHi. mDW 23135. Van Tyne, p. 234. Asks for DW's comments on the draft of his message to the Senate and declares that he wants to be known as a peacemaker.

[Aug 9–20?]   To [William Cabell Rives?]. ALS. NN. mDW 24022. Will send the book with the maps as soon as he can find it.

Aug 10   To Edward Curtis. ALS. NN. mDW 23140. Asks him to find some job for Vanbrogh Livingston as a favor for Mrs. Webster.

Aug 10   To Mrs. Edward Curtis. Printed. PC, 2: 142–144. Informs her: "C. H.——— of Vermont was made a Middy."

Aug 10   To William Cabell Rives. LS. DLC. mDW 23143. Sends him sealed packages of secret papers and a memorandum of General Winfield Scott.

Aug 10   To [William Cabell Rives]. ALS. DLC. mDW 23145. Regrets that it will not be practical "to get our treaty in today."

[c. Aug 10]   Recommendation from William Campbell Preston, for the Charleston *Southern Patriot*, the Columbia *Southern Chronicle*, and the Cheraw *Farmers' Gazette*—public printers (ALS with ANS by DFW. DNA, RG 59. mDW 53335).

Aug 11   From Gideon Barstow. ALS. NhHi. mDW 19915. Asks for the return of his papers of application for the consulate at Rio de Janeiro.

Aug 11   From Caleb Cushing et al. AL draft. DLC. mDW 23153. Asks that application be made to the British government for the release of Americans imprisoned on Van Diemen's Land.

Aug 11   From Edward Kavanagh. AL. DLC. mDW 23157. Believes that the Maine commissioners are succeeding in their efforts to counter prejudice against the treaty.

Aug 11   Application from Thomas McGuire (ALS. NhHi. mDW 23159).

Aug 12   From Charles Mason. ALS. DNA, RG 59. mDW 54759. Accepts appointment as chief justice of the Supreme Court of Iowa Territory.

Aug 12   From Francis Ormand Jonathan Smith. ALS. DNA, RG 59. mDW 56629. *Diplomatic Papers*, 1. Applies for compensation for individuals he hired "to adjust the tone and direction" of public opinion in Maine toward the boundary settlement; submits bill for own services, as well as those of assistants.

[Aug 13]   To Caroline Le Roy Webster. ALS. NhHi. mDW 23163. Van Tyne, pp. 602–603. Reports on his health and social activity in Washington.

Aug 13   From Edward Everett. ALS. MHi. mDW 23171. Reports developments in Britain regarding the boundary settlement; comments on "riotous assemblages" in the industrial districts of Britain.

Aug 13   Deed transferring property in Portage County, Wisconsin, from DW and wife to Herman Cope and Thomas S. Taylor. Copy. Deed Book A: 35. Register of Deeds, Columbia County, Wisconsin. mDWs.

Aug 15   To Silas Moore Stilwell. LS. NN. mDWs. Encloses a remission of fine for J. Howard Williams.

Aug 15   From George Evans. ALS. DNA, RG 59. mDW 55794. Makes inquiries concerning the watchmen for the northeast executive building.

Aug 15   Recommendation from Samuel Denison, for George F. Usher (ALS. MWalB. mDW 23178).

Aug 16   To Antonio de Larruez [Larrua]. LS. SpSAG. mDW 23180. *Diplo-matic Papers*, 1. Protests Spain's decision to deduct a sum for its *Amistad* claim from the installment now due the United States under the convention of 1834.

[Aug 16]   To Caroline Le Roy Webster. Copy. NhHi. mDW 23183. Van Tyne, p. 276. Discusses Caroline's purchase of carpets and his health; comments on the President's appearance and expresses fear over the consequence of another veto.

Aug 16   From Murdoch MacLean. ALS. DNA, RG 59. mDW 53429. Accepts appointment to print the laws in the Cheraw *Farmers' Gazette*.

Aug 16   From Samuel Weir. ALS. DNA, RG 59. mDW 53427. Accepts appointment to print the laws in the Columbia *Southern Chronicle*.

Aug 16   Application from J. S. Nevins—distribution of the census (ALS. MWalB. mDW 23186).

Aug 17   To John Plummer Healy. ALS. MHi. mDW 23188. *Diplomatic Papers*, 1. Expects the Ashburton treaty will be ratified despite opposition; asks him to arrange insurance for a barn at Marshfield.

Aug 17   To Stephen Pleasonton. LS. NcD. mDW 23192. Informs him that a particular charge in the account of Abraham P. Gibson, U.S. consul at St. Petersburg, is to be allowed.

Aug 17   To William Cabell Rives. ALS. DLC. mDW 23195. Forwards papers on the northeastern boundary.

Aug 17   To Nathaniel Leverett Rogers & Brothers. Copy. DNA, RG 76. mDWs. Encloses a letter on the subject of the laws and duties applied by the British government in the Bay of Islands.

Aug 17   From Washington Irving. ALS. MH-H. mDW 23197. Defends Reuben G. Beasley, consul at Havre, against charges.

Aug 17   From Henry P. Marshall (with AN by DW). ALS. MWalB. mDW 23201. Asks if the commission appointing E. A. Webster U.S. consul at Bombay has been forwarded to him.

Aug 17   From John Canfield Spencer. ALS. NhHi. mDW 23203. Suggests that the possession of Rouse's Point renders unnecessary an additional fort at Windmill Point.

Aug 17   From Caleb L. Swayze. ALS. DNA, RG 59. mDW 54862. Accepts appointment as U.S. attorney for Louisiana.

Aug 17   From Thomas S. Wilson. ALS. DNA, RG 59. mDW 54901. Accepts appointment as associate judge on the Iowa Supreme Court.

Aug 18   To Washington Barrow. Copy. DNA, RG 46. mDW 50229. Directs him to press the *Armstrong* claim and also that of James Hall against Portugal.

Aug 18   To Johan George Hülsemann. LS. DLC. mDW 23206. Extends official recognition to Daniel J. Desmond, provisional vice consul of Austria at Philadelphia.

Aug 18   To William Cabell Rives. ALS. DLC. mDW 23207. Reports that he has found no trace of Lattré's map.

Aug 18   To [Seth Weston]. ALS. NhHi. mDW 23209. *PC*, 2: 144–145. Gives instructions for work at Marshfield.

Aug 18   From John M. Lea. ALS. DNA, RG 59. mDW 54728. Accepts appointment as U.S. attorney for middle Tennessee.

Aug 18   Message transmitting treaty between the United States and the Republic of Texas. AD draft. NhHi. mDW 23213.

Aug 19   To [William McKendree Gwin?]. ALS. NhExP. mDW 23221. Asks what has become of John Francis Hamtramck Claiborne.

[Aug 19]   To William Cabell Rives. ALS. DLC. mDW 23222. Refers to pages in certain documents and thinks "we *have* just what Genl [John Ellis] Wool says we want."

[Aug 19?]   From William Cabell Rives. ALS. MHi. mDW 24033. Hopes for a favorable vote in the Senate on Aug 20 on the treaty.

Aug 19   Recommendation from Barker Burnell, for Isaac N. Coffin—indexer (ALS. MWalB. mDW 23224).

Aug 20   To [John Francis Hamtramck] Claiborne. ALS. NhD. mDW 23226. Agrees to see him at the State Department.

[Aug 20]   To [George Ticknor]. ALS. NhD. mDW 23228. *Diplomatic Papers*, 1. Declares: "The work [of the Webster-Ashburton Treaty] is done 39 to 9."

Aug 20   To [Seth Weston]. ALS. NhHi. mDW 23229. *PC*, 2: 145. Gives instructions for storing salt hay and asks what he thinks about building a barn.

Aug 20   Application from James A. Kelly, for the *Louisiana Chronicle*— public printer (ALS. DNA, RG 59. mDW 53274).

[Aug 20]   Editorial on Lord Ashburton's mission. AD. NhD. mDW 23231. *National Intelligencer*, Aug 20, 1842 (in part).

Aug 21   To Jeremiah Mason. Printed. *PC*, 2: 146. Reports that the Treaty of Washington has been ratified by a margin greater than expected.

[Aug 21?]   To William Cabell Rives. ALS. DLC. mDW 23236. *Diplomatic Papers*, 1. Credits Rives for "much of our success" with the treaty.

Aug 21   From John Tyler. ALS. DLC. mDW 23239. Tyler, *Tylers*, 2: 226. Informs him that the Senate has ratified Treaty of Washington.

[Aug 21]   To John Tyler. Copy. NhHi. mDW 23238. *Diplomatic Papers*, 1. Comments on the ratification of the Treaty of Washington.

Aug 21   From Andrew Talcott. ALS. DNA, RG 59. mDW 56797. Asks that $3,000 from the appropriation for the exploration and survey of the northeast boundary be remitted to the cashier of the Bank of America.

Aug 22   To William S. Derrick. LS. NjP-Sch. mDW 23241. Entrusts him with the exchange of treaty ratifications at London.

Aug 22   To Edward Everett. ALS. MHi. mDW 23244. Introduces William S. Derrick, who carries the ratified Treaty of Washington to England.

Aug 22   From Alexander Baring, Lord Ashburton. ALS. George C. Whipple, Jr., Carmel, N.Y. mDW 23249. Welcomes the news of the treaty's ratification and asks for copies of the finished papers to take with him.

Aug 22   From John Grant Chapman with enclosure: Resolution of Port Tobacco Whigs.   236

Aug 22   From Shobal Vail Clevenger. ALS. NhHi. mDW 23260. Retracts his criticism of George W. Greene, consul at Rome.

Aug 22   From Samuel C. Reid, Jr. Copy. DNA, RG 46. mDW 50230. Asks to be informed of the nature of any communication from Washington Barrow.

Aug 22   From James E. Wharton. ALS. DNA, RG 59. mDW 53417. Accepts appointment to print the laws in the *Wheeling Times and Advertiser*.

Aug 22   Recommendation from Zadoc Casey, for Q. C. Alexander (ALS. MWalB. mDW 23253).

[Aug 22] Editorial note on death of Isaac Rand Jackson. AD. NhD. mDW
23348. *National Intelligencer*, Aug 23, 1842.

[Aug 22] Editorial note on mission of William S. Derrick to England. AD.
NhD. mDW 23262. *National Intelligencer*, Aug 23, 1842.

[Aug 22] The Treaty of Washington (editorial). AD. NhD. mDW 23263.
National Intelligencer, Aug 23, 1842. *Diplomatic Papers*, 1.

[Aug 23] To Harriette Story White Paige. ALS. Mrs. Irvin McD. Garfield,
Southboro, Mass. mDWs. Encloses a letter of introduction for
her husband to Ashburton and thanks her for a gift of hand-
kerchiefs.

Aug 23 To Nathaniel Pitcher Tallmadge. Invitation. WHi. mDW 23271.

Aug 23 From James Gore King. ALS. DLC. mDW 23272. Curtis, 2: 140.
Invites DW to dinner in New York in honor of Ashburton.

Aug 23 From Charles March. ALS. NhHi. mDW 23274. Congratulates
DW on the successful negotiation of the treaty.

Aug 24 To Nicholas Biddle. ALS. DLC. mDW 23276. Proposes to visit
Biddle on his trip north.

Aug 24 To John Plummer Healy. 237

Aug 24 To Joseph S. Pagaud et al. Typed copy. NhD. mDW 23287.
Accepts honorary membership in the Union Literary Society of
Hampden-Sydney College.

Aug 24 To John Tyler. Printed. *PC*, 2: 146–147. *Diplomatic Papers*,
1. Praises the President's role in the recent negotiations.

Aug 24 From John Caldwell Calhoun. ALS. NjMoHP. mDW 23280. Requests a copy of the Cherokee Treaty of 1819.

Aug 24 From Benjamin H. Sheppard. ALS. DNA, RG 59. mDW 54830.
Accepts appointment as U.S. marshal for middle Tennessee.

Aug 24 Application from Charles Nichols—consul, Amsterdam (ALS.
MWalB. mDW 23285).

Aug 24 Recommendation from Samuel L. Hays, for Bazil Williamson—
distribution of census documents (ALS. MWalB. mDW 23283).

Aug 25 To Edward Everett. 238

Aug 25 To Edward Everett. ALS. MHi. mDW 23293. *Diplomatic Papers*,
1. Comments on his relations with Clay's supporters and with the
President; thinks of resigning and expresses interest in the London
mission; urges that Henry Stephen Fox be replaced in Washington.

Aug 25 To Carlton Hurd et al. AL draft. NhHi. mDW 23301. *PC*, 2: 147–
148. Recalls his days at Fryeburg.

Aug 25 To Silas Moore Stilwell. LS. NN. mDWs. Encloses the remission of
forfeitures and penalties against the ship *Sea*, John A. Delano,
master.

Aug 25 From James D. P. Ogden et al. (with Ogden to DW, Aug 26, 1842).
Printed invitation. DLC. mDW 23312. Invite DW to dinner to honor Lord
Ashburton.

Aug 25 Application from G. R. Fall, for the Jackson *Mississippian*—public
printer (ALS. DNA, RG 59. mDW 53270).

Aug 25 Recommendation from Joseph Leonard Tillinghast, for George F.
Usher (ALS. MWalB. mDW 23305).

Aug 26 To John Plummer Healy. 239

Aug 26 From James D. P. Ogden (enclosure: Ogden et al. to DW, Aug

25, 1842). LS. DLC. mDW 23310. Encloses an invitation to a public dinner to honor Lord Ashburton.

Aug 27   To Caleb Cushing et al. (with DW to Alexander Baring, Lord Ashburton, Aug 29, 1842). Printed. CaOOA. mDW 23322. Agrees to intervene with the British government on behalf of Americans imprisoned on Van Diemens Land.

Aug 27   To [James D. P. Ogden et al.]. Printed. *Boston Semi-Weekly Atlas*, Sept 7, 1842. Declines invitation to New York dinner in honor of Lord Ashburton.

Aug 27   To William Winston Seaton. Printed. Josephine Seaton, *William Winston Seaton* (Boston, 1871), p. 306. Invites him to share "a plain New England dinner" and to talk over the "future."

Aug 28   From Jeremiah Mason.   239

Aug 29   To Alexander Baring, Lord Ashburton (enclosures: Caleb Cushing et al. to John Tyler, Aug 10, 1842; DW to Cushing et al., Aug 27, 1842). Copy. CaOOA. mDW 23321. Asks him to recommend to the British government the pardon and release of the Americans now imprisoned on Van Diemen's Land.

Aug 29   To Nicholas Biddle. ALS. DLC. mDW 23320a. Proposes to meet Biddle and Robert Field Stockton on his way to New York.

Aug 29   To Harriette Story White Paige. ALS. Mrs. Irvin McD. Garfield, Southboro, Mass. mDWs. Reports that he will be coming to Boston soon and asks her to find him a cook for Marshfield.

Aug 29   From George S. Curson. ALS. DNA, RG 59. mDW 56475. Reports his arrival off Vera Cruz and his plans to continue on to Mexico City.

Aug 29   From James Renwick. ALS. DNA, RG 59. mDW 56799. Asks DW to honor a draft on the appropriation for the survey and exploration of the northeast boundary to meet contingent expenses.

Aug 29   From James Renwick. ALS. DNA, RG 59. mDW 56800. Asks to have the enclosed draft remitted to him.

Aug 29   From John Tyler. ALS. DLC. mDW 23323. Thinks Texas should ultimately bear expenses incurred by the United States on account of the Texas prisoners in Mexico.

Aug 29   Recommendation from William Wyatt, for the *Florida Journal*— public printer (ALS. DNA, RG 59. mDW 53272).

Aug 30   Deed transferring property in Eaton County, Michigan, from DW to Herman Cope and Thomas S. Taylor. Copy. Deed Book 5: 509–510. Register of Deeds, Eaton County, Michigan. mDWs.

Aug 30   Deed transferring land in St. Clair County, Michigan, from DW to Herman Cope and Thomas S. Taylor. Copy. Deed Book M: 312–313. Register of Deeds, St. Clair County, Michigan. mDWs.

Aug 30   Deed transferring property in LaSalle County, Illinois, from DW to Herman Cope and Thomas S. Taylor. Copy. Deed Book 11: 41. Register of Deeds, LaSalle County, Illinois, mDWs.

Aug 30   Deed transferring property in LaSalle, Whiteside, and Jo Daveiss counties, Illinois, from DW to Herman Cope and Thomas S. Taylor. Copy. Deed Book F: 462. Register of Deeds, Jo Daveiss County, Illinois. mDWs.

Aug 31   To Edward Everett. LS. MHi. mDW 23324. Introduces Francis Robert Rives, the newly-appointed secretary to the London legation.

Aug 31   From Edward Everett. LS. MHi. mDW 23330. Comments on

the outcome of the Ashburton negotiations; finds that his salary
has been reduced by the lowering of the exchange rate.

Aug 31   From Thomas Ritchie. ALS. DNA, RG 59. mDW 53419. Declines
appointment to print the laws in the *Richmond* (Va.) *Enquirer*.

Aug 31   Recommendations from Z. Collins Lee, for Richard M. Harrison—
distribution of the census (ALS. MWalB. mDW 23338); from James
William McCulloh, for Richard M. Harrison (ALS. MWalB. mDW 23340).

[Aug]   To Caleb Cushing. ALS. DLC. mDW 23343. Asks Cushing to return
some papers.

[Aug]   From John Tyler to DFW (with enclosures: *Detroit Daily Advertiser*,
Aug 16, 1842; Detroit *Constitutional Democrat*, Aug 17, 1842). ALS.
DNA, RG 59. mDW 53252. Asks that government patronage be taken
from the *Advertiser* and given to the *Constitutional Democrat*.

Aug [?]   Application from Isaac N. Coffin (ALS. MWalB. mDW 23346).

Sept 1   From Edward Everett. ALS. MHi. mDW 23351. Urges the appointment of Alexander Van Rensselaer as his secretary of legation; hopes
that DW will remain in the cabinet.

Sept 1   From George Hamilton. ALS. DNA, RG 59. mDW 53437. Accepts
appointment to print the laws in the *Natchitoches* (La.) *Reporter*.

Sept 2   From R. S. Elliott and C. McCurdy. ALS by Elliott, signed also
by McCurdy. DNA, RG 59. mDW 53531. Give notice that the *Pennsylvania Intelligencer* is now the exclusive property of C. McCurdy.

Sept 2   To Thomas Ritchie from DFW. Copy, endorsed by DW. NhHi.
mDW 23366. Insists that political considerations do not influence
the State Department's choice of publishers of the laws.

Sept 3   From Alexander Baring, Lord Ashburton.   241

Sept 3   Application from Marmaduke D. Johnson Slade, for the Tuscaloosa *Independent Monitor* (ALS. DNA, RG 59. mDW 53519).

Sept 3   To John Quincy Adams from DFW. Copy, with revision and
endorsement by DW. NhHi. mDW 23369. Responds to Adams's
contention that money to pay certain expenses of the U.S. legation
to Mexico was not constitutionally appropriated.

Sept 3   From Thomas Ritchie to DFW. ALS. DNA, RG 59. mDW 53421.
Disclaims any intention of impugning the State Department's
motives in its distribution of appointments to publish the laws.

Sept 4   To Daniel Fletcher Webster. ALS. NhHi. mDW 23381. Van
Tyne, pp. 277–278. Reports that Ashburton has sailed from New
York; insists that Adams is wrong about "the Mexican business"
and urges Fletcher to pay Waddy Thompson's bill.

Sept 5   To John Plummer Healy. ALS. MHi. mDW 23383. Promises
a maximum effort to "save" Massachusetts for the Whigs.

[Sept] 5   To Daniel Fletcher Webster. ALS. NhHi. mDW 23384. Van
Tyne, pp. 273–274. Asks for documents to enable him to reply to
the Portuguese minister; gives instructions for handling various
papers.

Sept 5   Recommendation from Mesquita LaParra & Co. et al., for Levi
Bixby (LS. NhHi. mDW 23388).

Sept 6   From John Quincy Adams to DFW. ALS. NhHi. mDW 23393.
Insists that a congressional resolution of Aug 31 appropriating

$6,000 for the U.S. mission to Mexico is unconstitutional and challenges DFW to cite legal precedents in defense of the resolution.

Sept 6 To John Quincy Adams from DFW. Copy. NhHi. mDW 23389. Cites legal precedents in support of the payment of money appropriated under the joint congressional resolution of Aug 31, 1842.

Sept 6 From William Crum. ALS by proxy. DNA, RG 59. mDW 53522. Reports his *Iowa City Standard* is missing two issues of the *National Intelligencer*.

Sept 6 Draft on DW for $157.08 payable to Richard Smith. ADS by DFW. MHi. mDW 39865.

Sept 7 To Daniel Fletcher Webster. ALS. NhHi. mDW 23395. Announces his arrival at Julia's and reports that all are well.

Sept 7 From Selah R. Hobbie. LS. DNA, RG 59. mDW 54486. Announces Benjamin Andrew's appointment as deputy postmaster for Cleveland.

Sept 7 From Andrew Talcott. ALS. DNA, RG 59. mDW 56802. States that he is ready to leave for Bangor and the St. John River, and reports having drawn $2,000 from the appropriation for the northeast boundary survey.

Sept 8 From Harrison Gray Otis et al. LS. MHAt. mDWs. *W & S*, 3: 111–112. Invite DW to a public dinner.

Sept 8 Draft on DW for $1,000 payable to C. H. Eldridge (with ANS by DW). ADS by Richard Smith. MHi. mDW 39867.

Sept 9 To Harrison Gray Otis et al. Printed. *W & S*, 3: 112. Accepts invitation but urges that the dinner be dispensed with.

Sept 9 To John Tyler (with copies of correspondence concerning the convention between the United States and the Kingdom of Sardinia). LS. DNA, RG 46. mDW 48381. Transmits copies of correspondence requested by a Senate resolution of July 24.

Sept 9 To Daniel Fletcher Webster. ALS. NhHi. mDW 23396. Asks him to acknowledge an Everett despatch and to send a copy of his most recent despatch to Cass.

Sept 10 From Selah R. Hobbie. LS. DNA, RG 59. mDW 54895. Announces Eli Wilcox's appointment as deputy postmaster at Middletown, Conn.

Sept 10 From Waddy Thompson. 241

Sept 10 Recommendation from William Pitt Fessenden, for William B. Gooch—consul, Port-au-Prince (ALS. NhHi. mDW 23400).

Sept 11 From [John Tyler]. Invitation [to Mrs. Letitia Tyler's funeral]. NhHi. mDW 23406.

Sept 13 To James Duane Doty from DFW. ALS. WHi. mDW 23408. Asks him to look after "this Jones affair" for DW; reports the State Department's authority to appoint publishers of the laws is now restricted to the District of Columbia.

Sep 13 From Robert M. Patterson to DFW. ALS. DNA, RG 104. mDW 57146. Asks to have a letter forwarded to John P. Brown at Constantinople.

Sept 14 From Nicholas Biddle. 242

Sept 14 From Joseph Williams. ALS. DNA, RG 59. mDW 54897. Acknowledges appointment as associate judge of the Supreme Court of Iowa Territory.

Sept 15   *To Charles Pelham Curtis.*   243
Sept 16   *To John Plummer Healy.*   244
Sept 16   From Edward Everett. ALS. MHi. mDW 23429. Paul Revere
Frothingham, *Edward Everett: Orator and Statesman* (Boston,
1925), pp. 228–229. Objects to Francis Robert Rives's appointment
as secretary to the London legation; comments on DW's political
position and his intimation of interest in the London mission.
Sept 16   From Edward Everett. LS. MHi. mDW 23440. *Diplomatic
Papers*, 1. Praises DW's skill in the negotiations with Ashburton and
thinks this is the time to press for a settlement of other controver-
sial issues; comments on the specific cases of various ships seized
by British cruisers.
Sept 16   From Edward Everett (enclosure: Everett to Lord Aberdeen,
Sept 16, 1842). Extract. DNA, RG 46. mDW 50389. Comments on
actions taken in the seizure cases of the ships *John A. Robb* and
Douglas.
Sept 17   To Charles Pelham Curtis. ALS. DLC. mDW 23444. W & S, 16:
383–384. Agrees reluctantly to a public meeting; notes the publica-
tion of his impressment and *Creole* letters.
[Sept 22]   From Selah R. Hobbie. LS. DNA, RG 59. mDW 54769. An-
nounces John Minge's appointment as deputy postmaster for
Petersburg, Va.
Sept 23   To Daniel Fletcher Webster. ALS. NhHi. mDW 23451. *PC*, 2:
149–150. Complains of ill health; refuses to intervene in Walter
Forward's case but will write to President regarding his own.
Sept 24   To James S. Wadsworth. ALS. DLC. mDW 23455. Declines in-
vitation to a function at Albany because of ill health and a prior
commitment.
Sept 24   To Daniel Fletcher Webster. ALS. George C. Whipple, Jr., Mt.
Carmel, N.Y. mDW 23459. Asks him to acknowledge a note from
Joaquin Acosta [?] and to send DW a translation.
Sept 26   To John Plummer Healy. ALS. MHi. mDW 23461. Asks him to
remit $700 to the Merchants' Bank of New York.
Sept 26   Application from Jesse Waln—customs inspector, Philadel-
phia (ALS. DLC. mDW 23467).
Sept 26   Recommendation from Joseph W. Jackson et al., for Edward J.
Hardin—attorney, Georgia (LS. MWalB. mDW 23465).
Sept 27   *From Jacob Harvey.*   244
Sept 27   From Eliza Buckminster Lee. ALS. NhHi. mDW 23472. Sends
him one of her books.
Sept 27   From Josiah Quincy. ALS. NhHi. mDW 23474. Praises
DW's role in the treaty negotiations and urges him not to resign
from the cabinet.
Sept 27   From James Renwick. ALS. DNA, RG 59. mDW 56804. Re-
ports having drawn $1,000 from the account for the survey of the
northeastern boundary.
Sept 28   From Robert Bowne Minturn et al. LS. NhHi. mDW 23478.
Van Tyne, p. 278. Urge him to remain in office.
Sept 28   Deed transferring property in Dane County, Wisconsin, from
DW to John Porter. Copy. Register of Deeds, Dane County,
Wisconsin. mDWs.

Sept 28   Deed transferring property in Rock County, Wisconsin, from DW to John Porter. Copy. Register of Deeds, Rock County, Wisconsin. mDWs.

Sept 29   Application from Morgan L. Ogden—indexer (ALS. MWalB. mDW 23479).

[Sept 30]   Notes for speech at Faneuil Hall, Boston, with AN by Harriette Story White Paige. AD. MH-H. mDW 23481.

Oct 1   From Edward Everett. ALS. MHi. mDW 23492. Reports a conversation with Aberdeen on the Ashburton treaty, the unresolved issues of Oregon, and two seizure cases; describes an excursion to Lincolnshire.

Oct 1   From J. C. Gevers. ALS. NhHi. mDW 23496. Announces his arrival in New York preparatory to assuming office as chargé d'affaires for the Netherlands.

Oct 1   From James Renwick. ALS. DNA, RG 59. mDW 56808. Transmits his account with the State Department.

Oct 1   Account of Folliot T. Lally with the U.S. Boundary Commission. Copy. DNA, RG 59. mDW 56810.

[c. Oct 1]   From William B. Gooch. ALS. NhHi. mDW 23499. Recommends the consolidation of the U.S. agencies at Port-au-Prince and Aux Cayes, Haiti.

Oct 2   To Daniel Fletcher Webster. ALS. NhHi. mDW 23501. *PC*, 2: 150–151. Reports that the Boston meeting went off as expected; comments on Tyler's standing in New England.

Oct 3   To Caleb Cushing. ALS. DLC. mDW 23505. Asks him to write Tyler on behalf of [Timothy?] Upham and to write to New Hampshire "about *another business.*"

Oct 3   From Nicholas Biddle. ALS draft. DLC. mDW 23508. Expresses delight with DW's Faneuil Hall speech and condemns the Whigs who are trying to drive him from power.

Oct 3   From Nicholas L. Goldsborough. ALS. MWalB. mDW 23519. Asks DW to return letters of recommendation for some appointment.

Oct 3   From Robert Gould Shaw. ALS. NhHi. mDW 23521. Regrets being absent from the Faneuil Hall meeting and praises DW's self-sacrifice for the public good.

Oct 4   To Daniel Fletcher Webster. ALS. NhHi. mDW 23524. Van Tyne, pp. 278–279. Thinks Tyler alone should be informed of Cass's request to return to the U.S.

Oct 5   To Daniel Fletcher Webster. Copy. MHi. mDW 23526. *W & S*, 16: 384. Defends his Faneuil Hall speech.

Oct 5   To Daniel Fletcher Webster. Copy. NhHi. mDW 23527. Van Tyne, p. 279. Sends English despatches and suggests that Cass's request to resign be given a cordial acceptance.

Oct 5   From John Canfield Spencer. Copy. DNA, RG 46. mDW 52090. Reports the release of a young boy by the Comanche Indians and suggests that arrangements be made with Texas authorities for returning him to his parents.

Oct 7   From Daniel Jenifer. ALS. NhD. mDW 23529. Comments on European reaction to the Washington Treaty; reports conversations with Austrian officials relative to that country's tariffs, especially on tobacco.

Oct 9   From James S. Calhoun. ALS. NhD. mDW 23537. Inquires about the reasons for his removal as U.S. consul at Havana.

Oct 11   From Peyton A. Southall. ALS. DNA, RG 59. mDW 56494. Reports the delivery of despatches to Waddy Thompson at Mexico City.

Oct 13   To [John Plummer Healy]. ALS. MHi. mDW 38475. Expects to go to Marshfield on Oct 19, if not sooner.

Oct 13   From Selah R. Hobbie. LS. DNA, RG 59. mDW 54777. Announces Miles Nash's appointment as deputy postmaster at Tallahassee, Fla.

Oct 15   To Daniel Fletcher Webster. ALS. NhHi. mDW 23553. Van Tyne, p. 280. Comments on reaction to his Faneuil Hall speech; reports on his stay at The Elms in Franklin.

Oct 15   From Amos Lane. ALS. NhD. mDW 23559. Comments on the Faneuil Hall speech and on Presidential politics.

Oct 15   *Memorandum of things to be put in the cellar.*   245

Oct 16   Application from A. G. Roussac—consul, Bombay (ALS. MWalB. mDW 23562).

Oct 17   From Edward Everett. ALS. MHi. mDW 23576. *Diplomatic Papers,* 1. Comments on the ratification of the treaty, on Oregon, and on Cass.

Oct 17   From George Griswold et al. LS. DLC. mDW 23584. *Madisonian,* Nov 2, 1842. Invite DW to a public dinner in New York.

Oct 18   Application from Ferdinand Henry Finck (Copy. NcD. mDW 23588).

Oct 19   *To Daniel Fletcher Webster.*   246

Oct 19   From Hezekiah Hawley. ALS. DNA, RG 59. mDW 54679. Accepts appointment as U.S. marshal for the Apalachicola District of Florida.

Oct 20   To [Hiram Ketchum?]. ALS. NhD. mDWs. Asks whether he is expected to accept the invitation to the New York dinner.

Oct 20   To Daniel Fletcher Webster. ALS. NhHi. mDW 23599. Van Tyne, pp. 281–282. Advises him not to show Derrick's note to the President for fear he will conclude that Everett has not pressed hard enough for an early exchange of the treaty ratifications.

Oct 20   To Daniel Fletcher Webster. Copy. NhHi. mDW 23601. Van Tyne, p. 282. Regrets that the negotiations with Mexico are not to be held in Washington.

Oct 20   To Daniel Fletcher Webster. ALS. NhHi. mDW 23602. Van Tyne, p. 282. Urges him to assure Tyler that he meant only to defend the exchequer plan, not to represent it as his own.

Oct 20   From William M. Blackford. ALS copy. DNA, RG 76. mDWs. Reports on the condition of property belonging to the U.S. legation at Bogota.

Oct 20   *From Edward Everett.*   247

Oct 20   Application from S. M. Cochran—consul, Maracaibo (ALS. MWalB. mDW 23605).

Oct 20   Recommendations from Edward Duvall and John R. Duvall, for S. M. Cochran (ALS by E. Duvall, signed also by J. R. Duvall. MWalB. mDW 23607); from Z. Collins Lee, for S. M. Cochran

(ALS. MWalB. mDW 23617); from James Shrigley, for S. M. Cochran (ALS. MWalB. mDW 23619).

Oct 20 To John Tyler from DFW with ANS by Tyler. ALS. DNA, RG 59. mDW 56633. Asks Tyler to sign an order to pay George Smith $100 on account, for services performed.

Oct 21 To Edward Curtis. ALS. NN. mDW 23621. Agrees to "some sort of a meeting," preferably after the New York elections.

Oct 21 Recommendations from Z. Collins Lee, for S. M. Cochran (ALS. MWalB. mDW 23627); from Richard A. Smith, for S. M. Cochran (ALS. MWalB. mDW 23630).

Oct 22 From George S. Curson. ALS. DNA, RG 59. mDW 56478. Reports that he is preparing to leave Savannah for Vera Cruz.

Oct 23 From Hannah F. Lee (enclosure: Mrs. Ruth G. Channing to Mrs. Lee, Oct 9, [1842]). ALS. NhHi. mDW 23632. Encloses a letter from Mrs. William Ellery Channing expressing her late husband's view of the necessity of DW's remaining in office.

Oct 24 From J. P. Reed. ALS. DNA, RG 59. mDW 53216. Inquires about the status of his appointment to publish the laws.

Oct 25 From Edward Stubbs to DFW. ALS. DNA, RG 59. mDW 56637. Urges that he persuade the President to rescind his order allocating four rooms now occupied by the State Department to the second comptroller.

Oct 26 To John Plummer Healy. ALS. MHi. mDW 20616. Sends letters for his perusal and suggests they may be shown to friends.

Oct 26 From Robert Hanna. ALS. DLC. mDW 23639. Calls DW's Faneuil Hall speech "a damper" and expects that it will draw the wrath of the Clay forces.

Oct 27 To [?] Greene. ALS. OCHP. mDWs. Thanks him for letter praising speech at Faneuil Hall on Sept 30.

[Oct 27] To John Plummer Healy. ALS. MHi. mDW 23641. Informs him that Mrs. Webster's ill health has forced a delay in his return to Boston.

[Oct] 27 To [Hiram Ketchum]. ALS. NhD. mDW 23643. States his intention of declining the invitation to the New York dinner.

Oct 27 To [?] Smith. ALS. NhD. mDW 23648. Wants to see him before going to Washington.

Oct 27 From Nicholas Biddle. ALS. DLC. mDW 23651. Reports hearing that Mr. Kiderlen is disreputable and quite unfit to be appointed U.S. consul at Würtemberg.

Oct 28 To George Griswold et al. Printed. *Madisonian*, Nov 2, 1842. W & S, 16: 386–388. Declines invitation to a public dinner in New York; reflects on his role in the recent negotiations with Ashburton.

Oct 28 From John Tyler. ALS. George C. Whipple, Jr., Carmel, N.Y. mDW 23653. Asks him to arrange an audience at whatever time is convenient for the Count de Colobriana (chargé d'affaires for Sardinia).

Oct 29 To [Nathaniel F. Williams]. ALS. NhD. mDW 23654. Promises to send him a draft on Oct 30.

Oct 31 From George S. Curson. ALS. DNA, RG 59. mDW 56479. Reports that the ship carrying him to Vera Cruz has stopped briefly at Havana to take on fuel.

Oct 31 From Francis Asbury Dickens to DFW. LS. DNA, RG 59. mDW 55159. Transmits a copy of John Beard's nomination as marshal for eastern Florida.

Nov 1 To [Seth Weston]. ALS. NhHi. mDW 23660. Van Tyne, pp. 673–674. Instructs Weston on work to be done at Marshfield.

Nov 2 From Samuel C. Reid, Jr. to DFW. Copy. DNA, RG 46. mDW 50232. Expresses dismay on hearing that Portugal is unlikely to rule favorably on the *Armstrong* claim.

Nov 3 To [Daniel Fletcher Webster]. ALS. NhHi. mDW 23669. Van Tyne, pp. 282–283. Reports his arrival in New York, where he expects to leave Mrs. Webster.

Nov 3 From Edward Everett. ALS. MHi. mDW 23675. *Diplomatic Papers*, 1. Reports comments from the London *Morning Chronicle* and his own conversations with Cass on the Treaty of Washington; discusses French affairs and the activity of Duff Green; insists his comments on pork, beef, and turnips have been misreported.

Nov 3 From William B. Gooch. ALS. NhHi. mDW 23686. Reports the expulsion of the U.S. agent at Port-au-Prince and suggests the consolidation of that agency with his at Aux Cayes.

Nov 3 From William Henry Seward. ALS draft. NRU. mDW 23684. Requests that Isaac Newton be given a letter of introduction to Edward Everett.

Nov 5 From Robert E. Hornor. ALS. DNA, RG 59. mDW 53525. Reports that he has sold the *Princeton Whig* to John T. Robinson.

Nov 6 To Edward Everett. ALS. MHi. mDW 23689. Introduces George W. L. Newton.

Nov 7 From George S. Curson. ALS. DNA, RG 59. mDW 56481. Expects to leave Vera Cruz for Mexico City this evening.

Nov 7 From Alexander Drysdale. ALS. DNA, RG 59. mDW 54600. Accepts appointment as U.S. attorney for Georgia.

Nov 7 Recommendation from Abbott Lawrence, for Ralph Emerson—consul, Havre (ALS. NhD. mDWs.).

Nov 8 From John Tyler. ALS. DLC. mDW 23699. Thinks both the *National Intelligencer* and the *Madisonian* ought to be selected to publish the treaty.

Nov 8 Application from John H. Noyes—indexer, Department of State (ALS. MWalB. mDW 23697).

Nov 9 Application from George Brown—diplomatic agent in Paraguay, or some post in Washington (ALS. DLC. mDW 23701).

Nov 9 Recommendations from Aaron Clark, for George A. Clark—bearer of despatches (ALS with AN by DW. MWalB. mDW 23705); from Charles Morris, for R. M. Hamilton—consul, Rio de Janeiro (LS. MWalB. mDW 23709).

Nov 10 To David Fairbanks. LS. NCorniCC. mDW 23713. Informs him that his passport has been forwarded to New York.

Nov 10 From John McElvain. ALS. DNA, RG 59. mDW 54753. Acknowledges appointment as U.S. marshal for Ohio.

Nov 10 From William S. Murphy (with William Hunter to Lemuel

Shaw, Sept 25, 1855). Copy. MHi. mDWs. Transmits official papers forwarded to him from Guatemala.

Nov 10   From Alexander Waugh. ALS. DNA, RG 59. mDW 54885. Accepts appointment as justice of the peace for Alexandria.

Nov 10   To Caleb Cushing from DFW. ALS. DLC. mDW 23711. Conveys DW's invitation to dinner.

Nov 11   Recommendation from John Reynolds to DFW, for the *Belleville* (Ill.) *Advocate*—public printer (ALS. DNA, RG 59. mDW 53535).

Nov 12   To Caleb Cushing. Invitation. NN. mDW 23714. Invites Cushing to dinner.

Nov 12   From Nicholas Biddle. ALS draft. DLC. mDW 23716. Advises him to remain in office so long as conscience will permit; discusses a corporate matter involving Moncure Robinson.

Nov 12   From George S. Curson. ALS. DNA, RG 59. mDW 56483. Reports having delivered despatches to Waddy Thompson.

[p/m Nov 13]   To John Plummer Healy. ALS. MHi. mDW 23717. Requests exact copies of his letters to Healy of Aug 24 and 26.

Nov 14   To Seth Weston. ALS. NhHi. mDW 39202. Inquires about affairs at Marshfield.

Nov 14   From John Hogan.   250

Nov 14   From John Beard to DFW. ALS. DNA, RG 59. mDW 54496. Accepts appointment as U.S. marshal for eastern Florida.

Nov 14   From Isaac H. Bronson to DFW. ALS. DNA, RG 59. mDW 54498. Reports that John Beard has assumed office as U.S. marshal for eastern Florida.

Nov 15   From Washington Barrow (enclosure: José Joaquin Gomes de Castro to Barrow, Nov 12, 1842). Extract. DNA, RG 46. mDW 50234. Reports bringing the *Armstrong* and *Hall* cases to the attention of the Portuguese government and doubts that stronger representations would be successful.

Nov 15   From Nicholas Biddle. ALS draft. DLC. mDW 27324. Suggests that DW write Sylvanus Thayer on a railroad project.

Nov 15   From Edward Everett. LC. MHi. mDW 23728. Introduces Albert Davy, former U.S. consul at Kingston-on-Hull.

Nov 15   From Shepard & Strong. LS. DNA, RG 59. mDW 53533. State that the ownership of the *Rochester Daily Democrat* has been transferred to Strong & Dawson.

Nov 15   Application from Josiah Butler—appointment to the Board of Exchequer (ALS. MWalB. mDW 23726).

Nov 15   From William Butler to DFW. ALS. DNA, RG 59. mDW 53527. Writes regarding compensation due the publisher of the Calhoun, South Carolina, *Highland Sentinel* for printing the laws.

Nov 16   To Stephen Pleasonton. LS. NhHi. mDW 23729. Authorizes payment of certain charges incurred by the U.S. consul at Valparaiso.

Nov 17   To Samuel Turell Armstrong. ALS. MHi. mDW 23732. Plans to make public the substance of his letters of Aug 24 and 26 to John Plummer Healy.

Nov 17   To Washington Irving (with DW to John Wade Damon, Dec 27, 1842). Extract. DLC. mDW 23957. Advises him on what action to take in a judicial dispute at Madrid between two Americans, John Wade Damon and Frederick Tudor.

Nov 17 From Edward Everett. LC. MHi. mDW 23734. Explains the delay in the exchange of treaty ratifications; expresses satisfaction with his new secretary; complains of Duff Green's unauthorized activity; urges DW to come to England as a special envoy; letter "not sent," according to Everett's endorsement.

Nov 17 From Pelham W. Hayward (enclosure: memorial of the Suffolk Life Insurance Company of Boston, Nov 17, 1842). ALS. DNA, RG 76. mDWs. Presents a memorial demanding redress from the Buenos Aires government for "an outrage" against two American vessels.

Nov 17 Application from Edward Kavanagh—northeast boundary commissioner (ALS. DLC. mDW 23737).

Nov 18 To Harriette Story White Paige. Printed. PC, 2: 152–153. Declares that a few days will tell whether he will remain in Washington or return to the North.

Nov 19 Recommendation from Thomas I. McLain et al., for the Warren, Ohio, *Trumbull County Democrat*—public printer (ALS by McLain, signed also by others, with AN by DW. DNA, RG 59. mDW 53513).

Nov 20 From George William Gordon. ALS with ANS by DW. NN. mDW 23748. Encloses a letter from Charles W. Cutter (not found) and recommends delaying a change from the *Boston Journal* to the *Gazette.*

Nov 21 To [Edward Curtis?]. ALS. NN. mDW 23750. Finds himself busy with "the Treaty & Genl Cass."

Nov 21 To John Plummer Healy (enclosure: introductory note for publication in the *Boston Courier*). ALS. NhHi. mDW 23751. W & S, 16: 388. Consents to the publication of his letter of Aug 24 to Healy and to the second, if necessary.

Nov 21 To Charles Anderson Wickliffe. ALS. KyLo. mDW 23755. Declines Captain Black's invitation for tomorrow.

[Nov 21] The Cabinet (editorial note, endorsed by Caleb Cushing). AD. NN. mDW 23824. *Madisonian*, Nov 21, 1842.

Nov 21 Application from Thomas C. Dubs—consul, Maracaibo (ALS. MWalB. mDW 23756).

Nov 22 From Nicholas Biddle. ALS draft. DLC. mDW 23761. Reports having begun an effort through the Philadelphia *Pennsylvania Enquirer* to build public support for payment of the state debt.

Nov 23 To Daniel Fletcher Webster. ALS. PPAmP. mDW 23763. Hopes to see him before long.

Nov 23 From Joseph Tinker Buckingham et al. LS. MB. mDW 23765. Invite him to deliver an address at the dedication of the Bunker Hill monument on June 17.

Nov 23 From John Canfield Spencer. Copy. DNA, RG 46. mDW 52094. Reports the recovery of another white boy from the Comanche Indians.

Nov 24   To Seth Weston. ALS. NhHi. mDW 23771. *PC*, 2: 153. Suggests that he start filling the ice house.

Nov 24   From Julia Webster Appleton. ALS. NhHi. mDW 23772. Reports on family activity.

[p/m Nov 24]   To Nicholas Biddle. ALS. DLC. mDW 38234. Urges Biddle to continue to write on some cause, probably the bank question or state debts.

Nov 26   To Marcus Duvall.   253

Nov 26   Application from William Frith Williams—consul, Bermuda (ALS. MWalB. mDW 23775).

Nov 28   To Joseph Tinker Buckingham et al. ALS. NhD. mDW 23777. Agrees to speak at the dedication of the Bunker Hill Monument.

Nov 28   To Edward Everett. ALS. MHi. mDW 23779. *Diplomatic Papers*, 1. Outlines the basis for negotiating with Britain concerning Oregon and U.S. commercial relations with the British colonies.

Nov 28   To Hiram Ketchum. ALS. NhD. mDW 25475. Advocates the postponement of the Whig national convention until May 1844.

Nov 28   To Harriette Story White Paige. ALS. Mrs. Irvin McD. Garfield, Southboro, Mass. mDWs. *PC*, 2: 156–157 Reflects on Thanksgiving; reports on activities in Washington.

Nov 28   To George Washington Warren. ALS. MHi. mDWs. Encloses his reply to the Bunker Hill Monument Committee.

Nov 28   From Humphrey Howe Leavitt. ALS. DNA, RG 217. mDW 57231. Asks that John McElvaine's bond be forwarded to the clerk of the U.S. district and circuit courts at Cincinnati.

Nov 28   Application from William Frith Williams (ALS. MWalB. mDW 23795).

Nov 28   Recommendations from Eliza Buckminster Lee, for Ralph Emerson (ALS. NhHi. mDW 23791); from Hezekiah F. Williams, for William Frith Williams (DS. MWalB. mDW 23793).

Nov 29   From Nathan Weston. ALS. DLC. mDW 23807. Asks that Webster and Tyler review his son's court martial sentence.

Nov 29   Application from William Frith Williams (ADS. MWalB. mDW 23809).

Nov 30   From Edward Everett. ALS. MHi. mDW 23813. Advocates vigorous opposition to the British government's assumption of sovereignty over New Zealand.

Nov 30   From Henry H. Williams. Copy. DNA, RG 206. mDWs. Asks that money due George Flood, late U.S. chargé d'affaires to Texas, be used to pay the expenses of returning his widow to the United States.

Nov 30   Recommendation from James W. Zacharie, for Alexander McGregor—consul, Campeche (ALS. MWalB. mDW 23817).

[Nov]   To Caleb Cushing. ALS. NN. mDW 23819. Invites him to dinner.

[Nov]   To Caleb Cushing. ALS. NN. mDW 23822. Asks him to stop by the State Department before calling on the President.

[Dec 1]   To [Edward Curtis?]. ALS. NN. mDW 23826. Wishes that a forthcoming editorial in the *Madisonian* on the Treaty of Washington might appear in the New York papers about the time of Cass's arrival.

Dec 1   To Daniel Fletcher Webster. Printed. *PC*, 2: 157. Asks him to return to Washington immediately and to bring Joseph M. Hernandez with him.

Dec 2   "The Treaty" (editorial). Printed. *Madisonian*, Dec 2, 1842. Curtis, 2: 147–149.

Dec 2   Check for $15 payable to [Edward] Kavanagh. DS. DLC. mDW 39869.

Dec 2   Check for $150 payable to [Edward?] Stubbs. DS. DLC. mDW 39870.

Dec 3   From Edward Everett.   253

Dec 3   From William Bennett Parker. ALS. DLC. mDW 23836. Calls DW's attention to his article on *"the Colonial Trade."*

[Dec 3]   The Message (editorial). AD. NhHi. mDW 20785. *Madisonian*, Dec 3, 1842. Van Tyne, pp. 242–245 (misdated December 1841).

Dec 4   From Francis Lieber. ALS. NhHi. mDW 23838. Requests a copy of the Webster-Ashburton correspondence and expresses admiration for DW's diplomatic letters.

[c. Dec 4]   "The Intelligencer and the President" (editorial). Printed. *Madisonian*, Dec 5, 1842. Curtis, 2: 207–209.

Dec 5   To John L. Graham. LS. NhD. mDW 23842. Requests that despatch agents be allowed inside the New York Post Office.

[Dec 5]   To Hiram Ketchum. ALS. NhD. mDW 23844. Reports having spoken to the President about John S. Maxwell as secretary to some European legation.

Dec 5   To Charles B. Penrose. LS. DNA, RG 206. mDWs. Recommends that the widow of the late George Flood, U.S. chargé to Texas, be granted a travel allowance for her return to the United States.

Dec 5   To Samuel C. Reid, Jr. Copy. DNA, RG 46. mDW 50237. Agrees to let him make copies of documents pertinent to the *General Armstrong* case.

Dec 5   Application from William Wood—bearer of despatches to Europe (ALS with ANS by DW. MWalB. mDW 23847).

Dec 6   To Stephen Pleasonton. LS. PPARA. mDW 23851. Approves, with specified exceptions, reimbursement of Charles Scott Todd for contingent expenses incurred as U.S. minister to Russia.

Dec 6   From [Lewis Cass]. AL draft. MiU-C. mDW 23853. Announces his return to the United States and reports having presented Henry Ledyard to the French foreign minister as the U.S. chargé d'affaires at Paris.

Dec 6   From Charles F. Mayer. ALS. NhHi. mDW 23854 Introduces Francis Mayer as one knowledgeable in Mexican affairs.

Dec 6   From Isaac Van Zandt. ALS. TxLT. mDWs. Announces his arrival and asks when he should present his official credentials as Texas chargé d'affaires.

[Dec 6]   The Exchequer (editorial). AD. NhHi. mDW 20988. *Madisonian*, Dec 6, 1842. Van Tyne, pp. 249–252 (misdated Jan 1842).

Dec 7   To William Campbell Preston. ALS. ViHi. mDWs. *W & S*, 16: 673–674. Expresses regret over Preston's resignation from the Senate.

Dec 7   Application from E. Augustus Ware, for the *Florida Journal*—public printer (ALS. DNA, RG 59. mDW 53515).

[Dec 7] Draft by DW of section of Presidential message re General Andrew Jackson's fine. AD. DLC. mDW 23856.

Dec 8 *To Henry Hubbard.*   255

Dec 8 *To [Seth Weston].*   255

Dec 8 *To Nathaniel F. Williams.*   256

Dec 9 From Henry G. Andrews. ALS. MWalB. mDW 23869. Transmits a proposal that a despatch agency be established on Malta and suggests his brother for agent.

Dec 10 To James William McCulloh. LS. DNA, RG 217. mDW 57228. Informs him of an adjustment to be made in the travel allowance to be given the widow of George Flood, late U.S. chargé d'affaires to Texas.

Dec 10 From David Hoffman and Charles F. Mayer. Copy. DNA, RG 206. mDWs. Transmits copies of documents relating to a claim by a Colonel Hackley to Florida lands.

Dec 10 Recommendation from John P. Richardson, for Beaufort T. Watts—secretary, Mexican legation (ALS. MWalB. mDW 23871).

Dec 10 Draft by DFW on DW for $1,000. ADS. MHi. mDW 39871.

Dec 12 To Francis Lieber. ALS. CSmH. mDW 23873. Thanks Lieber for his flattering letter and sends along his Ashburton correspondence.

Dec 12 To Nathaniel F. Williams. ALS. NhD. mDW 23874. Asks him to accept and return an item, probably a draft, which he promises to provide for.

Dec 12 From Thomas Fessenden et al. ALS by Fessenden, signed also by others. DLC. mDW 23876. Invite him to a dinner sponsored by the New England Pilgrims' Society of New York.

Dec 12 From James Graham. ALS. DLC. mDW 23878. Announces DW's election to honorary membership in the Democratic Tyler Club of New Orleans.

Dec 12 From John F. Mullowny. Printed. *Madisonian*, Feb 6, 1843. Reports his arrival at Tangier and the substance of his demands upon the bashaw.

Dec 12 From William Henry Russell. ALS. MWalB. mDW 23880. Accuses the Locofocos of conspiring for his removal as U.S. marshal for Missouri.

Dec 12 Check for $50 payable to self. DS. DLC. mDW 39873.

Dec 12 Recommendation from Lorenzo Draper et al., for John Frederick Scheibler—consul, Germany (LS. NhHi. mDW 23979).

Dec 13 To [Willie Person Mangum] (enclosure: report on the number of American seamen registered in the collection districts of the U.S. during the year ending Sept 30, 1842). LS. DNA, RG 46. mDW 49514. Transmits a report on American seamen, as required by law.

Dec 13 To Harriette Story White Paige. ALS. Mrs. Irvin McD. Garfield, Southboro, Mass. mDWs. Reports that he has presented the application of G. H. Paige for an appointment to the secretary of war.

Dec 13 Recommendation from Caleb Cushing, for James Auchincloss—consul, Glasgow (ALS. NN. mDW 23884).

Dec 14 To Richard W. Greene (enclosure: Senate resolution of Dec 13, 1842, re bankrupt law). Printed LS. RHi. mDWs. Asks for comments upon the bankrupt law.

Dec 14   To John McLean (enclosure: Senate resolution of Dec 13, 1842, re bankrupt law). LS. DLC. mDW 23886. Asks for his comments on the bankrupt law.

[Dec 14]   To [John Tyler]. AD. DLC. mDW 23889. Sends a draft of a Presidential veto message.

Dec 14   To U.S. Attorneys for the States and Territories. Copy. DNA, RG 46. mDW 49707. Requests suggestions for the modification or amendment of the bankrupt law.

Dec 14   To the U.S. Judges. Copy. DNA, RG 46. mDW 49708. Requests suggestions for the modification of the bankrupt law.

Dec 15   To D. B. Chapman. ALS. NhHi. mDW 23896. Regrets not having the time to answer Chapman's interrogatories.

Dec 15   To the Clerks of the U.S. District Courts. Copy. DNA, RG 46. mDW 49705. Asks for detailed information on the operation of the bankrupt law.

Dec 15   To [John Plummer Healy].   256

Dec 16   From Thomas Spicer. ALS. DNA, RG 46. mDW 49759. Reports on cases under the bankrupt law brought before the U.S. district court for Maryland.

Dec 17   To James Kent. ALS. NNC. mDW 23903. Sends a copy of his correspondence with Lord Ashburton.

Dec 17   To Samuel Putnam. ALS. MSaE. mDW 23905. *Historical Collections of the Danvers Historical Society*, 10 (1922): 25. Sends a copy of his Ashburton correspondence; congratulates Putnam upon his retirement from the bench.

[Dec 17]   From Charles D. Betts. ALS. DNA, RG 46, mDW 49718. Reports on actions in U.S. district court for southern New York under the bankrupt law.

Dec 17   From Francis Lieber.   257

Dec 17   To Caleb Cushing from DW & Caroline Le Roy Webster. AL in Caroline Le Roy Webster's hand. NN. mDW 23901. Invite Cushing to dinner.

Dec 18   From George M. MacRae. ALS. DNA, RG 59. mDW 54751. Acknowledges appointment as U.S. attorney for southern Florida and explains his delay in reaching Key West.

Dec 18   From Seth Weston. ALS. NhHi. mDW 23911. *PC*, 2: 159–160. Reports on farm activity at Marshfield.

Dec 19   To Thomas Fessenden et al. LS. MHi. mDW 23914. Van Tyne, p. 745. Declines invitation to dine with the New England Pilgrims' Society of New York; praises the virtues of the Pilgrims.

Dec 19   From Samuel Rossiter Betts (enclosure: statement of matters relating to bankruptcy applications in the southern district of New York). ALS. DNA, RG 46. mDW 49722. Makes detailed suggestions for the modification of the bankrupt law.

Dec 19   From Joseph C. Potts. ALS. DNA, RG 59. mDW 49744. Reports bankruptcy cases brought before the U.S. district court for New Jersey and suggests changes in the law.

Dec 19   From Millard Fillmore. LS. DNA, RG 59. mDW 55798. Asks that the State Department's contingent fund estimates be arranged by classification.

Dec 19   From Ogden Hoffman. LS. DNA, RG 46. mDW 49717. States
that his experience with the bankrupt law has been limited.

Dec 19   From Francis Hopkinson. ALS. DNA, RG 46. mDW 49746. Reports on cases brought before the U.S. district court for eastern
Pennsylvania under the bankrupt law.

Dec 19   From [John Mussey?]. AL incomplete. DNA, RG 46. mDW
49710. Details actions taken under the bankrupt law in the U.S.
district court for Maine.

Dec 19   Recommendation from Caleb Cushing, for Franklin Gage—
consul, Cuba (ALS. MWalB. mDW 23921).

Dec 20   From Francis Bassett (enclosure: report of the number of ap-
plications, etc., under the bankrupt law in the district court of the
United States in Massachusetts). ALS. DNA, RG 46. mDW 49715.
Transmits statement of Massachusetts bankruptcy cases.

Dec 20   From Peter V. Daniel. ALS. DNA, RG 46. mDW 49760. Thinks
the bankrupt law has had a detrimental effect and ought to be
repealed.

Dec 20   From Willard Hall. ALS. DNA, RG 46. mDW 49756. Points to
certain ambiguities in the bankrupt law.

Dec 20   From Robert C. Nichols. ALS. DNA, RG 46. mDW 49762. Con-
cludes that the bankrupt law has had a pernicious influence and
calls for its repeal.

Dec 20   From Samuel C. Reid, Jr. Copy. DNA, RG 46. mDW 50238. Requests a copy of a proceeding held at Rio de Janeiro in the *General
Armstrong* case.

Dec 20   Recommendations from Z. Collins Lee, for Edwin W. Ogden—
consul, Maracaibo (ALS. MWalB. mDW 23923); from J. S. Richardson et al., for Beaufort T. Watts (ALS by Richardson, signed
also by others. MWalB. mDW 23925).

[c. Dec 20]   From Charles D. Betts. ADS. DNA, RG 46. mDW 49796.
Details cases and actions taken in the U.S. district court for southern New York under the bankrupt law.

Dec 21   To George Ticknor. ALS. DLC. mDW 23928. Suggests that
Ticknor approach the *North American Review* on Lieber's idea for
an article on DW's diplomatic correspondence.

Dec 21   From Samuel Rossiter Betts. ALS. DNA, RG 46. mDW 49720.
Suggests amending the bankrupt law to provide for instances of
false representation or cheating.

Dec 21   From Nicholas Biddle. ALS draft. DLC. mDW 23930. Reports
his efforts to rouse public support for payment of the Pennsylvania
state debt.

Dec 21   From Nicholas Biddle. ALS draft. DLC. mDW 23931. Urges
DW to concur in Tyler's appointment of Frederick List as consul
to Würtemburg.

Dec 21   From William Leigh Brent. ALS. DNA, RG 46. mDW 49765.
Reports on cases brought before the U.S. district court for the District of Columbia under the bankrupt law.

Dec 21   From Calvin Colton. ALS. DNA, RG 59. mDW 53501. Gives
circulation figures for the weekly and daily editions of the Washington *True Whig*.

Dec 21   From Cornelius Darragh (enclosure: A. A. Irwin to Darragh,

Dec 20, 1842). ALS. DNA, RG 46. mDW 49751. Contends that the bankrupt law has been used most effectively by those least entitled to its benefits.

Dec 21   From Alexander Drysdale. ALS. DNA, RG 46. mDW 49768. Finds that experience with the bankrupt law in the U.S. district court for Georgia has been too limited to permit any just conclusions about its operation.

Dec 21   From George Glen. ALS. DNA, RG 46. mDW 49766. Reports on bankruptcy cases brought before the U.S. district court for Georgia.

Dec 21   From John Holmes. ALS. DNA, RG 46. mDW 49712. Suggests including *"moneyed or trading corporations"* in the bankrupt law and urges that the law be given a fair trial.

Dec 21   From John Beauchamp Jones. ALS. DNA, RG 59. mDW 53503. States that the circulation of the *Madisonian* is 4,000.

Dec 21   From James Kent. ALS. DLC. mDW 23932. *Diplomatic Papers*, 1. Comments on the Webster-Ashburton correspondence and criticizes Judge [Esek] Cowen's opinion in the McLeod case; reminisces about his childhood in Putnam County, New York.

Dec 21   From J. Booth Roberts. ALS. DNA, RG 46. mDW 49758. Reports on cases brought before the U.S. district court for Delaware under the bankrupt law.

Dec 22   From Charles Anthony. ALS. DNA, RG 46. mDW49820. Suggests changes in the bankrupt law that would make it more popular in Ohio.

Dec 22   From Millard Fillmore. LS. DNA, RG 59. mDW 55796. Asks for a detailed statement of the planned expenditures from the contingent fund.

Dec 22   From Joseph Gales & William Winston Seaton. LS. DNA, RG 59. mDW 53511. Give circulation figures for the daily and triweekly editions of the *National Intelligencer*.

Dec 22   From John H. Hanna. ALS. DNA, RG 46. mDW 49838. Reports on bankruptcy cases brought before the U.S. district court for Kentucky.

Dec 22   From Charles A. Ingersoll. ALS. DNA, RG 46. mDW 49797. Describes cases brought into U.S. district court for Connecticut under the bankrupt law.

Dec 22   From A. A. Irwin. ALS. DNA, RG 46. mDW 49807. Reports cases and actions in U.S. district court for western Pennsylvania under the bankrupt law.

Dec 22   From Francis Lieber. ALS. NhHi. mDW 23936. Praises DW's impressment letter and thinks he has elevated despatch writing to a literary art.

Dec 22   *From James Boyles Murray, with enclosure: DW's account.*   258

Dec 22   From Edward H. Prentiss. ALS. DNA, RG 46. mDW 49777. Reports bankruptcy cases brought before the U.S. courts in Vermont.

Dec 22   From Ashur Ware. LS. DNA, RG 46. mDW 49771. Comments on the operation of the bankrupt law.

Dec 22   Promissory note for $1,250 payable to Isaac P. Davis. DS. MHi. mDW 39874.

Dec 23   To the Congress of the United States. AL draft. NhD. mDW

23996. Submits a report on the commercial systems of other nations and suggests that a full-time position be created at the State Department to process trade data as it is received.

Dec 23   To John Tyler. LS. DNA, RG 46. mDW 49002. Declares that Lord Ashburton never suggested during the negotiations that the federal government assume or guarantee state debts.

Dec 23   From Charles Davis. ALS. DNA, RG 46. mDW 49778. Reports that popular sentiment in Vermont overwhelmingly favors repeal of the bankrupt law.

Dec 23   From John M. Lea. ALS. DNA, RG 46. mDW 49840. Comments on the bankrupt law and its effect in middle Tennessee.

Dec 23, 25   From Thomas B. Monroe. LS. DNA, RG 46. mDW 49561. Discusses the operation of the bankrupt law in Kentucky.

Dec 23   From Matthew Calbraith Perry. Copy. NhHi. mDW 23944. Thanks DW for the books sent to the Naval Lyceum at the Brooklyn Navy Yard.

Dec 23   From James Renwick. ALS. DNA, RG 59. mDW 56812. Reports having drawn $1,000 from the account for the exploration and survey of the northeast boundary; reports also that the Boundary Commission will hold a meeting in Washington.

Dec 23   From Henry M. Watts. ALS. DNA, RG 46. mDW 49748. Reports that the bankrupt law operates unequally in various U.S. court districts and urges that the Supreme Court be empowered to rectify "the incongruity of decisions."

Dec 24   To Edward Everett. LS. MHi. mDW 23946. *Diplomatic Papers,* 1. Introduces two representatives of the Hawaiian government and asks that they be assisted in obtaining guarantees of the islands' independence.

Dec 24   To Thomas Green. LS. ViHi. mDW 23948. Informs him that Archibald Green's bond as U.S. consul at Galveston has been accepted.

Dec 24   To Caroline Story White Webster. ALS. NhHi. mDW 23950. *PC,* 2: 162. Sends item to be put in her Christmas stocking.

Dec 24   From William Hatcher. ALS. DNA, RG 46. mDW 49834. Reports that no cases have been filed with U.S. district court for western Virginia under the bankrupt law.

Dec 24   From Thomas Irwin. ALS. DNA, RG 46. mDW 49806. Believes the bankrupt law has had a beneficial effect in western district of Pennsylvania.

Dec 24   From Andrew T. Judson. ALS. DNA, RG 46. mDW 49800. Reports that the bankrupt law has worked well in Ohio and has brought relief to many helpless debtors; recommends extending its provisions to corporations.

Dec 24   From Amos Kendall. ALS. DNA, RG 59. mDW 53509. Gives circulation figures for the Washington *Expositor.*

Dec 24   From B. T. Moore. ALS. DNA, RG 49. mDW 49600. Reports on cases brought before the U.S. courts for northern Alabama under the bankrupt law.

Dec 24   From Archibald Randall. ALS. DNA, RG 46. mDW 49811. Recommends some modification of the bankrupt law but feels its general effect has been beneficial in eastern district of Pennsylvania.

Dec 24   From Peleg Sprague. LS. DNA, RG 46. mDW 49784. Thinks creditors' rights under the bankrupt law ought to be strengthened; expounds on its effect in Massachusetts.

Dec 24   From Roger B. Taney. ALS. DNA, RG 46. mDW 49815. Sees no point in recommending amendments to the bankrupt law since Congress is now contemplating its repeal.

Dec 24   From Joseph Story. ALS. DNA, RG 46. mDW 49790. Comments on the bankrupt law and believes it has worked well on the whole.

Dec 24   Recommendation from Lucius Lyon, for Digby V. Bell—consul, West Indies (Printed. *Historical Collections. Collections and Researches made by the Michigan Pioneer and Historical Society*, 27, Lansing, 1897: 558–559).

Dec 26   From Walker Anderson. ALS. DNA, RG 59. mDW 49601. Describes the operation of the bankrupt law in west Florida; argues that it works to the disadvantage of the creditor.

Dec 26   From Samuel Rossiter Betts. ALS. DLC. mDW 23954. Praises highly DW's *Creole* letter.

Dec 26   From Alfred Conkling. ALS. DNA, RG 46. mDW 49530. Feels that "extreme generality" is the "all-pervading weakness" of the bankrupt law.

Dec 26   From Franklin Dexter. ALS. DNA, RG 46. mDW 49786. Discusses the shortcomings of the bankrupt law, as seen in Massachusetts.

Dec 26   From David Files. LS. DNA, RG 46. mDW 49843. Details applications and actions taken by the U.S. district court for southern Alabama under the bankrupt law.

Dec 26   From William A. Haywood. ALS. DNA, RG 49. mDW 49595. Reports no actions under the bankrupt law in the U.S. court in Raleigh because it failed to give the court original jurisdiction.

Dec 26   From Anson Little. ALS. DNA, RG 46. mDW 49544. Reports on bankruptcy cases brought into U.S. district court for northern New York.

Dec 26   From Isaac Samuels Pennybacker. ALS. DNA, RG 46. mDW 49826. Comments on the operation of the bankrupt law in U.S. district court for western Virginia.

Dec 26   From Ross Wilkins. ALS. DNA, RG 46. mDW 49553. Reports that the bankrupt law is working satisfactorily, free of the fraud he had feared might occur.

Dec 27   To John Wade Damon (enclosure: [DW] to Washington Irving, Nov 17, 1842). Copy. DLC. mDW 23957. Encloses a copy of the State Department's instructions to Irving respecting a legal controversy between Damon and Frederick Tudor.

Dec 27   To Pattison, Noe & Company. ALS. MHi. mDW 23959. Expresses thanks for a hat sent to Caroline Webster and sees it as evidence that American manufacturing needs only "just encouragement."

Dec 27   To the United States Senate. LS. DNA, RG 46. mDW 49703. Forwards responses to a circular letter sent out in compliance with a Senate Resolution of Dec 13, 1842, re the operation of the bankrupt law.

Dec 27   From Henry Y. Gray. ALS. DNA, RG 46. mDW 49836. Reports bankrupt cases brought into the U.S. district court for South Carolina.

Dec 27   From James L. Talbot. ALS. DNA, RG 46. mDW 49914. Encloses a statement of applications made under the bankrupt law in U.S. district court for western Tennessee.

Dec 27   Application from J. O. Cleveland—marshal, Missouri (ALS. MWalB. mDW 23960).

Dec 28   To [John Beauchamp Jones]. Copy. DNA, RG 59. mDW 54462. Instructs Jones to publish in the *Madisonian* private acts passed by Congress and Indian treaties, in addition to the orders, resolutions, etc. mentioned in his letter of appointment.

Dec 28   To Peyton A. Southall. LS. ViU. mDWs. Appoints him bearer of despatches to Mexico.

Dec 28   From George C. Bates. ALS. DNA, RG 46. mDW 49823. Reports that the bankrupt law has worked satisfactorily in the Michigan district court.

Dec 28   From Williams Burns. ALS. DNA, RG 46. mDW 49920. Reports applications, discharges, and cases still pending in U.S. district court for southern Mississippi under the bankrupt bill.

Dec 28   From Philip Richard Fendall. ALS. DNA, RG 46. mDW 49593. Reports on cases under the bankrupt law brought before U.S. district court in Washington, D.C.

Dec 28   From Matthew Harvey. ALS. DNA, RG 46. mDW 49781. Recommends repeal of the voluntary provisions of the bankrupt law, never popular in New Hampshire.

Dec 28   From Elisha M. Huntington. ALS. DNA, RG 46. mDW 49557. Reports no difficulty in executing the bankrupt law and sees no point in amending it.

Dec 28   From John Beauchamp Jones. ALS. DNA, RG 59. mDW 53505. Accepts appointment to print the laws in the *Madisonian*.

Dec 28   To Caleb Cushing from DFW. ALS. DLC. mDW 23962. Asks him to call on DW at seven.

Dec 29   To John Quincy Adams. LS. DLC. mDW 23964. Requests a $20,000 appropriation to provide for the joint boundary commission under the Treaty of Washington.

Dec 29   To [Edward Everett]. ALS. MHi. mDW 23968. *Diplomatic Papers*, 1. Outlines U.S. policy on the Sandwich Islands; criticizes Benton's "purported" speech on the Treaty of Washington; comments on Sparks's role in the negotiations and also on Massachusetts politics.

Dec 29   *To [Robert Perkins Letcher].*   260

Dec 29   From James W. Campbell. ALS. DNA, RG 46. mDW 49589. Reports on bankruptcy cases brought into U.S. district court for eastern Tennessee.

Dec 29   From John McLean. ALS. DNA, RG 59. mDW 49817. Recommends a repeal of the voluntary provision and an amendment of the bankrupt law to include banks.

Dec 29   Application from John Frederick Scheibler (ALS. NhHi. mDW 23975).

Dec 30   To Waddy Thompson. ALS. TxU. mDWs. Suggests that the

Mexican government might be approached with a proposal for ceding upper California to the United States.

Dec 30   From Henry Baldwin. ALS. DNA, RG 46. mDW 49548. Comments on the operation of the bankrupt law in Pennsylvania and throughout the United States.

Dec 30   From H[orace?] Bassett. ALS. DNA, RG 46. mDW 49555. Details applications and actions taken by U.S. district court for Indiana under the bankrupt law.

Dec 30   From M. B. Brown. ALS. DNA, RG 46. mDW 49916. Comments on the operation of the bankrupt law in Tennessee.

Dec 30   From Edward Curtis (with Robert A. Tucker to DW, c. Dec 30, 1842). ANS. MWalB. mDW 23992. Introduces Robert A. Tucker.

Dec 30   From Humphrey Howe Leavitt. ALS. DNA, RG 46. mDW 49818. Suggests changes in the bankrupt law.

Dec 30   From Smith Thompson. ALS. DNA, RG 46. mDW 49546. Argues that amending the bankrupt law would merely add to its ambiguity.

[c. Dec 30]   From Robert A. Tucker (enclosed with Edward Curtis to DW, Dec 30, 1842). ALS. MWalB. mDW 23992. Asks if William Frith Williams is to be appointed U.S. consul at Bermuda.

Dec 31   From Courtland Cushing. ALS. DNA, RG 46. mDW 49912. Favors making corporations issuing paper money subject to compulsory bankruptcy.

Dec 31   From Francis Preston Blair and John Rives. LS. DNA, RG 59. mDW 53507. Give circulation figures for the Washington *Globe* and *Congressional Globe*.

Dec 31   From Joseph Gales and William Winston Seaton. LS. DNA, RG 59. mDW 53499. Accept appointment to publish the laws in the *National Intelligencer*.

Dec 31   From A. H. Rutherford. ALS. DNA, RG 46. mDW 49921. Reports applications and discharges under the bankrupt law in the U.S. district court for Arkansas.

[Dec]   To William Campbell Preston. ALS. ViHi. mDWs. Extends an invitation to Mrs. Preston, but declines an invitation to dine with the Prestons because of a prior engagement.

[Dec]   To Daniel Fletcher Webster. ALS. NhHi. mDW 23994. Van Tyne, p. 286. Urges those who favor repeal of the bankrupt law to stand firm.

Dec   From Brantz Mayer. ALS draft. MdHi. mDW 24001. Analyzes the Mexican government's proposals for settling the claims of American citizens.

[Dec]   *From John Tyler.*   261

[Dec ?]   From John Tyler. ALS. DLC. mDW 24016. Asks for DW's thoughts on the election and land distribution bills which might be included in the Annual Message.

[1842]   From John Tyler. ANS. DLC. mDW 21154. Orders sending abroad the *Madisonian* and the New York *Union*, since he has "no desire to have papers placed in the hands of Foreign Ministers that are replete with abuse of me."

[1842]   From John Tyler. ALS. DLC. mDW 24038. Makes suggestions for the appointment of secretaries to the legations at Spain, Mexico, and Russia.

[1842] Receipt from John J. Crittenden for $100 received from the state department for public services. ADS. DNA, RG 59. mDW 56623.

[1842] Recommendation from S. DeWitt Bloodford, for a Mr. Benson— bearer of despatches (ALS. MWalB. mDW 20431).

[1842] Rules, Regulations, and Forms of Proceedings in Matters of Bankruptcy, in the District Court of the United States for the Kentucky District. Printed document. DNA, RG 46. mDW 49604.

[1842?] From John Tyler. ALS. NhHi. mDW 24036. Asks that some job be found for an applicant.

[1842?] Receipt for $350 paid George Smith by the state department for services on the frontier in 1841. AD by DW, signed by Smith. DNA, RG 59. mDW 56601.

[1842–1843] From John Tyler. ALS. DLC. mDW 24045. Encloses two letters from Duff Green.

[1842–1843] From John Tyler. ALS. DLC. mDW 24047. Comments on Latin American affairs.

[1842–1843] From John Tyler. AL. DLC. mDW 24050. Returns a letter, and comments that the Rothschilds do not seem "overly friendly" toward the United States.

[1842–1843] From John Tyler. ALS. DLC. mDW 24052. Writes concerning the Rothschilds' demand for payment on Van Ness's drafts.

[1842–1843] From John Tyler. ALS. DLC. mDW 24055. Returns "the paper and despatch" and thinks the Rothschilds are "rather scurvy fellows."

1843

Jan 1   From Joseph Eve.   262
Jan 1   Recommendation from Caleb Cushing, for Nathaniel Cheever— consul, Trinidad (ALS. MWalB. mDW 24057).
Jan 2   From Alexander Baring, Lord Ashburton. ALS. NhHi. mDW 24063. PC, 2: 162–164. Reports British criticism of the Treaty of Washington; expresses dismay at Tyler's remarks on the cruising convention and denies there is a conspiracy among capitalists to force a settlement of state debts by refusing credit to the federal government.
Jan 2   From Alexander L. Collins. ALS. DNA, RG 46. mDW 49972. Submits correspondence containing information on the bankrupt law; describes briefly the administration of the law in Wisconsin.
Jan 2   From [Edward Everett]. AL. MHi. mDW 24077. Diplomatic Papers, 1. Reports an exchange of views with Aberdeen and also with Ashburton on Oregon, U.S. trade with the British West Indies, and the idea of a new special diplomatic mission.
Jan 2   From Henry Gibson. ALS. DNA, RG 46. mDW 49591. Reports cases brought before U.S. district court for eastern Virginia under the bankrupt law.

Jan 3   To the United States Senate. LS. DNA. RG 46. mDW 49769.
Transmits additional responses to the State Department's circular
concerning the bankrupt law.

Jan 3   From Andrew A. Harwood. ALS. DLC. mDW 24085. Thanks him
for books sent to the U.S. Naval Lyceum at New York.

Jan 3   From Charles N. Jordan. ALS. DNA, RG 46. mDW 49922. Reports applications filed in the U.S. court for western Florida under
the bankrupt law.

Jan 3   From James F. Owings. ALS. DNA, RG 46. mDW 49976. Reports
applications made under the bankrupt law in the U.S. district court
for Illinois.

Jan 3   From Henry Potter. ALS. DNA, RG 46. mDW 49597. Describes
the administering of the bankrupt law in North Carolina and suggests some improvements.

Jan 4   From Thomas Douglass. ALS. DNA, RG 46. mDW 49924. Reports applications filed in the U.S. court for eastern Florida under
the bankrupt law.

Jan 4   From Edward Kent.   263

Jan 4   Recommendation from Christopher Morgan, for Joseph C.
Luther—consul, Rio de Janeiro (ALS. NhHi. mDW 24087).

Jan 5   From Montgomery Blair. ALS. DNA, RG 46. mDW 49913.
Admits to having had little practical experience with the bankrupt
law.

Jan 5   From Francis Preston Blair and John Rives. LS. DNA, RG 59.
mDW 53495. Accept appointment to print the laws in the Washington *Globe*.

Jan 5   From George R. Fairbanks. ALS. DNA, RG 46. mDW 49923. Reports on bankruptcy cases brought into the U.S. Superior Court
for eastern Florida.

Jan 5   From Robert W. Wells. ALS. DNA, RG 46. mDW 49978. Argues
that the bankrupt act is unconstitutional.

Jan 6   From Joel Eastman. ALS. DNA, RG 46. mDW 49904. States his
belief that the bankrupt law is gaining popular favor.

Jan 7   To John Tyler. LS. DNA, RG 46. mDW 49006. Transmits diplomatic correspondence pertaining to the *Caroline* incident.

Jan [7?]   From John L. Hayes. ALS. DNA, RG 46. mDW 49898. Reports
cases brought before U.S. district court for New Hampshire under
the bankrupt law.

Jan 7   From James Renwick. ALS. DNA, RG 59. mDW 56814. Transmits his account and vouchers for the quarter ending December 31.

Jan 8   From R. S. Birchett. ALS. DNA, RG 46. mDW 49925. Details petitions and actions taken in U.S. district court for middle Florida
under the bankrupt law.

Jan 8   Application from Price & Rohrer, for the *Mississippian*—public
printer (LS. DNA, RG 59. mDW 53488).

Jan 9   To John Quincy Adams. LS. MHi. mDW 24091. Van Tyne, p.
285. Recommends that $40,000 be appropriated for the mission to
China.

Jan 9   To Francis Asbury Dickens from DFW. ALS. DNA, RG 46. mDW
50090. Requests printed copies of the treaty with Peru now before
the Senate.

[Jan 9]   To John Plummer Healy.   264
Jan 9   To the United States Senate. LS. DNA, RG 46. mDW 49528.
Transmits additional responses on the operation of the bankrupt
law.
Jan 9   From Samuel Bulkley Ruggles.   265
Jan 9   From William A. Thompson. ALS. DLC. mDW 24103. Com-
mends DW for his role in the Ashburton negotiations and asks for
a copy of his Ashburton correspondence.
Jan 9   Application from Henry F. Fish—consul, Bermuda (ALS.
MWalB. mDW 24096).
Jan 9   Promissory note payable to Richard Smith for $14,726. Copy.
MHi. mDW 39876.
Jan 10   From William Miner. ALS. DNA, RG 46. mDW 49911. Reports
applications made in U.S. district court for Ohio under the bank-
rupt law.
Jan 10   Application from Henry F. Fish (ALS. MWalB. mDW 24105).
Jan 10   Receipt for $100 paid to Albert Smith. ADS. DNA, RG 59. mDW
56641.
[c. Jan 10]   From Philemon Dickerson. ALS. DNA, RG 46. mDW 49906.
Comments extensively on the bankrupt law.
Jan 12   To the United States Senate. LS. DNA, RG 46. mDW 49893.
Submits a report on U.S. imports for the months of July, Aug, and
Sept 1842.
Jan 12   From Nicholas Biddle. ALS draft. DLC. mDW 24113. Reports
that he has interests in Texas and asks what chances there are for
reconciliation between Texas and Mexico.
Jan 12   From John T. Pitman. LS. DNA, RG 46. mDW 49968. Details
cases brought before U.S. district court for Rhode Island under the
bankrupt law.
Jan 13   To Edward Everett. LS. MHi. mDW 24114. Introduces W. W.
Coriell and J. B. Newhall, who are traveling to Europe in the in-
terests of Illinois and Iowa.
Jan 13   From Charles B. Penrose. Copy. DNA, RG 206. mDWs. En-
closes a bond for Edward Porter, U.S. consul at Tabasco, Mexico.
Jan 14   From Justin Butterfield. ALS. NhHi. mDW 24115. Introduces
Chicago postmaster, B. William Stuart.
Jan 14   Recommendation from William H. Tuthill, for John C. Higgin-
son—marshal, Iowa Territory (ALS. MWalB. mDW 24117).
Jan 16   To John Macpherson Berrien. LS. DNA, RG 46. mDW 50052.
Replies to his request for information on Alexander Drysdale and
John McElvain.
Jan 16   From David Webster.   266
Jan 17   From John Otis. ALS. NhD. mDW 24121. *Diplomatic Papers*, 1.
Encloses the Maine commissioners' report but is unsure how it will
be received by the legislature; calls for a liberal settlement of the
"disputed boundary fund."
Jan 18   To the United States Senate. LS. DNA, RG 46. mDW 49896.
Transmits communications pertaining to the bankrupt law.
Jan 18   From Nicholas Biddle.   267
Jan 18   Applications from Henry F. Fish (ALS. MWalB. mDW 24125);
from William P. Hall—consul, Barcelona (ALS. MWalB. mDW

24129); from J. W. Holding—consul, Rio de Janeiro (ALS. NhHi. mDW 24132).

[Jan 19] To Caleb Cushing. ALS. NN. mDW 24220. Reports being "again disappointed about Baltimore"; mentions hearing from many quarters of Cushing's "admirable speech yesterday" on the bankrupt law.

Jan 19 From Peyton A. Southall. ALS. DNA, RG 59. mDW 56495. Reports a late arrival in Vera Cruz and his plans to leave for Mexico City.

Jan 19 From Joseph G. Totten. LC. DNA, RG 77. mDWs. States there is little prospect that an appointment can be made now to the U.S. Military Academy from the Massachusetts first congressional district.

Jan 19 Recommendation from George H. Walworth, for John C. Higginson (ALS. MWalB. mDW 24134).

Jan 20 To Willie Person Mangum. LS. DNA, RG 46. mDW 49926. Reports the names and compensation of State Department employees for 1842.

Jan 20 To Willie Person Mangum (enclosure: [report of expenditures], Jan 4, 1843). LS. DNA, RG 46. mDW 49931. Transmits an account of expenditures from the State Department's contingency fund for the half year ending June 30, 1842.

Jan 20 From John S. Dunlap. ALS. DNA, RG 46. mDW 49874. Encloses a statement of applications filed in U.S. District Court for Iowa under the bankrupt law.

Jan 20 From Francis Lieber. ALS. NhHi. mDW 24136. Comments on the significance of the Webster-Ashburton negotiations; inquires about the mission to China and hopes that Congress will make the necessary appropriation.

Jan 20 From Theodore H. McCaleb. ALS. DNA, RG 46. mDW 49863. Suggests alterations to the bankrupt law.

Jan 21 To Mrs. Jeremiah Smith. Copy. NhHi. mDW 24140. Van Tyne, p. 629. Encloses for her approval the draft of an epitaph prepared by himself and George Ticknor for Jeremiah Smith.

Jan 21 To John Tyler. LS. DLC. mDW 24142. Reports, in response to a Senate inquiry of January 19, that the British government has made no grant of land to Hudson's Bay Company in Oregon Territory.

Jan 23 To [Joseph Gales and William Winston Seaton]. ALS. NhD. mDW 24144. Doubts that he can send before Jan 24 "the matter *preliminary* to Lord Palmerstons articles."

Jan 23 To the United States Senate. LS. DNA, RG 46. mDW 49966. Transmits replies to the State Department's circular letters on the bankrupt law.

Jan 23 From George Evans. ALS. MWalB. mDW 24148. Claims but slight acquaintance with [James S.?] Williams.

Jan 23 From Richard W. Greene. ALS. DNA, RG 46. mDW 49984. Favors repeal of the voluntary feature of the bankrupt law and modification of the involuntary provisions.

Jan 23 From Peyton A. Southall. ALS. DNA, RG 59. mDW 56496. Reports his arrival in Mexico City.

Jan 23   Application from Eben Ritchie Dorr—bearer of despatches to
Chile (ALS. MWalB. mDW 24146).

Jan 23   Recommendation from James Grant, for John C. Higginson
(ALS. MWalB. mDW 21373).

Jan 23   Bond signed by Peter Force and another by Peter Force et al.,
pertaining to his existing contract to print government documents.
DS. DNA, RG 59. mDW 53544.

Jan 24   From Millard Fillmore. ALS. DLC. mDWs. Inquires about recent changes in Canadian commercial rules, especially regarding
the reexport of American processed grain to Great Britain.

Jan 24   From Charles H. Wiltberger. ALS. DNA, RG 59. mDW 54903.
Accepts appointment as justice of the peace for Washington.

Jan 24   Recommendations from Egbert S. Barrows, for John C. Higginson (ALS. MWalB. mDW 24149); from Francis James et al., for
Samuel Walker—superintendent of mason work, Patent Office
Building (ALS by James, signed also by others. DNA, RG 46. mDW
51636).

Jan 25   From Z. Collins Lee. ALS. DNA, RG 76. mDWs. Encloses affidavits relating to the barque *Mary* and asks that they be sent to
the U.S. minister in Brazil, where condemnation proceedings
against the ship are under consideration.

Jan 25   From Charles Mason. ALS. DNA, RG 46. mDW 49879. Explains the difficulty in obtaining information on the operation of
the bankrupt law in Iowa.

Jan 25   Recommendation from Edward Douglass White, for Joseph C.
Luther (ALS. NhHi. mDW 24151).

Jan 27   To Stephen Pleasonton. Copy. NNPM. mDW 24153. Approves,
with specified exceptions, reimbursement of Henry Wheaton for contingent expenses incurred at the Berlin mission.

Jan 27   To Seth Weston. ALS. NhHi. mDW 24155. *PC*, 2: 164–165.
Discusses business pertaining to his Marshfield farm.

Jan 27   Recommendations from Charles Ellis et al., for Henry F. Fish
(ALS by Ellis, signed also by others. MWalB. mDW 24160); from
Charles Joseph Perot et al., for Henry F. Fish (LS. MWalB. mDW
24158).

Jan 28   To [Willie Person Mangum]. AL. DNA, RG 46. mDW 49999.
Informs him that the accompanying packet (not found) was just
received from Europe.

Jan 28   To Silas Moore Stilwell. LS. NN. mDWs. Encloses the President's remission of fine for Charles Edwards and requests an
acknowledgment.

Jan 28   Recommendations from Edmund March Blunt, for Henry F.
Fish (ALS. MWalB. mDW 24161); from Isaac Dashiell Jones, for
Brantz Mayer—agent to Mexico for receiving money (ALS. MWalB.
mDW 24177).

Jan 29   To Edward Everett. LS. MHi. mDW 24179. *Diplomatic Papers*,
1. Reports that Oregon is becoming a political issue; recommends
a tripartite settlement of the Texas, California, and Oregon issues;
discusses prospects for a special mission to London; suggests Everett might be ideal for the mission to China.

Jan 29 From John Caldwell Calhoun. ALS. MWalB. mDW 24187.
Vouches for a Samuel Church.
Jan 29 Recommendation from Reuel Williams, for a Mr. Hancock—
consul, New Brunswick (ALS. MWalB. mDW 24189).
[c. Jan 29] From John Tyler. ALS. DLC. mDW 24816. Tyler, *Tylers*, 2:
261. Approves DW's letters to Everett and Thompson and agrees
that the Texas, California, and Oregon issues ought to be "introduced with the same treaty."
Jan 30 To John Quincy Adams. Copy. MHi. mDW 24191. *W & S*, 16:
392–393. Makes a suggestion regarding the bill which provides for
the mission to China.
Jan 30 To Edward Everett. ALS. MHi. mDW 24193. Encloses a note
from Tyler on China and states that Fletcher Webster would like
to accompany the China mission.
Jan 30 To Waddy Thompson. LS. NhD. mDW 24196. *Diplomatic
Papers*, 1. Asks Thompson to be more explicit in objecting to his
present secretary of legation; thinks it inexpedient to send an agent
to Yucatan; asks if he has sounded out the Mexican government
on a "matter."
Jan 30 From Samuel Prentiss. ALS. DNA, RG 46. mDW 49882. Thinks
the voluntary provision of the bankrupt law has had a generally
negative effect.
Jan 30 From Waddy Thompson. ALS. DLC. mDW 24203. *Diplomatic
Papers*, 1. Thinks the Monterey incident has made it inexpedient for
the present to discuss the cession of California with Mexico; complains at having his judgment countermanded and offers to resign;
complains also that money appropriated for his expenses has been
diverted to other uses.
[Jan 30] From John Tyler. ALS. DLC. mDW 24222. Tyler, *Tylers*, 2:
261–263. Refers to their earlier conversation regarding a treaty
with Mexico, and asks if Everett might like to go to China.
Jan 30 Application from John H. Sherburne—State Department post
(ALS. DLC. mDW 24200).
Jan 31 To Edward Everett. LS. MHi. mDW 24207. Introduces a Mr.
Lane, who will be traveling to Europe to study medicine.
Jan 31 From Edward Everett. LC. MHi. mDW 24208. Acknowledges
various communications on Liberia and promises to take up the
matter with the British government.
Jan 31 From Edward Everett. ALS. MHi. mDW 24213. Comments on
Liberia and on the map discovered by Sparks in the archives of the
French foreign office; reports a conversation with McGregor on the
proposed commercial treaty and on U.S. trade with China.
Jan 31 From Caleb Green. ALS. DNA, RG 46. mDW 49887. Reports on
bankruptcy cases in U.S. district court for western Louisiana; urges
that the court be authorized to hold three or four terms annually
instead of the one now allowed.
Jan 31 From John Plummer Healy.   267
[Jan] To the Publishers of the Laws of Session of 1842–1843. Copy.
DNA, RG 59. mDW 54460. Directs them to copy the laws, etc., as
printed in the *Madisonian*.
[Jan] From John Tyler. ALS. DLC. mDW 24226. Tyler, *Tylers*, 2: 267.

Thinks the U.S. has done enough in disavowing Commodore Thomas Ap Catesby Jones's act and that Don Juan N. Almonte's demand for his punishment goes too far.

[Jan?] From John Tyler. ALS. DLC. mDW 24228. Approves DW's suggestion concerning correspondence with Mexico on the Monterey incident.

[Jan?] From Charles Anderson Wickliffe (enclosure: Preston S. Loughborough to Wickliffe, Dec 18, 1842). ALS. DLC. mDW 24230. Forwards a letter from Preston S. Loughborough concerning allegedly derogatory remarks made against DW by John Jordan Crittenden.

[Jan–Feb] From John Tyler. ALS. DLC. mDW 24236. *Diplomatic Papers*, 1. Proposes sending the *Pennsylvania* to China, providing the appropriation is sufficient.

[Jan–May?] To Nathaniel F. Williams. ALS. NhD. mDW 25541. Asks Williams to make a quick trip to Washington.

Feb 1 From William Bates (with DW to John Quincy Adams, Feb 6, 1843). ALS. MHi. mDW 24276. Submits a petition from Wareham, Mass., in support of the exchequer plan.

Feb 1 From Edward Everett. ALS. MHi. mDW 24242. *Diplomatic Papers*, 1. Reports Aberdeen's disappointment with Tyler's comments on the northwest boundary and the cruising convention.

Feb 1 Application from David Hoffman—Austrian mission (ALS. DLC. mDW 24246).

Feb 1 Check for $20 payable to self. DS. DLC. mDW 39877.

Feb 2 Recommendation from Augustus Seymour Porter, for Henry F. Fish (ALS. MWalB. mDW 24249).

Feb 3 To Edward Everett. LS. MHi. mDW 24251. Introduces locomotive-builder Octavius A. Norris, who is planning a business trip to Europe.

Feb 3 From John James Audubon.   268

Feb 3 From Ambrose Dudley Mann. ALS. NhHi. mDW 24254. Reports European views of the American economy and finds that little is known in Europe of American institutions; declares that Britain has been forcefully affected by American power under the Tyler administration.

Feb 3 Check for $130.55 to [?] Wilson. DS. DLC. mDW 39878.

Feb 3 Recommendation from Truman Smith, for Henry F. Fish (ALS. MWalB. mDW 24257).

Feb 4 Recommendation from John L. Wilson, for George F. Usher (ALS. MWalB. mDW 24259).

Feb 5 "To the printer of the Madisonian." ALS draft (signed by DW with pseudonym). NhHi. mDW 24261. Responds in kind to allegory of Clay's presidential aspirations which appeared in the *Madisonian* of December 16, 1842.

Feb 5 From Nathaniel Pope. ALS. DNA, RG 46. mDW 49861. Promises lengthy comment on the bankrupt law should the movement for repeal fail.

Feb 5 From Jesse Waln. ALS. DLC. mDW 24273. Requests the return of a letter of recommendation and also DW's autograph.

Feb 5   Memorandum of a $2,000 loan from Caleb Cushing. ADS. DLC.
mDW 39879.
Feb 6   To John Quincy Adams (enclosure: William Bates to DW, Feb 1,
1843). ALS. MHi. mDW 24275. W & S, 16: 396. Encloses a letter
from one of JQA's constituents.
[Feb 6]   To [Jared Sparks]. ANS. MH-H. mDW 24278. States that he
has mislaid Sparks's expense account and asks for another copy.
Feb 6   To [Robert Charles Winthrop]. ALS. MHi. mDW 24279. Praises
Winthrop's speech and vote on the exchequer bill.
Feb 6   From Daniel Le Roy. ALS. NhHi. mDW 24283. Authorizes pay-
ment of John Chrystie's quarterly account and recommends his
continuance as despatch agent.
Feb 6   Recommendation from Pliny Merrick, for Joseph C. Luther
(ALS. NhHi. mDW 24285).
Feb 7   To George S. Curson. Printed. PC, 2: 166–167. Asks him to do
what he can for George Crittenden, imprisoned in Mexico for par-
ticipation in the Texas expedition "over the Rio Grande."
Feb 7   To John Plummer Healy.   269
Feb 7   To [Thomas Gibbs] Morgan. Printed. PC, 2: 167. Encloses a com-
munication to be forwarded to Waddy Thompson by the most expe-
ditious means available.
Feb 7   To Waddy Thompson. ALS. NcD. mDW 24295. PC, 2: 165–166.
Asks him to intervene with Mexican authorities for the release or
parole of George Crittenden.
Feb 7   Recommendation from Anthony Halsey, for Henry F. Fish (ALS.
MWalB. mDW 24298).
Feb 8   To Charles Anderson Wickliffe. Copy. DLC. mDW 24301. Recom-
mends P. Miner for postmaster at Wilkes Barre, Pa.
Feb 8   From Robert Perkins Letcher.   269
Feb 8   From Jared Sparks. ALS. NhD. mDW 24309. *Diplomatic
Papers*, 1. Reports he is writing an article for the *North American
Review* on the Treaty of Washington; expresses irritation at his
treatment in the Senate debate over the map controversy.
Feb 8   From Charles T. Whippo et al. ALS by Whippo, signed also by
others. NhHi. mDW 24312. Voice strong objection to the removal of
Joseph T. Boyd, postmaster at Newcastle, Pa.
[Feb 8]   From Charles Anderson Wickliffe. Copy. DNA, RG 28. Reports
requesting legislation which would empower the Post Office Department to make arrangements with Texas for the prepayment of
postage.
Feb 8   Recommendation from Peter A. Hargous, for Lewis Stanislaus
Hargous—for transmission of Mexican indemnity (ALS. MWalB.
mDW 24302).
Feb 9   To [Edward Curtis?]. ALS. NN. MDW 24316. Suggests that Curtis come to Washington immediately after the adjournment of Congress, when DW will give "a day" to certain subjects; gives whimsi-
cal instructions concerning food delicacies.
Feb 9   To Nathaniel F. Williams. ALS. NhD. mDW 24317. Promises to
send $1,000 but warns he may be obliged to draw on him again.
Feb 9   From George Ticknor.   270
Feb 9   From John Tyler. ALS. DLC. mDW 24324. *Diplomatic Papers*, 1.

Agrees with DW's disapproval of the Almonte letter concerning the
Monterey incident and thinks the United States has gone far
enough by disavowing the incident.

Feb 9   Recommendations from Caleb Cushing, for Edward R. Weir—
district attorney, Kentucky (ALS. MWalB. mDW 24319); from
Phineas White, for Thomas Woodhouse Stevens—consul, Europe
(ALS. NhD. mDW 24327).

Feb 10   From John P. Adams. Copy. DLC. mDW 24330. Accepts appointment as U.S. consul at La Guaira, Venezuela.

Feb 10   From Edward Everett. ALS. MHi. mDW 24332. *Diplomatic
Papers*, 1. Comments on the controversy in Britain over the Sparks
map.

Feb 11   From Preston S. Loughborough. ALS. DNA, RG 59. mDW
54745. Acknowledges appointment as U.S. district attorney for
Kentucky.

Feb 11   Bill from J. H. T. Werner, metal turner, for repairs, through
Feb 4, 1846. ADS. NhHi. mDW 40049.

Feb 13   From Robert Perkins Letcher.   271

Feb 13   From John Tyler. ALS. NhHi. mDW 24348. Tyler, *Tylers*, 2:
265. Asks whether he should appeal directly to Santa Anna for the
release of George Crittenden.

Feb 14   To Walter Forward (enclosure: Alphonse Pageot to DW, Feb 9,
1843). LS. DNA, RG 217. mDW 57209. Transmits a note received
from the French minister at Washington.

Feb 14   From John Tyler (enclosure: Tyler to George W. Summers,
Feb 14, 1843). ALS. DLC. mDW 24351. Encloses his reply to Summer's plea on behalf of Judge Anderson Hutchinson, captured during the Mexican raid.

Feb 14   Promissory note to Richard Smith—$4,000 payable at the Bank
of the Metropolis. DS. American Security Bank, Washington, D.C.
mDWs.

Feb 14   Recommendation from Nicholas Biddle, for Charles S. Fry—
appointment, U.S. Marine Corps (ALS draft. DLC. mDW 24350).

[Feb 15]   To [Caleb Cushing]. AN. NN. mDW 24454. Invites him for
whist and praises his speech on a bill to reduce congressional
salaries.

*Feb 15   To Caleb Cushing, with enclosure: to Charles Anderson Wick-
liffe, from DW and Caleb Cushing, Feb 15.*   272

Feb 15   To Edward Everett. LS. MHi. mDW 24358. Introduces the
Reverend J. B. Condit of Portland.

Feb 15   To Henry Ledyard. LS. RNR. mDW 24359. Introduces Condit.

Feb 15   To Robert Perkins Letcher.   273

Feb 15   To Jared Sparks (with ANS by Sparks). ALS. MH-H. mDW
24365. *Diplomatic Papers*, 1. Offers documents for Sparks's use in
preparing article on the Treaty of Washington; comments on the
map controversy.

Feb 15   From J. Francis Hutton to DFW. ALS. NhHi. mDW 24369.
Complains of the objections to Seth Driggs's appointment as U.S.
consul at Port-au-Prince and asks for the return of Driggs's papers.

[p/m Feb 16]   To Nicholas Biddle. ALS. DLC. mDW 24371. Promises to do what he can on behalf of Charles S. Fry's application for a commission in the Marine Corps.

Feb 16 To John Tyler (enclosure: copy of the commission given to DW to treat with Lord Ashburton, Aug 1, 1842). LS. DNA, RG 46. mDW 49057. Transmits document.

Feb 16 From Leverett Saltonstall. ALS. DNA, RG 76. mDWs. Encloses letter to himself from N. L. Rogers & Brothers, Salem merchants, concerning their goods left in New Zealand.

Feb 17 To Silas Moore Stilwell. LS. NN. mDWs. Requests an acknowledgment of the pardon for Samuel A. Suydam.

Feb 18 From James L. Edwards. ALS. DNA, RG 59. mDW 54612. Accepts appointment as commissioner of pensions.

Feb 18 From John Tyler. ALS. DLC. mDW 24375. Revises and approves a letter.

Feb 18 Recommendations from Charles Chapman, for Henry F. Fish (ALS. MWalB. mDW 24373); from John B. Eldridge, for Henry F. Fish (ANS. MWalB. mDW 24374).

Feb 20 To the United States Senate. Copy. DNA, RG 46. mDW 49859. Encloses correspondence relative to the bankrupt law.

Feb 20 From Washington Barrow (enclosures: W. Barrow to José Joaquin Gomes de Castro, Feb 9, 1843). Extract. DNA, RG 46. mDW 50239. Warns that the Portuguese government will continue procrastinating on the *Hall* and *Armstrong* cases until the United States assumes a "very decided tone."

Feb 20 From Seth Driggs. LS. NhHi. mDW 24377. Asks that an abstract of the charges against him be sent to J. Francis Hutton.

Feb 20 To Caleb Cushing from DFW. ALS. DLC. mDW 24379. Conveys an invitation to dine with DW and other guests.

Feb 21 To Robert Perkins Letcher.   274

Feb 21 From Jared Sparks. ALS. CtY. mDW 24388. *Diplomatic Papers*, 1. Inquires about navigation rights on the St. John River under the Treaty of Washington and comments on "the conflict of maps."

Feb 22 To [Willie Person Mangum]. LS. DNA, RG 46. mDW 49891. Transmits statements on passengers arriving from abroad at each U.S. collection district during 1842.

Feb 22 To the United States Senate. Copy. DNA, RG 46. mDW 49872. Transmits additional correspondence on the bankrupt law.

Feb 22 From Jared Sparks. ALS. DLC. mDW 24392. Comments on the map controversy; contends that DW acted correctly in withholding the maps from Ashburton.

Feb 22 House resolution requesting information regarding stationery, job printing, etc. DS. DNA, RG 59. mDW 55800.

Feb 23 From James Renwick (enclosures: list of surveying instruments in the possession of James Renwick, Feb 22, 1843; receipt for various articles, Sept 18, 1842). ALS. DNA, RG 59. mDW 56819. Transmits documents accounting for equipment used in the northeast boundary survey.

Feb 23 Senate resolution requesting information on books, etc., in the State, Treasury, War, Navy, and Post Office Departments. AD. DNA, RG 59. mDW 55804.

Feb 24   To Caleb Cushing. ALS. DLC. mDW 24396. *Diplomatic Papers*, I. Encloses papers for perusal by Cushing and John Quincy Adams, and strongly suggests that Congress authorize a special mission to England.

Feb 24   From John Jordan Crittenden. ALS. NjMoHP. mDW 24400. *Diplomatic Papers*, I. Expresses appreciation for efforts being made to win his son's release from imprisonment in Mexico; asks whether it is true that Waddy Thompson is returning to the United States.

Feb 24   From C[harles?] Stanton et al.   274

Feb 24   From Andrew Talcott. ALS. DNA, RG 59. mDW 56834. Reports having drawn $500 from the appropriation for the survey and exploration of the northeast boundary.

Feb 24   From John Tyler. ALS. DLC. mDW 24405. Asks for Aberdeen's letter to Everett of Dec 1841 and for the House resolution calling for any communications from Great Britain on the construction of the treaty.

[Feb 24]   From Charles Anderson Wickliffe. Copy. DNA, RG 28. mDW 57063. Asks DW about a diplomatic agent.

Feb 25   To Edward Everett. ALS. MHi. mDW 24407. *Diplomatic Papers*, I. Thinks Sir Robert Peel's and Lord Aberdeen's observations on Tyler's references to the cruising convention are based on error; sees doubtful prospects for a special mission to England; thinks of succeeding Everett for a year in London should he agree to go to China.

Feb 25   From Henry Stephen Fox. ALS. NhHi. mDW 24413. Reports having incorporated DW's memorandum into his despatch to Aberdeen and offers to send an amended version if he wishes.

[Feb 25]   From John Tyler. ALS. DLC. mDW 24461. Asks for Henry Stephen Fox's despatch; reports that Walter Forward has resigned, effective March 1.

Feb 25   Recommendation from Matthew St. Clair Clarke, for Charles Murray—despatch bearer to England (ALS. MWalB. mDW 24111).

Feb 26   To Joseph Gales and William Winston Seaton. ALS. NhD. mDW 24415. Sends editorial on the map controversy for publication in the *National Intelligencer*.

Feb 26   From John Tyler. ALS. DLC. mDW 24417. Tyler, *Tylers*, 2: 261. Criticizes the allusion to his message in Aberdeen's letter; states that he wants authority to send a special mission during the congressional recess and insists that strong language must be used with England.

[Feb 26]   "The Boundary Maps" (editorial). AD. NN. mDW 24421. Printed. *National Intelligencer*, Feb 27, 1843. *Diplomatic Papers*, I.

Feb 27   To John Prentiss. Printed. *New Hampshire Sentinel*. March 8, 1843. Denies having once said "Take care of the rich, and the rich will take care of the poor"; claims longtime support of independence for the "industrious classes."

Feb 27   From Nicholas Biddle.   275

Feb 27   From Edward Everett. LC. MHi. mDW 24430. *Diplomatic Papers*, I. Reports Peel appears cool toward a special mission and toward DW's suggestion for a tripartite treaty; reports the U.S. is suspected of seeking ascendancy in the Sandwich Islands through the American missionaries living there.

Feb 27   From Brantz Mayer. ALS. NhHi. mDW 24437. Asks to be informed of the substance of Waddy Thompson's objections to his continuance as secretary of legation in Mexico.

Feb 27   From Putnam I. Farnham & Co. ALS. DNA, RG 76. mDWs. Comment on depositions of four crewmen from the barque *Jones*, seized by the British in 1840.

Feb 27   Recommendation from John Todd Stuart, for William Pickering—despatch bearer to Europe. (ALS. MWalB. mDW 24439).

Feb 28   To John Jordan Crittenden. Copy. DLC. mDW 24441. *Diplomatic Papers*, 1. Reports having received no indication that Waddy Thompson plans returning to the United States.

Feb 28   From Alexander Drysdale. ALS. DNA, RG 59. mDW 54602. Accepts appointment as U.S. attorney for Georgia.

Feb 28   From James Renwick. ALS. DNA, RG 59. mDW 56838. Transmits his closing account for the exploration and survey of the northeast boundary.

Feb 28   From H[enry?] Shaw.   276

Feb 28   Receipt for $600, paid by DW to Albert Smith. ADS. DNA, RG 59. mDW 56642.

[Feb]   From John Tyler. ALS. NhHi. mDW 24459. *Diplomatic Papers*, 1. Declares that Peel's speech of February 2 makes it imperative that the Cass correspondence be published immediately.

[Feb]   From John Tyler. ALS. DLC. mDW 24463. Writes concerning Judge Anderson Hutchinson's case.

[Feb ?]   Remarks on the right of search. AD. NhHi. mDW 24456.

March 1   To Robert Bennie Cranston. Printed. George Champlin Mason, *Annals of the Redwood Library and Athenaeum* (Newport, R.I., 1891), p. 162. Reports that Robert J. Taylor's letter has been referred to the officers of Congress, who are responsible for distributing the American State Papers.

March 1   To Hiram Ketchum. ALS. NhD. mDW 24466. *Diplomatic Papers*, 1. Confides that he will leave the State Department and doubts that he will re-enter public life.

March 1   From Edward Everett. LC. MHi. mDW 24471. Relates a conversation with Aberdeen on Oregon, Mexico, the Sandwich Islands, and the problem of winning Parliament's approval of an extradition law.

March 1   Recommendation from David R. Porter et al., for Joseph S. Dixon—consul, Rio de Janeiro (LS. NhHi. mDW 24474).

March 2   To [Nicholas Biddle].   277

March 2   To [Seth Weston]. ALS. NhHi. mDW 24477. *PC*, 2: 167–168. Discusses plans for an addition to his Marshfield house.

[c. March 2]   To Hiram Ketchum. AL (signature removed). NhD. mDW 24044. Sees no objection to publishing [Hugh?] Maxwell's letter; promises to recommend N. Berry for U.S. consul at Lyons.

March 3   To John Tyler.   277

March 3   House resolution requesting information on retail and wholesale prices in foreign markets. Printed document. DNA, RG 59. mDW 55817.

[March 4?]   From Nicholas Biddle. ALS. DLC. mDW 24484. Asks:
"Why should you resign?" and invites DW to talk about it.

March 5   To Henry Willis Kinsman.   278

March 6   To Martin Sciple. LS. NhD. mDW 24494. Replies to an inquiry concerning the validity of the "Carver claim."

March 6   To Waddy Thompson. LS. ScU. mDWs. Asks him to seek the
release of [Joseph A.] Crew, captured during the Mexican attack
on San Antonio.

March 6   To [Seth Weston]. ALS. NhHi. mDW 24495. *PC*, 2: 168–169.
Gives instructions for work at the Marshfield farm.

March 6   From F. L. Claiborne. ALS. DLC. mDW 24497. Wants to buy
a pair of Leicester sheep from DW's flock.

March 6   From James Lawrence Day. Extract. DNA, RG 46. mDW
50247. Encloses a letter complaining of the detention of an American vessel by *H.M.S. Spy.*

March 6   From Reverdy Johnson. ALS. NhD. mDW 24500. Gives assurances of his respect for DW despite their recent differences of
opinion.

March 7   To John Tyler (with ANS by Tyler). LS. DNA, RG 59. mDW
56643. Requests authorization for advances to George Brown, U.S.
commissioner to the Sandwich Islands.

March 7   From Nicholas Biddle. ALS draft. DLC. mDW 24506. Sends
some item with the enjoinder that it be shown to no one but
Fletcher.

March 7   From Lewis Cass. AL draft. MiU-C. mDW 24508. Discusses
right of search.

March 7   From Duncan Kirkland McRae. ALS. DNA, RG 59. mDW
54757. Accepts appointment as U.S. attorney for North Carolina.

March 7   Recommendations from John McLean, for a Mr. Edwards—
despatch bearer to Mexico (ALS. MWalB. mDW 24562); from San-
derson Robert, for John L. Wilson—consul, Haiti (ALS. MWalB.
mDW 24564).

March 8   To Waddy Thompson. LS. TxU. mDWs. Asks him to see if he
can win the release of George C. Hatch and John Beardley from
imprisonment in Mexico.

March 8   From John James Audubon. ALS. Albert E. Lownes, Providence, R.I. mDWs. *The Auk,* 52 (April 1935): 166. Acknowledges
a $200 draft and expresses the hope that DW will dispose of his
Birds of America only in dire financial need.

March 8   From J. Florentin Cox. ALS. DNA, RG 59. mDW 54552. Accepts appointment as justice of the peace in Washington, D.C.

March 8   From Reverdy Johnson.   278

March 8   From James Madison Porter. ALS. DNA, RG 59. mDW 54803.
Accepts appointment as secretary of war.

March 8   Application from William B. Peck—surveyor, Oregon (ALS.
MWalB. mDW 24574).

March 9   To Edward Everett. Copy. DNA, RG 46. mDW 50445. Transmits a statement and letter relating to the *Jones* case.

March 9   To [Franklin Haven]. ALS. MH-H. mDW 24576. Reports that
he has sent Healy funds to take up his $1,000 note.

March 9   To John Paul Robinson. ALS. NNC. mDWs. Urges him to help return Caleb Cushing to Congress; so doing he will "act well for the country, & well for *yourself*."

March 9   From John Tyler. ALS. DLC. mDW 24582. Suggests that "notice" be given Charles Scott Todd, minister to Russia; Washington Barrow, chargé d'affaires to Portugal; William Baber, chargé to Sardinia; Allan Hall, chargé to Venezuela; and perhaps also to William Hunter, minister to Brazil.

March 9   From Charles Anderson Wickliffe. LS. DNA, RG 59. mDW 54669. Announces William Harden's appointment as deputy postmaster in Frankfort, Ky.

March 9   Recommendations from Henry W. Andrews, for John L. Wilson (ALS. MWalB. mDW 24578); from William John Duane, for a Dr. Conway—unspecified post (ALS. MWalB. mDW 24580).

March 10   To Edward Everett. AL draft. DLC. mDW 24584. LS with postscript in DW's hand. MHi. mDW 24597. *Diplomatic Papers*, 1. Discusses Everett's appointment as U.S. commissioner to China and insists he has no desire to succeed him in London.

March 10   To John Plummer Healy.   279

March 10   From William Alexander Duer. ALS. DLC. mDW 24610. Asks DW to take charge of arranging for the publication in London of his book on constitutional jurisprudence.

March 11   To Nicholas Biddle. ALS. DLC. mDW 24614. *Diplomatic Papers*, 1. Reports the President is subjecting everything to political purposes, especially his reelection; finds his influence in the administration has dwindled and anticipates measures which will make his position untenable.

March 11   To Jared Sparks. ALS. MH-H. mDW 24619. *Diplomatic Papers*, 1. Contends that winning the prior consent of Maine and Massachusetts was his "grand stroke" in the Ashburton negotiations; reports that the appropriations needed to implement the treaty have passed Congress by substantial majorities.

March 12   To Thomas B. Curtis. ALS. DLC. mDW 24626. *Diplomatic Papers*, 1. Denies that Everett's appointment as commissioner to China was made merely to make the London mission available to himself and declares that nothing could induce him to go abroad.

March 12   To Peleg Sprague. ALS. MDuHi. mDWs. Reports that appropriations for the Treaty of Washington have been approved by Congress.

March 12   To Seth Weston. ALS. NhHi. mDW 24634. *PC*, 2: 169–170. Discusses the reconditioning of an old pasture and asks him to make sure the boats are ready.

March 13   To Thomas B. Curtis.   280

March 13   From Richard Key Watts. ALS. DNA, RG 59. mDW 54883. Accepts appointment as justice of the peace in the District of Columbia.

March 13   Recommendation from Thomas W. Williams, for John J. Hyde (ALS. MWalB. mDW 24641).

March 14   To Caleb Cushing. ALS. DLC. mDW 24644. Urges that he advise Tyler against making removals in Massachusetts except on Cushing's recommendation.

March 14   To John Tappan. LS. MWiW. mDW 24646. Informs him that a despatch bag and box will be handed him for delivery to the secretary of the Board of Trade in London.

March 14   From Abel Parker Upshur. ALS. NhHi. mDW 24649. Encloses the draft of his instructions to Matthew Calbraith Perry for DW's perusal.

March 14   From William Waters. ALS. DNA, RG 59. mDW 54879. Accepts appointment as justice of the peace in Washington, D.C.

March 14   Application from Jesse E. Dow—compilation of the *Biennial Register* (ALS. MWalB. mDW 24647).

March 15   Recommendations from Hugh Birckhead, for John S. Lafitte—consul, China (ALS. MWalB. mDW 24651); from Courtland Cushing, for Richard H. Betts—consul, Matamoras (ALS. MWalB. mDW 24654).

March 16   To Lewis Cass. Printed. Curtis, 2: 197. Acknowledges Cass's letter of March 7.

March 16   To the Minister for Foreign Affairs of Hawaii. Copy (in Hawaiian). H-Ar. mDW 24659. Announces George Brown's appointment as U.S. commissioner to the Hawaiian Islands.

March 16   To [John Tyler]. LS. DNA, RG 59. mDW 56645. Requests authorization for advances to be made to Albert Smith.

March 16   To [John Tyler] (with ANS by Tyler and receipt for $1,000 received from Edward Stubbs, March 16, 1843). LS. DNA, RG 59. mDW 56647. Requests authority to draw $1,000 from the contingent fund for obtaining documents, etc., relating to Mexican claims.

March 16   From John Tyler. ALS. DLC. mDW 24665. *Diplomatic Papers*, 1. Expresses approval of the proposed extradition treaty with Prussia, providing it excludes "constructive crimes arising out of political offenses."

March 16   Receipt for $1,000 from Edward Stubbs. DS. DNA, RG 59. mDW 56648.

March 16   Recommendation from R. P. Crocker, for Stephen Powers—consul, Basel (ALS. MWalB. mDW 24662).

March 17   From Josiah Quincy. Press copy. MH-Ar. mDW 24687. Asks for the return of books and maps loaned the government by Harvard College.

March 18   To [Jared Sparks]. ALS. MH-H. mDW 24690. Van Tyne, p. 287. Replies to insinuations in the London *Morning Chronicle* by stating that his expressed confidence in the U.S. boundary claims was based on the treaty and not on the evidence of "the map."

March 18   From Ralph Randolph Gurley. ALS. DNA, RG 59. mDW 55742. Stresses the need for continuing U.S. support and protection of Liberia.

March 18   From Waddy Thompson. ALS. DLC. mDW 24694. *Diplomatic Papers*, 1. Reports on the pending release of George Crittenden and also on the treatment of other prisoners.

March 18   Recommendation from Zachrisson & Co., for Ernest Zachrisson—transmission of mail to the Pacific (LS. MWalB. mDW 24701).

March 19   From Albert Smith. ALS. DLC. mDW 24704. Discusses the

selection of someone to direct "the scientific corps" in the marking
of the boundary established under the Treaty of Washington.

March 20 To Edward Everett. LS. MHi. mDW 24706. Encloses issues
of the *Intelligencer* containing an article on the map Sparks found
in Paris.

March 20 To John Plummer Healy. LS. MHi. mDW 24714. Summarizes the question of Mexican claims, which he hopes Healy
will manage.

March 20 To [Albert Smith]. ALS. DLC. mDW 24719. Reports that
George Ashmun declines to serve with the boundary surveyors.

March 20 From George S. Curson. ALS. DNA, RG 59. mDW 56485. Reports having delivered his despatches to Waddy Thomson.

March 20 From Andrew Stevenson. ALS. DLC. mDW 24721. Introduces Thomas McIntosh, who is anxious to accompany Everett to
China.

March 20 From Charles Anderson Wickliffe. LS. DNA, RG 59. mDW
54877. Announces the appointment of postmasters for Albany and
Schenectady.

March 20 Power of attorney to Jacob Le Roy and Edward Le Roy re
the estate of Herman Le Roy. DS. NN. mDW 39880.

March 21 To Edward Webster. ALS. NhHi. mDW 24723. PC, 2: 171.
Advises him to accept the post offered by Albert Smith and to inform Smith also that there is mail for him at the Boston Post Office.

March 21 From Albert Smith. ALS. DLC. mDW 24727. Accepts appointment as commissioner under Article Six of the Treaty of
Washington.

March 21 From John Tyler. ALS. DLC. mDW 24729. Reports having
decided to appoint John G. Dischler U.S. attorney for Iowa.

March 21 Recommendation from James Madison Porter, for Pollard E.
Birckhead (Copy. NhHi. mDW 24725).

March 22 To Albert Smith. Copy. NhHi. mDW 24731. Indentifies the
U.S. Army officers who will assist in marking the boundary described in Article One of the Treaty of Washington.

March 22 From George Frederick Bown (enclosed with John I. De
Wolfe to DW, May 4, 1843). ADS. NhHi. mDW 25039. Petitions
against being replaced as consular agent in St. Johns, Newfoundland; recommends appointment of a consul for Newfoundland, and
suggests himself for the position.

March 22 From James E. Harvey. ALS. MWalB. mDW 24733. Requests
a copy or extract from William Campbell Preston's letter recommending him for a western appointment.

[*March 23*] *From Charles Pelham Curtis.* 281

March 23 From Charles Murray. ALS. DNA, RG 76. mDWs. Encloses
letters concerning claims by the heirs of [John] Paul Jones.

March 23 From Charles Anderson Wickliffe. LS. DNA, RG 59. mDW
54524. Announces James Brooks's appointment as deputy postmaster at Dayton, O.

March 24 To James Madison Porter. Copy. NhHi. mDW 24738. Calls
attention to the application of George Dana, Jr., for appointment
to the U.S. Military Academy.

March 24 To John Tyler (with ANS by Tyler; receipt for $1,000. [c.

March 24]). LS. DNA, RG 59. mDW 56649. Asks that the State Department's agent be authorized to advance him $1,000 from the con-
tingent fund.

March 24   From James Madison Porter. ALS. NhHi. mDW 24739. Gives
assurances that George Dana, Jr., will be appointed to the U.S. Military Academy.

[March 24]   Editorial on the Convention of 1824. Printed. *National
Intelligencer*, March 25, 1843.

[c. March 24]   Receipt for $1,000 (with ANS by Edward Stubbs, July
21, 1843). ADS. DNA, RG 59. mDW 56652.

March 25   To Henry L. Sheldon. LS. VtMiS. mDW 24741. Regrets being
unable to comply with Sheldon's request concerning the distribution
of the compendium of the Sixth Census.

March 25   From George S. Curson. ALS. DNA, RG 59. mDW 56488.
Reports on George Crittenden's situation, the release of Judge Anderson Hutchinson, and Waddy Thompson's delicate health and irritable mood.

March 25   Bill for seeds purchased from William Skirving, Liverpool.
Copy. NhHi. mDW 24838.

March 27   To Caleb Cushing.   282

March 27   To James D. Graham (enclosure: DW to Albert Smith,
March 22, 1843). Copy. DNA, RG 60. mDWs. Encloses his letter informing Albert Smith of Graham's appointment to head the scientific corps attached to the boundary expedition.

March 27   To [James Madison Porter]. Copy. DNA, RG 92. mDWs. Asks
him to detail two army officers, skilled in astronomy and surveying,
to the scientific corps assigned to the boundary expedition.

March 27   From Francis Bowen. ALS. NhD. mDW 24745. Encloses,
with comment, prepublication copy of Sparks' article on the Treaty
of Washington and asks about someone to write on American-
Mexican relations.

March 27   From Edward Kavanagh. LC. Me. mDW 24748. Writes concerning the compensation due Maine under the Treaty of Washington for the civil posse it maintained to deal with the boundary crisis.

March 28   From John Pope.   282

March 28   From John Tyler. LS. DNA, RG 59. mDW 55836. Authorizes
DW to exchange ratifications of the convention with Mexico of Jan
30, 1843.

March 29   To Edward Everett. ALS. MHi. mDW 24767. *Diplomatic
Papers*, 1. Denies Nathan Hale's view that Everett's appointment to
the China mission was intended to make room for him in London
and declares that he does not want to be sent on any mission.

March 29   To Edward Everett. LS. MHi. mDW 24771. Introduces the
Reverend Charles C. Beatty.

March 29   To Edward Everett. LS. Uk. mDW 24772. AL copy. MHi.
mDW 24708. *PC*, 2: 170–171. Points to difficulties in negotiating
a treaty of commerce with Britain; thinks Washington should be
the site of the negotiations.

March 30   To Albert Smith. Copy. NhHi. mDW 24775. Informs him
that five officers, not three as previously stated, will be assigned to
the scientific corps attached to the boundary commission.

March 30   From John J. Abert. Copy. DLC. mDW 24778. Names the officers who have been detailed to the boundary expedition.

March 30   From Jared Sparks. ALS. DLC. mDW 24782. Discusses his article on the Treaty of Washington; comments further on the map controversy.

March 30   From John Tyler. ALS. DLC. mDW 24786. States that he has decided to send George H. Proffit to Rio de Janeiro and asks that Proffit and the incumbent U.S. minister, William Hunter, be so informed.

March 30   From Charles Anderson Wickliffe. LS. DNA, RG 59. mDW 54620. Announces Joseph Ficklin's appointment as deputy postmaster in Lexington, Ky.

March 31   To Caleb Cushing. ALS. DLC. mDW 24788. Asks Cushing to wait for him in Massachusetts.

March 31   To Alphonso Taft. LS. DLC. mDW 24790. Encloses a copy of his Faneuil Hall speech for reference to his views on "relief of the states."

March 31   To Seth Weston. ALS. NhHi. mDW 24791. Van Tyne, p. 674. Asks Weston to have things in readiness for his arrival at Marshfield on April 7.

March 31   From Edward Everett. LC. MHi. mDW 20485. *Diplomatic Papers*, 1. Writes on map controversy.

March 31   From Crawford W. Hall. ALS. DNA, RG 59. mDW 54663. Accepts appointment as U.S. attorney for eastern Tennessee.

March   From Benjamin Glover Shields (enclosed with DW to Waddy Thompson, April 1, 1843) Copy. ScU. mDWs. Asks him to intercede for George C. Hatch, captured by the Mexicans at San Antonio.

[March ?]   To [?]. ALS incomplete. DLC. mDW 24019. Denies that appointing Albert Smith as boundary commissioner was intended to slight Edward Kent.

[March–May]   From John Tyler. ALS. DLC. mDW 21108. Advises concerning the appointment of U.S. consuls for Rotterdam and Matamoros.

April 1   To Jacob Idler. LS. NN. mDW 24820. Discusses Idler's claim against Venezuela.

April 1   To Waddy Thompson (enclosure: Benjamin Glover Shields to DW, March 1843). LS. ScU. mDWs. Asks him to seek the release or relief of George C. Hatch, captured during the Mexican raid on San Antonio.

April 1   From Moses C. Good. ALS. DNA, RG 59. mDW 54649. Accepts appointment as U.S. attorney for western Virginia.

April 2   To Francis Bowen.   284

April 2   To Albert Smith. ALS. DLC. mDW 24824. Discusses the work and personnel of the boundary commission; advises that he will be available in Boston for consultation.

April 3   To [Caleb Cushing]. ALS. DLC. mDW 24827. States that he expects to be in Boston on Thursday morning, April 6.

April 3   From Edward Everett. LC. MHi. mDW 24829. *Diplomatic Papers*, 1. Expresses misgivings about accepting the China mission and asks for time to think it over.

April 3   From Edward Harden. ALS. DNA, RG 59. mDW 54667. Accepts appointment as U.S. marshal for Georgia.

April 3   From William Skirving (enclosure: bill from William Skirving, March 25). ALS. NhHi. mDW 24834. Describes the order of seeds and a plow he is shipping to DW.

April 3   From Andrew Talcott. ALS. DNA, RG 59. mDW 56842. Encloses a bill from J. W. Glass, Jr., for expenses connected with the northeast boundary survey.

April 4   From Albert Smith. ALS. DLC. mDW 24839. States that in surveying the boundary he will carry out Aberdeen's and Webster's views.

April 5   To Edward Everett. ALS. MHi. mDW 24841. Introduces J. Smyth Rogers of New York.

April 5   From Nicholas Biddle, with enclosure: memorandum on DW's resignation.   284

April 6   From James Laurenson to DFW. ALS. DNA, RG 59. mDW 54726. Accepts appointment as justice of the peace for Washington, D.C.

April 7   From Francis Ormand Jonathan Smith, with enclosure: Smith to John Tyler, April 7.   286

April 7   From Alphonso Taft.   291

April 9   To Daniel Fletcher Webster. ALS. NhHi. mDW 24855. Van Tyne, p. 287. Reports his arrival in Marshfield; notes the discovery in New York of a map "important, to the right side."

April 10   From Daniel Fletcher Webster. ALS. NhHi. mDW 24858. Reports that the President has ordered that [William S.?] Murphy be provided a $2,500 outfit.

April 11   From Charles Anderson Wickliffe. ALS. DNA, RG 59. mDW 54546. Reports Enoch C. Chapman's appointment as deputy postmaster at Norwich, Conn.

April 13   To [Caleb T.?] Symmes. ALS. DLC. mDW 24862. Orders the next dividend on his shares paid to Seth Weston.

April 13   To Daniel Fletcher Webster. ALS. COMC. mDW 24864. Thinks Tyler erred in ordering an outfit for Murphy.

April 14   To Horace Mann. ALS. MHi. mDW 24867. Appoints him bearer of despatches and explains the conditions of the appointment.

April 14   From Henry St. George Tucker. ALS. NhHi. mDW 24871. Describes a British map found in the Richmond library which supports the American interpretation of the northeast boundary.

April 15   From George S. Curson. ALS. DNA, RG 59. mDW 56490. Reports preparing to embark at Acapulco for Callao.

April 15   To John Tyler from DFW with ANS by John Tyler, April 15, 1843. LS. DNA, RG 59. mDW 56655. Asks Tyler to authorize advances to Baring Brothers from appropriations under the secretary of state's control.

April 16   To Warren Delano.   294

April 16   To Daniel Fletcher Webster. ALS. NhHi. mDW 24877. Van Tyne, p. 288. Introduces Warren Delano, Jr., who wants Fletcher to stay with him during his visit to China.

April 16   From John G. Deshler. ALS. DNA, RG 59. mDW 54574. Accepts appointment as U.S. attorney in Iowa.
April 16   From George Folsom. ALS. NhD. mDW 24879. Thanks DW for his remarks to the New-York Historical Society on April 15 concerning the northeast boundary and asks for a copy for publication.
April 17   From John A. Bryan. LS. DNA, RG 59. mDW 54506. Announces Abraham J. Berry's appointment as postmaster at Princeton, N.J.
April 18   From James Duane Doty. ALS. DLC. mDW 24887. Reports that George Wallace Jones's suit has been settled in DW's favor.
April 18   From Edward Everett. ALS. MHi. mDW 24893. *Diplomatic Papers*, 1. Comments on the U.S. mission to China and his reasons for deciding not to accept it.
April 18   From Edward Everett.   295
April 18   From William Beach Lawrence. ALS. NhD. mDW 24906. Asks DW to select the most accurate among the newspaper reports of his remarks to the New-York Historical Society, for publication in the Society's proceedings.
April 18   From Isaac Leffler. ALS. DNA, RG 59. mDW 54732. Acknowledges appointment as U.S. marshal for Iowa.
April 18   From Charles Anderson Wickliffe. LS. DNA, RG 59. mDW 54570. Reports John B. Dawson has been appointed deputy postmaster at New Orleans.
April 19   Application from P. A. Sage & Company, for the Washington *German in America* and *German National Gazette*—public printers (LS. DNA, RG 59. mDW 53497).
April 20   To [?]. ALS. CtHi. mDW 2856. Acknowledges an invitation to meet his Baltimore friends on some convenient occasion.
April 20   From Nicholas Biddle.   295
April 20   From William Campbell Preston to DFW. ALS. DNA, RG 59. mDW 53493. Asks that the publisher of the Columbia, South Carolina, *Southern Chronicle* be paid for printing the laws.
April 20   From Jared Sparks.   297
April 21   To [Joseph] Travers. ALS. NhD. mDWs. Hopes he will come to Washington so that "some satisfactory and definite arrangement" may be made concerning DW's debt to him.
April 21   From Lawrence Kearney (enclosure: James P. Sturgis to Kearney, April 20, 1843). LS. DNA, RG 59. mDW 55749. Recommends changes in the U.S. consulate at Macao; notes the extensive involvement of American merchants in the opium trade and the difficulty of suppressing it.
April 21   From Isaac Leffler. ALS. DNA, RG 59. mDW 54734. Accepts appointment as U.S. marshal for Iowa.
April 22   To William Beach Lawrence (enclosure: note on northeastern boundary map). ALS. NHi. mDW 24917. *Diplomatic Papers*, 1. Encloses a note on the Oswald map for possible publication with DW's remarks to the New-York Historical Society on the northeast boundary.
April 22   To Francis Robert Rives.   297
April 22   From John W. Fenno. ALS. NhHi. mDW 24926. Encloses an

article on DW written by Edwin P. Whipple, brother of the applicant for U.S. consul at St. Johns.

April 23, 28   To Edward Everett. ALS. MHi. mDW 24908. *Diplomatic Papers*, 1. Discusses the China mission, special mission on Oregon, and his impending resignation.

April 24   To George Folsom. LS. NHi. mDW 24928. Reports that he is forwarding a corrected report of his remarks to the New-York Historical Society for publication.

April 24   To William Beach Lawrence. LS. NHi. mDW 24929. *Diplomatic Papers*, 1. Agrees with Peel that the evidence from the maps re the northeast boundary is inconclusive.

April 24   From Nicholas Biddle. ALS draft. DLC. mDW 24931. Declares: "None but the very blind can now avoid seeing the fate which lies before him unless he turns round."

April 24   From Thomas Chambers.   298

April 24   From John Tyler to DFW. LS. DNA, RG 59. mDW 55838. Appoints him secretary to the special mission to China.

April 25   To Edward Everett. AL draft. DLC. mDW 24936. LS. MHi. mDW 24944. *Diplomatic Papers*, 1. Comments on the map controversy and argues that the maps afford significant but inconclusive evidence as to the location of the boundary.

April 25   To Josiah Quincy. LS. MH-Ar. mDW 24952. Returns books and maps belonging to Harvard College and promises that the State Department will reimburse the college for missing items.

April 25   From Christopher Hughes. ALS. DLC. mDW 24954. *Diplomatic Papers*, 1. Reports the pleas of Dutch holders of American state bonds; notes the general odium in which American credit is held in Holland.

April 25   From Henry St. George Tucker. ALS. NhHi. mDW 24958. Discusses his findings on the northeastern boundary question.

April 25   From John Tyler. AL. DLC. mDW 24962. *Diplomatic Papers*, 1. Expresses support for an extradition treaty with France, providing it excludes political offenses.

April 25   Credentials for Daniel Fletcher Webster, secretary to the China mission. AD. DNA, RG 59. mDW 57033.

April 26   To Nathaniel Chapman et al. LS. PPAmP. mDW 24965. Acknowledges an invitation to the Centennial Anniversary of the American Philosophical Society.

April 26   To Edward Everett. ALS. MHi. mDW 22268. Asks that the enclosed be read to Aberdeen.

April 26   From Edward Everett. ALS. MHi. mDW 24970. Reports a conversation with Peel on the subject of a commercial treaty.

[April 26]   Editorial on the slave trade. AD. NN. mDW 24984. *National Intelligencer*, April 26, 1843.

April 27   To Edward Everett. LS. MHi. mDW 24974. Copy. Uk. mDWs. Curtis, 2: 165–166. Speaks critically of Horace Everett; outlines U.S. policy on the seizure of American vessels engaged in the slave trade, and encloses copies of *National Intelligencer* of March 25 and April 26.

April 27   To Edward Everett. LS. MHi. mDW 24979. Introduces Joseph Sampson.

April 27   To Washington Irving. LS. NhD. mDW 24980. Introduces
Charles Handy Russell.

April 27   To Henry Ledyard. LS. RNR. mDW 24981. Introduces Charles
Handy Russell.

April 27   To D. S. Swain. LS. Nc-Ar. mDWs. Promises to forward volumes for the University of North Carolina library.

April 27   To Andrew Talcott (with James D. Graham to Talcott, May
20, 1843). LS. MoHi. mDW 24982. Asks him to deliver instruments
to James D. Graham for the use of the joint boundary commission.

April 27   From Edward Everett. LC. MHi. mDW 24990. *Diplomatic
Papers*, 1. Reports Aberdeen's reaction to DW's observations on the
right of visit and search.

April 27   Receipt for $1,000 from Duff Green. DS. DNA, RG 59. mDW
56650.

April 28   To Samuel Rossiter Betts. LS. CtY. mDW 25000. Promises to
forward a set of the *Biennial Register*, as complete as possible.

April 28   To Edward Everett. ALS. MHi. mDW 25001. Reports that the
President will act only on Everett's "advice & direction."

April 28   To Edward Everett. ALS. MHi. mDW 25003. States that Duff
Green is again going to England on business.

April 28   To John Powell. LS. H. Bartholomew Cox, Oxon Hill, Md.
mDW 25006. Acknowledges Powell's letter assigning his claims
against Mexico to his brother Thomas Powell.

April 28   From Alexander Baring, Lord Ashburton. ALS. NhHi. mDW
25798. *PC*, 2: 190–193. Reports that British reaction to the treaty
is generally favorable, except for the extradition article.

April 28   From Putnam I. Farnham & Company. LS. DNA, RG 76.
mDWs. Summarize the history of the *Jones* case and appeal to the
U.S. government to correct "this monstrous wrong!"

April 28   From P. A. Sage and Alfred Schücking. ALS by Sage, signed
also by Schücking. DNA, RG 59. mDW 53090. Accept appointment
to print the laws in the *German in America* and the *German National Gazette.*

April 28   From David Sears et al. ALS by Sears, signed also by others.
NhD. mDW 25007. *National Intelligencer*, May 27, 1843. Stress
the importance of DW's remaining active in public affairs after he
leaves the State Department.

April 29   To Thomas B. Curtis. ALS. NhD. mDW 25010. *Diplomatic
Papers*, 1. Thinks G. T. Curtis has done him justice in a recent article; expects to be back "among you" within a month.

April 29   From Edward Kavanagh. LC. Me. mDW 25013. Writes concerning a resolution of the Maine legislature dealing with the disputed territory fund.

April 29   Special passport for William S. Campbell, U.S. consul for Rotterdam. DS. DNA, RG 59. mDW 57034.

[April]   To Caleb Cushing. ALS. DLC. mDW 25015. Asks him to be at
the President's by 7:30.

May 1   To Hiram Ketchum. Printed extract. *Seventy-second anniversary of the birthday of Daniel Webster, celebrated by a number of
his personal friends, at the Astor House . . . January 18, 1854* (New

York, 1854), p. 20. Reports he will be leaving the State Department within a few days "altogether against my own judgment."

May 1   *To [John Taylor].*   299
May 1   Special passport for John Parrott. DS. DNA, RG 59. mDW 57035.
May 2   To Edward Everett. LS. MHi. mDW 25029. Introduces David Leavitt of New York.
May 2   To John Canfield Spencer. Copy. DNA, RG 217. mDW 57204. Encloses a letter from the French minister at Washington requesting the refund of duties levied on a French ship at Portland.
May 2   From George Lethbridge Saunders. ALS. DLC. mDW 25030. Asks him to sit for a miniature.
May 2   To Edward Stubbs from DFW, (with receipt for vouchers, Feb 6, 1843). ALS. DNA, RG 59. mDW 56846. Encloses $600 for models and the daguerreotype to be charged to the fund appropriated for the China mission.
[May 2?]   To Richard Milford Blatchford. Printed. *PC*, 2: 222–223 (misdated April 29, 1846). Writes that next week he will throw off the burden of public responsibility.
May 3   To John Plummer Healy. ALS. MHi. mDW 25033. Asks him to attend to certain matters and to have the office ready for his arrival.
May 3   *To Mary Ann Sanborn.*   300
May 3   *To David Sears et al.*   301
May 3   Promissory note for $1,100 payable to Isaac P. Davis. DS. MHi. mDW 39884.
May 4   To Edward Everett. LS. MHi. mDW 25037. Introduces Henry D. Maxwell.
May 4   To Richard Smith. ALS. UPB. mDWs. Encloses a letter to [Edward?] Curtis, which Smith is to read and seal up; states "Mr Nicholls knows all about the Arkansas land"; asks for the discounting of Thomas Cookendorfer's $1000 draft.
May 4   From Edward Kavanagh. LC. Me. mDW 25043. Finds references to the disputed territory fund in a British despatch too vague for comment and suggests that the authorities in New Brunswick furnish additional explanation.
May 4   From Samuel Weir. ALS with AN by DW. DNA, RG 59. mDW 53491. Asks if he should continue publishing the laws in the Columbia *Southern Chronicle.*
May 4   From Charles Anderson Wickliffe. LS. DNA, RG 59. mDW 54761. Reports Jacob K. Mead's appointment as deputy postmaster at Newark, N.J.
May 4   From Charles Anderson Wickliffe. Copy. DNA, RG 28. mDW 57065. Discusses postage charged the Mexican consul at New York.
May 4   Recommendation from John I. De Wolfe, for George Frederick Bown—consul, Newfoundland (ALS. NhHi. mDW 25038).
May 4   From Edward Stubbs to DFW. ALS. DNA, RG 59. mDW 56567. Acknowledges DFW's check to pay for models and the daguerreotypes to be sent with the China mission.
May 5   Warranty deed transferring property in Marshfield, Mass., from DW to Joseph P. Cushman. Copy. Deed Book 210: 142. Register of Deeds, Plymouth County, Massachusetts. mDWs.

May 6   To Edward Everett. LS. MHi. mDW 25044. Introduces James H.
Behan of Norfolk, Va.

May 6   From Robert Myers. ALS. DNA, RG 59. mDW 54775. Accepts appointment as U.S. marshal for the Apalachicola District of Florida.

May 6   From James Madison Porter. Copy. DNA, RG 46. mDW 52124. Encloses a report by the superintendent of Indian Affairs at St. Louis.

May 6   From Andrew Talcott. ALS. DNA, RG 59. mDW 56848. Encloses expense account for services rendered the northeast boundary survey by
W. A. Eliason.

[May 8]   To Edward Curtis. ALS. NN. mDW 27519. Is sitting for portraits
by George P.A. Healy and George Lethbridge Saunders; will attend a lecture on China in the evening.

May 8   To Caleb Cushing. Copy. DLC. mDW 25045. Lists credentials and
other arrangements made to accommodate Cushing's mission to
China.

May 8   To Edward Everett. LS. ViU. mDW 25053. Introduces George F.
Leitch of New York.

May 8   To John Tyler. Copy. DLC. mDW 25054. Recommends Zachariah
Jellison for U.S. consul at Rio de Janeiro.

May 8   To John Tyler. ALS. DNA, RG 59. mDW 55571. *Diplomatic Papers*,
1. Resigns as secretary of state.

May 8   From Charles R. Belt. ALS. DNA, RG 59. mDW 54502. Accepts appointment as justice of the peace for Washington, D.C.

May 8   From Jesse E. Dow. ALS. DNA, RG 59. mDW 54596. Accepts appointment as justice of the peace in the District of Columbia.

May 8   From John Tyler. ALS. DLC. mDW 25059. Decides that Henry M.
Rector should be appointed U.S. marshal for Arkansas.

May 8   From John Tyler. Copy. DLC. mDW 25063. *Diplomatic Papers*, 1.
Accepts DW's resignation.

May 8   Special passport for Caleb Cushing. DS. DNA, RG 59. mDW 57030.

May 9   From Robert Gilmor et al. LS. DLC. mDW 25064. Invite DW to a
public dinner in his honor at Baltimore.

May 9   Application from John S. Lafitte (ALS. MWalB. wDW 25066).

May 9   Receipt for book borrowed from the Department of State library. DS.
UkLU. mDW 25068.

May 10   To [Edward Curtis?]. ALS. NN. mDW 25069. Reports that Caleb
Cushing has gone to Baltimore to wait for Fletcher; plans to leave Washington within a week.

May 10   To Mrs. Edward Curtis. Printed. PC, 2 : 172. Thanks her for note on
the barber's pole and describes preparations for his departure from
Washington.

May 10   To Nathaniel F. Williams. ALS. NhD. mDW 25070. Promises
to provide for an acceptance.

May 11   To Nathaniel F. Williams. LS. NhD. mDW 25072. Requests information on commerce passing through the port of Baltimore.

May 12   To Edward Everett.   303

May 12   To Edward Everett. ALS. MHi. mDW 25079. *Diplomatic Papers*,
1. Stresses the nonofficial character of Duff Green's trip to England;
reports the President's high regard for Everett; calls the Everett and
Irving appointments "the principal monuments of *my* administration of the Dept."

May 12   From Weston F. Birch. ALS. DNA, RG 59. mDW 54508. Accepts
appointment as U.S. marshal for Missouri.

[*May 12*]   *Editorial on DW's resignation as secretary of state.*   304

[May 12?]   To Nathaniel F. Williams. ALS. NhD. mDW 25165. Sends
him a $1,000 check and asks that the endorsed draft be returned.

May 13   From Josiah Quincy. ALS copy. MH-Ar. mDW 25089. Suggests
that the government furnish Harvard with other maps to replace
those which have been lost.

May 14   From Alexander P. Field. ALS. NhHi. mDW 25092. Asks to know
what charges have been leveled against him and gives assurances of his
loyalty to DW and to Tyler.

May 14   From Christopher Hughes. ALS. NhD. mDW 25095. Describes the
depressed state of American credit and national prestige in Holland.

May 15   To Albert Smith. ALS. DLC. mDW 25099. Reports on the arrangements he made for the payment of Smith's fees; asks if Edward might
visit his brother in Boston.

May 15   Agreement with Charles F. Sibbald and John Connell to
represent Sibbald's claim before the government. DS. NhHi. mDW
25101.

May 15   From Andrew Talcott (enclosure: inventory of camp equipage used
in the survey of the northeast boundary, May 15, 1843). ALS. DNA, RG
59. mDW 56850. Encloses an inventory of equipment on hand from the
northeast boundary survey.

[May 16]   To Edward Everett. LS. MHi. mDW 25104. Explains his reaction
to Aberdeen's note of Dec 21, 1841, regarding the right of visit and search.

[c. May 16]   Editorial on right of search. AD. NhD. mDW 24026. *National
Intelligencer*, May 16, 1843.

May 17   To [Edward?] Curtis. ALS. DLC. mDW 25118. Encloses an extract
from a letter recently received from Everett; reports he will be leaving
Washington this afternoon.

May 17   To Richard Smith. ALS. UPB. mDWs. States he is "ready to make
any assignment, or give any order" and asks him to send the proper
papers to the New York Custom House—DW will execute and return
them.

May 17   Promissory note from Charles Huntt to DW for $40. DS. NhHi. mDW
39886.

May 18   From Edward Everett. ALS. MHi. mDW 25123. Comments on Duff
Green's activity in London, complaining that it has placed him in an
awkward position.

May 19   To Nathaniel F. Williams. ALS. NhD. mDW 25130. States that William's acceptance for $1,000 has been "filled at 6 months."

May 19   Promissory note for $755.63 payable to Joseph Travers. DS. MHi.
mDW 39888.

May 22   To Isaac P. Davis. ALS. MWalB. mDW 25132. Promises to send him
copies of the Baltimore speech; calls for immediate publication of Davis's
letter and his reply as an explanation of "New England sentiments."

May 22   From John Tyler. Printed. *William and Mary Quarterly*, 18 (Jan
1910): 172–173. Believes Aberdeen erred in his interpretation of DW's
view of the right of search; comments on DW's objection to Dr. Martin's
appointment as chief clerk at the State Department.

May 22   From Jesse Lynch Williams et al. LS. NhD. mDW 25135. Invite him to ceremonies in celebration of the opening of the Wabash & Erie Canal.

May 24   From Waddy Thompson. ALS draft. TxU. mDWs. Protests the Treasury Department's decision to charge to his personal account a $6,000 draft for the expense of sending Texas prisoners home.

May 27   From Harrison Gray Otis et al. ALS by Otis, signed also by others. NhD. mDW 25137. Transmit resolutions of appreciation and also an invitation to a public dinner to be held in DW's honor at Faneuil Hall.

May 28   To Edward Everett.   306

May 28   To John Gibson Lockhart. ALS. NN. mDW 25145. Introduces Thurlow Weed.

May 30   From Joshua Bates.   306

May 31   From Edward Everett. ALS. MHi. mDW 25159. Comments on DW's resignation and the appointment of Cushing as commissioner to China; expects that Great Britain will disavow the occupation of the Sandwich Islands.

[May]   To [Caleb Cushing]. ALS. DLC. mDW 25163. Invites Cushing to dinner.

May 1843–March 1847   Memorandum of legal fees. AD. MHi. mDW 25167.

June 7   To Caleb Cushing. ALS. DLC. mDW 25188. Introduces Thomas Newbold Smith, who is going to China.

June 9   To Jesse Lynch Williams et al. ALS. InHi. mDWs. Declines an invitation to the opening of the Erie & Wabash canal; comments on the significance of the project.

June 15   To George Ticknor. ALS. NhD. mDW 39065. Requests a short conference with Ticknor.

June 17   From Judah Lee Bliss (with reply by DW, [Dec 1843] and memorandum by Bliss, Nov 10, 1852, and Nov 8, 1870). ALS copy. CtY. mDW 25257. Requests an autographed excerpt from DW's reply to Hayne.

June 17   From Edward Everett. ALS. MHi. mDW 25265. Reports that DW's remarks on trade in Baltimore became the occasion for a debate in the House of Commons; disagrees with DW's interpretation of the Oswald and Jay maps.

June 17   From John MacGregor.   307

June 18   From John Perkins Cushing. ALS. DLC. mDW 25277. Invites the ladies in the President's party and others to inspect his grounds.

June 19   Warranty deed transferring property in Marshfield, Mass., from DW to Charles P. Wright, Jr. Copy. Deed Book 210: 120. Register of Deeds, Plymouth County, Massachusetts. mDWs.

June 20   To John Tyler. ALS. NcD. mDW 25279. Reports the death of Hugh Swinton Legaré.

June 21   From Lewis Condict (with AN by DW). ALS. NhD. mDW 25280. Requests DW to use his influence to win the release of Israel Canfield from imprisonment in Mexico.

June 26   From Edward Everett. AL. MHi. mDW 25286. Reports a conversation with Aberdeen on discrepancy between DW's recollection and that of Lord Ashburton as to what had passed between them in reference to Aberdeen's letter to Everett of Dec 20, 1841; reports also conversing with William Ewart Gladstone on the idea of a commercial treaty; blames English abolitionists for delaying the enactment of an extradition law.

June 27   To Waddy Thompson. ALS. ScU. mDWs. Encloses a letter from
Lewis Condict and asks him to assist Israel Canfield.

June 28   To Francis Ormand Jonathan Smith. ALS. MeHi. mDW 25290. Asks
him to come to Boston to arrange some business and to discuss public
affairs.

June 28   Promissory note to Ebenezer Trescott for $308.46. DS (with signa-
ture crossed out). MHi. mDW 39890.

[June 29]   To John Plummer Healy. ALS. MHi. mDW 25292. Expects to be
in Boston by Sunday and asks that his mail be held there.

June 30   To Corcoran & Riggs. ALS. Riggs National Bank, Washington, D.C.
mDWs. Reports having drawn on them for $500 and asks if he may draw
up to $1,200.

July 3   To Edward Everett. ALS. MHi. mDW 25294. Introduces William P.
Winchester of Boston.

July 3   To John Tyler. Printed. Curtis, 2: 212. Explains his objections to Dr.
M[artin]'s appointment as chief clerk at the State Department and also
his reasons for not delivering the commission appointing "Mr. J———"
consul at Matanzas.

July 3, 1843–Jan 5, 1845   Account with Samuel Frothingham. DS. NhHi.
mDW 39985.

[July 4]   Resolutions regarding Webster and the temperance movement (with
Josiah Moore to Theodore Parker, Feb 17, 1853). Copy. DLC. mDWs.

July 8   To Francis Ormand Jonathan Smith. ALS. MeHi. mDW 25297. Reports that the change in a trial date has postponed his trip to Boston
and asks to meet him there on some later day.

July 8   From George S. Curson. ALS. DNA, RG 59. mDW 56493. Reports
having delivered the treaty with Peru for the adjustment of American claims to James C. Pickett, U.S. chargé d'affaires to Peru.

July 8   From John Tyler.   308

July 13   To the Emperor of China from John Tyler (based on draft by
DW). Printed. Fuess, *Cushing*, 2: 419–420. Extends greetings and
proposes that the United States and China negotiate a treaty of
commerce.

[July 19]   To John Plummer Healy. ALS. MHi. mDW 25303. Asks that a report that he is to address the Dartmouth alumni be denied in newspapers.

July 20   To Edward Everett. ALS. MHi. mDW 25306. Introduces Reverdy
Johnson, Jr.

July 25   To John Plummer Healy. ALS. MHi. mDW 25307. Asks him to
take care of some financial matters; reports he will be leaving for
Hanover, N.H., this afternoon.

Aug 1   To [?]. ALS. NhD. mDW 25309. Asks if John Taylor might buy some
property from the addressee's mother.

Aug 2   From Edward Everett. ALS. MHi. mDW 25315. Reports that no
progress has been made toward a commercial agreement with Great
Britain.

Aug 5   To John Eliot Thayer. ALS. MHi. mDW 25319. Asks that any retainer
arranged for with a Mr. Prentiss be paid to John Plummer Healy.

[p/m Aug 10]   To John Plummer Healy. ALS. MHi. mDW 38570. Complains of "slow progress" in the trial at Concord of *Commonwealth
v. Wyman*, 8 Metcalf 247 (1844).

Aug 10   From Reverdy Johnson. ALS. DLC. mDW 25320. Suggests they
meet for consultations on a case.

Aug 14   To [Josiah Moore].   310

[Aug 14]   To Caroline Le Roy Webster. ALS. NhD. mDW 25339. Comments on the progress of the case, *Commonwealth* v. *Wyman*, now
underway in Concord; asks that his horse and chaise be sent for
him at Hingham.

Aug 16   From Josiah Moore (with Moore to Theodore Parker, Feb 17,
1853). Copy. DLC. mDWs. Admits to authoring the Duxbury resolutions relative to DW's temperance habits; insists that he intended
no more than a moral rebuke, and not an expression of unneigh-
borliness or lack of respect.

Aug 19   To John Gray. ALS. MHi. mDW 25322. Discusses a case involving Gray and expresses doubts as to whether he should prose-
cute the claim.

Aug 21 18[43–48]   To Levi Brigham. ALS. NhD. mDWs. Orders
champagne.

Aug 24   From Waddy Thompson.   310

Aug 24   Draft for $25 payable to Richard Smith, for insurance on
DW's Washington house. ADS by Smith. MHi. mDW 39893.

Aug 25   From John Quincy Adams. LC. MHi. mDW 25329. Forwards a
letter from Joseph Hodges.

Aug 29   To Edward Curtis. ALS. NN. mDW 25324. Reports having
written Upshur regarding Albert Davy; states that he has been
relaxing and is now doing a "small business" at his office.

Aug 29   To John Tyler.   311

Aug 30   To Richard Smith. ALS. IEN. mDW 25337. Discusses payment
of property insurance and the possible sale of his Washington
house.

[Aug]   To [?]. Printed. F. B. Sanborn, *Henry D. Thoreau* (Boston,
1882), p. 91. Comments on his "miserable catarrh."

Sept 5   From Moses Stuart. ALS. NHi. mDW 25341. Urges DW to address a political meeting in Essex County.

Sept 5   Promissory note for $1,100 payable to Isaac P. Davis at the
Merchant's Bank. DS. MHi. mDW 39895.

Sept 10   To Charles Augustus Stetson. ALS. MiAlbC. mDW 25344. Reports being detained at Marshfield by his "annual influenza" and
asks that a room be reserved for him at the Astor House for the end
of the week.

[Sept 10]   To Caroline Story White Webster. ALS. NhHi. mDW 25353.
Van Tyne, p. 606. Reports that he and Mrs. Webster are in poor
health and asks if the christening of Harriette Paige Webster might
be postponed until the next Sunday.

Sept 15   To John Gray. ALS. NhD. mDW 25346. Declines to represent
Gray in some case.

Sept 18   To Hiram J. Hartwell. ALS. InHi. mDW 25347. States that
he will not leave New York for Philadelphia before the end of the
week.

Sept 18   To Hariette Story White Paige. Printed. *PC*, 2: 174. Discusses
afflictions of the family and thanks her for a book.

Sept 30   From Simeon Veazey et al. (with Rufus G. Lewis to George

Washington Nesmith). Printed LS. NhHi. mDW 25349. Ask DW to enter the presidential race.

[Sept?] From John Haven et al. Printed. *Boston Courier*, Feb 5, 1844. Request DW's permission to nominate him as presidential candidate.

[Sept?] From Rufus Piper et al. Printed LS. NhHi. mDW 25360. *Boston Courier*, Feb 5, 1844. Dublin citizens ask DW to become a presidential candidate.

[Sept?] From Alexander H. Stickney et al. Printed LS. NhHi. mDW 25363. *Boston Courier*, Feb 5, 1844. Somersworth citizens ask DW to become a presidential candidate.

[Sept?] List of Portsmouth, North Hampton, Hampton and Rye signers of letters from John Haven et al. requesting DW to be presidential candidate. Copy. NhHi. mDW 25356.

[Sept ?] To [George William Gordon] (enclosure: editorial on the *Western Statesman*). AL. NhD. mDW 25534. Asks him to copy an enclosed article on Clay's nomination and send it to the *Boston Journal* for publication.

Oct 1 To Harriette Story White Paige. ALS. Mrs. Irvin McD. Garfield, Southboro, Mass. mDWs. Reports on his activities.

Oct 1 Indenture for the lease of DW's Boston law office from Henry Greenough. Printed DS with MS insertions. MHi. mDW 39897.

Oct 2 From Nicholas Biddle. ALS draft. DLC. mDW 25366. Invites him to the dinner and exhibition of the Philadelphia Agricultural Society.

Oct 2 *From Robert Perkins Letcher.*   *313*

Oct 3 To [Edward Curtis?]. ALS. NN. mDW 25371. Discusses a legal matter and his plan for visiting Philadelphia.

Oct 3 From Edward Everett. ALS. MHi. mDW 25376. Reports on the official instructions given Henry Stephen Fox regarding the Oregon boundary; explains Peel's decision not to send a commissioner to Washington to negotiate a commercial treaty.

Oct 3 Draft for $1,000 payable to David A. Hall. LS. MHi. mDW 39898.

Oct 5 From Moses Stuart et al. Printed. *Boston Semi-Weekly Atlas*, Nov 11, 1843. Invite DW to address Whigs at Andover.

Oct 6 Draft on Thomas Cookendorfer—$1,000, payable to DW at the Bank of the Metropolis. ADS. MHi. mDW 39900.

Oct 9 From Nicholas Biddle. ALS draft. DLC. mDW 25380. Argues that DW should now return to his "old political associates."

Oct 9 From Edward Stubbs. ALS. DNA, RG 59. mDW 56568. Inquires about the compensation DW promised Peyton Southall for carrying despatches to and from Mexico.

Oct 12 From Edward Stubbs. ALS. DNA, RG 59. mDW 56569. Asks for vouchers for use in making up the account of "suspended charges" for the contingent fund.

Oct 13 From S. C. Phillips, J. W. Proctor, and F. W. Choate. Printed. *Boston Semi-Weekly Atlas*, Nov 11, 1843. Invite DW to the Essex County Whig convention.

Oct 14 To Thomas Lyman Dunnell. ALS. NhD. mDW 25383. Declines invitation to address the Providence Lyceum.

Oct 14 To Samuel Merrill. ALS. MAnP. mDW 25385. Promises to answer Merrill's communication soon.

Oct 15   *To Stephen Clarendon Phillips.*   314

Oct 16   To William Bayard. ALS. NNU-F. mDWs. Gives his legal opinion of an Alabama law incorporating "the Trading and Importing Company of Alabama."

Oct 16   To William Davis. Printed. *Niles National Register*, 65 (Oct 28, 1843): 141–142. Declines invitation to attend the Whig convention at Plymouth; discusses Massachusetts politics and the forthcoming election.

Oct 16   To Edward Everett. ALS. MHi. mDW 25389. Introduces William Bayard.

Oct 16   To John Plummer Healy. ALS. MHi. mDW 25391. Asks him to pick up some papers which have been sent to Rufus Choate.

Oct 17   To Moses Stuart et al. Printed. *Boston Semi-Weekly Atlas*, Nov 11, 1843. Accepts invitation to address the Whigs at Andover.

Oct 20   To J. B. B. Hale. LS. NhHi. mDW 25393. Explains the procedure by which Presidential electors are chosen in Massachusetts.

Oct 23   *To Robert Perkins Letcher.*   315

Oct 23   From Samuel Merrill. ALS. MAnP. mDW 25403. Acknowledges DW's acceptance of the invitation to the Andover meeting on Nov 9 and asks what time the official escort should meet him in Boston.

Oct 25   From Osgood Mussey. ALS. DLC. mDW 25404. Returns the paper DW asked him to prepare; asks him to bring other papers when he comes to Washington.

Oct 27   To Daniel Wright. ALS. Miss Lucy J. Bonney, Hanover, Mass. mDWs. Asks him to drive some oxen from Pembroke to Marshfield and encloses two bills for the seller, a Mr. Briggs.

Oct 29   To Edward Everett. ALS. MHi. mDW 25406. Introduces Henry Davis, Jr., of Syracuse, N.Y.

Nov 1   *To Seth Weston.*   317

[Nov 1]   *To Edward Curtis.*   319

[c. Nov 1]   *From John Tyler.*   319

Nov 2   From John Frost. ALS. DLC. mDW 25413. Reports that he is dedicating his *Pictorial History of the United States* to DW.

Nov 6   To Daniel Wright. Copy. NhHi. mDW 28884. Reports on trip to Brighton, cattle, and John Taylor, whom he saw.

Nov 7   From Robert Perkins Letcher. ALS. NhD. mDW 25415. Comments on Whig attacks on DW for remaining in the Tyler cabinet; gives assurances of Clay's and Crittenden's high regard and urges him to "come into the fight quickly."

Nov 10   To Nathaniel F. Williams. ALS. NhD. mDW 25442. Authorizes him to draw for the amount of an acceptance due Nov 19 and 22.

Nov 10   *To Nathaniel F. Williams.*   319

Nov 11   From Moses Stuart. ALS. DLC. mDW 25446. Calls the Andover speech one of DW's best efforts and thinks it explains clearly his reasons for remaining in the Tyler cabinet.

Nov 13   To Moses Stuart. ALS. MH-H. mDW 25450. W & S, 3: 158. Asks if he may dedicate the pamphlet edition of his Andover speech to Stuart.

Nov 14   To John Plummer Healy. ALS. MHi. mDW 25454. Asks that his letters be sent to him daily at Lowell.

Nov 15   To Mary Ann Sanborn. Printed. *PC*, 2 : 177. Expresses a desire to see her and her husband; reports on his plans for the winter.

Nov 15   From Moses Stuart. ALS. DLC. mDW 25456. Thanks DW for the dedication of the Andover speech and again highly praises it.

Nov 16   To Nathaniel F. Williams. ALS. NhD. mDW 25459. Promises to send a check despite the demands of his court engagement at Lowell.

Nov 17   To Edward Curtis.   320

Nov 20   To John Frost. ALS. PPL. mDWs. Thanks Frost for the dedication proposed for his *Pictorial History of the United States.*

Nov 20   From Samuel H. Perkins et al. LS. DLC. mDW 25463. Invite DW to a Thanksgiving dinner to be given by the Sons of New England in Philadelphia.

Nov 21   From Nathaniel Sawyer et al. Copy. DLC. mDW 25465. Ask for DW's views on restoring public credit.

Nov 23   From John Clark et al. ALS by Clark, signed also by others. MHi. mDW 25468. *Lowell Journal*, March 22, 1844. Ask him to sit for a portrait which will hang in some public hall in Lowell, Mass.

Nov 25   To Lewis F. Allen. ALS. TxSjM. mDWs. Offers to converse on the topics of Allen's letter; fears a "new commotion" should Tyler recommend the annexation of Texas.

Nov 25   To Hiram Ketchum. ALS. NhD. mDW 20720. Asks him to confer with Joseph W. Moulton on a legal matter.

Nov 25   To Samuel H. Perkins et al. Copy. MAnP. mDW 25472. Declines invitation to the Thanksgiving dinner planned by the Sons of New England in Philadelphia, but offers a toast to be read on that occasion.

Nov 25   To Jared Sparks. ALS. MH-H. mDW 25473. Agrees to show him the paper from which he made extracts in his speech at Andover.

Nov 30   To Joshua Bates.   320

Nov 30   To [Richard Milford Blatchford?]. ALS. NhExP. mDW 25482. Promises to answer his communication once he has seen the President's message.

Nov 30   To Edward Everett.   321

Nov   To James William Paige. Printed. *PC*, 2 : 176–177. Invites him on a "jaunt" to Marshfield.

Dec 2   To John Clark et al. Printed. *Lowell Journal*, March 22, 1843. Agrees to sit for a portrait; credits discriminating revenue laws for encouraging the growth of manufacturing cities like Lowell.

Dec 2   To Hiram Ketchum.   323

Dec 2   To Junius Spencer Morgan. ALS. NNPM. mDW 25494. Thinks that he might visit Morgan in Hartford but warns that he will not give an address.

Dec 2   To Nathaniel F. Williams. ALS. NhD. mDW 20778. Promises to mail him a check; states that he is sick with influenza but expects to see him in Baltimore in ten days.

Dec 5   From Richard Milford Blatchford. ALS. NhHi. mDW 25496. Reports the three transportation companies forming a line between Boston and New York have voted passes for DW, his wife, and servant.

Dec 8   To George Ticknor. ALS. NhD. mDW 25498. Hopes to see him on Tuesday.

Dec 9   To Charles Allen. ALS. MHi. mDW 25499. *W & S*, 16: 417. Predicts that propositions regarding Texas may come up in Congress and that southerners are likely to dominate the House Committee on Foreign Relations.

Dec 12   To Gordon L. Ford. ALS. NN. mDW 25502. *W & S*, 16: 416. Promises to look for a lost autograph album when he reaches Boston.

Dec 13   To Edward Curtis.   324

Dec 14   To Caleb Cushing. ALS. DLC. mDW 25507. Introduces George Frazer, who has commercial objects in China.

Dec 14, 1843–Nov 7, 1845   Account with Brigham & Son for wine and cheese, $312.31. AD. MAnP. mDW 39902.

Dec 15   To Rufus Choate. ALS. CSmH. mDW 25509. Agrees to give Francis Lieber letters of introduction to friends in Europe.

Dec 16   To Edward Curtis. Printed. *PC*, 2: 178. Promises to be in New York December 21 and to bring wine and a cusk.

Dec 18   To [David ?] Sears. Printed. *PC*, 2: 178–179. Asks for a bottle of wine to take with him to New York.

Dec 19   From Charles Allen.   324

Dec 21   Deed transferring property in the township of Bergen, Hudson County, New Jersey, from Francis Price and wife to DW. Typed copy. Register of Deeds, Hudson County, New Jersey. mDWs. Described as land and premises "on which the Weehauken Mountain House now stands," known also as the Pavillion property.

Dec 21   Bond to Francis Price for $9,000. Printed DS with MS insertions. MWalB. mDW 39988.

Dec 26   To Edward Everett. ALS. MHi. mDW 25514. Discusses William Taggard's claim on the British government and asks Everett to use his good offices on Taggard's behalf.

Dec 26   To Edward Everett. ALS. MHi. mDW 25518. Refers to his letter regarding Taggard's claim, and asks him to see Sir William Follett or show him the letter.

Dec 27   To John Plummer Healy. ALS. MHi. mDW 25521. Asks him to look up "my Franklin Pamphlet" and send it to Edward Curtis.

Dec 27   Agreement transferring 10,000 acres of land in Arkansas to Francis Price. ADS. NhD. mDW 40286.

Dec 28   From Edward Everett. LC. MHi. mDW 25523. Reflects on his daughter's recent death; reports DW's recent speeches have drawn notice in England; reports also a conversation with Aberdeen on the Oregon boundary.

[Dec]   To Judah Lee Bliss (enclosure: extract from reply to Hayne). ALS Facsimile. NHi. mDW 25531. Encloses a hand-copied passage from his speech as requested by Bliss.

[Dec ?]   To John B. Ayres (with ANS by Ayres, Dec 1843). ALS. NhD. mDW 25528. Asks him to "copy this, *confidentially*," identified by Ayres as a paper later used in the Girard case argument before the Supreme Court.

[Dec ?]   To Caroline Story White Webster. ALS. NhHi. mDW 39125.

PC, 2: 177–178. Agrees to dine with her, providing he may bring a dish of baked beans.

[1843?]   To Daniel Fletcher Webster. ALS. NhHi. mDW 21017. Reports that he can say nothing today.

[1843?]   To Daniel Fletcher Webster. ALS. NhHi. mDW 21019. Reports that "our business draws near a close" and advises Fletcher not to part with his house "till I see you."

[1843?]   To Robert Charles Winthrop. ALS. MHi. mDW 25543. Agrees to see Winthrop's friends and hopes to confer with Winthrop also.

[1843?]   To Robert Charles Winthrop. ALS. MHi. mDW 25545. Praises Winthrop's speech and requests a conference.

[1843–1844]   To Daniel Wright. ALS. MiAlbC. mDW 25552. Expects to go to Marshfield with guests and asks him to have the boat ready.

Index

The following abbreviations are used: BUS, Bank of the United States; DW, Daniel Webster; DFW, Daniel Fletcher Webster. Page-entry numbers between 327 and 534 refer to material in the Calendar. Numbers set in boldface type indicate pages where individuals are identified. Individuals identified in the *Dictionary of American Biography* are denoted by an asterisk immediately following the name. Those identified in the *Biographical Directory of the American Congress* are denoted by a dagger.